حقـــوق الأجيـــال القـــادمة
Rights of Future Generations

اقتراحـــــــات
Propositions

Adrian Lahoud, editor
Andrea Bagnato, coeditor

Sharjah Architecture Triennial

في الواقع، يقدّم لنا جايمز أسلافه بالفعل، ولكنه حريص على ألا يقدّم كلّ أسلافه، بل فقط أولئك الذين ناضلوا ضد الاستعباد.

حورية بوثلجة

The Congregation of the Damned

Adrian Lahoud

For the labour of the missing asks that our words dialogue with silence rather than seek contact. In the presence of their silence, the disappeared, these objects in excess, can make a demand on us. And it is our task to substantiate the distance that otherwise can make silence sound like inexorable oblivion.
—Walid Sadek, "Collecting the Uncanny and the Labour of the Missing"

The language of the triumphant was as different from the language of the conquered, as that of the living from the dead.
—Saidiya Hartman, *Lose Your Mother: A Journey along the Atlantic Slave Route*

LAWANG

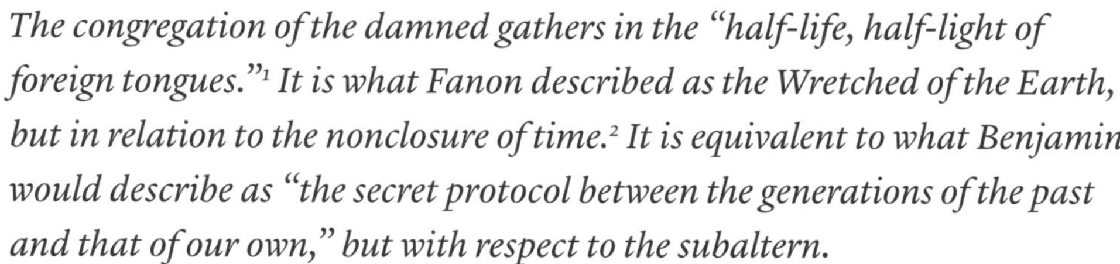

The congregation of the damned gathers in the "half-life, half-light of foreign tongues."[1] *It is what Fanon described as the Wretched of the Earth, but in relation to the nonclosure of time.*[2] *It is equivalent to what Benjamin would describe as "the secret protocol between the generations of the past and that of our own," but with respect to the subaltern.*

Veranda of a Sebop longhouse in the 1910s. The veranda is the main thoroughfare of the longhouse, subdividing the building along its main axis. Households occupy similarly sized rooms, arranged in a row facing the veranda. Each household has its own hearth and food preparation area. The deep roof is occupied by men during funeral rites and used for storage. Image from Charles Hose and William McDougall, *The Pagan Tribes of Borneo*, vol. 1 (London, 1912), plate 64.

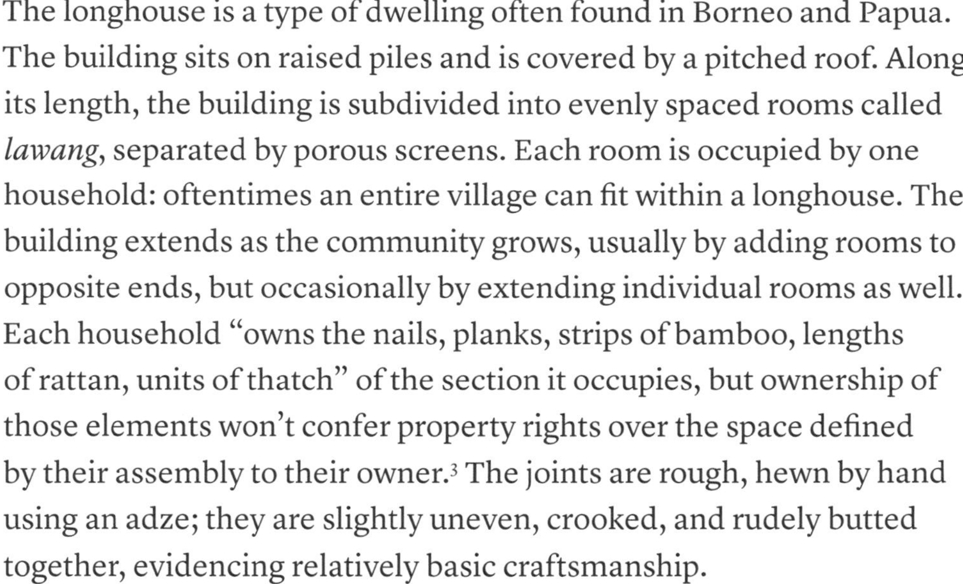

The longhouse is a type of dwelling often found in Borneo and Papua. The building sits on raised piles and is covered by a pitched roof. Along its length, the building is subdivided into evenly spaced rooms called *lawang*, separated by porous screens. Each room is occupied by one household: oftentimes an entire village can fit within a longhouse. The building extends as the community grows, usually by adding rooms to opposite ends, but occasionally by extending individual rooms as well. Each household "owns the nails, planks, strips of bamboo, lengths of rattan, units of thatch" of the section it occupies, but ownership of those elements won't confer property rights over the space defined by their assembly to their owner.[3] The joints are rough, hewn by hand using an adze; they are slightly uneven, crooked, and rudely butted together, evidencing relatively basic craftsmanship.

Describing the longhouse as an entire village in a single building is not quite right either. In fact, it is more like an entire village in a single room, at least from the perspective of people who are used to defining rooms by solid walls that enclose space. From the perspective of the inhabitants of the longhouse, however, neither "privacy" nor "room" depend on this kind of enclosure. More accurately still, in the encounter between these two perspectives, the very notion of a room equivocates.[4] Behavior between neighbors in the longhouse is regulated by a particular array of social codes. The codes don't depend on solid walls for their negotiation; indeed, they function perfectly well without walls, or, more precisely, they function *through* walls. In a trivial sense, the horizontal joints and vertical screens subdivide. More profoundly, the joints organize an etiquette of interaction between each household's behavior according to the intention, notification, and duration of the neighborly gaze—or the reason for looking, the communication of an intention to look, and the length of the look itself.[5] This prompts questions. Should members of neighboring households avert their eyes if overly curious? Are they reprimanded if they are? Do they look, but refuse to see?

To a stranger unfamiliar with longhouse life, the household space might seem to be devoid of privacy. It might feel to them like a very intimate, highly surveilled room, albeit a rather long one. But presumably this stranger's thinking, feeling, and looking was trained on spaces and bodies that made sense in the stranger's society—but that appear alien to the inhabitants of the longhouse. What would the inhabitants of the longhouse make of the stranger's home? Of its solid walls? Would they read the walls as evidence of neighborly distrust? After all, if these strangers trusted their neighbors, what would they need solid walls for?

It's impossible to know whether the forms of life that unfold in a longhouse are more trusting or less, since the very idea of "trust" is another site of comparative equivocation, just like "room" or "wall." It might be more precise to say that the wall and the joint pose the problem of neighborly relations in different ways. More importantly, this speculative comparison suggests that the difference between the materiality of architectural elements (walls, floors, joints, screens, partitions) and behaviors (glances, intentions, durations) is less reassuring, less essential than imagined. It is as if the relation between sociality and form were inherently plastic, interchangeable, and jurisgenerative.

This is another way of saying that there is no essential dimension to architecture beyond a collection of diverse elements and their cross contamination—not only the walls, floors, joints, screens, roofs, partitions, as some would have it, but also grounds, soils, earthworks, landmarks, trees, gardens, pathways, rivers and mountains, animals, songs, and spirits.[6] Architecture's claim to some inviolable, elemental essence, whether building, shelter, tectonics, or craft, is only even conceivable by denying the reality of human existence for countless others, only realizable through the subordination of others, only enforceable through the exercise of institutional authority and the power to include, depict, credit, and judge that comes with it.

The curation of the 2019 Sharjah Architecture Triennial was informed by writing on alterity, in particular the work of Eduardo Viveiros de Castro, Phillipe Descola, Ghassan Hage, Elizabeth Povinelli, and David Wengrow.[7] The experiment this approach set in motion had little to do with the inclusion of so called non-Western content, but was instead the provisional outcome of a practical and political problem: the encounter between different communities, institutions, curators, artists, and architects. Because these encounters are also sites of speculation involving the lives of others conducted according to complex, uneven power relations, basic ideas around curation and architectural exhibition making had to be put into question. The Sharjah Architecture Triennial's dissonant tone is motivated by the necessity of decolonizing a discipline plagued by ontological monotony, epistemological violence, and an ever more exploitative political economy—something that is nowhere more evident than in the exhibition complex itself. The sensorial poverty that all this reproduces in the field necessitates experiments in other kinds of feelings, other kinds of power, other kinds of being, of which the Triennial is simply one. These other kinds of feelings, power, and being coalesce around the multiplicity of meanings given to the words that make up the Triennial's title: Rights, Futures, and Generations.

TINDOUF

Informal Collective on Western Sahara, *Necessità dei volti – Fourth Extension*, 1999–2019, Sharjah Architecture Triennial, p. 275.
The Sahrawi Museum of Resistance is a unique event within the "shapeless empire" of archival practices: the only collection in the world meant to be returned rather than kept. Maintained in exile in Algeria and under occupation in Morocco, the snapshots were originally collected as evidence of a long-denied war. As the collection grew, it became clear to those collecting that the Moroccan soldiers were also victims of the Moroccan State. Image courtesy of the artists.

The congregation of the damned invokes knowledge of the past through non-standard means. Like a green screen conflating near and far, or a lenticular image holding past and present in a single frame, the congregation is present as the contamination of present experience—the inability of present experience to be present to itself.[8] *The conflict between other times and other spaces persisting in present time and present space might be the basis of a political strategy, it might be the appearance of a compositional problem, it might just be the mark of an anachronic character. Sometimes, it can become what Dread Scott describes as "a past that didn't exist trying to jam itself into the present."*[9]

In 1999, a group of artists and activists called the Informal Collective visited the Saharan desert towns of Tindouf and Smara to view the photo archives of the Saharawi Museum of Resistance. The photos had been left behind by Moroccan soldiers—conscripts from the proletariat and peasantry—participating in a military campaign against the Saharawi. The images depict the war and the Moroccan soldiers fighting it, their families, and their friends; they were collected over sixteen years by members of the Sahrawi People's Liberation Army and the Polisario Front. The photographs' current owners thus became "involuntary guardians" of another people's past, but only in anticipation of a future where they could be returned to the Moroccan soldiers or their families. The anticipated return of the images assigns another meaning to the conflict in Western Sahara, one in which the involuntary guardianship of the photos is paired with the reluctant conscription of the soldiers and acts as a promise of redemption. Or, to put it differ-

Farzin Lotfi-Jam, Felicity Scott, and Mark Wasiuta, *Media Habitat, c. 1975*, 2019, Sharjah Architecture Triennial, p. 258.
The self-presentation of the need for development and progress depended on the dissemination of cinematic techniques and filmmaking equipment. Images of skilled and unskilled labor formed a key component of the films produced by the UN, including numerous examples of architects who were seen as uniquely able to address the problems Habitat highlighted around settlement, shelter, and urbanization. Image courtesy of the artists.

ently, the archive is the expression of a yet-to-be-fulfilled solidarity between the past and the present.[10]

The installation *Media Habitat, c. 1975* examines an archive of 16mm films commissioned for Habitat 1, the UN Conference on Human Settlement held in 1976 in Vancouver. The artists digitally scanned one hundred of these films, cut them into individual clips, and tagged them according to content or cinematic technique. The result is a database presented in the form of a control room and organized around degrees of national development and recurring visual tropes. Initiated by the UN to "record the reality" of global urbanization, the Habitat project was designed to increase foreign aid by persuading states of its merit. The films—their commissioning, circulation, and legacy—marked the birth of a globalized "developmental paradigm" in the audio-visual register. This paradigm is forged through three processes: developmental imaging, temporal ordering, and semiotic tutelage.

At the level of content, *developmental imaging* combines depictions of irretrievable archaisms and nascent modernities. Consultants, experts, managers, technicians, architects, and planners acted like bureaucratic shepherds of a yet-to-be-modern people that mingled with vernacular architectures, peasants, and farm animals. Connecting the two realms were technologies meant to secure a nation's passage from the archaic stage to the modern one. At the level of form, the developmental image restages the *availability* of the Third World, especially its accessibility to experts as the precondition of its improvement.[11] The purpose of both was to reproduce the problem of development in strictly technical terms.

Each nation's improvement should be sequential and orderly, like a production line. Its meter played to a promise: images of a developed present were offered to those inhabiting a less developed past, to assure a more developed future. To entrain time, the Habitat films needed to entrain consciousness. The films teach, but who or what is being taught, and how? A new assemblage of landscapes, faces, bodies, gestures, cameras, and screens established a durable link between concerns like help, empathy, paternalism, and national pride. They taught that everyone is different, but different *in the same way*: national dress, national buildings, national food, national song, national dance.

The UN Habitat films are machinic agents of miseducation. Their effects continue to reverberate today, not least within the architectural exhibition, where reproducing the South as a not-yet-developed, not-yet-modern project awaiting architecture's "help" produces cultural capital that is banked in North American and European institutions as the precondition for further funding. The result is a paternalistic performance of moral virtue by architects, in which the South is used to lubricate yet another extractive economy. The artists' response to this is a warning to the audience (and curators)—a machinic resynthesis of the material that works to diagnose a new grouping of existing signs.[12] By decoding the corpus of films, organizing them according to dominant tropes, and making them accessible through a control room, the artists try to short-circuit the sociogenic work the UN initiative started and that the architectural exhibition inherits. The installation is an interruption in the afterlife of that inheritance presented to those on the factory floor.

YUCATAN

The congregation of the damned is the sensible, physical reaction to a war waged against history by the enemies of the future, where the difference between "something felt or done in response to an event" or a "chemical process involving the change of substance" can no longer be separately determined.[13] The congregation remetabolizes violence by assimilating its ruins. Ariella Aïsha Azoulay suggests that "imperial logics rely on disrupting intergenerational memories."[14] Because anything might remember, the imperial project must deploy every tactic and every tool to destroy intergenerational transmission, working simultaneously on biological, social, and cultural fronts. But from the perspective of the congregation everything remembers, and so the imperial project can never be completed.

The idea of an ancestor usually refers to parents, grandparents, great-grandparents and so on—moving backward in time, expanding in branching blood lines that trace descent through biological reproduction. Alongside them are others that hold common cause to reproduce social and cultural expectations and that are sometimes named "mother" or "father," "auntie" or "uncle," "brother" or "sister," depending on how biological and social forms of reproduction are distinguished. The common image of a family tree describes inheritance according to its biological dimension. As Alain Pottage reminds us, law deploys the idea of kinship through the notion of the family, using the image of a tree as the source of legitimacy to naturalize the legal order of genealogical descent.

> First, legal representations were absorbed into the "natural" order of botanical taxonomies, which were cast in the image of law's own notions of genealogical descent, and then law re-integrated this factitious image as the "original," or "natural" order of which it was just the cultural mirror-image.[15]

The biological family transmits in time what the institution of property possesses in space. In turn, the setting of the nuclear home encloses and privatizes feelings and affects between generations in order to secure that precious patrimonial cargo—inherited wealth. Under capitalism, the reciprocal relationship between family, property, and home dominates our understanding of intergenerational inheritance, and architecture plays a constitutive role. The Sharjah Architecture Triennial's theme, Rights of Future Generations, set out to trouble the dominance of such an idea of inheritance. Not only do colonial, imperial, and capitalist forms of domination depend on eliminating models of intergenerational inheritance that do not adhere to this type, they also depend on eliminating intergenerational life *as such*. Therefore, they will seek to deprive people of their own biological, social, and cultural history, since this history will rightly be seen as the primary means of resistance to their subordination.

In the time of slavery, descent posed a legal problem to the slave owning class. Through the legal notion of *partus sequitur ventrem*, Virginia's 1662 Slavery Act determined that a captive person's offspring was the heritable property of the slave owner. [16] The Act formalized the underlying logic of already existing practices of capitalist extraction and exploitation. If the biological potential of the enslaved female formed one site of violence, the ineliminable social generativity of the offspring formed another, since the estate of slavery depended on the *circulation and dispersal* of the enslaved (so as not to reproduce kinship in exile) as much as it did on the reproductive potential of the captive mother. As Hortense Spillers notes, "If 'kinship' were possible, the property relation would be undermined."[17]

So too with the settler colony, fixated on breeding and physiognomic traits. According to the policies enacted by A.O. Neville, the elimination of Indigenous peoples had a "proper" pace that was measured in generational time. As Chief Protector of Aborigines in Western Australia between 1915 and 1940 and the palliative servant of the

Fearing that the blood of mixed descendants would haunt White Australia for generations, the Australian government laid out a plan aiming at the destruction and annihilation of Aboriginal people and culture. From 1910 to 1970, up to one in three Aboriginal children were forcibly placed under the guardianship of the state in adoptive or foster families, religious or charitable institutions. The exact number of lives affected is unclear, because many removals were never recorded. Image from A. O. Neville, *Australia's Coloured Minority: Its Place in the Community* (Sydney, 1947).

state's genocidal program of deracination, Neville claimed to "smooth the dying pillow" of the "Native race."[18] In Australia, the theft of Aboriginal children from their parents, families, kin, and communities by the Australian Government, and their placement in non-Indigenous institutions or foster and adoptive families, remained official policy for most of the twentieth century, as it did in Canada and the United States. A total of sixty-seven definitions and 700 pieces of legislation attempted to define Aboriginality according to skin color and the proportion of "European blood"—which would in turn be used to decide whether Aboriginals would live on a reserve or among white society. These Aboriginal children, now adults, many of whom are still alive, are known as the "stolen generations."

Enslavement and settler-colonial deracination set out according to different purposes and moved toward different ends. In both cases, however, the transmission of intergenerational material, whether biological or social, became the object of intense and violent attention, since it was rightly seen as vector for biosocial care, kinship, and solidarity, and could not, therefore, be allowed to survive.

Cultural material was just as threatening: if intergenerational transmission could not be over coded, it had to be eliminated. Burning heralded colonial arrivals: on July 12, 1562, in the town of Mani in the Yucatán, Bishop Diego Delanda Calderón ordered hundreds of Mayan prisoners into the plaza where over 20,000 ritual items and codices, recording over 800 years of Mayan history, were incinerated on a bonfire, "finding in these books nothing more than the deceit of the devil."[19] Burning heralded colonial departures too: on the eve of Algerian independence, the dean and the head librarian of the University of Algiers set fire to the university library before leaving, destroying 500,000 books to prevent them from falling into the hands of those fighting for Algerian freedom.

Examples of looting, burning, bonfires, and destruction abound across present and former colonies.[20] As violent as these examples are, they represent only a fraction of the worlds affected and can only allude to the scale of destruction. Like a blind spot or an eclipse, empire fills the gap where an image used to be. The Sharjah Architecture Triennial was not only colored by the sense of these worlds passing, but also by the waning of whatever solace the documentation of such passing might have provided. The exhibition was not a response to intergenerational loss nor was it an answer. The responses to it are already everywhere anyway, and no answer will ever be adequate. It just started in the middle of it because there was nowhere else to start. In many ways, intergenerational loss is simply the precondition of work in the Global South, one that the exhibition tried to uninhabit as a strategic disfiguration of loss, organized by the forever open question: What has survived?

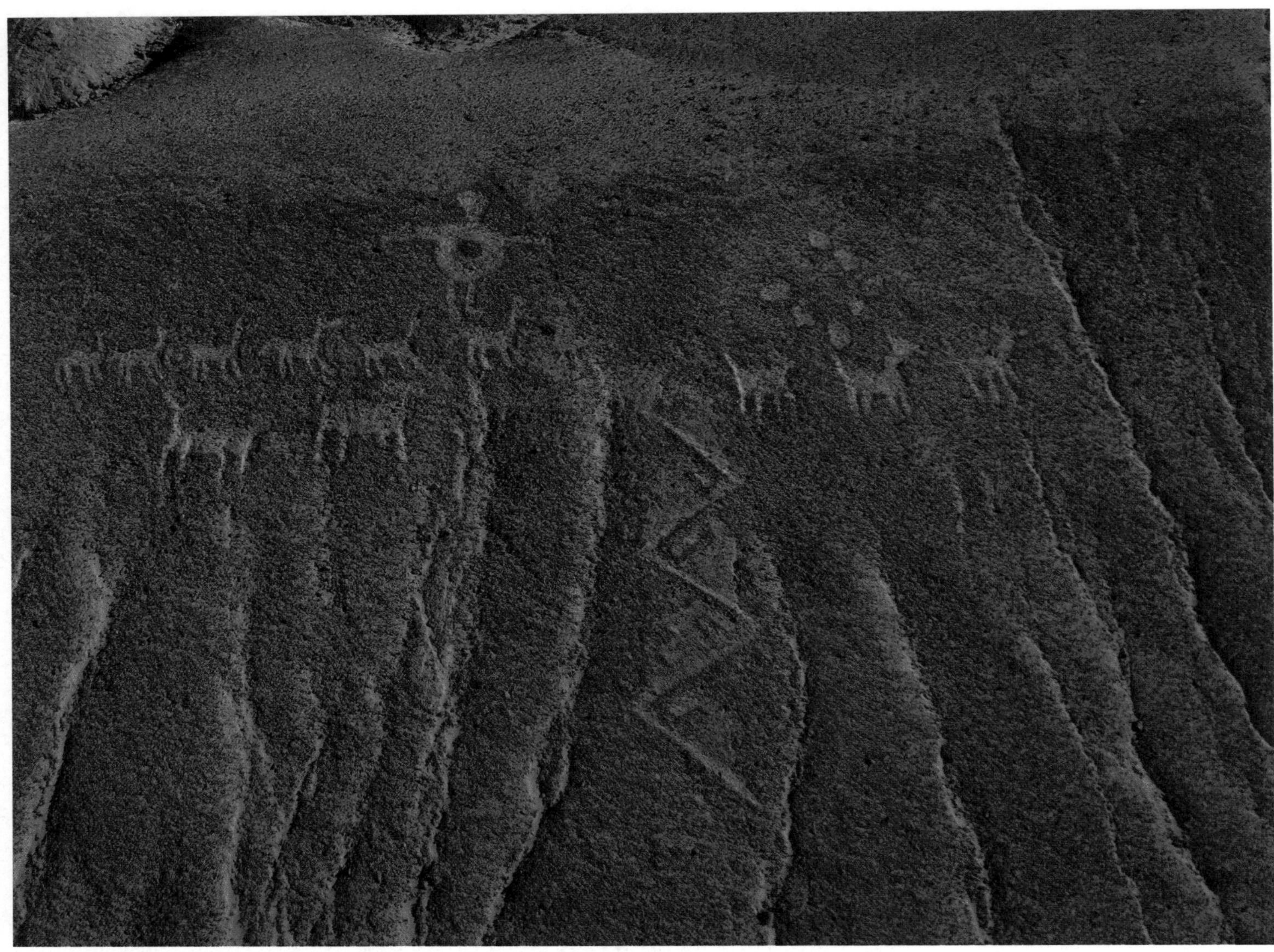

Alonso Barros, Gonzalo Pimentel, Juan Gili, and Mauricio Hidalgo, *The Atacama Lines*, 2019, Sharjah Architecture Triennial, p. 276.
Mining companies enclose and fence off geoglyphs to prevent them being driven over or damaged, thereby treating them as an artifact rather than seeing them as part of a continuous landscape of pathways, sequences, caravan routes. The density of geoglyphs, and thus the relevance of the landscape as heritage, becomes a key field of dispute between mining companies and indigenous populations. Photo courtesy of Fundación Desierto de Atacama.

THAKI

The congregation of the damned is an effect that modifies its cause. Like a glint that precedes the light it receives, the sign the congregation sends is invented by the presence of those who are ready for it, those who can't or won't recognize it because they know that recognition doesn't get them very far. Instead, they incorporate the sign through their own presence as preparation for the arrival of the past. In the middle of it, they retroactively confer on the past what looks to them like the offering of a communicative gift to the future that is us, here, now. Or to put it differently, nothing can be definitively lost, everything might have survived.

Along the mountainous slopes of abandoned caravan routes that cross the Atacama Desert in Chile are thousands of geoglyphs. These earth drawings are made by displacing rocks and stones to form depictions of humans, animals, mythological figures, and geometric shapes. The pathways joining modern Bolivia, Chile, and Argentina once formed a multiethnic network linking the peoples of the Andean Plateau and its saltpans to each other and to the world beyond. The geoglyphs of the Plateau were located on slopes so as to be seen by travelers

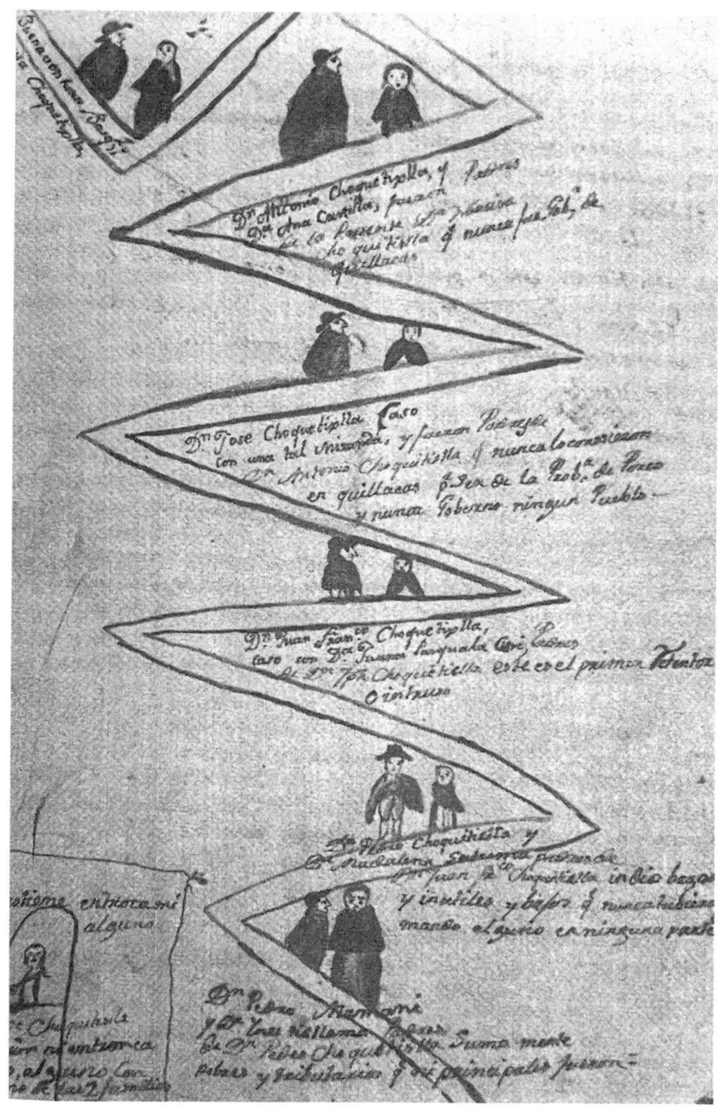

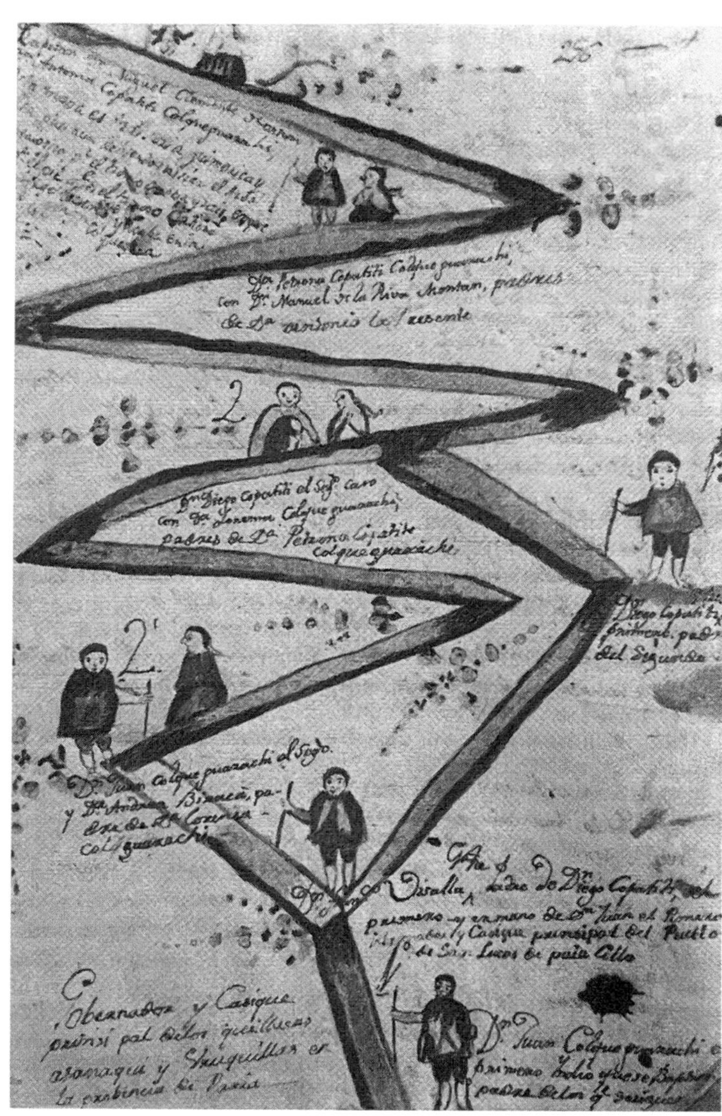

Schema of intergenerational transmission as a mountain path. The image on the left is the Choqueticlla family path, with the "pathless beggar" in the bottom left corner; the image on the right is the Colque Guarache family path. The staffs of office indicate the nobility of the Colque Guarache family line, in contrast to the ignoble Choqueticlla one. The images are to be read chronologically from bottom to top, suggesting an idea of genealogical ascent. Image from Thomas Abercrombie, *Pathways of Memory and Power* (Madison, 1998), p. 228.

snaking along the valley floors, but also scaled and positioned so as to be witnessed by supernatural beings and other geoglyphs. Transdesert routes were more than infrastructure for travel. The Aymaran people call them *thaki*, a word that describes a uniquely Andean form of social memory, in which named mountains and rivers act in sequence to elicit imagination in movement as ritual and oral performance. *Thaki* express an entire metaphysical system structured around the paths that lives take and the choices those lives make as they move. The social generativity of movement across the Plateau is elicited by the topographic and mnemotechnical ensemble of landforms, pathways, names, sightlines, sequences, and artifacts that make up Indigenous Andean architecture.

In his book titled *Pathways of Memory and Power: Ethnography and History Among an Andean People*, anthropologist Thomas Abercrombie includes two curious illustrations that point to the *thaki*'s intergenerational importance. Dating to 1804, they were drawn to support an inheritance claim in a litigation over property between the Guarache and Choqueticlla families. In depicting family lineage to resolve a property dispute, the drawings make a familiar appeal to genealogy. How they choose to depict it is another thing entirely. Instead of a family tree, the illustrations show the *thaki* in the shape of a path that zigzags up and down the face of a mountain. The lines and the figures drawn at each corner represent a sequence of names and actions to be recited and performed as the caravan passed through the landscape. They also represent an ancestral lineage, a path that threads through individual lives as a temporal-topographic sequence. These two illustrations weld European notions of filiation to Andean ideas of emplacement and social memory, arresting in both written and graphic form the physical and spiritual practices of moving through the desert landscape and the oral recitations and performances that accompanied movement. The documents mark a point of resistance to the predatory encroachments of Spanish colonization, but that is not all. In the bottom left-hand corner of the illustration depicting the Choqueticlla family, a lone figure stands outside the filial line of connection to ancestors. An annotation refers to him as a "pathless beggar." Strangely, to emphasize the state of being stranded outside of the social world, he is depicted *inside* a building.

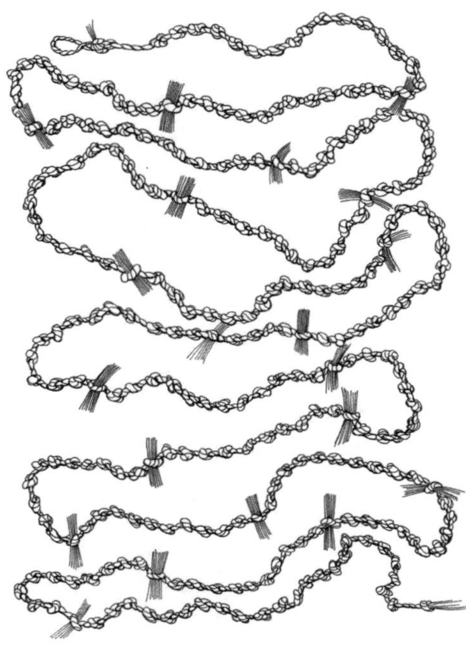

Schema of intergenerational transmission according to a Iatmul mnemonic cord, or *kirugu*. The cord begins with the series Night, First Journey, Maternal Womb, Prenatal Life, and ends with the series Day, Second Journey, Light, Postnatal Life, Father. In between are sites (Matsun Island) and secret names (of the Flying Fox). Image from Jürg Wassman, *Der Gesang an den Fliegenden Hund* (Basel, 1982), p. 113.

KIRUGU

The congregation of the damned assembles in a reenactment that comes before the event it repeats. The congregation is present because we are present, because we call it to assembly, because we call it to assembly through a presence that isn't present to itself. The congregation persists despite the war being waged against it, despite the temporal ordering this war reproduces. It persists because it has learned to uninhabit time—to exist instead within the aspect of time marked by what Dionne Brand has called "ancestral estrangement and filial longing."[21] *A future generation is not only a group of people that aren't here yet; it's the problem posed to the rest of us of how to exist in the time of their nonarrival, how to uninhabit this ever-present in an untimely way, like a temporal runaway, or to share in what David Scott describes as the social institution of time but in relation to catastrophe.*[22]

Andean, Australasian, Mesoamerican, and Amerindian peoples have often been described as having "oral traditions," with icons and symbols acting as prompts to memory, performance, or speech. A notable example is the Iatmul practice of recitation—found in many of the villages along the Sepik river in Papua New Guinea—where memorized lists of thousands of ancestors' names are passed down generation to generation. More than oral records of genealogy, these lists are the literal pathways of an ancestor's original migration. *Kirugu* is the name given to a length of cord whose knots represent a sequence of toponyms ordered according to this path. During song cycles, the cord's owner will pass the knots through their hand "like a rosary." Each knot designates "an episode relating to the life of the ancestors," with the larger knots indicating a name that can be uttered and small knots indicating names that should only be recalled in the mind of the owner.[23]

Because their vocalizations lack phonetic transcription into written form, the graphic traditions of oral societies are still seen as abortive, ultimately failed attempts to produce writing. This mistaken view is founded on a model of mental activity that is discreet, stilted, and mechanical: the recollection exists in the mind in its complete form, but because it sits along many other recollections, its retrieval depends on something "outside" of the mind to prompt that particular recollection into conscious perception—usually an icon, a symbol, or a glyph, or in this case, perhaps, a knot. The sign supports recollection through repetitive association. Its apprehension occurs because it triggers the *retrieval* of a fact, a name, or a story. Because they are seen from the viewpoint of "people with writing," graphic practices are erroneously understood in terms of how *reliably* they produce recollections—that is to say, how closely they adhere to a model of communication based on written language.

The anthropologist Carlo Severi claims that the very idea of an oral society is mistaken. For Severi, the material cultures and graphic traditions of these societies are not failed attempts to develop a form of writing. On the contrary, they represent a wholly independent technology of social memory and imagination. In his book *The Chimera Principle*, he argues that that the graphic icons, symbols, and illustrations of Andean, Australasian, Mesoamerican, and Amerindian societies are *incomplete* images posing the problem of their completion to the imagination.

Named after the mythical monster, these chimeras span two realms: one is visible to the eye, the other only to the mind. But the minds these chimeras are visible to are not enclosed in their individuality, not captured in their selfhood, not divorced from their environment. The chimera registers as lack in comparison to writing, but only from the perspective of individuals and selves that believe their minds to be theirs and theirs alone. The chimera's job is not to transcribe sound nor to prompt recollections, but to solicit the action of a shared imagination in the socially extended mind of the beholders—an immanent imagination that is collectively composed, and whose composition the chimeras worked to cultivate. By seeing signs as a mere inventory or list, the notion of recollection turns memory into a stock. But the incomplete chimerical sign does not prompt retrieval of a stock: it *disturbs*, *splits*, *cajoles*, *provokes*, and *taunts* thought into action, according to the imaginative necessity of shared social improvisation.

In the West, the imagination, much like dreaming, is a predominantly private and asocial affair. On the contrary, here we find a deprivatized and socialized understanding of the imagination as shared cultural artifact—albeit one whose meaning and durability depends on the creative practice of its members in ritual contexts of imaginative exercise.[24] If Severi were wrong and there really were societies "without writing," then we should also allow that there were societies devoid of dreams and imagination too.

NGURRARA

The congregation of the damned is the unbound coexistence of all the oppressed people that have died, that are still here, and that are yet to be born. The congregation persists in the radiance of everything everywhere. In each case the question is: How does the life of a form pass through the form of a life? Sometimes the form resides in rebellions and other rituals of reenactment, calling forth what Saidiya Hartman describes as the "revenants of a dismembered past."[25] Sometimes the form is expressed as the passage of gestures surreptitiously hosted: expressions that were theirs are now yours, for a time.[26]

Ngurrara Canvas II, 1997, Sharjah Architecture Triennial, p. 294.
Graphic registration of ancestors: The testimony given by Nanjarn Charlie Nunjun, Nyangarni Penny K-Lyon, Nada Rawlins, and Yukarla Hitler Pamba at the 1992 plenary hearing in Pirnini, Australia. The Warla Jila, a waterhole, is painted as a blue form enclosed by deep green, with a series of white lines radiating out of it. The *jila* is located in the middle of a salt flat; the lines represent the subtle pathways worn into the salt flat by hundreds of years of traffic, as communities converged on the *jila* from the surrounding desert. Still from *Putuparri and the Rainmakers*, directed by Nicole Ma (Madman Films, 2015).

On May 10, 1997, in Pirnini, on the edge of Australia's Great Sandy Desert, forty Indigenous artists assemble around the perimeter of a painting. The canvas lies flat on the rust-colored earth like an iridescent carpet. It has been painted as proof of tenure in a Native Title land claim measuring over 80,000 square kilometers. Standing to one side, near a row of white Toyota Land Cruisers, are representatives of the State and Federal Governments who have travelled to Pirnini to hear the artists' testimony. As the plenary session begins, old men and women walk over to the painting one by one. As their turn to speak arrives, the artists stand on the part they have painted and talk about their country in their own language. The translation of their testimony appears straightforward, consisting of short statements addressed to the tribunal chair and the other artists: "This is my father's country," or "this is my country."[27] They describe their parents, grandparents, and great-grandparents. They name the *jila* (waterholes) depicted in the painting and describe having to work at the cattle stations arranged along the Canning Stock Route. At the conclusion of each person's testimony, there is some applause, until another artist stands to take their place.

If the artists present evidence so that it conforms to the tribunal's understanding of their tradition and origin, the state can, through the delegated authority of the tribunal, elect to grant them title over the land. In other words, to secure *their right* to *their land*, the artists will be asked to dramatize the very thing that white settler society sought to eradicate.[28] Despite being the original inhabitants of this land, despite the state stealing it from them, the state now calls for evidence which it expresses as a series of demands addressed to the artists: *Who are you? Where are you from? Who do you come from?*

But what, in the eyes of the tribunal, counts as evidence of their tradition? How does Fred Chaney (the deputy chair of the Native Title Tribunal) recognize what the painting "says"—if indeed it can be said to speak—beyond the kinds of statements made by the artists as they stand on it? From the perspective of the white settler state, testimony depends on the self-possession of the speaker and the impression of logical consistency in their speech. The state tries to negate the dissipation of the self and the asynchronic time of the dreaming by ordering the witness, by calling the witness to order many selves into one. But here in the desert, the state's call to order becomes porous, the cordon the state tries to tape around the self can't complete the work of enclosure because the painting the cordon surrounds shimmers like a portal between realms, between other bodies standing in other times and other places. The *words* of the artists' answers are diligently recorded by the tribunal's scribe, but the totality of their enunciation confounds documentation and escapes translation. It resounds through their assembly. It ripples through the rounds of shared silence and laughter that pass between them. The forty artists respond to the liberal desire for alterity by making a painting as proof, by testifying on it, by holding the tribunal on country. They convene a polyphony in response to attempted enclosure. That ancestral chorus refuses the evidentiary paradigm to better evidence their own incommensurability—and in that momentous gesture of incomplete presence, which is also a withdrawal, they offer an invitation to white Australia to join them.

For the time being, the artists' ability to pass on social memory has survived the ravages of contact with *kartiya* (white people). Despite the virtuosity of their collective performance and the remarkable legal verdict that stemmed from it, the future is far less certain. Already, the sense of resignation among senior members of the community is hard to shake. Though both struggles for land rights take place in extractivist states, the difference between Chile and Australia is five hundred years of colonialism versus a people that had their first contact with whites in their present lifetimes. During the opening of the Sharjah Architecture Triennial, two desert peoples—the Ngurrara and the Atacameno—met for the first time. The Ngurrara learned that their friends in the Atacama, to prevent the encroachments of copper and lithium mining companies, now depend on satellites and drones. They also depend on archaeologists and anthropologists, who—working from the physical traces of the geoglyphs—attempt to rescue the meaning of their own enigmatic chimeras, now absent in the lived practices and imagination that once lent them sense and connection to the world.

The congregation of the damned is intergenerational resistance under global occupation. Because capitalism is racialized according to extractive processes that convert life worlds to resource zones. Because the destruction of the biosphere occurs through the colonization, subordination, and sacrifice of Black and Brown bodies. Because the basis of that dominance is an endless war against the dead. Therefore what Françoise Vergès describes as the "architectures of the damned" are technologies of uninhabitation. The only thing the architecture of the damned shelters is its porosity to other times and other places, the only thing it encloses is the issue of a call to assembly. Its form is a refrain that entrains life, like a life that entrains form as escape from the occupiers' grasp. Worlds leak through their roofs. Histories tunnel through their walls. Mountains escape plantations.

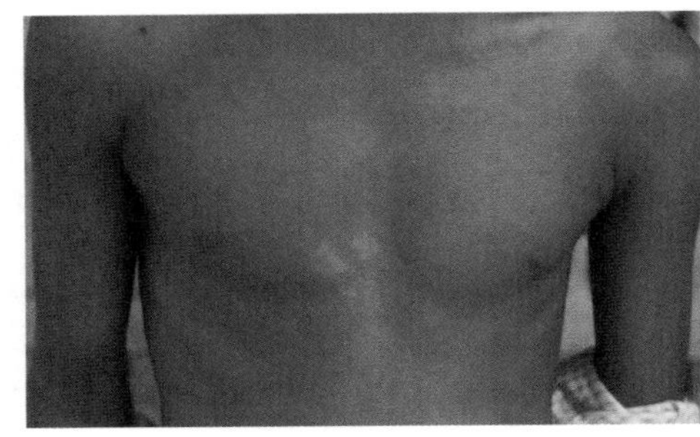

Graphic registration of ancestors: "Hypopigmented macule on chest of an Indian youth who, as a child, said he remembered the life of a man, Maha Ram, who was killed with a shotgun fired at close range. The coroner's report on Maha Ram's death confirms that the wound corresponds to the form of the birthmark." Ian Stevenson, "Birthmarks and Birth Defects Corresponding to Wounds on Deceased Persons," *Journal of Scientific Exploration* 7, no. 4 (1993), p. 405.

In his performance titled *Natq* at the Sharjah Architecture Triennial, Lawrence Abu Hamdan was in dialogue with Yousef Al Jawhary. Born in 1967, but dead by 1984, Al Jawhary, a fighter in the Lebanese Civil War, is now reincarnated in the figure of Bassel Abi Chahine, born only three years after the death of his former self. For Abu Hamdan, Bassel's recounting of his memories as Yousef is *natq*, an Arabic term that describes a form of speech that is "impossible to explain by any means except re-incarnation" because it recalls events that could not have been witnessed any other way. Reincarnation is a form of inheritance where the soul, the memories, or the physical attributes of a deceased person are passed on to another individual at birth. Transmigration, or the passage from a perished body to a newly alive one, can take many years.

The formal cessation of the Lebanese Civil War heralded by the 1989 Taif Accord was followed by the Amnesty Law of 1991, which retroactively exempted combatants from legal responsibility—effectively exonerating them from prosecution for the tortures, rapes, mass murders, forced disappearances, and unlawful detentions committed during the war. Amnesty, derived from the Greek *amnēstía*, indicates forgetfulness, leaving things behind or unmentioned. With respect to justice, forgetting is memory's precondition: we forget, so as to get on with the work of remembering well. Time need be suspended long enough to remedy past wrongs, but not longer, since remembering is what retroactively justifies the injustice of forgetting—and amnesty without transitional justice is just impunity. In the Lebanese State, the post-Taif absolution of combatants was nothing more than a class consolidating its impunity, as the torturers, rapists, and murderers, along with their sponsors and patrons, still hold power. Enacted by those same leaders on behalf of the special status they hold each other in, and in relation to the extreme vulnerability they have produced in the Lebanese people, the amnesty protects and reinforces the walls of impunity that prevent the maimed, the disappeared, and the detained from making claims to justice. In a context absent of truth, dignity, remedy, or reparations, Bassel Abi Chahine's reincarnate testimony tunnels through the walls of impunity that protect criminals from trial.

According to Abu Hamdan, among Lebanon's Druze community every soul transmigrates, but "only a few remember the passage." Importantly, "the more violent, unexpected, and transgressive the death, the more one life's memories leak into the next."[29] Reincarnation is the symptom of the prolongation of suffering, a sign of the return of the disappeared and the displaced. Reincarnation points to the fact that there are intergenerational transmissions of memories that are karmic, traumatic, and aleatory as much as there are blood filiations that are biologically determined, reproductive, and territorial. Reincarnation proposes an alternative order of kinship as inheritance that is transversal, one in which the memory of the other persists in you—*as* you—making you always more than one.

In his 1997 book *Reincarnation and Biology: A Contribution to the Etiology of Birthmarks and Birth Defects*, the psychiatrist Ian Stevenson examined the birthmark as a sign of the persistence of ancestors, and he too suggested that especially traumatic memories act as a kind of trigger for recollection in later lives. Drawing from case studies in Burma, Brazil, Sri Lanka, Thailand, Lebanon, and Nigeria, he suggested that there is a high correlation between the shock to consciousness presented by the moment and the mode of death and the chances of a wound appearing in the next life—as if trauma were able to weave some unknown thread between bodies, each generation passing its encrypted message to the next, who must learn how to decipher it again.

THE PATHLESS BEGGAR

In "a non-world no ancestor will haunt," the congregation inherits an itinerant power.[30] *It deflects language through momentary negations and subjunctive modifications of the master's grammar, like a dissident or vagabond, to make space for equivocation. Equivocation concerns nothing but sense, or what is implicit in the presupposition without being stated, as the expression of a practice of resistance to domination. Errant and uninsured, the call to assembly multiplies sense to loosen the proposition's hold on feelings that exist prior to the naming of feelings or the description of a state of affairs.*

In *The Long Revolution*, Raymond Williams suggests that each generation trains the next according to its own general cultural pattern. In time, the succeeding generation frees itself from this pattern to establish its own. When ancestors have passed, future generations can only recall the past through the documents left behind. For Williams, accessing the past in this way is necessarily limited, since the lives that lent cultural documentation its sense have passed—something he terms "selective tradition." The lines that connect the present to the past are provisional and subject to change, which he describes as a "continual selection and reselection of ancestors." Williams was trying to set out a theory of political change taking place at the very threshold of recognition. Because living and feeling differ generationally, each generation's immersion in its own structure of feeling shapes its interaction with other generations.

Williams's generational structure is ordered and synchronic—affects escape the enclosure of the individual and leak into the social group, in part through the interaction that social group has with its predecessors through "recorded communication that outlives its bearers." The difficulty, however, is knowing what has been left behind, let alone what counts as "cultural." For Williams, the structure of feeling emerges as two or three contemporaneous generational groups select and reselect cultural material from their noncontemporaneous predecessors—but also, more interestingly, through their collective immersion in a structure of feeling. There is something crucial in his proposition, which is the idea of *contagious* feelings and affects that liberate intergenerational transmission from its often neurotic enclosure in notions of individuality or family.[31] The selection and deselection of ancestors is the work of making and unmaking a multiplicity by making and unmaking what "ancestor" means, and therefore what *we* mean.

Williams's promise of selecting ancestors that are not originally—which is to say, not biologically or socially—yours is a potent political concept. But the communion with ancestors that this promises demands more than the synchronic idea of "selection" can provide. Five years after Williams developed the idea of a selective tradition in the *The Long Revolution*, C. L. R. James wrote a text called "The Making of the Caribbean People," which he presented in the summer of 1966 at the Second Montreal Conference on West Indian Affairs. Toward the conclusion of his address, James says: "These are my ancestors; these are my people. They are yours too, if you want them."[32] Fifty-one years later, an echo of Williams's and James's generational refrain returned in the presentation of a document titled "Uluru Statement from The Heart," authored by delegates of Australia's First Nations, which sought to begin a truth-telling process and instate permanent Indigenous representation in Australia's Parliament. Djunga Djunga Yunupingu, a senior Gumatj ceremony man, referred to the document as "a gift for the Australian people. If you want it and if you do recognise it."[33] There could be so much to say about these two qualifiers, these two preconditions: "if you want it" and "if you recognise it." What to make of this intergenerational refrain which is *conditionally* offered as the most profound gift? Our ancestors can be your ancestors, our history and traditions be yours, not according to a logic of exchange but according to a practice of communion in shared struggle with the dead, whose sole guiding principle is decolonization. This call, then, is an invitation of unjustifiable generosity—but being ready to receive the gift entails a reckoning. In her essay in this volume, Houria Bouteldja notes that "while C. L. R. James indeed offers his ancestors, he is careful not to offer 'all' of them—only those who have struggled against slavery. He isn't offering an ideological, ethnic, or biological filiation, but a political, anti-colonial one."[34]

HARRAGA

Everything is a sign of something else waiting to be registered as a trace. The congregation is the dormant mark of the survival of everything that has perished.[35] *The present biosphere is the product of violent extraction from Black and Brown bodies and their lands. The scientific models used to study the etiology of climate involuntarily track the disavowed, postmortem circulation of Black and Brown bodies as changes in the land, the ocean, and the atmosphere. These models introduce something entirely novel into the idea of the future: a rigorous counterfactual, which is to say a permanent reenactment of alternatives for the paths our lives will take and the consequences of choices our lives will make as we move. As such, they are more than a representation of possible futures and possible pasts—they become the remainder through which the present rehearses the possibility of another future and, by doing so, remakes itself.*

Harraga is the Arabic term used to describe the path of migrants leaving the Maghreb. It can be translated as "those who burn." Literally, it refers to the act of destroying or leaving identification documents behind before attempting to cross the Mediterranean. The identification document that is burned is, before anything, a mark of violence. What burns is not a verified name and a photograph—it is a portrait of one's position within a global ordering of incarceration, displacement, and extermination. Even the dead are not spared, as the struggles to identify and repatriate loved ones after death at sea demonstrate. In many instances, identification is impossible, and people remain missing. But the nonidentified body is still a body, even in its decomposition, in its multiplication, and its dilution in the sea. The body as environmental concentration confounds mourning insofar as mourning depends on "knowing whose body it really is and what place it occupies."[36] The violence of *not knowing what, or who, or where, or how*, of being unable to locate, identify, repatriate, or bury the dead might mark the extinction of both the mourner and the mourned. Like the disidentification of the passport's ritual destruction, the nonidentification of the dead sanctifies the environment according to what Walid Sadek describes as the labor of the missing. In turn, this

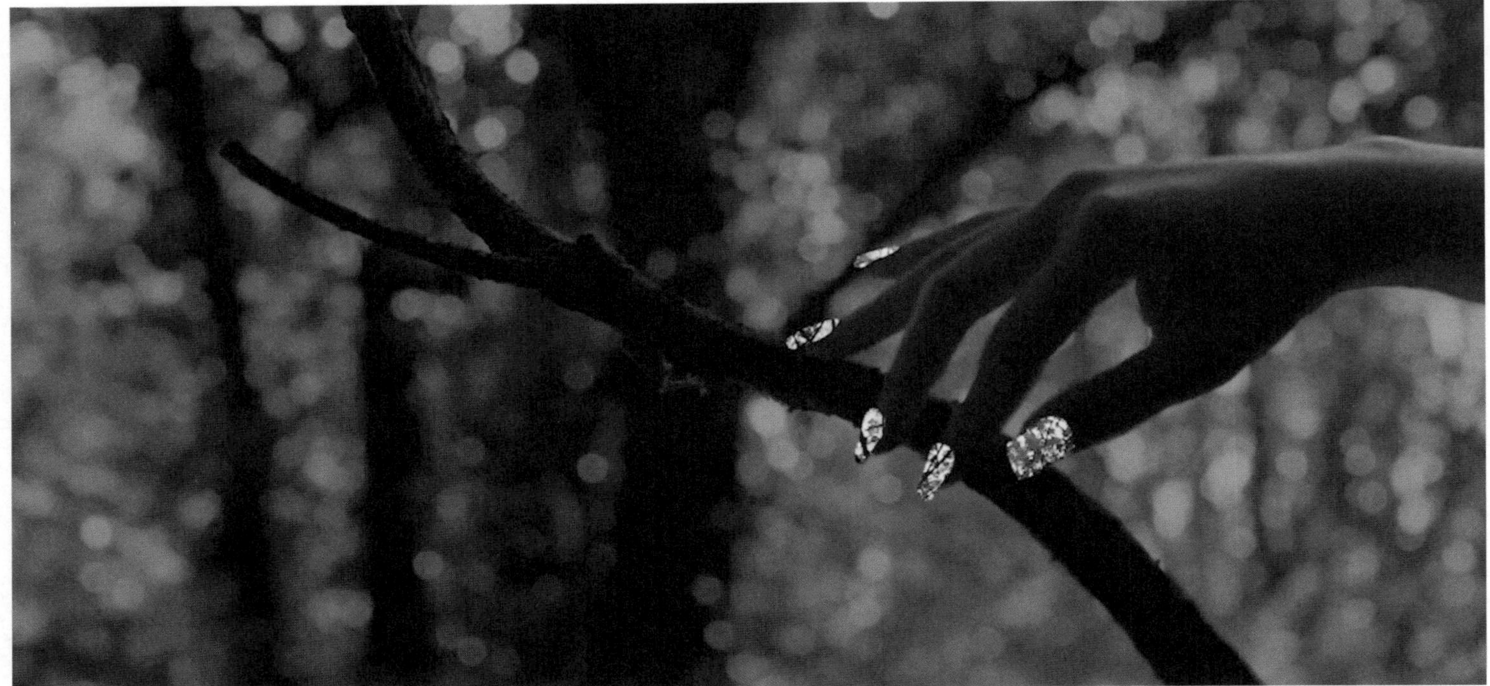

The Otolith Group, *Infinity minus Infinity*, 2019, Sharjah Architecture Triennial, p. 266.
Images courtesy of the artists. In the opening scene, a hand strokes a tree branch. The fingernails are painted green, and chroma-keyed in postproduction to be replaced by footage from another shot. In film, the sequential ordering of scenes moves forward and backward in time through montage. Montage retains the unity of the scene within a continuous temporal order. *Infinity minus Infinity* points to a copresence of different times and spaces through the generalization of the idea of a screen as portal, one that registers on the surface of objects already in the frame.

labor intensifies environmental relations according to a power of alliance that confounds simplistic notions of identity and place.[37]

The fantasy of some fundamental discontinuity between the past and present of racial colonial subjugation depends on separating the resource as extracted from the resource as transformed. In her essay "Ancestral Claims," Denise Ferreira da Silva states that greenhouse gases are the present expression of the energy expropriated from human bodies and the earth. Past expropriation persists in present circulation.[38] The *longue durée* of power expropriated from bodies marks, in the energetic register, what Christina Sharpe's notion of "residence time" marks in the physiochemical one.[39] Residence time names the persistence in oceans of the traces of bodies drowned in the Middle Passage and the Mediterranean, measured in millions of years. Sharpe and Ferreira da Silva invite us to disfigure loss around historical trauma as environmental persistence. Both recall, though in an inverted form, the short story by Italo Calvino titled "Blood, Sea." Calvino's story takes the form of a dialogue between blood cells separated into bodies that are travelling in a car on an excursion through the Italian Alps. He writes:

> The conditions that obtained when life had not yet emerged from the oceans have not subsequently changed a great deal for the cells of the human body, bathed by the primordial wave which continues to flow in the arteries. Our blood in fact has a chemical composition analogous to that of the sea of our origins.[40]

The private sea we have inside was once outside, because the blood we carry used to be shared ocean. Calvino suggests that this is the chemi-

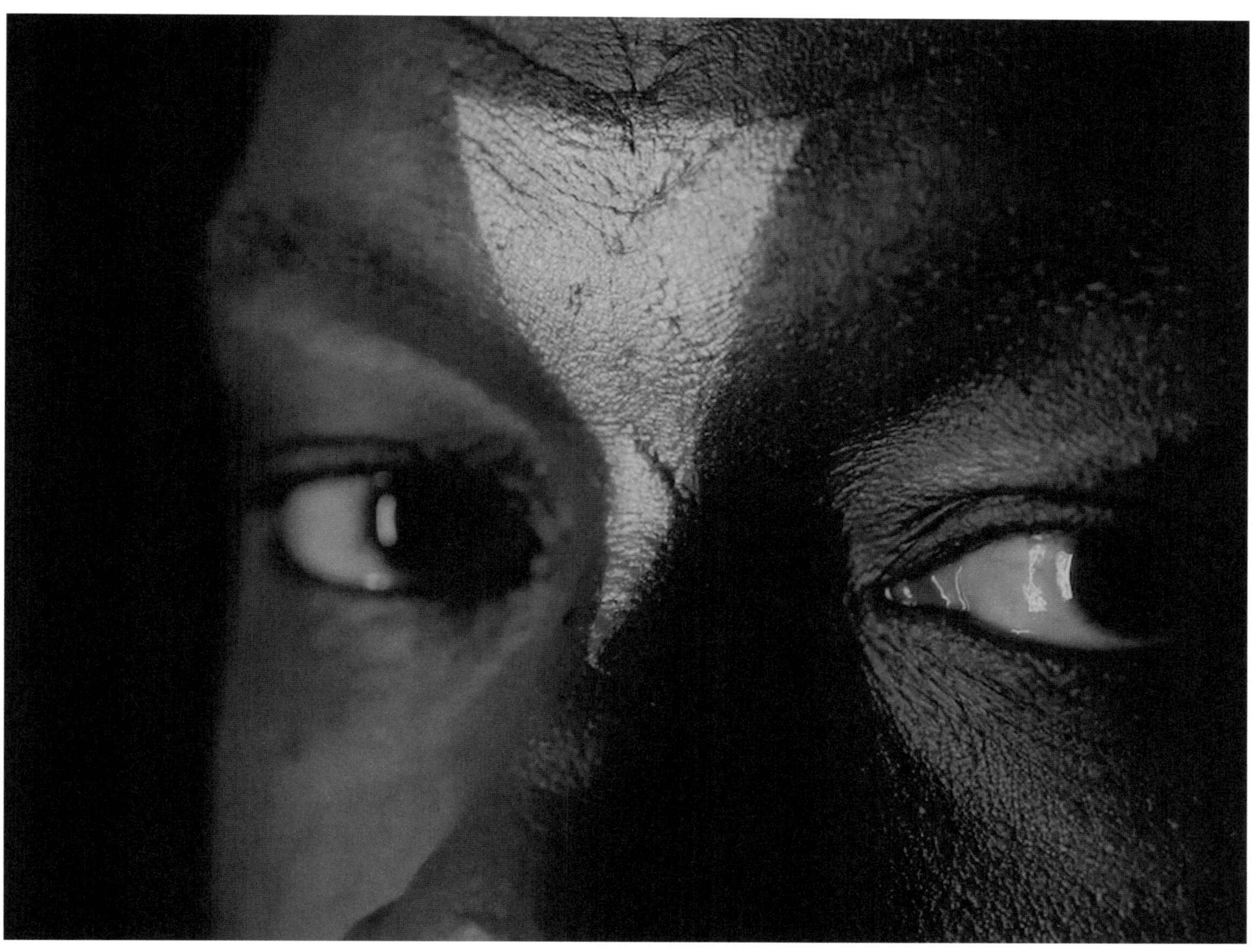

The Ajna or "third eye," here marked by a luminous triangle, acts as one of the trans-temporal portals in the film. Associated with enlightenment and precognition, the third eye holds different dimensions in co-existence, bypassing communication in a strictly aural or visual register and creating the possibility of anachronic diegesis where multiple scenes coexist in a single frame.

cal evolutionary basis for our longing for intimacy. The ocean grieves its separation into individual bodies. If, for Sharpe, seawater is a vector for the corrosion and decomposition of bodies which spans millions of years, for Calvino it is the primordial basis for human blood—in an evolutionary arc also spanning millions of years, but in the opposite direction. The presence of primeval oceans in human blood is recounted as the privatization of a communal inheritance, the violent separation of an original plenitude. "Blood, Sea" therefore refers to the conjunction of two liquid signs. Blood (locked within individual bodies) stands in for the purity of the filial line, while sea represents a primordial sociality: "All blood would finally be our blood."[41] At the story's conclusion, there is a violent car accident. Blood from each body spills out of its owner onto the road, reunited again in the crumpled metal.

The language of the triumphant is as different from the language of the conquered as the living's from the dead's. But whoever aims to rescue the dead from their purgatory in oceans and ash, ice cores and soil, must first be ready to receive them as the basis of their own survival. The readiness to receive someone's ancestors is *environmental relation as anticolonial struggle*. The struggle begins with an acknowledgment of the multiple forms these relations take and a

Samaneh Moafi with WORKNOT!, Mhamad Safa, Maria Bessarabova, Platform 28, and residents of Mehr in Dowlatabad, Esfahan, *Parable of Mehr*, 2019, Sharjah Architecture Triennial, p. 282.
The project proposes a series of interventions in the lifeworld of the Mehr, a public housing project for more than two million families in Iran initiated by the government of Mahmoud Ahmadinejad. Through modifications in domestic layout, furnishings, cooking utensils, and lighting, new opportunities for collective, homosocial solidarity are created around shared rituals. Alongside these interventions, a social-media communication strategy deploys aural, visual, and rhythmic elements to link and coordinate new activities across the territory of Mehr. Photo by Marco Cappelletti.

permanent state of equivocation in regard to the differences between them as an ethical-political project.

The Sharjah Architecture Triennial's inclusion of devotional sonic practices like Al Ahly Thikr Jamaah, the Mazaher ensemble, and Dewa Alit and Gamelan Salukat presented a call to assembly as the art of receiving, selecting, and reselecting ancestors. It could be found in Kelman Duran's sampling of Big Rube's verse in "Liberation": "And the ground is dry / But the roots are strong, so some survive." It was in the twin suns of the Otolith Group's *O Horizon* and the Mleiha Fort in the Sharjah desert, or the affirmation of gathering under a solitary tree as the site of study. Sometimes it's just a frequency, the particular intensity of a yellow or a green, a pathway in the desert, a cord in a hand, a birthmark on your skin, or maybe just a joint in a wooden floor. Calling the congregation to assembly is a process of constituting refrains through our bodies and imagination in our environment. The Triennial was an attempt to embody, in the curation, setting, content, and political economy of the exhibition— that is to say, in its environment and the bodies and objects within it—forms of solidarity with the dead able to shake the very idea of a future and a generation, making a chronological error out of the former, and a noncontemporaneous alliance out of the latter. In saving the dead and the missing from inexorable oblivion, perhaps the living do not only translate between incommensurable languages, but also embody and incorporate the past

Godofredo Pereira, *Ex-humus*, 2019, Sharjah Architecture Triennial, p. 309.
The performance explores the history of political exhumations in Latin America in terms of disputes over resources, extractivism, and the disempowerment of the dead. Pereira writes: "If the dead are the true owners of the land, could it be because they are in continuity with the soil, the rivers, the trees. After all, it is under the ground where roots grow making common cause across the living and the non-living, and if so we need to care for the dead because environments speak through them, we need to care for the dead because our ancestors are not only of the past but also of the future and we need to care for the dead because their voice is the song of the revolutions to come." Photo by Talie Eigeland.

in a process of ongoing reenactment. Reenactment liberates the past's expression in the present as the retroactive effect of a sign's reception. In that action, the congregation is called to assembly as the invention of the person or thing that sends the sign and the person or thing able to receive that sign. And those signs are everywhere. They are everything. The congregation of the damned is unbounded because there is no a priori limit on what might in the future be received, no limit on what might, therefore, be retroactively produced as the past's gift to the future. "These are my ancestors; these are my people. They are yours too, if you want them."

Bouchra Ouizguen, *Corbeaux*, 2014–2019, Sharjah Architecture Triennial, p. 310.
A horde of women dressed in black moves around in silence, before their shrieks and jerking make all notions of time and space disappear. Drawing on Persian literature from the ninth and twelfth centuries, Ouizguen's interest is for an era when the figure of the madman or madwoman had its place in the community. Memories of long nights of trance are summoned up via moving figures, imbibed with the Isawa and Hmadcha rituals of the Marrakech regions. Photo by Talie Eigeland.

Adrian Lahoud was the curator of the Sharjah Architecture Triennial 2019, titled *Rights of Future Generations*. Focusing on the Middle East and Africa, his work critically examines concepts of scale and shelter in architecture in light of emancipatory urban and environmental struggles. He is dean of the School of Architecture at the Royal College of Art, London.

This essay is indebted to conversations with too many people to name, but especially to Lawrence Abu Hamdan, Hoor Al Qasimi, Andrea Bagnato, Alonso Barros, Kodwo Eshun, Denise Ferreira da Silva, Charles Heller, Valerio Massaro, Moad Musbahi, Edwin Nasr, Ngurrara Artists and community, Godofredo Pereira, Gonzalo Pimentel, Jasbir K. Puar, Dread Scott, Paulo Tavares, Anjali Sagar, Gayatri Spivak, David Wengrow, and Kasia Wlaszczyk.

1 Homi K. Bhabha, *The Location of Culture* (New York, 1995), p. 139.

2 "If so, then there is a secret agreement between past generations and the present one. Then our coming was expected on earth." Walter Benjamin, "On the Concept of History," in *Selected Writings: Volume 4, 1938–1940* (Cambridge, MA, 2006), p. 390.

3 Christine Helliwell, "Good Walls Make Bad Neighbours: The Dayak Longhouse as a Community of Voices," *Oceania* 62, no. 3 (1992).

4 See Peter Metcalf, *The Life of the Longhouse: An Archaeology of Ethnicity* (Cambridge, 2010).

5 Helliwell, "Good Walls Make Bad Neighbours."

6 In the main exhibition at the 2014 Venice Biennial of Architecture, Rem Koolhaas famously identified fifteen "elements of architecture."

7 "Anthropology is not a discipline that studies exotic human societies; it is rather one that accepts no other scientific tool than the capacity of the subject of science to embrace ways of feelings, thinking, and acting that first seemed completely unacceptable to her . . . Otherness is not the object of anthropology; it is its instrument." Patrice Maniglier, "Anthropological Meditations: Discourse on Comparative Method," in Pierre Charbonnier, ed., *Comparative Metaphysics: Ontology after Anthropology* (London, 2017), p. 110.

8 See Ghassan Hage, *The Diasporic Condition: Ethnographic Explorations of the Lebanese in the World* (Chicago, 2021).

9 Dread Scott, in conversation with Adrian Lahoud and Lawrence Abu Hamdan, Ashkal Alwan, Beirut, 2021.

10 "The movement from the present to the past—metalepsis strictly speaking—as, for example, in having the present be an effect of a past cause or an answer to a past claim or need, necessarily involves a parallel prolepsis—what I will call a metaleptic prolepsis—wherein one moves from the past back to the present: the past anticipated its effect, response or fulfilment in a present, a present which was 'future' for it, but is present now." Timothy Bahti, "History as Rhetorical Enactment: Walter Benjamin's Theses 'On the Concept of History,'" *Diacritics* 9, no. 3 (1979).

11 See Stefano Harney, Fred Moten, *All Incomplete* (Colchester, 2021).

12 Gilles Deleuze, *The Logic of Sense* (New York, 1997), p. 237.

13 Hannah Landecker, "Food as Exposure: Nutritional Epigenetics and the New Metabolism," *BioSocieties* 6, no. 2 (2011).

14 Ariella Aïsha Azoulay, "Open Letter to Sylvia Wynter: Unlearning the Disappearance of Jews from Africa," *The Funambulist* 30 (June 2020).

15 Alain Pottage, "Our Original Inheritance," in Martha Mundy, Alain Pottage, eds., *Law, Anthropology, and the Constitution of the Social: Making Persons and Things* (Cambridge, UK, 2009).

16 Jennifer L. Morgan, "*Partus sequitur ventrem*: Law, Race, and Reproduction in Colonial Slavery," *Small Axe* 22, no. 1 (2018).

17 Hortense Spillers, "Mama's Baby, Papa's Maybe: An American Grammar Book," *Diacritics* 17, no. 2 (1987).

18 "Bringing Them Home: Report of the National Inquiry into the Separation of Aboriginal and Torres Strait Islander Children from Their Families," Australian Human Rights Commission (1997), p. 10, https://humanrights.gov.au/our-work/bringing-them-home-report-1997.

19 Diego de Landa, *Relación de las Cosas de Yucatán* (Mexico City, 1986), pp. 31–32.

20 See for example Shoehi Sato, "Operation Legacy: Britain's Destruction and Concealment of Colonial Records Worldwide," *Journal of Imperial and Commonwealth History* 45, no. 4 (2017).

21 Dionne Brand, *A Map to the Door of No Return: Notes to Belonging* (Toronto, 2011), p. 61.

22 David Scott, "The Temporality of Generations: Dialogue, Tradition, Criticism," *New Literary History* 45, no. 2 (2014).

23 Jurg Wassmann, "The Politics of Religious Secrecy," in Alan Rumsey, James F. Weiner, eds., *Emplaced Myth: Space, Narrative, and Knowledge in Aboriginal Australia and Papua New Guinea* (Honolulu, 2001), p. 54; Carlo Severi, *The Chimera Principle: An Anthropology of Memory and Imagination* (Chicago, 2015), p. 75.

24 Matthew Spellberg, "On Dream Sharing and Its Purpose," *Cabinet* 67 (Spring 2019–Winter 2020).

25 Saidiya Hartman, *Scenes of Subjection: Terror, Slavery, and Self-making in Nineteenth Century America* (Oxford, 1997), p. 72.

26 "The ruins, which are small rituals, aren't absent but surreptitious, a range of songful scaring, when people give a sign, shake a hand." Moten, Harney, *All Incomplete*, p. 46.

27 *Putuparri and the Rainmakers*, directed by Nicole Ma (Madman Films, 2015).

28 See Elizabeth Povinelli, *The Cunning of Recognition: Indigenous Alterities and the Making of Australian Multiculturalism* (Durham, 2002).

29 Lawrence Abu Hamdan, *Natq*, performance at Sharjah Architecture Triennial, November 10, 2019.

30 Édouard Glissant, *Poetics of Relation* (Ann Arbor, 1997), p. 37.

31 "Contagions are autonomous, unregulated, their vicissitudes only peripherally anchored by knowable entities. They invoke the language of infection and transmission, forcing us to ask, how does one catch something whose trace is inchoate or barely discerned? . . . Contagions thus complicate even the most complex articulations of affiliation; that is, contagion returns the process of affiliation to indeterminacy and contingency." Jasbir K. Puar, *Terrorist Assemblages: Homonationalism in Queer Times* (Durham, 2007), p. 172.

32 C. L. R. James, *Spheres of Existence: Selected Writings* (London, 1980), p. 191

33 Helen Davidson, "Garma Festival: Indigenous Sovereignty Would Be a Gift for all Australians," *The Guardian*, August 3, 2018, https://www.theguardian.com/australia-news/2018/aug/04/garma-festival-indigenous-sovereignty-would-be-a-gift-for-all-australians.

34 Houria Bouteldja, p. 72 of the present volume.

35 Amade M'charek, "Harraga: Burning Borders, Navigating Colonialism," *The Sociological Review* 68, no. 2 (2020).

36 Jacques Derrida, *Specters of Marx: The State of the Debt, the Work of Mourning and the New International* (New York, 2006), p. 10.

37 See Godofredo Pereira's ongoing project "Ex-humus" on the animating power of dispute over identity or cause of death in processes of exhumation.

38 Denise Ferreira da Silva, p. 176 of the present volume.

39 Christina Sharpe, *In the Wake: On Blackness and Being* (Durham, 2016), p. 41.

40 Italo Calvino, "Blood, Sea," in *t zero* (New York, 1969), p. 39.

41 "Thus the native discovers that his life, his breath, his beating heart are the same as those of the settler." Frantz Fanon, *The Wretched of the Earth* (New York, 1963), p. 45.

Breathing Exercises

Françoise Vergès

How can we convey the precarity, fragility, and vulnerability of human life and of the conditions that support human life—the purity of air and water, care and tenderness, transmission and memory, light and shade, habitat, refuge and security, a place to lay one's head, dreams, love, to nourish and be nourished—while avoiding the ideology of protectionism that ends up policing poor and non-white communities, increasing incarceration and imperialism? How can we imagine an antiracist, feminist, and decolonial politics of protection that takes into account precarity, fragility, and vulnerability? How can we protect the right to breathe, which Achille Mbembe describes as a "universal right?"[1] How do we repair a damaged planet, maltreated by centuries of colonialism and racial capitalism, founded on the promethean promise of man's total mastery over the biosphere? Antislavery, anti-racist, decolonial, feminist, indigenous, and abolitionist approaches to teaching and learning have amassed a library of strategies for social organization and intergenerational transmission. It is an incomplete library as strong and relentless as the preceding colonial effort to erase voices and words. One of the first aims of these pedagogies is to teach us how to unlearn the learned alienation from ourselves and our surroundings, the alienation that trains us to approach the world as made of objects to manipulate and discard. It drills into our minds an ideology of mastery over the world and instills the promethean promise that man's destiny is to extract from and exhaust both humans and the earth. The pedagogies in this library propose an ethics of protection that encompasses all aspects of human life and opposes the power and monopoly given to the institutions of the liberal patriarchal and militarized state not only to protect, but also to educate. The state has monopolized the politics and practices of protection through walls, borders, laws, and police, while fabricating through the very same instruments ever greater vulnerability and precarity to disease, poverty, pollution, exploitation. It has fabricated the right to intrude in family life, to disrupt kinship, to arrest, and imprison.

The intertwined logics of monocultures and mining, segregating architecture, and authoritarian schooling have constructed a toxic entanglement of racism, sexism, and exploitation. The interruption of intergenerational forms of living and transmission has been central to the state's strategies of isolation and separation. Against these assaults, peoples of color have developed pedagogies of unlearning to preserve intergenerational transmission and to keep the power of imagination alive.

Unlearning as a strategy to protect future generations from colonial destruction includes: rituals that allow an individual to reenter the community through welcoming and renaming; ceremonies of cleansing; caring practices for trauma, for depression, for physical and psychic wounds. "We revolt because we can't breathe," Frantz Fanon wrote.[2] We can't breathe because the air is made irrespirable, because racism makes the air poisonous. If to be born human is to be born vulnerable, in need of care and protection to overcome contingency and precarity, racial/patriarchal capitalism transforms these conditions into fragilities that threaten the very possibility of life, of breathing. Breathing is not equally distributed; it is not a given; lungs can be damaged at birth. Decoloniality as an exercise teaches us how to remove the poison from our minds and bodies, to train our lungs to survive, so that we can revolt.

Ibiye Camp with Emmy Bacharach and David Killingsworth, *The Sacred Forests of Ethiopia*, p. 269.

Decolonial answers make a force out of instability and root themselves in the fragile and the ephemeral in order to transmit the sources of resistance needed to imagine a future. But libraries have been burned, objects have been looted, tongues have been cut, graves desecrated, cities erased from the Earth. If mourning has become a familiar state of mind, there are still traces, fragments of the knowledge preserved through manual and oral memory.

The 2019 Sharjah Architecture Triennial presented an architecture of the damned. Be it the moving habitat that developed on the *chars* of Bangladesh—islands that emerge then disappear at the will and whim of the Padma, Meghna, and Jamuna Rivers—be it the thousands of geoglyphs that trace ritual paths in the deserts of northern Chile, the sacred forests of Ethiopia, or the maps of Aboriginal land, they add to the library of knowledge and teaching that mixes words, rituals, songs, signs, and communal history and memory. The architecture of the damned demonstrates that there is no manual work without a theory, without a philosophy of making, without abstract thought. Its library provides alternative epistemologies to those that have been recognized as knowledge by the elites. It contains what has been hidden from the colonizer's ravenous gaze and has to be deciphered and recovered—texts and words that were seen as nonsense or babbling by colonizers, songs that were heard as noise, rituals that were described as backward, objects that were seen as coarse and without beauty. While contradictions exist (resulting from intergenerational and gendered conflicts or differences in status), refusing domination and the search for a collective resolution are a constant effort.

"We couldn't mention the name of someone else's country because we come from another place, from [a] different country. That is really the Aboriginal way of respecting copyright. It means that you can't steal the stories or songs or dances from other places," the Aboriginal artist Tommy May said to explain how the Ngurrara communities constructed the *Ngurrara Canvas*. He adds: "We can't show white people everything. If you tell everybody, it is like selling your country. You can give a little bit, but not too much."[3] These regimes of visibility and invisibility, dissimulation and unveiling, eschewal and juxtaposition, of construction through straw and stone, and of sharing space with respect for the other, offer a grammar of knowledge and rights (to speak, to act, to intervene) that predate rights as they have been understood by the West, with its requirement of embracing abstract individualism (the one performed by the white male property owner). Decolonial strategies developed around truth and dissimulation, transparency and opacity, the half-said/half-unsaid rhetoric, the pretense of not understanding what was said or done while listening or looking closely to turn the colonizer's weapons back on himself.

The gestures of offering a glass of water, tea or coffee, food and refuge weave a social world where words are not necessary. These are the gestures currently criminalized by European states in the name of protecting the nation from foreigners. If war has always meant that keeping one's door open is no longer possible, colonialism has normalized entering people's homes without being invited—with the argument that they need to be civilized. Most cultures see in this entitlement the embodiment of what Aimé Césaire called the *ensauvagement* of Europe, the process whereby "colonization works to decivilize the colonizer, to brutalize him in the true sense of the world, to degrade him, to awaken him to buried instincts, to covetousness, violence, race hatred and relativism."[4] In Kanaky-New Caledonia, Kanaks observed that French settlers never considered that they had to "do the custom" (*faire la coutume*), to execute precise rites that carry precise names—*doing* being central because it entails an active performance of a series of acts essential to enter the Kanak world. Gifts, the most important of which are traditionally coins and yams, allowed the exchange of words.

The recognition of precarity and vulnerability as an ethics of protection must be distinguished from their implementation on a global scale. Ruth Wilson Gilmore's powerful summary of racial capitalism as the production of a "group-differentiated vulnerability to premature death" brings to light how much death is conditioned by the joint brutality of racial capitalism, heteronormativity, legacies of slavery, colonialism, and capitalism.[5] Precarity and vulnerability were made into instruments of domination through obedience and subordination.[6] The world of slavery was a world of social and premature death, and postslavery colonialism has extended that model to the present day. Groups, communities, and peoples continue to be made vulnerable to premature death, as they are deprived of clean water, clean air, decent housing, access to good education and health services, forced to work until their bodies are exhausted, dying much earlier than the bourgeois male and female bodies. Neoliberalism and hyperconsumption have accentuated and normalized precarization.

Though, as we conceptualize contingency, "the possibility arises at the same time of being able to leave and start something new:

the potentiality of exodus and constituting," we shouldn't ignore the conditions and forces that transform this contingency into an accrued exposure to premature death.[7] For migrants, refugees, populations living in camps or war zones, women confronted to femicide in their everyday lives, children whose childhood status is denied, the homeless, the poor, the racialized, Black, and indigenous peoples, to leave and start anew constitutes an inherent condition of their existence, a condition framed by brutality and violence. Leaving and starting anew cease to become choices. Confronted with an increased fabrication of vulnerability, we must turn to the responses and strategies by communities under assault to avoid a feeling of impotence and total dispossession. The very possibility of "future generations" rests on this undying power of resistance. The word may sound hollow, since it has been commodified, but we need to remind ourselves that, in the darkness of oppression, there are always voices that say: "One day, we will be free!"

Alonso Barros, Gonzalo Pimentel, Juan Gili, and Mauricio Hidalgo, *The Atacama Lines*, p. 276.

NOT TO BREATHE

We live in times of house arrests, of racial and identity-based profiling, of calls for soil and blood. And in these times, to be able to breathe has become the exigency around which calls for justice, equality, dignity, and respect for life have coalesced. Never has the act of breathing *in itself* been so much at the forefront of anti-racist movements as a call to change the way we inhabit the Earth—Black Lives Matter, Palestinian Lives Matter, Mexican feminists, indigenous fights for land, Afro-Brazilian feminists. From the United States to Palestine, France to Brazil, South Africa to India, and Australia to Kenya, deaths are accumulating, as a result of police officers who squeeze the lungs of those they arrest until they exhale their last breaths. The planetary dimension of suffocation reveals that, as described by Mbembe, "In its dank underbelly, modernity has been an interminable war on life," and that "all these wars on life begin by taking away breath."[8]

To prevent someone from breathing is at once an act that aims to silence and to kill. The inability to breathe describes the suffocating and asphyxiating atmosphere imposed by slavery, colonialism, and police states, as well as the act of killing itself. In *Plantation Memories: Episodes of Everyday Racism,* Grada Kilomba engages in an analysis of the muzzle that was imposed by slave owners on enslaved subjects: "The mask sealing the mouth of the Black subject prevents the white master from listening to those late truths she/he wants to turn away, 'keep at distance,' at the margins, unnoticed and quiet."[9] Voices eventually elevate from the mask; they break forms of political suffocation with a sharp edge. To prevent one from breathing is also a weapon of torture and death. Gas chambers, waterboarding, tear gas—they are all conceived and deployed so that people are deprived

Ngurrara Canvas II, p. 294.

of air. Security forces across the world, which have never been so well protected and armed, are more than ever imbued with the imperative to injure, maim, kill, and rape as quickly as possible. In addition to water trucks, grenades, live or rubber bullets aimed at the chest, eye, face, and hand, and other military technologies of pacification, we are now faced with the image of an indifferent police officer who, live on camera and throughout a painful duration, is resting his knee on George Floyd's neck.

TO SUFFOCATE

Throughout 2019 and the first months of 2020, huge fires ravaged California, Amazonia, Central Africa, and Australia, sending ash clouds for miles around and into distant mountain peaks, obscuring the sky and the sun, and covering trees and soil. High flames devoured everything in their path. The lands became ashen and silent. When we learned on April 3, 2020, as the COVID-19 pandemic was already spreading across the world, that the fires ravaging the Chernobyl region were not sparing the exclusion zone around the former nuclear plant, we had the feeling that a terrible misfortune was awaiting us, and that we would not be able to escape it. Literature is often more able to evoke the inevitable consequences of this all-consuming drive for human domination than reports from experts. In *The Emissary,* novelist Yoko Tawada tells the story of a century-old writer, Yoshiro, and his teenage great-grandson, Mumei, to evoke the terrible ramifications of an environmental catastrophe whose origins remain unexplained. Japan's children no longer survive infancy, they have difficulty breathing; they are helpless and must be protected by the older generation such as Yoshiro's, who seem to be bestowed with eternal life. Each day sees the children's life expectancy shorten—eating an orange is a mortal danger. It is a world where all certainty—geographic, social, geological, or biological—has disappeared. Nothing can be taken for granted: Tokyo's climate goes from scorching to freezing in a matter of seconds. Even death is no longer guaranteed. If the elderly cannot die, death is no longer a moment of transforming the dead into ancestors, and the concept of future generations is erased. An ecological catastrophe has interrupted intergenerational transmission.

The economy of suffocation means the destruction of both planetary and human lungs. The legacies of the 1956 mercury poisoning in Minamata, Japan, of Agent Orange sprayed over Vietnam between 1961 and 1971, and the 1984 explosion of the Union Carbide pesticide plant in Bhopal, India, are just three examples of catastrophes made by twentieth-century racial capitalism.

If greed and predation were the driving forces of European capitalism and colonization—during the slave trade and in its postslavery configuration—they are now more than ever at the foundation of an economy that theorist and activist Sayak Valencia qualifies as "gore capitalism." She defines it as follows: "Gore capitalism refers to the undisguised and unjustified bloodshed that is the price the Third World pays for adhering to the increasingly demanding logic of capitalism. It refers to the many instances of dismembering and disembowelment, often tied up with organized crime, gender and the predatory use of bodies. In general, this term posits these incredibly brutal kinds of violence as tools of necro-empowerment."[10] Violence is the systemic and structural basis of racial capitalism and patriarchy—though, as Jasbir Puar has shown, we should speak of *violences* rather than *violence,* as there are forms and gradations within violence. Their grouping under the encompassing term "violence" leads to abstraction; it naturalizes violence and prevents the analysis of the multiple ways through which the state disables bodies. To Puar, the liberal answers to violence reinscribes the disabled body in an individualistic discourse and practice—resilience, repairing the body to erase the sources and causes of violences.[11]

Thus, when nationalist forces speak of "protectionism," we translate and hear "racism." Femicides, assassinations of indigenous activists, violence against the elderly and children, or police violence are nowhere near diminishing. While these actions differ from one country to another, it is clear that inequalities and injustices have considerably worsened, contributing to the conditions of precarity produced by the globalization of capitalism and its racist structures. Such forms of violence have shed a bright light on the fact that governments have historically differentiated between those who benefit from social protection and continue to enjoy this privilege and those who, having been framed as disposable, as resistant to "normal living" by their very nature, are now not only exposed to the virus, but also continue to be criminalized for their behavior.

TO CONTAMINATE

The COVID-19 pandemic was a foretold disaster. We quickly understood we were living not only a sanitary crisis, but also a political and historical moment, which was by no means due to chance. The term *crisis* itself must be used with caution. COVID-19 became a global disaster when Western populations became affected and deaths among its populations ran into the thousands. We can bet that if the pandemic had ravaged Haiti, Syria, or Congo, for instance, the narrative of a "global crisis" would have been muted. For decades, scientists have alerted governments to the risks posed by the proliferation of zoonoses leading to interspecies transmissions, by the increase in conditions favoring infectious diseases, and by the defunding of research into these diseases. Neoliberal racial capitalism has led us to the edge of the abyss—rising seas, melting glaciers, devastating cyclones, droughts, and floods, polluted air and water—all the while instituting and legislating violence. Under its laws, breathing has become a class and racial privilege, and there are now more premature deaths in the world from air pollution than from any other cause. Hurricane Katrina in 2005, the women burned alive at Rana Plaza in 2013, the lands and racialized communities devastated by chlordecone in the West Indies, by the gold industry in Guyana, the nickel industry in Kanaky, the extraction of uranium in Niger, of cobalt in Congo, the mines in South America, Australia, Madagascar: the causes and consequences of these disasters have been covered by state lies and corporate impunity. This brings to light a *posthuman* condition (Western philosophers have conceptualized it as a postmodern condition, but in fact it was produced by European modernity). The measures taken by governments to reduce contamination have shown again that protection from disease and maiming is not a universal right. Not only has the death rate from COVID-19 been higher among poor and racialized communities—Black, indigenous, migrant, refugee, and imprisoned populations—because they do not have easy access to care, do not have medical coverage, or suffer from high rates of comorbidity, but also because their jobs put them at greater risk. The history of colonialism and pandemics, of science and racialization, shows that socioeconomic conditions structure biological ones.

In the Global South, peoples have a deep understanding of why and how racial capitalism has brought epidemics. They have seen how casually Europeans used chemicals in the soils, injected viruses into Black and indigenous populations, and practiced forced sterilizations and abortions on women of color. I often think that H. G. Wells's *Island of Doctor Moreau,* in which a mad scientist experiments to create human-like hybrid beings from animals via vivisection, can be read as a leading text of promethean mastery. I am from Réunion Island, where, from 2005 to 2006, the Chikungunya epidemic (a virus carried by mosquitoes) affected close to 40% of the population and led to 300 deaths. Among the casualties, we should also count those who became disabled, and the impact on plants and the soil following the spraying of pesticides. Though the first cases appeared in February 2005, the French State refused to take the epidemic seriously, claiming that the following winter would beat the virus, and that it was the population's lack of hygiene that explained the high rate of contamination.

The Chikungunya epidemic demonstrated the links between deforestation in the countries of the Indian Ocean Rim, the multiplication of zoonoses produced by neoliberalism, hyperconsumption, and tourism, the weakening of public health services as a result of imposed austerity measures, medical research focused on diseases affecting white men in the north, and governmental contempt. The high rate of mortality was explained by the prevalence of comorbidity (diabetes, hypertension, obesity) among the population of Réunion, illnesses which are directly linked to poverty, racism, and coloniality. The government applied drastic and brutal measures, asking the army to spread insecticides in gardens and streets. Afterward, the inhabitants reported that they stopped seeing butterflies, birds, and chameleons in their gardens, and that they suffered from migraines and allergies.

When world governments announced measures to stop COVID-19, I was not surprised to see the police given greater prerogatives to control racialized communities—those forced to go to work because they fulfill the essential functions for bourgeois society to continue as usual (cleaning, caring, delivering, transporting, etc.). It was no surprise either to see impoverishment and hunger spread while the circulation of goods to maintain a certain standard of living had to continue. The clauses of the racial contract and the sexual contract were visible to all those who wanted to see.

TO INHABIT

If no one can justify denying the peoples of the Global South access to technologies which have long facilitated the lives of societies in the Global North—a reality exacerbated by inequalities and injustices that were produced historically in order to maintain relationships of dependence—the fact remains that the present situation requires no less than an imaginative leap on a planetary level. To ask oneself questions pertaining to the rights of future generations, when the notion of the future itself is being put to the test, demands we rid ourselves of binary thinking and promethean illusions. It instead suggests a pedagogy of transmission, repetition, and imitation that—as any parent will testify—is anchored in the human condition. It suggests crafts where the apprentice will learn to look, smell, touch, taste, until the hand, the ear, the eye, the nose acquire a memory of the gesture: when workers no longer need to look into their box of bolts because their fingers recognize the one they need; when sailors and *dhow* captains locate currents through the color of the sea; when women are able to grow vegetables in the desert by retracing the paths of undercurrents of water in the sand or knit without looking at their fingers. These pedagogies nourish a theory where the gesture is not foreign to the thought and therefore encourage us to imagine a decolonized and anti-racist theory of environmental and reproductive justice, of the rights of indigenous peoples, of queer and trans people, and of vulnerability and fragility. As a little girl, I spent a lot of time in the kitchen offering my help for any kind of small work: sorting rice, lentils, and beans, cleaning salads and herbs, crushing ginger and garlic, slicing onions and tomatoes—anything that allowed me to stay in the kitchen. I was fascinated by the process whereby meat, vegetables, and spices would acquire a specific color, shape, smell, and taste. But when I was asking the woman who cooked when to add onions, turmeric, or tomatoes, for instance, she always answered, "You look and you see." She never said, "After two minutes, when the onions are brown," but "You look and see." I still look and see when I cook and tell my friends when they ask for a recipe, "You will see when to add this or that." I was learning to trust the touch, to know when spices were good or not, and that visits to the market were indispensable. Manual and crafts workers know the importance of mobilizing the senses to enrich abstract teaching that their discipline requires. Some years ago, I was in Chiang Mai among a group of scholars accompanying doctoral students researching crafts as humanities. Groups were organized to spend a full day in a workshop (silver, stone or wood carving, weaving and indigo making). I chose weaving and went with a friend and five students to a village two hours away from the city. Women weavers were expecting us and each student was assigned to one of them. The elder and most respected weaver offered to teach me. We communicated by gestures, look, and touch. She showed me how to set the weft on a very simple weaving frame. I was unable to even do one entire length of weft, breaking thread after thread which the elder patiently reconnected. I became impatient and decided I no longer wanted to learn. Very simply, I was vexed that I could not "do" such a "simple" thing. Ten minutes later, I came back, chastened and ashamed of myself. I, who talked of decolonial pedagogy, of the power of repetition and imitation, could not handle failure! My attitude was insulting. The elder patiently started again to show me how to set the weft, but it was when I finally suspended rational calculation (she does this, then that) and trusted my fingers to imitate her fingers' "dance" that I could do my weft and then weave. Her knowledge was at once abstract, theoretical, practical, and physical. She expressed her annoyance at my clumsiness but was never patronizing. She was an incredible pedagogue, a woman of color who would never be considered a teacher in the hegemonic educative system—but thanks to her patience, she brought me back to a way of learning that I had partly lost through years of academia. The hours spent learning to weave reminded me that I had taught myself how to sew through repetition, imitation, failures, and overcoming difficulties, that I could undo an entire sewn piece to correct a mistake, and that learning to transform a flat surface into a volume was a source of great joy.

The Global North, which has mostly lost this anti-capitalist and anti-extractivist pedagogy, has to impose an exclusively technological relation to matter and to the world in order to expand its hegemony. As neoliberalism has brought in this logic to non-Western countries, the importance of anti-extractivist pedagogies is growing. It feeds the political theories of global reparation and abolitionism which confront us with multiple temporalities of reparation, of a past, a present, and a future in need of repair, so that generations to come can meet their basic needs. The politics of reparations and abolitionism were brought to the fore following the public lynching of George Floyd on May 25, 2020, which not only triggered anger at the impunity of the police and the state, but also pushed forward a collective demand that memorial inscriptions in cities be revised, and that colonial statues disappear. The 2020 movement for the fall of imperialist statues began on May 22, 2020, in Fort-de-France, Martinique. A group of young Martiniquais toppled two statues of Victor Schoelcher (May 22 celebrates the day in 1848 when the enslaved proclaimed *themselves* free, refusing to wait for the arrival of the Commissioner of the Republic who had been expected to apply the February 27 decree of abolition). Two young Black women took public responsibility for the toppling of the statues. Facing the camera, they quietly and firmly told the police, the judiciary system, and the state why they had taken part in this act. "Schoelcher is not our savior," they proclaimed, voicing a series of demands for justice in education, health, and the economy, and denouncing racism. To them, the statues reflected a world built by the ancestors of the white men in power today, guaranteeing them a space in which they could exert and display their power and arrogance. They lived in "their" cities, cities of conquerors, of men who crushed the insurrections of the oppressed, and who took vengeance with cruelty on those who had dared to challenge their power; men who went to the four corners of the world to exploit, dispossess, rape, steal, and plunder, so that their sons were born with privileges which were in no way owed to their talents or skills. They did not pull down the statue of a slaver or a slave owner, or the author of openly racist texts, but of an antislavery French republican. They showed that colonialism and racism survived in the republic, that French abolitionism has not brought freedom or equality but neocolonialism. Their gesture was powerful—and yet, in the media, in academic conversations, in calls for papers on the falling down of statues, it is the June 6 toppling of the Edward Colston statue in Bristol that stands as the beginning of the 2020 movement. I am not claiming Martinican copyright nor origins over toppling of offensive statues, but I am asking why one anti-racist gesture enters history and another doesn't. What is it in the anti-hegemonic act of a young Martinican that cannot be inscribed and recognized even by those who would call themselves allies? How do we constitute our own decolonial archives? How do we account for the abundance of anti-racist gestures, for their creativity, for the spaces they open so we all can breathe better?

We, artists, refugees, exiles, poor, Blacks, Muslims, trans, are claiming the right to live in these cities and to be able to decide collectively on that which surrounds us, to walk in the streets, squares, and gardens without encountering the representations of those who have defended a racist, sexist, xenophobic, and murderous ideology, and who believed that humanity should be divided between those whose lives matter and those whose lives don't. *We want to breathe.*

To topple these statues is to reflect on the cultural memory we want to build around our public spaces. It is the present that should determine which statues, which forms of representation usually found in public spaces, which fights and actions we want to honor. We want less monumental statues and ironic diversions, less ephemeral installations, murals, and "memory forests"; what we need are representations rooted in collectivity. The imagination must be at the service of a shifting and dynamic memory, creations that exist between the past and the future, such as the giant geoglyphs of the Atacama Desert, or ones that reach toward futurity. The rights of future generations are already being written and expressed in the slogans of young people who see their livelihoods threatened by the selfishness and greed of a caste. These slogans echo millennial demands for justice, freedom, and equality, but they also contain aspirations for a world where everyone can breathe freely, and where everyone can feel protected by communities whose principles are to take care of the Earth, to reach out, to offer water and food to those who need it, and who are fighting exploitation, racism, and state-sanctioned murder. And from there, to engage in experimentations that hold a respect for the land and for nature, for forms of coexistence, and for collective living.

Translated from the French by Edwin Nasr

Françoise Vergès is a political theorist, feminist, and decolonial activist. She convenes workshops and works with artists of color. *A Decolonial Feminism* (2021), *The Wombs of Women* (2020), *Resolutely Black: Conversations with Aimé Césaire* (2020), and *Monsters and Revolutionaries* (1999) are among her books that have been translated into English.

1. Achille Mbembe, "Le droit universel à la respiration," *Seneplus*, April 6, 2020, https://www.seneplus.com/opinions/le-droit-universel-la-respiration (accessed June 20, 2020).
2. Frantz Fanon, *Black Skin, White Masks* (New York, 2008), p. 201.
3. In Adrian Lahoud, ed., and Andrea Bagnato, ed., *Rights of Future Generations: Conditions* (Berlin, 2019), pp. 16–21.
4. Aimé Césaire, *Discourse on Colonialism*, trans. Joan Pinkham (New York, 2001), p. 35.
5. Ruth Wilson Gilmore, *Golden Gulag: Prisons, Surplus, Crisis, and Opposition in Globalizing California* (Berkeley et al., 2007), p. 28.
6. See Isabell Lorey, *State of Insecurity. Government of the Precarious*, trans. Aileen Derieg (London, 2015).
7. Ibid, p. 21.
8. Achille Mbembe, "Le droit universel à la respiration" (see note 1).
9. Grada Kilomba, *Plantation Memories: Episodes of Everyday Racism* (Münster, 2008), p. 21.
10. Sayak Valencia, *Gore Capitalism* (Los Angeles, 2018), p. 20.
11. See Jasbir K. Puar, *The Right to Maim: Debility, Capacity, Disability* (Durham, NC, 2017).

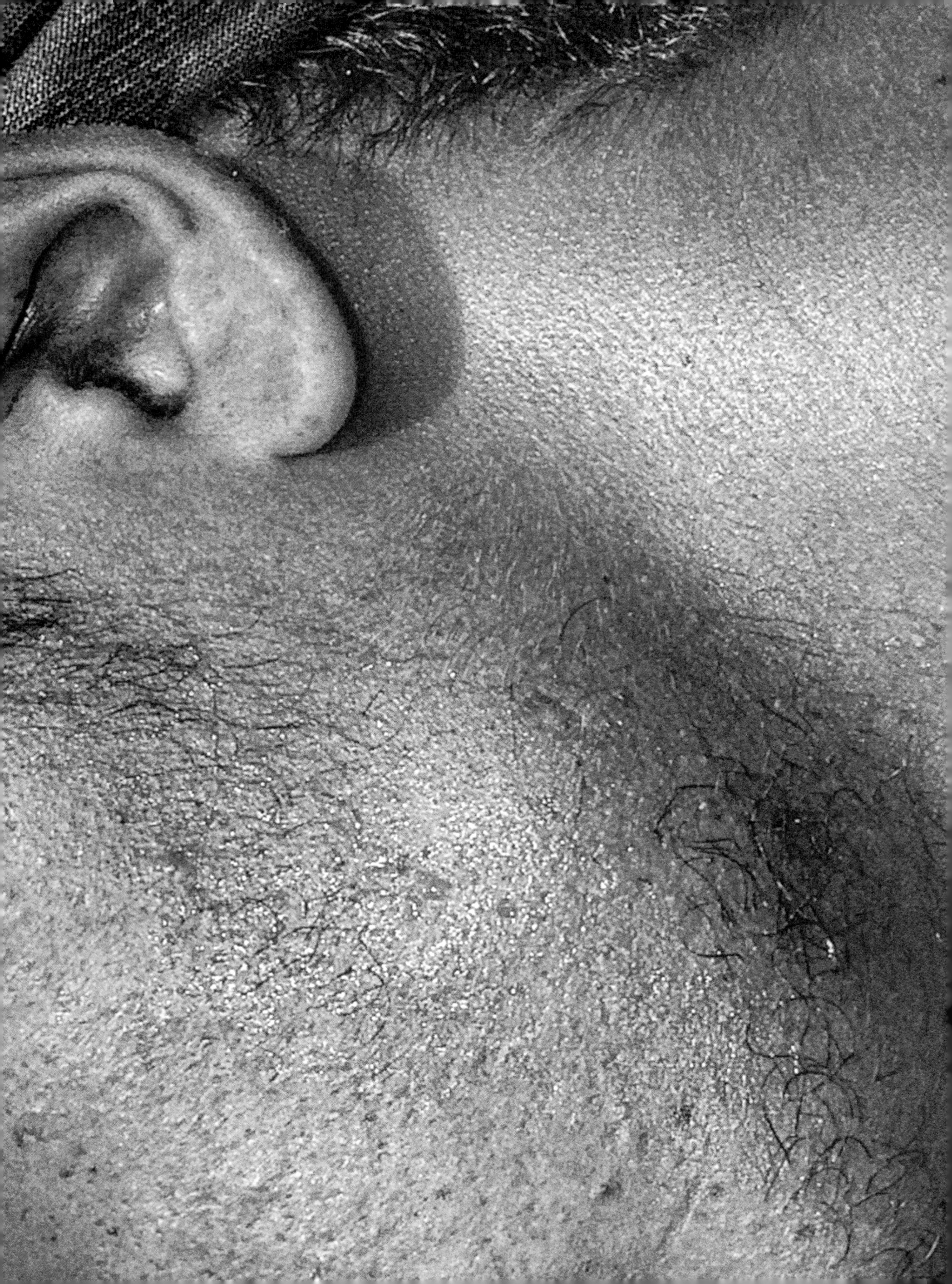

An Open Letter to Hannah Arendt

Ariełla Aïsha Azoułay

Dear Hannah,

I know this letter is an interruption—and I apologize for that. But there are some thoughts I would like to share with you. I need to discuss citizenship with you. We both spent years on this question. I started as a student of your texts. I used them to unlearn the identity I was given in the factory of empire and embraced them as a substitute for the absent voice of the "elders" who had failed to protect their children from the state's assembly line, where children are prepared to become citizens in its own image. I unlearned my Israeli citizenship through companionship with Palestinians who were denied theirs. Your writings gave me the confidence to bend political theory away from its imperial attachments, and instead to fabulate the existence of a worldly sovereignty in Palestine pre-1948. I made myself into a co-citizen of this fabulated Palestine, and *The Human Condition* made it possible. When, more than a decade and a half ago, in my book *The Civil Contract of Photography,* I refused to recognize photographers as owners of their images, emphasizing the always-crowded event of photography and the rights of the photographed, I described what I was doing as a form of "historical fiction."[1] With time, I refused to acknowledge the existence of the major pillar of historical work—the *past*—and I came to see my work as a kind of "potential history," or what Saidiya Hartman calls "critical fabulation."[2]

From the moment I understood that my name should have been Aïsha, my Algerian grandmother's name which my father never uttered, I felt an unfamiliar pain alongside an unexpected fury. An unattended, intergenerational wound that I didn't know existed erupted. For years, I felt defined by one imperial project, that of the colonization of Palestine. But suddenly, I was transposed to another, the French conquest of Algeria in 1830. At the center of this conquest was an enigma: Who were my ancestors before they were turned into citizens of the French Republic? What did the French want to destroy when they first called the people they colonized "indigenous," only to later deny them that condescending status and their older modes of living, and force them to become French citizens?

In some sense, it feels too late for such an exploration. My father, who was born in Algeria—he left in 1949, at the age of twenty-seven—died, and I have no one close to me to ask about the life there that I didn't live. I used to say that I have nothing "Algerian"—objects, memories, tastes, songs, habits, language—and now I'm revolting against myself for the years I spent without revolting against this imperial fiction, this story that I was never Algerian. How can one remember what was not transmitted? Is it lost forever? Is this how it seemed to my father when the Crémieux Decree, which deracinated his ancestors from their indigenous condition and made them citizens

Left: Postcard from Algeria, ca. 1910. Author's personal collection.
Right: Pierre-August Renoir, *Noce juive d'après Delacroix* (The Jewish Wedding), ca. 1875. Oil on canvas, 108 x 145 cm. Worcester Art Museum / Bridgeman Images.

It is unknown when exactly this photograph was taken, nor is it known when it was printed on a postcard. The postcard was purchased in Algeria and mailed to France (seemingly in 1910, from what can be read of the postal stamp). One may speculate that the photograph predates 1870, when polygamous formations were outlawed as part of the effort to civilize Jews so that they could fit into French citizenship. But this is a trap. The violent imperial campaign of uprooting Algerian Jews from their "premodern" world entailed separating them from Muslims, and dismantling shared indigenous practices and modes of sustenance. But the aim of turning them into "modern" French citizens was a long process that had many opponents among the colonizers, who were looking for evidence of the Jews' disloyalty or incompatibility with citizenship. After 1870, in spite of their new status of citizens, Algerian Jews were often reproached and persecuted for being "still Arab" in their manners and modes of life.
In 1875—barely five years after Algerian Jews were made French citizens—Renoir made a copy of

of France, was abrogated? When their citizenship was taken, what remained of indigeneity for those who had moved to the cities was for the most part a penalty regime. They were switched from one law to the other (*loi indigène*). Many of their indigenous modes of life were already lost and prohibited, others were made "past," "uncivilized." Some of the objects which this indigeneity consisted of are probably in the basements of French or European museums, and I intend to find them.

Had I read your text "Why the Crémieux Decree Was Abrogated" earlier, I would have challenged my father with details.[3] But I didn't—I couldn't. I came to your Jewish writings last. For years, I avoided engaging with "Jewish" things in my own scholarship. Even when I was studying the citizenship model shaped by the French Revolution, I skipped the extension of citizenship to the Jews in France at the wake of the revolution and focused on the model's mechanisms of excluding, and belatedly including, Black people and women. In retrospect, I think my refusal to engage with Jewish things was a kind of displacement. It was also a protection I needed from Judaic Studies' (self?) appointment to produce and represent the history of the Jews as a relatively cohesive subject, with internal hierarchies between the groups it claims to represent through its entanglement with Israel Studies and Holocaust Studies. I also think this protection, or displacement, prepared me to finally call for my ancestors, and to ask them to side with me as I try to remember who they were before they were

Eugène Delacroix's 1839 painting of a Jewish wedding in Morocco (where Jews were not given French citizenship). The painting is a telling example of the visual attempt to capture and display the truth of the Jews as "still Arabs" and still mingling with them. It is as if it were visually saying: "See what the Jews are hiding underneath their civil gown." Similarly, the five women and their many children captured in the postcard tell another truth about the Jewish family and its unruliness in the eyes of an emerging global capitalist market: North-African Jews resist leaving the polygamous household, which would enable the economy to thrive. And yet, in the racial capitalist visual market, such an image could be, at once, a proof that the Jews were a lost cause, unworthy of the citizenship that had been granted to them, and a profitable token of exoticization. The postcard displays a mode of life that imperialism was trying to bring to an end—yet a rare, surviving specimen could readily be commercialized. We do not know what the terms of the exchange were that brought the members of this large family to exit their home and pose for the camera, what role the circulation of such postcards played in the ending of their resistance.

buried under two successive colonial projects. If, at the end of the day, the Jews had not capitulated to a belief in citizenship (twice!)—Algerian Jews in France, and Jewish people in Palestine—I would not have had to distance myself from "Jewish" things. I would not have to do the work of calling my ancestors; their voices would have already been wrapped around me.

I am one of those "Oriental Jews," as you described them in your letter to another European, Karl Jaspers, when you wrote, "they speak only Hebrew, and they look Arabic."[4] Most people don't read me as an Arab-looking person—as much as I can understand what you meant by it—nor do I have any inheritance from the Jews who originated from North Africa. In fact, I don't seem to fully belong to Mizrahi Jews as a group, whose identity was defined by the Israeli regime. While we share origins in North Africa, my father's migration from Algeria to Israel in 1949 preceded the Zionists' brutal provocation to the Jews of North Africa to migrate to Palestine, now Israel. My father was not part of this Zionist-provoked mass migration, and was therefore not subjected to the humiliation and exploitation of his peers, who migrated as an identified group, the Mizrahim. In fact, from the eyes of the French citizen my father had trained himself to be, he also saw his peers as "Oriental Jews" and distanced himself from this group in Israel, as well as from his life in Algeria. He imposed this generational rupture, and my mother supported it. I'm left to mourn its supposed irreversibility. But now that the name Aïsha is mine again, I'm ready to attend to this intergenerational colonial wound, visible in anti-imperial scar maps that can be traced on the bodies of those people whose families voluntarily-forcibly migrated. Have you heard their song calling for the abrogation of border decrees?

The solidarity and care with which you wrote your text on Algerian Jews and Muslims, and your deep engagement with the fraught history of the extension of French citizenship to the Jews, allowed me to stop—for the first time, I think—judging my father for embracing French citizenship. He believing it would facilitate his escape from the colonizers' gaze that he subsequently interiorized: a mental acrobatics that prepared him to unproblematically adopt another colonizer-citizen position that awaited him in Israel. It's now impossible for me to continue omitting the "Jewish" element in my work—understood not as a given identity but as a colonial fabrication, part of the campaign of delineating groups of people for their professed religion and deracinating them from their world to make them available for displacement. I can no longer omit from my father's migration from Algeria to Israel the decades of deracination that made leaving one's home forever even conceivable.

In lieu of the memoir and letters that he didn't write, I used your text on the abrogation of the Crémieux Decree to speculate about his life in Algeria pre- and post-Vichy regime. It not only helped me piece together the little I knew of our family life there, but also, more importantly, understand the deeper reason for my reticence to engage with the history of the "Jews." Such history requires recognition of the existence of the "Jews" as a category in and of itself, one whose rich and diverse transgeographical histories were subsumed by colonial and imperial projects to emphasize their national belonging—or unbelonging—and to minimize the price they were forced to pay when identified as somehow separate from their world. This world of which they were a part was turned, by the very same gesture, into a non-Jewish world in a way that made their deracination acceptable. The production of the unhyphenated "Jew"—not the Algerian-Jew, the Egyptian-Jew, the Palestinian-Jew, but just the "Jew"—became the source of a malaise. The name Aïsha guides me through the colonizer's labyrinth of destroyed worlds, erased identities, and new promises of colonial citizenship. Lose your father, maybe, but why lose one's female ancestors, witches like Sycorax, to a character in Shakespeare's *The Tempest*? Or the powers of another Algerian witch whose name didn't survive when, in 1541, she advised the ruler of Algiers not to surrender to Charles V's invasion plot, and whose skills and talents didn't rest until the latter's fleet was wrecked?

Why abandon my dreams?
did I already encounter
the person
or the people
I can confidently
trust them with?[5]

One month after the French High Commissioner in Algeria's Ordinances on Jewish Rights were published on March 14, 1943, you wrote your text on the Crémieux Decree, in which you show that, though the Vichy regime officially ended in Algeria, its policies continued to be endured. While one of the decrees reads as a restoration of the Jews' rights—"All legislative and administrative acts, subsequent to June 22, 1940, which include discriminations for reason of being Jewish, are null and void"—you point to another contradicting decree that proclaims that "the decree of October 24, 1870 [the Crémieux Decree], concerning the status of the native Israelites of Algeria is abrogated." I'm not sure where exactly my father was at this moment. I assume that, with the end of the Vichy regime, he was liberated from the concentration camp in Bedeau and, soon after, recruited to the Free French Army, as they needed soldiers from the colonies to win the war and preserve the empire against decolonization, for which colonized peoples all over the world were struggling.

I have no doubt that advocating for the restoration of citizenship for the Jews was the right thing to do. I am, however, grateful that your account of the restoration of citizenship doesn't take the 1870 Crémieux Decree as its point of departure, but rather the *sénatus-consulte* act from five years earlier. This earlier decree invited both Jews and Muslims to become French citizens so long as they renounce their autonomy and agree to no longer be governed according to their religious laws. As you report, "Neither native Jews nor native Muslims, however, showed themselves very eager to ask for French citizenship."[6] In fact, less than 200 Muslims and 152 Jews applied for citizenship. With this in mind, no one should continue to say that, in 1870, all the Jews were made citizens without first emphasizing that it was against their will. I know this even though neither my father nor my grandmother told me about it. That they later complied is a different story that cannot be approached in a linear way. It is as if their compliance binds me still.

You describe, rather uncompromisingly, the inherent cynicism of the French decision to transform Jews into citizens in 1870, which had allowed for a fabrication of a new cohort of citizens to help the French recover from its defeat in the Franco-German War and the political crisis that followed, but also against the 1871 Mokrani Revolt, when 250 tribes rose up against French colonial power in Algeria: "It was, therefore, of no small importance to the government to have about 38,000 loyal Frenchmen in the colony at time when trouble obviously lay ahead." I love this turn of phrase—even if unintentional—where you seem to reverse the dynamics involved in the granting of citizenship. Though it is usually described as a gift extended to the governed, you say that, by accepting citizenship, it is the governed who are instead granting a gift to the colonizing power. Your account reveals who was actually given a gift and whose interests were served by it. Let's be clear: with a single decree consisting of only a few lines, the French government received 38,000 loyal French citizens! As much as I love your clarity here, I hate the French. Their use of the Jews for their own needs is just the beginning of the catastrophe they unleashed. What the French did at that point was begin the countdown to the termination of Jewish life on the African continent.

Everywhere, colonial powers divided local populations into groups, cultivating different interests in each so that these groups would be set against each other and dance to the colonizer's tune. Within most of the groups, the colonized were trained as soldiers so as to oppress their own people. In the case of Jewish Algeria, educators and rabbis were recruited to monitor the conversion of Jews into French secularism and to oversee their deracination from Muslim, Berber, and Arab cultures and traditions. Citizenship was not a gift but a weapon.

Not surprisingly, though, the man for whom this decree is named, Adolphe Crémieux, a Jewish lawyer and Minister of Justice in the French parliament, was also one of the founders and leaders of the École Israelite Universelle, a Paris-based network of Jewish schools throughout the Mediterranean. The school's mission, like other imperial boarding schools across the colonial world, was to produce a new man and woman. In this case it was a new Jew, one that would fit into Christian French secularism. This project of human engineering was led by French colonial actors alongside the participation of French Jews who, at that time, had already pledged allegiance to the French empire. To fully grasp the instrumentality and brutality of citizenship, we must imagine the Jews in Algeria not as an already-diasporic group in exile—the "Jews"—but instead as part of the indigenous populations of North Africa who were colonized in 1830. As I cannot recall ever having come across such a simple sentence in the many different books that I read about the colonization of Algeria—that French colonization in Algeria meant the *French colonization of Algerian Jews*—I had to wait until I was able to write it myself. As soon as it is said, the progressive imperial narrative that frames citizenship as a blessing collapses.

For you to then write that the second reason for the extension of citizenship to the Jews "lay in the fact that the Jews, unlike Muslim natives, were closely linked to the mother country through their French brethren," entails having to ignore or deny that in 1865, when the *sénatus-consulte* was issued, the imperial manipulation of the body politic, in France as well as in Algeria, had already started. The logic and practice of creating what we should call *internally deracinated groups* was already entrenched. When I read this now, I want to shout loudly and shake you by the shoulders in order to wake you up. I want to ask you how it is possible that, even with your deep understanding of the otherness of Jews living in Algeria and of the world they shared with Muslims, you could still fall into the trap of attaching a colonized group—the "Jews"—to "the mother country through their French brethren?" It is only by cleansing the "Jews" of their indigeneity and their world that such brotherhood between European and Algerian Jews could be invented, at the expenses of centuries of brotherhood with Muslims. In the French context, where many of the Jews were not allowed to live within town walls, or were allowed to practice only a few occupations considered humiliating such as moneylending, peddling, or cattle-trading, the struggle of certain Jewish communities in France to be accorded citizenship could be, and indeed was, perceived as a triumph.[7] But to make of that necessity a virtue, and of that accommodation a standard for all forms of relations? Your oversight here upsets and obsesses me.

In *The Origins of Totalitarianism,* you brilliantly captured the essence of imperialism by arguing that "expansion as a permanent and supreme aim of politics is the central political idea of imperialism," and recognized in the "expansion for the sake of expansion" a totalitarian recipe.[8] I wonder why you missed the expansive nature of the type of citizenship that was invented by imperialism, as well as the role it played in facilitating processes of territorial expansion? You seem very close to recognizing it when you discuss the Crémieux Decree—its promulgations, abrogation, and restoration—not only in relation to the Jews, but also in regard to the French body politic that considered the decree as "a beginning and a way to attract the Arabs by the privileges it gave to its citizens."[9] But then, in the next passage, you seem to buy into the imperial assumption of the universal nature of citizenship and believe that it represents a progressive stage of governance, even after uncovering its manufactured origins. Let me give you an example from your discussion of women. You start by explaining that the Muslims' refusal to "renounce their personal status (which, similarly to the Jews, permitted polygamy and the denial of rights to women)" led to the failure of the French policy of assimilation, but then you unjustifiably frame the French as caring for women's rights: "French civil law and the French penal code have their bases in the equality of the sexes."[10]

It is unclear to me what brought you to depict the French as more progressive and to substitute varieties of human relations with a single linear model that measures stages of political development. I would not raise this, I would not be so upset with your oversight, if it weren't for the fact that your writing taught me how to unlearn citizenship and reject its poisonous promises. Is it too much to say that I feel betrayed, that I want to know why, but also to ask if, you have betrayed yourself as well?

The Jews in Algeria were not only "Arab-speaking Jews," as you describe them. They spoke Judeo-Arab, Ladino, Judeo-Berber, Tamazight. You knew that they shared much more than a language with the Muslims; in fact, it would even be more accurate to assert that much of what they shared was not *across* those two categories—"Muslim" and "Jew"—but existed prior to their differentiation as two separate identities. Sometimes, even in the span of a single sentence, your writing shows this irreconcilable tension in concepts. You write that the Jews "were not very different from the customs of their Arab surroundings," only to then take on the viewpoint of the French colonizer: "[These customs] did not appear to the French as typical of the Jewish people, but rather bad habits of a small portion of that people, somehow led astray—habits that could easily be corrected by the majority of the same people." This tension is hard to miss.

A few weeks ago, I reached out to my cousins who were born in Algeria and migrated to France in 1962, when Jews could no longer stay there. I met with them once or twice when I was in my early twenties and still didn't know a word of French. I wrote to them asking about my father's life in Algeria and about our grandmother's name, Aïcha. Don't ask me now why I misspelled the name and replaced the "c" with "s"—it will deviate us too much from the story I'd like to share. Here is what my cousin wrote in reply: "The first name AICHA comes from a very rich woman who lived in Oran. Grandmother said that this woman had bracelets from the wrists to the elbow!!! This woman held that grandma carries her first name. Who was this woman I do not know."
You should not be surprised that I knew nothing about this other Aïcha, since you already know by now how long it took me to learn about our grandmother's real name. My Ariadne's thread is woven from three strands. The first is a vague memory of my father once saying that he had a third grandmother. I don't remember the details—or maybe there weren't any?—except that he was unable to explain his kin relationship to this woman. He did mention something about "outside of marriage." The second is related to another detail I heard recently from my cousins about my grandmother: "She made twenty-one trips to Paris to see her daughters, and six to Israel" (all of which took place in one decade, the 1950s, prior to the charter flights era), adding: "Granny was proud

of this first name because she said that she [the other Aïcha] had blessed her, and that she would always have money for her, especially when she went to buy plane tickets to see her daughters or Roger [my father]."

I still don't know who this third grandmother was. I believe she was my great-grandfather's second wife. As polygamy was eradicated from the towns—my family lived in Arzew and Oran—and Jews were already made citizens, the exact kin relation of Aïcha, this third grandmother, had to be concealed for her to continue acting as part of a family unit whose members were tied together by love, financial aid, and other forms of supports that made my grandmother feel blessed by her presence. The third is also related to something my cousins wrote to me in their first reply to my email. Unprompted by me, they volunteered their understanding of the irregularities surrounding marriage: "Mixed marriages were prohibited, and men were beaten up and women ostracized from society." Such irregularities were produced by a system of regulations that contradicted existing kin formations that didn't conform to the French heteropatriarchal family unit. In this climate, I suspect that the memory of broader pre-French family networks was transmitted as a memory of problems or irregularities regarding marriage.

If you're wondering why I'm telling you about this third grandmother, it's because you discuss polygamy as a major factor fueling the resistance of the indigenous population in Algeria, Jews and Muslims alike, to French citizenship. And, demonstrating the flickering understanding you have of Jews' worldliness in North Africa prior to colonization, and your later use of the already-exiled identity, "Jews," you don't assume polygamy to be indicative of a backward model of relationship. Instead, you explain polygamy as a social model of sustenance and protection against the oppression of the landless class. Women, you explain, were the main source of "manpower" for the *fellah,* and the only one he could afford in "hiring." As you imply, "these French colonialists, mostly large landowners whose prosperity depend upon cheap native labor and sympathetic government officials," had a direct interest in breaking these polygamous formations and have unprotected individuals available for them to exploit. Not only could women be exploited as cheap labor in those lands that settlers appropriated, but they would also end up losing the structures of mutual aid, care, and protection that members of the broader family unit provided to each other. But then you switch from recognizing the worldliness of Algerian Jews to viewing them with a colonizer's eye. From the *fellahin* you move to city dwellers and briefly write that in the towns "polygamy has almost disappeared."[11] "Almost disappeared" is a familiar imperial song announcing as *already done* that which it aims to still achieve. I cannot prove this (yet), but I think that this second Aïcha, whose name was given to my grandmother born two decades after the Crémieux Decree, was part of an expanded, indigenous family unit no longer allowed to exist among those who were made "Jews" and "French." In some interesting legal cases that were brought to court, Jews were denounced for faking dates and kin relationships in documents, so as to camouflage their resistance to the law prohibiting polygamy. The almost disappearance of polygamous family units is another way to describe the almost disappearance of the shared modes of being-in-the-world of Arab Muslims and Arab Jews.

Imperialism's "almost disappeared" formations create taboos, topics on which one cannot talk without being suspected of antifeminism, conservatism, or backwardness. Hence my gratitude for the transmission of the possibility to study polygamy on its own terms in Algeria, as a family formation common to Jews and Muslims, and as a sociopolitical formation of partnership and care. If from the late eighteenth century onward, Jews' assimilation is always, as you wrote in an earlier essay, "assimilation to *enlightenment*," then their assimilation as a group must have preceded via the assimilation of a smaller group of scholars who could no longer speak of the polygamous family as a sociopolitical formation of protection and mutual aid without being treated as uncivilized, antifeminist, and anti-Enlightenment thinkers. Nor could they suggest that perhaps the rights women enjoyed prior to the assimilation to *enlightenment* might have been greater than those under the patriarchal property regime of bourgeois monogamous marriage. Scholars who dared to defend this formation would have appeared as failures of assimilation, and this had to be avoided at any price. French people of Jewish origins thus arrived in Algeria as messengers of the French Revolution's enlightenment, mandated to promote a doubled *mission civilisatrice*: to assimilate Arab Jews into "Jews," and prepare them for the culminating point of true assimilation, which is that of becoming European.

You could not know, at the time of writing, of Judith Surkis's research on polygamy and sovereignty in French Algeria, or Joshua Schreier's research into the documents some of these French-Jewish messengers of the Enlightenment left behind. A mesmerizing picture emerges from them. When rabbinical authority was "overruled" in Algeria by the Consistoire Central de France, a Napoleonic institution, the focus of the local rabbis' activity shifted from charity work and ritual service to policing women's lives by eradicating polygamy and divorce—a way to distance the new "Jews" from their brethren Muslims. We ought to think about this assimilation as a kind of "culturecide" initiated by settler-colonials and executed by European Jews—to eradicate Arab-Jewish lifeways and assimilate them into a deracinated "Jewish" identity, from which they would be offered the "gift" of European citizenship. This racism by European Jews toward Oriental Jews, prevalent from the mid-nineteenth century onward, was not yet studied as part of imperialism's racializing apparatuses.

But your work helped us see that it might be, even if you didn't realize it yourself. You depict this aggressive reeducation campaign that targeted local rabbis and used their authority in indigenous Arab-Jewish communities. You describe the French colonizers who lured freshly assimilated "Jews" in France to perform their newly acquired Frenchness by publicly "emphasizing their differences from Eastern Judaism." French Jewry, represented by the Paris Consistoire Central, could assume responsibility for overruling native rabbis, and even guarantee for the rapid assimilation of Algerian Jewry. Accordingly, when the Crémieux Decree was issued, "the Parisian Consistoire was given legal power to appoint all Algerian rabbis. . . . The schools of the Alliance Israélite Universelle, together with the active policy of the Consistoire, assimilated the native Arab-speaking Jews in a relatively short time and changed them into loyal French citizens." There is no other way to describe this except as a colonial attack on an indigenous mode of life. With the scattered records of the indigenous opposition to enter under the French law and embrace the bargain it involves, I call to read the language of the 1870 Crémieux Law—"the native Jews of the departments of Algeria are declared French citizens"—as the ultimate sanction in a campaign of repressing this refusal and opposition to citizenship.

When you wrote your text in 1943, you didn't have to explain what the "personal status" was that indigenous people had to renounce in order to become citizens. You make clear, however, that it was not the only thing the indigenous were required to renounce. I want to clarify this point for those who will read my open letter to you: "personal status" was a colonial imposition, a status given to the indigenous along with colonization, *allowing* them to continue to respect Islamic or Judaic laws under the new French law. This meant that the system of rights under which they were born and lived for centuries prior to French colonization was detached from the world of which it was part. It was made into a united set of laws amendable by French governors who could decide if, when, and how the local population can be governed by it. This misleadingly glorious moment of turning the Jews into citizens is inextricably tied to the moment in which they were not longer permitted to be-in-the-world as Jews, when the path disallowing them from being Algerian Jews was already laid before them. When citizenship is conceived as something that is being given under certain circumstances to one group of people, it is not surprising to see that under different circumstances it is taken away. Thus the French citizenship of Jews in Algeria was revoked in 1940, renewed in 1943—and detached from the world in which it was first imposed when, in 1962, Algerian Jews were expected to leave their homeland on the basis of that very citizenship. This is not incidental to imperial citizenship but rather scripted in it. In 1943, against these undercover Vichy generals who ruled Algeria and withheld citizenship and legal rights from Algerian Jews, you didn't simply advocate the restitution of citizenship. Instead, you cared enough to tell the history of this citizenship from the point of view of those oppressed by it, even before they themselves felt oppressed by its removal.

Talking to my dead ancestors—those who were born before 1830, before European citizenship was brought to their Judeo-Arab world as part of the imperial technology of conquest—deepened my understanding of the harmful role of citizenship in reducing the diversity and heterogeneity of Jewish life around the world in general, and in North Africa in particular. When becoming citizens in France, Jews had to prove their loyalty to the state that granted them citizenship, but which could also take it away from them. Cultural and political assimilation, and policing other Jews' assimilation, became the proof of loyalty. Had they not been required to prove their loyalty, the tragedy that started with the colonization of Algeria in 1830 and the slow destruction of the Arab world in which Jews felt at home would have been recognized in continuity with the genocidal colonization of other parts of Africa in the nineteenth and twentieth centuries. The memory of this tragedy would not have been so easily exchanged for a fable about the glorious European emancipation of the Jews in and beyond Europe. At the end of World War II, the same fable facilitated the displacement and integration of Jews—from Europe and later from the Muslim world—to Palestine, into another project of colonization that plays a major role in the perpetuation of Euro-American global imperial power. There, as citizens of a new state, and in the name of the same European type of differential citizenship, they took part in the ongoing destruction of Palestine.

I cannot end this letter without asking you: Have you ever thought about the role European Jews played in destroying the life-world of Arab Jews?

Yours,
Aïsha

Ariella Aïsha Azoulay is professor of modern culture and media and comparative literature at Brown University. Her books include *Potential History – Unlearning Imperialism* (2019), and *The Civil Contract of Photography* (2008). She is also a film essayist and a curator of archives and exhibitions. Among her films are *Un-documented: Undoing Imperial Plunder* (2019) and *Civil Alliances, Palestine, 47-48* (2012); among her exhibitions is *Errata,* at the Tapiès Foundation (2019).

1. Ariella Azoulay, *The Civil Contract of Photography*, trans. Rela Mazali and Ruvik Danieli (New York, 2008).

2. See Ariella Azoulay, *Potential History: Unlearning Imperialism* (London, 2019) and Saidiya Hartman, "Venus in Two Acts," *Small Axe: A Caribbean Journal of Criticism* 12, no. 2 (2008).

3. Hannah Arendt, *The Jewish Writings* (New York, 2008).

4. Hannah Arendt to Karl Jaspers in *Correspondence: Hannah Arendt, Karl Jaspers, 1926–1969*, ed. Lotte Kohler and Hans Saner (New York, 1996), p. 43.

5. Paraphrasing Abdellatif Laâbi's poem "In Front of the Mirror" from his book *Presque Riens* (Montreuil, 2020), p. 13.

6. Arendt, *The Jewish Writings*, p. 246.

7. On the occupations of the Jews before and after the revolution see Zosa Szajkowski, "Notes on the Occupational Status of French Jews, 1800–1880," *Proceedings of the American Academy for Jewish Research, 1979–1980*, Vol. 46/47, Jubilee Volume.

8. Hannah Arendt, *The Origins of Totalitarianism* (Orlando, 1975), p. 125.

9. Arendt, *The Jewish Writings*, p. 249.

10. Ibid, p. 248.

11. Ibid.

12. Ibid, p. 246.

Ancestors of Choice: Toward a Decolonial Genealogy

Houria Bouteldja

Of all the human soul's needs, none is more vital than this one of the past.
—Simone Weil, *The Need for Roots*

To immigrate is to change one's genealogy.
—Malika Sorel-Sutter, *Décomposition française*

The COVID-19 pandemic and the global health crisis it initiated continue to engender consequences on societies of the Global North. Largely due to advanced capitalist states' colossal means and their quasi-monopoly on the nuclear weapons industry, until now these societies had been relatively spared from the effects of economic crises, epidemics, and natural catastrophes, which primarily affect countries in the Global South. The signs of our newfound fragility have begun to manifest and unfold in time within the past twenty years, marking a decisive end to our impunity and invulnerability.[1] As such, the 9/11 attacks were the first warning shots of global-scale crises to come, an event of transformative magnitude that has sounded the death knell of the West's impunity. Since then, within the borders of Empire we have encountered various epidemics (Creutzfeldt-Jakob disease, H1N1 influenza, and others), nuclear accidents, terrorist attacks on European soil, and a major economic crisis in 2008 that led to the emergence of major social movements (the Indignado*s* in Spain, the Occupy Movement in the United States, the yellow vests in France). Though somehow unprecedented in scope, the current pandemic is but an additional signal of the impending decline of this civilizational era. At this stage, pessimists will fear the violent and devastating reactions of the wounded monster. Optimists of the Gramscian variant, on the other hand, will locate an opportunity to witness the latter's continued decline—might they even dare formulate an end to the logic of capitalist forms of extraction and profit altogether? If we are to hold on to that optic, it then becomes imperative to oppose extractive logics, and thus urgent to configure and embody alternative modes of being. We could lean on the Marxist model of emancipation, which provides us a key to undoing the logic of capitalism through a materialist lens, but it will most likely prove insufficient. Donna Haraway invites us, rather intuitively, to "stay with the trouble." She might be right; we might have to learn to cohabitate with risk and insecurity. But this will also prove insufficient. The present juncture urges us instead to engage in a totalizing cultural revolution—an upheaval based on perspective, the replacement of the current political lexicon by a new one to make a clean sweep of the liberal ideology that serves as a compass for people-consumers, and which must be urgently disposed of.

Let's observe the scene: The peoples of the Global North are in the process of having their immunity stripped from them, while the peoples of the Global South are revolting against decades of postcolonial state oppression in every corner of the world. The racial pact that once allowed the white proletariat to form a pact with the ruling classes is crumbling in real time as a result of capital's insatiable appetite for profit. We might be holding a strong hand at the moment! We know that, within these conditions, setting the stage for fascism will be privileged over all else, and especially over the possibility of a revolutionary momentum. But the latter can no longer do without the decolonial perspective. If Haraway is right to invite us to stay with the trouble, she can't afford to forget that peoples of the Global South have indeed been staying with the trouble since 1492. The task at hand will thus consist in recognizing this ancient trouble and its deeply anchored roots, as well as recognizing the struggles and afterlives of the ancestors of those who continue to inhabit this trouble in its contemporary form. In order for this task to take effect, we will need to answer certain questions. In France, colonial ideology has long imposed on communities of color a mythical filiation with the "Gauls." This filiation has been duly rejected by anticolonial struggles and decolonial thought; however, as "whitened" or "assimilated" communities, have we indeed been able to escape said filiation? To what extent are we not descendants of Vercingetorix or General de Gaulle? Conversely, the whites in France massively buy into this postulate. But are they truly the descendants of the Gauls? To what extent are they not the descendants of Geronimo, of Toussaint Louverture, or even or the Emir Abdelkader? Are we allowed to choose our ancestors? If we are to adhere to C. L. R. James's thought, the answer would be a resounding yes: "These are my ancestors, these are my people. They are yours too if you want them."[2] When Sartre proclaims: "Liberate France from Algeria," we are invited to interpret this slogan as follows: that France can only be free once Algeria is free, or even that the French will only be free once the Algerians are. James's invitation can seem so vertiginous in its sheer generosity that it opens up unknown horizons. Indeed, how do we transform the defeats of some into victories for all? And how do we recalibrate our imaginary of defeated historical figures so as to turn them into victors of the past five centuries?

The digitally recorded killing of George Floyd in Minneapolis was a seismic event of a rarely equaled magnitude, and its shockwaves propagated toward most Western democracies. As a result, anti-racist mobilizations have occurred wherever we find a massive presence of postcolonial subjects—in part as an expression of solidarity with Black people living in the United States, as well as to denounce the forms of systemic racism they, as non-white inhabitants of white metropolises, are themselves victimized by. These spontaneous outbursts have come to unveil what decolonial movements had been emphasizing for numerous years: the common thread among imperialist nation-states lies in the racial pact that unites the white proletariat and the national bourgeoisie against a racialized underclass condemned to face structural discriminations, arbitrary forms of policing, and biased criminal justice systems. The COVID-19 pandemic has acutely corroborated this reality—in the US, France, and the United Kingdom, it is in fact non-whites who have most succumbed to the virus, either as a result of poor treatment, negligence, and malnutrition, or because they form the majority of workers deemed "essential" to the economy and have thus failed to benefit from confinement measures. Each imperialist nation-state has its underclass, be it composed of Black, Pakistani, Latinx, Caribbean, Native American, or Arab and Muslim subjects. The conjuncture brought forth by George Floyd's killing has come to further reveal the existence of an incoming political potential located within Empire, one capable of upending the Left-Right divide and the class struggle between the white proletariat and the (trans)national bourgeoisie that has sustained it. The anti-racist mobilizations that followed, by amplifying the political agency of a new demographic within a white world, have come to articulate a struggle of "social races"—a struggle which at once unsettles old political systems as well as lays bare antagonisms within the proletariat. This is to say that, while the existence of a class struggle remains undeniable, we can't deny that there also exists within the working class a statutory struggle between whites and non-whites. Decolonial movements and thinkers have said this time and time again: any and all revolutionary processes are bound to fail as long as race hasn't been abolished. In fact, we are unable to envisage the end of capitalism except through the unification of oppressed classes—and race is the knot that precludes the constitution of a united historical bloc.

Put schematically, capitalism was shaped by the power politics of nation-states, and nation-states have since continued to accumulate power to destroy and conquer through modern capitalism. Now, imagine race to be one of the pillars of this "geopolitical logic of power," due simply to a hierarchical division having played out on a global scale between dominant nations—competing among themselves—and dominated nations—the hunting ground of the former. This point is crucial because race is the knot that constitutes the alliance between the modern state and capital; it is around race that capitalist valorization and the power politics of nation-states are tied. Thus state personnel (high-ranking officials, chiefs of police, military staff, etc.) "encounter" capital through race. By following their autonomous, national-racial logic, state administrations serve capitalist interests. They carry out these interests by pursuing a policy of imperial power, i.e., by continuing to assert "national" economic interests, through trade as well as diplomatic and military agreements. This is what France does with its arms industry and its large groups specialized in aeronautics and nuclear power. It is what France does through Françafrique. Then, on its national soil, the colonial continuity of the nation-state becomes undeniable and manifests itself through the very *materiality* of the state apparatus: it is the history of its police and prefectures, intelligence services, ideological and media systems, and the Republican school (*l'école républicaine*). All these apparatuses more or less reproduce a logic of separation of the population between whites and others. This logic of separation is constitutive of the modern nation-state and, as Abdelmalek Sayad and Étienne Balibar have admirably argued, the nation inevitably produces "foreigners."[3] The universality of human rights has always held exceptions, as imperialist nation-states continue to demonstrate by conducting predatory policies in the Global South. However, by reproducing the logic of race, the state's personnel subsequently reinforce hierarchies that are themselves exploited by capital. Descendants of the colonized are the last to be employed and the first to be dismissed. The system generates a reserve of cheap labor which can, for example, conveniently face "uberization," fulfilling the dream of all bosses to make work flexible. This brings us to the last point: if this labor force is easier to exploit, it is because the racial logic of the nation-state tends more toward the economic and legal protection of white proletarians than that of their non-white counterparts. It also implies that the white working-class movement tends to spontaneously rely on republican legality and trust the neutrality of the state or, rather, to at least consider that the welfare state is the "decent" side of the state, as opposed to its nastier authoritarian and sectarian side. But for non-whites, the "decent" side of the state also strives to domesticate them. Even social workers, unemployment agencies, child protection officers, and physical and mental personnel abide by modalities of social control. We can then conclude that the logic of race undoubtedly strengthens apathy and inertia within social movements. Since white supremacy is the knot that ties capital to the state, untangling this knot among the oppressed would allow for the radicalization of social movements. Opposing capital should also translate into opposing the state. This opposition to the state can be channeled through decolonial struggles, but the latter's efficacy would not be as impactful if it weren't itself based on a powerful political theory—or, to put it another way, on a thought and praxis *of its own*. When we have to cross swords with the white Left—our privileged ally and, therefore, our primary adversary—it becomes imperative to provide ourselves with an "ideological capital" able to rob the white Left of its cultural hegemony. Such hegemony might have been won at the end of World War II, but continues to be lost to white neoconservatism, even fascism. To win this battle, we need to pave the way for a cultural revolution. This revolution will be intrinsically decolonial, or it will not be at all.[4]

A Beninese friend recently told me: "The risk with their history of integration and their famous 'our Gallic ancestors' is that tomorrow we will end up saying 'our ancestors the slave owners.'" It is important to reflect on this fear. Cecil Rhodes in South Africa, Edward Colston in Bristol, Victor Schoelcher in Martinique, Jean-Baptiste Colbert in France: the act of toppling colonial statues, which has been playing out for a few years now and has intensified since the killing of George Floyd, ultimately denies the integrationist fatality of the Gallic myth. There are decolonial forces in France and in the West that are resisting this integrationist injunction, especially when they aim to dismantle the symbols of colonial and slave-holding systems. This is a notable advancement because dismantling is neither marginal nor anecdotal. They are the expression of a decolonial consciousness in construction, capable of identifying the ideological base of white power rooted in the law of the strongest and on the narratives of conquerors—historical figures whose virtue is not so much to exalt the past as to confirm the present world order and, we fear, to prepare for the future. Thus, unbolting is no longer a purely symbolic act. By taking action to restore historical truth and to impose the point of view of the wretched of the earth, toppling statues becomes a powerful political act capable of competing with the official myths, perhaps even of shattering them. However, it does not erase the risk of assimilation, which first takes on the face of integration.

In my book *White, Jews, and Us: Toward a Politics of Revolutionary Love,* I write: "I am not innocent. I live in France. I live in the West. I am white. Nothing can absolve me of this." The relationship of non-white subjects to a white nation-state is of an inherently integrationist nature. Their presence is explained by the needs of the employers and the bourgeoisie but, as they live in France, it benefits from the social gains of the white proletariat. They are integrated in the country's social pact, despite occupying a subaltern position in the social totality. They are neither white nor the wretched of the earth. They are postcolonial subjects, the "indigenous of the republic" (*indigènes de la République*). However, it must be understood that, since they are no longer part of the wretched of the earth, they have been whitened. If that is the case, how are they to repudiate their Gallic ancestors? The fact is that they form, alongside the "native" French, a "national community" that guarantees them a certain standard of living, as well as social, syndical, and political structures that protect their rights. And if that is the case, how are they to dissociate from their Gallic ancestors, who are part and parcel of a mythology that itself constitutes the ideological foundation on which the French nation-state rests and reproduces its supremacism? The pertinence of my Beninese friend's hypothesis is therefore confirmed. If we were truly the heirs of the Gallic, then how come we aren't also the heirs of slave owners, since we also benefit, even as indigenous people, from the reaping of colonial conquests? To put it another way, integration *barbarizes* us.[5] We are worse than the simple heirs of the mythical Gauls; we are in fact, as my friend fears, the effective heirs of the slave owners.

In contrast, the vast majority of whites who glorify their phantasmagorical Gallic ancestors never seem to recognize themselves in indigenous struggles, and even less in their emancipatory figures. They are irremediably foreign to their history and their identity. When they hear of Toussaint Louverture, they think, at worst, that he has deprived them of Haiti or, at best, that he has liberated slaves. At no time has the idea that this separatist—who left an indelible mark on the history of France—may have transformed them as a people ever crossed their minds. Neither would be the case with the Algerian National Liberation Front (FLN), the writings of Frantz Fanon, or the poetry of Aimé Césaire. However, the struggles of slaves and colonized peoples not only transformed France and the French, but objectively debarbarized them. Not to the point of civilizing them, surely, though it did play a considerable part in laying the groundwork for it. At the heart of the barbarization of the indigenous people and the debarbarization of the whites, we can locate a potentially effective struggle against the national, racial, and imperialist pact of the French Republic. The effectiveness with which both the debarbarization of the whites *and* of indigenous people can arise directly depends on the progress of the decolonial movement. The more the counterrevolution regains ground, the more processes of barbarization will prove fatal. However, the progress of the decolonial movement is creating a real panic. France has been going through an acute moral and political crisis for a few years; I would even call it a crisis of meaning. This observation can be extended to all countries on the planet, but in particular to the old liberal democracies which constitute the most advanced capitalist states. I would say that we are facing a major crisis in the white, Western world, unable to digest and cope with the end of its empire. This is why I conclude the introduction to my book with the following question: "What can we offer white people in exchange for their decline, and for the wars that will ensue?" Answering this question is a challenge and can only come about through a real political alternative. In essence, I would say that we need to conceive a narrative of totality, or even design a utopia. But this can only materialize if a clear filiation is established between us and the ancestors that we have chosen. To put it more bluntly, there can be no projection into the future if we do not sort out which ancestors deserve to figure in our pantheon.

Signs of a looming crisis can presently be located in the Macron government's repression of the yellow vests (*gilets jaunes*) movement, or in increased forms of police brutality, and even in the surreal and hysterical debates that have been spawning around the Islamic veil. They can also be found in the Left's own crisis and its inability to produce political alternatives. The Left is fragmented and unable to unify popular classes, while the Far Right deploys itself politically as a mirror to what is currently happening all over Europe. Moreover, this crisis is manifesting through the decline of French elites. Let's take a closer look at two major "intellectual" figures of neoconservative discourse in France: Éric Zemmour and Alain Finkielkraut. Both of them are Jewish, one of Algerian origin and the other German. I insist on their origin because they are two historic victims of white supremacy that have converted into defenders of this same supremacy. To understand the mechanics of this conversion, it is important to understand that they, in fact, renounced their ancestors to adopt those of their executioners. This isn't without consequence on their political positioning. Indeed, the position they occupy today in the political spectrum marks a break in filiation, one that can also be engaged with as a form of treason, if we are in the camp of persecuted Jews, or of "assimilation," if we are in the camp of the neoconservative republican ideology. The latter, at the moment, has the wind in its sails, to the detriment of a progressive camp in ruins, fractured by Islamophobia and Eurocentrism, and completely incapable of unifying popular classes through class-based solidarity.

The two media intellectuals, both of whom are champions of the French neoconservative camp, agree with former French president Nicolas Sarkozy when he said in 2016 that "when you become French, your ancestors are the Gauls."[6] Zemmour adds: "To be French, you have to accept Napoleon as your ancestor and Joan of Arc as your great-grandmother." He explains: "I'm nostalgic for the time when France dominated Europe, and I understand real nationalists like Putin or Trump. I understand Putin very well when he says: 'Whoever does not regret the break-up of the Soviet Union has no heart.' To me, whoever does not regret the Napoleonic Empire is not really French. I long for the greatness of my country."[7] Since then, he has inexorably slipped toward embracing neofascist discourse, going so far as to excuse the Marshal Pétain, known mainly for having made a pact with Hitler in 1940 and having collaborated with the Nazis: a page in the history of France that the Republicans see as a mere "parenthesis," "an accident," but which any decolonial would see as constitutive of colonial history. Finkielkraut, on the other hand, has interpreted Sarkozy's declaration through subtler terms, claiming: "Our ancestors, we offer them to everyone."[8]

This neoconservative proposition strangely resembles that of C. L. R. James, itself decolonial. Not unlike the West Indian revolutionary intellectual, Finkielkraut is offering us "his" ancestors. It is quite troubling. But the trouble subsides as soon as the fog starts to clear. In fact, while C. L. R. James indeed offers his ancestors, he is careful not to offer "all" of them—only those who have struggled against slavery. He isn't offering an ideological, ethnic, or biological filiation, but a political, anticolonial one. Meanwhile, Finkielkraut offers all of his ancestors without any distinction: from Vercingetorix to Charles de Gaulle and his Algerian war, via Robespierre and the French Revolution; Napoleon, Europe's executioner; Thiers, the butcher of the Commune of Paris, and even Pétain, the Nazi collaborator. He thus makes himself the cantor of a memory to the glory of the "French spirit," wiping away social and political contradictions and giving pride of place to the myth of an eternal and dominating France. In fact, Sarkozy and Finkielkraut's proposal is diametrically opposed to that of James: one is characterized by its colonial and identitarian nationalism, the other by its revolutionary essence. While the former convenes a broad political spectrum that extends from France's neoconservatives to its socialists, the latter struggles to settle within the current political landscape; it is wedged between a republican Right and a Far Left that still dismisses race as an analytical and political category. Even Jean-Paul Sartre—who died both an anticolonialist and a Zionist—wasn't ready to take the final step toward his dewhitening, and the Far Left ends up reproducing the logic of race, perhaps without being aware of it. It is especially apparent in their choice of historical references. Unlike the French elites, they will always prefer Rosa Luxemburg to Joan of Arc, and Louise Michel to Victor Hugo. They also have their blind spots because they prefer Robespierre to Toussaint Louverture, despite the fact that the Haitian revolution has prolonged and reinforced the French Revolution by dismantling colonial and slave-holding systems, the foundations of an imperialist republic-in-the-making. By failing to comprehend and engage with James's proposition, white revolutionaries deprive themselves of the soul of their potential ancestors, and also of their power. As for us decolonials, the devotees of revolutionary love, we give thanks to C. L. R. James and his generosity and open our arms to his ancestors to make them members of our pantheon, while hoping for one thing only: that his ancestors recognize us as their worthy heirs.

Translated from the French by Edwin Nasr

Houria Bouteldja is a founding member of the Parti des Indigènes de la république (PIR), a decolonial political organization based in France. She has written numerous essays on decolonial feminism, racism, autonomy, and political alliances as well as articles on Zionism and state Philo-Semitism. She is the author of *Whites, Jews and Us: Towards a Politics of Revolutionary Love* (2017). She recently resigned from the PIR, but remains committed to decolonial activism.

1. I say "our" because I do not externalize myself from the West. I live there, so I am a part of it.

2. C. L. R. James, *Spheres of Existence: Selected Writings* (Wheeling, IL, 1980), p. 187.

3. Étienne Balibar and Immanuel Wallerstein, *Race, Nation, Class: Ambiguous Identities* (London, 2010).

4. This paragraph is based on a speech delivered on May 25, 2016. See Houria Bouteldja, "Pouvoir politique et races sociales," Parti des Indigènes de la République, June 20, 2016, http://indigenes-republique.fr/pouvoir-politique-et-races-sociales/ (accessed November 20, 2020).

5. I borrow this term from Césaire to underline both that barbarization is first and foremost the barbarization of Europe and the colonizer, but also a relative barbarization of non-whites living in Europe. It is a notion that must be distinguished from "barbarity," which describes a state of nature—as does "savagery"—and which borrows from the register of the Far Right; barbarization, on the other hand, is a social and historical process inherent in processes of integration into Western modernity. See Houria Bouteldja, "White Innocence and the Barbarisation of the Racialised: Letting the Sleeping Monster Lie," Parti des Indigènes de la République, January 29, 2020, http://indigenes-republique.fr/white-innocence-and-the-barbarisation-of-the-racialised-letting-the-sleeping-monster-lie (accessed November 20, 2020).

6. Joseph Bamat, "France's Sarkozy Trumpets 'Gaulish ancestry' as he Chases Far-right Votes," France 24, September 20, 2016, https://f24.my/2cEzc (accessed November 20, 2020).

7. Éric Zemmour (@zemmoureric), "Pour devenir français, il faut penser que Napoléon est son ancêtre et que Jeanne d'Arc est son arrière-grand-mère," Twitter, October 23, 2019, https://twitter.com/zemmoureric/status/1187068598004699137; "Éric Zemmour répond à l'invitation de Louis Aliot en campagne pour les municipales de 2020," Made in Perpignan, September 24, 2019, https://madeinperpignan.com/eric-zemmour-repond-a-linvitation-de-louis-aliot-en-campagne-pour-les-municipales-de-2020 (accessed November 20, 2020).

8. Alain Finkielkraut, interview by Élisabeth Lévy, "L'esprit de l'escalier," Radio RCJ, November 27, 2016.

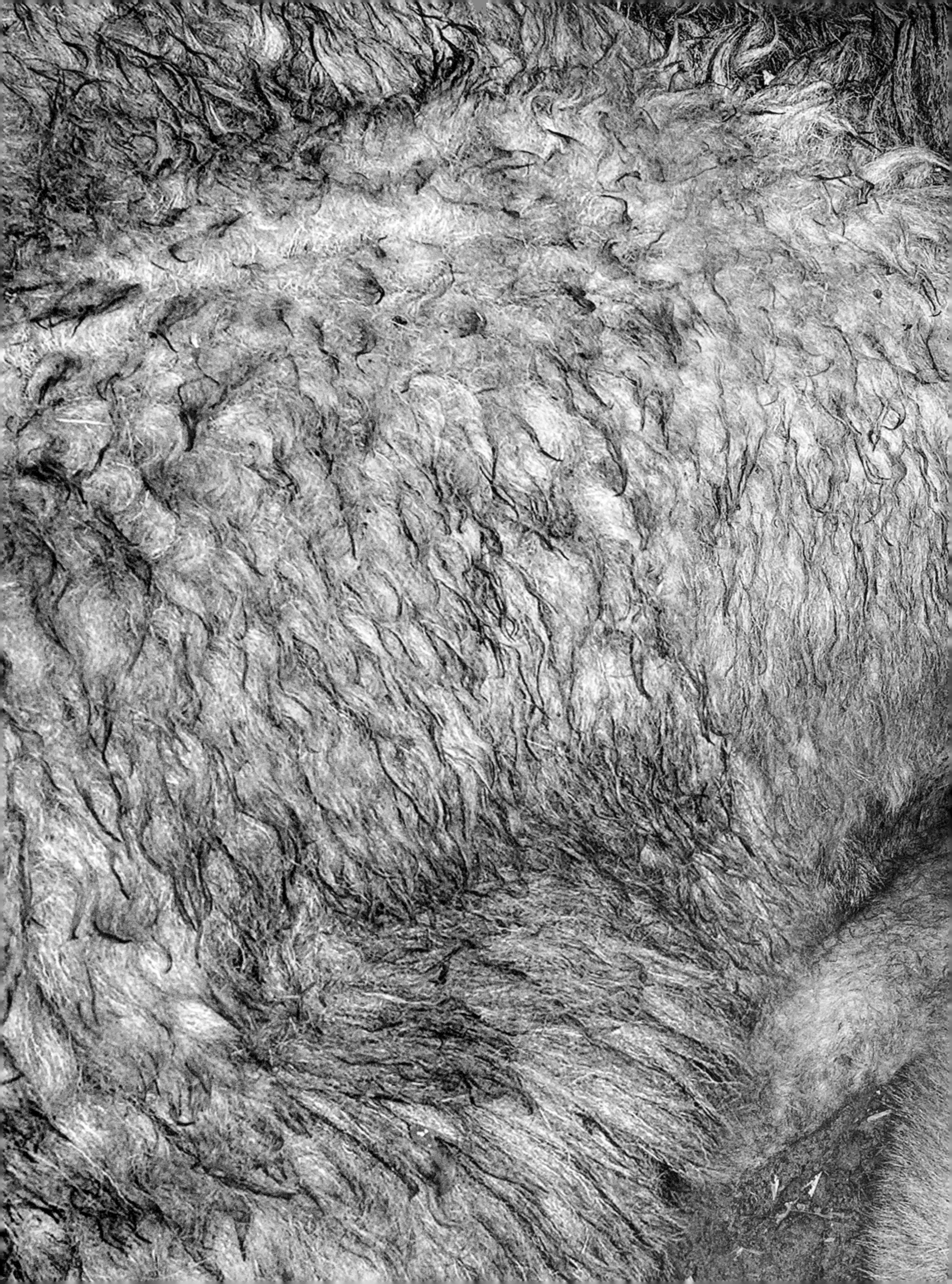

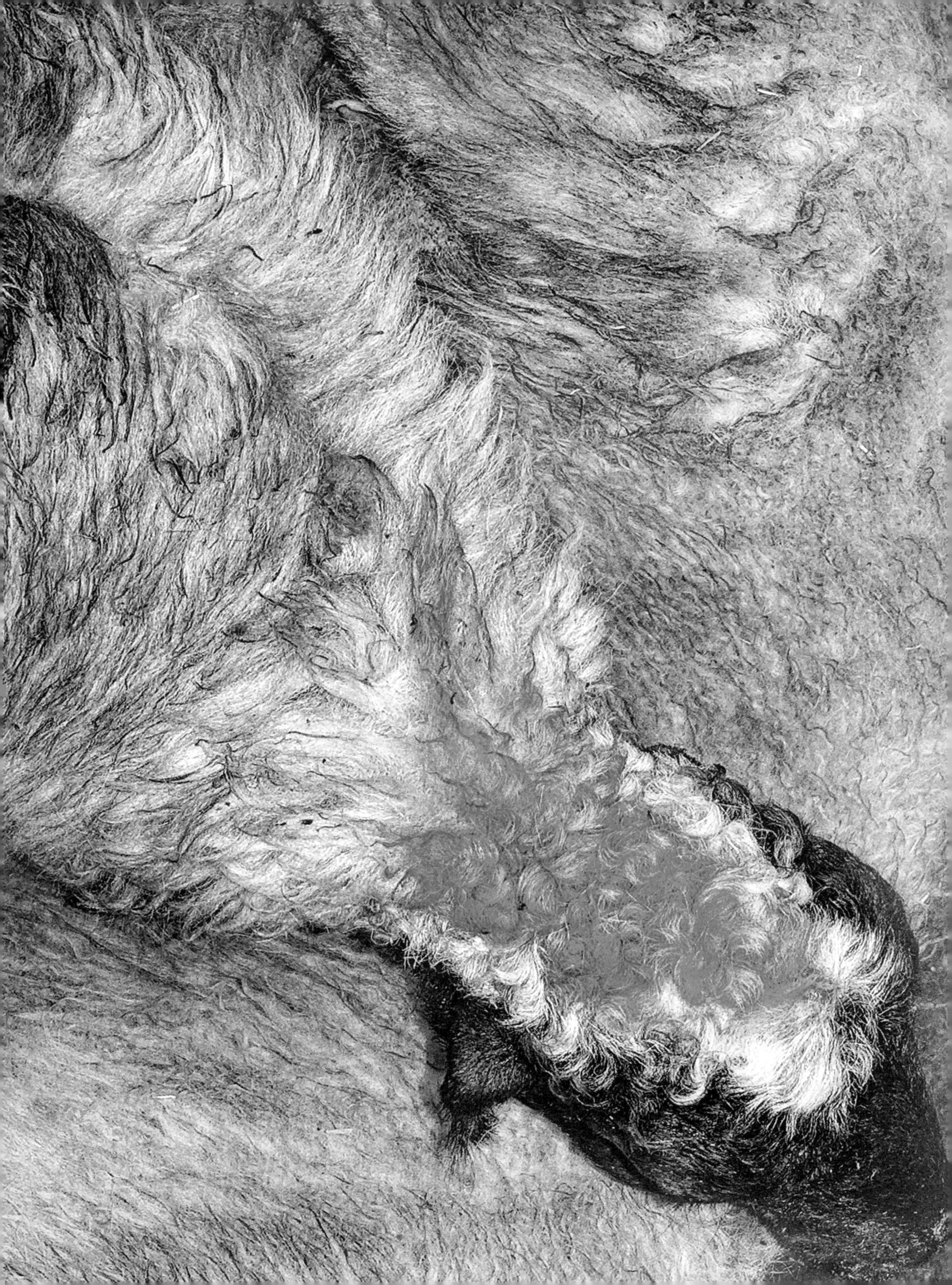

Transcript: Biospheres of War

Ghassan Abu-Sittah
Jehan Bseiso
Jasbir K. Puar
Francesco Sebregondi
Helga Tawil-Souri

In 2014, the United Nations projected that Gaza would be uninhabitable by the year 2020. Now that that year has passed, what does that prediction mean? Since the Great March of Return began on March 30, 2018, more than 8,000 protestors have been shot by Israel Defense Force snipers and sustained lower limb injuries, usually requiring multiple surgeries and, in many cases, amputation. Using visual materials, experimental video art, modeling, and sound, architect Francesco Sebregondi and queer theorist Jasbir K. Puar projected Gaza beyond the spectacle of humanitarian visual economies to show biopolitical practices of maiming and containment in daily life. Their joint installation situated maiming in its multiscalar, temporal, generational, and spatial forms, complicating the exceptionalism of Gaza. It also shed light on the elasticity and porosity of the blockade, its uneven and ever-changing modulation of flows, designed not only to restrict goods and people, but also to control the act and idea of movement itself. What escapes the blockade, however, is no less than multiple horizons of unyielding resistance and the future lives of return. On November 10, 2019, Puar and Sebregondi were joined in Sharjah by Ghassan Abu-Sittah, Jehan Bseiso, and Helga Tawil-Souri to discuss the situation on the ground in Gaza. A transcript of the conversation was also published in Jadaliyya *on March 30, 2020.*

FRANCESCO SEBREGONDI As many of you will know, since March 30, 2018, thousands of Palestinians in Gaza have been gathering at different points along a thick, militarized fence that separates Israel from the Gaza Strip. They are protesting their indefinite confinement within the regime of the Gaza blockade, which has been ongoing since 2007. They are also protesting and calling for the end of the seventy-one-year-long occupation of Palestine, and they are claiming their right to return to the land they belong to. As of today, the response from the Israeli military has been to shoot over 8,000 unarmed protesters with live ammunition, at least 1,200 of whom will be crippled for life.

Our project tries to interrogate what is at stake in these protests. It tries to look at what is happening, but also how and where it is happening. It tries to unpack both the structure of power that is deployed at the level of the blockade itself, understood as a system of containment of a population that is considered unworthy, as well as the shifts in the modalities of power that are displayed in the brutal repression of these protests, themselves a response to the blockade. But, perhaps even more importantly, what the project tries to question is the people of Gaza's unyielding capacity to resist. We are trying to address Gaza no longer as a merely humanitarian emergency that would require our distant attention, but also as a reserve of political imagination: as a place from which to think and to oppose any discourse claiming that an extremely advanced technological apparatus of power may be able to cancel a form of resistance and to annihilate a liberation struggle that has been ongoing for, again, seventy-one years. Jasbir will speak about how we have analyzed and studied the modalities of power that we are describing and opposing, somehow, in this project, as well as the reasons why we have invited these guests specifically.

JASBIR PUAR Since 2014, I started to notice that a lot of discussions on the violence of Gaza were organized around the question of civilian deaths. In this notion of collateral damage, death was disarticulated from disability. What is the productivity of that disarticulation? What kinds of goals does it serve? I started thinking about the tactic of deliberate maiming. It is a tactic that has become very visible in the recent protests (dubbed the Great March of Return), but we can actually trace it earlier, to the first Intifada—if not before. We can trace it to the West Bank, and to other locations such as Kashmir. One of the goals of the project was to deexceptionalize Gaza in relation to these practices, and to think more generally about how the violence of the nation-state is not just organized through letting-live or making-die, but also through perpetual injuring and the productivity of perpetual injuring.

We can see what is happening in Gaza now as the acceleration of a tactic of deliberate maiming, but we can also start thinking about how that tactic has been submerged in a narrative about living and dying as the primary modulation that nation-state violence is embedded in. The first goal for us was to return to the question of a liberation project, of a liberation movement, which is really important because the language coming out of Gaza right now is organized around humanitarian aid and human rights discourse, which translates everything into a kind of economic project as opposed to a political one. The second goal, just to reiterate, was to deexceptionalize Gaza historically, geopolitically—both in relation to the West Bank, East Jerusalem, and the Golan Heights, but also in terms of settler colonialism more generally. To paraphrase Patrick Wolfe's formulation around settler colonialism: the settler-colonial state is invested in genocide through annihilation or assimilation. One of the things I have been interested in is thinking about debilitation and perpetual injuring as another facet of genocide.

The third aim that I think was important to the project was the following: the 2020 prediction came up when I started looking at Gaza in 2014, so, six years ago. It seems like a long time. As time has gone on, what does it mean that 2020 is upon us and Gaza is apparently unlivable? What are the thresholds of livability that are constantly shifting? The blockade itself is a kind of elastic formation that is constantly expanding and shifting and allowing things to move in and out. It is not so much about a finite relationship to movement, but about the constant modulation of movement itself; it controls the notion of what movement is and what it constitutes.

The last thing I will say is that a biopolitical fantasy around maiming is that resistance can be stripped, that it can be annihilated, and that there is a point at which resistance cannot reorganize itself. We really wanted to expose the fantasy as such.

GHASSAN ABU-SITTAH My thirty-year journey in terms of working with war wounds started during the first Intifada in Palestine, but then expanded in the region to Iraq and Syria. It has left me with a few points that I would like to share. The first is this idea that wars are not temporal events. Wars create an ecology, a biosphere, in which people will live permanently, even after the political component of the war ends. This biosphere contains within itself the destruction of social relationships and the destruction of the built environment that was created to protect people. That destruction creates channels of injury and reinjury that will enslave or imprison people within this biosphere for generations to come. We can see southern Iraq as an example. Southern Iraq, the Basra area, and the areas that are demonstrating at the moment really have not had war for a long time, but the destruction—and the intensity of the destruction—by the first and second American invasions and the years of blockade created that ecology.

The most interesting, or the most obscene in its ingenuity, of these ecologies is Gaza, because you have created a hermetically sealed space in which you are able to titrate people's lives, and really the aim is to keep them in that zone between an incomplete life and the absence of total death. You do that titration in the siege by allowing different components of life to come in, or by denying them. It literally is like a chemical equation: when you are titrating life, you are bringing in more hours of electricity or withdrawing hours of electricity, you are bringing in the infrastructure for sewage and water treatment or you are withdrawing it, you are allowing food or not. We know that from the WikiLeaks papers—the Israelis were talking about putting people in Gaza on a very strict diet, so there is actually a calorie control and formula that the Israelis employ when they allow food, medication, and medical personnel in.[1] And then the components of death: you control the number of cancer patients who are permitted to leave Gaza, allowing it to vary between 20% and 40% rejection rate. And then, during the negotiations on deescalation with Hamas, you throw in the offer of a cancer hospital in Gaza. Then you realize that actually what you are doing is titrating this condition. Then you have these waves of war on Gaza that Ariel Sharon called "mowing the lawn."[2] The aim of these waves is to even out the bumps in the system, since you are able to inflict more in terms of death than you are able to control through the siege. Which brings us to the Marches of the Return.

In the Marches of Return, 0.01 percent of Gaza's population was injured within a year, which is a huge number when you think about a place with a population of two million.

The second phenomena was the intimacy of sniper fire. You do not have a process in which injury, maiming, or mutilation is a byproduct of the ordnance; with snipers, you are able to decide exactly where the bullet will go, even down to which limb. The decision to create this body of disabled young men—seven thousand so far, that we know of clinically—that you are consigning to a two- to three-year period of up to ten surgeries that will leave them, eventually, with a degree of disability, leaves you with the question of why you would want to do this.

If you step back to the origins of the Zionist movement, what differentiates Zionist colonialism from, let's say, Apartheid colonialism in South Africa, is that in South Africa you needed Black labor as part of the natural resource of the country. Zionist capital does not need Palestinian labor; therefore you need to use the body of the colonized in a different way—you need to harvest the body in a different way. And you harvest the body in Gaza differently by creating disability so that, economically, you benefit from being the only conduit of international aid, but, politically, you are able to transform a national liberation question—an anticolonial question—into a question of humanitarian aid. So, Gaza is no longer about the refugees, and the ethnic cleansing of 1948, and the denial of Palestinian rights. Gaza is about how many doctors you have allowed in, how many doctors you have not allowed in, how many hours of electricity you will let in. So, you are able to harvest the bodies, not in the way other colonialists have harvested the body for labor, but rather harvest the body for political capital.

Let's step back and look at the wound. These wounds become part of the struggle between the colonized and the colonizer. The wound, particularly because it is in its most vicious form when it is shot by the sniper, becomes the biological manifestation of the hegemony of the colonizer over the body of the colonized. It is the permanent narrative of the relationship between the colonized and the colonizer. But, at the same time, the colonized, the wounded, almost reaffirm their ownership of the wound by giving it a narrative of resistance. And so, rather than what the Israelis intended it to be—what, they, in Arabic, call كي الوعي, which means "branding," in the sense you brand cattle—the struggle of the colonized and the wounded becomes to own the narrative of the wound as a form of generating a consciousness of resistance. It is as if they were saying, "This is my biological manifestation of the struggle against the colonized, of the struggle against the siege." This is in no way belittling the physical pain and the clinical suffering, but it is about the struggle around the wound as a space in which consciousness becomes a battleground that is being played out between the colonized and the colonizer.

JEHAN BSEISO Where Gaza is concerned, if the last ten years are any indication then the very idea of a future, like our patients' legs, is amputated. That is exactly why we need to keep talking about it and not only providing medical care. I would like to refer to Gloria Anzaldúa, the Chicana writer and theorist, who writes: "To survive the Borderlands / you must live *sin fronteras* / be a crossroads."[3] So, for Gaza to survive, it needs to continue to be a crossroads, even if it is a crossroads of the macabre, a crossroads of surveillance, a crossroads of violence, a crossroads of pain, because it can also be a crossroads of solidarity and resistance.

I represent a very practical organization today. MSF/Doctors Without Borders has been on the ground in Gaza since 2000. We treat hundreds of people and, since the March of Return started in March 2018, we have treated half of those wounded by Israeli gunfire and live ammunition, most of them in the lower limbs. Our surgeons talk about bones turning into dust; complex, very serious injuries that Dr. Abu-Sittah knows very well. Infection is already a problem, but, in Gaza, infections resistant to antibiotics are rearing their ugly heads as well.

We were talking yesterday about what we can learn from Gaza. Unfortunately, some of the lessons that we, as a medical, humanitarian organization are learning from Gaza are very painful ones: about how you can treat people with critical injuries in a very low-resource setting, about how you can keep pumping people with antibiotics but they cannot heal—which says a lot about the body and, again, links with Jasbir's work on maiming. What does recovery look like in Gaza today, when we cannot even get wounds to close, when our patients suffer recurring infections, and when sometimes we treat entire families for gunshots? It is really difficult, and it has created a new "normal."

In March 2019, one year after the March of Return protests started, our teams were ready to prepare for what we call mass casualty preparedness: hundreds of people come into the corridors for us to triage and we provide the care for those who need it most. Fortunately, on the anniversary of the March of Return, "only" four people were killed and sixty-four were injured. The fact that our teams report being relieved that four people were killed and sixty-four injured by live ammunition is horrendous and unacceptable. Right now, what we can say is that Gaza needs to continue to be a living present, not only through the provision of medical care, but also by breaking the silence and breaking the oblivion. If architecture can be an archive, then so can medical witnessing and data. This is a little bit uncomfortable and it is definitely new. Medical data becomes a narrative tool, a witnessing tool. It can no longer be just numbers, it can no longer be just people and injured and nameless patients; it needs to be stories, even for an independent organization like Doctors Without Borders.

I will end by saying that in Gaza, we also face the limitations of humanitarian action. My colleagues have described the impossibility of looking at this as just a humanitarian crisis, one where the prison doors open to let in some assistance and close again. In 2012, our teams left Libya because we publicly declared that we refuse to patch up victims between torture sessions. What do we do in Gaza today? Do we leave Gaza? I would say no, because we are providing really urgent medical care, but our complicity in a system by working in the prison is something that is very much on our minds and in our debates as an organization.

HELGA TAWIL-SOURI As far as I know, the only place on Earth where people are pushed down to a humanitarian level is Gaza. If you think about it, humanitarianism, for all of its faults, for all of its misleading, for all of its horrors, itself is usually supposed to pull people up. In Gaza, humanitarianism pushes people down. In Gaza, people have been pushed down to this humanitarian level, whether we are thinking about it infrastructurally, psychologically, or biologically. The maimed body is a very real thing, but it is also representative of a different kind of maiming, of what we talk about when we talk about Gaza. I have spent the better part of fifteen years thinking and writing about Gaza and Palestine, and all I can tell you is that Gaza is absolutely not gentle on the soul to think about. It is a beautiful place. Gaza is like sparkling eyes, the smell of fresh strawberries, the smell of fresh fish, but also the smell of shit flowing down the streets; the contradictions are just astounding. But if you could try to capture every word, every thought, every process that Gaza inhabits, I think you would need a new vocabulary. At least for me, it has become impossible to tell the story of Gaza. So, I very much appreciate these different kinds of attempts to think of a new vocabulary to explain something that is really unexplainable.

How else can you grasp that, by 2020, a place is uninhabitable? First of all, it is already uninhabitable, and so, okay, thank you very much UN for telling us so, but what the fuck are we supposed to do about that? It is very angering. And this is maybe the thing, I do not think that one can speak of a place like Gaza without actually getting angry. There is always this kind of response: "What are we going to do?" And, "How can we help?" And so on, and that is a wonderful thing, but I think there also needs to be room for a kind of expression of the absolute. Again, I feel like I just do not have the words anymore to explain Gaza.

I generally work on infrastructure, and specifically on telecom infrastructure, which sounds incredibly boring. But, if you think about it, we are supposed to be wireless and we move around the world, we are all free and mobile and so on, but not in Palestine. In Palestine, things like fiber optic cables follow the territorial limitations that Israel has built around Palestine. So, what does it mean to think about a state that has a very limited or, if you want, maimed infrastructure? How can you even think of it? What kind of state are you allowing to be produced that cannot even control something like the technological connection between people, let alone the physical or geographical one?

FRANCESCO SEBREGONDI An idea driving the project that we have developed for the Triennial is to approach Gaza as a kind of extreme, and paradigmatic, urban form: one whose project is that of managing, or dealing with, an undesired population, a population that has been framed as such. This project is carried out through practices of maiming that maintain a level of vulnerability across a population of two million people—let us be reminded of this, a fast-growing population of two million people—and through practices of containment that are aimed at confining a population within a specific, defined territory. Looking at this urban form as a machine, as a functioning assemblage, in fact looking at its architecture, really brings to the fore the fact that some of the most advanced experimentation with regards to both spatial and biopolitical technologies are at work there. I think that this is why Gaza is a place that we simply cannot ignore or forget when thinking about the urban future more generally. That is, at the same time as certain idealized urban futures are being incubated, we have places such as Gaza, where a dark urban future has already materialized, whose aim is to maintain and contain a population outside of the sphere of society. I think, as architects, we need to address the existence of this project that is most directly materialized in Gaza today.

JASBIR PUAR I would be interested in talking more about the social life with the wound. The field of disability studies is driven by Euro-American understandings of the exceptional nature of disability. A place like Gaza, and most places in the Global South, complicate that understanding of disability as exceptional; it is actually endemic. And so, when we start thinking about how disability rights intersect with the right to maim, what is that relationship? How does the rights project fail a place like Gaza, along with many places in the Global South? What is that social life of the wound in relation to disability? Is it completely evacuated? Is it something that cannot be acknowledged? In some sense, a social model of disability has to disarticulate maiming from the social model and naturalize it as something that cannot be recuperated, not material for a rights project. So, you have contradictions in Gaza as well; you have a Paralympic team that is very successful, you have BBC documentaries about amputated soccer players—all of these recuperative models of disability that human rights frameworks can entertain—and then you have this other understanding of the wound as a form of resistant anthology. Maybe that is a framing question, or maybe not, but I just wanted to bring in the global context of a form of humanitarianism that is organized around this idea that disabled bodies should be bodies that are empowered, in a very specific way.

GHASSAN ABU-SITTAH When you look at this idea that Gaza, in a few months' time, will become "officially" uninhabitable, one thing strikes me in particular. On the eve of the movement of the American embassy to Jerusalem in May 2018, 3,000 were wounded in four hours. And being there, on that day, one of the things that shocks you—and I had seen it almost accumulating—is the rate of reinjury. So, which one of the wounds in the particular individual should you be addressing now? I had patients who had been injured in the same limb as in 2004 or 2008. Or patients who had been injured in other wars and then have come back as injured again. And so, that is within the same body. Then, the wound becomes a social phenomenon. How do people maneuver this relationship of the wounded family, of multiple members of the family having wounds? One of the things that I do is provide clinical advice to humanitarian organizations like MSF on planning projects. I have been working on a project on streamlining amputee services in Gaza. Two problems: if you are a child that loses a limb, the body, the stump, continues to grow, and continues to grow disproportionately; so the bones usually outgrow the soft tissues and they need multiple surgeries as they grow up. The statistic that is shocking is that in 2006, just during the Gaza wars as such—not the incursions or the little air raids in between—1,300 people lost limbs, and became amputees who require prosthetics. If you look at the people who needed secondary amputations—in the case of a failure of the reconstructive process—you are looking at 2,000 to 2,500 people.

This social phenomenon in a very close society means that, as Helga said, you really need to discover not only new language, but, as a clinician, new ways of thinking about things. Reconstructive surgery is really a boutique service; I have trained in the National Health Service in the UK to spend eight hours on a case. But what do you do when you have epidemic numbers of reconstructive cases, where you cannot spend eight hours—because you cannot spend eight hours times 7,000, each of which will need nine surgeries? If you start multiplying the number of hours, you see the scale of epidemiology that you see in infectious diseases, in diarrhea, in Ebola; you see an intentional infliction of a physical disablement. This means to start reimagining medical care on a scale that nobody else has dealt with, to look for data where none exists, except in World War I. I mean, that is the scale that we are looking at. Between 4:00 p.m. and 8:00 p.m. on May 14, 2018, 3,000 were injured. It literally felt like what you would feel if you had been in World War I, with waves of thousands of patients. Six and seven per ambulance were being brought in at the same time. Gaza pushed the limitations of our understanding, and the limitations of language, and the limitations of scientific knowledge in terms of that kind of infliction of suffering, for no reason other than that Israel designed this project, has always wanted to create politicide, i.e., the annihilation of Palestinians as a political body, and are happy to skirt as close as they need to skirt to genocidal policies to achieve politicide. What is happening in Gaza, this concept of how many people you can squeeze into the smallest plot of land, and the smallest conditions of habitability, is that kind of urge for politicide and the willingness to pursue genocidal policies to achieve it.

JEHAN BSEISO I would like to make two small comments. Jasbir, you mentioned the Paralympics and things like that which remind us that the body in Gaza is not disabled, it is also recovering. And you mentioned the importance of situating the body within disability rights and empowerment discourse. I agree completely, but I also want to highlight that that discourse cannot remove the wound—and the disability—from the politics in which it occurred. We see a little bit of a self-critique of the organization which I am part of, where we tell the story of the disability but not the context around it, and I think that is very, very important to keep in mind, and I say it as a reminder also for us. Telling the stories of disability is also telling the stories of Gaza and fighting against oblivion, because maiming outlasts media cycles; we see that deaths and killing are more interesting for the media, are more interesting for coverage. But thousands of amputees—nobody is interested in covering their stories anymore, and that is quite concerning.

HELGA TAWIL-SOURI One of the things that I think about when I listen to my copanelists, or colleagues, or friends up here is, we often think about Gaza as contained or maimed in different ways, and there is always that question of whether one can really imprison, collapse, squeeze, contain—there are so many other words that I could use—people and a population, and to what extent. At the same time, I think it is helpful to zoom out to different scales, geographic or temporal. What if we think about Gaza not just from the perspective of a body, or a national body, even, but from an environmental scale? Gaza is also an environmental disaster that is being created and propagated.

Jasbir's and Ghassan's work brings up the question: What kind of future are we actually enabling? It is almost incomprehensible to us to try to figure out what it means to live with a maimed limb. I mean, God forbid, you do not want that to happen to you, but it is not completely inconceivable to imagine what it would be like to live with a phantom limb or a prosthetic. But, what if you move up the next level? What does it mean to live in a maimed family, in which you have multiple wounds of one person, multiple wounds of a family, in which you will then also have the wounds of the building, and of the village, and of the city? And if you move up even more in scale, to a whole nation and in a national sense—not national belonging but, at least, a national project of some sort. And, to keep moving, zoom out and to think about: What does that mean for the future? Not just simply on an individual or a family, or on a social or on a national level, but on this much larger global scale. And so, the tension is to talk about Gaza in a very specific way. There is a part of me that wants to disagree with Gaza as an example, Gaza as a metaphor, Gaza as a paradigm, and so on, but at the same time recognize that it really does function in that way. Is that the kind of future that we are creating in different places? Whether it is Chile, or Hong Kong, or Sudan, or wherever else you kind of see these "mini-Gazas." And, then, what does it mean to think about these at different timescales?

JASBIR PUAR One of the things that we tried to focus on—but really is about the future in ways that we cannot predict—is the idea of the wound as family. What kinds of gender relations are being reorganized and rethought in the context of a predominantly male population being unable to work in the same ways? What happens to women as caretakers? There is also the question of the wound that grows. Young people being wounded and having a wound that grows are understood as having a stunted body in terms of medical thresholds and metrics. What does it mean to be foreclosed from a certain kind of adulthood, which is also a certain gendering; in order to be male or female, you have to be understood as a gendered adult in some sense. So, these are the questions about the rights of future generations and futurity. But I also think that these are the spaces that we cannot yet know, that are going to be spaces where resistance cannot be stripped—new ways of living, and living in what is understood as unlivable.

Ghassan Abu-Sittah has worked as a war surgeon in Syria, Iraq, South Lebanon, and during the three wars in the Gaza Strip. He has published extensively on war injuries.

Jehan Bseiso is executive director of Médecins Sans Frontières Lebanon. She is also a poet and writer, and her book *I Remember My Name* won a Palestine Book Award in 2016.

Francesco Sebregondi is an architect and a research fellow at Forensic Architecture since 2011. He is completing a PhD at the Centre for Research Architecture, Goldsmiths, University of London.

Helga Tawil-Souri is an associate professor in media, culture, and communication, and Middle Eastern and Islamic Studies at New York University.

1. The Associated Press, "Israel Used 'Calorie Count' to Limit Gaza Food During Blockade, Critics Claim," *The Guardian,* October 17, 2012, https://www.theguardian.com/world/2012/oct/17/israeli-military-calorie-limit-gaza (accessed January 28, 2021).

2. Mouin Rabbani, "Israel Mows the Lawn," *London Review of Books* 36, no. 15 (July 31, 2014), https://www.lrb.co.uk/the-paper/v36/n15/mouin-rabbani/israel-mows-the-lawn (accessed January 28, 2021).

3. Gloria Anzaldúa, "To Live In the Borderlands Means You," in *Borderlands/La Frontera: The New Mestiza* (San Francisco, 1987), pp. 194–95.

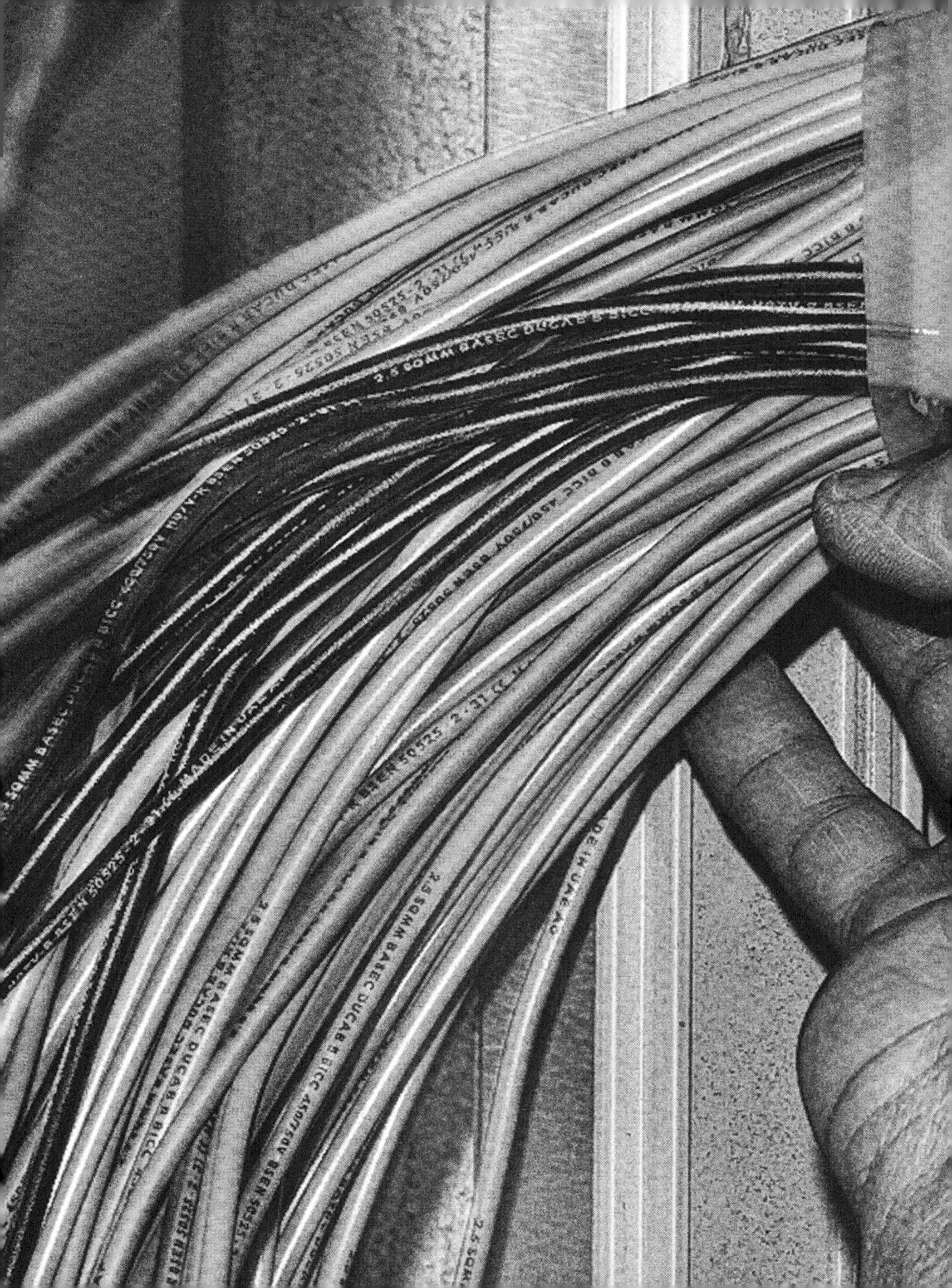

2.5 SQMM BASEC DUCAB B BICC
BSEN 50525 2.31
MADE IN UAE
450/750V

Combat Breathing, Redux

Jasbir K. Puar

During the first two years of the Great March of Return in Gaza, from 2018 to 2020, over 7,000 protesters were shot in the lower limbs. Many of these injuries have required amputations, multiple surgeries, or have developed wound resistance due to insufficient antibiotics.

NADIA'S LEG

> My friend . . . Never shall I forget Nadia's leg, amputated from the top of the thigh. No! Nor shall I forget the grief which had molded her face and merged into its traits forever. I went out of the hospital in Gaza that day, my hand clutched in silent derision on the two pounds I had brought with me to give Nadia. The blazing sun filled the streets with the color of blood. And Gaza was brand new, Mustafa! You and I never saw it like this. The stone piled up at the beginning of the Shajiya Quarter where we lived had a meaning, and they seemed to have been put there for no other reason but to explain it. This Gaza in which we had lived and with whose good people we had spent seven years of defeat was something new. It seemed to me just a beginning. I don't know why I thought it was just a beginning. I imagined that the main street that I walked along on the way back home was only the beginning of a long, long road leading to Safad. Everything in this Gaza throbbed with sadness which was not confined to weeping. It was a challenge: more than that it was something like reclamation of the amputated leg![1]

Ghassan Kanafani's short story "Letter from Gaza," written in 1956, speaks to a *longue durée* of maiming. The text forces a reckoning with the endlessness of intergenerational Palestinian injury; there is no afterlife of violence. A history of Israeli maiming of Palestinian bodies could have many beginnings, whether of the Nakba, the 1967 occupation, or then-Defense Minister's Yitzhak Rabin's infamous "break their bones" policy during the first intifada. But Kanafani portrays a different symbolic imaginary of the "amputated leg," of his niece "Nadia's leg" as the advent of a Gaza that is "brand new." "It seemed to me just a beginning": this Gaza "throbbed with sadness which was not confined to weeping"; the "blazing sun" and the "color of blood" are one and the same.[2] Kanafani's protagonist hails the amputated leg as more than a wound, mark, or biological manifestation of the colonizer/colonized relationship. The scene of crisis and grief in the hospital room genuflects to a vibrant political consciousness that respects sadness with few tears, that cultivates the life-giving energy of a sun that eventually sets but also rises again. The narrator's rousing reorientation is not a predictable call for resilience, nor does it solicit the empathic humanitarian gaze. Rather, the amputated leg signifies the unqualifiable momentum of collective subjectivity that is inherently in excess of, and therefore escapes, the strategic aims, calculations, and desires of the biopolitical state to strip Palestinian bodies of all vitality and resistance.[3] In this brand-new Gaza, there is no prothesis or rehabilitation that can redress the missing limb. The amputated leg is shadowed by its absent twin, the phantom limb. In this case, the phantom limb does not ache for wholeness, but rather demands the return of Palestinians to their 1948 homes. If the image of Nadia's leg signals the resistance to occupation, the phantom limb of this amputation is no less than liberation itself.

In 2018, Gaza became the theater of explicit maiming; no longer accidental or incidental but intentional in its scale and intensity, witnessed and sanctioned by global audiences. In the interstices of diagnostic and speculative realms of analysis and theorizing, how do we reorient the spectacle of maiming as the apex of sovereign power to the open horizons of Palestinian resistance?

"It seemed to me just a beginning" might be an appropriate description of *Future Lives of Return,* an installation I coauthored with Francesco Sebregondi at the Sharjah Architecture Triennial that attempted to convey the complexities of resistance in Gaza. In 2018, newspapers had been rife with photos of scores of men injured in the lower limbs during the Great March of Return, some with crutches or wheelchairs, some amputated. The theater of humanitarian crisis had been sealed with these and other empathy-inducing images of pain, images, as Nitasha Dhillon notes, "already decided in advance," which convey more about humanitarian saviors than of the photographed Palestinians.[4] Even those representations that showed the protesters resisting in myriad forms were folded into the "resilience" narrative. Despite aiming to counter it, the pornographic documentation of the ravages of Israeli State power tends to performatively reiterate this violence by tutoring publics in the value of the Israeli body as national property more so than conveying the realities of Palestinian resistance.

To short-circuit libidinal investments in the suffering body, even those marshaled to solicit humanitarian affects, we resisted the impulses of the evidential. There were no photos of wounds nor portrayals of the wounded, no representations of walls or borders, no images of Israeli soldiers, no documentaries. That is not to say that we did not use evidential materials, but rather that we sought to deploy these materials beyond the contexts of their immediate apprehension and consumption, illuminating the semiotic excess of images that exceed the presentation of logic, proof, and empiricism. Communicating maiming in Gaza without images caught in the binary of victimhood and transcendence became a primary guiding philosophy, as did a commitment to shift from perspectives "on Gaza" and "about Gaza," to "of Gaza" and from Gazans.

Leading with the above passage from Kanafani's "Letter from Gaza," *Future Lives of Return* sought to convey multiple Gazan perspectives from a location that is usually presented as a contained, homogenized entity. The installation was composed of art, photography, data charts, and a closing film that connected Gaza to other liberation struggles titled *Training in the Practice of Freedom*.[5] A centerpiece model of the Great March encampments depicted the spatial intimacies of the protests, to honor the myriad communal rituals, quotidian activities, and care work undertaken there: reading circles, cooking, medical support, tire burning, kite flying, singing. Unlike forensic models that seek precision tracking of elements in a Cartesian space along a timeline, our model foregrounded intensities and durations: the sense of collectivity expressed in the density of bodies, the charge of solidarity given in their orientation and their motion, the feelings of conviviality formed in the inclination of these bodies to each other. A four-speaker sound installation, *Perceptual Siege,* enveloped the exhibition with protest noises, the narrative voices of the wounded, and an audio terrain of enclosure. Sound artist Dirar Kalash did not aim to replicate the sensorial stratum of "being there," but rather to wrap the experience of the exhibition in the confines of "being here," a mix of textures that haptically inform but also assault the senses.

Video pieces from Gazan artists were another mode of thickening an assemblage of perspectives. The eight videos we selected necessarily reflect the material conditions of the blockade. The equipment necessary to produce moving image work is widely accessible thanks to mobile phones. Gazan artists use portable, transferable media to circumvent the contained conditions of production; like avatars in a biosphere of war, the work circulates because they cannot. These largely nonrepresentational pieces refuse the gaze of the documentarian and the humanitarian. Instead, they illuminate different notions of movement: the porosity of the blockade, the sea as horizon, the shuttling of refugee existence, shuttling between "waiting" and "fighting."[6] These videos highlight and challenge mobility restrictions on the colonizer's terms and also imagine, and thus extend, what movement is on their own terms. In other words, there is a refusal to allow the blockade to define all horizons of mobility.

The ActiveStills Collective is comprised of Israeli and Palestinian photographers who have been documenting the violence of Israel's settler colonial occupation since 2005.[7] Working across and against the Green Line, the work of ActiveStills provided a multifaceted archive that allowed us to evaluate the relationships between the

Left: *Transit* (Taysir Batniji, 2004) marks the movements to and from Rafah, the border crossing with Egypt. Scenes of waiting with luggage and other belongings are juxtaposed with images of airports and checkpoints. Using slides gives the viewer a sense of show-and-tell, inviting the viewer into a prior mode of showing others vacation pictures or family photos. © VG Bild-Kunst, Bonn 2022.

Right: *Port Hour* (Salman Nawati, 2010) projects the porosity of the blockade through imagery of the sea, the beaches, the fishing boats. The sea is part of the blockade structure and also an escape from it. Through a reworked parkour, the obstacles to overcome are not the burnt-out detritus of war but the crafts of fishing and the geospatial demands of the ocean. The protagonist reshapes the boundaries of the sea, emphasizing the elasticity of bodies in reorganizing resistant capacities.

banal and the spectacular, the images that circulate and those that do not. After reviewing thousands of photographs, we chose thirty-one photographs to convey the ordinary rather than the extraordinary: the makeshift medical clinics, the decimated olive trees and homes, the wheelchair abandoned at the checkpoint, the festive activities at the Great March encampments, the ubiquity of female activists at protests.

But the immanent critique of spectacle does not foreclose its theatrical return—we were, after all, creating an exhibition, replete with the attendant dilemmas that subtend extractive economies of display. We chose one "award-winning" photograph that had gone viral in the early months of the Great March, that of Saber al-Ashqar taken on May 11, 2018. Al-Ashqar is a double amputee in a wheelchair, wielding a slingshot with his right arm. Behind him are billowing clouds of smoke and the backsides of two female protesters. This photograph went viral in large part because of the empowerment discourse it plays into: the disabled body can protest, can have agency and vigor. But the scene is not necessarily an exceptional one in Gaza, so we anchored this photograph alongside others showing mundane daily activities informed by debilitation. Resituating viral imagery, the spectacular, in the context of the banal is a crucial strategy for muddling the terrains of visibility and what Édouard Glissant hails as the colonized's "right to opacity."[8] Exposing the humanitarian gaze for its partiality to "tragic icons of disability," this resituating deflates the contingency of that desire; what seems spectacular from the outside is revealed as an everyday occurrence.[9] Because the wheelchair has become the universal symbol of disability worldwide, this resituating also displaces the wheelchair as a/the primary prothesis, calling attention instead to the corporeal empowerment of the slingshot.

Pivoting away from telling stories about humanitarian crisis to telling stories about Palestinian liberation meant attending to the *longue durée* of maiming, especially to the different temporal scales that stretch well before and well beyond the impact of the sniper's bullet on flesh and bone. We followed the reserves of political imagination and ingenuity that remained beyond the reach of the biopolitical state

Left: Basma Alsharif wrestles with going to Gaza in her experimental film *Deep Sleep* (2014). Refusing mobility as rigidly prescribed by modernity, *Deep Sleep* moves between dream-like states, hypnosis, fantasy, and reality, and between Malta, Athens, and Gaza. Alsharif is present only as a subconsciousness, moving not only between spaces, but also through historical time. Ancient ruins are juxtaposed with the ruins of war: What makes a place one of civilization?

Right: *Bath Time* (2012) takes the viewer on a whimsical trip of interspecies bathing. In late 2009, a Gazan zookeeper, unable to replace a lost Zebra, painted a donkey with stripes. Multimedia artist Sharif Waked rescripts what is a common evening ritual for children—it's bath time, time for washing up. We see a donkey with painted stripes in a stark white bathtub with tiled white walls. As the bath progresses, his camouflage slowly washes away.

and transcended its dominant representational forms. It confronted us with the truth that the risk of being killed or maimed was not the epitome of the Freudian "death drive" inappropriately ascribed by journalists, nor a fetishization of martyrdom (in part remaindered from the seemingly incommensurate life-death paradigms of suicide bombers), but really just the fodder for a certain kind of living, nothing more than a demand for just forms of life, the persistence of which refuses the biopolitical fantasy that resistance can ever be extinguished.

MAIMING

We can think of maiming on two registers which sometimes overlap or intersect: literal and metaphorical. Literal practices of incapacitating bodies occur through a variety of corporeal assaults, be it the targeting of limbs by snipers, the calibration of caloric intake and drinkable water, or the production of never-ending spectrums of trauma. The metaphorical uses of maiming—not always thoughtfully uttered—deploy tropes of debilitation to refer to damaging conditions, e.g., "crippling Gaza's economy." The two merge at what at first appears to be the "event" of maiming, the conditions for which are being created well before and long after the actual moment of injury, due to overall environmental and infrastructural debilitation. Maiming "outlasts media cycles."[10] Modulated between asphyxiation and suffocation, in Gaza the life trajectory of a maiming is multiscalar in temporal and spatial terms, prompting one to wonder: What/where is the "real" wound? In this dual usage, maiming is not confined to an assault against the human biological form; it is rather a precondition that dictates the humanness or its lack thereof accorded to the body and to populations. Maiming is thus not only something that "happens" to a body; rather, it is folded into the ontology of resistance, of what it means to live "under occupation."

Chokepoints regulate, or titrate, food, electricity, medical supplies, water, cement, other building materials, but also doctors' visas, humanitarian aid workers, and infrastructure. The data that are

Left: *Governor's Game* (Mohamed Abusal, 2018) offers a meditation on construction, destruction and reconstruction, a parable for the Right to Return. It opens with what appear to be small pieces of stone being assembled by hands on a white tablecloth. Increasingly, we discern the flesh and seeds of a pomegranate, a Palestinian national fruit of sorts, being reconstructed. Referencing the commons of the domestic, *rumman* (pomegranate) symbolize both the process of dissembling and reassembling that characterizes the dual temporality of refugee existence, as well as gesturing to the geopolitical stakes of domestic banality.

Right: *Daggit Gazza* (Hadeel Assali, 2013) juxtaposes scenes of making *daggit* in a kitchen to the sound of a phone conversation—between men—about the war. The audio conversation links Gaza to relatives in Houston, Texas, while the topic of the siege of Gaza conveys the stressors on domestic spaces. In this sense, the purported "private" of domestic space is the public of Palestinian resistance; there is no distinction.

collected on these quantities constitute the metrics of dividualization. The dividual is digital, a composition of data points that do not privilege a normal/abnormal binarization, but rather render a series of relations to statistical norms that inform titration as a technology of control. The process of dividualization is enacted through titration, such that the experience of life is funneled into banal yet brutal empiricisms about health, infrastructure, reproduction—anything that can be capacitated and debilitated through monitoring and modulating.[11] Titration is a type of "security mechanism" that generates "the code of a dividual material" to variably distribute and modulate time and again the elements central to livable lives, ostensibly to "optimize a state of life."[12] In the case of Gaza specifically (and Palestine more generally), these security mechanisms informing the logistics of containment are not about optimizing a state of life, but rather about the "minimization of undesired mobility."[13] By maintaining a population in a state of perpetual injury, sustaining chokehold technologies of enclosure, and calculating these metrics of maiming, the digital coordinates of the dividual, not the individual, become the primary target of inhumanist biopolitics.

Projections in 2012 stated that by the year 2020 Gaza would become uninhabitable.[14] 2020 is here and some 1.8 million Gazans remain, suggesting that thresholds of livability are less about a universal understanding of humanistic existence and more about constantly redefining what constitutes the livable. Titration is a form of modulation by degree that tempts a change in kind, approaching thresholds that only cohere retroactively. The livable/unlivable binary is usurped by the generating of incremental degrees of being. To convey a sense of how titration works, we presented a series of charts inspired by the straightforward gravitas of W. E. B. Du Bois's "Data Portraits."[15] Our charts distilled the congestion of statistics on the blockade released by humanitarian aid and human rights organizations. Twenty-four charts represented information on the availability of potable water, daily hours of electricity, the ratio of injuries to deaths over the years, destruction of hospitals, frequency of patient transport and visa allotments, the regulation of fishing zones, flows of goods, the destruction of agriculture, and the release and containment of Internet bandwidth.

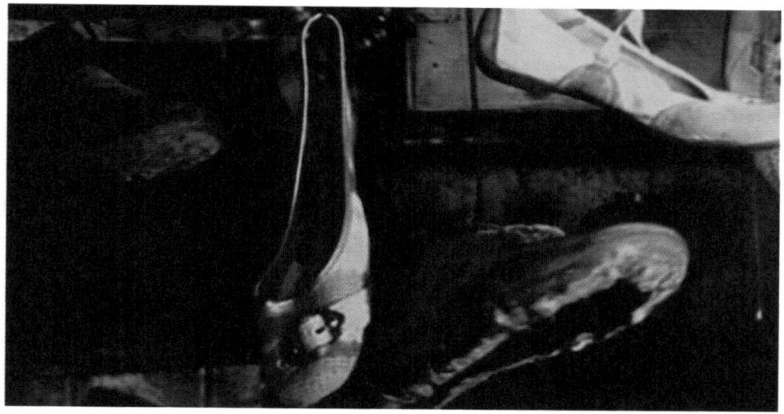

Left: *Light From Gaza* is a long meditation on the quotidian uses of electricity and the spectrum of technology that is absorbed into the unconscious of the user. Mohamed Harb's film denaturalizes electricity and excavates the extent to which it recedes into the "natural" of daily life without thought, taken for granted, in contexts where electricity is uncontested as a collective social good or not withheld as a form of collective punishment. Harb reminds viewers of the second-by-second reliance on electricity through numerous appliances and apparatuses that sublate this reliance. Rendering beautiful scenes of light and darkness through the shortage of electricity, the aesthetics of load-shedding, there is here an implicit mocking of the contemporary obsession with light sculptures.

Right: Salman Nawati's *Scenario* (2013) opens with a number of pairs of shoes, men's and women's, ballet slippers to boots, hung from a ceiling, as if in an open-faced market stall. At first swaying in the breeze to sanguine music, the shoes are suddenly attacked and disappear, one by one, as the music turns aggravated and jarring.

The blockade of Gaza is therefore elastic. It functions not only as an enclosure of movement but also as control over what movement is and what it can be imagined to be. Thresholds of the un/livable are infinitely recalibrated through the porosity of the blockade through a logistical governmentality that seeks to regulate the idea of movement itself. Defiantly redefining movement through, not despite, the uncertainties generated by this heaving blockade, Gazans rethink mobility as this indistinguishable interface between inner and outer: or, mobility as a Möbius strip.

REMOTE OCCUPATION TO INTIMATE SNIPING

The colonizer's capacity to maim is typically interpreted as a process of "dehumanizing" the target, but this argument presumes a process of colonial "othering" that is daunting for the Semite, whose racial "other" is, it could be said, already within. Israeli soldiers' descriptions of sniper targeting suggest there is an additional proprioceptive process akin to sensing, sifting, sorting.[16] Dividualizing does not break down or dismember the body—knees, ankles, limbs— but rather never recognizes these disparate elements as part of a composite in the first place. The target becomes not the Palestinian, not even the Palestinian limb, but simply the/a limb. There is the intimacy of proximity here—snipers and protesters are not far from each other, their faces, sometimes their eyes meet. But one learns not to see the limb as missing a/the body. This intimacy is what allows, rather than thwarts, seeing a human arm or leg as "a part" that floats free of the human form, available to the sniper as perceptually decoupled from the body. The intimacy that is produced with the part has as its corollary the situatedness of the rest of the individual's body. This relational frame of sight dividuates by "unseeing" the body as a composite. Soldiers tally the limbs they have conquered at the end of each day.[17]

The individual is humanized in order to register grievances within human rights frames (never politically feasible or effective for Palestinians) and dehumanized in order to be killed. The dividual is a ground zero analysis of fragments that are not of a whole, of bodily metrics, and of para- and sub-individual capacities. The composite of the body is irrelevant; it is unimportant that it exists. While the maimed individual is (fantasized as) available for empowerment and prosthetic technologies/apparatuses, *the dividual is a communicated expectation* rather than an ideologically-driven figure and relies on soliciting training on the plasticity of parts. Dividualization is an important factor in how Palestinians are targeted because it is a dividual and not the individual that is the desired formulation driving an inhumanist biopolitics, a biopolitics that moves from humanity to pure capacities and their metrics.

The libidinal economy of picking off bodies—nay, lower limbs—one by one fuels a kind of affective renewal of settler subjectivity, a sadism that revels in the performative repetition of massacre. That is to say, it is not satisfying enough to massacre (a mass) just once, or now and again. Rather, to sustain this sadism not only must the numbers add up to a massacre; each act of sniping is a massacre unto itself.

Sniping therefore acts as source material for renewing settler colonial subjectivity and entitlement that has (temporarily) exhausted the utility of aerial bombing, drones, and other forms of remote-controlled violence. The oscillation between intimate and remote modalities of violence suggests settler ambivalence about both proximity to and difference from the colonized. Maiming is the reiterative performative of the (founding?) event of settler colonialism that contributes to its enduring structure. The words of Kanafani's narrator echo here: "It seemed to me just a beginning."[18] In the case of Palestine, we could surmise that the right to maim is one precondition for settler colonial occupation. Patrick Wolfe has importantly argued that settler colonialism is a structure, not an event, stressing that elimination of the native is not accomplished only via one-off genocide.[19] The endless repetition of the founding moment renders porous the limits of the event in time, such that event and structure are no longer opposed, nor do they disappear each other. These events of maiming compose the debilitating structure of settler colonialism, a recursive structure.

Sniper tactics have been tested with regularity in the refugee camps in the West Bank from at least the first intifada. What is the tactical value of using snipers now? In the context of the remote-control occupation of Gaza, sniping indicates an unleashing of sovereign power that is sanctioned and conducted with impunity in front of a nonengaged international audience. This is a shift from 2014. Sniping is a progressive stage in the renewed potency of sovereign power that continues and will continue to search and root around for its limits. Maiming in this instance is not a strategy to avoid the glare of the international community by keeping the death toll low, as might have been the case in the past. It is actually about producing the spectacle of disability—Palestinian maiming—that signals a life not worth living, contra the liberal fantasy that a disabled life is a life worth living. This is the audacity of the Israeli biopolitical state, to demonstrate that maiming, not (only) killing, is the epitome of sovereign power. Sniping is an act of precision without any pretense that maiming is an inescapable consequence of war; precision maiming shifts injury from unavoidable to intentional.

Snipers use a range of ammunition: "live" ammunition, rubber bullets, illegal dum-dum bullets, all of which are considered nonlethal.[20] "Nonlethal" is a placebo term, meant to pacify, nullify, or minimize the impact of violence. The designation of lethality can shift depending on who is the user, the distance between user and target, and how the ammunition is used. The distinction between lethal and nonlethal weapons is a technical and legal valuation, but it is one that also organizes a narrative of harm spatially and temporally. It keeps our attention on the distinction between life versus death, allowing for the exploitation and leverage of the obscured hinge between injury and death. Concern remains on whether a weapon will kill in an attempt to deflect questions about what happens to those who are injured. This distinction also minimizes the event of injury so that the before and after, the life trajectory of a maiming, is effaced. What does it mean to use nonlethal weapons in Gaza where the medical infrastructure is so decimated? Nonlethal injuries can become, if not lethal, certainly what has been called in Palestine a "permanent disability"—which is really a euphemism for a permanent injury, a wound that never heals. There are also subdistinctions of less lethal, less-than-lethal, nondeadly, pain-inducing. Tear gas is nonlethal and yet the effects of long-term exposure to tear gas might count as "less-than-lethal" rather than legitimately nonlethal. These gradations belie temporal anxieties: How soon do you die? How proximate is death?

HOME INVASIONS

The problem of gender is at the center of maiming and yet largely unremarked upon in most accounts of the March, be they mainstream or progressive news outlets, NGO reports, or even medical data. Why are all the images, photos, and news coming from Gaza all of men, and crowds of men? Is this an elision of who occupies public and protest spaces? But this frame resuscitates the public/private divide so prized by second-wave feminists and thoroughly deconstructed by feminists of color. A complex enmeshment of the public of the protests, the private of the domestic, and their asymmetric gendering becomes visible when foregrounded through the effects of maiming.

Beyond a surface reading of emasculation, the delimiting of manual labor, and the presumed "burden" that the disabled put on kin structures and women, what is maimed masculinity and how is it tethered to or relieved from the representational politics of gender? And is there something like a maimed femininity? If we pivot from the theater of masculine injury, of fetishized martyrdom, most maiming in Gaza still happens to women, girl children, and bodies that are deemed illegible to the male-female binary. Women endure chronic forms of violence involving domestic violence, sexual assault, and intimate partner abuse. While the scene of maiming is masculine, violence against women is calibrated with injuries and deaths of the siege, waxing and waning in relation to maiming of men, a perverse relation of the domestic to the war. From a feminist point of view, the end of the siege/attack/maiming does not mean that violence abates for women. That is to say, often times when the protests end, the violence at home begins.[21]

These two scenes of violence, one with snipers, the other with kin, are both scenes of intimacy. The wound is a narrative of resistance that marks family, kin, and homosociality. Male homosocialities of the wound, having access to heroic triumphalism, create fraternal affiliations while simultaneously fragmenting or putting strain on familial filiations. Female homosocialities are weighted differently. They do not carry the same heroism; shame and victimhood are the scripts at hand. Are not these scripts, however, anchored within and emanating from the vantage of nationalist masculinity? There is every reason to believe that female homosocialities far exceed them. Shrouded by these public scenes of masculine heroism are prolific spaces of becoming where "the goods"—Claude Lévi-Strauss's term for women as objects of exchange between men—"refuse to go to market." What happens when "the goods get together?" This is to ask, what convivial kith and kin are possible when the strictures of heteronormativity are so tight that it cannot perceive beyond itself that the goods/women are "maintain[ing] among themselves another kind of trade?"[22]

Maiming men is in effect a multifold erasure of women, exacerbating or layering the already positioned female body as wives, mothers, and daughters in any revolutionary struggle: women are symbolically integral, yet materially subjugated.[23] What intentional maiming amplifies in this classic conundrum is the thickening of "vast amounts of extra and exhausting" reproductive labor, affective and pragmatic, as the caretaking of injured and incarcerated male family members falls to women.[24] Women's participation in political protesting and organizing is thus delimited, thereby reinforcing the masculism of the national struggle and, along with it, traditional gender roles.[25] The ideological work of counterinsurgency maiming is profound: if the family is a unit of resistance, maiming is an assault on the family, not only as a cultural formation but more trenchantly, Hadeel Badarneh notes, as an economic formation, suturing even tighter the economic dependency on the colonizer and deepening vulnerability.[26] Maiming intensifies the division of time and space required for social reproduction, as women take on not just more unpaid labor but also more waged/paid labor, as the surplus labor pool is depleted of young men. The heteronormative family unit is compromised, yet gender roles are reified, especially through ideals of "national heroism" and martyrdom.[27] These are the conditions which give rise to a political and social environment where gender-based violence happens, sometimes with impunity.[28]

Through this circuitry of magnified, gendered social reproduction and the violence underpinning it, the maiming of men is at once an assault on masculinity yet a double maiming on women, who have to work more and may also be subject to (more) sexual and gender violence, not to mention forms of corporeal debilitation that accrue to any (overworked) laborer. Furthermore, the Israeli State benefits from the subjugation of Palestinian women (recall the woman question of the decolonization era) and queers (the homosexual question that is instrumentalized in pinkwashing discourses) in part to justify its colonizing mandate.[29] If on one side the colonizing state revels in its superiority vis-à-vis gender and the supposed backwardness of Palestinian women and the society (men) that oppress them, on the other side it solicits, as Badarneh explains, the "dismantling of social cohesion to serve its demographic benefit, preventing reunification and pushing for a reduction in birth rates."[30] Colonialism exploits the dialectic between the rupturing of heteronormative family cohesion and the reentrenchment of rigid gender binaries.

Maiming, therefore, is not just a bodily assault but also a phenomenon that reorganizes social orders. It delimits not just corporeal resistance (attempting to strip the ontological resistance of the body), but also the horizons of liberation, through the short-circuiting of organizational vitality and growth. But when we focus only on how the laboring body is drained of the capacity for organizing, for politics, for resistance, we reify an ontology that positions resistance as somehow external to the body. Structurally, care and mutual aid economies are not necessarily distinct from the networks of support and the labor of social reproduction, but rather they are embedded in those activities and forms of resistance that already sustain quotidian existence.

"Stunting" is a medical term to describe children who are not thriving according to normative metrics; it is also a process of ungendering, which Nadera Shaloub-Kevorkian has called "unchilding."[31] This unchilding forecloses normative (adult) masculinity ("manhood") and femininity ("womanhood") and as such reorganizes relations of masculinities and femininities while simultaneously opening possibilities for multiple genderings.[32] Are dividuated bodies ungendered? Is dividuating an ungendering or nongendering modality of power? The intersection of stunting and maiming is also an ungendering process, suggesting the life trajectory of a maiming for a stunted youth to be one of wounds progressing with the maturing/aging of the body, requiring "continuous surgical needs." The injury evolves with "the stunted body."[33] The wound does not submit to repair or heal, but rather grows with the body.

The saturation of spatial and temporal stratum in Palestine is achieved in part by the use of technologies of measure to manufacture a "remote-control" occupation. Instead of home evictions, raids, and demolitions, we can perceive a different version of Israeli "home invasions" through the maiming and stunting of domestic space and the heteronormative family unit demarcated within it.[34] The public sphere, classically defined, is focused on as the site of titration, modulation, and elasticity of a threshold of livability. The reshaping of the domestic occurs through this dissolution of privates from publics; the demarcation of rigid gender binarization is not a casual or even tactical byproduct of maiming. It is, perhaps, its ultimate aim: to tax the social fabric of Palestinian lives and the collective capacities for resistance, for pleasure, for dreaming.

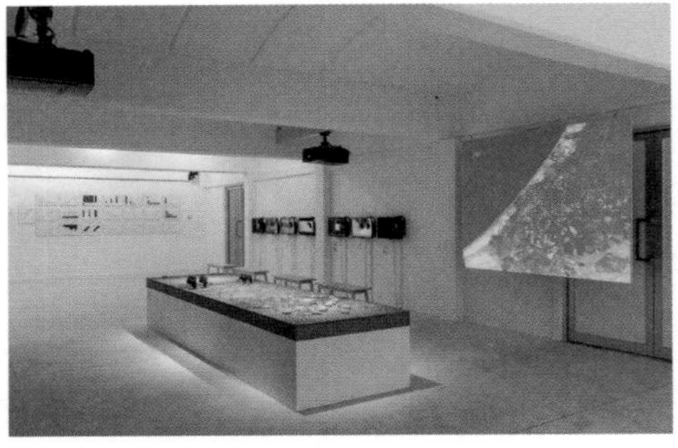

Francesco Sebregondi and Jasbir K. Puar, *Future Lives of Return*, p. 263.

COMBAT BREATHING

> I went out into the streets of Gaza, streets filled with blinding sunlight. They told me that Nadia had lost her leg when she threw herself on top of her little brothers and sisters to protect them from the bombs and flames that had fastened their claws into the house. Nadia could have saved herself, she could have run away, rescued her leg. But she didn't.[35]

> There is not occupation of territory on the one hand and independence of persons on the other. It is the country as a whole, its history, its daily pulsation that are contested, disfigured, in the hope of a final destruction. Under these conditions, the individual's breathing is an observed, an occupied breathing. It is a combat breathing.[36]

We re/turn to Frantz Fanon to remind ourselves that we have been here before and we know this combat breathing, where the "very possibility of respiration becomes the ultimate challenge."[37] Was combat breathing ever a metaphor? What matters is that now it is everything but a metaphor: our dying planet suffocating under smog, New Delhi under climate lockdown, aboriginal lands of Australia on fire, the San Francisco Bay Area awakening to dark red skies: the atmospherics of suffocation. It is the chokeholds of Gaza and the checkpoints of Palestine. It is the knee on the Black neck and the ravages of COVID-19

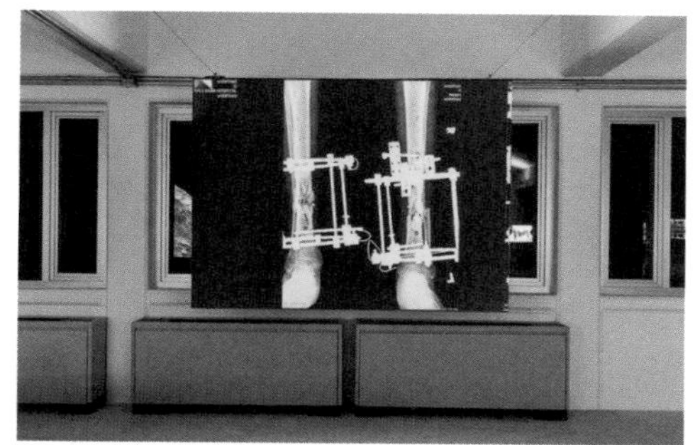

on the Black communities. "I can't breathe" is of the lurid theater of police brutality against Black bodies and the collective consciousness of the planet on the brink of many revolutions. The mask, the knee, the chokehold, the carbon dioxide emissions, the pellet bullets, the "nonlethal" weapons: these are the prostheses, the witnesses, the perpetrators of combat breathing. Nadia's leg, too, is inseparable from the collective insurgency against the blockade of Gaza. In Chinese medicine, the lungs are the organ of grief; they function as the interface between internal and external such that both disappear; they are, in essence, the body's Möbius strip. "I can't breathe" is therefore also a mournful wail, a call of grief, and grieving of the organic flow of life and movement.

The spectacle of maiming is hardly proprietary to Gaza. The circuitry of maiming loops most forcibly to the blinding of insurgents with pellet bullets in Kashmir; tear gas canisters route us to the US-Mexico border. Deexceptionalizing Palestine also foregrounds links with Puerto Rico, Flint, New Orleans, and other locations where, as with Gaza, the "natural disaster" is not only the opportunity for a business plan; disaster is the business plan.

From Gaza and from any conflict zone, perhaps even from any Global South location, the world does not appear as an able-bodied one; the contours of normativity are not universal. Histories of violence focalized through death renders apparent certain narratives. What histories are yet to be written with wounding as the focus? They would trace maiming, and more pointedly the hinge between maiming and death, to see how it is maximized as a state technology. In 2010, the Indian government switched the ammunition in occupied Kashmir to "nonlethal" pellet bullets. In Chile, more than 300 protestors suffered from ocular trauma due to eye injuries between October 2019 and March 2020. In June 2020, journalists have been shot in the eyes and protestors have been indiscriminately wounded in the US uprisings protesting George Floyd's murder. To grasp and expose the sovereign right to maim is to register that, from the vantage of the biopolitical settler colonial state, things are happening *exactly as they should*.

It is worth thinking through the linked symbolic economies of targeting eyes and targeting lower limbs. The first might be read as the destruction of the literal capacity to see and also the capacity to envision new political horizons. The second portends to hinder mobility needed for social reproduction and to resist, but also attempts to curtail the ability to participate in movement, to control what movement is and can be. The solidarity actions from disparate parts of the world that are returning the spectacle of maiming to the maimers, reclaiming the right to maim as the right to be maimed, are inspiring. In response to the Israel Defense Forces shooting of journalist Muath Amarneh in the eye, photographs of children in classrooms, fellow journalists, and protesters with one eye covered, by hands, by signs, by eyepatches, in Chile, Bolivia, Hong Kong, as well as in Palestine, went viral. These images going viral signal a global exposure of the sovereign right to maim, a refusal to pretend any longer that the humanitarian alibi of "sparing life" by injuring instead of killing will be tolerated.

"I can't breathe" is the outing of the maimed body that resists, that will be otherwise whole. From the 2014 Ferguson to Gaza protests we have the mantra, "When we breathe, we breathe together." More than emblematic of Black-Palestine solidarity, this injunction demands a world where nobody takes the first breath, or the last.

Jasbir K. Puar is professor and graduate director of women's and gender studies at Rutgers University. She authored the books *The Right to Maim: Debility, Capacity, Disability* (2017) and *Terrorist Assemblages: Homonationalism in Queer Times* (2007), and is currently completing a collection of essays on duration, pace, mobility, and acceleration in Palestine titled *Slow Life: Settler Colonialism in Five Parts.*

1. Ghassan Kanafani, "Letter from Gaza," Marxists.org, May 2014, https://www.marxists.org/archive/kanafani/1956/letterfromgaza.htm (accessed November 17, 2020).

2. Ibid.

3. See Jasbir K. Puar, *The Right to Maim: Debility, Capacity, Disability* (Durham, NC, 2017).

4. Nitasha Dhillon, *From Occupation to Decolonization*, Ph.D. diss. (University of Buffalo, 2020), p. 36.

5. MTL Collective, *Filming as Training in the Practice of Freedom*, YouTube video, 1:25:29 min, uploaded by "IRI Institute of Radical Imagination," November 2, 2020, https://instituteofradicalimagination.org/2020/11/02/filming-as-training-in-the-practice-of-freedom-mao-mollona-mtl-collective-amin-husain-nitasha-dhillon (accessed November 17, 2020).

6. Nasser Abourahme, "'Nothing to Lose but Our Tents': The Camp, the Revolution, the Novel," *Journal of Palestine Studies* (autumn 2018).

7. See https://www.activestills.org.

8. Édouard Glissant, *Poetics of Relation*, trans. Betsy Wing (Ann Arbor, 2006), p. 189.

9. Neel Ahuja, "Animal Death as National Debility: Climate, Agriculture, and Syrian War Narrative," *New Literary Studies* 51, no. 4 (2020).

10. Ghassan Abu-Sittah et al., "Biospheres of War," p. 85 of the present volume.

11. Ghassan Abu-Sittah, "The Virus, the Settler, and the Siege: Gaza in the Age of Corona," *Journal of Palestine Studies* (2020).

12. Michel Foucault, *Security, Territory, Population: Lectures at the Collège de France 1977–78*, trans. Graham Burchell (London, 2011), p. 246.

13. Francesco Sebregondi, "Power, Logistics, Interface: The Case of Gaza," Research Values 2018, December 13, 2017, https://researchvalues2018.wordpress.com/2017/12/13/francesco-sebregondi-power-logistics-interface-the-case-of-gaza (accessed November 17, 2020).

14. "Gaza in 2020: A Liveable Place?," Report by the United Nations Country Team in the occupied Palestinian territory (August 2012), https://www.unrwa.org/userfiles/file/publications/gaza/Gaza%20in%202020.pdf (accessed January 20, 2021).

15. See Whitney Battle-Baptiste and Britt Rusert, *W. E. B. Du Bois's Data Portraits: Visualizing Black America* (New York, 2018).

16. See Hilo Glazer, "'42 Knees in One Day': Israeli Snipers Open Up About Shooting Gaza Protesters," *Haaretz*, March 6, 2020, https://www.haaretz.com/israel-news/.premium.MAGAZINE-42-knees-in-one-day-israeli-snipers-open-up-about-shooting-gaza-protesters-1.8632555 (accessed November 17, 2020).

17. Ghassan Abu-Sittah, interview by Perla Issa, "There Is No International Community," *Journal of Palestine Studies* (2018).

18. Kanafani, "Letter from Gaza" (see note 1).

19. Patrick Wolfe, "Settler Colonialism and the Elimination of the Native," *Journal of Genocide Research* (December 2006).

20. See Paul Rocher, *Gazer, mutiler, soumettre: Politique de l'arme non létale* (Paris, 2020).

21. Rema Hammani, Andaleeb A. Shehadah, eds., "Navigating Through Shattered Paths: NGO Service Providers and Women Survivors of Gender-Based Violence," UN Women Research Paper (September 2017), https://palestine.unwomen.org/en/digital-library/publications/2017/12/gbv-research17.

22. Luce Irigaray, *This Sex Which Is Not One* (Ithaca, 1985), p. 196.

23. Ann McClintock, "The Angel of Progress: Pitfalls of the Term 'Post-Colonialism,'" *Social Text* (1992).

24. "On the Media of Counterinsurgency and the Targeting of Decolonize this Place," *Verso Books Blog* (March 11, 2020), https://www.versobooks.com/blogs/4593-on-the-media-of-counterinsurgency-and-the-targeting-of-decolonize-this-place (accessed January 9, 2021).

25. The relationship between social reproduction and women's participation in revolutionary movements has long been discussed; here I follow Dhillon, *From Occupation to Decolonization* (see note 4).

26. Hadeel Badarneh, "The Economy of Desires in Late Capitalism: Reading in the American and Palestinian Context," *Anemones* (2018).

27. Ibid.

28. UN Women, "Navigating Through Shattered Paths" (see note 21).

29. On the effects of pinkwashing on Palestinian queers, see the work of al-Qaws for Sexual and Gender Diversity in Palestinian Society, directed by Haneen Maikey.

30. Badarneh, "The Economy of Desires in Late Capitalism" (see note 26).

31. Nadera Shalhoub-Kevorkian, *Incarcerated Childhood and the Politics of Unchilding* (Cambridge, UK, 2019).

32. These questions follow the work of Hortense Spillers on the "ungendering" of enslaved black women and C. Riley Snorton's rereading of Spillers. In different veins, both scholars ask what is produced by the foreclosures of a gendering that coheres through anti-blackness. For Spillers, what she calls "an American grammar" cannot recognize the kin formations forged through enslavement. Snorton suggests that generative fluidities might be opened from this foreclosing of gender from blackness in the way of transgressive, nonbinary, and fungible corporealities. Following Spillers, who ruminates on how gender is displaced from the domestic space to the slave ship, we might think about what gender is in containment and blockade, under siege, when domestic space is undone. Hortense Spillers, "Mama's Baby, Papa's Maybe: An American Grammar Book," *Diacritics* (Summer 1987); C. Riley Snorton, *Black on Both Sides: A Racial History of Trans Identity* (New York, 2017).

33. Abu-Sittah, "There Is No International Community" (see note 17).

34. For research and analysis on the impact of house demolitions on women and gender-based violence, see Hanan Abu-Ghosh, "The Impact of House Demolitions on Gender Roles and Relations: We Will Come Back to Build in the Same Place, We Are Here and We Will Stay Here," *Women's Affairs Technical Committee – Ramallah* (2014).

35. Kanafani, "Letter from Gaza" (see note 1).

36. Frantz Fanon, *A Dying Colonialism*, trans. Haakon Chevalier (New York, 1965), p. 65.

37. Joseph Pugliese and Suvendrini Perera, "Combat Breathing: State Violence and the Body in Question," *Somatechnics* (2011).

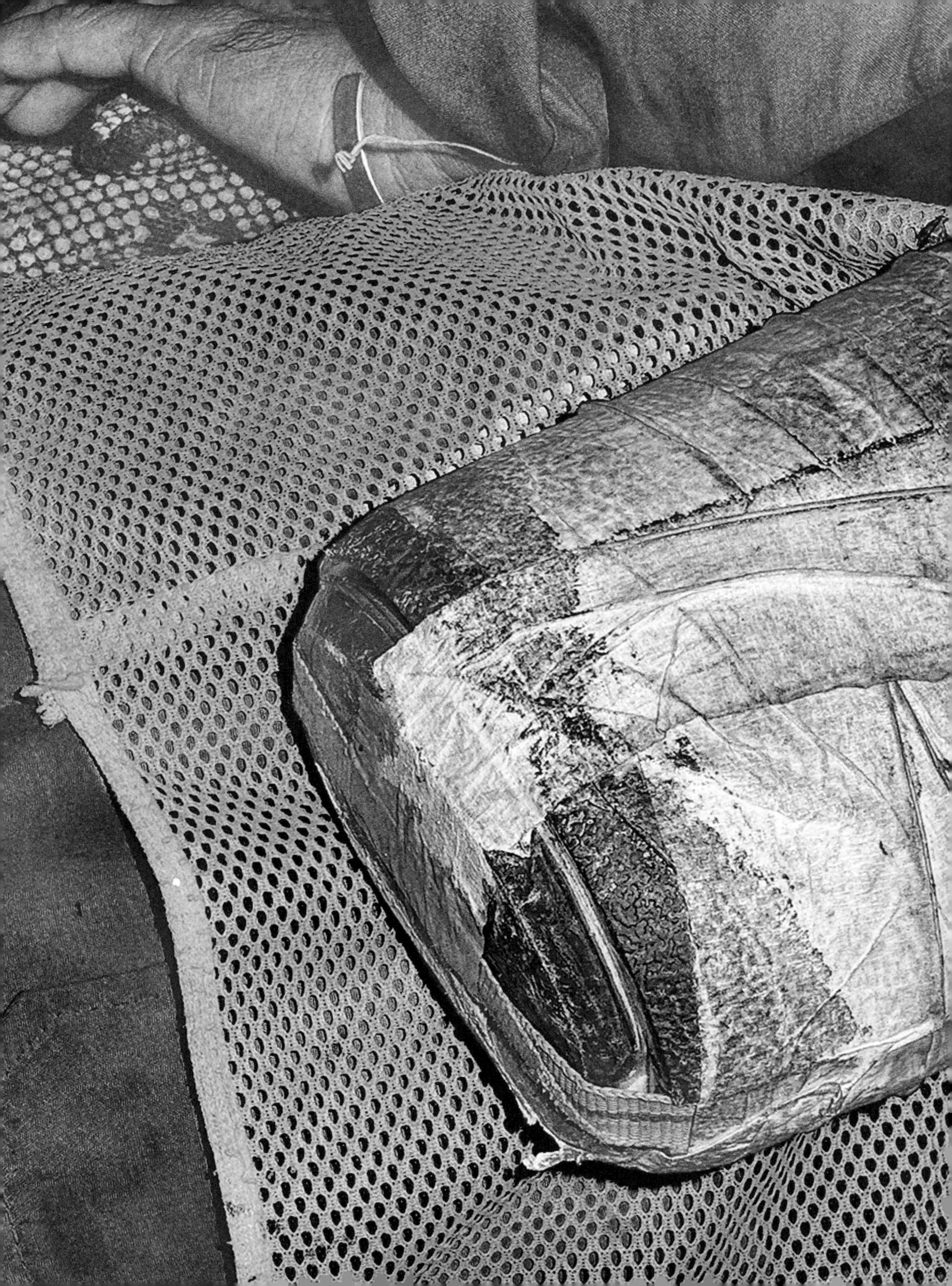

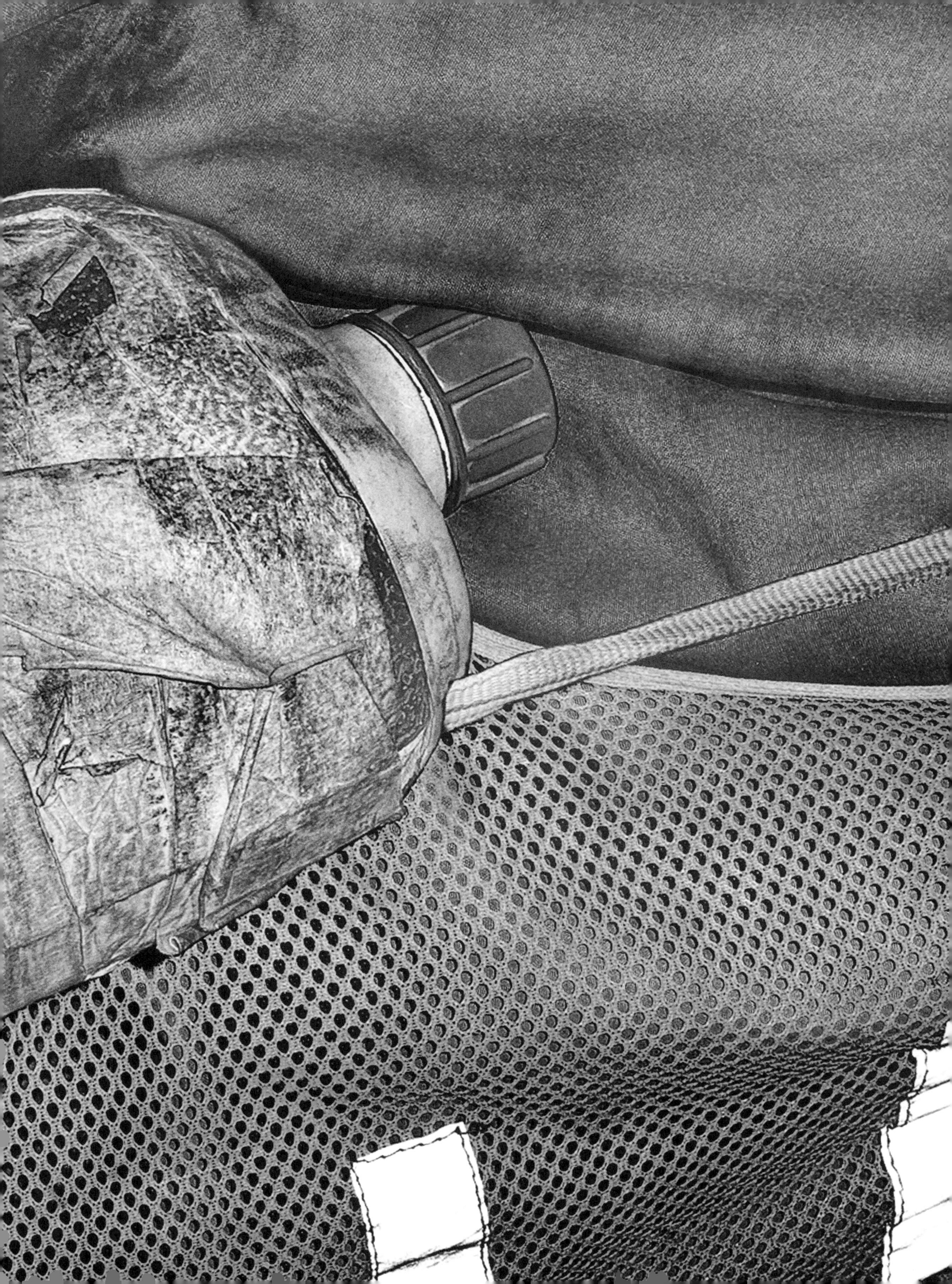

Embracing Destruction

Nadia Abu El-Haj

Jerusalem, sometime after the War of 1967: a construction crew was digging at the site of my grandfather's hotel. They opened up the ground and came upon a mosaic beneath their feet. If the Israel Antiquities Authority got a whiff of its existence, construction would be stopped, at the very least temporarily. Far more troublesome, my grandfather could lose his land. This was East Jerusalem. Classifying a place as an "antiquity site" was one known means of land seizure. My grandfather told the workers to cement over the find immediately.

As I remember it, my father told me that story, though I'm not entirely sure. Perhaps it wasn't about my grandfather at all. It might have happened to a family friend. Regardless, the scenario is neither implausible nor uncommon in East Jerusalem. For Palestinians living under Israeli rule, the underground portends an existential threat. *Depth Unknown,* an installation by Dima Srouji in the first Sharjah Architectural Triennial in November 2019, unpacks that threat.[1] Focusing on the Palestinian village and archaeological site of Sebastia, it speaks of a phenomenon that has long been a powerful weapon in the arsenal of Zionist settler-nationhood.

Excavations at Sebastia—located at what is believed to be the biblical city of Samaria, the capital of the Northern Kingdom during the second Iron Age—commenced in the early twentieth century under the auspices of a Harvard University team.[2] These digs were one instance of a broad, scientific-qua-religious quest: during the late nineteenth century, European and American explorers-cum-geographers came to Palestine in search of the biblical past. Driven by a Protestant theological imaginary, they sought to establish the historicity of the Bible, and they began by locating its events and stories on the contemporary landscape. Such cartographic practices presented Palestine as a concrete, coherent, and visibly historic place, produced it as a sustained object of scientific inquiry, and established the intellectual grounds for excavations to come. By the early twentieth century, surface level surveys gave way to excavations, and biblical archaeology came into its own as a distinct discipline: the underground was made to reveal truths—and *forms* of truth—hitherto not visible or available on the land's surface.

If Protestant practitioners dug to establish the veracity of Christian theology, the Jewish Palestine Exploration Society (during the British Mandate) and Israeli archaeologists (after 1948) dug in search of empirical evidence of the biblical accounts of Israelite and Jewish settlement and sovereignty in ancient Palestine. Archaeological facts would substantiate a nationalist project; that is, they would verify the truth of an ideology that framed colonial settlement in Palestine as a project of national return. Excavating was part and parcel of an ongoing practice of conquest through which a Jewish-sovereign presence on the land, past and present, would be established, rendered visible in concrete form. Mapping, surveying, and excavating assembled material-symbolic facts that "revealed" the land's identity as the Jewish national home *by definition,* often prior to, and in anticipation of, the actual settlement or seizure of specific places within it.

History, as sensibility, fervor, and pursuit, was essential to (the birth of) nationalisms in the nineteenth century, and Zionism was no exception.[3] For its part, archaeology was a distinct iteration of the modern historical imaginary and practice of history, and it spoke to a project of *settler*-nationhood in a particularly powerful way. Archaeologists do far more than generate narrative accounts of the past. They do not "go to" archives and sort through documents that ended up there, whether by intention or by chance.[4] Much like ethnographers in Bronisław Malinowski's methodological directive, archaeologists produce the historical archive on which their narratives are based.[5] More specifically, they uncover *material* things out of which not just stories but also novel landscapes and architectures are made.[6]

Dima Srouji with Dirar Kalash, Silvia Truini, Nadia Abu El-Haj, and Omar Jabareen, *Depth Unknown,* p. 284.

In excavating Palestine's ancient past, the Jewish Palestine Exploration Society and, subsequently, Israeli archaeological institutions sought to establish the nation's origin story and its rights to sovereignty *in this particular place,* and they did so by assembling objects that stood as evidence of a prior Israelite and Jewish presence and sovereignty. Not only was the identity of the Jews as a historic people at stake; so too was the identity of the land. With biblical stories setting the parameters of the scholarly search, archaeologists embedded an Israelite/Hebrew identity within a landscape whose ownership was deeply contested from the start. Archaeology (re)inscribed a specific biography of the land; a story of its lost Israelite and Hebrew past was made to appear, and, as "evidenced" by this history, the land itself, not just the people, had a right to become once more what it always already was.

Settler colonizers imagined the lands they conquered as *terra nullius,* as hollow space. In response, one powerful anticolonial gesture has been to recuperate the past, to establish a history of the "prior." What communities, states, and histories were forged on and through the land that settlers declared empty? In support of legal battles over indigenous land titles, or in political struggles to stop the expropriation of land by mining companies (to take but two instances), producing evidence of deep and longstanding life-worlds on these lands has been one way of trying to hold settler-nations to account. Artistic representations and counter-cartographic projects challenge ideologies of *terra nullius.*[7] So too might a counter-archaeological sensibility—mapping "the architectural imaginary of the constantly shifting Palestinian ground, making visible disregarded strata, displaced objects, and the entangled narratives of Palestine." As *Depth Unknown* asks: "What would the ground of Palestine say, if it were allowed its own, independent voice?"[8]

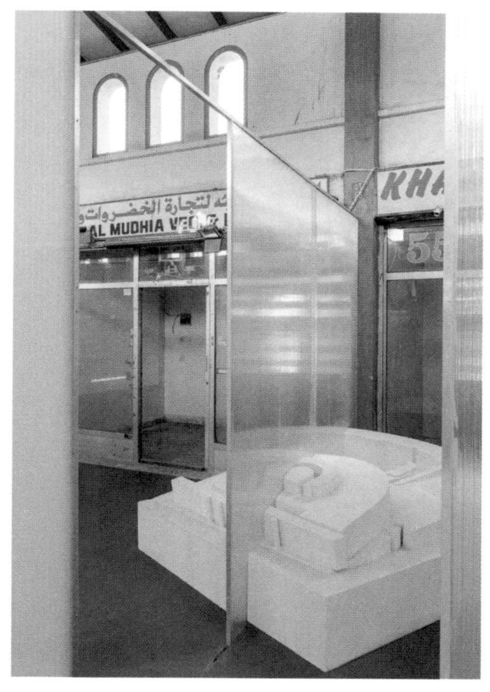

Yet, Palestine was never imagined as *terra nullius* in the same way as other settler colonies were. In speaking for the land, the Zionist settler imaginary told a story of Israelite/Jewish indigeneity.[9] It staked its exceptionalism (this is *not* a colonial project, in other words) on an originary claim rooted in (a belief in) an ancient Israelite conquest and sovereign presence. Evidence for that claim was forged by digging down—far enough down—into the earth. If Palestine was *terra nullius* on its surface, a civilizational history was embedded in its underground.

Contesting this project of settler-colonialism poses particular kinds of problems, then. When the settler appropriates the status of the indigene, what might a felicitous counterclaim look like? One might harken back to an even earlier origin story: this is the Land of Canaan. One might frame a deep and enduring history—all of it—as part of not just a Palestinian self, but of a global cultural heritage.[10] Alternatively, one might reject a deep history and turn instead to the histories of villages destroyed in 1948, documented, at least in part, on the basis of oral accounts.[11] Or one might follow the historian's desire for the archive by documenting the story of Palestinian dispossession and resistance.[12]

Writing in the 1990s, the late anthropologist Michel-Rolph Trouillot explored the various kinds of historical silences produced by "the archive," engaging in a then-widespread conversation in postcolonial scholarship.[13] Yes, as postcolonial scholars argued, the (colonial) archives silenced the histories of the colonized. But, Trouillot insisted, there is more than one way in which archives produce silences, and they need to be pried apart and responded to in specific ways. In *Silencing the Past,* he retells the story of "a former slave turned colonel, a forgotten figure in the Haitian Revolution," an instance in which available evidence in the archives can be "repositioned" in order to generate a new narrative. He rereads the story of the "discovery of America," showing "how the alleged agreements about Columbus actually masks a history of conflicts," which, once uncovered in the archives, allows us to reframe that story as a process rather than as a singular "event." In the case of the Haitian Revolution, Trouillot identifies a different kind of silence. Not just retrospectively, but as the events unfolded, the Haitian Revolution was "unthinkable" for Europeans, "an impossible history." Revolution is an act of politics; slaves were not "man," ergo slaves were not capable of this distinctively human act. This particular silence indexes an ontological impasse; that is, that particular capacities belong to some forms of being and not to others.[14]

The question of whether Palestinians were civilized enough, capable of national consciousness, or whether they possessed a right to a nation-state of their own, echoes through the project of Jewish settlement in Palestine, even if this was not an ontological impasse of the same order that Trouillot describes.[15] But I want to take up the question of ontology in a different register: What if we stretched the question of ontological possibility and impossibility beyond Trouillot's focus on historical actors and considered the ontological status of evidence itself? In other words, I want to think about the relationship between the epistemological status of evidence—how reliable, credible, or authoritative is it?—and its myriad forms: as documents, as material traces or objects, and as the memories and oral accounts of particular subjects, for example. What evidence is there, or *what might count (be authorized) as evidence* of an (enduring) Arab/Palestinian presence in and right to this place? Eyal Weizman has argued that the "mode of operation of contemporary colonialism is to erase the traces of its own violence," and that was certainly true of the Israeli State during and after the 1948 War, when 472 Palestinian villages were destroyed. That act sought not only to make return seemingly impossible, but also aimed to cleanse the landscape of material traces of other claims to belonging, ownership, and sovereign right. Digging down through stratum after stratum, so too did Israeli archaeology destroy material cultural remains of "others"—other religious, cultural, and civilizational claims, other forms of life—on its way down to the biblical scene, leaving, as Dima Srouji puts it, a void in its wake.

"Is it possible that the antonym of 'forgetting' is not 'remembering,' but *Justice?*" the historian Yosef Hayim Yerushalmi asks.[16] In Yerushalmi's question, we hear a torque of the modern historical sensibility that first emerged in the nineteenth century: it is no longer only that the past—as memories, documents, objects, or genes, even—defines who we *really are.*[17] In its late twentieth and early twenty-first-century iteration, remembering the past is framed as a decidedly ethical act, and it characterizes a powerful Euro-American, post-Holocaust sensibility: we must not forget lest (the) evil (of the Holocaust) be repeated.[18] There is no possibility of a future—a radical future, that is—without first reaching into and recuperating traces of a (silenced, repressed, unconscious, or erased and destroyed) past. In Weizman's words, "Confronting denial is important because denial, in all its multiple forms, is the condition of possibility for violence to be perpetrated in the future."[19]

History, of course, is never simply a matter of "what happened"; it is made, at one and the same time, of sociohistorical processes and their narrativization, as Trouillot insists. With regard to the question of Palestine, Edward Said argued in 1984, an enduring fight for "the permission to narrate" has been central to the struggle against Zionism. The Nakba—the expulsion of 750,000 Palestinians from their villages and cities during the 1948 War—was widely discussed among Palestinians themselves. In living memory, people knew what had happened to them, to their parents, their grandparents, to their towns and villages and life-worlds, even as Israeli politicians and historians continued to deny that reality. While documented and recounted by Palestinian scholars, for decades after the 1948 War, this other history was not just erased on the ground; it was silenced and dismissed—not just in Israel but throughout the Euro-American world.

With the declassification in 1978 of documents pertaining to Israel's "War of Independence," the facts were to change.[20] Israeli historians gained access to previously unavailable documents and a few began to rewrite the history of their state. On the basis of this novel documentary evidence, they challenged hegemonic narratives regarding the founding of the Israeli State. Most fundamentally, historians such as Benny Morris and Ilan Pappé, to name but two, argued that Palestinians did not leave their homes at will or under orders from Arab regimes; they were driven out, expelled by Zionist military forces during the war. There were disagreements among these so-called New Historians and on the part of Palestinian scholars who continued to challenge them: Was the expulsion intentional, preplanned, and essential to the establishment of the Jewish state? Was it an "event" that unfolded during the chaos of war? Nevertheless, the basic parameters of that "new" history became widely accepted in the Israeli academy, even in the Israeli public domain. During its "War of Independence," Zionist military brigades perpetrated substantial violence and harm against the land's Palestinian population, a largely civilian population expelled so that the Jewish state could be established and its borders expanded. By the mid-1980s, this scholarship seemed to portend a promise. The facts were out there; archival evidence demonstrated what Palestinians had already known. Post-Zionism was emerging as a term and a politics. Might the facts on the ground also change? Might a Palestinian historical narrative become more widely intelligible, more authoritative? Were we at a turning point in the Palestinian struggle against the settler state?[21]

Beginning in the early years of the new millennium, teams sent by the secretive security department of Israel's Ministry of Defense began to pore over documents in Israeli archives to remove them from the public domain. Formerly available—that is, previously declassified—documents were resealed into vaults of state security.[22] "Hundreds of documents have been concealed as part of a systematic effort to hide evidence of the Nakba," Hagar Shezaf of the Israeli daily *Haaretz* reports.[23] In fact, the main document on the basis of which Benny Morris published his seminal 1986 essay, "The Birth of the Palestinian Refugee Problem, 1947–1949," has disappeared. Shefaz posed the following question to Yehiel Horev, former head of the Ministry of Defense's security department: "Benny Morris has already written about the document, so what's the logic of keeping it hidden?" Horev responds:

> I don't remember the document you're referring to, but if he quoted from it and the document itself is not there [i.e., where Morris says it is], then his facts aren't strong. If he says, "Yes, I have the document," I can't argue with that. But if he says it's written there, that could be right and it could be wrong. If the document were already outside and were sealed in the archive, I would say that that's folly. But if someone quoted from it—there's a difference of day and night in terms of the validity of the evidence he cited.[24]

The status and authority of the written word returns with a vengeance here. In the absence of the original document, what could possibly count as proof? Documents, in this ontology, are objects whose presence or absence makes a difference. They transform a statement from disputable to a matter of fact.[25]

Horev is not wrong: as material objects, as presumably objective, official documents have an epistemological authority that is not conferred on Palestinian accounts and memories; Palestinians, in their very being, are presumptively unreliable witnesses to their own experiences of colonization and war. Nevertheless, the relationship between matters of fact and matters of power and politics is more complex than he suggests. Simply put, even in the face of facts, whether in the memories and narratives of Palestinian refugees or in the declassified documents, the Nakba remains an impossible history: the facts may be out there, but no recognition of their political significance, and as such, no political transformation has followed suit. By the early 2000s, Benny Morris had turned from a reluctant post-Zionist to a staunch defender of the 1948 War. All nations are founded in violence; Israel is no exception. It had to be done, he declared, and in taking that position, he was far from alone.[26]

Several years after Morris's recantation, a prominent, left-leaning Israeli columnist published a journalistic account of the past and present of Israel, its founding, and its contemporary political impasses. *My Promised Land: The Triumph and Tragedy of Israel* is also Ari Shavit's own reckoning with the violence against Palestinians on which the State of Israel was built.[27] Lydda, a small city in central Palestine, stands at the heart of the book; its inhabitants, like the vast majority of Palestinians throughout the land that was to become Israel, were expelled during the 1948 War. But the story of Lydda is even more morally complex. This particular Palestinian town endured a massacre. How does a liberal subject grapple with and reconcile himself to that?[28]

Lydda, in Shavit's narrative, stands for a tragic inevitability that was not recognized by the Jewish settlers until it was too late. "Lydda is our black box," he writes. "In it lies the dark secret of Zionism. The truth is that Zionism could not bear Lydda . . . if Zionism was to be, Lydda could not be. If Lydda was to be, Zionism could not be." For a good fifty years, Zionism "succeeded in hiding from itself the substantial contradiction between the Jewish national movement and Lydda. . . . Then, in three days in the cataclysmic summer of 1948, contradiction struck and tragedy revealed its face."[29] Palestinians would have to be forced to leave if the Jewish state was to be born.

That fact does not lead to any substantive (auto)political critique, however. It appears as an unfortunate truth for which there is no (good) answer and certainly no political resolution. In Shavit's hands, Lydda is represented as a "tragedy," at once unavoidable and a sign of the Jewish settlers' (if only partial) fall from grace: with the massacre in Lydda, Zionism lost its innocence. But even as Shavit chooses to focus on Lydda because of the massacre, this act of extreme violence is not really the point: the massacre might have been avoided, but its conditions of possibility—that is, conquest and expulsion—were not. "Do I turn my back on the Jewish national movement that carried out the deed of Lydda?" Shavit asks, rhetorically.

> Like the brigade commander, I am faced with something too immense to deal with . . . for when one opens the black box, one understands that whereas the small mosque massacre could have been a misunderstanding brought about by a tragic chain of accidental events, the conquest of Lydda and the expulsion of Lydda were not accidents . . . the choice is stark: either reject Zionism because of Lydda, or accept Zionism along with Lydda.[30]

Shavit chooses to "stand by the damned."[31]

Yehiel Horev may be a little too frightened of the power of documents. Recuperating the silences of the archives might not make much difference at all. To rely on a distinction made by the philosopher Stanley Cavell, "knowing" is not the same as "acknowledging." The stories that the declassified (and now partially reclassified) documents tell are widely "known" today. The facts are, by and large, accepted among the Israeli Jewish public, and by the American liberal establishment that so enthusiastically embraced Shavit's book. But they are not *acknowledged*. They do not emerge as matters of public concern and action.[32] At one and the same time, the story of Lydda demonstrates that Israel was founded on the violence of conquest and expulsion (and massacres) of its Palestinian population—in living memory—and insists that there was no other choice.

Remembering has no relationship to justice here. No longer silenced, no longer forgotten, no longer erased (there is material evidence, after all), the catastrophe of 1948 carries no ethical or political force. If there is an arc of history in Shavit's and Morris's political reckonings, it does not bend toward justice. Yes, the war that Palestinians have long remembered and that Palestinian historians have documented on the basis, among other sources, of the testimony and memories of its survivors, is true. And yet, the Nakba is not a history worthy of repair. In other words, even if one can come to some general agreement about the "facts," even if one interprets, at least in large part, "what happened" in the same way, those facts may still fail to rise to a matter of public concern. That would require an ethical and political choice, and that choice has a far more tenuous relationship to questions of epistemology (to knowing, to how we know) than those of us on the Left might like to believe.

Forgetting is the opposite of justice, sometimes. At other times, destroying the historical trace might be precisely what justice demands. Had my grandfather not cemented over the mosaic, he may well have lost his land and livelihood, and for the second time.[33] Had the site of biblical Samaria never been identified and excavated, the town of Sebastia—in this retrospective fantasy, just another Palestinian town with no particular biblical significance, one not located near an antiquity site—might not be encircled by Jewish settlements and might not have remained under direct Israeli rule.[34] The void, in short, is not always such a bad thing. At times, justice may require both erasure and forgetting.

There may well be intrinsic ethical reasons for insisting on recovering other traces, other pasts, and there may be powerful desires for acts of recuperation regardless of their consequences. But to insist that forgetting is the opposite of justice is to operate within a political calculus and rationale that misses a powerful contemporary configuration of (colonial) power. In Israel/Palestine, settler-nationhood no longer depends on the suppression of the historical trace, of "truth." It operates through the embrace of a far more brazen and explicit seizure of power: yes, the Nakba, but no, we—Israelis—don't care.

Nadia Abu El-Haj is Ann Whitney Olin Professor of Anthropology at Barnard College and Columbia University and codirector of the Center for Palestine Studies at Columbia. Among her books are *Facts on the Ground: Archaeological Practice and Territorial Self-Fashioning in Israeli Society* (2001) and *Combat Trauma: Imaginaries of War and Citizenship in Post 9/11 America* (2022).

1. See the *Depth Unknown* project website, https://depthunknown.com (accessed November 5, 2020).

2. George Andrew Reisner Jr. led excavations of Samaria in 1908–1910, during which time he was assistant professor of Egyptology at Harvard University. Those excavations were followed up in 1931–1935, under the leadership of John W. Crowfoot, head of the British School of Archaeology of Jerusalem (BSAJ). The 1931–1935 excavations were a joint project of the BSAJ, the London-based Palestine Exploration Fund, and Harvard and Hebrew Universities. See William F. Albright, *The Archaeology of Palestine* (New York, 1960).

3. See Benedict Anderson, *Imagined Communities: Reflections on Origin and Spread of Nationalism* (New York, 2006). On Zionism, see Yael Zerubavel, *Recovered Roots: Collective Memory and the Making of Israeli National Tradition* (Chicago, 1994).

4. For an incisive reading of the archive and archival practices, see Carolyn Steedman, *Dust: The Archive and Cultural History* (New Brunswick, NJ, 2002).

5. In his introduction to *Argonauts of the Western Pacific,* Malinowski lays out a scientific method for ethnographers: he tasks anthropologists not just with collecting specific kinds of data, but also with keeping records in such a way that a later scholar would be able to go back over the evidence, similar to how laboratory scientists (purportedly) replicate experiments. Bronisław Malinowski, *Argonauts of the Western Pacific* (Long Grove, IL, 1984).

6. See Nadia Abu El-Haj, *Facts on the Ground: Archaeological Practice and Territorial Self-Fashioning in Israeli Society* (Chicago, 2001), Chapter 7.

7. See, for example, the case of the Ngurrara Canvas II, exhibited at the Sharjah Architecture Triennial, and the counter-cartographic project Ground Truth, created by the Israeli nonprofit organization Zochrot in cooperation with Forensic Architecture. In using the terms "counter-cartographic" and "counter-archaeological," I draw on Eyal Weizman's work in "counter forensics." That is, if the history of forensics has been a state project, in counter-forensics, "a state is the alleged criminal." Eyal Weizman, *Forensic Architecture: Violence at the Threshold of Detectability* (New York, 2018), p. 30.

8. Dima Srouji, *Depth Unknown* project website, https://depthunknown.com (accessed November 5, 2020). Practices of contemporary indigenous politics often move well beyond this kind of "counter" practice; they call for radically different forms of knowing and living. In doing so, some radical, indigenous political projects pose epistemological and ontological challenges to a post-Enlightenment "common sense" not recognized in counter practices that work to flip the gaze, but which don't challenge the basic grammar of the projects they resist—scientific or political. See Elizabeth Povinelli, *The Cunning of Recognition: Indigenous Alterities and the Making of Australian Multiculturalism* (Durham and London, 2002) and Vanessa Agard-Jones, "What the Sands Remember," *GLQ* 18, no. 2–3 (June 2012): 325–46.

9. See, for example, Marc Daalder, "Jews as an Indigenous People," *Jewish Currents,* August 28, 2017, https://jewishcurrents.org/jews-as-an-indigenous-people (accessed November 5, 2020); see also Matthew Gindin, "Are Both Jews and Palestinians Indigenous to Israel?" *Forward,* May 24, 2017, https://forward.com/scribe/372978/are-both-jews-and-palestinians-indigenous-to-israel (accessed November 5, 2020).

10. For example, the Palestinian Authority lobbied UNESCO to declare Sebastia a World Heritage Centre; it is currently under consideration (see the UNESCO World Heritage Centre Tentative List, http://whc.unesco.org/en/tentativelists/5718 [accessed January 25, 2020]). Lobbying for its recognition as a World Heritage Site is another way of contesting Israel's claim to the site as a site of national significance for the modern Jewish state.

11. See Walid Khalidi, *All that Remains: The Palestinian Villages Occupied and Depopulated by Israel in 1948* (Washington, DC, 1992). See also the collection of "memorial books" on Palestinian villages at Columbia University Center for Palestine Studies, http://palestine.mei.columbia.edu/palestinian-village-histories-geographies-of-the-displaced (accessed January 25, 2020).

12. See for example Walid Khalidi, *From Haven to Conquest: Readings in Zionism and the Palestine Problem until 1948* (Beirut, 1971); Ibrahim Abu Lughod, *The Transformation of Palestine: Essays on the Origin and Development of the Arab-Israeli Conflict* (Chicago, 1971); and Yazid Sayigh, *Armed Struggle and the Search for State: the Palestinian National Movement, 1949–1993* (New York, 1997).

13. Michel-Rolph Trouillot, *Silencing the Past: Power and the Production of History* (Boston, 1995).

14. Trouillot argues that in some respects that impossibility endures. Standard historical accounts of the "Age of Revolution," that is, the years 1776–1843, fail to include the Haitian Revolution as a pivotal turning point in European and world history. "What we are observing is archival power at its strongest, the power to define what is and what is not a serious object of research and, therefore, of mention," ibid, p. 99.

15. The question of whether or not colonized peoples were capable of self-rule was, of course, endemic to nineteenth- and twentieth-century colonialisms. Nevertheless, even if less civilized than their European counterparts, natives were not *property*; they were not, strictly speaking, "not man."

16. Yosef Hayim Yerushalmi, *Zakhor: Jewish History and Jewish Memory* (Seattle, 1996), p. 117.

17. See Nadia Abu El-Haj, *The Genealogical Science: The Search for Jewish Origins and the Politics of Epistemology* (Chicago, 2012).

18. As Joan Wallach Scott recounts, "U.S. Associate Supreme Court Justice Robert Jackson, the chief prosecutor at Nuremberg, promised to document and punish the 'sinister influence' of National Socialism in a way that would make it at once *unforgettable* and *unrepeatable,*" *On the Judgment of History* (New York, 2020), emphasis added.

19. Eyal Weizman, *Forensic Architecture: Violence at the Threshold of Detectability* (New York, 2017), p. 134.

20. Under Israeli law, classified documents are declassified after thirty years.

21. The late 1980s, of course, mark the moment of the First Intifada, which began in 1987. That movement on the ground generated an optimism among Palestinians, at least early on, that a political solution (imagined as a two-state solution) would be achieved.

22. For a similar effort to remove already declassified documents from the public domain in the US post-9/11 see Joseph Masco, *The Theater of Operations: National Security Affect from the Cold War to the War on Terror* (Durham, NC, 2014).

23. Hagar Shezaf, "Burying the Nakba: How Israel Systematically Hides Evidence of 1948 Expulsion of Arabs," *Haaretz.com,* July 5, 2019, https://www.haaretz.com/israel-news/.premium.MAGAZINE-how-israel-systematically-hides-evidence-of-1948-expulsion-of-arabs-1.7435103 (accessed November 5, 2020).

24. Ibid.

25. There was, perhaps, an intermediate moment in Israeli society between the declassification of the archive—and Said's demand that Palestinians have a "right to narrate"—and this effort to make "the facts" disappear. In the 1990s, when Yossi Sarid was Minister of Education, there was a call, however brief, to allow history textbooks to place Palestinian narratives alongside Israeli ones. We have our narrative, Palestinians have theirs. They can exist and be read side by side, but without any demand that one takes a stand. "Their" account does not deny the validity of "ours." That is, you have your narrative; we have ours.

26. See Ari Shavit, "Survival of the Fittest? An Interview with Benny Morris," reprinted on *Counterpunch,* January 16, 2004, https://www.counterpunch.org/2004/01/16/an-interview-with-benny-morris (accessed November 5, 2020).

27. Ari Shavit was a prominent columnist at *Haaretz* from 1995 to 2016, when he was forced to resign after sexual harassment allegations surfaced as part of the #MeToo movement.

28. The book was publicized for an American audience with a chapter Ari Shavit published in *The New Yorker,* "Lydda, 1948: A City, A Massacre, and the Middle East Today," October 21, 2013 issue. It was published to wide acclaim in the US and reviewed as a profound and sincere ethical exploration of the state of Israel by one of its most prominent liberal columnists. For reviews see Leon Wiesseltier, "The State of Israel," *The New York Times,* November 21, 2013, https://www.nytimes.com/2013/11/24/books/review/my-promised-land-by-ari-shavit.html (accessed November 5, 2020), and Jonathan Freedland, "The Liberal Zionists," *The New York Times,* August 14, 2014, https://www.nybooks.com/articles/2014/08/14/liberal-zionists (accessed November 5, 2020).

29. Shavit, ibid, pp. 108–09.

30. Ibid, p. 131.

31. Ibid.

32. Stanley Cavell, *Must We Mean What We Say? A Book of Essays* (New York, 1969).

33. My grandfather's business was in what became West Jerusalem in 1948. He lost everything and started over after an employee snuck through the armistice line to retrieve a bill of sale for rugs that had been imported to the port in Aqaba, Jordan. It was on the basis of that one stock of merchandise that he started over in East Jerusalem after the war.

34. Under the Oslo Accords, Sebastia was placed in Area C, the region of the West Bank that remains under direct Israeli control. These spaces are carved out to protect Jewish settlements.

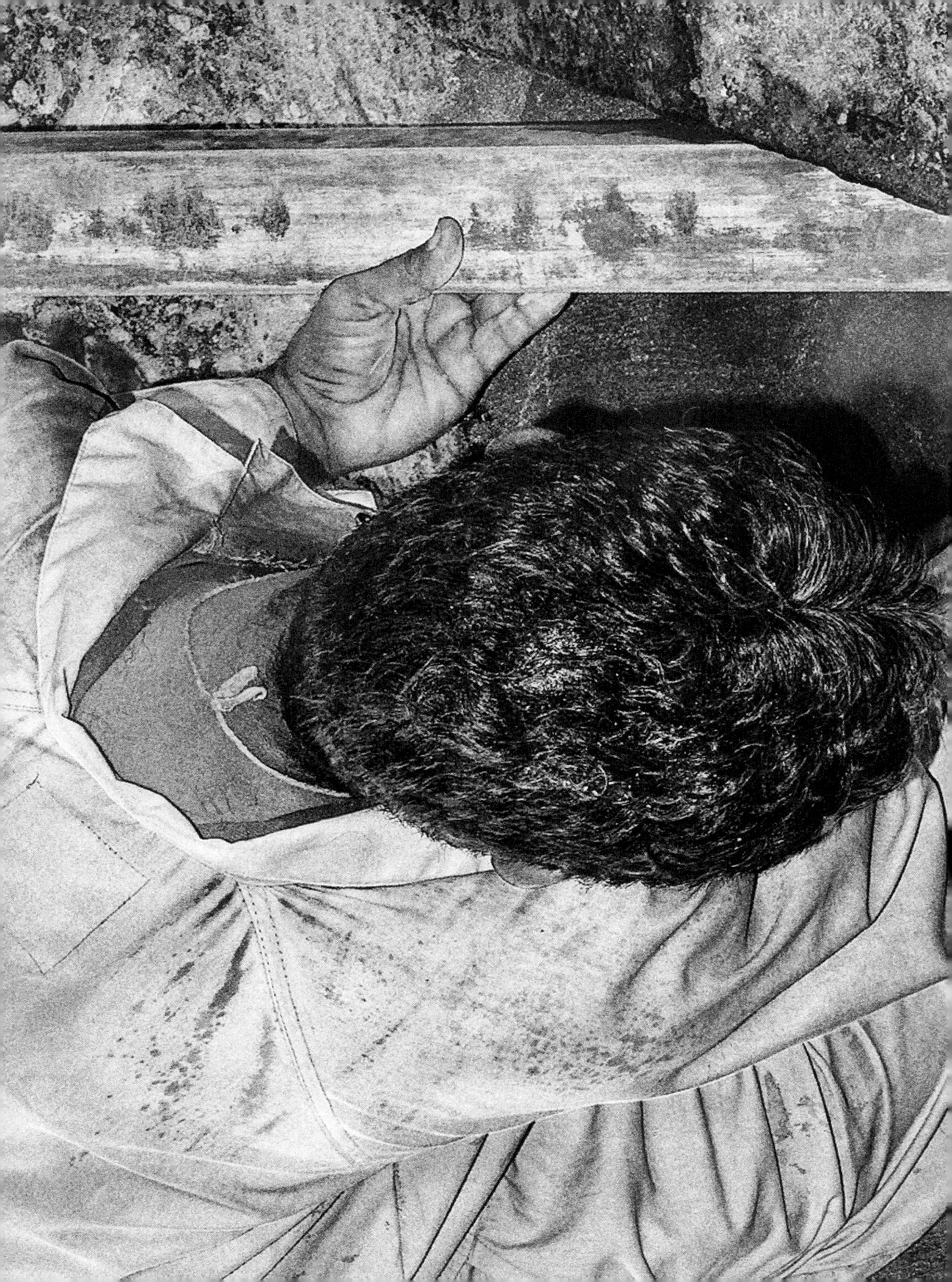

Education and the Incalculable

Gayatri Chakravorty Spivak

The following text is the transcript of a lecture delivered in Sharjah on February 8, 2020.

What is it to supplement? It is to open up the claim to totality of any formation—art, for example, or, for that matter, architecture. It is also to introduce something dangerous, the incalculable. In this case, the incalculable is the ungeneralizability of the subaltern.

Who is the subaltern? It is a member of a small group on the fringes of history. Today, we can say that the largest part of the electorate in so-called democracies, who only serve as body count and have no right to citizenship, belong to collectivities of small subaltern groups. They need to be generalized if efforts such as ours are to work.

How can the subaltern be generalized? Through working to insert them into citizenship. Citizenship is to claim rights, for sure, but it is also the ability to think about the welfare of other people. This is why it is not enough just to establish educational structures. The privileged must give sustained time and skill to the education of the texture of minds damaged by historical crimes—sometimes damaged millennially, as in the case of the caste system—thus to supplement art and architecture. As I said to the World Economic Forum when I was a member of its Committee on Values: "Real knowledge depends on cooking the soul with slow learning, not the instant soup of a one-size-fits-all toolkit. The world is not populated by humanoid drones. You cannot produce a toolkit for 'a moral metric,' or if you do you will be disappointed."

Who needs this education most? Everyone, of course. Otherwise most of the world would keep on thinking that bribe culture and rape culture are simply normal. But the specific need is located in the largest sector of the electorate in so-called democracies, made up of the victims of class apartheid in education—and also, of course, in the very top layer of superpowers. I am fortunate enough to be active with my time and skill in both these sectors. At Columbia University in the City of New York I have been teaching for more than thirty years. Before that, in the 1970s and 1980s, I taught at such powerful institutions as Emory University in Atlanta, and the University of Texas in Austin—not as a native informant for South Asia, but in the dominant language and German, French, and English literatures, and the politics of culture. Equally, I have been an active teacher and teacher trainer among the landless illiterates—so-called untouchables and tribals—for just about thirty-five years. Top and bottom of society. At the top, I try to prevent writing "green" work into what I call sustainable underdevelopment—sustaining cost-effectiveness, profit maximization, marketability at the maximum, and "green" at the minimum. I also try to train them to imagine the mind machine of those whom they are thinking to "help." To be equal is not to be the same. Different histories produce different mindsets.

At the bottom, I try the difficult task of devising a pedagogy that will insert the intuitions of democracy into the children of the abysmally poor. As I said above, citizenship and voting should not be just my rights, but also the rights of other people. It is very hard to instill this into the very poor—and yet, they vote, and the future of unborn generations depends on the voter habitually intuiting both of these ends of being a citizen. This is the contradiction at the heart of democracy, without which it cannot play—the contradiction between liberty, my rights, and equality, for those who do not resemble me at all.

Marina Tabassum Architects, *Inheriting Wetness*, p. 270.

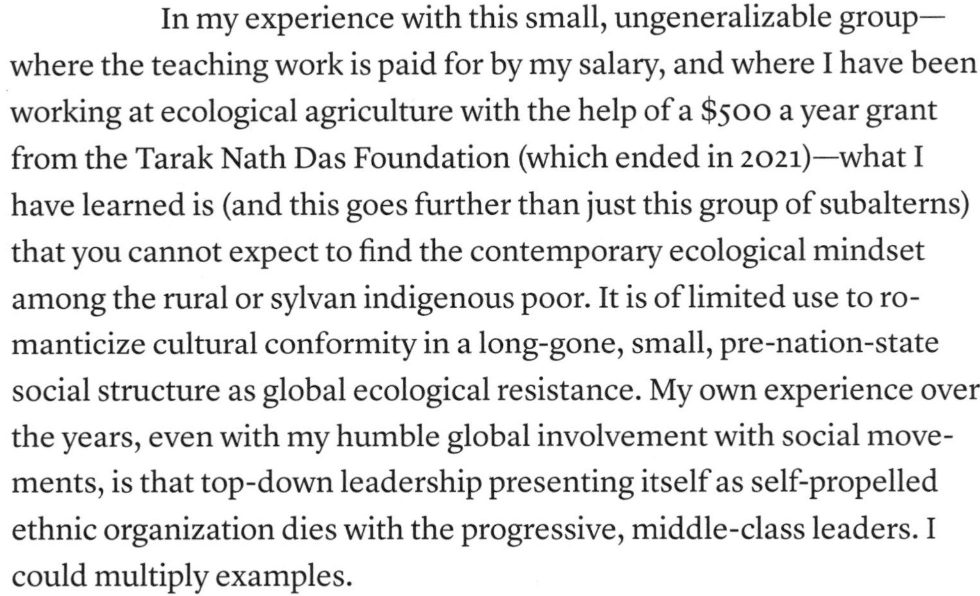

In my experience with this small, ungeneralizable group—where the teaching work is paid for by my salary, and where I have been working at ecological agriculture with the help of a $500 a year grant from the Tarak Nath Das Foundation (which ended in 2021)—what I have learned is (and this goes further than just this group of subalterns) that you cannot expect to find the contemporary ecological mindset among the rural or sylvan indigenous poor. It is of limited use to romanticize cultural conformity in a long-gone, small, pre-nation-state social structure as global ecological resistance. My own experience over the years, even with my humble global involvement with social movements, is that top-down leadership presenting itself as self-propelled ethnic organization dies with the progressive, middle-class leaders. I could multiply examples.

The subalterns' intelligent assessment of multiparty democracy is that the parties are like competitive football clubs: those who promise most, and perform least, win. Also, they understand that violence and intimidation are logical parts of elections. To quote my student Rambhandari Lohar, a nine-year-old practicing English conversation with me, "elections are a game." When asked to explain to me in Bengali what he meant by "game," his answer was "মারামারি," fighting.

I have already asked, who is the future generation? I now want to ask, why rights alone? Today, the Anthropocene demands that we think of the human as both poison and medicine. It would be medicine for the victims. As an example, I mention the Rohingyas, an ethnic group that, according to the United Nations, is being genocidally exterminated by the military government of Myanmar, using rape and sexual violence as weapons of genocide. I am obliged to mention them whenever I speak in public. Not incidentally, India is also active against the Rohingyas. Nasir Uddin, professor of political science at the University of Chittagong in Bangladesh, has done hundreds of hours of interviews with them, and, from their descriptions of their own condition, has concluded that their existence is "subhuman." Being human as medicine rather than poison—this is the philosophical premise of human rights at the inception of the Bill of Rights in the eighteenth century. We need to restore the value of being human to the Rohingya—the

human as medicine. The women Nasir Uddin interviews speak in detail about their suffering, but do not produce a "life is subhuman" remark. I have marked their presence by a picture of a mother by the famous photographer Shahidul Alam, to let the eyes speak, although I am troubled that I am obliged to show women silent because I wanted a convenient quotation.

Poison can be turned into medicine by learning the dosage—one might draw an analogy with natural and positive law. For lack of time, I cannot develop the analogy, but I mark the moment. Here is a song about dosage: "Think man later, as a second step." The guy singing, Santosh Karmakar, is not a subaltern; he is a landowner, and a high school teacher.

> Life is the truth of the world / look and fill your eyes.
> The human being is true above all else.
> Think that / that man is above all else / after the first truth / that biodiversity comes first.

In the first line, "life" stands for the word *pran,* which is used to translate the "bio" of "biodiversity." In the second line, he quotes a famous tag from the fifteenth-century Bengali poet Chandidas. We all know that Karmakar's injunction in the song—biodiversity first, human second—is hard to follow for the human being in general. That is because the defining human affects are violence, fear, greed. "Family values" are greed dressed up as love. With globalization, when the social contract of the state is no longer necessary, the emphasis on citizenship is falling further apart, as we know—all over the world. By contrast, human rights keeps the definition of itself as inalienable, an effect without a cause which can turn into a cause with an effect pretty easily. And, in the current conjuncture, this gives us nothing more than support for openly nonsecular—read faith-based—political discourse. With education corporatized and an emphasis on science, technology, engineering, and mathematics, what we are witnessing is a return of the irreducible humanity of greed, fear, and violence. This is the human, and the differentiation of the human into medicine and poison, or the differentiation of self and world, must be thought within this return. And in this process we must ask: What is the relationship between being human and being a citizen? Is it simply a matter of claiming one's own rights, or thinking about the rights of others? When human rights are protected within "sustainable underdevelopment"—as I said, sustaining the maximum cost-effectiveness with the minimum of development, implicitly operating as insertion into the circuit of capital without subject-formation—the idea of the rights of others cannot be produced in the beneficiaries. This is my lesson for students at the top. I want to go by way of a riddle invoked by W. E. B. Du Bois in a 1906 speech, and a powerful novel by Tillie Olsen, the daughter of parents active in the 1906 Revolution in Russia, titled *Tell Me a Riddle*. Here is Du Bois speaking in 1906, in front of what he calls "a smug Hampton." These remarks are particularly significant because the history of Hampton Institute in Virginia is deeply involved with the Black Reconstruction. In the early days, support for the Institute came from the Freedmen's Bureau, the "socialist" oasis which was blasted by the desert sands of a racialized capitalism, the story of which is told with great passion in Du Bois's *Black Reconstruction in America*. But we are getting ahead of ourselves. In 1906, Du Bois says:

> I speak . . . to you young teachers for two great reasons: first . . . because I am a teacher . . . but secondly and chiefly, because you are the type and representative of that fateful class through whom the great army of tomorrow's men are learning the riddle of the world, the meaning of life and the life worth living.[1]

What is the riddle? That the self-interested subaltern must be moved to the impassioned, impersonal love of a generalizable humankind. Over against this is Tillie Olsen's protagonist—a dying woman, an old woman, journeying from her home to her hospital bed.

She had participated in the 1905 Revolution in Russia, and then gone down the path of marriage and migration to the United States. It is as if the woman, grown old in a more "normal" trajectory, shows us the violence of reproductive heteronormativity, of the expectations from a grandmother who must not care about humanity, but only about grandchildren—the sheer, unremarkable violence of the everyday, a gendered everyday that unhinges the mind by a commonplace denial of entry into the public sphere.

As the protagonist moves toward death, Olsen weaves passages, sometimes dreamlike, that lay out this conflict poignantly. The protagonist is scolded because she has scared her son-in-law, a rabbi, when she says about herself in delirium: "At once go and make them change. Tell them to write: Race, human; Religion, none." And the husband's response: "Look how you have upset yourself, Mrs. Excited Over Nothing." Now she can think of the killing cancer as "*being able at last to live within, and not move to the rhythms of others,* as life had forced her to: denying; removing; isolating; taking the children one by one; then deafening, half-blinding—and, at last, presenting her solitude."[2] Now she can think of her activist days as "*hunger; secret meetings; human rights; spies; betrayal; prison; escape*—interrupted by one of the grandchildren."[3] Olsen writes:

> Her breath was too faint for sustained speech now, but still the lips moved:

... As a human being responsibility
... Dogma dead war dead one country.[4]

She's allowed to say this because she is dying, and she is not supposed to be just a woman looking after her family.

If you succeed, the formerly oppressed become suboppressors, said Paulo Freire in the *Pedagogy of the Oppressed*.[5] Therefore I would like to invoke what I said in 1997 to the Swiss NGO that was wanting to change its task from saving Holocaust survivors to saving refugees and asylum seekers.

> Planetary imaginings locate the imperative in a galactic and para-galactic alterity—so to speak!—that cannot be reasoned into self-interest. How can we provide adequate justification for giving care, for considering the capacity to help others as a basic human right? How can we inscribe responsibility as a right rather than an obligation? This is a paradox that has troubled intellectuals and philosophers as well as cultural leaders through the ages. Ground-level Islam, in my part of the world, combines right and responsibility in the tremendous concept or figure of *al haq*. *Haq* is the "para-individual structural responsibility" into which we are born—that is, our true being. Indeed, the word "responsibility" is an approximation here, for this structural positioning can also be approximately translated as "birth right." Whether it is right or responsibility, it is the truth of my being, in a not quite English sense, my *haq*. Thus your goal, in spite of all appearances, cannot reduce itself to merely integrating the underclass immigrant into this economic dynamic. Think, therefore, the planet as the merely imagined proper receiver and transmitter of imperatives. I want it to be understood that I am not speaking for Islam or indeed any named religion. It so happens that I have linguistic access to how the youngest people of the Book institutionalized the practice and thus began its effacement. How ethics separated itself from the law in the history of Islam has been recorded. And, like most cultural logics institutionalizing responsibility, Islam has historically allowed the woman to take the other's part within it. What is new here is that the dominant is educated persistently to attempt, at least, to suspend appro-

> priation in its own interest in order to learn to learn from "below," to learn to mean to say—not just deliberately non-hierarchically, as the US formula goes—I need to learn from you what you practice; I need it even if you didn't want to share a bit of my pie; but there's something I want to give you, which will make our shared practice flourish. You don't know, and I didn't know, that civility requires your practice of responsibility as pre-originary right.

Let me now summarize the points I have so far made: 1) Generalization of the subaltern into citizenship. 2) Citizenship is not merely to claim rights (liberty) but also to think other people (equality). 3) Textural teaching, or soul-cooking, into this contradiction at the top and the bottom. 4) Democracy is football clubs. 5) The need for human rights subject formation. 6) The review of the loss of idealism in the postrevolutionary world.

I can now move on to my last movement: supplementing architecture and art with hands-on, democratic, quality education, not just income production or STEM disciplines. Please remember: to supplement is to expand totality and to introduce the incalculable.

First, a few words on supplementing architecture—"housing gendered minds," words uttered at a conference called Housing the Majority at Columbia GSAPP. I am not an architect, said I, I am a teacher of the humanities. My idea of "majority" is the largest sector of the electorate in places like continental Africa and India. As such, I am not directly involved with sub-proletarian urban housing, but rather with the landless illiterate rural population of India, and the urban-rural interface in Nigeria. The urban is determined by the volatility of the rural. In the Indian context, the subaltern build clay houses, the government provides cheap latrines—not much in demand. My task is to rearrange desires so that a desire to use latrines may be produced rather than uselessly imposed. Is this "housing?" In some ways, it is, because large projects of giving brick habitats to randomly selected villagers seem not to have anything to do with a sense of place. As for the corner of Africa that I "know," the work by those with whom I am allied is to rearrange desires so that a return to land becomes even more viable.

My interest has been in the fact that there is no effort at subject-formation—making up the "I" that will use these things—among the beneficiaries. I have recently defined "development" as "the economic transition into the circuit of capital with insufficient attention to subject formation." In the classes of which I speak there is no subject formation about housing—although the government has, for some time now, propagated, in my area, these brick habitat projects,

Nidhi Mahajan, *Silences and Spectres of the Indian Ocean*, p. 286.

left to the building imagination of the locals. The housing materials are supposed to be given to the BPL, a creolized subaltern word whose "correct" English meaning—Below the Poverty Level—is neither known nor needed. Since I will speak of gender soon, I will give you an example of this creolization—incidentally, an informal word that determines the formal, of which I have written elsewhere. When you are arranging your son's marriage you are APL (above poverty level), says Ujjwal Lohar, a local. In other words, this is a well-off family, give a big dowry. When you are arranging your daughter's marriage, he continues, you are BPL. In other words, we can't give too much of a dowry, forgive us. The English initials are creolized, lexicalized into the local. The brick habitat cannot of course be given to the real BPL, who are barely alive—so an artificial BPL, favored by the party in power, gets housing.

The rest of my remarks are made in the understanding that, in building the house, we house the body. Hence latrines. They are offered but not used. A planning commission lady in India (when India had a planning commission) made a widely shared joke, uncomprehending: "We offered them latrines or cell phones, and they took cell phones." Class difference is speaking here.

Who would want to use the latrines built a few hundred yards from one of my schools, when the children are used to sitting under the sun? When the child wants to be excused, s/he goes in the fields. They must *want* a variety of consumerism based on preventive health desire, much harder to produce, except disease by disease, affectively.

My best teacher in the red sari now uses the latrine (attached to my room, with an outside door) in my absence. I don't know when exactly this happened. And how did she respond, a few years ago? In answer I quote a paragraph from a talk called "Situating Feminisms" I have given in Beijing, Berkeley, Delhi, Milan, New York. Our class reaction to it is embarrassment. Many questions were asked about many parts of my talk, but never was this paragraph touched.

> A man walks with me down a path strewn with human waste, and says with ill-concealed pride: "Our toilets are free." When his mother is afflicted with cholera, or a male coworker's son with hepatitis, for lack of education the man and the coworker cannot use the free National Health Service. But I can, so it is possible for me to show, by explaining the difficult prose of the World Health Organization into the regional language, that they are paying the price of their free toilets, and will continue to do so.
> When a capable woman teacher—who regularly teaches the books in the state curriculum outlining

oral-fecal disease—is asked why she doesn't use the toilet (2,800 rupees paid for by me for her own use) added to her dwelling, she remarks, "The men here are very courteous. They do not go near the fields which they know are being used by women for defecating." Now this is a different kind of argument—gender solidarity through acknowledgment of gendered division of bodily affect. This is not a question of obeying hygienic principles. In my case, this has been rearranged through the use of caste shame by class mobilization through relatively recent European colonization. Am I simply interested in creating a "middle class" through the use of caste obedience? Then let's not accuse the elitists. This is not premodern to modern on the way to the postmodern—this is an acknowledgment of the relief map of modernity calling for epistemological activism, leading toward slow but real changes, supplementing necessarily feudal problem-solving through learning to learn from below.

I had just heard a brilliant paper by a Dr. Binni in Baroda on the caste distribution of shame in the context of the women's Channar rebellion and other related resistances in Kerala. I had heard the teacher lengthily lectured by a male Delhi University historian because she had dared to cite Foucault. She is an epistemological activist for the historiographers, and I hope I will learn more from her in the future. In the caste Hindu marriage, *Lajjaharan,* or the removal of shame, is one mark of being married. When I strip in the Euro-US gym locker room, I am married to colonial history through the rearrangement of caste shame, which was harnessed to a modernity sequentially and teleologically computed so that I can lead today. Yet that is still employing a sexual difference that doesn't acknowledge the plurality of genders.

Architecture, housing the majority, must become interdisciplinary here. This is a profound epistemic change—how to know your body as an object—involved with developing a preventive attitude toward health. The change is also connected not merely to literacy but to complex education, so that the collusion of doctors, the medical profession, and the pharmaceutical industry cannot completely destroy the poor, for whom a diagnosis is never considered necessary.

Finally, art. A first example, related to Marina Tabassum's project and my rural school experience. I do not usually build school buildings. I wait until a particular school has been able to operate for a year or so, following our principles of teaching, in basic thatched shacks provided by local self-government and then collect funds to build the building. The first such building had been built on government public land by eminent domain. At a certain point, I declared that another school was ready for a building. Imagine my surprise, when I next visited the school, to encounter this document. So-called untouchable outcasts, themselves technically landless, had donated the 720 square-foot area enclosed by the four mud huts they inherited from their parents. This was the first time in history that a landless outcast had given land to a Brahmin—myself—and a white Englishman—the former student whom I was trying to train (in vain) to take my place when I died. I told myself not to be sentimental when I saw this surprising document, restrained my tears, and accepted it as normal. The rearrangement of desires, indeed! The subaltern had claimed and obtained agency, on their own.

A nice story, except that the most capable teacher, because of whose teaching the school building had been erected, had to be dismissed by me subsequently because she was working for the Hindu fundamentalists, and accepting payment from both them and me, using my schoolroom to teach their material. And she so intimidated the outcasts in the hamlet—because her caste-Hindu family, although low on the totem pole of caste, had lorded over these outcasts for some time—that they could not send their children to the school when I got a new teacher, out of fear. When this went on for many months, I was obliged to close the school, and give away the building that I had built on the land to them.

By now, this change in subaltern agency has been accepted as a rule by the entire group, without any guidance or insistence from me at all. The thing to notice in the document is that some of the holdings are so small that the computer has not been able to record it as anything but 00.00! Again, a touching story, except that these same people, fighting among themselves according to party lines, had accused my supervisor—a fellow villager—of two unbailable offenses: sexual molestation and attempted murder! These are typically the offenses that all interparty violence among the subalterns generate for accusation. The charges are still not dismissed. So, the task of rearranging desires goes on, however affectively fulfilling may be the certain details of the visual culture that we can extract from our experiences!

A second example, related to Nidhi Mahajan's work. In the mangrove forests of the southern part of West Bengal, Tushar Kanjilal established the Tagore Society for Rural Development in the 1960s. Certainly the face of the area has been changed by Tusharda's indefatigable work. He died recently, and he wrote what follows:

However, for Dinu giving education was sacred. He used to call it a *puja*—a worship service.

Head teacher and students' guardians told Dinu he would have a formal retirement ceremony. Dinu said what would he retire from—who will stop me from doing the rest of the work? Dinu still goes to school every day if a teacher is absent, he takes the class and keeps his sacred pursuit moving. Many don't like this. He has nothing to say against anyone. The absence of any effort to build the children as healthy, capable, strong human members of a society imagined by him gives him pain.

The village has a higher secondary school. The election of an administrative committee is on the agenda. Both sides have come prepared with truncheons, bombs, guns. In that atmosphere the thing that is sure to die is education. Dinu ran there like a madman. He stood between the two sides and pleaded with both sides to be at peace. He didn't know that in this changed world, education, humanity, dependence upon each other—such a society that had been indicated by great men for a good life—that day was over. Now from schools to the central government, state government—everywhere it is the greed for power that drives people and in that drive human beings perhaps become inhuman.

A few hours later I got the news that Dinu had been beaten up. I ran to the hospital, by then Dinu was dead. I do not believe in the soul, nor in the next life. Therefore I don't feel like fulfilling my duty by wishing peace for Dinu's soul. I wish for one thing, that this death should not be in vain. Only that in the near or distant future, a thousand unarmed Dinus will become a wall between violent polarities.

With this hope "that in the near or distant future, a thousand unarmed Dinus will become a wall between violent polarities," we can end for the moment.

Gayatri Chakravorty Spivak is a literary theorist and feminist critic, and an activist in rural education and feminist and ecological social movements. She is professor in the humanities at Columbia University and the recipient of twelve honorary doctorates. Among her books are *In Other Worlds: Essays in Cultural Politics* (1987) and *A Critique of Post-colonial Reason: Towards a History of the Vanishing Present* (1999).

1. W. E. B. Du Bois, *The Education of Black People* (New York, 1973), p. 5.
2. Tillie Olsen, *Tell Me a Riddle* (New York, 1956), pp. 60–69, emphasis added.
3. Ibid, p. 95.
4. Ibid, pp. 105–09, italics in original.
5. Paulo Freire, *Pedagogy of the Oppressed*, trans. Myra Bergman Ramos (New York, 2006).

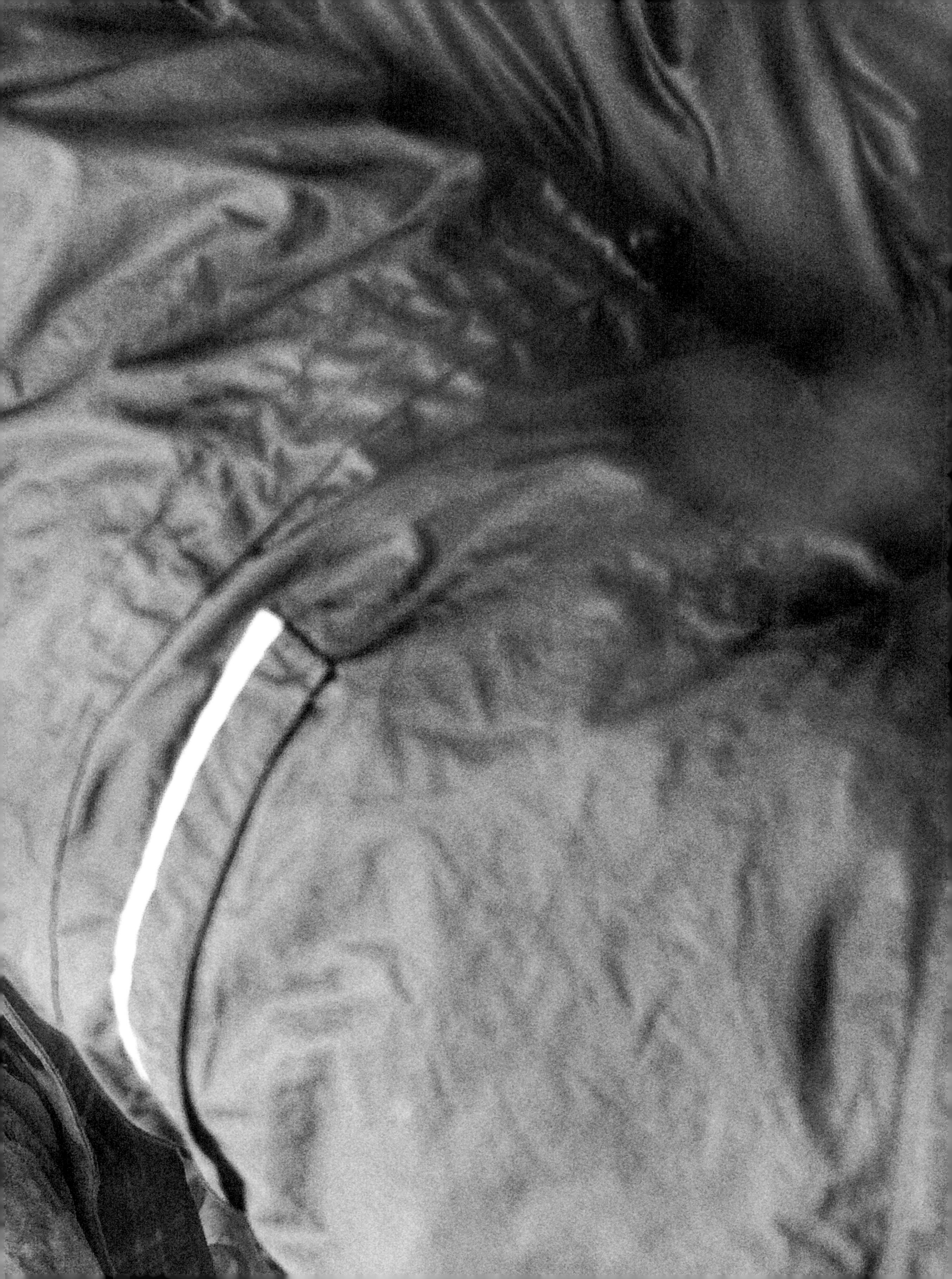

Transcript: Forms of Afterlife

Sepake Angiama
Kodwo Eshun
Esi Eshun
Denise Ferreira da Silva
Salah Hassan
Anjalika Sagar

On November 10, 2019, Anjalika Sagar and Kodwo Eshun (The Otolith Group) were joined by Esi Eshun, Denise Ferreira da Silva, and Salah Hassan for a discussion moderated by Sepake Angiama.

SEPAKE ANGIAMA

I first came across Salah through his writings in *Nka – Journal of Contemporary African Art,* which was important for me as a young cultural producer in London trying to make sense of exhibitions like *Africa95,* and in thinking about how to continue a connection to a place where I was not born but I identify as being from. He will take us on a journey through three significant moments within Sudanese history in relation to the Black Radical Tradition.

These moments have also been highlighted in the film made by The Otolith Group, which formed in 2002. Their practice takes us through a number of different media, including film and performance, using a science-fiction aesthetic to explore places or imaginaries that we have not yet formed. In the project titled *Infinity Minus Infinity,* they have been in an ongoing conversation with Denise Ferreira da Silva, who also joins us. I am excited to think about the forms that are reiterated within the quality of the film, but also in the deep thinking around Blackness. We are also joined by Esi Eshun, who was a collaborator of The Otolith Group on the conceptual framework of the film and its storytelling.

SALAH HASSAN

In response to Adrian Lahoud's question on how does one claim other people, how does one claim humanity—a reference to C. L. R. James—I originally thought about presenting a paper I wrote called "The Caribbean In Me." As a Sudanese person who has lived more than half of his adult life in the United States and is part of African and African-American studies, it was natural for me to be attracted to the Black Radical Tradition—characters like James, Frantz Fanon, George Padmore, Sylvia Wynter, Eric Williams, Aimé Césaire, Édouard Glissant, and Cedric Robinson.

Most of the names I have mentioned are from the Caribbean or of Caribbean origin living in the diaspora. This led me to think: Why the Caribbean? Why have these small islands produced giant thinkers who influence me? I found the answer in Glissant's writing. He talks about the Caribbean as small islands where all cultures of the world meet—the British Empire, the enslaved population, and the indigenous population—making it more global than Europe itself. He proposed another way of thinking about the world, moving from the continental to what he called the "archipelagic": thinking of the world as a constellation of archipelagos.

In a way, this allows for a reclaiming of humanity. As we move away from the geoformal unit to thinking about the whole world as being in a state of what Glissant calls "creolization," it is not only those of us from the Third World to be affected by Europeans—but European modernity is revealed as owing much of its inheritance to other peoples. Glissant says that big empires always crumble and small countries survive, which is interesting as we witness the crisis of capitalism and its efforts to renew itself. What have I learned from the Black radical tradition that will link me to the story of the recent Sudanese Revolution and what it has meant in the world?

One of the elements that I find interesting is that capitalism has been a racialized system from the beginning. Aimé Césaire said in his critique of universalism that there are two ways to lose oneself: "walled segregation in the particular, or dilution in the universal." (To give you an example from the Middle East, what would be the logic for capitalism, if not its extreme racialization, to concentrate on one country like Israel to the detriment of the whole Arab population, and to continue the exceptionally violent treatment of the Palestinian people?)

For many, in the Arab world and globally, the 2018–2019 Sudanese Revolution has been exceptional. What did suddenly emerge in Sudan that attracted the attention of the world? First, it was a highly organized form of revolution. Second, it was peaceful and nonviolent, following other traditions of nonviolent struggle like the Civil Rights Movement. There was also the strong female participation: more than half of the people in the streets were women. But there is nothing exceptional about all this if you consider the history of resistance and civil societies in Sudan. The reasons for the surprise is instead what the late Kenyan scholar Ali Mazrui called "multiple marginalities." Sudan is at the edge of the Arab world and of Africa; we are at the margins of both, although if we think in an archipelagic way, we are actually at the center, as the meeting place.

There is a long history of radicalism and social movements in Sudan. From the 1940s, the Communist Party organized trade unions and the civil society. The leadership of these radical groups distinguished itself from radical Marxism across the globe by critiquing Soviet Communism. They connected intellectually with the Black and the Arab world—communist leader Abdel Khaliq Mahjub wrote about African socialism and translated the poetry of Aimé Césaire—and played an important role in vernacularizing and localizing the radical tradition. There is a book called *Six Years of Underground*, or *Sitt Sanawaat Taht al-'Ard*, written in 1964, which mentions the types of engagement used by demonstrators today. The weapon of the general strike, *al-idraab al-'am*, the weapon of *al-'asyaan al-madani*, civil disobedience, were outlined, thought of, and experimented with not only in 1964, but also in a subsequent revolution in 1985. We could claim that Sudan has the "copyright" to the Arab Spring in that sense—in the way it is a people's movement, it is from the ground up, and it invented its own weapons.

But why the participation of women? From the 1940s there was a strong women's movement in Sudan. You might have heard of Fatima Ahmed Ibrahim, or the formation in the late 1940s and early 1950s of the Sudanese women's union, *al-Ittihad al-Nisa'i*. The right to vote was gained in Sudan before any other Arab country, and women were elected in the first and second parliament (women parliamentarians are appointed across the Arab world, rather than elected). One could therefore say that the struggle for democracy, freedom, and human rights in Sudan has its roots in movements that were more inclusive than others.

I will end by saying that what is exceptional about this movement, in my view, if you compare it to the Arab world, is that it is anti–Muslim Brotherhood. In Sudan there was a Muslim Brotherhood coup that led to thirty years of dictatorship, meaning that the figures who were in power were originally from the Muslim Brotherhood. In other countries they have always remained in the margins or in the opposition. (In Egypt, one of the tactics of fear that is used in any uprising is the possibility of a return to the Muslim Brotherhood domination that was seen in the election of Mohamed Morsi, the first Egyptian president to be elected democratically.) This is the story of my people, you can claim it too. There are lots of lessons to learn, since social movements sometimes have a domino effect: there are links and exchanges (you can see it now in Iraq, Lebanon, Chile, and others). What makes Sudan highly organized is that it has a leadership, called the Sudanese Professionals Association, made up of doctors, engineers, university professors, and working-class groups. In 2013, this group of people met and predicted that there would be change. They did not want to be caught off guard, so they drafted a highly detailed program for a transition. It has limitations—but I will leave it there.

SEPAKE ANGIAMA Our talk is framed today by the title "Forms of Afterlife." One of the departure points that you touched upon is the Trinidadian writer C. L. R. James, who has written extensively on the history of Black radical acts as well as the international communist movement. You allude to the idea of the Global South being framed as a kind of archipelago, where islands are spaces of creolization. I wanted to ask you, do you see Sudan creating an island mentality—not necessarily being understood as part of Africa? Is it in this sense that you were alluding to an archipelagic way of thinking?

SALAH HASSAN I am often asked in the West, "Are you African or Arab?" I feel comfortable moving between the two. I celebrate the most positive legacies of the

Arab world and of the Black intellectual tradition. This has also been a central question for artists and writers. Most of those who come from a Left tradition identify as Afro-Arab, which they think of as a hybrid identity. There is a school of philosophy, poetry, and literature in Sudan called *Madrasa al-Ghaab wal-Sahra'*, or the School of the Bush and the Desert. They took geographic elements of Sudan as a symbol of its hybridity, because the map of Sudan moves from the desert to the equatorial forest.

One of the first epic poems written by Sudanese poet Mohammed Abdul-Hayy is called *Sinnar: A Homecoming*, or *Return to Sinnar*. It is modeled, I believe, after Aimé Césaire's *Cahier*. You see in *Return to Sinnar* the first Islamic kingdom in the context of the southern part of Sudan in which Arabic, African, and Islamic traditions meet. This is the melting pot from which the Sudanese nationalist movement later emerged.

SEPAKE ANGIAMA I would like now to talk about *Infinity Minus Infinity*. Anjalika, you are going to talk about the notion of matter, thinking about the material qualities of the film.

ANJALIKA SAGAR I am going to lay out some of the different forms of thinking around politics that led to the making of this film. The intention behind it was to create a space as an atmosphere or feeling of Blackness, almost like a state of folded delirium where time is moving and shaping itself according to different ways of seeing, feeling, and hearing. I also want to talk about the fear behind our choice to make this film. In London, experiencing what was going on in the world at large and a techno-fascist inscription of enclosure on multiple levels—in our bodies, lives, hearts, and minds—I began to realize what it feels like to be colonized. To feel that in the middle of my so-called progressive London made me realize that something needed to be done, in the way that we can do it as artists. I understood that people from the Caribbean, the Windrush Generation, were being forcibly removed after being invited by Britain during the Commonwealth era to come and work. I talked to people who had worked in the Underground for forty years, people who have families in England but are being sent "back."

This strikes at the heart of work by people like Stuart Hall, Margaret Busby (who first published C. L. R. James), Olive Morris, Diane Abbott, John La Rose, and many others. The anti-racist struggle in Britain comes from a long history of multiethnic rebellion that has been in place as long as racial capitalism has been in place. What is this as a resistant aesthetic? What kind of resistant aesthetic can allow us to think around a work in order to remain free of forms of capture that entire series of enclosures demand of us?

The other aspect of this film was the idea, formally, that the senses (meaning our haptic relation to the world) are being colonized, in terms of cognitive capitalism entering the body. What does it mean to feel colonized through techno-fascism? How do we revive the senses but also reveal them as occupied? This comes out of the previous film we made, *O Horizon,* which looks at the Tagorian relationship between pedagogy and decolonization in Bengal at the beginning of the 1900s. Tagore asked students to engage with their hands, their minds, their bodies in a space of thinking around the sonic and the physical, as a way to revive the spirit of revolution against 200 years of the British occupation of India. Another aspect was the idea of the film essay as free jazz (I think Arthur Jafa said this), which led me to think about a different approach to editing—going through the body rather than going through a montage with one image after another. I was thinking about the idea of polyphony and about Glissant, the way he uses song, vocality, and poetics, and I thought about having his passages exchanged between Elaine Mitchener and Dante Micheaux could put Glissant's poetry through another level of creolization, one which could allow for the creolization of the film to take place. Though polyphony was important, so was class, race, gender, and the planetary. I was thinking about how to bring the planetary into a state of consciousness where Blackness is no longer about being the category, but disidentifying from it.

ESI ESHUN

I am going to talk about some of the overlapping issues in the film, besides Windrush, that we were thinking about when making it. We are talking about moments of apparent revolution and liberation, and how those have carried through into the present day, how there are always layers of meaning and understanding that permeate the way we receive information from the dominant strata of society. One of the influences for the film was Kathryn Yusoff's book *A Billion Black Anthropocenes or None,* which we were all reading at the time it was first conceived. The book makes comparisons between the birth of the discipline of geology and the birth of colonialism, and considers how matter relates to Black human beings—Black bodies—and the minerals that were extracted from the earth. She posits that both were subjected to extractive technologies and articulates clearly how these two factors are implicated in climate change.

Yusoff focuses on a particular moment in time which geologists term the Orbis Spike. It occurred in 1610, with the decimation of the Carib population—the native population of the Caribbean—and the repopulation with Black slaves. She argues that the change in flora and fauna that occurred, due to the arrival of new groups of people and new species of plants and animals, changed the biospheric nature of the environment.

Another aspect that was key to the film was slavery and the notion of compensated emancipation.

Slave plantations functioned as pitiless laboratories in which to test the capacities of human bodies as forms of biological, biochemical, or bioengineered batteries, charged with powering a relentless regime of production and annihilation through systematic mechanisms of violence. Slaves functioned as raw material, the equivalents of the minerals used for battery capacitors; they were used to fuel the plantation economy and thus the wider industrial system in which they played a part.

As the biological equivalent of the mineralogical elements, whose extraction formed the impetus of capitalism and then slavery, slaves were considered by the system that maintained them as forms of inert, largely inexpressive matter, incapable of the type of abstract thinking that would mark them out as fully human. In order to maintain the myth of their nonhuman status, regulatory systems of enclosure and control over the spatial-temporal capacities of slaves were maintained by regimes of physical, psychic, philosophical, and juridical violence upheld by numerous apparatuses of the state and its derivatives.

The ostensible terminus of this regime was in 1833, with the abolition of slavery across the empire—primarily in the Caribbean islands and, to a much lesser extent, in Canada and South Africa. While the favored myth of abolition has held that a handful of Christian campaigners succeeded in persuading Parliament to liberate slaves through the sheer force of their moral authority, the truth, as ever, is rather more complex. Instead of negotiating freedom for slaves, the campaigners achieved only a partial victory, brought about in no small part by recognition on the part of the powerful West Indian slave-owning lobby that the economic validity of slave ownership had been compromised in the face of other, more lucrative forms of free trade.

And what really happened, as has only recently become public knowledge (thanks to the archival work done by Catherine Hall and Nicholas Draper at University College London), is that in order to agree to release their slaves, the owners had to be paid £20 million in compensation, which in today's money is roughly equivalent to £16–17 billion. The owners, needless to say, were already among some of the richest families in Britain, and hence the world: families steeped in the aristocracy, in merchant banking, in shipping, families who then as now control flows of capital around the world. Among these families were the Barings and the Barclays.

These slave owners became the recipients of grossly inflated sums of money in compensation for the loss of their slave property, the inventory of which was meticulously logged on ledger sheets with the purpose of claiming the future earnings they would never accrue. At no point, of course, were the former slaves given compensation for the injuries *they* had sustained over centuries. Instead, they were summarily bound to undertake a further six years of unpaid labor, known as apprenticeship, in which they worked for free for their former owners, only now redefined as bosses. So disproportionate was the wealth of the families of former slave owners that when it came to light in 2017 that British taxpayers had been paying off the interest accrued to the debt ever since, it came as a shock, but not as a great surprise.

SEPAKE ANGIAMA

I think that the questions of value and matter are pertinent to the film in relation to thinking about the social and political struggle that we are currently seeing in various uprisings across the world. In the film, you also touch on the relationship between ecological collapse, financial collapse, and the notion of "returning" people who had settled in Britain. Kodwo, I wonder if you could open this up a little more.

KODWO ESHUN

Part of what we are witnessing at the moment is not so much the making of the Caribbean peoples but the unmaking of the Caribbean peoples. In an essay that Denise Ferreira da Silva wrote in 2017, which had a major influence on our thinking, she asks: "Why don't black lives matter?" The question there is how to understand Blackness, how to understand lives, and how to understand matter. What is the matter that does not matter?

The so-called hostile environment policy carried out by the Conservative government—legislated in the 2014 Immigration Act—allows for a juridical assemblage of the deprivation of citizenship. People of the Windrush Generation, who came to the UK in the 1940s and 1950s to rebuild the decaying industrial infrastructure of the empire, are being systematically deprived of their citizenship. This is part of the making and unmaking of citizenship within a wider imperial project, which includes the deportation of refugees to Iraq, Syria, Afghanistan, and Sri Lanka. Since 9/11, it is effectively an ongoing imperial project of deportation, detention, sanctioning, deprivation, and dispossession on a mass but covert scale throughout the UK.

This question of the hostile environment opens onto the broader question of why Black lives do not matter. We wanted a particular language with which to think through the matter of Black lives and the hostile environment, one that could do justice to the gravity of these questions. Yesterday we watched a compelling performance by the Egyptian collective HaRaKa, and they talked about the notion of aesthetic justice. What are the aesthetics that can do justice to these questions? What we are talking about are the forms of life of the afterlife, or the life of forms of the before and afterlife of slavery.

In 1960, Richard Wright said that the conditions of slavery and segregation gave the Negro artist an intellectual, bitter moral prominence. I would say that the question of Black lives that do not matter and the hostile environment gives certain Black feminists a bitter moral prominence. Under the conditions of the hostile environment, the thinking, writing, and research of figures like Denise Ferreira da Silva, Saidiya Hartman, Christina Sharpe, Hortense Spillers, Sylvia Wynter, and many others attain a certain forcefulness because they put pressure on the received ideas required to understand the stakes. They help us to form an aesthetic that can respond to the crisis at hand. Part of the project was to dramatize these questions.

One concept we looked at was Saidiya Hartman's notion of the chorus. In her new volume *Wayward Lives, Beautiful Experiments,* she says that if you go back to the Greek etymology of "chorus," it means "the dance within an enclosure." She says that the chorus—and specifically she refers to the chorine: the female chorus—is a figure that recreates the Black Radical Tradition at the level of the assembly and at the level of the plural. That is what we tried to do: we tried to think through the question of the matter of Black lives under the aesthetics of the chorus.

SEPAKE ANGIAMA

Denise, toward the end of the film we are taken through an equation which always results in a neutral response (a zero). I wondered if you could talk more about these equations in relation to blackness and your thinking through why Black lives do not matter.

DENISE FERREIRA DA SILVA

Before I talk about the equation of value, I wanted to refer to two quotes which I have used in my writings. One is from the Zapatistas' Second Declaration of the Lacandon Jungle, in which they mention being in the mountains and talking to their dead. They ask which path they should choose, and the dead respond: "For everyone, everything . . . Until it is so, there will be nothing for us." The other is a quote from Frantz Fanon in which he writes: "Our historic mission is to sanction all revolts, all desperate actions, all those abortive attempts drowned in rivers of blood." I hope those resonate as I talk about the equation of value and some of the things that were in my mind as I was writing it.

The equation of value is primarily a way in which I try to activate the disruptive capacity of Blackness—the challenge it presents to modern thought and modes of existing, that which works within the category of

Blackness but it is not subsumed by it. This is the capacity to explode all forms and categories: mathematical, conceptual, but hopefully also institutional and practical. The equation is a tool of what I call "Black Feminist Poethics," which I locate fully within the Black Radical Tradition for many reasons, but mostly because it takes up the task of Black studies as it has been named by C. L. R James and Cedric Robinson: the dismantling of Western civilization.

I also name this task decolonization, or the end of the world *as we know it*. This task demands the restoration of the total value expropriated from native lands and slave bodies. (I use "native lands" as a phrase that signals that the task is a moment of the anticolonial project, which can be traced to when the first indigenous Americans and the first inhabitant of the Maluku Islands, all of what is today Mozambique, resisted European attempts at appropriating their lands and bodies 500 years ago.) Total value is not something to be measured, determined, or delimited in any way—it is everything. Not what was or has been, but what has become and what it made possible; that is, every cent, building, cell, brick, every particle that constitutes anything that now exists and has facilitated the reproduction and accumulation of capital anywhere on this planet. This is what I mean that it is also the end of the world *as we know it*. But why Blackness?

The point of departure here was these endless instances of total violence—racial violence—deployed by the state everywhere against Black persons. I take this otherwise unacceptable, excessive deployment of force as a sign that Blackness as a siphon holds all other possible ways of existing and thinking that need to be crushed so that modern thinking and existing become possible. As such, it suggests forms of afterlife outside blood and kinship relations. It signals other kinds of thinking before, against, and beyond categorizations, which relate to what Salah said about Sudan. This is the categorization that is refused in the claim made by the Zapatista dead, and it is also present in Fanon's naming of "our historical mission."

The turn to how Blackness hosts these other ways of thinking in the world has been inspired by many interventions in Black feminist thought, in particular Hortense Spiller's idea of "female flesh ungendered." Spillers claims the tortured, wounded, Black, female, native body as the site of a figuring of the crimes and ethical violations of slavery and conquest. More specifically, I pursue Spiller's question of whether the wounds—the markings of violation—are passed to future generations. This figure is what inspires the equation of value and other experiments that I have been doing lately.

The question of value figures a confrontation without staying in the moment of opposition and, as such, departs from Marx's dialectic. Instead, when I place Blackness against life, the movement is one of annihilation or, as I describe elsewhere, "negativation." This move releases other possibilities without naming them, including life. Life is the most important signifier of the ethical problem that rules in the post-Enlightenment period. The movement is one of breaking the determinations that give life its ethical supremacy, and which are designed to inspire an image of the world which would precede any conception and practice of existence that does not reproduce the modern point of departure. The modern point of departure is a separation of the human from the world, which sets up the world as an object to be conquered, mapped, and appropriated, and the praxis and methods that enable extraction from, and extinction of everything that is not considered "human."

SEPAKE ANGIAMA You raise an important point, which is held within indigenous thinking, of a nonseparation between the body and the earth as matter—it is something I feel resonates within the film itself. I wanted to pick up on the flesh of geology within the film. It strikes me every time I watch the film, because it is that moment of thinking about the connection between the earth, the matter of the earth, and the body. I was interested to know what has influenced the shift in your thinking about matter as not separate from the earth—the human and nonhuman in relation.

ANJALIKA SAGAR In Advaita Vedanta philosophy there is the idea that subject and object are not separate. This is deeply held within the structure of tantric thinking, where there is a sense of a constant folding with the material world. One learns through one's relation to everything in the cosmos because fundamentally we are all one. This involves a practice which is in the yoga sutras, in Ayurveda, and in Hindu philosophies. I was interested in what that practice is in my life and in general. In the film, I also wanted to think about what it is to reanimate ourselves in matter in the present. How do we reanimate into the planet again with responsibility and a sense of sustainability?

ESI ESHUN For me, one of the key, unspoken points of the film is an attempt to render a notion of animism, that everything in nature lives and is a conflation of matter and energy. Within the film we have forms that take on multiple forms. They do not belong to individual or social categories, and they permeate several dimensions and time frames at once. These figures also speak from what Kathryn Yusoff calls "geologic subjectivity," which is speaking in terms that might be applied to matters of the earth.

One of the characters whom I play has several heads and is a personification, in many ways, of the earth. There is a continuity between matter and energy, which in some way this film is attempting to address in its form, without seeking to apologize for it. These are forms of thinking that are specific to non-Western frameworks, and the West tends to have a condescending view of them. By placing them at the center of the film, you cease to make them something to question or to apologize for—you are immersed within that world, within that frame. Part of what the film is doing is allowing you to put preconceptions aside for a while and enter into space you might not normally choose to enter.

SEPAKE ANGIAMA Adrian challenged us to describe what he referred to as "the life after," and the kind of moment that precedes the "after." What do we consider life, this vital force or breath? The Triennial as a whole asked us to think beyond our present moment or our present future to consider ancestry, but also generations looking back, in order to reshape a possible future moment. I want to thank our speakers this afternoon for helping us to move through ways of thinking about forms of life.

Sepake Angiama is the artistic director of Iniva in London. She was previously head of education for Documenta 14, and cocurator of the 2019 Chicago Architecture Biennial.

Kodwo Eshun and Anjalika Sagar are the founders of The Otolith Group. Their moving images, audio works, performances, and installations engage with the legacies and potentialities of diasporic futurisms.

Esi Eshun is an artist and researcher. Her work investigates some of the socioeconomic, psychological, and philosophical contradictions of colonialism and its continuing significance.

Salah M. Hassan is director of The Africa Institute of Sharjah, and Goldwin Smith Professor of African and African Diaspora Art History and Visual Culture at Cornell University.

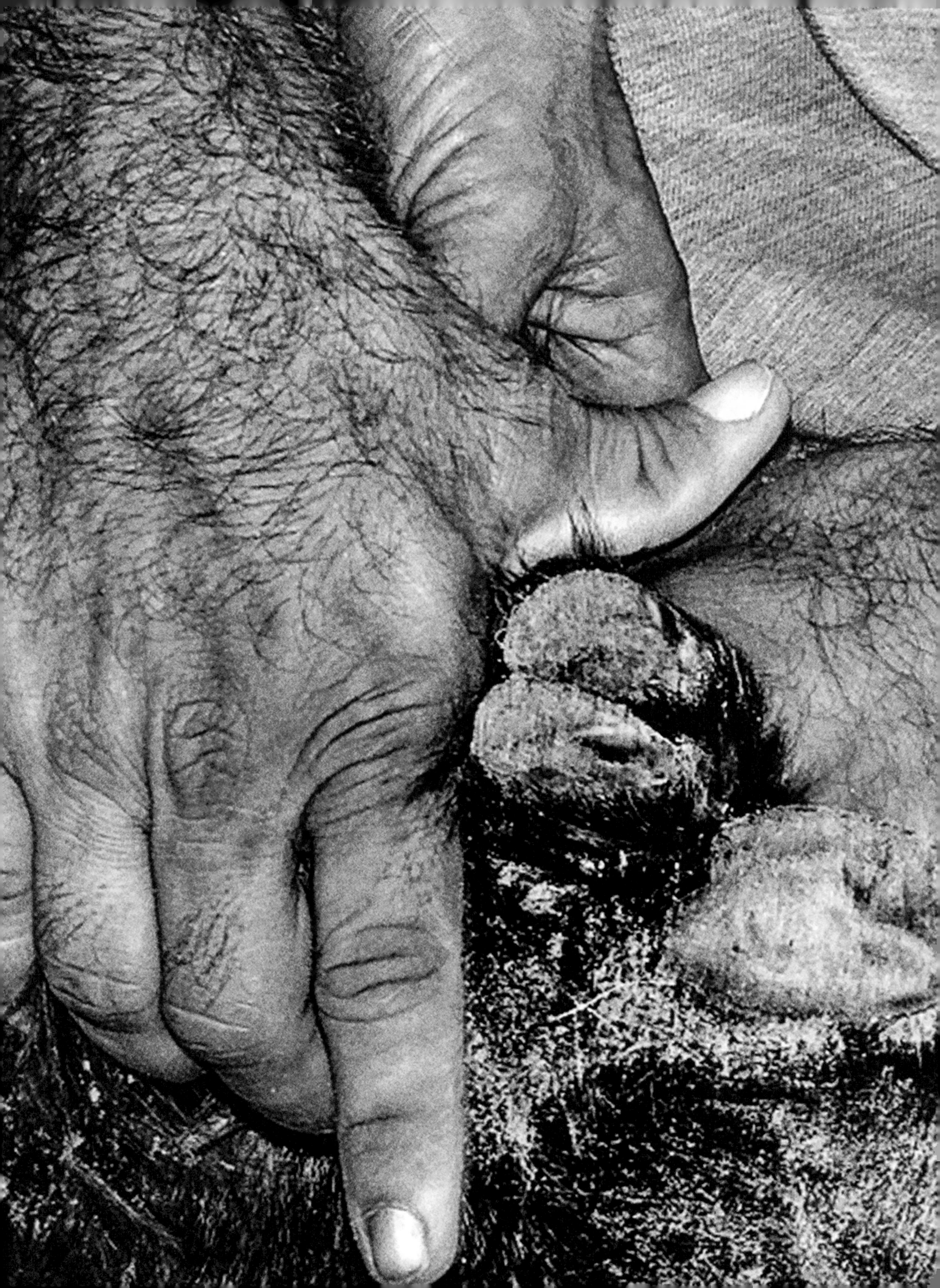

Nubian Historiography and the Eternally Beating River of Return

Alia Mossallam

During an introduction to a performance held in California in 1987, renowned Nubian singer Hamza Alaa El Din demonstrated an aspect of the very particular relationship between nature and the sounds of his percussion instrument, the *daf*.[1] Holding it up for a demonstration, he said:

> "I believe every drum plays the sounds of the four elements. This one is water."
> He then struck the center of his *daf*, producing a deep echoing sound.
> "This one is earth."
> He then struck the side of the *daf* with his palm, creating a flat, consistent beat.
> "This one is fire."
> He then flicked the edges of his *daf* with his fingers, creating a quick, accelerating melody.
> "And this one is air."
> He swished the palm of his hand around the rim of his instrument.
> "Now, when you let your drum play *you*, you can feel all those four elements. Please, allow me."[2]

With that, he began to beat his *daf*, as the audience heard each of the elements, and then experienced them, at times overlapping, at others multiplying together in consecutive waves of sound to the hauntingly beautiful melody of "Himayala," a children's ditty.

Between January 2010 and 2018, I recorded various interviews, meetings, events, and gatherings in Nubian villages in my attempt to understand and document how histories can be "sung." Here, I reflect on both the content of these songs—*what* they tell us about experiences of migration—and the songs as a method—*how* they tell these histories.

Throughout the building of the Aswan High Dam—completed in 1970, a cornerstone of Gamal Abdel Nasser's brand of Arab socialism—at least 100,000 Nubians were displaced from their villages; at least 50,000 of them were resettled to the north of the dam, in the Egyptian deserts of Kom Ombo. The history of that resettlement is drowned in the din of the Nasserist ideological drive and high modernist propaganda, which made the building of the dam seem a necessity in the popular imaginary. The dam was framed and propagated as an emblem of the revolutionary postcolonial moment of the 1960s: a source of electricity, water, and a chance at modernity for all; a metanarrative that targeted Nubian communities themselves, as Gamal Abdel Nasser addressed them, promising a life of prosperity after the building of the dam.[3]

The process of resettling Nubian communities itself was almost completely overshadowed by the international efforts dedicated to the relocation of the ancient Egyptian temples that dotted Nubian villages at the time. While absent from official historical narratives, stories of the experience of displacement, the sentiments toward it, and life before and after it are evoked in Nubian songs. They are preserved within families and village communities, and retold in gatherings, events, and bedtime stories. This history forms an inheritance and a legacy that are intertwined with these communities' relationship with nature and music.

WATER: HISTORY AS A RIVER

In thinking of popular historiography, particularly that surrounding the building of a dam, it is useful to think of the river as a metaphor for how history flows. Like the river, popular historiography flows across boundaries—Nubian stories of migration covered the region between Egypt and Sudan, long before borders were clearly demarcated through migrations north and south of the Aswan High Dam. Stories about migration are not limited or arranged according to temporal boundaries either. Songs cover migration from the building of the Aswan reservoir in 1902 and tell of the accumulated experiences of resettlement and loss rather than differentiating clearly between events and periods of time.

It is important to remember that, though it may seem like it, the river is not opposite to the dam—nor is it trapped behind it, rendered stagnant. Popular historical narratives flow "through" the dam, at times providing counter-histories (stories that oppose the official narration of the experience of dam building), and at others, linking lived experience to the dam itself (as many Nubians worked on the dam or believed that it might carry promise for their communities). Thus, we see how ideas flow across boundaries, how narratives flow through generations. We perceive a history embodying multivalence and fluidity, rather than a chronological historiography that offers a streamlined and opaque narrative.

In my first visit to the Nubian village of Gharb Suhail in 2010, I was introduced to musician and cook Chef Shaaban. He happened to be the nephew of Ahmed Sidqi Selim, a renowned singer who put Gharb Suhail on the map as far as Nubian cultural history went. For me to understand what the dam meant to Nubians at the time, Shaaban insisted, I had to listen to Sidqi's songs.

The first song that Chef Shaaban sang to me is one that uses the Nile as a metaphor, titled "Dayman nasrebu ya Nil," which means "Always triumphant, oh Nile." Sidqi was a legendary Kanzi-language singer, whose songs became iconic of the period of the dam's building and preceding migration.[4] His fame peaked in the 1960s and was comparable to that of Abdel Halim Hafez and Umm Kulthum in orating the nationalist projects of the 1952 Nasserist revolution. His songs are remembered for having "prepared" Nubia for the dam. In "Dayman nasrebu wo Nil" (1960), he starts with the stanza:

> Always triumphant, oh Nile,
> You have always triumphed us (Nubians),
> And provided a great source of life for us;
> Be the same power to Nasser as you have been to us,
> Don't let him down.

This stanza is sung as an opening call and is not accompanied by music. Sidqi is then joined by a chorus, as is the singing style in most Nubian gatherings, and the deep beat of the *daf* described by Hamza Alaa El Din in the opening lines. The beat echoes that of a steady flow, cheered on by the chorus and pushed forward by their words, as they encourage the Nile to continue flowing and thus to continue triumphing, beating stronger and stronger in unison, singing and moving faster as the song nears its end. By calling on the Nile to support Nubians, Sidqi refers to migrations past, beyond the building of the dam—the migrations of 1902, 1913, and 1933, each of which took place either during the building or the subsequent heightening of the Aswan reservoir. The Nile is also called upon to support "Nasser," indicating Gamal Abdel Nasser, who was ironically celebrated in this and many of Sidqi's songs leading up to the building of the dam.

The Nile in this song is a force that has triumphed over Nubians despite one migration after another. The promise is that with *this* migration, which was to happen in 1964, the Nile may also bring Nubians the bounties of the High Dam:

> You who when drunk from one is never the same,
> Triumph us as you always have,
> Bring fertility, light and metal . . .

Other of Sidqi's songs carry many of the 1952 revolution's ideas and emblems. "Tay tay tay" encourages its listeners to travel the world and claims that, since Nubians had now become part of *al wihda al arabiyya* (Arab unity), they would have a home in many Arab countries all around the world. Terms or concepts such as *al wihda al arabiyya,* which are emblematic of Nasserist, pan-Arab revolutionary discourse, appear in the song in their Arabic form, rather than in Kanzi.

The Nile thus carries more than just water from its source in the south; in that period, it was sung in order to carry ideas from the north (the dam) as well. A philosophy of the Nasserist revolution produces a language that constitutes a Gramscian "common sense" and thus becomes the basis of a hegemonic idea—the justification of the dam becomes plausible to everyone.[5] Terms such as *al ishtirakiyya* (socialism) and *al nasr* (victory) were brought by the Nile into their understanding of the world the dam created, and contributed to the belief that the move would bring them closer to an urban modernity that promised integration and prosperity.

These songs carry that which is no longer visible: how people actually moved from living in their village communities by the Nile to the arid conditions of their unroofed houses in the Kom Ombo desert. Households received brochures and publications containing alluring pictures of stoves and taps with running water. Comic books as early as 1960 featured strips of Nubian children happily growing in prosperous, bountiful villages on the other side of the "migration." Gamal Abdel Nasser addressed the Nubians himself in a visit to the old villages at the start of works on the dam in January 1960. In this memorable speech (he was the last Egyptian president to visit Nubia and address the Nubians), he promised them that with the dam, with their migration, they would no longer be marginalized peasants—they would become workers, themselves builders of the new nation. They would have better access to education and become part of the revolution. The displacement held promise. But no one mentioned that they would be settled away from the Nile, without flowing water, to houses without roofs and in impoverished living conditions.

Emotions toward the move were mixed. The majority were devastated to leave, but felt it necessary; a minority of youth believed it may better their lives as a community. The arrival to Kom Ombo was a devastating shock to all. Where there was once water, there would now be endless stretches of desertic landscapes and exposure to the sun, and where there should have been integration, there was in fact more isolation.

EARTH: LYRICAL MAPS AND MIGRATORY BIOGRAPHIES

Around forty villages were moved to Kom Ombo during the construction of the dam. However, they were not resettled in the same geographic order; rather, they were arranged haphazardly, with many Upper Egyptian villages and tribes that preexisted in Kom Ombo interspersed in the new settlements. The "new" villages ended up preserving their original names, all the while being suffixed with the word *tahjir*: Eneiba became Eneiba-Tahjir, and Adendan became Adendan-Tahjir. *Tahjir* is the Arabic word for displacing or migrating—implying a perpetrator who migrates the migrated—in present continuous form. A reminder, with every mention of the village's name, that this was not the original one, but a resettled version of it, and that its inhabitants maintained a constitutional right to return to the original village.

In a visit to Eneiba-Tahjir in 2018, I asked about the use of the term *tahjir* when speaking to Waguih Hassan, an intellectual and activist who had himself been resettled in his late teens. I wondered if the term *tahjir* was used in this grammatical present-continuous tense because the experience of displacement was one whose repercussions were continually and continuously felt, until the present. He said it was possible, but that a more plausible explanation for this would be that there was no word for *tahjir* in Nubian languages. The experience was simply coined in the form it was communicated to them. *Tahjir bilaad al Nuba* (the resettlement of Nubian lands) resulted in people being moved from Eneiba to Eneiba-Tahjir, another land and perhaps even a temporary one. The process maintained an identity and meaning for the original Eneiba—a land to be returned to.

Some *tahjir* songs included the list of the names of the villages in their original geographical order along the Nile's banks, creating a sort of lyrical map that one can learn by heart. Among these songs is "Sandala," which describes the journey of a boat carrying various village communities migrating to the new lands. The song starts by calling out the names of each village, followed by *Guballah ayuhh* (head there, yes!) indicating where the *Sandal* (a Nile sailing boat) is heading. The first time I heard it, I registered the description of villages that I was sure were not resettled to Kom Ombo, north of the dam, but rather to Sudan in the south. This was when I was told that the song was also intoned throughout previous experiences of displacement, during the heightening of the Aswan reservoir in 1913 and 1933 before the Egyptian-Sudanese borders were clearly demarcated. At first, imagining the songs as archives, I asked for those "that only spoke of the 1964 displacement," but I was then told there was no way to ascertain that any displacement song was written only for 1964. *Tahjir* songs were songs of *tahjir,* and they carried within them the experience itself, regardless of the historical circumstances they were referring to.

As the song proceeds, it describes the passengers waving goodbye to reciprocating palm trees, empty of the birds that have already migrated, and bidding farewell to the cats and dogs they were not allowed to take with them, and which instead took shelter in the homes that had been left behind. It sings, "the tears flow like the river," but the call for the destinations breaks the tone of loss once again, only to resume.

Singing the songs thus evokes a map, so that any child can recall the order of the villages before the displacement. But this was also a biographical map, showing not only where Nubian communities came from, but also the experiences through which these communities were forged. The songs are layered, and in singing or listening to *tahjir* upon *tahjir* upon *tahjir,* we realize that what was significant about this history was not when it happened, but that it continues to happen.

During my trip to Gharb Suhail, I was introduced to Zizi, a girl who was my contemporary and always interested to listen to the songs I recorded and reflect on them with me. Eventually, Zizi and I became friends, and I was taken in by her family in the small village where I lived for most of my time researching in 2010.[6] This village was never displaced, and the entirety of its residents were from one family, Zizi's mother's. Her father, on the other hand, came from Abu Simbel, which was completely drowned in 1964. He promised to take me to his family in the displaced villages of Abu Simbel and Ballana-Tahjir, but before that, there was one important trip to be made. He took us on a boat trip in the reservoir behind the dam, Buhairat Nasser (Lake Nasser), or Buhairat al-Nuba (Lake Nubia), as the Nubians called it. There he instructed that I draw a map, as he indicated every spot where a village once was and now lay submerged below us. In some places there was no trace, in others there would be traces of land: what he indicated was once the top of a mountain, for instance. Before visiting the *tahjir* villages of Kom Ombo, he believed I should first understand where they once were.

Later, when Zizi and I made the trips to Abu Simbel-Tahjir and asked about songs about displacement, we were told that I was in fact looking for songs like "Wo hanina." We started with a visit to the house of the eldest of Zizi's aunts, who invited many others to come so they could share their stories. As one *khalla* (aunt) introduced me to the other, they would say, "She's a researcher, looking for songs like 'Wo hanina.'" But no one would sing the song itself. It became like a code, a genre for the particular kind of songs I was looking for, songs that either described the displacement experience or lamented the migration upon arrival.

Eventually, I managed to find the song, sung by Sayyid Jayyir, a singer born in 1930s Abu Simbel. Sung in Fadjiki, the language of most displaced Nubians, it speaks of a man who returned to visit his submerged village to find only its highest mountain peaks visible over the water. As he stood on it, a bird came to him and beratingly asked, "What do you return for now, stranger?" I was told that the song was highly emotive, and that Gamal Abdel Nasser's security apparatus did not allow people to sing it in gatherings for fear of what mobilization may result from an overflowing of emotions.

Guilt was the deepest emotion I encountered, beyond loss, when talking about the displacement. It seemed to finally reconcile the memory of some people's belief in the possibilities of the move, and the realization that they had been conned, and that they should have perhaps resisted leaving. Anger about the displacement and how it was carried out was more prevalent among the younger generations, those who were born into the lands of *tahjir* and had to build a life and identity despite the displacement. Being born into a marginalized minority, and being of a Nile-born Nubian culture without having access to the Nile, is doubly disadvantaging.

In the late 1990s, singer Khidr al-Attar (born in 1962 in the village of Ibrim) started performing a daring song, which he called "Ismi hinaak," or, "My Name Is There." This song was not only confrontational but was also sung in Arabic, which allowed al-Attar to target a whole new audience: younger Nubians who were united by their understanding of Arabic, and possibly also the broader Egyptian public.

> My name is where
> My axe is; there.
> My name is there, and my homeland is there . . .
>
> A history of Nuba, they tried to erase,
> On the day we parted with our dear place.
> But our history is inscribed deep in stone
> By a people who shook the earth with strength of will alone.
> My name is where my axe is; there.
>
> Come, oh Nubī and Nubiyya,
> Beat the drums of our return.
> Beat the drums of the next migration,
> For when have we ever bowed to humiliation?
> My name is where my axe is; there.
>
> There are martyrs, oh people, behind the dam,
> They imposed upon us a migration so bitter,
> When they told us Kom Ombo was a paradise to be gained;
> While we walked in it, for years estranged.
> There are martyrs, oh people, behind the dam . . .
>
> . . . And marks of shame on the foreheads of that generation.[7]

It seems it was then strategic for this song to be performed in Arabic—for the younger generations to object, to be openly bitter, to demand that Nubians return to their original lands. The song thus becomes a confrontational cry against an unjust displacement by a generation subject to the *dhul,* or humiliation of a shameful past, and an unpromising future.

This song is very different to the others: in language, in tone, in confrontation. In another stanza, Khidr al-Attar sings of "a mark of shame stamped on the foreheads of our forefathers," referring to the generations who "left" their villages. Instrumentally, it does not have the flow of Ahmed Sidqi's songs, nor the consistent jubilant or melancholic beat of the *daf* that are found in folk songs such as "Wo hanina" and "Sandaliyya." Instead, it included a varied range of instruments and mixers typical of more contemporary forms of music making, but also one that reflected the exposure—to the rest of Egypt in language, and to Sudan in musical style and technology—toward a coming out into the world. This was a song that mobilized.

After the 2011 revolution, the drums for return did indeed beat higher. Mobilizations that had started in the late 1990s, and the change in rhetoric of the early 2000s when the call for a "right to return" emerged, culminated in organized pressure until return was deemed a constitutional right in 2013. Article 236 of the Egyptian Constitution of 2014 states Nubians' right to return and the state's responsibility to develop the original villages and establish an authority to ensure the process is carried out successfully. However, in the same year, Egypt's military state declared lands near the Sudanese border, including Nubian villages, military property, and in 2016 a decree allowed the sale of those lands including the village of Toshka. The right to return was constitutionally guaranteed, but the lands had become off-limits.

In response, "caravans of return" were organized by Nubian activists. They attempted to challenge the decree by organizing a march to the former Nubian villages of Toshka and Farkhund, only to be stopped and besieged for a week by Egyptian authorities. In September 2017, a renewed call for action, *al eid fel Nuba ahla,* was developed by artists and intellectuals inviting people to join them in a peaceful musical march in Aswan to sing for the right to return. This time, the response was ruthless. Organizers of the march were arrested and came to be known as *mu'taqali al dufuf,* "the duffuf (plural of *daf*) detainees." The threat of songs of return being performed to the rhythm of the daf in the streets of Aswan, and rippling across them, wasn't something the authorities would risk or tolerate.

WIND: STRUGGLES, INTIMATE AND PROFOUND

This was not the first time that Nubian communities had risen up to call for their rights. Nafissa Zarrar's family, whom I had met in Abu Simbel-Tahjir, gave me scans of her late brother's personal documents, insisting they would help with my research. In his youth he had worked on the Aswan reservoir before he moved to Alexandria in the 1920s, only to become one of the mobilizing forces behind a movement demanding compensation on behalf of the Nubian community for the inundation of their lands after the reservoir had been heightened in 1933.

The documents included minutes of meetings he had attended or convened, to brainstorm ways that the state could be confronted. In 1933, there were meetings for petitions demanding compensation for inundated lands. Little is known of these petitions, outside of a few academic sources. Little is known of the 1933 movements, or of the attempts to mobilize in 1967 and 1968 a call for Nubian communities' right to return. The latter were dismissed with *la sawt ya'lu fawqa sawt al ma'rakah,* or, "All voices are subordinate to the voices of the battle," indicating the Six-Day War of 1967. (In the late 1960s, the term *tahjir* eventually came to refer to the situation of migrants from the Suez Canal, as 750,000 residents from Suez were resettled throughout Egypt. One *tahjir* eclipsed the other.)

Although an archive of the 1933 petitions is not publicly accessible in Egypt, in Nubian villages it can be located through stories of descendants, and in Nafissa's case, her brother's paper trail. This history may seem dispersed in the absence of a central archive, but it is a history that is central to Nubian communities, and it is dispersed equally in everyone's consciousness. Of all the recordings I made during my different visits and stays in Nubia, my favorite remain the interviews with Nafissa. She had a sense of humor and a quick wit, despite her being almost ninety when we met. As was typical in interviews I had with the elderly, many members of her family were there. The recording is laced with many layers of laughter, and a March wind that was inconsistent in strength but persistently there, like a transparent curtain repetitively billowing over our conversation. The emotional proximity, the intimacy of the shared history somehow prevails over the events the songs refer to.

In one particular interview, Nafissa sings a lullaby that reassures her young son that now, in the lands of *tahjir,* there was nothing to fear, for the spirits of the Nile are no longer a threat to him, and swimming at night is thus no longer dangerous. These Nile spirits were a common Nubian myth and dictated the relationship with the Nile. Nafissa explained that, though they depended on the Nile spirits and their blessings for luck and support, in marriage, birth, and even death, some of them were vengeful and to be feared. Walking by the Nile at night was considered dangerous, for example, as unappeased Nile spirits could kidnap or drown a person. Here in Abu Simbel-Tahjir, on the other hand, there were no Nile spirits, only *jinn. Jinn* were spirits who lived on land and, Nafissa explained, "Despite being Muslim like us, they are no help at all, and cannot be trusted." The double-edged relationship of fear and dependency that had existed with Nile spirits could not be built with the land spirits.

This provoked one of many moments of snickering by the younger girls among us. Although much of Nafissa's experiences and relations with her old village are dictated by the supernatural and metaphysical, they are powerful markers of her sense of place. These histories are less visible than a dam, but they are no less substantial. Relations with Nile spirits fill Nubian folk stories, but they also dictate how people lived in villages that they believed they shared with other beings. These spirits defined the inhabitants' relationship with their lands, their daily rituals, and unspoken laws, such as where to walk and when. They were part of a larger community.

Listening to the recordings, Nafissa's wrinkled voice, breaking as she attempts to stretch it melodiously, immediately reminds me of her beautiful face, the smell of musk, and the sound of the wind in their courtyard. In some "supernatural way," Nafissa's memories have become my own. It is hard to imagine how she lightens the intensity of experiences of displacement, linking them to her struggle to cohabitate with different spirits. It is her light, witty spirit and the laughter and wind that fills this interview that has come to define my research experience, the experience of the migration that has, by some inexplicable inheritance, become part of my own repertoire: my understanding of struggle, life, music, and history, my appreciation of the value of wind, laughter, warmth, and wonderful company as fuel for struggle and continuity.

To relay the experience of the displacement of Nubian communities without iterating my encounters would only be passing on half the knowledge I have acquired. Ahmed Shawkat's struggle against the heightening of the reservoir of 1933 cannot be told without Nafissa's spiritual and metaphysical losses due to the migration, nor can it be told without my relationship to Zizi, with whom I spent the months of my ethnographic research. The experience of the dam as I relay it is thus a story within a story within a story. These stories are intergenerational, told by and through intergenerational relationships, rippling vertically through time. The experiences are also interrelational, a history that ripples through relationships across and beyond familial ties, just as they ended up with me, and through me, into this written medium. The story is not separate from its teller, nor from the context of its telling, itself a way of knowing and telling.

NOW, LET YOUR DRUM PLAY YOU . . .

In looking at how people document their experiences of larger historical events, we witness a history that is oppositional but not contrary, and one that is not just parallel to but interlaces through hegemonic, overarching narratives. Nubian songs, like the Nile, capture and embody "flow" by singing of geographies that transcend national boundaries, of an experience beyond marked epochs of time, of a force of nature that no longer flows in resettled villages. These songs should be thought of as a link between the past and the present, a vessel through which experiences continue to radiate and echo, and as a source of history told in several languages, as a storytelling technique and a haunting. They tell us more than just "important" historical events and movements. Rather, they carry the kernels of ideologies, the sound of a disappeared river, and the many emotions associated with migration. They drive and mobilize toward more just futures. The structure of sound that a song represents allows for a structure of many feelings and a multivalent history that can never be told in one, straightforward narrative. But that history cannot be accessed by "reading into" the song—it must be felt. In other words, you must let the music play *you*.

Alia Mossallam is a writer and cultural historian. As a EUME fellow of the Alexander von Humboldt Foundation in Berlin, she is writing a book on the visual and musical practices of the builders of the Aswan High Dam and the Nubian communities displaced by it. She founded the site-specific public history project "Ihky ya Tarikh," and has taught at the American University in Cairo, Cairo Institute of Liberal Arts and Sciences, and the Freie Universität in Berlin.

1. The *daf,* the frame drum central to Nubian music, is also known as *duff* or *tar*.
2. This and the other songs referenced in this essay may be listened at https://linktr.ee/rfgen
3. In a speech addressing Nubians in January 1960, Gamal Abdel Nasser promises a life of "happiness, freedom and prosperity" after the dam. The speech can be accessed at http://www.nasser.bibalex.org (accessed March 5, 2021).
4. Nubian communities are either speakers of Kanzi, also known as Mattokki (spoken in villages closer to Aswan), or of Fadjiki (spoken in villages closer to Sudan, in the south, most of which have been resettled by the building of the dam); only a minority are Arabic speakers.
5. Nasser's philosophy relates to what Antonio Gramsci termed "spontaneous philosophy," not merely a system of beliefs that reflects a specific class or government interest, rather a philosophy that is "proper to everybody." This philosophy is contained in: (1) language itself, which is a totality of determined notions and concepts and not just of words grammatically devoid of content; (2) "common sense" and "good sense," and (3) popular religion, and therefore also in the entire system of beliefs, superstitions, opinions, ways of seeing things and of acting that are collectively bundled together under the title "folklore." Nasser's ideology and rhetoric drew on elements of spontaneous philosophy and was itself eventually internalized as "common sense." See Antonio Gramsci, *Selections from the Prison Notebooks* (New York, 1971), p. 323.
6. The name of the village has been intentionally omitted for the purposes of confidentiality.
7. *Nubī* and *Nubiyya* are the masculine and feminine form of the word "Nubian," respectively.

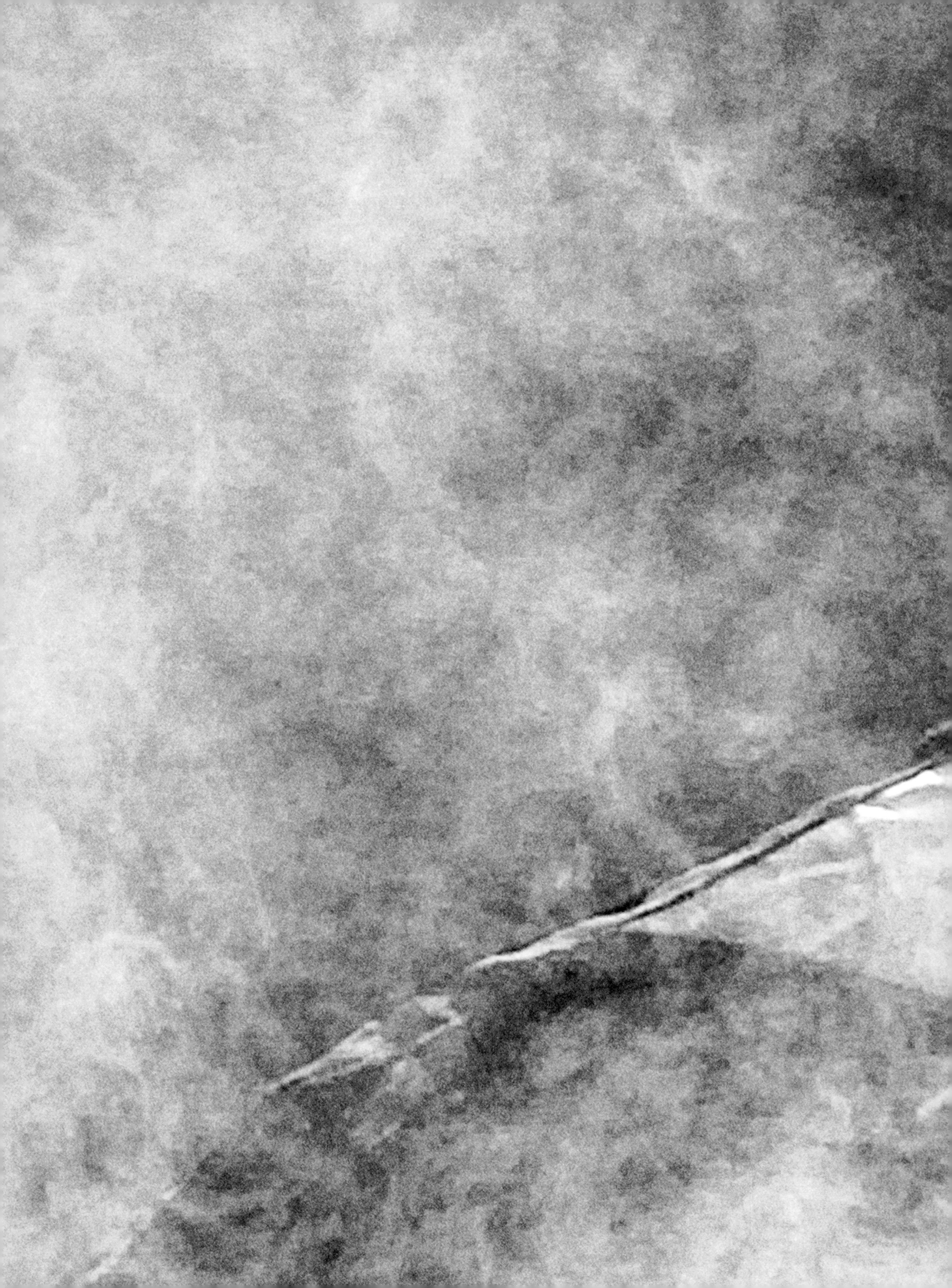

Acoustic Necrophagy

Moad Musbahi

During the French occupation of Algeria at the end of the nineteenth century, a cry echoed from al-Hamel, a village 200 kilometers south of Algiers, to the colonial regime's office in the capital. The background of this piercing tone centered on an inheritance dispute. It concerned two descendants of a Sufi sheikh, the spiritual leader Sidi Mohammed bin Abi al-Qasim—his daughter, Lalla Zaynab, and her first cousin, Mohamed bin al-Hajj Muhammed.[1] The property in question was a title, that of leader of the *zawiya* of al-Hamel, a religious seat that provided executive and spiritual privilege across three administrative divisions or *départements*. This was a vast territory with a sizable population and was thus of paramount importance to the colonial regime's interests. The indigenous community was split, with many finding Mohamed too worldly and his traits too impious for successful leadership. In the contestation that ensued, Lalla Zaynab wielded both her local religious credentials and a far-reaching savviness in French bureaucracy; she penned a series of tactical letters articulating her cousin's disrepute, evoking the chaos that might unfold were he to get the title.[2] The regional French administrator, Major Crochard, favored the male cousin, finding fault with the daughter's gender. He wrote in 1897 that her femininity would make her amenable to anti-French sentiment and incapable of effective administration.[3] This preference was characteristic of the colonial regime, which had long been having trouble when attempting to control Sufi centers under female leadership.[4] The dispute was brought before the head of the French judiciary, the *procureur-general*, after Lalla Zaynab had hired a French lawyer, Maurice L'Admiral, to petition those at the helm of the hierarchy about the misconduct of the local *Affaires indigènes* office (and Crochard by extension).[5] An act of such boldness spoke of the awareness she accumulated while traveling with her father and in the conversations with the many political refugees and pilgrims that had passed through the *zawiya* over the years (the seemingly provincial site of al-Hamel was in fact a crucial node for the exchange of information). News from distant locales was a precious resource, which Lalla Zaynab successfully used to subvert the challenges to her position within the spiritual hierarchy.

But the event that decided the matter, after which the community firmly rallied around her, does not belong to the colonial order. In popular memories that persist to this day, a story is recounted of a sonic event that swept over and swelled the ranks of Lalla Zaynab's following. In a moment of distress, distraught with all that was happening, she went to lay and take refuge at her late father's resting place. Slumped at his tomb in a state of supplication, her eyes began to tear. Her heightened emotional state produced a stress on the larynx, turning a whimpering phonation into a continuous pitch—a cry. The act called forth her dead father, who—it is recounted—spoke to the crowd and declared her as the rightful heir. The declaration cemented the succession. Lalla Zaynab mobilized her status as a pious figure bent down in humility, a daughter endowed with genetic privilege, and a voice capable of divine revelation. And it is in this latter quality, in the status of a body and its potential for musicality, that this story is pertinent.

Succession was determined through the voice of the dead, a voice made possible by Lalla Zaynab's phonotraumatic act of crying.[6] The event highlights how the corporeal can be a sonic medium. The body's ability to host a composition is limited by physical constraints; when the limit is surpassed through a sacrificial offering, as in Lalla Zaynab's cry, time collapses.[7] The ritual of crying exposes the way that both space *and* sound can host, and be hosted, in their interpolative enactments and structural formations. During her subsequent time as the head of the *zawiya,* she was known for having a hoarse voice—what modern medicine would define as dysphonia, a syndrome characterized by an abnormal audition, sounding unlike oneself. She ultimately died due to internal bleeding of the throat only a few years later. The final sacrifice: her passing away, a consequence of the divine offering made through the loss of her voice.

THE NECK

Social relatedness in Arabic (*qara'ba*) is etymologically tied to the neck (*raqaba*)—as the distance between the head and the chest and as the quality of the social relation between people. In its anatomical function, it connects the vocal and visual capacities, the eyes and the mouth, with what sustains them, the heart and the lungs. The neck is orthopedically distinct from the rest of the spinal column as it is capable of extra articulations, made possible by the shape of the seven vertebrae that compose it. In the dark history of slavery on the Arabian Peninsula, the freedom "of one's neck" was the abolitionist sign of one's newly allotted rights as a freed person.[8] One bends one's head down as a sign of respect to those older than oneself, or whose authority reigns over one. The acute angle of the neck's incline indicates the relative standing between people, while its elevation enables one to survey the surroundings (in Arabic, the neck is also related to the word used to denote the one who keeps guard, *raqab*). The neck can be understood as a vital link, elevated platform, and, by the same token, gatekeeper.

Within modern anatomy, the neck is subdivided into regions called "triangles," which group the complex assembly of nerves, blood vessels, muscles, and lymph nodes into arbitrary clusters for isolated examination and surgery.[9] Conceptually, such triangular associations find a parallel in the anthropological unit of the heteronormative family—the three points between mother, father, and eldest child. From this base unit, descent is aggregated and inheritance distributed. Knowledge of one's ancestors is called the science of *usul,* which is the plural form of the word *asl*. Without an *asl*, a thing or person is awaiting rootedness—or rather, they are understood as awaiting a future in which they can be placed and read against other things. The condition of having *asl* is the ability to locate things or people in a universal relation.

Knowledge of one's descent is not enough to provide a history—it needs to be animated by the historical consciousness of the people concerned. Being morally compelled to remember, one has to continually visit graves and narrate stories so as to be able to create a *ta'rikh*, or record of histories, and thus to accumulate the *usul*. These histories, *taw'rikh*, comprise lists of names and locations compiled into ancestral anthologies and genealogical dictionaries. As *taw'rikh* are predicated on travel and connection with others, knowledge of one's *usul* is ultimately determined by their relative mobility to access histories, or to host those that can impart them. In this way, *usul* is not only a record of the past—it is almost not a record at all—but a protocol from which future action can be considered. As book-objects and their accompanying rituals of oral narration, *taw'rikh* have given rise to an architecture for safekeeping and to stage their performative requirement. Recalling the destination from an intergenerational memory, people would journey to these buildings across long distances. At times, one's *usul* would reach back hundreds of years, yet ancestors were made present and proximate in the moment of their evocation.

Despite the importance of many such books, ancestral relations were also articulated from memory. One maintains the genealogical remembrance of their *ta'rikh* through an unconditional form of hospitality. Drawing people, goods, and spiritual blessing, the architecture associated with them was enmeshed in an order that was transnational and intergenerational in the utmost sense—a historic destination and a prospective resource.

THE HAND

The perils encountered across the Sahara required a swift method of travel to avoid fraught encounters and called for an extended fellowship to accompany the voyage. The norms of conduct and any guarantees were formalized, for the safety of travelers, in the *zawiya*. Built with the logic of a fortress, it was an architecture that afforded protection for its itinerant benefactors. The *zawiya* of al-Mahmura in Janzour, a town west of Tripoli, has many features that are common across this building typology. It has been in existence since 1228 (1823 CE). The thickness of its perimeter wall was designed to withstand raids from all cardinal points and also provided natural insulation from the extreme temperatures of the desert environment. The outward-facing elements were unadorned, and the only sign of their upkeep was in the glossy veneer of adobe or, at times, whitewash that reached half the height

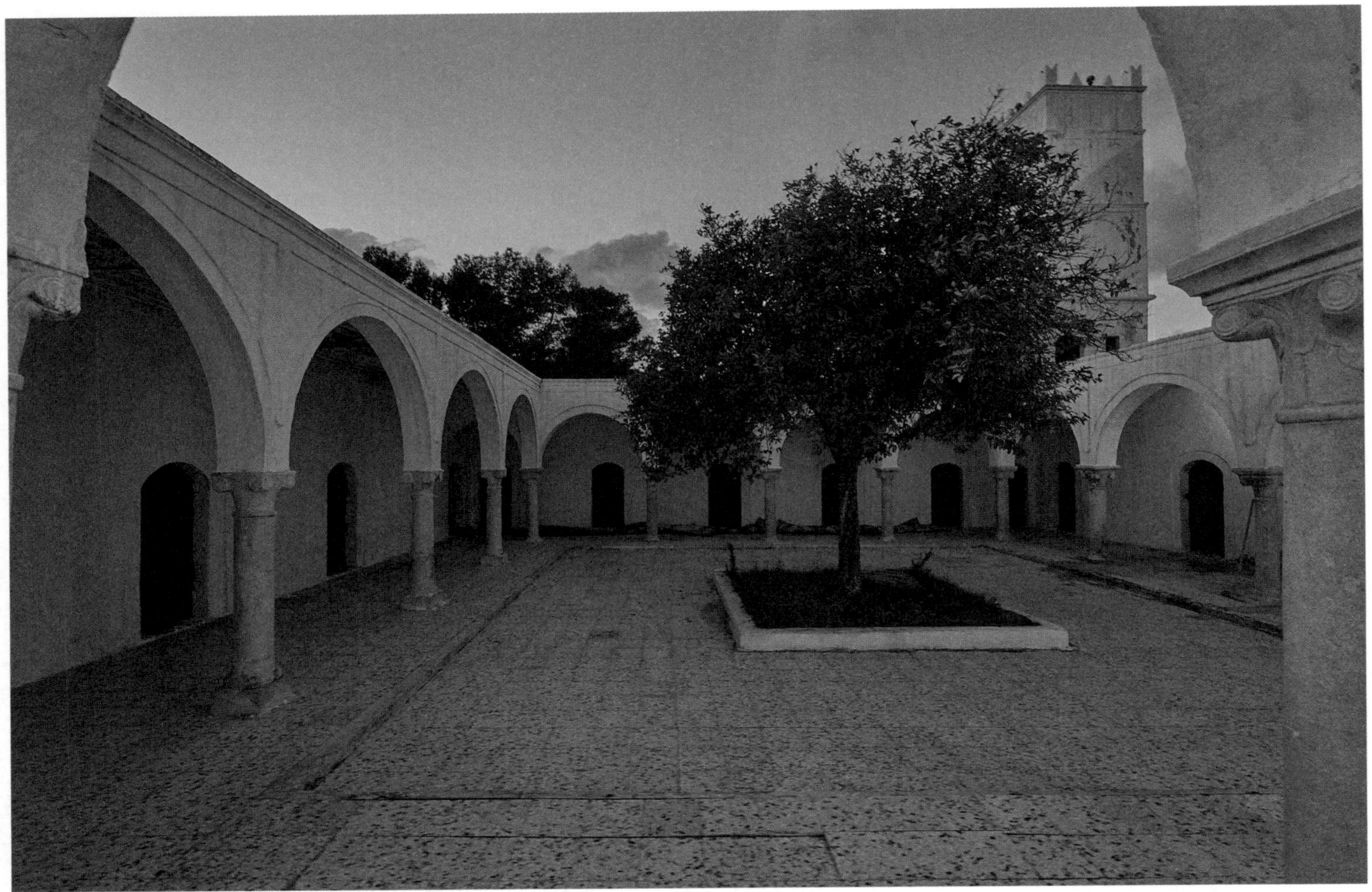

The main courtyard of the *zawiya* of Mahmura, Janzour, Libya, 2018. Photo by the author.

of the wall. The continual process of maintenance signaled the labor provided by the inhabitants of the *zawiya,* whose presence was thus visible to foreign arrivals. In contrast with the perimeter wall, the main entrance was usually decorated with calligraphy, a break in the façade that extended far above the height of the wall. The actual opening was a low, solid door that led to a small passage, leading the guest down a long corridor into the central courtyard.[10] The *zawiya* indicates the vital presence of water. In gaining access, a guest is able to quickly quench their thirst—but the layout of the corridor and courtyard would limit the water quantity one could use. For the mercantile class that was in good standing with the custodians, there was usually a second courtyard, arranged so as to allow a caravan, its extended entourage, and animal convoy to replenish and hydrate sufficiently. This adjacent structure, squatter and set lower into the ground, also contained dry storage rooms arranged around the courtyard. Each room was subdivided into compartments, some with small windows for ventilation and others perfectly closed for the preservation of perishable goods. The volume of the compartments was measured through the Islamic unit of the *sa'*, the amount contained in four handfuls of grain. A single *sa'* was the charitable payment required during the two holidays of Eid. The breadth of one's palms thus determined the capacity of the depot—a form of bodily accountancy that left its imprint upon the architecture. The act of payment, the counting of produce, finds a coun-

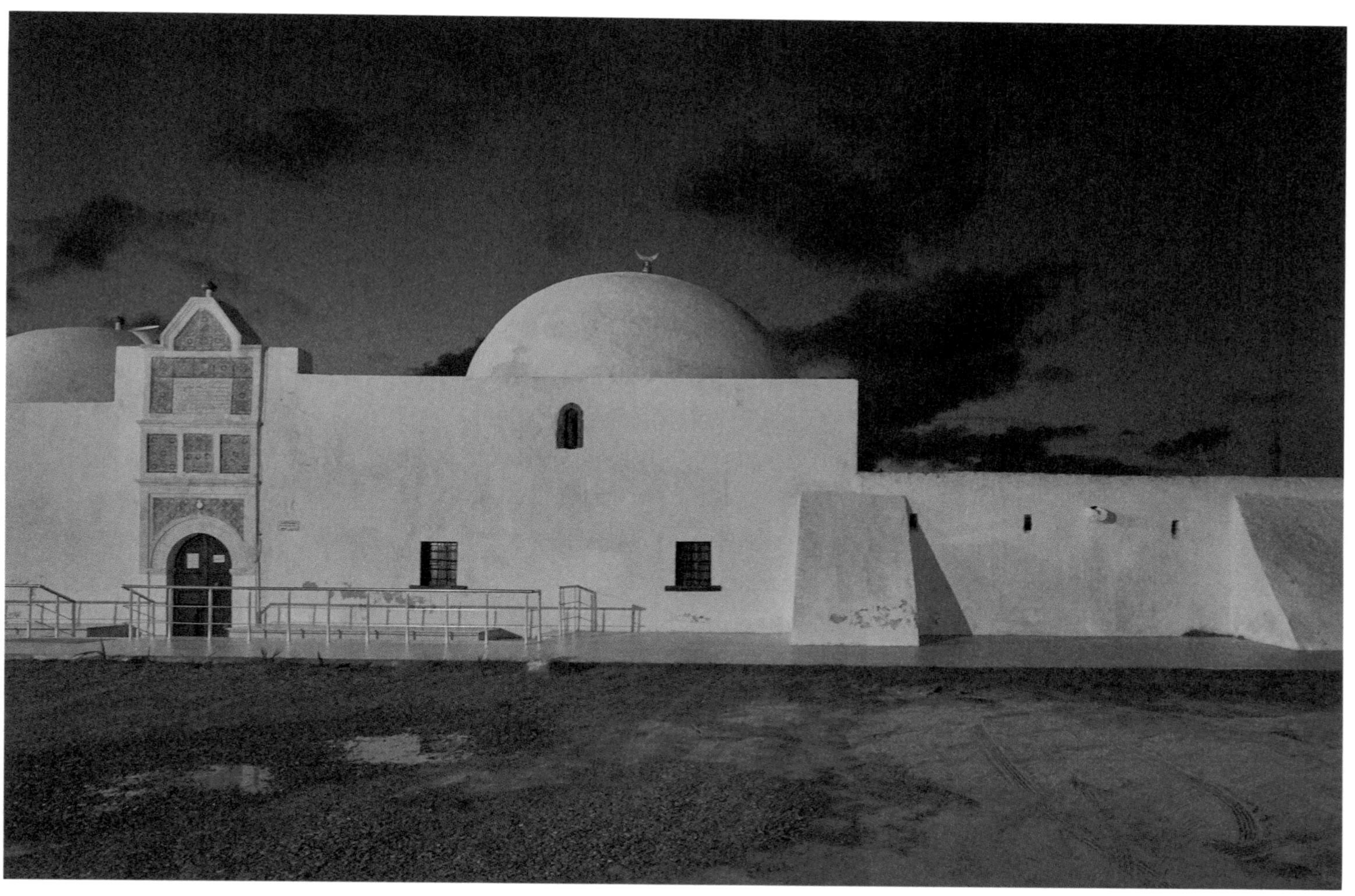

The main entrance of the *zawiya* of Mahmura, Janzour, Libya, 2018. Photo by the author.

terpoint in the act of praying: the hands as supply and supplication. As a point in a network of coordination, trade, and mediation among various peoples, the corporeality of the *zawiya* continually animates the respective pasts of those who arrived before.

To meet the demands of hospitality, the *zawiya* had rooms for visitors and travelers and a larger hall for collective prayer. The central courtyard revolved around a single tree, typically an almond or orange—a visual marker of the seasonal cycles and a provision of shade for activities to be undertaken in the view of all. Designed to be maintained by both its immediate inhabitants as well as the migrants who passed through, the *zawiya* was governed as a household. The surrounding land was placed under the care of the spiritual leader of the *zawiya,* in agreement with the families of the area, but divisions of inheritance and patronage based on kinship and lineage were continually subject to strong contestation. The leader would carefully mediate over endowments and local disputes between aggravated parties.[11] Would-be jurists traveled to *zawiyat* to gain admittance to the class of a respected teacher (one gains the authority to write Islamic religious rulings, or *fatwat,* through a license issued by an already established jurist). As a space of contact between a state or transnational apparatus and the local population, the *zawiya* fixes law to space. Far from being remote, the encounter with this architecture becomes a single moment in a vast, manifold, and heterochronic network of times and places across overlapping sovereignties and jurisdictions.

The discovery of a well or spring were acts of divine provenance; it is in the witnessing of, and association with, such events that one is deemed worthy of a pious following, and such stories are relayed with meticulous detail. It is in this tradition that a *zawiya* is founded by a learned figure who taps into the ground's hydrological possibility and then educates their newly attracted following. The territorial distribution of *zawiyat* is a measure, a *namus* of the land, as they are found near sites of environmental affordance.[12] The founder is buried, after death, at the site of consecration, which thus becomes a place defined through interment and remembered for its teaching methods. The burial of the holy remains transforms an unmapped, "cornerless" space into a pedagogical destination—an area bound by a set of corners, giving scale to what constitutes the sacred; a line with enough kinks to delimit the inside from the outside. The religious significance of the *zawiya* is taken a step further, as the founder's remains also gain the power of *baraka*—a word that when literally translated as "blessing" loses the materiality it has in Arabic. It is only in the physical proximity with the material remains that one is able to gain access to this blessing. Even when remains are not always directly seen or touched, the faith in their material presence is what sustains the ties between a community of believers. The term *zawiya* is literally translated as "corner," and in this sense it is first and foremost the architecture that surrounds and furnishes the tomb. This edifice augments the practice of prayer as it is also a space of teaching, where the learning inherited from and directed by the dead animates their resting place. This pedagogical dimension raises the remains above the threshold of perceptible audibility; it operates as an extended echoic chamber, allowing them to be heard.

The primacy of oral instructions within the Arabic tradition stems from the Quran, the spoken document turned evidentiary paradigm of Islam. As the cornerstone that Islamic knowledge emerged from, the power of the Quran lies in its seeming immutability and inalterability, which is the source of its authority. Its genesis into written form took place only years after the Prophet's death in 632 CE, and most crucially not as a text to be simply read silently but as a book of diction. As a manual to instruct on the precise use of breath and the place of the tongue, it was a pedagogy of annunciation. The speech the archangel Gabriel recited to the Prophet was passed from mortal mouth to mortal mouth, until the caliph ʻUmar, the first religious ruler after the death of the Prophet, deigned it to be made into a book.

The reception of the Quran as an instrument of imperial synchronicity can be evidenced in the tombstone record. Across the inscriptions upon the stones of the dead, one can track the vocal inflections of the verse, the variance, and variability between statements and their similitude from the sixth century until the end of the eighth.[13] Inscriptions are used to assess the spread of Islam in the early years of its dissemination as they indicate the extent to which the faithful were buried and thus how far they had traveled from ground zero of revelation. They contain verses, biographical data of the deceased, and lines of prayer that are typically written in the imperative, instructing the visitor to perform certain tasks.[14] These are not mere signs to prompt a passive reading but a ritual guidance that transforms the encounter into an interceding act, beseeching the divine in favor of the deceased. The tomb creates an utterance, a sonic space of instruction: "He is the one who created you from clay and specified your finite term upon it."[15] Death is ritually evoked by prostration, by bending the leg into an anatomical corner. The knee returns the body back to the earth. The proximity of the body of knowledge, as signified by the interred corpse, and the body of the traveling scholar is tied to the spoken vibrations resonating between them. The *zawiya* is a designation not only of a built form, but also an aggregation and expansion of these epitaphic instructions. A seemingly isolated and immovable architectural type, it speaks to a form of geographical and temporal interconnectedness. It is a concrete space where the process of learning and the display of its outcome are brought together.

THE KNEE

The knee is what gives the leg the potential for transportation: a fleshy fold that creates mobility, the bare mechanics of migration. The set of bones and hard cartilage, held afloat in an elastic sea of tendons, shift the body from an upright orientation into a posture of humility—providing the ability to bow down before the divine. The knee, *rakaba* in Arabic, is used for the calculation of prayer: a *rak'a* is the set of movements defining the five-daily ritual of *salat*. This duty was influenced by the length of the journey believers had partaken in: if someone was considered to be "on the road," they reduced the number of *rak'at* performed. Memorialized within the muscular fiber, the frequency of kneeling thus became an indication of one's past migratory activity.

Both pleading for forgiveness (prayer) and appealing for shelter (after a journey) are made possible through the bent leg; they are brought together in the act of supplication. This ritual practice highlights the material dimension of prayer and the place of its performance. It relates to the figure of the suppliant in Ancient Greek tragedy: crouching down, one puts oneself in a place of debasement and enters a chthonic state of near-death. Through this mimicry of the dead, the supplicatory performance exposes "the 'place' of supplication as that of the glosso-somatic terror of a threshold-experience between life and death or as the exception of a living-death, the uncanny dread one feels when experiencing the unknown as one's own."[16] A "glosso-somatic" event is, then, what defines a space of contact between this world and the afterlife. This liminal position, made possible by the knee, is given sacred significance in Islam as the elevated form of prayer that can only occur at the place of the dead. "Supplication" has two possible Arabic translations—*dua,* the asking for mercy and blessing, and *tawasil,* a word that designates the time and place of getting to know a previously unknown person. Sitting at the confluence of the two, the *zawiya* affords hospitality and establishes a triangular economy composed of guest (student), host (teacher), and space (school) of convergence.

The *zawiya* hosts a pedagogical practice of speaking and being spoken to. Its curriculum is divided into two categories: Quranic studies and *'ilm,* "scientific study," delivered in two spaces called, respectively, *Qur'aniyya* and *'alamiyya*. The distinction between them is made in sonic terms, through the rules governing the speech that is permissible within each space. The former follows the system of *qira'*, a type of vocal recital in which the speaker is not permitted to modify the words that they receive; it is a method of accurate reproduction. In the latter, the system is termed *riwaya,* and the transmitter has a license to alter the text. A well-known proverb by the scholar Ibn Muqbil says, "I sent out the verses crooked so that the transmitters can straighten them out for their delivery." In the encounter between these two forms of speech, the *zawiya* becomes an architecture of acoustic difference, where the polyphony of place and personhood determines what can be heard. Literally translated as "corner," the *zawiya* is a geometry of sonic amplification, where an acute angle reflects and focuses sound onto a receptive audience. It allows one to hear history and converse with the dead.

EPILOGUE

In many sects of Islam, the burial position is that of a person praying, lying down on the right side, propped up vertically so that their left shoulder is pointing away from the ground. Just as one prays facing Mecca, one is buried facing its direction. This positioning is meant to keep the corpse in the correct alignment as the stages of death set in—a perpetually sacred orientation as decomposition begins. After the body is placed in the soil it releases fluids high in ammonia that initially kill the surrounding vegetation—a destructive act by the buried remains. The spread of the fluids defines the limit of what is referred to in forensic anthropology as the "cadaveric decomposition island"—an initial demarcation of the dead person's (ecological) influence. Subsequently, bacteria, fungi, and insects begin their visitation. A common practice in Libya and Tunisia, with variants across the Islamic world, is the placement of rice, pumpkin seeds, and other small dry foods upon the topsoil of the deceased, as part of Islam's routinized obligation to visit ancestors. This expands the community of species that come and pay rites of respect.

This condition of the corpse as a site of possibility finds a ritual parallel in the concept of *baraka,* as the dead's blessing represents possibilities for the suppliant's earthly concerns. The cycle of bodily hospitality is a process of death producing life, a continual act of becoming. The species that derive their sustenance from the decaying corpse are called "necrobiome"—a collective of beings in an everlasting pilgrimage across a known and rewarding geography. They partake in a sacred maintenance of the most essential order of the world's necrophagic metabolism and renewal, an upkeep that weaves and implicates all dimensions of existence—the human, more than human, territorial, and environmental.

The concept of an acoustic necrophagy is a provocation to take seriously an interrelation of things beyond their normative categories or formal capacities, to not see the secular as distinct from the sacred, to locate the aural in the visual, to witness the past within the present. It is a way "to un-organise, un-form, un-think the world, towards the Plenum."[17] In the work of Leibniz, the plenum can be seen as a mode of thinking that construes and considers "[that] everybody is affected by everything that happens in the universe, to such an extent that he who sees all can read in each thing what happens everywhere, and even what has happened or what will happen, by observing in the present what is remote in time as well as in space."[18] The plenum is a theory that refutes the existence of an absolute vacuum; it imagines that the world is extensively and totally filled. The plenum inspires "a description of existence as marked by virtuality: matter imaged as contingency and possibility and rather than necessity and determinacy."[19] Breaking down space-time dualism, it is a way to view the world as an energy that is embedded within all things and determined by all other things across all time. The plenum finds a parallel in quantum physics' model of the phonon, a measure of elementary excitation present in all matter. The phonon is modeled as a quasi-particle and the smallest unit of sound; long-wavelength phonons give rise to the noises detectable by human ears.

The phonon locates sound as the common principle of exchange, the vital medium that makes possible the imagining of the universe as a whole. The scholar and poet Ibn Arabi wrote: "Like a lyre in which the movement of one string makes all others vibrate and thus evokes the secret harmonies of related concepts."[20] He far predated quantum physics and Leibniz, but one finds a striking resonance. Ibn Arabi proposed a Sufi Islamic theology that considered the universe as composed of the cosmic breath of an "unarticulated Being," a constant celestial droning. He determined that "divine 'breath' is pure being, so everything that exists is Divine speech, a cosmic array of words," and that human speech is but a lone and limited articulation of this breath.[21]

As described earlier, the Quran is a sonic event, the etched inscription turned speaking witness of the existence of the One. It is the defining oratory act from which things are derived and find their order, a foundational prism of phonatory conceptualization. It exists within a tradition where the self is but a word articulated by its creator, defining a world that is composed by subjects of speech, as speech, and connected through speech: "All of the world is endowed with rhythm, fastened by rhyme, on the Straight Path."[22]

This importance of the vocalic as a way of being in the world provides a clue to comprehend a space such as the *zawiya*. Sound reveals the building as being beyond simply property or form; it is, instead, something that connects what might at first seem distant from it. The sonic medium places the body in space and then marks the body as a site of social processes that exceed its limit, in the threshold between the planes of existence. A practice of acoustic necrophagy defines sounding as fathoming, as the continuous listening to the constellation that engulfs us all. A voicing out against the confines of historical silence. The *zawiya* becomes, in this understanding, a glosso-somatic corner of care that punctures time, or rather collapses temporality back onto itself—a triangular economy that provides protection, hospitality, and pedagogy, evidencing an architectural potential for a more equitable dialogue through the generations.

Moad Musbahi was part of the curatorial team of the Sharjah Architecture Triennial 2019. His research investigates migration as a method for cultural production and political expression. He curated *In Pursuit of Images* (Architectural Association, 2020) and has shown his work at Jameel Art Center and Beirut Art Center. He worked in Libya for the UNHCR and Red Crescent, and was recently in residency at Gasworks, London.

1. "Lalla" is the Arabic honorific equivalent to the title "Our Lady."

2. From an 1897 letter by Major Crochard, cited in Julia A. Clancy-Smith, *Rebel and Saint: Muslim Notables, Populist Protest, Colonial Encounters (Algeria and Tunisia, 1800–1904)* (Berkeley, 1994), p. 340, note 91.

3. Ibid., note 96.

4. Cited in Jamil M. Abun-Nasr, *The Tijaniyya: A Sufi Order in the Modern World* (Oxford, 1965), p. 88. The first French investigation of the matter in 1917 revealed that in the region of Tunis there were eighteen women in positions of spiritual authority. It is also important to note that gender did not figure in the local communities' decision for supporting Lalla Zaynab.

5. Cited in Allan Christelow, "Algerian Islam in a Time of Transition," *Maghreb Review* 8, nos. 5–6 (1983): 125.

6. Clark Rosen and Thomas Murry, "Phonotrauma Associated with Crying," *Journal of Voice* 14, no. 4 (2001): 575–80.

7. This finds a counterpart in the Ancient Greek *organon,* the word for both "[biological] body" and "[musical] instrument."

8. Quran 90:13.

9. For example, the Carotid Triangle, Anterior Triangle, Submental Triangle, and Muscular Triangle. Note that the latter of these regions actually has four sides, but the naming persists.

10. A field trip to Janzour was made possible by Nasir Zahaf and my numerous "cousins," whom I would like to thank for their guidance in gaining access.

11. The legal contestations over the property of the *zawiya* is elaborated in Judith Scheele, *Smugglers and Saints of the Sahara: Regional Connectivity in the Twentieth Century* (Cambridge, UK, 2012).

12. *Namus* is the classical Arabic equivalent of the ancient Greek *nomos.* It actually relates more to the notion of virtue than geography, but alludes to the latter. Discussed in Rana Issa, "The Arabic Language and Syro-Lebanese National Identity Searching in Buṭrus Al-bustānī's Muḥīṭ Al-Muḥīṭ," *Journal of Semitic Studies* 62, no. 2 (Autumn 2017): 465–84.

13. See Hasan al-Faqih, *Mawaqi' athariyya Tihama,* vol 1, *Mikhlaf 'Asham* (Riyadh, 1992), p. 353 and p. 388, and Arthur Jeffery, *Materials for the History of the Text of the Qur'an* (Leiden, 1937), p. 76 and p. 262. Variability in this sense is understood as deviation from what is utilized in the Uthmanic Codex due to localized changes, not on the larger debate around polygenesis of the Quran that has been convincingly refuted by recent scholarship.

14. 'Abd al-Tawab, *Steles islamiques,* vol 1, see the section on Aswan from ca. 820 to ca. 870 for numerous examples.

15. Quran 6:2.

16. Thanos Zartaloudis, "*Hieros anthropos* – An Inquiry into the Practices of Archaic Greek Supplication," *Law and Humanities* 13, no. 1 (2019): 63.

17. Denise Ferreira da Silva, "Toward a Black Feminist Poethics: The Quest(ion) of Blackness Toward the End of the World," *The Black Scholar* 44, no. 2 (2014): 86.

18. Gottfried Wilhelm Leibniz, *Leibniz: Philosophical Essays* (Indianapolis, 1989), p. 221. Da Silva draws on Leibniz to think the plenum as a way to locate the power of Blackness and its ongoing violation.

19. Ferreira da Silva 2014 (see note 18), p. 94.

20. Ibn Arabi quoted in Annemarie Schimmel, *As Through a Veil* (New York, 1982), p. 16.

21. Oludamini Ogunnaike, "The Presence of Poetry, the Poetry of Presence," *Journal of Sufi Studies* 5, no. 1 (2016): 58–97, 68.

22. Ibn Arabi quoted in Denis McAuley, *Ibn Arabi's Mystical Poetics* (Oxford, 2012), p. 45.

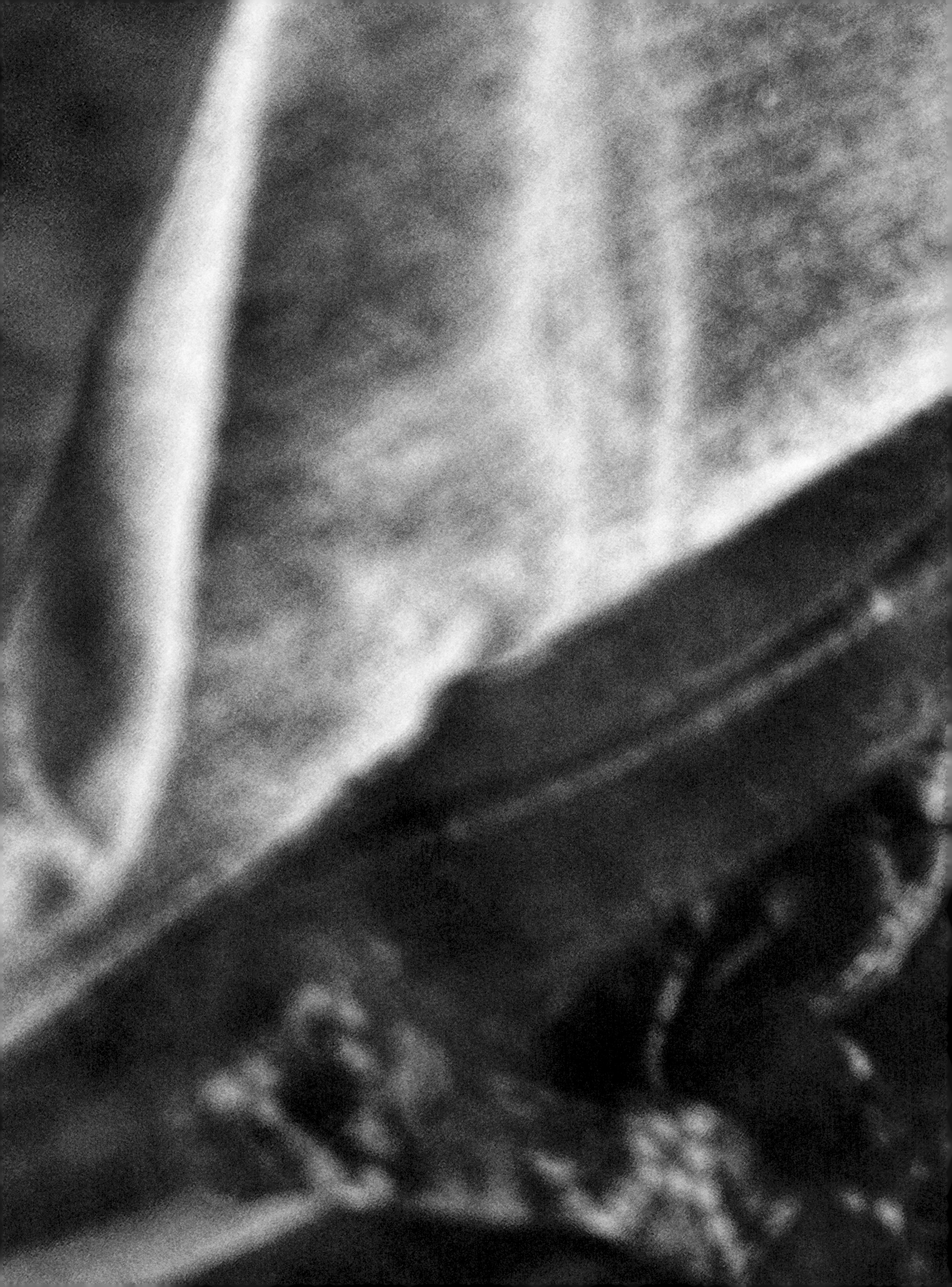

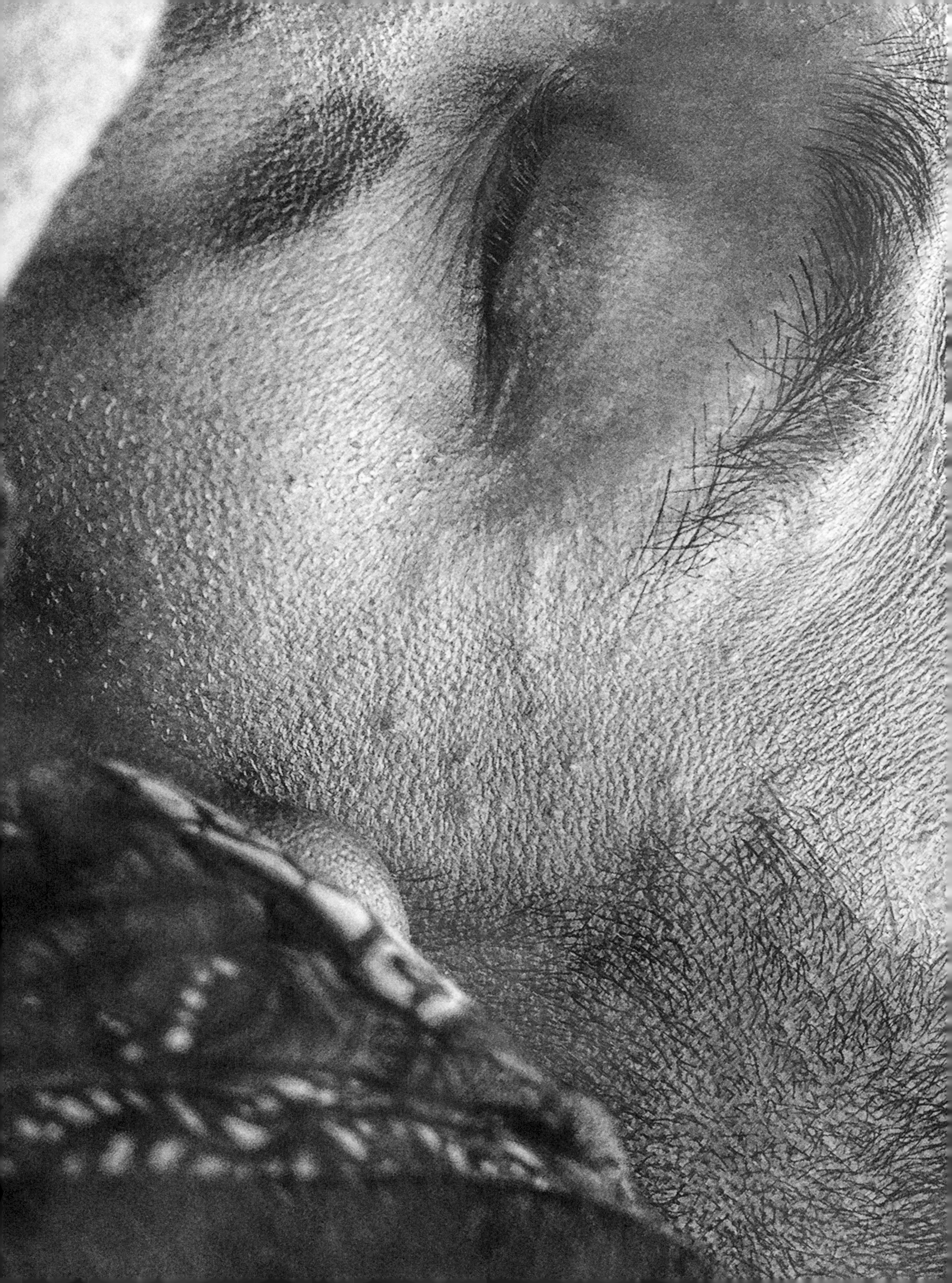

Ancestral Claims

Denise Ferreira
da Silva

Species Man did not shape the conditions for the Third Carbon Age or the Nuclear Age. The story of Species Man as the agent of the Anthropocene is an almost laughable rerun of the great phallic humanizing and modernizing Adventure, where man, made in the image of a vanished god, takes on superpowers in his secular-sacred ascent, only to end in tragic detumescence, once again. Autopoietic, self-making man came down once again, this time in tragic system failure, turning biodiverse ecosystems into flipped-out deserts of slimy mats and stinging jellyfish. Neither did technological determinism produce the Third Carbon Age. Coal and the steam engine did not determine the story, and besides the dates are all wrong, not because one has to go back to the last ice age, but because one has to at least include the great market and commodity reworldings of the long sixteenth and seventeenth centuries of the current era, even if we think (wrongly) that we can remain Euro-centered in thinking about "globalizing" transformations shaping the Capitalocene.
—Donna Haraway, "Tentacular Thinking: Anthropocene, Capitalocene, Chthulucene"

If it is thus conceded that one must go beyond a given concept in order to compare it synthetically with another, then a third thing is necessary in which alone the synthesis of two concepts can originate. But now what is this third thing, as the medium of all synthetic judgments? There is only one totality in which all of our representations are contained, namely inner sense and its a priori form, time. The synthesis of representations rests on the imagination, but their synthetic unity (which is requisite for judgment), on the unity of apperception. Herein therefore is to be sought the possibility of synthetic judgments, and, since all three contain the sources of a priori representations, also the possibility of pure synthetic judgments, indeed on these grounds they will even be necessary if a cognition of objects is to come about which rests solely on the synthesis of the representations.
—Immanuel Kant, *Critique of Pure Reason*

When considering the global catastrophes of the past decade or so, it seems that only a reorientation can respond to them; only a radical shift (perhaps a demolition) of the underground and the crumbling of the intrastructures of thinking, I find, may allow for the kind of transformation needed to appreciate the challenges that will be faced by the generations to come. As I attempt to outline the itinerary—the path that Black Feminist Poethics signal—my starting point is decolonization—the restoration of the total value extracted from Native Lands and expropriated from Slave Labor.[1] For decolonization is the only possible signifier/signified for anything that can be taken as a descriptor for what so many mean by "social justice" or "global justice"—or, more directly put: decolonization as a demand hosts the most urgent ethical-political issues. Any shift in thinking that prepares the terrain for the emergence of descriptors of existence capable of addressing today's global catastrophes will have to begin with decolonization; that is, it will have to start by acknowledging and confronting colonial and racial subjugation as constitutive of and active in the current global circumstances. Not as that from which such catastrophes derive—as the past of this present or the cause of these effects—but as that which is operative in all of them.

Which catastrophes? Which ethical-political issues? Let me mention four. First, there is an ongoing juridical-economic strategy, which I will call "criminality." It is a decades-long practice which takes the form of increasing rates of incarceration and of state-authorized killings, all justified by criminality (of the "gang banger," of the "terrorist," of the "illegal immigrant") and facilitated by private economic entities (privately owned prisons and detention centers, war mercenaries, and builders of walls). I am referring to Black and Latinx persons in the United States, but also to Muslim populations caught in the wars in the Middle East and the African continent; I am also referring to drug-related armed conflict throughout Latin America and the Caribbean. Second, and related, there is the unprecedented displacement of populations in the Global South, such as Europe's "refugee crisis," which the world began to take note of about five years ago but has been going on for much longer. A "crisis" that, most people forget, is related to the same local and regional wars I mentioned before—armed conflicts that do not interfere with labor expropriation, which seem to facilitate further land expropriation and the extraction of minerals so dear to global capital. This "crisis" is inseparable from the devastation of livelihoods provoked by development strategies, which seem to be returning the economies in the Global South to extraction and agriculture—this time around in the hands of multinational corporations. Let us not forget Europe's response to the "refugee crisis," which has been causing the death of so many Black and brown persons from former European colonies, has consolidated the corporate-security state and the return of lethal white identity politics. Third, there is the latest global crisis, the COVID-19 pandemic, which, true to form, in less than one year has proven deadlier to the Black, Latinx, and Indigenous populations of North America, and will, for sure, wreak havoc in the former colonies of the Global South. Fourth, no less dramatic in its expression—as seen in the recent fires on the West Coast of the United States—there is global warming, and our sheer incapacity to make sense of it. A thinking that takes into account all four developments—criminality, displacement, the pandemic, and global warming—and that situates them jointly unfolding in a global context must, I find, begin with the view that decolonization is the only relevant ethical principle of our times.

Why is this the case? Why is the connection between these four issues not given immediately, and why is decolonization the only appropriate ethical-political response to them?[2] If we are to attend to the demand for decolonization and appreciate its ethical force, a shift at the level of principles or a reconfiguring of the *transparent I* must occur underground and intra-structurally. As a contribution to the groundwork necessary for appreciating the demand for decolonization and for contemplating the fundamental reorientation it requests, I provide a description of the moments at which such an operation must first occur, namely a description of existence ("deep implicancy"). As I have done elsewhere, instead of providing a definition, in the following commentary of global warming I outline what happens to thinking when deep implicancy describes its intra-structural level, that is, the unspoken basis for gathering what happens and what exists.

ORDER OF NATURE

My point of departure here is how the Kantian "I think," the "unity of apperception" mentioned in the opening quote, is inscribed in the grammar and lexicon that constitute descriptions of what happens and what exists, both human and more than human. When considering how Kant's version of the subject operates at this level, as the figure of determinacy, it is important to note that it does so underground and intra-structurally—in the onto-epistemological pillars (separability, determinacy, and sequentiality) and descriptors (formality and efficacy). That it does so is a consequence of the precondition for knowledge, that of *given* order (that is, nature) which undergirds the Kantian program. Here I am referring to what Kant calls the "law of the specification of nature," which "assumes in behalf of an *order of nature* cognizable for our understanding in the division that it makes of its universal laws when it would subordinate a manifold of particular laws to these."[3] Being the sole and fundamental guide of judgment, this principle is the precondition for determinative scientific statements, reflective aesthetic statements, and imperative ethic statements. A crucial step in the direction of thinking needed for an adequate anticolonial analysis of the global context is to expose how the "I think" is at work in the very descriptive terms that compound our discourse. Let us consider those critical approaches to global warming that correctly consider colonial extraction, widespread agricultural production, and the needs of industrial capital as central to the creation of the conditions leading to an increase in greenhouse gases. The terms Donna Haraway comments on in the opening quote, "Anthropocene" and "Capitalocene," work correctly to attribute global warming to the human, to the way the conditions of human existence have impacted the planet. When doing so, however, in the attribution of determinacy, they establish a chain of efficacy that does not allow for an appreciation of how colonial extraction and expropriation are at work in the process. This is the case because of the way formality and efficacy operate intra-structurally in the "empirical" or "material" conditions that the terms Anthropocene and Capitalocene are designed to capture. On the one hand, formality is at work in how the Kantian "I think" is presumed in the procedure developed for establishing the ages of the Earth, which inscribes linear time onto the planet and allows for the naming of the phases of its history. The existing techniques and tools set the Earth's age at about 4.6 billion years. The first 600 million years are not yet officially named, it seems, due to a lack of the kind of evidence (bacterial life) that allowed for the naming of the following four billion years. Formality, one of the onto-epistemological descriptors that sustain claims to knowledge with certainty, maps the "I think" onto the planet because the naming procedure employs the methods, concepts, and formulations of the science of life.[4] On the other hand, efficacy is the primary onto-epistemological descriptor in analyses of global warming that register the beginning of a new phase in the Earth's existence, whether it is called Anthropocene or Capitalocene: that is, whether or not it results from shifts brought about by large-scale economic activities, all of which are dependent on extraction and labor expropriation. To put it differently, human economic activity is identified as the efficient cause in both cases; the difference is that "Capitalocene," as Haraway indicates, takes on a critical perspective in regard to the "I think," which is unexamined in "Anthropocene."

What if, instead of naming yet another geological age and rendering human exceptionality the final explanation for what we know results from economic activities, one attended to those activities? Humans have led to a rise in temperature that can/will cause the destruction or extinction of the planet's living inhabitants. At the most basic level, the food we eat and the fossil fuel used in our vehicles are culprits in this deadly energy flow, which is nothing but an increase of heat. Heat, the

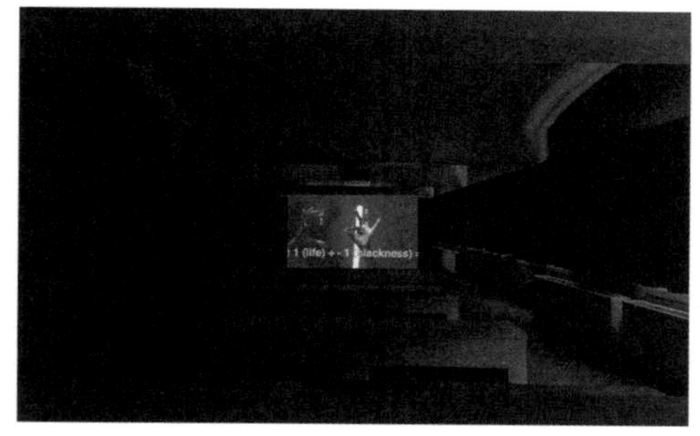

The Otolith Group, *Infinity minus Infinity*, p. 266.

transfer of internal kinetic energy, is what is at work in global warming. Heat flows from flesh to flesh by contact, radiation, or mediation. Everything that exists emits electromagnetic radiation, as long as its temperature—or rather, a measurement of its average internal temperature—is greater than absolute zero (which, as far as I have learned, has only been achieved through the intervention of scientists in a laboratory). Internal kinetic energy, which depends on mass and speed, can be transformed into any other form of energy. And how to attend to these activities without the onto-epistemological intra-structure of the "I think" and its ordered world? What if, instead of describing the economic activities that cause global warming in terms of efficacy, one considered all that enters in them—labor, raw materials, and instruments of production—in terms of their materiality? More precisely, I am interested in proposing a description of what happens in the very process of generating greenhouse gases. That is, in the transformation or transduction of potential energy (labor) or internal kinetic energy (calor) that takes place when something is applied to provoke an alteration in something else (labor), or when something exists alongside everything that is already in existence (calor).

LAND

With such a proposition, I move to introduce the outline of an argument: that decolonization provides us with an ethical basis for demanding the kind of juridical and economic changes necessary to challenge the dominance of state-capital and inspire a shift away from extraction (of lands and resources), which results in the displacement, dispossession, and death that forces the racial others of Europe to leave their homes. Even without a good grasp of what is at work in global warming, everybody knows that it results from the emission and accumulation of greenhouse gases—carbon dioxide, methane, and nitrous oxide—which have raised the temperature of the lower layer of the Earth (troposphere). The rise in temperature results from these gases' absorption and emission of infrared radiation. The accelerated accumulation of greenhouse gases has to do with an increased extraction of matter from the Earth, in the form of fossil fuels and soil nutrients to feed crops and livestock. The accumulation of gases, then, is inseparable from the expropriation of land and of the labor necessary to access fossil fuels and soil. Whether we locate the efficient cause earlier, with the emergence of agriculture, or in the late eighteenth century with the Industrial Revolution, there is no question that a certain concentration of means of production and of access to raw materials corresponds to the excess of greenhouse gases. I don't need to say much to support the point that coloniality—that is, the mode of governance that relies on the deployment of total violence to ensure the expropriation of the internal energy of lands and bodies—has facilitated this concentration for over 500 years now. It is then not unreasonable to point to the fact that the accumulation of these gases also expresses (materially) the extent and intensity of the concentration of expropriated internal (kinetic) energy facilitated by coloniality and the juridical-economic mechanism of state-capital. As for evidence of the intensity and extent of this expropriation of internal energy, it is sufficient to recall the levels of dispossession found in the Global South, or the never-ending wars in the African continent, the Middle East, Afghanistan—colonial conflicts that do not interfere with the extraction of natural resources.

Land, including the waters and other more-than-human inhabitants, exists as potential energy (chemical, gravitational, etc.). How to think in such a way that violates the linear separation and progression given by space and time? Well, think about how the equivalence between matter and energy presented by Albert Einstein materialized in the bombs tested in the Marshall Islands. In my view, this is about an image of existence without the presumption of separability. If we think, at the same time, that something has been extracted, and that Indigenous claims to land are not only a claim to possession (which is the logic of economic value I mentioned earlier) but are ancestral claims (as Indigenous epistemologies already assume)—we can think that Indigenous people are the water (bodies composed by water, and also by everything that grew on the land because of the water: plants, fish, birds). It is also possible to think that what has been extracted has not disappeared in consumption. Actually, if we think of "change" in terms of phase transition (the same matter changing into solid, liquid, gas, plasma) and transduction (one form of energy turning into another, as a microphone transforms sound waves into electrical waves) we can say that the bodies of their ancestors were composed of what grew because of those waters; when the water was extracted, parts of them were taken elsewhere. This is an ancestral claim; it cannot be measured because it is everything.

In the case of water extraction, two things can be contemplated at once: first, extraction and the total violence that enables it (ongoing theft of economic dispossession); and second, what I call re/de/composition, the fact that the water remains materially as bodies, trees, and all the other things that exist. We can think that the wealth that has been accumulated by the descendants of the occupiers, of the settlers in these lands; the wealth that was sent back to Europe in the form of objects but also of raw materials that entered the initial accumulation of capital, as industrial capital; the stolen wealth that has been transformed in so many ways, is also composed of that water. What has been extracted remains transduced into money, and now into these virtual financial objects that prevail in global capital.

If we take both matter and energy into account, we can think of the restoration of the extracted total value along different lines. It is not the return of a possession that can be monetized. It is the return of a constitutive part of the expropriated Indigenous community (like the return of a limb). Because the wealth yielded by what was extracted entered in the composition of what exists not only in Europe but everywhere, the return is also a homecoming of sorts; it is the actualization of a deep implication that already exists. So, restoration cannot be monetized; it cannot be calculated and addressed as a loss (or a gain). Thinking without linearity, without its onto-epistemological pillars (separability, determinacy, and sequentiality) and descriptors (formality and efficacy) and its ways of creating meaning allows for another appreciation of the call for decolonization by Indigenous peoples and the demand for reparations for Black persons. What has been demanded is a restoration of something that never completely disappeared and that has also made them/us part of all that exists.

Denise Ferreira da Silva is professor and director of the Social Justice Institute-GRSJ at the University of British Columbia, Vancouver, and adjunct professor of curatorial practice at Monash University Art, Design and Architecture, Melbourne. She is the author of *Unpayable Debt* (2021), which examines the relationships among coloniality, raciality, and global capital from a Black feminist perspective.

1. This description of decolonization accepts the liberal and historical materialist account of labor as well as of production. I offer an alternative account in Denise Ferreira da Silva, *Unpayable Debt* (Berlin, 2021).

2. There are, of course, many reasons why. Let me briefly comment on a theoretical one, which is that the prevailing logics for arguments for anything that could be taken as substantive (corrective and not only protective) justice, whether understood as "social" or "global," are distribution and recognition. Unfortunately, I don't have time to revisit either John Rawls's theory of distributive justice or Charles Taylor's articulation of recognition as the principle under multiculturalism—or their critics. I will mention only that the sharpest critiques begin precisely with shifting the attention to social (racial, gender, sexual) and colonial subjugation. On the former, see Iris Marion Young, *Justice and the Politics of Difference* (Princeton, 2012); on the latter, see Glen Coulthard, *Red Skin, White Masks* (Minneapolis, 2014).

3. Immanuel Kant, *Critique of the Power of Judgment* (Cambridge, UK, 2001), p. 72; emphasis added.

4. Formality uses the biological classificatory system that the French naturalist Georges Cuvier designed in the early nineteenth century. In it, the organic form of the European (Caucasian) "race" governs (as the model and the most perfect living formation) the understanding of the forms and functions of other living things. Hence, the unnamed phases/layers of the planet are so because they cannot be separated according to living things, which are, in turn, knowable because of the different degrees of complexity of their organisms, which allows for the determination of their genera, species, etc. And, after Cuvier's comparative anatomy was combined with Darwin's theory of natural selection, more-than-human living beings also acquired a place in a temporal sequence that charts the development of life that, as a figuring of G. W. F. Hegel's Spirit, is both the efficient and the final cause of the particularity of the parts and the movements of living things. For an in-depth analysis of the science of life and an elaboration of this argument, see Denise Ferreira da Silva, *Toward a Global Idea of Race* (Minneapolis, 2007).

أحيـــــانًا يكون النسيان نقيض العدالة.
وفي أحيانٍ أخرى، يكون محو الأثر التاريخي
هو تحديدًا ما قد تتطلبه العدالة كي تتحقّق.

نادية أبو الحـــاج

تمارين على التنفّس

فرانسواز فرجيس

ترجمه عن الإنكليزية فريق الأركلوغ

أن نفكّك ما تعلّمناه

كيف بمقدورنا أن ننقل هشاشة الحياة البشرية ووهنها وشروط وجودها المتقلقلة — المتمثّلة في نقاء الماء والهواء، الرعاية والحنان، الذاكرة وتناقل الخبرات، الضوء والظلّ، المأوى والأمان، أماكن للاستراحة، الأحلام والحب، أو منح الرعاية وتلقّيها — وفي الوقت ذاته أن نتجنّب الإيديولوجيا الحمائية وما تُفضي إليه من رقابة بوليسية على المجتمعات الفقيرة غير البيضاء وتزايد الاعتقالات وتعاظم الإمبريالية؟ كيف يُمكننا أن نتخيّل سياسات للحماية لا تشوبها العنصرية ولها طابعٌ نسوي ومناهض للاستعمار تأخذ في اعتبارها هذا الوهن والهشاشة والقلقلة؟ كيف يُمكننا حماية الحقّ في التنفّس، كما صاغه أخيل مِبمبي، بدوره «حقٌّ للجميع»؟[1] كيف يُمكننا أن نصلح كوكبًا أفسدته قرونٌ من الاستعمار والرأسمالية العنصرية المبنية على الوعد البروميثيّ بسيادة البشر المطلقة على الغلاف الحيوي؟ لقد تمكنّت المقاربات المناهِضة للعبودية والعنصرية والاستعمار ومقاربات السكان الأصليين وأنصار إلغاء السجون والمقاربات النسوية للتعليم والتعلّم عبر السنوات من مراكمة مجموعة كبيرة من الاستراتيجيات للتنظيم الاجتماعي وتوارث الخبرات عبر الأجيال. وهي وإنْ كانت استراتيجيات غير مكتملة إلا أنها تتمتّع بنفس قوّة المساعي الاستعمارية السابقة لها في شموليّتها لمحو الأصوات والكلمات. أحد مساعي هذه الاستراتيجيات هو تفكيك ما تعلّمناه من اغترابٍ عن أنفسنا وعن محيطنا، ذلك الاغتراب الذي يجعلنا نختبر العالم كعالم من أشياء تُستهلك ثم تُلفَظ. يدرّبنا ذلك الاغتراب على إيديولوجيا السيادة المطلقة على العالم، ويرسّخ فينا وعدًا بروميثيًّا بأنّ قدر الإنسان هو استنزاف الأرض ومَنْ عليها حتى النفاذ. بالمقابل، تُقدّم هذه الاستراتيجيات التربوية إطارًا أخلاقيًّا للحماية يشمل كل أوجه الحياة البشرية، ويجابه مؤسسات الدولة الأبوية الليبرالية المُعسكَرة في احتكارها لا للحماية وحسب بل وللتربية أيضاً. فالدولة تحتكر صياغة سياسات الحماية وتطبيقها عبر الحوائط والحدود والقوانين والشرطة، في حين أنها تنتج على نحو مقابل وبالأدوات ذاتها المزيد من الهشاشة والاعتلال في مواجهة المرض والفقر والتلوّث والاستغلال. تمامًا كما منحت لنفسها الحقّ في انتهاك الحياة العائلية وتمزيق أواصر القربى والحقّ في التوقيف والاعتقال.

صاغ المنطق المشترك للاسترراع أحادي المحصول والتّعدينَ والعمارة التميزية والتعليم السلطوي أساسَ علاقةٍ خبيثةٍ بين العنصرية والتمييز الجنسي والاستغلال. فتعطيل أشكال العيش المشترك وتوارث الخبرات عبر الأجيال هي مكوّنات أساسيّة في استراتيجية الدولة للعزل والفصل. وفي مواجهة هذا العدوان، طوّرت الشعوب غير البيضاء استراتيجيات تربوية لتفكيك ما تعلّموه والحفاظ على توارث الخبرات بين الأجيال وتعزيز قوة الخيال. تتضمّن سيرورة تفكيك التعلّم كاستراتيجية لحماية الأجيال القادمة من دمار الاستعمار طقوسًا تسمح للأفراد بالانخراط المجتمعي مجدّدًا عبر إعادة التسمية، وطقوسًا للتطهّر، وممارسات لرعاية من يعانون آثار الصدمة أو الاكتئاب أو الجراح النفسية والجسدية. كما كتب فرانتز فانون، «نثور لأننا لا نستطيع التنفّس».[2] لا نستطيع التنفّس لأنّ الهواء لم يعد صالحًا للتنفس، لأنّ العنصرية تُسمّم الهواء. إن كانت إنسانية المرء تقتضي أن يُولد هشًّا وبحاجة للرعاية والحماية، فالرأسمالية الأبوية العنصرية تُحوّل هذه الهشاشة إلى خطر يهدّد أبسط متطلبات الحياة وحق التنفّس بحدّ ذاته. فالتنفس ليس متاحًا بالتساوي؛ ولا هو من المُسَلّمات إذ يمكن للرئة أن تكون معطوبةً عند الولادة. تُعلّمنا مناهَضة الاستعمار كيف نزيل السُمّ من عقولنا وأجسامنا وأن نمرّن رئتينا على البقاء كي نستطيع أن نثور.

تُحوّل الأجوبة الديكولونيالية عدم الاستقرار إلى قوّة، وتُجذّر نفسها في الهشّ والمؤقت كي تنقل الموارد اللازمة لتخيّل المستقبل. لكن المكتبات حُرقت والأغراض نُهبت والألسنة قُطعت والمقابر دُنّست والمدن مُحيت من على وجه الأرض. إذا أصبح الحِداد حالةً ذهنية مألوفة، ما تزال هناك آثار وبقايا للمعرفة محفوظة في الذاكرة اليدوية والشفهية. قدّم ترينالي الشارقة للعمارة للعام 2019 أمثلةً على عمارة خاصّة بالأشقياء. سواء أكانت في المساكن المتنقّلة على الجزر النهرية في بنغلاديش التي تتشكّل موسميًا حسب مجاري تيّارات الأنهر الثلاثة جامونا وميغنا وبادما — تُدعى الواحدة من هذه الجزر «تشار» — أو في التشكّلات المنقوشة على الأرض التي تقتفي مسارات شعائرية تاريخية في صحارى شمال تشيلي أو في الغابات المقدّسة في إثيوبيا أو في خرائط سكّان أستراليا الأصليين، كل ذلك يشكّل إسهامًا في مكتبة ضخمة من المعارف والتعاليم تختلط فيها الكلمات والطقوس والأغاني والإشارات والذاكرة والتاريخ المجتمعي. توضّح عمارة الأشقياء هذه أنه ليس من عملٍ يدوي من دون نظرية، من دون فلسفةٍ للصنع، من دون فكرٍ مجرّد. تزوّدنا هذه المكتبة بإپستمولوجيات بديلة لتلك التي تعتبرها النُخب معارف مشروعة. وتحوي ما خُفي على أنظار المستعمِر النهمة من معارف لا بدّ من استعادتها وفكّ شيفرتها، وما استعصى على فهمه من نصوص وكلمات

ظنّها المستعمِر محض لغوٍ ورطانة، وأغانٍ وقعت على مسامعه كضجيج، وشعائر وصفها بالبدائية، وأشياء بدت في نظره فظّة ولا جمال فيها. وفي حين تستمرّ التناقضات (الناتجة عن الصراعات الجندرية والجيلية والفروق في المكانة) فإنّ رفض التسلّط والبحث عن حلول بديلة هو مسعىً مستمرّ.

يشرح الفنان تومي ماي المنتمي إلى السكان الأصليين لأستراليا كيف ينسج مجتمع نغورارا بساطهم الخرائطي: «لم نستطع الإجهار بتسمية البلاد الأخرى، فنحن ننحدر من مكانٍ آخر، من بلدٍ مختلف. هذه هي طريقة السكّان الأصليين في احترام حقوق الملكية الفكرية. لا يمكنك أن تسرق قصةً أو أغنيةً أو رقصةً من مكانٍ آخر». يتابع ماي: «لا يمكننا أن نُري البيض كل شيء. فإذا أخبرت الجميع، تكون كمن باع بلده. يمكنك أن تخبرهم ببعض التفاصيل، لكن ليس الكثير منها».[3] إنها أنظمة جلاء وخفاء، إنها أنظمة توريَة وإبانة، أنظمة تحاشٍ وتراكُب، أنظمة بناء بالقش والحجر، وأنظمة مشاركة المكان مع احترام الآخرين، كل هذه الأنظمة تقدّم قواعد للمعرفة والحقوق (الحقّ في أن تتكلّم وتفعل وتتدخّل)، وهي حقوق تسبق الحقوق بمفهومها الغربي الذي يعتنق الفردية المجرّدة (التي يمثلها صاحب المِلْك الأبيض). لقد تبلورت الاستراتيجيات الديكولونيالية حول مفاهيم الحقيقة والتورية، والشفافية والموارِبة، وخطاب ما يقال نصفه ويُستشفّ نصفه الآخر. كل هذه تدّعي عدم الفهم وهي تواجه المستعمِر ممعنةً فيه النظر لأجل تصويب سلاحه على صدره هو.

تنسج لفتات مثل تقديم كوبٍ من الماء أو الشاي أو القهوة أو الطعام والمأوى شبكةً من العلاقات الاجتماعية تغدو فيها الكلمات غير ضرورية. تجرّم الدول الأوروبية هذه اللفتات حاليًّا بحجّة حماية الوطن من الأجانب. وإذا ما كانت الحرب تعني دائمًا أنه لم يعد بالإمكان إبقاء الأبواب مفتوحة، فإنّ الاستعمار قد شرعن تاريخيًا الدخول إلى بيوت الناس دون استئذانهم تحت ذريعة حاجتهم للتحضّر. ترى أغلب الثقافات الشعورَ بهذا الاستحقاق تجسيدًا لما سمّاه إيمي سيزار «وحشنة أوروبا» *L'ensauvagement de l'Europe* وهي العملية التي «ينزع فيها الاستعمار هالة الحضارة عن المستعمِر، محوّلا إياه إلى وحش بالمعنى الحقيقي للكلمة، ينحطّ به ويوقظ غرائزه المدفونة: الجشع والعنف والكراهية العنصرية ونسبية المبادئ».[4] في كاناكي-كاليدونيا الجديدة، لاحظ الكاناكيّون أنّ المستوطنين الفرنسيين لا يأبهون بـ«مراعاة الأصول» *faire la coutume* أي بتأدية شعائر محدّدة لها أسماءها المحدّدة. لأداء الفعل هنا مكانة أساسية لأنه ينطوي على إتمام سلسلة من الشروط الضرورية كي تصبح جزءًا من عالم الكاناك. فتبادل الهدايا بين الكاناكيين، الأهمّ بينها تقليديًا هي العملات والبطاطا الحلوة، هي شرط لتبادل الحديث والكلام.

يجب أن نميّز بين الاعتراف بالحالة المتقلقلة والهشاشة باعتبارها إطار أخلاقي للحماية وبين إرسائه على نطاق عالمي. يسلّط التلخيص المؤثّر الذي تطرحه روث ويلسون-غيلمور للرأسمالية العنصرية كصناعة لـ «التفاوت في قابلية الموت المبكّر بين المجموعات المختلفة الضوء على الموت بوصفه نتيجة شَرطية لوحشية الرأسمالية العنصرية والجنسانية المعيارية وتراث العبودية والاستعمار والرأسمالية.[5] فالرأسمالية تُحوّل الهشاشة والوهن إلى أدوات للسيطرة من خلال الإخضاع والتطويع.[6] وإنْ كان عالم العبودية عالمًا من الموت المبكّر والموت المجتمعي، فقد أطال الاستعمار في مرحلة ما بعد العبودية من عمر هذا العالم في وقت لاتزال فيه الجماعات والمجتمعات والأفراد عرضة للموت المبكّر بسبب الحرمان من الماء والهواء النظيفين والسكن الملائم والتعليم والخدمات الصحيّة الجيدة والاضطرار للعمل إلى حدّ الإنهاك الجسدي فالموت أسرع من نظرائهم البورجوازيين. إذًا، فاقمت النيوليبرالية والاستهلاك المتطرّف من هذه الهشاشة واستقرارها كحالٍ طبيعي.

إلا أنه وبينما ننظر إلى هذا الوضع على أنّه وضع طارئ من حيث «أنّ إمكانية تجاوزه تتوقّف على قدرتنا على الخروج من الواقع الحالي والتأسيس لواقعٍ مغاير»، لا يجب أن نتجاهل الشروط والقوى التي تُحوّل هذا الوضع الطارئ إلى مراكمةٍ للمخاطر والموت المبكّر.[7] فبالنسبة للمهاجرين واللاجئين ومن يعيشون في مخيّمات اللجوء أو مناطق الحروب، والنساء ممّن يواجهن مخاطر القتل بشكل يومي، والأطفال مكتومي القيد، والمشرّدين، والفقراء ومن يتعرّضون للتمييز العنصري والسود والسكان الأصليين، تُشكّل الهجرة وبدء حياتهم من جديد سؤالًا وجوديًا محفوفًا بالعنف والوحشية. هنا لا تعود الهجرة وبدء حياة جديدة خيارًا طواعيًا. وفي مواجهة المزيد من صنع الهشاشة لا بدّ أن نعود إلى الاستراتيجيات التي طوّرتها المجتمعات المستضعفة للتغلّب على الشعور بالعجز والاستلاب التام. هنا سنجد أنّ إمكانية وجود «أجيال قادمة» بحدّ ذاتها تتوقّف على هذه القوّة الممانعة التي لا تبيد. قد تبدو الكلمة جوفاء لأنها سُلّعت مرارًا، إلّا أننا بحاجة لتذكير أنفسنا أنه ومن ظلام القمع ستظلّ هناك أصوات تقول «يومًا ما سنكون أحرارًا».

ألّا نتنفس

نعيش عصر الإقامات الجبرية والتوقيف على الهوية ودعاوى التراب والدم.[8] وفي هذا العصر تصبح القدرة على التنفّس ضرورةً تتضافر حولها العدالة والمساواة والكرامة واحترام الحياة. لم يكن فعل التنفّس بحدّ ذاته، وبكونه دعوة لتغيير الطريقة التي نعيش بها على كوكب الأرض، أبدًا في مقدّمة الحراكات المناهضة للعنصرية كما هو الآن — حراكات مثل حياة السود مُهمّة [Black Lives Matter] وحياة الفلسطينيين مُهمّة وحراك

النسويات المكسيكيات ونضالات السكّان الأصليين من أجل الأرض والنسويات الأفرو-برازيليات. من الولايات المتحدة إلى فلسطين، من فرنسا إلى البرازيل، من جنوب إفريقيا إلى الهند، ومن أستراليا إلى كينيا، يتراكم الموت على يد عناصر شرطة جاثمين على صدور المعتقلين حتى يلفظوا أنفاسهم الأخيرة. يكشف لنا انتشار هذا الاختناق على نطاق الكوكب، كما يصف مبيمبي، أنّ «الحداثة، في أخمص أعماقها، هي حربٌ متواصلةٌ على الحياة»، وأنّ «كل هذه الحروب على الحياة تبدأ بسلب الأنفاس».[9]

أن تمنع شخصًا من التنفس هو فعلٌ يهدف إلى الإسكات والقتل. تؤشّر عدم القدرة على التنفّس إلى الجو الخانق والغاصّ الذي تفرضه العبودية والاستعمار والدول البوليسية تمامًا كما يؤشّر فعل القتل نفسه. في كتابها مذكّرات المزرعة: فصول من العنصرية اليومية *Plantation Memories: Episodes of Everyday Racism* تتناول غرادا كيلومبا بالتحليل الكمّامة التي كان يفرضها الملّاك على عبيدهم قائلةً: «يحجب تكميم الأفواه السوداء أسماع السادة البيض عن الحقائق المتأخّرة التي يريدون 'درئها وإبقائها بعيدةً'، على الهامش، غير ملحوظة وخافتة».[10] في النهاية ترتفع الأصوات من خلف الكمّامات وتخترق بنصالها الاختناق السياسي. أن تمنع المرء من التنفّس هو أيضًا سلاحٌ للتعذيب والقتل. فغرف الغاز والإغراق بالماء إلى حدّ الاختناق والغاز المسيّل للدموع، كلها وسائل لحجب الهواء عن الناس. أصبحت قوى الأمن حول العالم، والتي لم تكن أبدًا محصّنة ومسلحةً بهذا الشكل، مخوّلة أكثر من ذي قبل للإيذاء والتشويه والقتل والاغتصاب. بالإضافة لخراطيم المياه والقنابل والرصاص الحيّ أو المطّاطي المصوّب إلى الصدور والعيون والوجوه والأيادي إلى جانب تقنيات عسكرية أخرى لامتصاص غضب الجماهير، أصبحنا اليوم في مواجهة صورة شرطي غير مكترث يُمعن في الضغط بركبته على رقبة جورج فلويد على الهواء مباشرةً.

أن نختنق

خلال العام 2019 والأشهر الأولى من العام 2020 اجتاحت سلسلةٌ من الحرائق الضخمة غابات كاليفورنيا والأمازون وإفريقيا الوسطى وأستراليا باعثةً بغيومٍ من الرماد لفّت قمم الجبال البعيدة وحجبت السماء والشمس وتغشّت الأشجار والأرض. التهمت ألسنة اللهيب الضخمة كل شيء في طريقها حتى أرمَدت الأرض وسكتت. وبينما كانت جائحة كورونا قد عمّتْ العالم، اكتشفنا في الثالث من نيسان/أبريل من العام 2020 وصول الحرائق إلى محيط المنطقة العازلة حول مفاعل تشيرنوبل السابق. استشعرنا كارثةً وخيمة تحيق بنا ولا مفرّ منها. عادةً ما يكون الأدب أقدَر من تقارير الخبراء على استدعاء العواقب الحتمية لهذه الغريزة القاهرة لسيادة البشر. في رواية المرسال *The Emissary* تخبر الروائية يوكو تاوادا قصّة الكاتب يوشيرو ابن المائة عام وحفيده الأكبر المراهق موماي لتتناول من خلالها العواقب الوخيمة لكارثةٍ بيئية تظلّ مجهولة الأسباب. في الرواية يموت أطفال اليابان في مهدهم بسبب صعوبة التنفّس، لذا تجب حمايتهم ومساعدتهم من قِبَل الأجيال الأكبر مثل يوشيرو، الذين يبدون وكأنهم يتمتّعون بالخلود بينما تقصر أعمار الأطفال المتوقعة مع كل يوم يمرّ. ترسم الرواية عالمًا اختفت فيه كل الثوابت — الجغرافية منها والاجتماعية والجيولوجية والبيولوجية — ولا شيء مسلّمٌ به، فأكل البرتقال أصبح خطرًا مميتًا، وطقس طوكيو يتحوّل من الحرّ اللافح إلى البرد القارس في ثوانٍ معدودة، وحتى الموت لم يعد أمرًا مضمونًا. فعندما لا يموت الكبار، لا يعود الموت لحظةً تحوّل الموتى إلى أسلاف، وبالتالي يُلغى مفهوم الأجيال القادمة. عطّلت الكارثة البيئية تناقل المعارف بين الأجيال.

اقتصاد الاختناق يعني تدمير رئة الكوكب كما رئة سكّانه. آثار التسمّم الزئبقي في ميناماتا باليابان في العام 1956، ورشّ مبيد العامل البرتقالي فوق فيتنام بين عامَي 1961 و1971، وانفجار معمل يونيون كاربايد للمبيدات الزراعية في بوبال بالهند عام 1984 هي ثلاثة أمثلة على كوارث أنتجتها الرأسمالية العنصرية خلال القرن العشرين. وإذا كان الجشع والافتراس هما القوّة الدافعة للرأسمالية والاستعمار الأوروبيين — أثناء تجارة العبيد وفي تنويعاتها الأخرى ما بعد إلغاء العبودية — فهما الآن قوام اقتصاد يرقى إلى ما تسمّيه المفكّرة والناشطة ساياك فالنسيا «رأسمالية الأحشاء المبقورة». وهو مصطلحٌ «يشير إلى سفك الدماء السافر وغير المبرّر الذي يقع دفعه على عاتق العالم الثالث كثمن للامتثال لمنطق الرأسمالية المُستفحل والمتطلّب، كما يشير إلى الحالات العديدة لقطع الأوصال وتمزيق الأحشاء التي تقترن عادةً بالجريمة المنظّمة والجندر والاستغلال الجائر لأجساد البشر. بشكلٍ عام، يطرح المصطلح هذه الأنواع الوحشية من العنف بدورها أدوات توظّف الموت من أجل السلطة».[11] العنف بالتأكيد هو القاعدة النظامية للرأسمالية العنصرية والأبوية، إلّا أنه وكما تُظهر جَسبير بوار، هناك أشكالٌ وتدرّجات كثيرة للعنف، يؤدّي اختزالها كلّها بكلمة «عنف» إلى نوعٍ من التجريد المخلّ الذي يجعل من العنف أمرًا طبيعيًا ويعرقل تحليل الأشكال المتنوّعة التي تعطب بها الدولة أجساد البشر. بالنسبة لبوار، فإن ردود الفعل الليبرالية على العنف تعيد تضمين الجسد المعطوب في الخطابات والممارسات الفردانية — كالمرونة وإعادة تأهيل الجسد المعطوب كطرقٍ لمحو أسباب العنف وجذوره.[12] لذا عندما تتحدّث القوى القومجية عن «الحمائية» فإنّ ما نسمعه هو «العنصرية». في الوقت ذاته لا يبدو قتل النساء واغتيال النشطاء من السكّان الأصليين والعنف ضد المسنّين والأطفال وعنف الشرطة وكأنه ينحسر بأي حال. قد تختلف مستويات ذلك من بلدٍ لآخر، إلّا أنه

من الواضح أنّ الظلم واللامساواة في تزايدٍ مستمرّ، بما يفاقم أوضاع الهشاشة التي تنتجها عولة الرأسمالية وبُناها العنصرية. تسلّط هذه الأشكال من العنف الضوء على حقيقة أنّ الحكومات فرّقت تاريخيًّا بين الذين يتمتّعون بالحماية الاجتماعية وينتفعون بها، وأولئك الذين يمكن إهمالهم ممّن تراهم غير مؤهّلين؟ لعيش «حياة طبيعية» بسبب طباعهم المتأصّلة وبهذا لا تتركهم الدولة في مهبّ خطر الفيروس وحسب، بل وتُمعن في تجريم أفعالهم اليومية كذلك.

أن نلوّث

كانت جائحة الكورونا كارثةً تمّ التنبؤ بها مسبقًا. أدركنا سريعًا أننا لا نعيش أزمةً صحّية بقدر ما نعيش حدثًا تاريخيًّا وسياسيًّا مفصليًّا لا يمكن أن يكون بفعل الصدفة، حتى أنّ لفظ «الأزمة» بحدّ ذاته يجب أن يُستعمل بحذر لوصفه. أصبح فيروس الكورونا جائحةً عالمية عندما أصبحت أعداد الإصابات والوفيات في البلدان الأوروبية تناهز الآلاف. ولو كانت الجائحة قد ضربت هاييتي أو سوريا أو الكونغو على سبيل المثال، فإنّ حديث «الأزمة العالمية» لم يكن ليُسمع. على مدى عقود ظلّ العلماء يحذّرون الحكومات من تقاعسها عن دعم الأبحاث العلمية حول انتشار الأمراض الحيوانية المنشأ ومفاقمة الظروف المواتية لنقل العدوى بين أجناس مختلفة من الكائنات. ومن حيث تدفعنا الرأسمالية العنصرية النيوليبرالية إلى حافّة الهاوية — مع ارتفاع منسوب مياه البحار وذوبان القشرة الجليدية والأعاصير المدمّرة ومواسم الجفاف والفيضانات وتلوّث الماء والهواء — فإنّها لا تتوقّف في الوقت ذاته عن مأسسة وشرعنة العنف. وفي ظلّ قوانينها، يصبح التنفّس امتيازًا طبقيًا وعرقيًا، خاصّةً إذا ما علمنا أنّ تلوّث الهواء هو المسبّب الأول للوفيات المبكّرة حول العالم. إعصار كاترينا في العام 2005، واحتراق النساء أحياء في حادثة رانا بلازا عام 2013، وخراب الأراضي والمجتمعات بتأثير الكلورديكون في جزر الهند الغربية، وبسبب تعدين الذهب في غايانا، وبسبب صناعة النيكل في جزر كاناكي، واستخراج اليورانيوم في النيجر، والكوبلت في الكونغو، والعمل في مناجم أميركا اللاتينية وأستراليا ومدغشقر: أسباب كل هذه الكوارث وتبعاتها قد غطّاها تواطؤ الحكومات وحصانة الشركات. يبرز هذا كله تعقيدات وضعنا ما بعد الإنساني (أنتج الفلاسفة الغربيون مفهوم ما بعد الإنسانية لتعريفها كحالة ما بعد الحداثية، إلا أنّ المفهوم صنيع ابنٌ للحداثة الأوروبية). فقد أظهرت الإجراءات التي اتخذتها الحكومات للحدّ من تناقل العدوى أنّ الحماية من المرض والتشويه ليست حقًّا للجميع. لم تكن أعداد الوفيات بسبب الكورونا في المجتمعات الأكثر فقرًا والأكثر تعرّضًا للعنصرية — السود والسكان الأصليين والمهاجرين واللاجئين والمعتقلين — أكبر لأنّ تلك المجتمعات لا تتمتّع بتوافر الرعاية والضمان الصحّي أو لأنها تعاني من ارتفاع في معدّلات الاعتلال المرضي المتزامن، بل أيضًا لأنّ عملهم يضعهم في مهبّ الخطر. يظهر تاريخ الاستعمار والجائحات والتفرقة العنصرية بذرائع علمية أنّ الأوضاع الاجتماعية والاقتصادية تؤثّر على بنية الأوضاع البيولوجية.

وفي الجنوب العالمي، تفهم الشعوب بشكل أعمق كيف ولماذا تنقل إليهم الرأسمالية العنصرية الأوبئة. فقد خَبِروا عن قرب كيف يستعمل الأوروبيون المواد الكيميائية على التربة ويحقنون مجتمعات السود والسكان الأصليين بالفيروسات ويجبرون النساء غير البيضاوات على الإجهاض والتعقيم القسري. غالبًا ما أفكّر في رواية هـ. ج. ويلز «جزيرة الدكتور مورو»، والتي يمكن اعتبارها رائعةٍ أدبية عن السيادة البروميثية على الطبيعة، وفيها يُجري طبيبٌ مجنون تجاربه الجراحية على حيوانات حيّة لإنتاج كائنات هجينة شبيهة بالبشر. في جزيرة ريونيون، التي أنتمي إليها، أصيب ما يقارب 40% من سكان الجزيرة بوباء الشيكونغونيا (وهو مرض وبائي فيروسي ينتقل بواسطة البعوض) بين عامي 2005 و2006، ما أسفر عن وفاة 300 شخص. لا يجب أن ننسى في عداد الضحايا من أصبحوا معاقين ولا يجب أن ننسى أيضًا أثر رشّ المبيدات على النباتات والتربة. ورغم ظهور الإصابات الأولى في شباط/فبراير 2005 رفضت السلطات الفرنسية أخذ الوباء على محمل الجدّ بزعم أنّ قدوم الشتاء كفيلٌ بالقضاء على الفيروس وأنّ مستويات النظافة الشخصية المتدنّية عند السكان المحليين هي السبب في الانتشار الواسع للوباء.

أظهر وباء الشـيكونغونيا العلاقة بين التصحّر في بلاد حوض المحيط الهندي وبين انتشار الأمراض الحيوانية المنشأ بفعل النيوليبرالية والاستهلاك المتطرّف والسياحة وإضعاف الخدمات الصحّية العامّة نتيجة الإجراءات التقشّفية المفروضة وتركيز الأبحاث على الأمراض التي تصيب الرجل الأبيض في الشمال العالمي فضلًا عن تواطؤ الحكومات. فُسّر المعدّل المرتفع للوفيات على خلفية شيوع الاعتلال المرضي المتزامن (السكّري والضغط والبدانة) بين سكان ريونيون، أي أنّ المرض مرتبطٌ بشكلٍ مباشر بالفقر والعنصرية والاستعمار. اتخذت الحكومة إجراءات صارمة وغاشمة فطلبت من الجيش رشّ المبيدات الحشرية في الحدائق والشوارع. أبلغ الكثيرون بعدها عن اختفاء الفراشات والطيور والحرباوات من حدائقهم وعن إصابتهم بالحساسيات والصداع النصفي.

عندما أعلنت الحكومات عن اتخاذ إجراءات لمواجهة كورونا، لم يدهشني منح الشرطة صلاحيات أوسع للسيطرة على المجتمعات التي التمييز العنصري الممنهج — أولئك المجبَرون على العمل لتلبية الحاجات الأساسية لدى المجتمع البورجوازي حتى يتمكّن من الاستمرار بشكلٍ اعتيادي (كالتنظيف والرعاية والتوصيل والنقل، إلخ). لم يكن مفاجئًا أيضًا أن أرى تزايد الفقر

والجوع بينما لا يتوقف تداول السلع حفاظًا على مستوىً معيّن للمعيشة. كانت بنود العقد العنصري والجنسي واضحةً لكل من رغب في مطالعتها.

أن نسكن

إذا لم يكن ثمّة تبرير لحرمان شعوب الجنوب العالمي من الحصول على أصناف التكنولوجيا التي أسهمت طويلًا في تيسير سبل العيش لمجتمعات الشمال العاملي — وهي حقيقةٌ فاقمتها المظالم التاريخية لاستبقاء علاقات التبعية بين الشمال والجنوب — لا يزال الوضع الراهن بحاجةٍ لما لا يقلّ عن قفزةٍ خيالية على مستوى الكوكب برمّته. عندما يسأل المرء نفسه أسئلةً تتعلق بحقوق الأجيال القادمة، وعندما يصبح مفهوم المستقبل نفسه محلّ تساؤل، يعني ذلك أنّه علينا التخلّص من التفكير بالتقابلات الثنائية والأوهام البروميثية. ويعني أنه ينبغي لنا اعتناق منهجية تربوية مبنية على التناقل والتكرار والتقليد التي هي — وكما سيؤكّد لنا وليّ أمر أي طفل — متجذّرة في الوجود الإنساني. بل يلمّح إلى حِرَف يتعلّم فيها التلميذ المُتدرّب بواسطة النظر والشمّ واللمس والتذوّق حتى تُكوّن اليد والأذن والعين والأنف ذاكرتها الخاصّة وهي ذاكرة الإيماء: بحيث لا يعود الحِرَفي بحاجة للنظر داخل صندوق عدّته ليعرف أي خردة يحتاج، لأنّ أنامله ستقوده إليها؛ وحيث يستدلّ بحّارة سفن الداو على التيّارات من لون البحر؛ وحيث يمكن للنساء زراعة الخضروات في الصحراء باقتفاء مسارات المياه الجوفية تحت الرمال؛ أو يمكنهنّ النسج بدون النظر إلى أصابعهن. تُغذّي هذه المنهجيات التربوية نظرية مفادها أنّ الإيماء ليس دخيلًا على الفكر، وتشجّعنا على تخيّل مفاهيم مناهضة للعنصرية والاستعمار وداعمة للعدالة البيئية والإنجابية ولحقوق السكّان الأصليين ومجتمع الكوير والعابرين(ات) والمجتمعات الهشّة والمهدّدة. أمضيت وقتًا طويلًا في طفولتي في المطبخ أساعد بما أقدر عليه: تنقية الأرز والعدس والحبوب، تنظيف مكوّنات السلطة والأعشاب، طحن الزنجبيل والثوم، وتقطيع البصل والبندورة — وأي شيء يسمح لي بالبقاء في المطبخ كطفلة. كنت مندهشةً لكيفية اكتساب اللحم والخضروات والتوابل ألوانًا وأشكالًا وروائح ونكهات بعينها. إلا أنني عندما كنت أسأل الطاهية متى يجب أن أضيف البصل أو الكركم أو الطماطم (على سبيل المثال)، كانت تجاوبني دائمًا «أنظري تعرفي». لم تُجب أبدًا «بعد دقيقتين، عندما يحمرّ البصل تمامًا». ولا أزال إلى اليوم أطهو بالنظر والملاحظة، وأجيب صديقاتي وأصدقائي حين يسألونني عن وصفةٍ معينة «ستعرفون متى تضيفوا هذا أو ذاك». تعلّمت أن أثق باللمسة، وملاحظة إذا ما كانت نوعية التوابل جيّدة أم لا، وأنه لا غنى عن الذهاب إلى السوق. يعرف الحِرفيون والصنّاع اليدويون أهمية تحفيز الحواسّ الذي تتطلبه حِرفهم لإثراء التعليم التجريدي. قبل سنوات، كنت في تشيانغ-ماي ضمن مجموعة من الأكاديميين بصحبة عدد من طلبة الدكتوراه الباحثين في الحِرف بصفتها فرعًا من العلوم الإنسانية. كان الطلبة مقسّمين إلى مجموعات بحيث يقضي كل منها يومًا كاملًا في واحدة من الورش الحرفية (الفضّة والنقش على الحجر أو الخشب والنسيج وصناعة صبغة النيل). اخترت النسيج وذهبت مع إحدى الصديقات بصحبة خمسة من الطلاب إلى قرية تبعد ساعتين عن المدينة. كانت الناسجات في استقبالنا وتولّت واحدة منهن الإشراف على كل متدرّبة. عرضت أكبرهنّ سنًا ومكانةً بينهنّ أن تعلّمني. تواصلنا بالإشارة والنظر واللمس. شرحت لي كيفية ضبط لُحمة القماش على هيكل نول بسيط. لم أستطع إكمال قطعة واحدة من القماش، أقطع درزة بعد أخرى بينما تعيد الناسجة المسنّة وصل ما قطعت بصبر وتؤدة. نفذ صبري وقرّرت ألا أواصل التعلّم. ببساطة كنت ممتعضة لأني لم أستطع «إنجاز» شيء بهذه البساطة. بعد عشر دقائق، عدتُ صاغرةً بعدما راجعت نفسي. أنا، التي لطالما تحدّثتُ عن المنهجيات التربوية الديكولونيالية وقوّة التكرار والتقليد، لم أستطع أن أتحمّل الفشل! كان تصرّفي هذا مهينًا. بدأت الناسجة المسنّة تشرح لي مجددًا وبصبر كيفية ضبط اللُّحمة، إلا أنني عندما توقّفت أخيرًا عن الحسبان العقلاني لكل شيء (أفعل هذا أولًا ثم ذاك إلخ). وبدأت أثق بتقليد أصابعي لأصابعها وهي «ترقص» حتى تمكّنت من ضبط اللُّحمة ومن ثمّ النسج. كانت فطنتها التقنية مجرّدة ونظرية وعملية ومادّية في الوقت ذاته. عبّرتْ عن انزعاجها من تعثّر حركاتي إلا أنّ نبرتها لم تكن مستعلية قَط. كانت مربيّة مدهشة، امرأة غير بيضاء لم تكن لتُعتبر أستاذة ضمن النظام التعليمي المهيمن — إلا أنّها وبفضل صبرها، أرجعتني إلى طريقة للتعلّم كنت قد نسيتها جزئيًا خلال سنواتي في الأكاديميا. ذكّرتني الساعات التي قضيتها في تعلّم النسج أني فيما مضى علّمتُ نفسي الحياكة عبر التكرار والتقليد والفشل وتجاوز الصعوبات، حتى أنني أستطيع أن أعيدَ حياكة قطعة كاملة لأُصلح خطأً صغيرًا، وكم كانت القدرة على تحويل قطعة قماش قماش مسطّحة إلى رداءٍ قابل للبس تبعث على البهجة .

كان لا بدّ للشمال العالمي، الذي فقد إلى حدٍّ كبير هذه المنهجيات التربوية الناهضة للرأسمالية ولاستخراج الموارد الطبيعية، أن يفرض علاقة آلية حصرًا مع المادّة والعالم كي يوسّع هيمنته. وفي حين صدّرت النيوليبرالية هذا المنطق إلى خارج الغرب، إلا أنّ أهمية المنهجيات التربوية المناهِضة لاستخراج الموارد في تزايدٍ مستمرّ. تُغذّي هذه المنهجيات النظريات السياسية للإلغاء والتعويض عن العبودية والتي تواجهنا بأطرٍ زمانية متعدّدة للاستدراك؛ أطرٍ لجبر ما أفسده الماضي والحاضر والمستقبل، بحيث تتمكّن الأجيال القادمة من ضمان حاجياتها الأساسية. جُلبتسياسات الإلغاء والتعويض عن العبودية هذه إلى الواجهة

في أعقاب جريمة إعدام جورج فلويد شنقًا علنيًا في 25 أيار/مايو 2020 الأمر الذي لم يُثِر الغضب في مواجهة حصانة الشرطة والدولة من العقاب وحسب، بل ودفع أيضًا بموجة مطلبية لمراجعة صياغة النصوص تحت النُصب التذكارية وإزالة التماثيل الكولونيالية من الفضاء العامّ. بدأ الحراك المُطالب بإزالة تماثيل الشخصيات الإمبريالية في 22 أيار/مايو 2020 في فور دو فرانس عاصمة جزر المارتينيك حين قام مجموعة من الشباب بإسقاط تمثال مفوّض الجمهورية الفرنسية فيكتور شولشير (22 أيار/مايو يوافق ذكرى إعلان العبيد تحرير أنفسهم عام 1848، استباقًا لوصول شولشير الذي كان من المفترض أن يطبّق مرسوم إلغاء العبودية الصادر 27 شباط/فبراير من ذلك العام). أخذت شابّتان سوداوان على عاتقهما المسؤولية القانونية لإسقاط التمثال. أخبرت الشابتان الشرطة والنظام القضائي بهدوءٍ وحزم أمام الكاميرا، لماذا قرّرتا الاشتراك في هذا العمل. أعلنتا «شولشير ليس منقذنا»، مصرّحتَيْن بسلسلةٍ من المطالب حول العدالة في مجال التعليم والرعاية الصحّية والاقتصاد وإدانة العنصرية. بالنسبة لهما كان التمثال انعكاسًا لعالم بناه أسلاف الرجل الأبيض المُتربّع على رأس السلطة اليوم، بما يضمن له إظهار وممارسة سلطته وغطرسته. عاشت الشابّتان في مدن هذا الرجل؛ مدن أجداده الغزاة المستعمرين الذين قمعوا ثورات المقهورين وانتقموا بكل شراسة ممّن رفعوا الصوت ضدّ سلطانهم؛ مدن رجالٍ جابوا أرجاء الأرض للاستغلال والسلب والنهب والاغتصاب والتخريب حتى يولَد أبناؤهم بامتيازات لا تعود أبدًا إلى مواهبهم ومهاراتهم. لم تسقط هاتان الشابّتان تمثالًا لمستعبد أو مالك عبيد أو مؤلّف نصّ عنصري سافر، بل لجمهوريّ فرنسي مناهضٍ للعبودية. أظهرتا أنّ الاستعمار والعنصرية استمرّا حتى في ظلّ الجمهورية، وأنّ إلغاء العبودية لم يجلب الحرية أو المساواة بل جلب النيوكولونيالية الجديدة. كانت تلك لفتةً قوية، إلا أنه في الإعلام وفي المناقشات الأكاديمية وفي دعوات لكتابة الأبحاث حول إزالة التماثيل، كان إسقاط تمثال إدوارد كولستون بمدينة بريستول في السادس من حزيران/يونيو هو الحدث الذي تصدّر حراك العام 2020 واُعتبر انطلاقته. لا أدّعي الأسبقية للمارتينيكيات لبداية الحراك من أجل إسقاط التماثيل العنصرية، إلا أنني أتساءل لمَ تدخل التاريخ لفتة مناهضة العنصرية دون لفتة أخرى مماثلة. ما هو ذلك الشيء الذي قد يجعل فعلًا مقاومًا لشابّةٍ مارتينيكية يغيب عن انتباه أو اهتمام أولئك الذين يسمّون أنفسهم حلفاء؟ كيف يمكننا أن نصوغ أرشيفاتنا بصيغةٍ ديكولونيالية؟ كيف يمكننا أن نفسّر كمية المواقف المناهضة للعنصرية، أن نلتفت لإبداع هذه المواقف، وأن نعتدّ بالفسحة التي تفتحها أمامنا حتى نستطيع جميعًا أن نتنفّس بشكلٍ أفضل؟

إننا نطالب نحن الفنانون، اللاجئون، المنفيّون، الفقراء، السود، المسلمون، العابرون(ات) بحقّنا في الحياة في هذه المدن وبحقّنا الجماعي في صياغة محيط يليق بنا؛ أن نمشي في الشوارع والميادين والحدائق دون أن نصادف تجسيدات مناصري العنصرية والذكورية وكراهية الأجانب وغيرها من الإيديولوجيات القاتلة الذين لطالما آمنوا بأن الإنسانية ينبغي أن تنقسم بين أناس تحمل حياتهم أهمية وآخرين لا تحمل حياتهم أهميّة البتّة. نريد أنْ نتنفّس.

يدعونا إسقاط هذه التماثيل لنتفكّر في الذاكرة الثقافية التي نرغب بتكوينها حول فضاءاتنا العامّة. الحاضر هو ما يجب أن يحدّد أي تماثيل وأي أشكال من التجسيد ينبغي أن تتواجد في الفضاء العام والحاضر، وهو ما يحدّد أي نضالات وأي أفعال ينبغي أن نحتفي بها. نريد قدرًا أقلّ من التماثيل العملاقة والإلهاءات الفنية الساخرة، ونريد كمًّا أقل من التركيبات الفنيّة الزائلة والجداريات و«الغابات التذكارية». التجسيدات التي نريدها حقًّا متجذّرة في الجماعيّة. ينبغي للخيال أن يكون في خدمة ذاكرة ديناميكية متحرّكة وفي خدمة إبداعات تتواجد بين الماضي والمستقبل، كما التشكّلات الأرضية في صحراء أتاكاما، أو إبداعات أخرى تصبو إلى رؤى مستقبلية أخرى. صارت حقوق الأجيال القادمة تُكتب بالفعل ويعبَّر عنها في شعارات الشباب ممّن تهدّد أرزاقهم أنانية النُخب وجشعها. تُرَدِّد هذه الشعارات صدى مطالب جيل الألفية بالعدالة والحرية والمساواة، إلا أنها كذلك تنطوي على تطلعات لعالم يتنفّس فيه الكل بحرية ويتمتّع فيه الكل بالأمان كجزء من مجتمعات ثوابتها الاعتناء بالأرض ومدّ يد العون وتقديم الماء والطعام لمن يحتاجونه، مجتمعات تحارب الاستغلال والعنصرية والقتل برعاية الدولة. ومن ثمّ تنخرط في تجارب تُولي الاحترام للأرض والطبيعة، وتجارب في أشكال التعايش والعيش الجماعي.

1 Achille Mbembe, "Le droit universel à la respiration," *Seneplus* (April 6, 2020), https://www.seneplus.com/opinions/le-droit-universel-la-respiration

2 Frantz Fanon, *Black Skin, White Masks* (New York, 2008), p. 201.

3 In Adrian Lahoud ed. and Andrea Bagnato, co-ed., *Rights of Future Generations: Conditions* (Berlin, 2019), pp. 16-21.

4 Aimé Césaire, *Discourse on Colonialism*, trans. Joan Pinkham (New York, 2001), p. 35.

5 Ruth Wilson Gilmore, *Golden Gulag: Prisons, Surplus, Crisis, and Opposition in Globalizing California* (Berkeley et al., 2007), p. 28.

6 See Isabell Lorey, *State of Insecurity. Government of the Precarious*, trans. Aileen Derieg (London, 2015).

7 المصدر نفسه، ص. 21

8 الاصطلاح الأصلي بالألمانية "Blut und Boden" وهو شعار سياسي يشير إلى مفهوم النقاء العرقي والوطني في الإيديولوجيا النازية. [المترجم]

9 Achille Mbembe, "Le droit universel à la respiration."

10 Grada Kilomba, *Plantation Memories: Episodes of Everyday Racism*, (Münster, 2008), p. 21.

11 Sayak Valencia, *Gore Capitalism* (California, 2018), p. 20.

12 Jasbir K. Puar, *The Right to Maim: Debility, Capacity, Disability* (Durham and London, 2017).

رسالة مفتوحة إلى حنّة أرندت

أرئيـــــــلّا عائشـــة أزولاي

ترجمه عن الإنكليزية فريق الأركِلوغ

عزيزتي حنّة،

أعلم أنّ في رسالتي شيئًا من التطفّل، لذلك سامحيني. ولكنّ عندي بعض الأفكار التي أودّ أن أطلعكِ عليها. أرغب في التحدّث إليكِ عن المواطَنة. فكلتانا أمضت سنوات من البحث في هذه المسألة. بدأتُ دارسةً لنصوصكِ. استعنتُ بها كي أمحوَ ما تعلّمتُه عن الهويّة التي علّبني فيها مصنع الإمبراطوريّة، واعتنقتُها كبديل عن غياب صوت «الكبار» الذين أخفقوا في تجنيب صغارهم خطّ إنتاج المواطنين في صورة الدولة. نبذتُ هويّتي الإسرائيليّة في صحبة فلسطينيين(ة) حُرموا(نَ) من هويّتهم(هِنّ). منحتني كتاباتكِ الجرأة كي أحيّد النظريّة السياسيّة عن ارتباطاتها الإمبرياليّة وكي أتخيّل بدلًا من ذلك وجود نمط مستقلّ من المعيشة في فلسطين ما قبل 1948. جعلتِني مواطنة في فلسطين المتخيَّلة تلك بفضل كتابك *The Human Condition* (الوضع البشري). وعندما رفضتُ الاعتراف بالمصوّر كمالكٍ للصورة الفوتوغرافيّة وأصررتُ على اكتظاظ الحدث الفوتوغرافي وعلى حقوق أصحاب الصور في كتابي *The Civil Contract of Photography* (العقد المدني للفوتوغرافيا) قبل عقد ونصف، اعتبرتُ ممارساتي في حينه شكلًا من أشكال «الخيال التاريخي».[1] ومع الوقت، توصّلت إلى رفض الماضي عمادًا رئيسًا في العمل التأريخي وتوصّلتُ إلى رؤية مشروعي على أنه «تاريخ محتمل» أو ما تطلق عليه سعديّة هارتمان مفهوم «الخُرافة النقديّة»[2]. [critical fabulation]

لحظة أدركتُ أنّ اسمي كان ينبغي أن يكون عائشة، على اسم جدّتي الجزائريّة الذي لم ينطقه والدي قط، انتابني غضب مباغت وألم لم أعهده من قبل. جرح مجهول غير مندمل بين جيلين قد نُكئ. أمضيتُ سنوات كثيرة وأنا أشعر بأنني أسيرة الانتساب إلى مشروع إمبريالي هو استعمار فلسطين. ثمّ وفي طرفة عين، أصبحتُ جزءًا من مشروع ثانٍ هو الاحتلال الفرنسي للجزائر في العام 1830. يخبّئ هذا الاحتلال لغزًا: من كانوا أسلافي قبل أن يصبحوا مواطنين في الجمهوريّة الفرنسيّة؟ ما الذي أراد الفرنسيّون هدمه عندما أطلقوا على الشعوب التي استعمروها صفة «السكّان الأصليّين» قبل أن ينتزعوا منهم هذا التصنيف الاستعلائيّ ويسلبوهم تقاليدهم في العيش ويجبروهم على التحوّل إلى مواطنين فرنسيّين؟

أشعر إلى حدّ ما أنّ فرصة طرح هذه الأسئلة قد ولّت. فوالدي المولود في الجزائر والذي غادرها ابن سبعة وعشرين ربيعًا عام 1949 قد مات ولا أقارب لديّ لأسأله عن الحياة التي لم أعشها هناك. لطالما أصررتُ على أنّ لا صلة لي بالجزائر — لا متاع ولا ذكريات ولا نكهات ولا أغانٍ ولا عادات ولا لغة — وها أنا الآن أتمرّد على ذاتي التي أمضت كلّ تلك السنوات خاضعة للكذبة الإمبرياليّة، كذبة أني لم أكن جزائريّة قطّ. كيف للمرء أن يتذكّر ما لم يتوارد إليه؟ وهل يضيع إلى غير رجعة؟ أهكذا خُيّل لوالدي عندما أُلغي قانون كريميو الذي اقتلع جذور أجداده من تلك الأرض وجعلهم مواطنين فرنسيّين؟ لم يتبقّ للذين انتقلوا إلى المدن من أصالتهم بعد نزع الجنسيّة عنهم سوى المنظومة العقابيّة. أحيلوا من قانون إلى آخر (قانون الأهالي). سبق أن فقدوا قسمًا يسيرًا من أنماط معيشتهم الأصليّة أو مُنعوا من ممارستها فيما نُبذ القسم الآخر منها بحجّة أنّه «بائد» أو «همجي». وعلى الأرجح لا تزال بعض الأغراض من مقوّمات الحياة الأهليّة تقبع في أقبية المتاحف الفرنسيّة أو الأوروبيّة، وأنا أنوي البحث عنها.

لو أنّني أبكرتُ قراءة نصّك «لماذا أُبطلَ قانون كريميو» لكنتُ واجهتُ أبي بالتفاصيل.[3] لكنني لم أقرأه، لم أستطع. أرجأتُ قراءة كتاباتك اليهوديّة إلى الآخر. تحاشيتُ لسنوات الانخراط في المسائل «اليهوديّة» في أبحاثي الأكاديميّة، حتّى عندما كنت في طور دراسة نمط المواطنيّة الذي تشكّل بتأثير الثورة الفرنسيّة. أهملتُ الأجزاء التي تتحدّث عن فرض المواطنة على اليهود في فرنسا غداة الثورة وحصرتُ اهتمامي في آليّات استثناء السود والنساء منها قبل أن يُعاد دمجهم بها في مرحلة متأخّرة. عندما أنظر إلى الوراء، يُخيّل لي أنّ رفضي الانخراط في المسائل اليهوديّة هو تعبير عن نوع من الانزياح. لقد كان ذلك بمثابة تحصين ضروري من تنصيب الدراسات اليهوديّة (ذاتها؟) كمنتج لتاريخ اليهود ومتحدّث عنه باعتباره، أي هذا التاريخ، موضوعًا متّسقًا نسبيًّا، خصوصًا بالنظر إلى التراتبيّات الداخليّة بين الجماعات التي تدّعي هذه الدراسات تمثيلها وتقاطعاتها مع الدراسات الإسرائيليّة ودراسات الهولوكوست. وفي اعتقادي أيضًا أنّ هذا الحذر أو الانزياح قد هيّأني لاستدعاء أسلافي وحثّهم على الاصطفاف معي في محاولتي لاسترجاع هويّاتهم قبل أن يردمها مشروعان استعماريّان متعاقبان. فلو نجح اليهود في رفض الانصياع لعقيدة المواطنة (لمرّتين على التوالي!) – بصفتهم يهودًا جزائريّين في فرنسا وشعبًا يهوديًّا في فلسطين – لما اضطررتُ إلى أخذ المسافة من المسائل «اليهوديّة». ولما كنتُ مُجبَرة على استدعاء الأسلاف بل كان لا بدّ لأصواتهم أن تدثّرني الآن.

أنا واحدة من أولئك «اليهود المشرقيّين» الذين ذكرتِهم في رسالتكِ إلى مواطن أوروبي آخر هو كارل جاسبرز عندما كتبتِ أنّنا «عبريّو المنطَق، عربٌ في الهيئة».[4] قلّة من

الناس يشبّهونني بالعرب – إن كنتُ فهمتُ مقصدكِ – كما أنّني لا أحمل أي إرث من يهود شمال أفريقيا. في الواقع، لا أبدو أنني أنتمي إلى اليهود المزراحيم كما عرّفهم وصنّفهم النظام الإسرائيلي. ففي حين أنّنا نتشارك في الجذور والمنشأ إلّا أنّ هجرة والدي إلى إسرائيل في العام 1949 كانت قد سبقت عمليّات الاستفزاز الضارية التي مارسها الصهاينة لحثّ يهود شمال أفريقيا على الهجرة إلى فلسطين التي هي إسرائيل اليوم. لم يشترك والدي في الهجرة الجماعيّة بتحريض صهيوني لذا لم يتعرّض للإذلال والاستغلال كسائر أقرانه من الذين هاجروا تحت لواء الجماعة الهويّاتية المعروفة بالمزراحيم. واقع الحال أنّ والدي كان ينظر إلى أقرانه، من موقع المواطن الفرنسي وهو دورٌ درّب نفسه على إتقانه، على أنّهم «يهود مشرقيّون» وقد نأى بنفسه عنهم في إسرائيل كما في الجزائر. فرضَ هذه القطيعة الجيليّة وأيّدتها أمي. وبقيتُ أنا أندب استحالة العودة. أمّا الآن وقد استعدتُ اسمي عائشة، فأنا على أتمّ الاستعداد لتضميد هذا الجرح الاستعماري الجيلي المطبوع في خرائط الندوب التي خلّفتها مناهضة للاستعمار والتي يمكن تتبّع آثارها على أجساد أفراد تلك العائلات التي أُجبِرت على الهجرة الطوعيّة. هل سمعت أغنيتهم المطالبة بإلغاء اتّفاقيّات الحدود؟

إنّ حسّ التضامن والمراعاة اللذين أستشفّهما من كتابتكِ عن يهود ومسلمي الجزائر، وانكبابك التامّ على دراسة التاريخ الحافل لعمليّة تجنيس اليهود ليصيروا مواطنين فرنسيّين، يمنعانني الآن — ولأوّل مرّة على ما أظنّ — من لوم والدي على تقبّله الجنسيّة الفرنسيّة واعتقاده أنّها ستيسّر له الإفلات من نظرة المستعمِر التي استبطنها في المحصّلة. هكذا أعدّته تلك البهلوانيّات الذهنيّة لاتّخاذ موضع المواطن-المستعمِر الذي كان ينتظره في إسرائيل بلا تردّد أو مساءلة. لم يعد في وسعي الآن أن أواصل إغفال العنصر «اليهودي» في مجال عملي، لا بوصفه هويّة مسلَّمة بل لكونه فَبركة استعماريّة وطرفًا في حملة لتصنيف مجموعات من البشر وفق معتقداتهم الدينيّة وانتزاعهم من عوالمهم لكي يكونوا مهيّئين للإحلال. لم يعد في وسعي أن أُسقط من سيرة هجرة والدي من الجزائر إلى إسرائيل عقودًا من عمليّات الاستئصال التي جعلت مغادرة أرض الأجداد إلى غير رجعة أمرًا قابلًا للتصوّر.

لجأتُ إلى كتاباتكِ عن إلغاء قانون كريميو نيابةً عن المذكّرات والرسائل التي لم يخطّها والدي علّني أتخيّل كيف كانت حياته قبل وبعد نظام فيشي. أعانتني تلك الكتابات على تركيب بعض الملامح من حياة عائلتي هناك استنادًا إلى التفاصيل القليلة التي أعرفها، والأهم أنّها أعانتني على فهم السبب الأعمق لتحفّظي على الانغماس في تاريخ «اليهود». فهكذا تاريخ يتطلّب الإقرار بوجود «اليهود» بصفتهم فئة مستقلّة في حدّ ذاتها، وكونهم مجموعة امتصّت المشاريع الاستعماريّة والإمبرياليّة تواريخها التعدديّة الغنيّة والعابرة للجغرافيا بهدف التأكيد على انتمائهم القومي — أو لا انتمائهم — ولتخفيض الثمن المفروض عليهم دفعه مقابل هويّة منفصلة عن عالمهم. وقد انقلب عالمهم ذاك الذي كانوا جزءًا من نسيجه بفعل الحركة عينها وآل إلى عالم معادٍ لليهود، ما سهّل تقبّلهم لعمليّة اقتلاعهم من أرضهم. بات إنتاج «اليهودي» بالمطلق بديلًا عن «اليهودي» المنسوب — اليهودي الجزائري، اليهودي المصري، اليهودي الفلسطيني — مصدرًا للاضطراب والضيق. يرشدني اسم عائشة عبر متاهة العوالم المدمَّرة على يد المستعمِر وعبر الهويّات المحذوفة والوعود الجديدة بالمواطنة الاستعماريّة. أخسرُ والدي، ربّما، ولكن لمَ أضحّي بالساحرات التي عرفتها جدّاتي شبيهات سيكوراكس في «عاصفة» شكسبير؟ لمَ أضحّي بتلك الساحرة الجزائريّة المنسيّة التي أشارت على حاكم الجزائر ألّا يستسلم لمخطط غزو الملك الفرنسي تشارلز الخامس في العام 1541 والتي سخّرت كلّ علومها ومواهبها لتحطيم مراكب الغازي؟

كي أتخلّى عن أحلامي
يلزم بدْءًا أن أجدَ
الفرْدَ
أو الشَّعْبَ
الذي أستودِعُها إيّاه
بكُلّ اطْمِئْنان[5]

كتبتِ عن قانون كريميو بُعيد شهر واحد من إصدار المفوّض السامي الفرنسي في الجزائر الأحكام المتعلّقة بحقوق اليهود في 14 آذار/مارس 1943 حيث بيّنتِ استمرار سياسات نظام فيشي بالرغم من سقوطه رسميًا في الجزائر. ففي حين أقرّ أحد هذه المراسيم بإعادة حقوق اليهود — «جميع التشريعات القانونيّة والإداريّة الصادرة بعد 22 حزيران/يونيو 1940 والتي تتضمّن التمييز ضدّ اليهود ملغيّة وباطلة» — تتحدّثين عن مرسوم آخر مناقض يقضي بأنّ «مرسوم 24 تشرين الأوّل/أكتوبر 1870 [أي قانون كريميو] المتعلّق بوضع الطائفة الإسرائيليّة في الجزائر لاغٍ.» لا أدري أين كان والدي في تلك اللحظة. أرجّح أنّه كان قد أُفرج عنه من معسكر الاعتقال في بيدو وتمّ تجنيده بُعيد ذلك في الجيش الفرنسي الحرّ الذي كان بحاجة إلى جنود من أبناء المستعمَرات لينتصر في الحرب وكذلك لمواجهة حركات التحرّر الوطنية، التي كانت شعوب المستعمَرات في كلّ أنحاء العالم تناضل في صفوفها، كي يحافظ على الإمبراطورية الفرنسية.

لا شكّ أنك كنتِ صائبة في مناصرتكِ لمسألة إعادة المواطنة لليهود. ولكنّني ممتنّة لك بالأخصّ على عدم استنادكِ إلى قانون كريميو 1870 كمنطلق لحجّتك في الدعوة إلى استعادة

المواطنيّة بل إلى مرسوم مجلس الشيوخ (*sénatus-consulte*) الذي صدر قبله بخمس سنوات. فقد دعا هذا المرسوم السابق كلًّا من اليهود والمسلمين إلى أن يصبحوا مواطنين فرنسيّين مقابل تخلّيهم نهائيًّا عن استقلالهم وعن الاحتكام إلى شرائعهم الدينيّة. وكما توردين «لم يندفع السكّان المحليّون سواء من المسلمين أو اليهود سعيًا للمواطنيّة الفرنسيّة.»[6] لم يتخطّ عدد المتقدّمين بطلب الجنسيّة المائتي مسلم و152 يهوديًّا. من هنا، لم يعد جائزًا القول إنّ ما حدث عام 1870 كان تجنيسًا لليهود من دون التشديد على أنّه تمّ بغير إرادتهم. أعرف هذه الحقيقة حق وإنْ لم يخبرني بها والدي أو جدّتي. أمّا امتثالهم لاحقًا ورضوخهم لهذه السياسات فهو مسألة أخرى لا تجوز مقاربتها بمنطق خطّي. وكأنّني ما زلتُ مقيّدةً بامتثالهم لذاك.

تتكلّمين بلهجة حاسمة عن السخرية الضمنيّة في القرار الفرنسي القاضي بتجنيس اليهود في العام 1870 والذي أتاح فبركة جماعة من المواطنين لمساعدة فرنسا على التعافي من هزيمتها في حربها مع الألمان ومن الأزمة السياسيّة التي نشأت عنها، وأيضًا على مجابهة ثورة المُقراني التي خرجت فيها 250 قبيلة ضدّ الاستعمار الفرنسي للجزائر في العام 1871: «لذا كان من المهمّ جدًّا بالنسبة للحكومة أن تكتسب 38 ألف مواطن فرنسي مُوالٍ في المستعمَرة تحسّبًا للقلاقل التي كانت تلوح في الأفق.» كم أحبّ انتقاء الألفاظ هذا — حتّى وإن لم يكن مقصودًا — كأنّك تعكسين ديناميّات مَنح المواطنة. ففي حين يُشار إلى المواطنة عادةً على أنّها عطيّة الحاكم للمحكوم، ترين أنّ قبول المواطنة هو عطيّة المحكوم للقوّة المستعمِرة. فروايتكِ تبيّن مَن أنعم على الآخر بالعطيّة وأي مصالح خدمتها تلك المنحة. إذًا فلنوضّح المسألة: لقد اكتسبت فرنسا في قرار واحد بمجرد بضع عبارات 38 ألف مواطن فرنسي مُوالٍ لها! كم أحبّ وضوحكِ، وكم أكره الفرنسيّين. لم يكن استغلالهم لليهود في سبيل مصالحهم إلّا بداية الكارثة والعدّ العكسي لإنهاء أنماط الحياة اليهوديّة في القارّة الأفريقيّة.

عمدت قوى الاستعمار أينما حلّت على تفرقة الشعوب المحلية إلى فئات وجماعات وغذّت التناحر فيما بينها خدمة لأهوائها ومصالحها. ودرّبت داخل كلّ جماعة من الجماعات، مجموعة من العسكر لقمع إخوانهم وأبناء شعبهم. أمّا في حالة يهود الجزائر، فقد تمّ تجنيد المعلّمين والحاخامات للإشراف على اعتناق اليهود للعلمانيّة الفرنسيّة وعلى اقتلاعهم من البيئات الثقافيّة والاجتماعيّة الإسلاميّة والعربيّة والبربريّة. لم تكن المواطنة عطيّة بل سلاحًا.

ولا عجب في أن يكون أدولف كريميو، المحامي اليهودي ووزير العدل في البرلمان الفرنسي الذي سُمّي القانون باسمه، واحدًا من مؤسّسي المدرسة الإسرائيليّة العالميّة وأحد مديريها، وهي شبكة مقرّها باريس تضمّ مجموعة من المدارس اليهوديّة الموزّعة على أنحاء منطقة المتوسّط. وقد اضطلعت تلك المدرسة، شأنها شأن سائر المدارس الداخليّة الإمبرياليّة في أرجاء العالم الاستعماري، بمهمّة تنشئة الرجل والمرأة الجديدين. وفي هذه الحال، كان الهدف تنشئة اليهودي(ة) الجديد(ة) القادر(ة) على التأقلم في النظام العلماني المسيحي الفرنسي. تولّى قيادة هذا المشروع للهندسة البشريّة مجموعة من المستعمرين الفرنسيّين بمعاونة يهود فرنسيّين سبق أن بايعوا الإمبراطوريّة الفرنسيّة. ولإدراك أداتيّة مشروع التجنيس ومدى وحشيته، يجب التفكير باليهود في الجزائر لا كجماعة شتاتيّة في المنفى — أي بوصفهم «يهودًا» في المقام الأول — بل باعتبارهم طائفة تنتمي إلى شعوب شمال إفريقيا الأصليّة التي أُخضِعت للاستعمار عام 1830. ولأنّني لا أذكر أنّني صادفتُ عبارة من البساطة والوضوح تصف الاستعمار الفرنسي للجزائر بأنّه استعمار فرنسا لليهود الجزائريّين، كان عليّ أن أنتظر اللحظة التي تؤهّلني لكتابتها بنفسي. فمجرّد قول هذه العبارة كفيل بتقويض السرديّة الإمبرياليّة التطوريّة التي تصوّر المواطنة على أنّها مكرمة من المستعمِر.

أمّا أن تعودي بعد كل هذا لتكتبي أنّ السبب الثاني لجعل اليهود مواطنين فرنسيّين «هو أنّهم بخلاف السكّان المسلمين ارتبطوا بعلاقة وثيقة مع موطنهم الأمّ من خلال أبناء ملّتهم من الفرنسيّين»، فإنّ ذلك يستتبع إهمال أو إنكار أنّ السيطرة الإمبرياليّة على الكيان السياسي في فرنسا والجزائر كانت قد أحكمت بالفعل في العام 1865 عندما صدر قرار مجلس الشيوخ وأنّ فكرة إيجاد ما يجب أن نطلق عليه الجماعات المستأصَلة من الداخل كانت قد ترسخت قولًا وممارسة. تنتابني رغبة بالصراخ وأنا أقرأ هذا الآن، أريد أن أهزّكِ من كتفيكِ كي أوقظكِ. أريدكِ أن تخبريني كيف أمكنكِ بالرغم من فهمكِ العميق «لغيريّة» يهود الجزائر وللحياة التي تَشاركوها مع المسلمين، كيف أمكنكِ أن تقعي في فخّ وصل فئة مستعمَرة، أي «اليهود»، بـ«موطنهم الأمّ من خلال أشقّائهم الفرنسيين؟» إذ لا سبيل لإيجاد رابطة الأخوّة هذه بين الأوروبيّين واليهود الجزائريّين على حساب قرون من التآخي مع المسلمين إلّا من خلال تطهير «اليهود» من أصولهم وعالمهم. يصحّ النظر إلى نضال بعض الجماعات اليهوديّة للحصول على المواطنة على أنّه انتصار بلا شكّ، خصوصًا في السياق الفرنسي حيث مُنع الكثير من اليهود من الإقامة داخل أسوار المدينة أو حُصروا بممارسة عدد قليل من المهن الوضيعة كالربا والبيع المتجوّل وتجارة المواشي.[7] ولكن أن يتحوّل هذا الاضطرار إلى مزية وأن تصبح معيارًا لجميع أشكال العلاقات؟ زلّتكِ هذه تثير غضبي وتوجّسي.

في «أصول الشموليّة»، تدركين ببراعة كُنْه الإمبرياليّة في قولكِ إنّ «التوسع كهدف نهائي وأسمى للسياسة هو المغزى السياسي للإمبريالية» وتحدّدين الصيغة الشموليّة

على أنّها «التوسّع من أجل التوسّع».[8] وإذ ذاك أعجب كيف فاتتكِ الماهية التوسعيّة لنمط المواطنة الذي ابتدعته الإمبرياليّة والدور الذي لعبه في تسهيل عمليّات التوسّع الجغرافي؟ تكادين تدركينها في سياق تحليلكِ لقانون كريميو — متطرّقةً إلى إصداره وإلغائه ومن ثمّ إعادته إلى حيّز التنفيذ — ليس فيما يتعلّق باليهود فحسب بل بالكيان السياسي الفرنسي الذي رأى في هذا القانون «فاتحة ووسيلة لاجتذاب العرب بفضل الامتيازات المتّصلة بالمواطنة.»[9] لكنّك لا تلبثين في المقطع التالي أن تسلّمي بالادّعاء الإمبريالي القائل بالطبيعة الشاملة للمواطنة وأنّها تمثّل مستوى تقدميًّا من الحكم بالرغم من تبيانكِ لجذورها المصطنعة. سأعطيكِ مثالًا من حديثكِ عن النساء. فأنتِ تردّين أسباب فشل سياسة الإدماج الفرنسيّة إلى رفض المسلمين «التخلّي عن أحوالهم الشخصيّة (التي تتيح لهم أسوة باليهود تعدّد الزوجات وإنكار حقوق النساء)»، ولكنّك ومن دون أي مبرّر تعمدين إلى إظهار الفرنسيّين في صورة المعنيّين بحقوق النساء: «يرتكز القانون المدني والقانون الجزائي الفرنسي على المساواة بين الجنسين.»[10] لا أفهم ما الذي حدا بك إلى تصوير الفرنسيّين على أنّهم الأكثر تطوّرًا واستبدال تنويعات العلاقات البشريّة بنموذج أحاديّ خطّي يقيّم مستويات التطوّر السياسي. ما كنت لأثير هذا الموضوع أو لأمتعض حتّى لولا أنني مدينة لكتاباتك في تمرّدي على ما تلقّنته عن المواطنة ورفضي لوعودها السامّة. هل أبالغ إن قلتُ إنّني أشعر بالخذلان وأريد أن أعرف السبب، وأن أعرف ما إذا كنتِ قد خذلتِ نفسكِ كذلك؟

لم يكن اليهود في الجزائر مجرّد «يهود ناطقين بالعربيّة» كما تصفينهم. فقد كانوا يتكلّمون اللغات العربيّة-اليهوديّة واللادينو والبربرية-اليهوديّة والأمازيغيّة. تعلمين أنّهم تشاركوا مع العرب ما هو أبعد من اللغة، بل يصحّ التأكيد على أنّ أغلب ما تقاسموه ليس ذا صلة بما هو «مسلم» أو «يهودي» بل يعود إلى زمن سابق على خلق التمايز الهويّاتي بين هاتين الجماعتين. أحيانًا، تنمّ كتاباتك عن تضارب مستعصٍ في المفاهيم حتّى في متن الجملة الواحدة. فتقولين إنّ اليهود «لم يختلفوا كثيرًا من حيث العادات عن محيطهم العربي» لتعودي مجدّدًا فتتبنّين منظور المستعمِر الفرنسي عندما تضيفين: «بدت [هذه العادات] للفرنسيّين غير مطابقة لعادات الشعب اليهودي، وإنّما عادات سيّئة لمجموعة صغيرة من ذلك الشعب التي ضلّت طريق الهداية والتي يمكن إصلاحها بسهولة من قبل الأكثريّة من أبناء ملّتها.» التناقض بين المقولتين واضح ولا يمكن إغفاله.

تواصلتُ قبل بضعة أسابيع مع أبناء خالتي الذين وُلدوا في الجزائر وهاجروا إلى فرنسا العام 1962 بعدما أصبحت حياة اليهود في الجزائر مستحيلة. كنت قد التقيتهم مرّة أو مرّتين وأنا في مطلع العشرينات وكنت لا أفقه حرفًا في اللغة الفرنسيّة. كتبتُ إليهم أسألهم عن حياة والدي في الجزائر وعن اسم جدّتي عائشة. لا تسأليني كيف أخطأت في تهجئة الاسم وأبدلتُ حرف c بحرف s فذلك سيحرفنا بعيدًا عن بيت القصيد. إليكِ ما وردني منهم ردًّا على أسئلتي: «الاسم الأوّل Aicha نسبة إلى امرأة ثريّة جدًّا كانت تعيش في وهران. كانت جدّتي تخبرنا أنّ الأساور الذهبيّة كانت تلفّ ذراعيها من المعصم إلى المرفق!!! وقد اختارت هذه المرأة جدّتي لتحمل اسمها الأوّل. من تكون تلك المرأة. لا أدري.»

لا تستغربي جهلي التامّ بعائشة الثانية، فأنتِ تعلمين كم من الوقت استغرقني كي أتعرّف إلى اسم جدّتي الحقيقي. خيط أريادني الخاصّ بي مجدول من ثلاث خصلات. الأولى ذكرى بعيدة مبهمة يذكر فيها والدي أنّ له جدّة ثالثة. لا أذكر التفاصيل أو ربّما لم تكن هنالك أي تفاصيل سوى أنّه لم يستطِع أن يفسّر نوع القرابة التي تربطه بتلك المرأة. قال شيئًا عن رابطة «خارج الزواج». الخصلة الثانية تتعلّق بتفصيلة أخرى سمعتها من أبناء خالتي عن جدّتي: «قامت بإحدى وعشرين رحلة بالطائرة إلى باريس لزيارة بناتها وستًّا إلى إسرائيل» (جميعها في غضون عقد واحد من الزمن في الخمسينيّات أي قبل رواج تأجير الرحلات الجويّة) مضيفين: «لقد كانت جدّتي فخورة بهذا الاسم لأنّها [عائشة الأخرى] قد باركتها وكانت تعطيها المال دائمًا ولا سيّما عندما كانت تنوي السفر لزيارة بناتها أو روجيه [والدي].»

لا زلت لا أعرف من تكون هذه الجدّة الثالثة ولكنّني أعتقد أنّها كانت الزوجة الثانية لجدّي الأكبر. وبما أنّ تعدّد الزوجات كان قد حُظر في المدن — كانت عائلتي تقيم بين أرزيو ووهران — وفي وقت كان اليهود قد تحوّلوا إلى مواطنين فرنسيّين، فقد توجّب إخفاء صلة القرابة الحقيقيّة مع عائشة كي تتمكّن من الاستمرار في العيش في كنف العائلة حيث الحبّ والدعم المادّي والأشكال الأخرى من الرعاية التي أنعمَت بها على جدّتي. أمّا الخصلة الثالثة فلها علاقة بأمر أورده أبناء خالتي في أوّل ردّ لهم على رسالتي الإلكترونيّة. تبرّعوا من تلقاء نفسهم بإيجاد تفسير للتجاوزات المتعلّقة بالزواج: «كانت الزيجات المختلَطة محرّمة وكانت عقوبتها الضرب المبرح للرجال والنبذ الاجتماعي للنساء.» لم تكن تلك التجاوزات إلّا نتيجة لمنظومة من الأحكام الرافضة لتشكيلات النسب والقربى التي لا تتّسق مع النموذج العائليّ الغيريّ الأبويّ الفرنسيّ. في هذا المناخ، أعتقد أن الذاكرة المتعلّقة بشبكات العلاقات العائليّة في زمن ما قبل الحقبة الفرنسيّة قد تواتر إلينا في صيغة اختلالات وتجاوزات في روابط الزواج. إن كنتِ تتساءلين لمَ عساني أخبركِ عن جدّتي الثالثة، فذلك لأنكِ تطرّقتِ إلى تعدّد الزوجات كأحد العوامل التي أشعلت رفض سكّان الجزائر الأصليّين سواء من اليهود أو من المسلمين لقبول الجنسيّة الفرنسيّة. وبالنظر إلى فهمكِ الضئيل لأحوال معيشة اليهود في شمال إفريقيا قبل الاستعمار واستخدامكِ اللاحق لمصطلح

«اليهود» كهويّة منفيّة، فإنّكِ لا ترين في الزواج المتعدّد دلالة على نمط متخلّف من العلاقات. على العكس من ذلك، تبرّرين تعدّد الزوجات بوصفه نموذجًا اجتماعيًّا يؤمّن الاستمراريّة والحماية من الاستغلال الواقع على طبقة غير الملّاكين. فقد كانت النساء، على حدّ تعبيركِ، المصدر الأساسي «لليد العاملة» بالنسبة إلى الفلّاح والوحيد الذي يطيق تكلفة «استخدامه». وتلمّحين إلى وجود مصلحة مباشرة لدى «الفرنسيّين المستعمرين، وأغلبيّتهم من كبار ملاك الأراضي الذين راكموا ثرواتهم عن طريق استغلال العمالة المحليّة الرخيصة بالإضافة إلى المسؤولين الحكوميّين المؤيّدين هم»، في القضاء على هذه الأنساق الأسريّة المتعدّدة بهدف تجريد الأفراد من منظومة الحماية وجعلهم أكثر عرضة للاستغلال. إذ لا يقتصر الأمر على استغلال النساء في العمل في الأراضي التي استولى عليها المستوطنون بأجر زهيد، بل ينتهي بهنّ المطاف أيضًا بفقدان بنى التعاضد والرعاية والحماية التي توفّرها الوحدة الأسريّة الموسّعة لأفرادها. ولكنّكِ تعودين فتتبنّين نظرة المستعمِر بعيدًا عن الإقرار بأنماط معيشة اليهود الجزائريّين. تنتقلين من الفلّاح إلى سكّان المدينة فتشيرين باقتضاب إلى أنّ «ظاهرة تعدّد الزوجات قد أوشكت على الزوال».[11] لِعبارة «أوشكت على الزوال» هذه رنّة إمبريالية مألوفة غايتها التغني بأمرٍ لم ينجز بعد بينما يُتناول وكأنّه تحقق بالفعل.

قد لا أمتلك أي دليل لإثبات التالي (حتّى الآن) ولكنّني على قناعة بأنّ المرأة الثانية التي تُدعى عائشة، والتي حملت اسمَها جدّتي المولودة بعد عقدين من صدور قانون كريميو، كانت واحدة من أفراد الأسرة الموسّعة من السكّان الأصليّين والتي لم تعد نموذجًا مقبولًا في أوساط «المهوّدين» «المفرنَسين». وهنالك أمثلة ذات دلالة من دعاوى قانونيّة في المحاكم تدين يهودًا متّهمين بتزوير تواريخ وعلاقات نسب في الوثائق الرسميّة لإخفاء عصيانهم لقانون منع تعدّد الزوجات. من هنا فإنّ لحظة التلاشي شبه التامّ للنماذج الأسريّة المتعدّدة ما هو سوى طريقة أخرى لوصف القضاء شبه التام على أنماط العيش المشتركة بين العرب المسلمين والعرب اليهود.

يخلق التعبير الإمبريالي «أوشك على الزوال» محرّمات وموضوعات يصعب الكلام فيها من دون مواجهة الاتّهام بمعاداة النسويّة وبالمحافظة والرجعيّة. لذا أدين لك بالامتنان لطرحكِ إمكانيّة البحث في مسألة تعدّد الزواجات في الجزائر ضمن سياقه بوصفه تكوينًا أسريًّا شائعًا لدى اليهود والمسلمين ونمطًا اجتماعيًّا سياسيًّا من أنماط الشراكة والرعاية. وإن كان إدماج اليهود منذ منتصف القرن الثامن عشر فصاعدًا بمثابة حركة «لإدخال اليهود في التنوير» كما كنتِ قد كتبتِ في مقالة سابقة، فلا شكّ أن تكون قد سبقته عمليّة إدماج مجموعات أصغر عن طريق الباحثين الذين لم يعد بإمكانهم الحديث عن الأسر ذات الزيجات المتعدّدة كتكوين اجتماعي سياسي للحماية والتعاضد من دون الوقوع في اتّهامات بالهمجية ومعاداة النسويّة والتنوير. كما لم يعد بإمكانهم الإشارة إلى احتمال تمتّع النساء ما قبل الإدماج في عصر التنوير بحقوق أوسع من تلك التي تقدّمها منظومة الملكيّة الأبويّة من خلال الزواج الأحادي البرجوازي. ومن يتجرّأ على الدفاع عن ذاك النسق يُنظر إليه على أنّه قد فشل في الاندماج ويجب تجنّبه بأي ثمن. هكذا وصل الفرنسيّون من أصول يهوديّة إلى الجزائر كرسُل تنويريّين للثورة الفرنسيّة لنشر الحضارة على وجهين: إدماج العرب اليهود في جماعة «اليهود» وتهيئتهم لبلوغ المرحلة النهائيّة من الإدماج الحقيقي بجعلهم أوروبّيين. لو قدّر لكِ أن تطّلعي على بحث جوديت سوركيس عن تعدّد الزوجات والسيادة في الجزائر تحت الاستعمار الفرنسي وأنت تكتبين، أو على بحث جوشوا شراير في الوثائق الخاصّة التي خلّفها بعض مرسَلي التنوير الفرنسيّين اليهود، لارتسمت لك صورة شديدة العجب. عندما ألغى المجلس المركزي في فرنسا الذي يعود تأسيسه إلى العهد النابليوني، المرجعيّة الحاخاميّة في الجزائر، تحوّل الحاخامات المحلّيون من ممارسة أعمال الخيريّة والشعائريّة إلى التحكّم بحيوات النساء عبر القضاء على ممارسات تعدّد الزوجات والطلاق كوسيلة لإقصاء «اليهود» الجدد عن أبناء جلدتهم من المسلمين. يجدر بنا النظر إلى هذا النوع من الإدماج كضرب من الإبادة الثقافيّة شنّه المستعمِرون الاستيطانيّون ونفّذه اليهود الأوروبيّون ضدّ أنماط الحياة العربيّة اليهوديّة بهدف إدماج العرب اليهود في الهويّة «اليهوديّة» المجرّدة من أي انتماء كي يُمنحوا من بعدها «هبة» المواطنة الأوروبيّة. ولم تكن هذه الممارسات العنصريّة السائدة منذ منتصف القرن التاسع عشر من قبل اليهود الأوروبيّين تجاه اليهود المشرقيّين قد حلّت موضع الدراسة بعد كجزء من منظومات إنتاج الهويّات العرقيّة الإمبرياليّة.

إلّا أنّ عملكِ قد أتاح لنا أن نرى ذلك ممكنًا حتّى وإنْ لم تعي ذلك. فأنتِ تصوّرين هذه الحملة الشرسة لإعادة تثقيف الحاخامات المحلّيين واستغلال سلطتهم داخل المجتمعات اليهوديّة العربيّة. تصفين كيف استدرج المستعمِرون الفرنسيّون «اليهود» حديثي الاندماج في فرنسا إلى المجاهرة «مغايرتهم لليهوديّة الشرقيّة». وقد تولّى اليهود الفرنسيّون الممثّلون بمجلس باريس المركزي مسؤوليّة إلغاء صلاحيات الحاخامات المحليين وضمان الإدماج السريع لليهود الجزائريّين. وبناء على ذلك، «أُعطي مجلس باريس السلطة القانونيّة لتعيين جميع الحاخامات الجزائريّين»، بعد صدور قانون كريميو، «وعمدت مدارس الاتّحاد الإسرائيلي العالمي بدعم من سياسات المجلس إلى إدماج اليهود الناطقين بالعربيّة في وقت قصير نسبيًّا وحوّلتهم إلى مواطنين فرنسيّين مخلصين».[12] ما من سبيل لوصف هذا النوع من

الممارسات سوى بالهجمة الاستعماريّة على أنماط الحياة المحلّية الأصليّة. وبالعودة إلى الوثائق المتناثرة والتي تشهد على رفض السكّان الأصليّين الانضواء تحت مظلّة القانون الفرنسي والصفقة المتّصلة به، أدعو إلى قراءة نصّ قانون كريميو للعام 1870 «جميع الإسرائيليين الأهالي في أقاليم الجزائر قد أصبحوا مواطنين فرنسيين» باعتباره يمثّل القصاص الأفظع في سبيل قمع الرفض والمعارضة للمواطنة.

عندما كتبتِ نصّكِ عام 1943، لم تكن هنالك حاجة لشرح المقصود «بالأحوال الشخصيّة» التي أُجبر السكّان الأصليّون على التخلّي عنها كي يصبحوا مواطنين. ولكنّكِ توضحين أنّها لم تكن الأمر الوحيد الذي أُجبروا على التخلّي عنه. دعيني أوضّح هذه النقطة لمن سيقرؤون هذه الرسالة المفتوحة إليكِ: لقد كانت «الأحوال الشخصيّة» تدبيرًا استعماريًا، وضعيّة قانونيّة يصنّف على أساسها السكّان الأصليّون المستعمَرون تتيح لهم الاستمرار في احترام شعائرهم الإسلاميّة أو اليهوديّة تحت سلطة القانون الفرنسي الجديد. معنى ذلك أنّ منظومة الحقوق التي ولدوا وعاشوا في كنفها لقرون قبل مجيء الاستعمار قد باتت منفصلة تمامًا عن العالم الذي كانت تنتمي إليه. تحوّلت هذه المنظومة إلى مجموعة موحّدة من القوانين تحت إشراف الحكّام الفرنسيّين الذين يملكون صلاحيّة اتّخاذ القرار في شأن شروط وحيثيّة وكيفيّة تطبيقها على السكّان المحلّيين. ولا يمكن فصل لحظة الانتصار المخادعة هذه والتي شهدت تحوّل اليهود إلى مواطنين عن اللحظة التي فقد فيها اليهود الحقّ في الوجود، فقد مهّد لها حرمانهم من حقّهم في أن يكونوا يهودًا جزائريّين. عندما نبني تصوّرنا عن المواطنيّة كشيء يُمنح تحت ظرف معيّن لمجموعة من الناس دون سواهم، لا يجب أن نُفاجأ عندما نجدها تُنزَع منهم في ظروف مختلفة. هكذا انتُزعت الجنسيّة الفرنسيّة من يهود الجزائر عام 1940 ثمّ أُعيدت إليهم عام 1943 ثم نُزعت من سياقها الأصلي عندما دُعي اليهود الجزائريّون إلى مغادرة موطنهم في العام 1962 بحجّة هذه الجنسيّة. ليس هذا بالحادث العرضي بل هو في صميم مفهوم المواطنيّة الإمبريالي. وفي العام 1943، لم تكتفي أنتِ بالدفاع عن حقّ استعادة الجنسيّة في مواجهة جنرالات فيشي المتخفّين الذين حكموا الجزائر وحجبوا مواطنيّة اليهود الجزائريّين وحقوقهم القانونيّة، بل جهدتِ لسرد تاريخ هذه المواطنة من وجهة نظر المضطهَدين حتى من قبل أن يدركوا مظلوميّتهم جرّاء حرمانهم منها.

حديثي مع أجدادي الأموات — أولئك الذين وُلدوا قبل عام 1830 أي قبل أن تفرض تكنولوجيا الغزو الإمبريالي المواطنة الأوروبيّة على العالم اليهودي العربي — ساهم في تعميق إدراكي لمدى إضرار مفهوم المواطنة بالتعدّدية والتنوّع في الحياة اليهوديّة حول العالم بشكل عامّ وفي شمال أفريقيا بشكل خاصّ. لقد كان على اليهود الحائزين على الجنسيّة الفرنسيّة أن يثبتوا ولاءهم عن طريق الاندماج الثقافي والسياسي ومراقبة إدماج اليهود الآخرين للدولة التي منحتهم تلك المواطنة والتي تمتلك في الوقت عينه سلطة انتزاعها منهم ساعة تشاء. لولا أن فُرض على اليهود إثبات ولائهم لكانت بانت المأساة التي افتتُحت باستعمار الجزائر عام 1830 والتدمير التدريجي للعالم العربي الذي شكّل موطنًا لليهود بصورة أوضح كامتداد للاستعمار الإبادي الذي ضرب الأجزاء الأخرى من إفريقيا في القرنين التاسع عشر والعشرين، ولما كانت طُمست ذاكرة هذه المأساة بسهولة مقابل أسطورة تحرير الأوروبيّين لليهود في أوروبا وخارجها. تلك الأسطورة عينها التي يسّرت تهجير اليهود في نهاية الحرب العالميّة الثانية من أوروبا ولاحقًا من العالم الإسلامي إلى فلسطين وإدماجهم فيها، أي إلى مشروع استعماري ثانٍ لا يزال يؤدّي دورًا أساسيًا في تكريس السلطة الإمبرياليّة الأورو-أميركيّة العالميّة. هناك، بصفتهم مواطنين في دولة جديدة شاركوا ولا يزالون في التدمير المستمرّ لفلسطين باسم تلك المواطنة الأوروبيّة التمييزية من نفس النمط. لا يسعني أن أختم هذه الرسالة من دون أن أطرح عليكِ هذا السؤال: هل فكّرتِ يومًا بدور يهود أوروبا في تدمير معيشة اليهود العرب وعالمهم؟

المخلصة،
عائشة

1 أرئيلا أزولاي، *The Civil Contract of Photography*، ترجمه عن العبرية ريلا مازالي وروفيك دانييلي، نيويورك 2012.

2 انظروا أرئيلا أزولاي، *Potential History: Unlearning Imperialism*، لندن 2019 وسعديّة هارتمان، "Venus in Two Acts," *Small Axe: A Caribbean Journal of Criticism* vol. 12 no. 2 (2008): 1-14.

3 Hannah Arendt, *The Jewish Writings* (New York, 2008).

4 Hannah Arendt to Karl Jaspers in *Correspondence: Hannah Arendt, Karl Jaspers*, 1926-1969, eds. Lotte Kohler and Hans Saner (New York, 1996), p. 43.

5 * من قصيدة "أمام المرآة" لعبد اللطيف اللعبي الواردة في ديوانه *Presque Riens* (نُتف لا غير، مونتروي 2020) ص. .13 نقلها إلى العربية من الفرنسيّة محمد خماسي كما نُشرت في جريدة العربي الجديد، 28 تشرين الثاني/ نوفمبر 2020.
https://www.alaraby.co.uk/culture/ أمام-المِرآة
[المترجم]

6 Arendt, *The Jewish Writings*, p. 246.

7 للمزيد حول المهن التي مارسها اليهود قبل الثورة الفرنسية وبعدها، انظروا:
Zosa Szajkowski, "Notes on the Occupational Status of French Jews, 1800-1880," *Proceedings of the American Academy for Jewish Research*, 1979–1980, Vol. 46/47, Jubilee Volume

8 Hannah Arendt, *The Origins of Totalitarianism* (Orlando, FL, 1975), p. 125.

9 Arendt, *The Jewish Writings*, p. 249.

10 المصدر نفسه، ص. 248.

11 Hannah Arendt, *The Jewish Writings* (New York, 2008).

12 المرجع السابق ص. 246.

في اختيار أسلافنا: نحو سلالة ديكولونيالية

حورية بوثلجة

ترجمها عن الإنكليزية زياد دلال

«من بين كلّ احتياجات روح الإنسان،
تبقى أهمّها حاجتنا للماضي.»
—سيمون فايل

«الهجرة هي تغيير الفرد لسلالة نَسَبه.»
—مليكة سورل-صاتر

تستمرّ جائحة كورونا والأزمة الصحيّة التي سبّبتها بالتأثير على مجتمعات عالم الشمال. لحدّ الآن، كانت هذه المجتمعات قد تمكّنت - بفضل الإمكانيات الهائلة لحكوماتها الرأسمالية واحتكارها الجزئي لصناعة الأسلحة النووية - من تجنّب نتائج كلّ من الأزمات الاقتصادية، والجوائح، والكوارث الطبيعية التي تعصف ببلدان عالم الجنوب أولًا وغالبًا. بدأت علامات هشاشتنا الجديدة تتجسّد وتظهر مع مرور الزمن في آخر عشرين سنة، معلنة بنهايةً حتميةً لحصانتنا ومناعتنا.[1] على هذا النحو، كانت هجمات 11 أيلول أولى الطلقات التحذيرية للأزمات العالمية القادمة، حيث أنها كانت حدثًا ذا قوّة تغييرية يدقّ ناقوسَ الهلاك لإحساس الغرب بالحصانة. منذ ذلك الوقت واجهنا داخل حدود الإمبراطورية الغربية أوبئة مختلفة (مرض كروتزفيلد جاكوب، وفيروس الإنفلونزا H1N1، وغيرها من الأوبئة)، وحوادث نووية، وهجمات إرهابية في الداخل الأوروبي، وأزمة اقتصاديّة كُبرى عام 2008 أدّت إلى ظهور حركات اجتماعية كبيرة (حركة الإندغنادوس في إسبانيا، وحركة احتلال وول ستريت في الولايات المتحدة، وحركة السترات الصفراء في فرنسا). بالرغم من نطاقه غير المسبوق، الوباء الحالي ما هو إلّا إشارةً إضافيةً للتدهور الوشيك لهذه الحقبة الحضارية. في هذه المرحلة، سيخاف المتشائمون من ردود فعل عنيفة ومدمّرة لهذا الوحش الجريح. في الجهة المقابلة، يرى المتفائلون من المذهب الغرامشيّ فرصة لمشاهدة احتضار هذا الوحش- وهل يجرؤون على صياغة نهاية المنطق الرأسماليّ المبنيّ على انتزاع الربح؟ إذا كنا نريد أن نسير مع هذه النظرة فمن الضروري أن نواجه ونعادي المنطق الانتزاعيّ، وبناءً على ذلك، يصبح من الضروري أن نهيّئ ونجسّد طُرقًا بديلة للوجود. بإمكاننا الاعتماد على المذهب الماركسيّ للتحرّر، الذي يقدّم لنا مفتاحًا لفكّ المنطق الرأسمالي بطريقة ماديّة. ولكن هذا لن يكون كافيًا على الأغلب. تدعونا دونا هاراواي، بشكلٍ حدسيّ، أن «ألا نبارح العناء.» وقد تكون على حقّ: قد ينبغي علينا أن نتعايش مع الخطر وانعدام الأمان، ولكن هذا أيضًا سيُثبت أنه غير كافٍ. الظرف الحالي يحثّنا على الانخراط في ثورة ثقافيّة شاملة الطبع : إنه شغب مبنيّ على منظور معادٍ للاستعمار يستبدل معجمنا السياسيّ الحالي بمعجمٍ جديد يناطح الأيدولوجيا الليبرالية التي تعمل كبوصلة لدى الشعوب بصفتها مستهلكين والتي يجب أن نتخلّص منها عاجلًا.

دعونا نرصد المشهد: يتمّ تجريد شعوب عالم الشمال من مناعتهم، بينما تثور شعوب عالم الجنوب في كل مكان ضدّ القمع الذي اتخذته حكومات ما بعد الاستعمار منهجًا لها. يتفتّت حاليًا الميثاق العرقي الاجتماعي الذي سمح للبروليتاريا البيضاء بالتحالف مع الطبقة الحاكمة جرّاء جشع النظام الرأسمالي. ولكن قد تكون أوراقنا رابحة في هذه اللعبة. نعرفُ أنّ التمهيد للفاشية في هذه الأوضاع سيكون عنده الأفضلية فوق كل شيءٍ آخر، وخاصّةً فوق زخْم الحركات الثورية. ولكن هذه الحركات الثورية لا تستطيع أن تستغني عن المنظور المعادي للاستعمار، أيّ المنظور الديكولونيالي. إذا كانت هاراواي على حقّ بدعوتها ألا نبارح العناء، فهي لا تستطيع نسيان أنّ شعوب العالم الجنوبي كانوا وما زالوا يعايشون العناء منذ عام 1492. بالتالي، المهمّة الآن هي الاعتراف بهذا العناء القديم ورصد جذوره الراسخة. كما أنّه علينا الاعتراف بالنضالات والصراعات التي خاضها أسلاف مَن لا يزالون يعايشون هذا العناء في شكله الحالي. من أجل المضي في هذه المهمّة، علينا أن نطرح ونجيب عن بعض الأسئلة. في فرنسا، لطالما فرضت الأيديولوجيا الاستعمارية نَسَبًا أسطوريًا [mythical filiation] على المجتمعات المتعدّدة عرقيًا تصلهم بشعوب بلاد الغال. كما ينبغي، رُفض هذا النسب من قِبل الفكر المعادي للإستعمار والصراعات الديكولونياليّة. ولكن، هل استطعنا فعلًا، كمجتمعات تمّ «استيعابها» و«تبييضها،» أن ننجو من هذا النسب؟ إلى أي درجة نستطيع إنكار كوننا أحفاد القائد الغاليّ فارسانجيتوراكس [Vercingetorix] وشارل ديغول؟ في المقابل، يقتنع بيض فرنسا بهذه الفرضية. ولكن هل هم حقًا أحفاد شعوب بلاد الغال؟ ألا نستطيع أن نعتبرهم أحفاد جيرونيمو وتوسان لوفرتور، أو حتى الأمير عبد القادر؟ هل نستطيع أن نختار أسلافنا؟ إذا التزمنا بفكرِ س. ل. ر. جايمز، فالجواب حتمًا سيكون نعم. «هؤلاء أسلافي، هؤلاء شعبي. وهُم أسلافكم وشعبكم إذا أردتم.»[2] عندما يعلن سارتر: «حرّروا فرنسا من الجزائر،» فنحن مدعوون لتفسير هذا الشعار كما يلي: لا تتحرّر فرنسا إلّا من خلال حريّة الجزائر، أو حتى:

الفرنسيون لن يكونوا احرارًا إلّا عندما يصبح الجزائريون أحرارًا. تبدو دعوة جايمز مهولة ومُدوخِة في سخائها لدرجة أنها تفتح علينا آفاقًا مجهولة. بالفعل، كيف نقلب هزائم البعض إلى انتصارات للجميع؟ وكيف نعيد تصوّرنا لشخصيات تاريخية كانت تُعتبَر مهزومة طوال القرون الخمسة الماضية لنحوّلهم إلى منتصرين ؟

كان مقتل جورج فلويد المسجّل في مدينة مينيابوليس حدثًا مزلزلاً ذا قوّة نادرة. بثّ هذا الحدث موجات صدمية لسائر المجتمعات الديمقراطية الغربية. ونتيجةً لذلك، رأينا مظاهرات معادية للعنصرية في كل بلدٍ يوجد فيه حضور حاشد لذوات ما بعد الاستعمار [postcolonial subjects] — ويرجع هذا جزئيًا إلى رغبتهم في التعبير عن التضامن مع السود الذين يعيشون في أمريكا، بالإضافة إلى تنديدهم بشتّى أشكال العنصرية المنهجية التي يقعون ضحيّتها كسكّان من ذوي البشرة غير البيضاء في المتروبول الأبيض. أتت هذه الفورات العفوية لتكشف ما كانت تشدّد عليه الحركات الديكولونياليّة: أي أنّ الخيط المشترك بين الدول الإمبريالية هو التعاهد العرقيّ بين البروليتاريا البيضاء والبورجوازية القوميّة ضدّ طبقة مُستضعفة حُكم عليها بمواجهة التمييز الهيكليّ الهرميّ، والعمل البوليسي التعسّفي، والمنظومة القضائية المنحازة ضدّهم. لقد أكدّت جائحةُ فيروس كورونا هذا الواقع بشدّة. في الواقع نجد أنّ معظم من أصيب بالمرض في الولايات المتحدة، وفرنسا، والمملكة المتحدّة هم من ذوي البشرة غير البيضاء. وذلك إمّا بسبب سوء العلاج أو الإهمال، أو سوء التغذية، أو لأنهم يشكّلون أكثرية الطبقة الكادحة التي تُعتبر ضرورية لقوام الاقتصاد، ممّا يحرمهم من فوائد إجراءات الإغلاق الشامل. لكلّ دولة امبريالية طبقة مستضعفة، سواء أكانت مؤلّفة من السود، أو الپاكستانيين، أو اللاتينيين، أو الكاريبيين، أو الأمريكيين الأصليين في الولايات المتحدة، أو العرب والمسلمين. الظرف الذي خلقه قتل جورج فلويد جاء ليكشف عن وجود إمكانية سياسية في داخل العالم الإمبريالي، وهي إمكانية تقدر على قلب التقسيم اليمين-اليسار والصراع الطبقي بين البروليتاريا البيضاء من جهة والبورجوازية الوطنية أو البورجوازية العابرة للحدود الوطنية من جهة أخرى. جاءت الحركات المعادية للعنصرية لتصوغ صراع «الأعراق الاجتماعية» [social races] عبر إبراز القوّة السياسية لديمغرافيا جديدة في العالم الأبيض. هذا الصراع يزعزع الأنظمة السياسية القديمة ويكشف العداوة داخل صفوف البروليتاريا في آن. وهذا يعني أننا لا نستطيع إنكار وجود صراع ذي صفة قانونية بين البيض وغير البيض ضمن الطبقة العاملة، وهذا بالرغم من واقع الصراع الطبقي، الذي لا شكّ فيه. لقد عبّر عن هذا الأمر المفكّرون والحركات الديكولونياليّة مرّة بعد مرّة: كلّ عملية ثورية أيًّا كانت ستفشل إذا لم يُلغَ مفهوم العِرق. بل لا نستطيع أن نتصوّر نهاية الرأسمالية إلا من خلال توحيد الطبقات المضطهدة. والعرق هو العقدة الذي تستبعد تشكيل كتلة تاريخية موحّدة.

يمكننا صياغة هذا بشكلٍ توضيحي: تشكّلت الرأسمالية جرّاء سياسة القوة التي تتّبعها الدول القومية، ومنذ ذلك الحين استمرّت هذه الدول بتراكم القوّة من أجل التدمير والاحتلال عن طريق الرأسمالية الحديثة. فلنتصوّرْ الآن أنّ العرق هو أحد أركان «منطق القوّة الجيوسياسية» [geopolitical logic of power]، وهذا جرّاء التقسيمات الهرميّة التي توالتْ على النطاق العالمي بين الدول المُهيمِنة، التي تتنافس بين بعضها البعض، على حساب الدول المُهيمَن عليها، والتي بدورها تقع فريسة سهلة للدول المهيمِنة. هذه نقطة مهمّة لأنّ العرق هو العقدة التي يؤسَّس من خلالها التحالف بين الدولة الحديثة ورأس المال. إنّ التقييم الرأسمالي وسياسة القوّة التي تتّبعها الدول القومية يتصلان ببعضهما البعض عبر التصنيف العرقيّ. لذلك، يتعرّف موظّفو الدولة (المسؤولون، مدراء القوى الأمنية، أركان الجيش، الخ) على رأس المال عبر العرق. يخدمُ هؤلاء الموظّفون المصالح الرأسمالية عبر اتباعهم المنطق القومي-العرقي المستقلّ والخاصّ بهم. يخدمون هذه المصالح عبر اتباعهم سياسات القوّة الإمبريالية، ممّا يعني استمرار تأكيدهم على المصالح الاقتصادية القومية عبر اتفاقيات تجاريّة ودبلوماسيّة وعسكريّة. هذا ما تفعله فرنسا من خلال شركاتها الكبرى المتخصّصة في الطيران والطاقة النووية وصناعة الأسلحة وكذلك هو ما تفعله عبر سياستها تجاه مستعمراتها الإفريقية السابقة المعروفة بفرانسأفريك [*Françafrique*]. لذلك، لا شكّ في استمرارية العلاقة الاستعمارية على الأراضي الفرنسية نفسها، ولا شكّ في أنّها تتوضّح عبر ماديّة جهاز الدولة: وهذا نفسه تاريخ شرطتها، ومحافظاتها، وأجهزتها المخابراتية، وأنظمتها الأيديولوجية ووسائل إعلامها، ونظام المدرسة الجمهورية الخاص بها [*l'école républicaine*]. كلّ هذه الأجهزة تعيد إنتاج منطق التمييز الذي يفصل السكان إلى فئتين: بيض وغير البيض. هذا المنطق التمييزي هو منطق تأسيسيّ للدولة القومية الحديثة. وكما يقول عبد المالك صياد وإتيان باليبار بشكلٍ رائع، إنّ الوطن ينتج الأجانب.[3]

لطالما تضمّن المفهوم الكوني لحقوق الإنسان استثناءات، كما تبرهن الدول الامبريالية حين تستمرّ بسياساتها المفترسة في عالم الجنوب. ولكن، موظّفو الدولة يعزّزون الهياكل الهرمية الرأسمالية، والتي بدورها تعيد إنتاج المنطق العرقيّ. وكما هو الحال دائمًا، يكون أحفاد الشعب المُستَعمَر آخر من يُوظَّف وأوّل من يُطرد. يُنتجُ النظامُ عمالةً احتياطيةً رخيصةً تتدهور عبر انتشار سوق العمل المؤقت على غرار نمط شركة أوبر، ممّا يحقّق أحلام كل مدير يريد أن يجعل العمل قابلا للطي. وهذا يصل بنا

إلى آخر نقطة: إذا كانت هذه القوى العاملة سهلة الاستغلال، هذا لأنّ منطق الدولة القومية العرقيّ يراعي حقوق البروليتاريا البيضاء الاقتصاديّة والقانونية ويحميها أكثر منه لحقوق العمال ذوي البشرة غير البيضاء. وذلك يعني أنّ حركة الطبقة العاملة البيضاء تعتمد تلقائيًا على النظام القانونيّ وتثق بحياد الدولة، أو بالأحرى، يعتبر أفرادها أنّ دولة الرفاهية هي الجانب الحنون للدولة، على عكس جانبيها السلطويّ والطائفي المقزّزيْن. ولكن بالنسبة لغير البيض، يسعى هذا الجانب اللطيف إلى ترويضهم. حتّى الاختصائيون الاجتماعيون، ووكالات البطالة، وموظّفو وكالة خدمات حماية الطفل، والعاملون في قطاعيْ الصحّة والطبّ النفسي يلتزمون بأشكال الرقابة الاجتماعية. يمكننا الاستنتاج أنّ المنطق العرقيّ يعزّز اللامبالاة وركود الحركات الاجتماعية. بما أنّ استعلاء البيض يمثّل العقدة التي تربط رأس المال بالدولة، فحلّ هذه العقدة بين صفوف المضطهدين يفتح الطريق أمام هذه الحركات الاجتماعية لتصبح حركات راديكالية. مقاومة رأس المال يجب أن تُترجم أيضًا إلى مقاومة الدولة. من الممكن توجيه معارضة الدولة عبر بوصلة الحركات الديكولونياليّة، ولكن فاعليّة هذه الأخيرة لن تكون مؤثرّة إذا لم تعتمد على نظريات سياسية متينة . أو، بعبارة أخرى، لن تكون هذه الحركات قوية إذا لم تعتمد على فكرٍ وتطبيقٍ خاصّ بها. عندما يتعيّن علينا أن نُشهر سيوفنا في وجه اليسار الأبيض، الذي هو حليفنا صاحب الامتيازات وبالتالي خصمنا الأساسي، يصبح من الضروري أن نوفّر لأنفسنا «رأس مال أيديولوجي» قادر على انتزاع الهيمنة الثقافية منه. ربّما تكون هذه الهيمنة قد اكتُسِبت عند نهاية الحرب العالمية الثانية، ولكن منذ ذلك الحين، تستمرّ خسارتها أمام المحافظين البيض الجدد، وحتى أمام الفاشية. لكسب هذه المعركة، نحتاج أن نمهّد الطريق لثورة ثقافية. هذه الثورة ستكون في جوهرها ديكولونيالية وإلا لن تكون على الإطلاق.[4]

أخبرني صديق بنينيّ مؤخرًا: «الخطر الكامن في تاريخهم المبنيّ على الاندماج وعلى مقولتهم الشهيرة، 'أسلافنا الغاليّين' هو أنّنا سنجد أنفسنا غدًا قائلين، «أسلافنا، ملّاك العبيد.» من المهم التفكير في هذا الخوف وأخذه بعين الاعتبار. سيسل رودس في جنوب افريقيا، إدوارد كولستون في بريستول، فكتور شولشر في مارتينيك، جان بابتيست كولبير في فرنسا: إن عملية الإطاحة بالتماثيل والمقامات الاستعمارية، التي بدأت منذ سنوات عديدة وتكثّفت حدّتها منذ مقتل جورج فلويد، تنكر في نهاية المطاف قدريّة أسطورة الاندماج الغاليّة. هناك قوى معادية للاستعمار في فرنسا والغرب تقاوم هذه الوصيّة الاندماجية، وخاصةً عندما تهدف هذه القوى إلى تفكيك رموز أنظمة الاستعمار والاستعباد. يعدّ هذا تقدّمًا ملحوظًا لأنّ إزالة التماثيل والمقامات ليست عملًا هامشيًا أو طريفًا إنّما هو تعبير عن وعيٍ ديكولونيالي قيد الإنشاء. ومن شأن هذا الوعي أن يحدّد الأساس الأيديولوجي وراء نفوذ البيض المتجذّر في قانون البقاء للأقوى وسرديات الغزاة: وهُم شخصيات تاريخية لا تكمن فائدتها في تمجيد الماضي فحسب بل كذلك في تعزيز النظام العالميّ الحاليّ والتهيئة للمستقبل، الأمر الذي يُخشى منه. إذًا، لم يعد هذا التفكيك عملًا رمزيًا. من خلال اتخاذ إجراءات لاستعادة الحقيقة التاريخية وفرض وجهة نظر «معذّبو الأرض،» يصبح عمل إسقاط التماثيل عملًا سياسيًا قويًا قادرًا على منافسة الأساطير الرسمية، بل وربما قادرًا على تحطيمها. ولكن بالرغم من ذلك، فهذا لا يمحو خطر الاستيعاب الذي يأخذ أوّلًا شكل الاندماج.

أقول في كتابي البيض، واليهود، ونحن: نحو سياسة الحب الثوريّ: «لستُ بريئة. أعيش في فرنسا. أعيش في الغرب. أنا بيضاء. لا شيء يمكنه أن يعفيني من هذا.» علاقة الذوات غير البيضاء بالدولة القومية البيضاء هي بطبعها علاقة اندماج. نفسّر وجود هذه الذوات عبر حاجات أرباب العمل والبورجوازية. ولكن بفضل عيشهم في فرنسا، فهم يستفيدون من مكاسب البروليتاريا البيضاء الاجتماعية. لقد دُمجوا في ميثاق البلاد الاجتماعيّ، وذلك بالرغم من احتلالهم مكانة اجتماعية تابعة [subaltern] في المجتمع ككلّ. لا هم بيض ولا هم معذبّو الأرض. هم ذوات ما بعد الاستعمار، «سكّان الجمهورية الأصليون» [*indigènes de la République*]. ما يجب فهمه هو أنه تمّ تبييضهم لأنهم لم يعودوا ينتمون إلى معذَبو الأرض. وإذا كان هذا هو الحال، فكيف لهم أن ينبذوا أسلافهم الغاليين؟ الحقيقة هي أنهم يشكّلون، إلى جانب الفرنسيين «الأصليين»، مجتمعًا وطنيًا يضمن لهم مستوًى معيشيًا معينًا، فضلًا عن البنى الاجتماعية والنقابية والسياسية التي تحمي حقوقهم. فكيف يفصلون أنفسهم عن «أسلافهم الغاليّين» الذين هم جزء لا يتجزّأ من الأساطير التي تشكّل في حدّ ذاتها الأساس الأيديولوجي الذي تقوم عليه الدولة القومية الفرنسية وتستخدمه لإعادة إنتاج استعلائها؟ بهذا نؤكّد وجاهة طرح صديقي البنينيّ. إذا كنّا حقًّا خلفاء الغاليين، فكيف لا نكون ورثة ملّاك العبيد، خاصةً وأنّنا نستفيد من غنائم الغزوات الاستعمارية، بالرغم من كوننا سكانًا أصليين. بعبارة أخرى، الإدماج يجعلنا برابرة.[5] نحن أسوأ من أن نكون ورثة الغال الأسطوريين. في الحقيقة، نحن بالفعل، كما يخشى صديقي، ورثة ملّاك العبيد.

في المقابل، يبدو أنّ الغالبية من البيض الذين يمجّدون أسلافهم الغاليين الخياليين لا يرون أنفسهم في نضالات السكّان الأصليين، أو حتى في شخصياتهم التاريخية التحرّرية. إنّهم مغتربون عن تاريخهم وهويّتهم بشكلٍ لا يمكن إصلاحه. عندما يسمعون عن توسان لوفرتور، إنّما يعتقدون في أسوأ الأحوال

أنه حرمهم من جمهورية هاييتي، أو في أحسن الأحوال، أنّه حرّر المُستعبدين. ولكن لا تخطر على ذهنهم فكرة أنّ هذا الانفصالي الذي ترك بصمة لا تُمحى في تاريخ فرنسا قد غيّرهم كشعب. وهذا هو الحال أيضًا مع علاقتهم بجبهة التحرير الوطني الجزائرية، أو كتابات فرانتس فانون، أو شعر إيمي سيزير. ومع ذلك، فإنّ نضالات المُستَعبَدين والمُستَعمَرين لم تغيّر فرنسا والفرنسيين فحسب، بل أدّت، بشكلٍ موضوعيٍ، إلى تجريدهم من بربرتهم. وإن لم يؤدِّ هذا إلى تحضّرهم الكلّي، فإنه وضع الأسس لهذا التحضّر. في صميم هاتين العمليتين، أي بربرة السكان الأصليين من جهة، ونزع بربرة البيض من جهة أخرى، يمكننا تحديد ملامح النضال ضدّ الميثاق القومي والعرقي والامبريالي للجمهورية الفرنسية. تعتمد فاعلية هذا النضال الذي يطمح إلى نزع بربرة البيض والسكّان الأصليين سويًا على تقدّم الحركة الديكولونياليّة. كلّما استعادت الثورة المضادة قوّتها، كلّما ازدادت عمليات البربرة فتكًا. ولكن تقدّم الحركات الديكولونيالية بات يخلق حالة ذعر حقيقية. تعيش فرنسا منذ بضع سنوات أزمة أخلاقية-سياسية حادّة. بل أكاد أسمّيها أزمة معنى. يمكن أن تنسحب هذه الملاحظة على جميع بلدان العالم، ولكنها تنسحب بالأخصّ على الديمقراطيات الليبرالية القديمة التي هي أكثر الدول الرأسمالية تقدّمًا. وأقول إننا نواجه أزمة كبرى في العالم الغربي الأبيض الذي يواجه صعوبة في استيعاب واقع نهاية إمبراطوريته والتعامل معه. لهذا أختم مقدّمة كتابي بالسؤال التالي: «ما الذي يمكن أن نقدّمه للبيض في مقابل تراجعهم، وفي مقابل الحروب التي قد تنشب؟» الإجابة على هذا السؤال تحدٍّ، ولا يمكن أن يُستجاب له إلا من خلال بديل سياسيّ حقيقي. أعتقد جوهريًا أننا بحاجة إلى تأليف سردية شاملة، أو حتى إلى تصميم يوتوبيا. ولكن هذا لن يتحقّق إلا عبر إثبات نسب واضح بيننا وبين أسلافنا المُختارين . بصراحة، ليس بالإمكان أن نتصوّر المستقبل من دون توضيح مَن مِن بين أسلافنا يستحقّ أن يُضمّ إلى مقبرة عظمائنا أي البانثيون الخاصّ بنا. نرى علامات الأزمة القادمة في قمع حكومة ماكرون لحركة السترات الصفراء، أو في تزايد ارتفاع وتيرة وحشيّة الشرطة، أو حتى في النقاشات السريالية والهيستيرية حول مسألة الحجاب الإسلامي. كما نرى علامات الأزمة في أزمة اليسار نفسه وعدم قدرته على إنتاج بدائل سياسية. اليسار بات متشرذمًا وغير قادر على توحيد الطبقات الشعبية، في حين ينتشر اليمين المتطرّف سياسيًا كمرآة لما يحدث في أوروبا. بالإضافة إلى ذلك، فإن هذه الأزمة تتجلّى أيضًا عبر تراجع النخب الفرنسية. دعونا نلقي نظرة فاحصة على مثقفَيْن أساسيَيْن في خطاب تيار المحافظين الجدد في فرنسا: إريك زمّور وآلان فينكلكروت. كلاهما يهوديان، الأوّل من أصل جزائريّ والثاني من أصل ألمانيّ. أشدّد على أصلهما لكونهما بهذا الأصل ضحيتين تاريخيتين لاستعلاء البيض تحوّلا إلى مدافعيْن عن هذا الاستعلاء بعينه. لفهم آليّات هذا التحوّل، من المهمّ أن نفهم أنّهما، في الواقع، تخلّيا عن أسلافهما من أجل تبنّي أسلاف جلّاديهم. هذا لا يخلو من عواقب على تموضعهما السياسي. بالفعل، فإنّ الموضع الذي يشغلانه في النطاق السياسي اليوم تشير إلى قطيعة في النسب التي من الممكن التعامل معها إمّا كشكل من اشكال الخيانة إذا كنا جزءًا من الطرف اليهودي المضطهد، أو كشكل من الاستيعاب إذا كنّا نميل إلى طرف الأيديولوجية الجمهورية للمحافظين الجدد. في الوقت الحالي، يتزايد نفوذ هذا الأخير، وذلك على حساب المعسكر التقدميّ المدمَّر والممزَّق بسبب الإسلاموفوبيا والمركزية الأوروبية، كما أنّه غير قادر على توحيد الطبقات الشعبية من خلال التضامن الطبقي. ينتمي هذان المثقّفان الإعلاميان إلى معسكر المحافظين الجدد في فرنسا، كما أنهما يتفقان مع الرئيس الفرنسي السابق نيكولا ساركوزي وهو يقول: «عندما تصبحون فرنسيّين، فإنّ أسلافكم هم شعب الغال.»[6] يضيف زمّور: «لكي تكون فرنسيًا، عليك أن تقبل نابليون كجدّك الأكبر وجان دارك كجدّتك الكبرى.» ويتابع: «أحنّ إلى الزمن الذي هيمنت فيه فرنسا على أوروبا، وأتفهّم القوميين الحقيقيين أمثال بوتين وترامب. أتفهّم بوتين جيدًا عندما يقول: ’كلّ مَن لا يحنّ لأيام الاتحاد السوفيتي ليس عنده قلب.‘ بالنسبة لي، كل من لا يحنّ للإمبراطورية النابليونية ليس فرنسيًا حقيقيًا. وأنا أشتاق إلى عَظمة بلادي.»[7] منذ ذلك الحين، تبنّى زمّور الخطاب الفاشي الجديد بعناد، وذهب بعيدًا به، إلى حدّ إعفاء الماريشال فيليب بيتان المعروف أساسًا لعقد اتفاق مع هتلر في عام 1940 وتعاونه مع النازيين. هذه صفحة في تاريخ فرنسا يعتبرها الجمهوريون بمثابة حادث عرضي أو جملة اعتراضية، ولكنها بالنسبة للحركة الديكولونيالية مكوّن تأسيسي للتاريخ الاستعماري. من ناحية أخرى، فسّر فينكلكروت تصريح ساركوزي من خلال عبارة أكثر مكرًا، قائلًا: «أسلافنا، نقدّمهم للجميع.»[8]

يشبه اقتراح المحافظ الجديد هذا بشكلٍ غريب اقتراح س.ل.ر جايمز الديكولونياليّ. على غرار المثقّف الثوري من جزر الكاريب، يقدّم لنا فينكلكروت أسلافَه. وهذا مقلق. ولكن هذا القلق يزول حالما ينقشع الضباب. في الواقع، يقدّم لنا جايمز أسلافه بالفعل، ولكنه حريص على ألا يقدّم كلّ أسلافه، بل فقط أولئك الذين ناضلوا ضد الإستعباد. لا يقدّم لنا نَسَبًا إيديولوجيًا أو عرقيًا أو بيولوجيًا، بل يقدّم نَسَبًا سياسيًا معاديا للاستعمار. في الوقت نفسه، يقدّم فينكلكروت كلّ أسلافه من دون تمييز، من فارسانجيتوراكس إلى شارل ديغول بحربه ضدّ الجزائر، مرورًا بروبسبيار والثورة الفرنسية، ونابليون، جلّاد أوروبا، وتيير، جزّار كومونة باريس، وحتى بيتان، العميل النازيّ. بذلك،

يجعل نفسه قائدًا لجوقة التغنّي بذكرى مجد «الروح الفرنسية،» ماحيًا التناقضات الاجتماعية والسياسية ومانحًا أسطورة فرنسا الخالدة المهيمنة مكان الصدارة. في الواقع، اقتراح ساركوزي وفينكلكروت مخالف تمامًا لاقتراح جايمز: الأوّل يتميّز بقوميّته الهويّاتية الكولونيالية؟، أمّا الأخير فيتميّز بجوهره الثوريّ. إذا كان الأوّل يجمع كافّة الأطياف السياسية في فرنسا التي تمتدّ من المحافظين الجدد إلى الاشتراكيين، فالثاني يكافح من أجل الاستقرار في المشهد السياسي الراهن ويجد نفسه محشورًا بين طرف يمينيّ جمهوريّ وطرف يساري متشدّد لا يزال يرفض العِرق كفئة متمايزة تصلح للتحليل السياسي. حتى جان-بول سارتر، الذي كان عند وفاته معاديًا للاستعمار وصهيونيًا في آن، حتى هو لم يكن مستعدًّا لأتخاذ الخطوة الأخيرة نحو التخلّي عن بياضه [de-whitening]. وفي النهاية، يعيد اليسارُ المتشدّدُ إنتاج المنطق العرقيّ، ربما دون أن يعي ذلك. وهذا واضح في اختيار هذا اليسار لمراجعه التاريخية. على عكس النخب الفرنسية، فإنهم يفضّلون روزا لوكسمبورغ على جان دارك ولويز ميشيل على فكتور هوغو. كما عندهم نقاط العمى الخاصّة بهم إذ يفضّلون روبسبيار على توسان لوفرتور، بالرغم من أهميّة الثورة الهاييتية التي عزّزت الثورة الفرنسية وأطالت بأمده من خلال تقويضها لمنظومتيّ الاستعمار والاستعباد، اللتين هما من أسس الجمهورية الامبريالية قيد التشكيل. بعدم فهمهم لاقتراح جايمز وعدم الاستجابة له، يحرم الثوّار البيض أنفسهم من أرواح أسلافهم المحتملين، كما يحرمون أنفسهم من قوّتهم. بالنسبة لنا، نحن الذين نعادي الاستعمار، والمخلصون للحب الثوريّ، فنحن نشكر جايمز على كرمه، ونفتح أيادينا لأسلافه من أجل ضمّهم إلى البانثيون الخاصّ بنا، ونرجو شيئًا واحدًا فقط: أن يقبلوا بنا أسلافه بصفتنا ورثتهم الجديرين.

1 أتحدّث بصيغة المتكلّم لأنني لا أُخرج نفسي من عالم الغرب. أعيش هنا، فإذًا، أنا جزء منه.

2 س. ل. ر. جايمز، أفلاك الوجود: كتابات مختارة، 1980، ص. 187

3 Étienne Balibar and Immanuel Wallerstein, *Race, Nation, Class: Ambiguous Identities* (London, 2010).

4 هذه الفقرة مأخوذة من خطاب أُلقيَ في 25 ايّار 2016. انظروا:
Houria Bouteldja, "Pouvoir politique et races sociales," Parti des Indigènes de la République, June 20, 2016, http://indigenes-republique.fr/pouvoir-politique-et-races-sociales/ (accessed November 20, 2020).

5 أستعير هذا المصطلح من إيمي سيزير للتأكيد على أنّ البربرية تكون أوّلا وقبل كلّ شيء، بربرة أوروبا والمستَعمِر، ولاحقًا تكون، بشكلٍ نسبيّ، بربرة غير البيض الذين يعيشون في أوروبا. يجب تمييز هذه البربرة من فكرة الهمجية التي تصف الحالة الطبيعية، والذي يكون مرادفها الوحشية، والتي تأتي من معجم اليمين المتطرّف. على خلاف ذلك، البربرة تدلّ على العملية التاريخية الاجتماعية الكامنة في عملية الاندماج في الحداثة الغربية. انظروا: حورية بوثلجة "البراءة البيضاء وبربرة العرق: عدم إيقاظ الوحش." *Parti des Indigènes de la République*, January 29, 2020, http://indigenes-republique.fr/white-innocence-and-the-barbarisation-of-the-racialised-letting-the-sleeping-monster-lie (accessed November 20, 2020).

6 Joseph Bamat, "France's Sarkozy Trumpets 'Gaulish ancestry' as he Chases Far-right Votes," France 24, September 20, 2016, https://f24.my/2cEzc (accessed November 20, 2020).

7 Éric Zemmour (@zemmoureric), "Pour devenir français, il faut penser que Napoléon est son ancêtre et que Jeanne d'Arc est son arrière-grand-mère," Twitter, October 23, 2019. https://twitter.com/zemmoureric/status/1187068598004699137; "Éric Zemmour répond à l'invitation de Louis Aliot en campagne pour les municipales de 2020," Made in Perpignan, September 24, 2019, https://madeinperpignan.com/eric-zemmour-repond-a-linvitation-de-louis-aliot-en-campagne-pour-les-municipales-de-2020 (accessed November 20, 2020).

8 Alain Finkielkraut, interview by Élisabeth Lévy, L'esprit de l'escalier, Radio RCJ, November 27, 2016.

حقوق الأجيـــال المقبلة: مقترحات نـــدوة: الغلاف الحيويّ للحــرب

ترجمه عن الإنكليزية فريق الأركِلوغ

قدّرت هيئة الأمم المتّحدة في العام 2014 أن تتحوّل مدينة غزّة إلى مكان غير صالح للسكن بحلول العام 2020. والآن وقد حانت السنة، ما المغزى من هذا التقدير؟ منذ انطلاقة مسيرة العودة الكبرى في 30 آذار/مارس 2018، تعرّض أكثر من 8000 متظاهر لإصابات بالرصاص في الأطراف السفليّة جرّاء القنص على أيدي جيش الدفاع الإسرائيلي، الأمر الذي تطلّب إخضاع الضحايا لعمليّات جراحيّة متعدّدة وصلت في كثير من الحالات إلى بتر الأطراف. يستعين المعماريّ فرانشسكو سِبريغوندي والمنظّرة الكويريّة جَسبير ك. پوار بالموادّ البصريّة وفنّ الفيديو التجريبيّ والنمذجة والصوت لإعادة صياغة مشهد غزّة بعيدًا عن استعراضيّة اقتصاد الصورة الإنسانيّة بهدف تسليط الضوء على ممارسات السياسة الحيويّة [biopolitical] في التشويه والاحتواء في الحياة اليوميّة. يؤطّر عملهما التركيبيّ المشترك فعل التشويه واضعًا إيّاه ضمن أنماط زمنيّة وجيليّة وكمّية ومكانيّة متعدّدة القياسات، ما يضفي عمقًا على استثنائية واقع غزّة. كما يلقي الضوء على سمات الحصار المِطواعة ومساحاته المَساميّة، وضبط معايرته[1] المتفاوتة ودائمة التغيّر والمصمّمة للتحكّم لا بحركة الموادّ الأساسيّة والبضائع والناس فحسب، بل أيضًا للسيطرة على فعل ومفهوم الحركة نفسها. ومع ذلك، ما يفلت من قبضة الحصار يفتح آفاقًا عديدةً للمقاومة الراسخة ويُبشّر بحيواتٍ قادمة لحقّ العودة.

في 10 تشرين الثاني/نوفمبر 2019، انضمّ إلى سبريغوندي وپوار كلّ من غسّان أبو ستّة وجيهان بسيسو وهيلغا طويل-سوري لمناقشة الواقع الميداني في غزّة. نُشِر نصّ هذا الحوار في موقع «جدليّة» في 30 آذار/مارس 2020.

فرانشسكو سبريغوندي

كما يعلم العديد منكم(ن)، يحتشد الآلاف من الفلسطينيّين في غزّة منذ يوم 30 آذار/مارس 2018 في نقاط عدّة على امتداد السياج الأمنيّ السميك الذي يحاصر قطاع غزّة ويفصله عن إسرائيل. يحتجّ المحتشدون على حبسهم إلى ما لا نهاية تحت نظام حصار غزّة المستمرّ منذ العام 2007. كما يحتجّون على احتلال فلسطين الذي يدخل عامه الحادي والسبعين مطالبين بإنهائه وبحقّ العودة إلى الأرض التي ينتمون إليها. فكان ردّ الجيش الإسرائيليّ استهداف ما بلغت حصيلته حتى هذه اللحظة 8000 مصاب من المتظاهرين والمتظاهرات العزّل بالذخيرة الحيّة والتسبّب بعاهات مستديمة لنحو 1200 شخص من بينهم(ن) على الأقلّ.

مشروعنا هو محاولة للتحرّي في القضايا التي تضعها هذه الاحتجاجات على المحكّ. نسعى من خلاله إلى النظر إلى ما يحدث ومتابعة كيفيّة ومكان حدوثه. كما يستجلي قوامَ البنية السلطويّة المكرّسة على مستوى الحصار بصفته نظامًا يهدف إلى تطويق واحتواء مجموعة من السكّان المحرومين من استحقاق المواطنة، إضافة إلى فهم تحوّلات أنماط ممارسة السلطة المتمثّلة في القمع الوحشيّ لهذه الاحتجاجات التي تأتي في الأساس كردّ فعل على الحصار. ولكن، لعل السؤال الأهمّ الذي يسعى المشروع إلى طرحه هو ذاك المتعلّق بثبات مقاومة أهل غزّة للحصار. أي أنّنا نسعى إلى معالجة قضيّة غزّة لا بوصفها وضعًا إنسانيًّا طارئًا يستجلب اهتمامنا من بعيد، بل أيضًا باعتبارها مدّخرًا للمخيّلة السياسيّة ومنطلَقًا للتفكير ولمعارضة أي خطاب يدّعي أنّه من شأن أي جهاز تكنولوجي شديد التطوّر إلغاء أشكال المقاومة كافّة والقضاء على نضال التحرير المتواصل منذ واحد وسبعين عامًا.

ستتحدّث جسبير عن كيفيّة دراستنا وتناولنا التحليليّ لأنماط السلطة التي نعمد إلى توصيفها ومعارضتها بشكل ما في سياق هذا المشروع، إضافة إلى الأسباب التي أدّت بنا إلى دعوة هؤلاء الضيوف بعينهم.

جَسبير پوار

منذ العام 2014، بدأت ألحظ أنّ معظم النقاشات حول العنف في غزّة يتمحور حول مسألة قتل المدنيّين، إذ يتولّى استخدام مفهوم «الأضرار الجانبية» فكّ الارتباط بين الموت والإعاقة. ما الذي ينتجه هذا الفكّ الدلاليّ بين المسألتين؟ وأي الأهداف يخدم؟ بدأت أتأمّل في نمط التشويه المتعمَّد الذي بات من الممارسات الجليّة في التظاهرات الأخيرة (التي تُعرف اليوم بمسيرة العودة الكبرى)، ونستطيع تتبّع هذا النوع من الممارسات في سياق الانتفاضة الأولى إن لم نأخذ بعين الاعتبار مراحل أسبق. يمكننا أن ننسب بداياته إلى الضفّة الغربيّة ومن هناك إلى أماكن أخرى مثل كشمير. ومن أهداف هذا المشروع نزع صفة الاستثنائيّة فيما يتعلّق بهذه الممارسات عن غزّة والتفكير بصورة أعمّ بكيفيّة انتظام عنف الدولة-الأمّة لا من خلال منح الحياة أو إنزال الموت، بل وأيضًا من خلال السعي الدائم للإيذاء وجدوى هذا السعي.

يمكن أن نعتبر ما يحدث في غزّة الآن تسارعًا لنمط التشويه المتعمّد، ويمكننا أيضًا أن نبدأ بالسؤال عن كيفيّة طمس هذا النمط داخل ثنايا السرديّة المحدّدة لثنائيّة الحياة والموت بصفتها الإطار الأساسي لعنف الدولة-الأمّة.

وقد كان أول أهدافنا أن نعود إلى مسألة المشروع التحرّري والحركة التحرّريّة، وهو سؤال في غاية الأهميّة بالنظر إلى اللغة المصدَّرة إلينا من غزّة حاليًّا والمنتظمة حول خطاب المساعدات الإنسانيّة وحقوق الإنسان الذي يترجم كلّ شيء إلى صيغة مشروع اقتصاديّ على طرف النقيض من المشروع السياسيّ. أمّا هدفنا الثاني، ، فقد كان نزع صفة الاستثنائيّة عن غزّة سواء تاريخيًّا أو جيوسياسيًا وبعلاقتها مع الضفّة الغربيّة والقدس الشرقيّة وهضبة الجولان، وكذلك في إطار الحديث عن الاستعمار الاستيطانيّ بصفة أعمّ. لقد عرّف باتريك وولف الاستعمار الاستيطانيّ بما معناه أنّ الدولة الاستعماريّة الاستيطانيّة تتوخّى الإبادة الجماعيّة إمّا من خلال الإجهاز أو الإدماج. أمّا عن نفسي، فأنا مهتمّة بالتفكير أيضًا في الإيهان والإيذاء المتواصل بصفتهما وجهًا آخر للإبادة الجماعيّة.

أمّا الهدف الثالث الذي أجده على قدر بالغ من الأهميّة فهو الآتي: عثرتُ على توقّعات الأمم المتحدة المذكورة بادئ القول عندما بدأتُ أبحث في شأن غزّة في العام 2014، أي قبل ستّ سنوات. يبدو الأمر الآن وكأنّه من الماضي البعيد. لو أخذنا بعين الاعتبار مرور كلّ هذا الوقت، ما معنى أن تحلّ علينا سنة 2020 وأن تكون غزّة مكانًا غير صالح للعيش؟ ما هي هذه الحدود المتغيّرة أبدًا لتعريف ما هو صالح للمعيشة؟ فما الحصار سوى تكوين مطّاطيّ يتمدّد ويتغيّر باستمرار آذنًا بحركة الأشياء صوب الداخل تارّة وصوب الخارج تارّة أخرى. فالحصار، إذًا، لا يدلّ على محدوديّة الحركة بقدر ما يدلّ على التغيير المتواصل لنظام الحركة ووتيرتها، أي أنّه يتحكّم بتعريف مفهوم الحركة وما تنطوي عليه.

وسأختم بالقول إنّ ممارسة التشويه تقوم في مخيّلة السّياسة الحيويّة على توهّم أنّه في الإمكان تجريد فعل المقاومة من فاعليّته أو سحقه كليًّا. أي أنّ ثمّة مرحلة تعجز بعدها المقاومة عن إعادة تنظيم نفسها. وقد أردنا بشدّة أن نفضح هذا التوهّم.

غسّان أبو ستّة

بدأتُ رحلتي في التعامل مع إصابات الحروب في فلسطين منذ 30 عامًا مع اندلاع الانتفاضة الأولى. طالت الرحلة فيما تلا واتّسعت لتصل مناطق أخرى في الجوار فشملت كلًّا من العراق وسوريا. تبلورت خلال هذه الرحلة أفكار عدّة بودّي مشاركتكم إياها. الفكرة الأولى هي أنّ الحروب ليست أحداثًا تجري في زمن محدود. تُحدث الحروب إيكولوجيا[2]، وتخلق غلافًا حيويًّا يعيش الناس ضمنه بصورة دائمة حتى بعد زوال المكوّن السياسيّ للحرب. ينطوي هذا الغلاف الحيويّ على هدم العلاقات الاجتماعيّة وتدمير البيئة العمرانيّة التي شُيّدت لحماية الناس. يُنتج ذلك الدمار وسائله للإيذاء المرّة تلو الأخرى في سبيل استعباد الناس أو احتجازهم داخل هذا الغلاف الحيويّ على مدار أجيال. جنوب العراق مثال على ذلك. لم يشهد جنوب العراق، أي منطقة البصرة وغيرها من المناطق التي تشهد اليوم الاحتجاجات الشعبيّة، الحرب منذ زمن طويل، غير أنّ وحشيّة دمار الاجتياحَيْن الأميركيين، الأول والثاني، إضافة إلى سنوات الحصار قد ساهما في إحداث تلك البيئة.

أمّا الأدهى والأكثر صفاقةً فهو الأوضاع الإيكولوجيّة في غزّة. إذ أنّهم أوجدوا هناك فضاءً محكَم الإغلاق يمكنكَ فيه معايرة حياة الناس عن طريق إبقائهم في برزخ ما بين حياة ناقصة وغياب الموت التامّ. وتتمّ عمليّة المُعايرة هذه أثناء الحصار من خلال السماح بإدخال بعض مقوّمات الحياة أو حظرها فيتحوّل الأمر تمامًا إلى معادلة كيميائية: عندما تقوم بمعايرة الحياة فأنت تتحكّم بمدّ المزيد من ساعات التيّار الكهربائيّ أو تقنينها، وتسيطر على تشغيل شبكة البنى التحتيّة للصرف الصحّي ومعالجة المياه أو تعطيلها، وتسمح بإدخال الغذاء أو تمنعه. تنبّئنا وثائق ويكيليكس بمحادثات الإسرائيليّين حول نيّتهم فرض حمية غذائيّة صارمة على أهل غزّة، بحيث أنّ هناك صيغة ما للتحكّم بكمّ السعيرات الحراريّة عند سماحهم بإدخال الغذاء أو الدواء أو الفِرَق الطبيّة.[3] تتبع ذلك معايرة الموت من خلال الحدّ من أعداد مرضى السرطان الذين يُسمح لهم بمغادرة غزّة بحيث تتراوح نسبة رفض طلبات مغادرة القطاع بين 20 إلى 40 في المائة. وبعد ذلك، يُلقي الإسرائيليون ضمن سلّة المفاوضات مع حماس على شروط التهدئة مقترحًا بإنشاء مستشفى لعلاج السرطان في غزّة. ومن ثمّ تدرك أنّ ما تفعله هو في الواقع عمليّة معايرة لهذا الوضع القائم. تتخلّل ذلك موجات من التصعيد العسكريّ ضدّ غزّة كان شارون قد أطلق عليها تسمية «جزّ العشب». وتهدف هذه الموجات إلى إزالة العراقيل والشوائب في آلية الحصار لأنها تحصد قتلًا أكثر ممّا بمقدورها أن تتحكّم به في محاصرة القطاع. وهنا نأتي إلى مسيرات العودة. أُصيبَ في مسيرات العودة هذه نحو 0.01 في المائة من سكّان غزّة خلال عام واحد، وهذه نسبة ضخمة جدًّا علمًا أنّ مجمل عدد سكّان القطاع لا يتجاوز المليوني نسمة.

أمّا الظاهرة الثانية فهي دقّة الإصابات برصاص القنّاصة. ففي القنص، لا مجال لاعتبار الإصابة أو التشويه أو الإعاقة نتيجة اعتباطيّة ناجمة عن العتاد، إذ أنّ القنّاص قادرٌ على تحديد موضع اختراق الرصاصةِ الجسدَ بل الطرفَ الذي يصوّب عليه بدقّة متناهية. عندئذٍ يتساءل المرء عن الدافع وراء هذا النوع من الممارسات الذي يخلّف سِربًا من الشبّان المعطوبين – سبعة

آلاف حالة موثّقة سريريًا حتى هذه اللحظة – المحكوم عليهم بسنتين إلى ثلاث سنوات من العلاج وما قد يصل إلى عشر عمليّات جراحيّة لينتهي بهم المطاف بنسب متفاوتة من العجز أو الإعاقة الجسديّة.

إذا عدنا إلى جذور الحركة الصهيونيّة، نجد أنّ الفارق بين الاستعمار الصهيونيّ واستعمار الأبارتهايد في جنوب أفريقيا على سبيل المثال هو أنّ الحاجة لعمالة السود في هذه الأخيرة كانت تشكّل جزءًا من مقدّرات البلد الطبيعيّة. أمّا الرأسماليّة الصهيونيّة فلا تحتاج إلى العمالة الفلسطينيّة ما يستدعي إيجاد استخدام آخر للجسد المستعمَر أو طريقة أخرى لجني نِتاج هذه الأجساد. وتُجنَى الأجساد في غزّة عبر إلحاق الأذى بها وإعاقتها فتستفيد الرأسماليّة الصهيونيّة على الصعيد الاقتصاديّ من كونها القناة الوحيدة للمساعدات الدوليّة، بينما تنجح على الصعيد السياسيّ بتحويل قضيّة التحرّر الوطنيّ، أي قضيّة مناهضة الاستعمار، إلى مسألة تقتضي بتأمين المساعدات الإنسانيّة. عندها، لا تعود لغزّة علاقة بقضيّة اللاجئين ولا بالتطهير العرقيّ الذي وقع في العام 1948 ولا بانتهاك حقوق الفلسطينيّين. قضيّة غزّة اليوم متعلّقة بعدد الأطبّاء الذين يُسمح لهم بالدخول وعدد الأطبّاء الذين يُمنعون وعدد ساعات المدّ بالتيّار الكهربائيّ. أي أنّها تجني الأجساد، لا بإخضاع العمالة كما فعل المستعمِرون الآخرون، بل بجني رأس المال السياسيّ منها.

لنرجع خطوة إلى الوراء ونعاين الجرح. تغدو هذه الجروح جزءًا من الصراع بين المستعمَر والمستعمِر. ولأنّ الإصابات برصاص القنّاصة هي من الجروح الأكثر ضراوة، تصبح هذه الجروح دليلًا حيويًّا على هيمنة المستعمِر على جسد المستعمَر. هي السرديّة الثابتة للعلاقة بينهما. ولكن في الوقت عينه، هي ملك المستعمَر الجريح الذي يوكّد ملكيّته هذه بأن يسبغ على الجرح سرديّة المقاومة. وهكذا وبدلًا من السماح للإسرائيليّين بتحقيق مبتغاهم بواسطة ما يسمّونه بالعربيّة عمليّة «كيّ الوعي»، بمعنى الوصم كما هو معروف في تربية الماشية، يتّخذ نضال المستعمَرين والمَكلومين منحى السعي إلى امتلاك سرديّة الجرح كشكل من أشكال توليد الوعي بالمقاومة. وكأنّهم يقولون: «هذا هو التمظهر الحيويّ لنضالنا ضدّ المستعمِر وضد الحصار». لا يقلّل ذلك بأي شكل من الأشكال من شدّة الألم الجسديّ والمعاناة السريريّة، ولكنّه ينظر إلى الصراع حول سرديّة الجرح هذه كمساحة يتحوّل فيها الوعي إلى ساحة المعركة بين المستعمِر والمستعمَر.

جيهان بسيسو

فيما يتعلّق بغزّة، وبالقياس إلى السنوات العشر الماضية، تبدو فكرة المستقبل مبتورة كحال سيقان مرضانا هناك. ولهذا السبب بالذات، يتحتّم علينا ألّا نكتفي بتقديم الرعاية الطبيّة، بل علينا أن نتكلّم عنها بصوت عالٍ وألا نتوقّف. أودّ هنا أن أستشهد بالكاتبة ومنظّرة الشيكانا غلوريا أنزالدو [الأمريكيّة من أصل مكسيكي] وهي تقول: «كي تنجو في المناطق الحدودية / عليك أن تحيا بلا حدود / أن تكون الملتقى».[4] إذًا، كي يستمرّ نبض غزّة في الحياة، لا بدّ لها أن تتحوّل إلى هذا التقاطع أو الملتقى حتى وإن كانت ملتقىً لما هو مريع ومترصّد وعنيف ومؤلم، لأنّها في الوقت عينه تشكّل ملتقى للتضامن والمقاومة. أمثّل اليوم منظّمة عمليّة جدًّا هي منظّمة «أطبّاء بلا حدود» العاملة في غزّة منذ عام 2000. قدّمنا العلاج لمئات المصابين منذ انطلاقة «مسيرة العودة» في شهر آذار/مارس 2018. عالجنا نصف الجرحى الذين أُصيبوا بالرصاص الإسرائيلي والذخيرة الحيّة، ويعاني معظمهم من إصابات في الأطراف السفليّة. يخبرنا جرّاحونا عن العظام التي تفتّتت إلى غبار: إصابات بالغة التعقيد والخطورة بات الدكتور حاج يألفها جيّدًا. أمّا الالتهابات، وهي من المضاعفات الشائعة، فقد بدأنا نشهد منها في غزّة أنواعًا مقاومة للمضادات الحيويّة.

كنّا نتكلّم بالأمس عن العِبَر التي يمكن استخلاصها من الأوضاع في غزّة. للأسف، تعلّمنا بدورنا منظّمة طبيّة إنسانيّة تعمل في الميدان هناك دروسًا أليمة جدًّا عن كيفيّة معالجة ذوي الإصابات البالغة بأشحّ الموارد، وعن كيفيّة الاستمرار في ضخّ المضادات الحيويّة في أجساد الجرحى على الرغم من عدم تماثلهم للشفاء. تُنبئنا تجاربنا بالكثير عن طبيعة الجسد وتتقاطع خلاصاتها مع بحث جسبير في فعل التشويه. ما هو حال التعافي في غزّة اليوم ونحن نعجز عن لأم الجروح بينما يعاني مرضانا من الالتهابات المتكرّرة أو تخضع عائلات بأكملها للعلاج من الإصابات بالرصاص؟ أمرٌ صعبٌ للغاية ولكنّه أصبح جزءًا من الحياة الاعتياديّة.

عشيّة الذكرى السنويّة الأولى لاحتجاجات مسيرة العودة في آذار/مارس 2019، استعدّت طواقمنا الطبيّة لاستقبال أعداد كبيرة من المصابين في ساعاتٍ وجيزة: يرد مئات الأشخاص إلى أروقتنا حيث يتمّ فرزهم لنقدّم الإسعاف الفوريّ للحالات الأكثر حرجًا. ولحسن الحظّ، لم تشهد سنويّة مسيرة العودة «سوى» أربعة قتلى و64 جريحًا. من المروّع بل وغير المقبول أن نسمع طواقمنا تعبّر عن ارتياحها لمقتل أربعة أشخاص فقط وإصابة 64 آخرين بالرصاص الحيّ. ولكن ما يمكننا قوله الآن هو إنّ غزّة تستحقّ مواصلة الحياة وتضميد حاضرها، لا من خلال توفير الرعاية الطبيّة فقط بل أيضًا من خلال كسر جدار الصمت والنسيان. وإن كان للعمارة أن تشكّل أرشيفًا، فكذلك الشهادات والبيانات الطبيّة. وهذه وظيفةٌ جديدة ومربكةٌ بعض الشيء، إذ تتحوّل البيانات الطبيّة إلى أداة للسرد وإدلاء الشهادة. لم يعد بإمكاننا التعامل مع البيانات الطبيّة بصفتها مجرّد أرقام وأعداد

من الجرحى المجهولين، بل بات علينا، حتى كمنظّمةٍ مستقلّة مثل «أطبّاء بلا حدود»، أن نروي قصصهم.

أختم بالإشارة إلى أنّنا نواجه في غزّة محدوديّة العمل الإنساني. يتحدّث زملائي عن تعذّر مقاربة الوضع في غزّة من منطلق الأزمة الإنسانيّة حيث تُفتَح أبواب السجن بين الحين والآخر لإدخال بعض المساعدات ومن ثمّ تُغلَق من جديد. في العام 2012، غادرت طواقمنا ليبيا لأنّها أعلنت صراحة رفضها تضميد جراح الضحايا في الفواصل بين جلسات التعذيب. ماذا نفعل في غزّة اليوم؟ هل نغادرها؟ أجيب بـ لا لأنّ الرعاية الطبيّة التي نقدّمها ملحّة للغاية. لكنّنا نفكّر ونتناقش كثيرًا داخل المنظّمة حيال مقدار تواطئنا مع النظام من خلال العمل داخل السجن.

هيلغا طويل-سوري

بحسب معرفتي، غزّة هي المكان الوحيد في العالم الذي يُدفع فيه بالناس إلى مستوى الاعتماد الكلي على المساعدات الإنسانيّة، هذا في حين يُفترض بالعمل الإنسانيّ أن يرتقي بهم، على الرغم من علّاته وتضليله ومآسيه. إلّا أنّ المساعدات الإنسانيّة في غزّة تحط من شأن الناس سواءً على المستوى النفسيّ أو الحيويّ أو على مستوى البنى التحتيّة. إنّ التشويه الجسديّ هو حقيقةٌ واقعة ويمثّل بالمقابل نوعًا آخر من التشويه يتلازم مع حديثنا الدائم عن غزّة. لقد أمضيت زهاء 15 عامًا وأنا أفكّر وأكتب عن غزّة وفلسطين، وباستطاعتي أن أؤكّد لكم أنّه عملٌ يستنزف الروح ولا يرأف بها. جميلةٌ غزّة. تشبه بريق العينين وعبق الفراولة والسمك الطازج وحتى نتن المجارير الطافحة في الشوارع، إنّ التناقضات فيها مذهلة. ولكنّ المفردات تخونني إنْ حاولت تسجيل كلّ كلمة وكلّ فكرة وكلّ سيرورة تشهدها غزّة. أقلّه أتحدّث عن نفسي حين أقول إنني أصبحت أجد مهمّة رواية قصّة غزّة مستحيلة. لذا، أنا ممتنّة لهذه المحاولات لصياغة معجمٍ جديدٍ من المفردات لوصف ما يفوق الوصف.

كيف السبيل إذًا لاستيعاب أن غزّة ستصبح غير قابلةٍ للسكن بحلول العام 2020؟ أوّلًا، غزّة ليست صالحةٍ للسكن بالفعل. شكرًا للأمم المتّحدة على إبلاغنا، ولكن كيف عسانا أن نتصرّف حيال ذلك؟ أمرٌ يبعث على الغضب. وهنا لبّ القضيّة، إذ لا أعتقد أنّه يمكن الحديث عن مكان مثل غزّة دون أن يغمرك الشعور بالغضب. ويأتيك الجواب دائمًا على شاكلة: «ماذا سنفعل؟» و«كيف نستطيع مساعدتكم؟» وما شابه من أسئلة، وهذا أمرٌ رائع. ولكنّي أظنّ أننا بحاجة إلى إفراد مساحة للتعبير عن المطلق. وأكرّر، بتّ أشعر أنني فقدت المُفرادت الملائمة لوصف غزّة.

يتركّز عملي بشكل عامّ على مجال البُنى التحتيّة ولا سيّما في الاتّصالات، ما قد يبدو غايةً في الملل. ولكنّ الأمر مختلفٌ في فلسطين حيث لا وجود للشبكة اللاسلكيّة كما لا نمتلك حريّة التنقّل حول العالم. في فلسطين، تخضع كابلات الألياف البصريّة للحدود الجغرافيّة التي فرضتها إسرائيل على فلسطين. فما معنى التفكير في مفهوم الدولة فيما بنيتها التحتيّة محدودة، أو، إن شئتم، مُشوَّهة؟ بل كيف ومن أين نبدأ؟ أي دولةٍ هذه التي نسمح بإنتاجها وهي عاجزةٌ عن التحكّم تقنيًّا بخدمات الاتصال ، فما بالك بالتلاقي الجغرافي والحيّ؟

فرانشسكو سبريغوندي

من بين الأفكار التي أسّست مشروعنا الذي طوّرناه للترينالي هو مقاربة غزّة بصفتها تكوينًا حضريًّا نموذجيًّا بإفراط، ويقوم على مخطّط لإدارة أو معالجة كتلة سكّانيّة غير مرغوب بها وقد تمّت موضعتها في هذا الإطار. ويُنفَّذ هذا المخطّط عبر ممارسات التشويه التي من شأنها أن تُبقي كتلة من السكّان يقارب تعدادها المليونيّ نسمة – لنتذكّر دائمًا أنّها كتلة سريعة التنامي – عند مستوى هشاشة مدروس، وذلك عبر ممارسات الاحتواء التي تؤدّي إلى احتجاز هذه الكتلة السكّانية داخل بقعة جغرافيّة محدّدة. بالنظر إلى هذا التكوين الحضريّ بوصفه آلية وتركيب فعّال، وبالنظر إلى عمارته أيضًا، يتضّح لنا أنّ هذا المكان هو مسرح بعض الاختبارات الأكثر تطوّرًا في مجال التكنولوجيّات المكانية والسياسة الحيويّة. من هنا، أعتقد أنّ لا مجال لإغفال أو إهمال مكان مثل غزّة عند محاولة استشراف المستقبل الحضريّ بصورة أعمّ. أي أنّه وبالتزامن مع رعاية سيناريوهات مثاليّة عن المستقبل الحضري في بيئات حاضنة، تقدّم لنا غزّة النموذج المتجسّد لمستقبل حضريّ قاتم يستوي باحتجاز كُتل سكّانيّة بعينها وإقصائها خارج نطاق المجتمع. وأرى أنه علينا كمعماريّين أن نواجه هذا المشروع الذي أخذ يتشكّل مباشرةً وعلى أرض الواقع في غزّة أكثر من أي مكان آخر اليوم.

جسبير پوار

أنا معنيّة بالحديث عن الحياة الاجتماعيّة من خلال التعايش مع الجرح. يخضع حقل دراسات الإعاقة لمفاهيم أورو- أميركيّة عن الطبيعة الاستثنائيّة للإعاقة. لكن الواقع في مكان مثل غزّة، بل وفي معظم الأماكن في الجنوب العالميّ، يزيد من تعقيد مفهوم الإعاقة بوصفها استثناء، فالإعاقة هناك متوطّنة. وبالتالي، ماذا يمكننا أن نقول عن العلاقة الناشئة من التقاطع بين حقوق المُعاقين والحق بتشويه الجسد؟ كيف يخذل المشروع الحقوقيّ غزّة وغيرها من الأماكن في الجنوب العالميّ؟ كيف هي تلك الحياة الاجتماعيّة المتعايشة مع الجرح بالنسبة إلى مفهوم الإعاقة؟ أهي مُفرَغةٌ من المعنى؟ أم عصيّة على الاعتراف بوجودها؟ لا بدّ

للنموذج الاجتماعيّ للإعاقة أن ينفكّ عن فعل التشويه بطريقة أو بأخرى، وأن يطبّع الإعاقة باعتبارها وضعًا غير قابل للتعافي وغير صالح لخطاب المشروع الحقوقيّ. من هنا فإن غزّة حافلةٌ بالمفارقات: لدينا منتخب الألعاب البارالمبيّة[5] اللامع بنجاحه ووثائقيّات البي بي سي عن لاعبي كرة القدم مبتوري الأطراف وغيرهم من نماذج التعافي التي تحتفي بها وتستوعبها أطر العمل الحقوق-إنسانيّة. في المقابل، لدينا المفهوم الآخر للجرح بوصفه سِجلّا لتدوينات المقاومة. لعلّ ذلك السؤال مدخلنا ولعلّه غير ذلك. ولكنّه بودي أن أضيف إلى النقاش نبذة عن السياق العالميّ الذي ساهم في إبراز نمط من العمل الإنسانيّ يتمحور حول ضرورة النظر إلى الأجساد المعاقة بدورها أجسادًا مُمَكَّنة ولكن بطريقة محدّدة دون سواها.

غسان أبو ستّة

ثمّة هاجس ينتابني حينما أعيد تأمّل مسألة تحوّل غزّة في غضون شهور من الآن «رسميًّا» إلى مكان غير قابل للسكن. عشيّة نقل السفارة الأميركيّة إلى القدس في أيار/مايو 2018، أصيبَ 3000 شخص في أربع ساعات فقط. ومن الأمور المروّعة التي شهدتها أثناء تواجدي هناك في ذلك اليوم كان الارتفاع المضطرد لنسبة الإصابات المتكررة؟ لدى الفرد الواحد. إذًا، أيّ من تلك الجروح في الجسد الواحد ينبغي أن تعالج الآن؟ كنت أعالج مرضى بإصابات جديدة في مواضع إصابات قديمة بعضها يعود إلى العام 2004 أو 2008 في نفس الأطراف. وكنت أعالج مرضى آخرين أصيبوا في حروب سابقة ثمّ عادوا إليّ مصابين مرة أخرى. وهذا كلّه ضمن مساحة الجسد الواحد. كيف يدير الناس علاقاتهم وسط عائلات جريحة، عائلة واحدة فيها عدد من الأفراد الجرحى والمصابين؟ يشمل مجال عملي تقديم الاستشارات العلاجيّة للمؤسّسات الإنسانيّة من أمثال «أطبّاء بلا حدود» في سياق تخطيط مشاريعها. وقد عملت على مشروع يهدف إلى تيسير الخدمات لمبتوري الأطراف في غزّة. ولدينا مشكلتان: إن كان المصاب طفلًا، سيواصل جسمه النموّ بالترافق مع نموّ الطرف المبتور وإنّما بشكل غير متكافئ ممّا يؤدّي إلى نتوء العظام عبر أنسجة الطرف المبتور ويستدعي ذلك تدخّلات جراحيّة عدّة خلال مراحل النمو الجسمانيّ. ثمّة إحصاء صادم يشير إلى أنّ عدد الإصابات التي أدّت إلى بتر الأطراف في العام 2006 أثناء الحروب على غزّة قد بلغت 1300 إصابة، ولا يشمل الرقم التوغّلات العسكريّة وغارات الطيران الوجيزة التي تخلّلتها، وبات جميع هؤلاء المصابين بحاجة إلى الأطراف الاصطناعيّة. ويرتفع هذا العدد إلى ما بين 2000 و2500 إذا ما شملنا الأشخاص الذين يحتاجون إلى عمليّات بتر ثانويّة، أي في حال حدوث أي فشل في السيرورة الاستبنائيّة.

كما قالت هيلغا، لا تتطلّب هذه الظاهرة الاجتماعيّة المتمادية في مجتمعٍ شديد الترابط مثل غزّة، ابتكار لغةٍ جديدةٍ فحسب، بل تحتاج من وجهة نظري الاختصاصيّة بصفتي معالج، إلى مقاربات جديدة. تندرج الجراحات الاستبنائيّج في عداد الخدمات المتميّزة بل المرفّهة. وقد تدرّبتُ في هيئة الرعاية الصحية الوطنية (NHS) في المملكة المتّحدة على تخصيص ثماني ساعات لمعاينة كلّ حالة. ولكن ما العمل عندما تواجهك حالات تستدعي الجراحات الاستبنائيّة بأعداد وبائيّة حيث لا وقت يتّسع لسبعة آلاف حالة مضروبة في تخصيص ثماني ساعات في تِسع عمليّات جراحيّة استبنائيّة لكلّ منها؟ فما إنْ يباشر المرء حساب مضاعفات عدد الساعات، تتّضح أمامه درجة الانتشار الوبائيّة للإصابات التي تضاهي انتشار الأمراض شديدة العدوى كالإسهال والإيبولا، ويبدأ بالتنبه إلى أنّ هناك تعمُّد في التسبّب بالإعاقة الجسديّة. يدعونا ذلك إلى إعادة تصوّر دور الرعاية الطبيّة على مستوىً لم يُشهد له مثيل منذ الحرب العالميّة الأولى والبحث عن معطيات لم تجمع بعد. هذا هو هول المشهد الذي نحن بصدده. بين الساعة 4 والساعة 8 من يوم 14 أيّار/مايو 2018، أُصيبَ 3000 شخص. كان الوضع فعلًا أشبه بالحرب العالميّة الأولى حين كانت أفواج المصابين تتوافد بالآلاف. كانوا يأتون ستّة أو سبعة في سيّارة إسعاف واحدة. لقد تخطّت تجربة غزّة حدود تصوّراتنا وحدود اللغة والمعرفة العلميّة في ما يتعلّق بطبيعة إلحاق الأذى والتعذيب، لا لسبب سوى أنّ إسرائيل قد وضعت هذا المخطّط سعيًا لتحقيق غايتها في الإبادة السياسيّة، أي القضاء على الفلسطينيّين كجسمٍ سياسيّ، ما يعني استعدادها للاقتراب من سياسات الإبادة الجماعيّة قدرَ الحاجة لبلوغ هذه الغاية. ويتمثّل سعيها الملحّ للإبادة السياسيّة والاستعداد لممارسة السياسات الإباديّة في سبيل ذلك المسعى في ما يحدث الآن في غزّة من زجّ هذا الكمّ من الناس في أصغر رقعة من الأرض وفي أضيق الظروف المعشيّة.

جيهان بسيسو

لديّ ملاحظتان صغيرتان. جسبير، لقد ذكرتِ الألعاب البارالمبية وهذه من الومضات الصغيرة التي تذكّرنا بأنّ جسد غزّة ليس مُعاقًا بل هو أيضًا جسدٌ في طور التعافي. ولقد أشرتِ إلى ضرورة مَركزة الجسد في خطاب حقوق المُعاقين وتمكينهم. وأنا موافقةٌ تمامًا، ولكني أودّ أن أشدّد في المقابل على أنّ هذا الخطاب لا يستطيع أن ينتزع الجرح – والإعاقة – من السياق السياسيّ الذي سوّغ له. في كلامي بعض من النقد الذاتي حيال المؤسّسة التي أنتمي إليها حيث يرتكز عملنا إلى سرد الحدث الذي أدّى إلى الإعاقة ولكنّنا نغفل الحديث عن السياق، وهذه ملاحظة بالغة الأهميّة يجدر بنا أن نبقيها في أذهاننا تذكيرًا لنا جميعًا.

إنّ توثيق تجارب التعايش مع الإصابة والإعاقة وسردها هو جزء لا يتجزّأ من سرد قصص غزّة ومقاومة النسيان، لأنّ العيش مع الإعاقة يتجاوز موجات التغطية الإعلاميّة فيما تولي وسائل الإعلام الصدارة لأخبار الموت والقتل. في المقابل، تلقى أخبار الآلاف من ذوي الأطراف المبتورة اللامبالاة وهذا أمر مقلق.

هيلغا طويل-سوري

من الأمور التي تطرأ على ذهني وأنا أصغي للمشاركين معي في هذه الندوة أو لزملائي وأصدقائي هنا الآتي: كثيرًا ما نتحدّث عن غزّة بوصفها مكانًا محاصرًا أو مشوّهًا بأكثر من طريقة، في حين أنّ السؤال الثابت هو عن مدى إمكانيّة احتجاز أو تدمير أو حشر أو احتواء – ثمّة تعابير كثيرة يمكننا استخدامها هنا – شعب بأكمله. في الوقت عينه، أظن أنّه من المفيد أن ننظر إلى الموضوع من أبعاد ومستويات مختلفة سواء جغرافيًّا أو زمانيًّا. ماذا لو قاربنا موضوع غزّة لا من منظور الجسد، أو الجسد الوطن حق، بل من منظور بيئيّ؟ فالوضع في غزّة هو أيضًا في طور الكارثة البيئيّة المتفاقمة والآخذة في الاتّساع.

يطرح عمل جسبير وغسّان سؤالًا عن طبيعة المستقبل الذي نمهّد له. قد يستعصي علينا أن ندرك معاناة الذين يعيشون بطرف مبتور. أعني، لا سمح الله، لا أحد يتمنّى أن يتعرّض لذلك غير أنّنا لسنا مجرّدين تمامًا من القدرة على تخيّل نوع الحياة في ظلّ التعايش مع الآلام الشبحيّة أو الأطراف الاصطناعيّة. ولكن ماذا لو ذهبنا إلى أبعد من ذلك؟ ما معنى أن يحيا المرء في عائلة مبتورة حيث الجسد الواحد مثخن بالجراح والعائلة مثخنة بجراحها كذلك، وحيث تتفتّح أيضًا وسط كلّ هذا جراح كل سكان البناية فالقرية فالمدينة؟ وأبعد، ماذا يحدث للوطن، لا بمعنى الانتماء فقط بل على الأقلّ في ما يتعلّق بمشروع وطنيّ ما. واذا أوسعنا زاوية النظر أكثر، إذا خرجنا إلى النطاق الأعمّ: ما تأثير كلّ هذا على المستقبل؟ السؤال هنا لا ينطبق على الفرد أو العائلة، ولا على المستوى الاجتماعيّ أو الوطنيّ بل على المستوى العالميّ الأشمل. وبالتالي، يتمركز التجاذب حول الطريقة المحدّدة التي نريد أن نتحدّث بها عن غزّة. جانب منّي يرفض غزّة الأمثولة أو المجاز أو النموذج، وفي الوقت عينه هي كذلك بالفعل. هل هذا هو المستقبل الذي نبنيه في أماكن مختلفة؟ لدينا «غزّات» صغيرة هنا وهناك، سواء في تشيلي أو هونغ كونغ أو السودان أو في أي مكان آخر. ما معنى أن نفكّر بهذه السياقات على مقاييس زمنيّة مختلفة؟

جسبير پوار

من الأمور التي سعينا للتركيز عليها، مع أنّها تكمن بالنسبة إلينا في الآتي/المستقبل، أي علم الغيب، هو فكرة الجرح كعائلة. ما نوع العلاقات الجندريّة التي قد يُعاد تشكيلها ويعاد النظر فيها في ظلّ مجتمعٍ يعجز معظم ذكوره عن مزاولة العمل بالشكل الاعتياديّ؟ وماذا يحلّ بالنساء وبدورهنّ الرعائيّ؟

ثمّ ماذا عن الجرح الآخذ التعمّق؟ يُعدّ الشباب الذين تعرّضوا للإصابات في سنّ مبكّرة من ذوي الأجساد غير مكتملة النمو بحسب المحدّدات والمقاييس الطبّية. ما معنى أن يُحرَم المرء من البلوغ، وأن يُحرم من الجندرة بشكل ما، فلِكي يكون الشخص ذكرًا أو أنثى لا بدّ له أن يطابق تصوّرًا ما عنه كشخص بالغ ومُجندر. هذه أسئلة تطال حقوق الأجيال المقبلة والمستقبل برمّته. إلا أنني أعتقد كذلك أنّها تفرد فضاءات للمقاومة لا سبيل بعد إلى تحديد معالمها، ولكنّها مقاومة لا يمكن انتزاعها من الوعي، هي أساليب جديدة للعيش، بل للحياة حيث يُخيّل إلينا أنّ لا قابليّة للحياة داخله.

1 انظروا https://depthunknown.com (accessed November 5, 2020)

2 قاد جروج أندرو رايزنر الكشوف الحفريّة في السامرة بين عامي 1910-1908 وهي الفترة التي عمل فيها كأستاذ مساعد للمصريّات في جامعة هارفارد. تمّ استئناف هذه الكشوف الحفريّة بين عامي1935-1931 بقيادة ج. و. كروفوت رئيس كلية الآثار بالقدس. أُجريت هذه الكشوف بالتعاون بين كلية الآثار وصندوق استكشاف فلسطين بلندن وجامعة هارفارد والجامعة العبرية. انظروا William F. Albright, *The Archaeology of Palestine* (New York, 1960)

3 * ارتأينا استعمال كلمة "عبراني" خلال النص لوصف جماعات يهودية قديمة حقيقية أو مُتخيّلة عوضًا عن "بني إسرائيل" لاقتصار الأخيرة على مجال دلالي محدود بالقصص الإبراهيمي. [المترجم]

4 انظروا Benedict Anderson, *Imagined Communities: Reflections on Origin and Spread of Nationalism* (New York, 2006). وحول الصهيونية، انظروا Yael Zerubavel, Recovered Roots: Collective Memory and the Making of Israeli National Tradition (Chicago, 1994)

5 لقراءة أكثر استفاضة حول الأرشيف والممارسات الأرشيفيّة، انظروا Carolyn Steedman, *Dust: The Archive and Cultural History* (New Brunswick, NJ, 2002)

6 في مقدمة كتابه *Argonauts of the Western Pacific* يُفصّل مالينوفسكي منهجًا علميًّا لعمل الإثنوغرافي، ويلقي على عاتقه مسؤولية جمع أنواع بعينها من البيانات، وكذلك حفظ تفاصيلها في سجل يمكّن من سيلحقه من أنثروبولوجيين من مراجعة البيانات في مرحلة لاحقة، بنفس الطريقة التي يعيد بها (فرضيًّا)

تنفّس قتالي، استعادةٌ

جاسبير ك. پوار

ترجمه عن الإنكليزية فريق الأركلوغ

خلال العاميْن الأولين اللذين نُظّمت فيهما مسيرة العودة الكبرى في غزة، تحديداً بين عامي 2018 و2020، أصيب أكثر من 7000 متظاهر بطلقاتٍ نارية في أطرافهم السفلية. تدهور كثيرٌ من هذه الإصابات ليستلزم بتر الأطراف المصابة أو خضوعها لجراحات عدّة، وتفاقم بعضها إلى جروحٍ مستديمة جرّاء نقص المضادّات الحيوية.

ساق ناديا

يا صديقي!

أبدًا لن أنسى ساق ناديا المبتورة من أعلى الفخذ. لا، ولن أنسى الحزن الذي هيكل وجهها واندمج في تقاطيعه الحلوة إلى الأبد. لقد خرجت يومها من المستشفى إلى شوارع غزة وأنا أشدّ باحتقارٍ صارخ على الجنيهين اللذين أحضرتهما معي لأعطيهما لناديا. كانت الشمس الساطعة تملأ الشوارع بلون الدم. كانت غزة، يا مصطفى، جديدةً كل الجِدّة. أبدًا لم نرها هكذا أنا وأنت. الحجارة المركومة على أول حيّ الشجاعية، حيث كنّا نسكن، كان لها معنى. كأنما وُضعت هناك لتشرحه فقط. غزة هذه، التي عشنا فيه، ومع رجالها الطيبين سبع سنوات في النكبة كانت شيئًا جديدًا. كانت تلوح لي أنها....أنها بدايةٌ فقط. لا أدري لماذا كنت أشعر أنها بدايةٌ فقط. كنت أتخيّل أن الشارع الرئيسي، الذي أسير فيه عائدًا إلى داري لم يكن إلا بدايةً صغيرة لشارعٍ طويلٍ طويل يصل إلى صفد. كل شيءٍ كان في غزة هذه ينتفض حزنًا على ساق ناديا المبتورة من أعلى الفخذ، حزنًا لا يقف على حدود البكاء. إنه التحدي. بل أكثر من ذلك. إنه شيء يشبه استرداد الساق المبتورة![1]

تتناول قصة غسان كنفاني الموجّهة لصديق طفولته مصطفى الذي غادر غزة البعد الزمني الطويل للتشويه والإعاقة.[2] يفرض النص جردة حسابٍ على القارئ، واضعًا إياه إزاء لانهائية الجرح الفلسطيني العابر للأجيال. فليس هناك من حياةٍ أخروية للعنف فهو لا ينتهي. يمكننا أن نروي تاريخ التشويه الإسرائيلي للأجساد الفلسطينية انطلاقًا من بداياتٍ عديدة، سواء بدأنا بالنكبة أو باحتلال عام 1967 أو بسياسة «هشّموا عظامهم» بحسب التعبير الشائن لوزير الدفاع الإسرائيلي إسحق رابين إبان الانتفاضة الأولى. إلا أنّ كنفاني يرسم مخيلةً رمزية مختلفة لـ «الساق المبتورة» لابنة أخيه ناديا باعتبارها بداية لتاريخ غزة أخرى «جديدةٍ كل الجِدّة». ما لاح لكنفاني على أنه «بدايةٌ فقط» وانتفاض غزة «حزنًا....لا يقف على حدود البكاء» و«الشمس الساطعة» و«لون الدم» هي كلها الشيء ذاته.[3] يشيد كنفاني بالساق المبتورة بوصفها أكثر من مجرد جرح أو علامة أو تجلٍّ بيولوجي للعلاقة بين المستعمِر والمستعمَر. يتراجع مشهد الأزمة والأسى في غرفة المستشفى لصالح وعيٍ سياسي نابض. قد يبكي حزنًا، إلا أن حزنه يستنبت طاقةً مفعمةً بالحياة؛ طاقة شمس قد تغرب، إلا أنها لن تلبث أن تشرق من جديد. تغييره المثير لوجهة الخطاب هو أكثر من مجرّد دعوة أخرى مكررة للصمود والتحمّل أو استجداء التعاطف الإنساني. بالأحرى يستعمل كنفاني الساق المبتورة ليشير إلى زخمٍ لا يمكن توصيفه لذاتٍ جماعية تتجاوز الأهداف والحسابات الاستراتيجية للدولة الحياسية[4] [the biopolitical state] ورغبتها في تجريد الأجساد الفلسطينية من حيويتها وقدرتها على المقاومة.[5] في هذه الغزة الجديدة كليًّا ليس من ثمّة طرف اصطناعي أو إعادة تأهيل من شأنها أن تعوّض عن الطرف المفقود. بل تقف الساق المبتورة في ظل صنوها الغائب، الطرف الشبحي. ولا يتحرّق إلى الطرف الشبحي سعيًا للتكامل، بل للمطالبة بعودة الفلسطينيين إلى بيوتهم التي هُجّروا منها عام 1948. إذا كانت صورة ساق ناديا المبتورة رمزًا لمقاومة الاحتلال، فليس الطرف الشبحي لهذا البتر سوى التحرير ذاته.

في العام 2018 أصبحت غزة مسرحًا لممارسة التشويه بشكل سافرٍ ومتعمّد في مقداره وقسوته. تشويهٌ يشهده ويُقرّه جمهورٌ عالمي. عبر التحليل والتنظير التشخيصي والاستشرافي، كيف نُعيد توجيه النظر لمشهد التشويه هذا من كونه أوج السلطة السيادية للاحتلال إلى كونه أفقًا مفتوحًا للمقاومة الفلسطينية؟

«كانت تلوح لي أنها بداية فقط» يُمكن أن تكون هذه العبارة وصفًا جيدًا للتجهيز الفني «الحياة المستقبلية للعودة»، الذي قمت بإنتاجه بالتعاون مع فرانشسكو سبريغوندي ضمن ترينالي الشارقة للعمارة، وحاولنا فيه أن نعبّر عن تعقيدات المقاومة في غزة. في العام 2018 امتلأت الصحف بصور أشخاص أصيبت أطرافهم السفلية في مسيرة العودة الكبرى، بعضهم يستند على عكّازات أو مُقعدٌ على كراسٍ مدولبة وبعضهم الآخر بُترت أطرافه. تمّمت هذه الصور، مع صورٍ أخرى مؤلِمة مثيرة للتعاطف، مشهد الأزمة الإنسانية. كانت الصور «المقرّرة سلفًا» تبرز جهود فرق الإنقاذ أكثر مما تبرز معاناة الفلسطينيين المصوَّرين.[6] غطّى خطاب «الصمود» حتى على الصور التي أظهرت المقاومة من منظور مختلف. رغم أنّ هذه الصور كانت تستهدف بالأساس

فضح بطش الدولة الإسرائيلية، إلا أنّ التوثيق البورنوغرافي للألم والمعاناة جاء ليعيد إنتاج هذا البطش أداتيًّا عبر تنبيه الجمهور إلى قيمة الجسد الإسرائيلي كمِلك قومي عوضًا عن نقل حقائق المقاومة الفلسطينية.

لكي نقطع السبيل على هذا الاستثمار الشهواني في صورة الجسد المُعذّب، حتى في تلك الصور التي أُعدت لاستجداء المشاعر الإنسانية، حاولنا تفادي إغراء الإثباتي. لم يكن هناك لا صور للجروح ولا للجرحى، ولا لحوائط أو حدود، ولا صور لجنود إسرائيليين، لم يكن هناك من ثمّة جماليات وثائقية. لا يعني هذا أننا لم نستعمل موادًا وثائقية وإثباتية، إلا أننا عمدنا إلى توظيف هذه المواد فيما هو أبعد من السياقات المباشرة لإدراكها واستهلاكها، مسلطين الضوء على الفائض السيميوطيقي للصور التي تتجاوز تمثيل المنطق والدليل والممارسة الإمبريقية. بالنسبة لنا أصبح الحديث عن التشويه في غزة دون صور مقيّدة بثنائية الضحية والتسامي على الألم الفلسفة التي توجّه عملنا، كذلك كان الالتزام بتجنّب المنظور التقريري «حول غزة» و«عن غزة» واستبداله بـ «لغزة» ومن قِبل الغزّاويين.

انطلاقًا من الفقرة السابقة من نص غسان كنفاني، سعى مشروع «الحياة المستقبلية للعودة» لتوصيل وجهات نظر مختلفة من غزة، من موقعٍ عادةً يتمّ تصويره ككيان محدود ومتجانس. تألّف التجهيز الفنّي من أعمال فنية وفوتوغرافية ورسوم بيانية وفيلم ختامي بعنوان «تدريب على ممارسة الحرية» يصل غزة بنضالات التحرر المختلفة حول العالم.[7] كان محور العمل نموذجًا مجسّمًا لمخيّمات مسيرة العودة الكبرى يصوّر التفاصيل الحميمية الدقيقة للتظاهرات، ويحتفي بالطقوس اليومية لا سيّما الفعاليات الاجتماعية كحلقات القراءة والطبخ والدعم الطبّي وحرق الإطارات وتطيير الطائرات الورقية والغناء. بعكس المجسّمات التي تنطلق من قاعدة البحث الجنائي وتسعى للتقصّي الدقيق لإحداثيات المشهد في الفضاء الديكارتي ومفاعيله على امتداد محور الزمن، يولي مجسّمنا أهميةً خاصة لحدّة الأحداث وآمادها: رؤية روح الجماعة في احتشاد الأجساد، والتماس طاقة التضامن في حركتها وتماوجها معًا، والشعور بالبهجة مع تجاذب هذه الأجساد إلى بعضها. في الوقت ذاته أحاط تجهيزٌ فنيّ بعنوان «حصار إدراكي» يتألف من أربع مكبّرات صوتية بفضاء العرض، غامرًا إياه بأصوات من جلبة التظاهر وحكايات الجرحى واصطخاب حالة الحشر. لم يشأ فنان الصوت ضِرار كلش أن يعيد التراتب الحسّي لشعور «التواجد هناك» في قلب التظاهرة، بل عمد إلى اكتناف المعرض بقيود «التواجد هنا» في قلب فضاء العرض، مستخدمًا خليطًا من المواد يُثري الحواس، وإن كان يجتاحها أيضًا.

كذلك أسهمت أعمال الفيديو التي أنتجها فنانون من غزة في إثراء هذا التركيب المتنوّع من وجهات النظر. الفيديوهات الثماني التي اخترناها تعكس بالضرورة الأوضاع المادية للحصار، خصوصًا بعد أن أصبحت متطلبات إنتاج الفيديو متاحةً على نطاقٍ واسع بفضل الهواتف المحمولة. يستخدم الفنانون الغزّاويون وسائط محمولة قابلة للتناقل للتغلّب على صعوبات الإنتاج تحت الحصار. تمكّن الوسائط تناقل العمل الفنّي تحديدًا لأن منتجيه لا يمكنهم الحركة. ترفض هذه الأعمال غير التمثيلية النظرة الوثائقية والإنسانية. عوضًا عن ذلك تسلّط الضوء على المفاهيم المختلفة للحركة: مساميّة الحصار أي قابليته للاختراق والبحر كأفق وتقلّب طبيعة وجود اللاجئين بين «انتظار» و«صراع».[8] تتحدّى هذه الفيديوهات القيود التي يفرضها المستعمِر على الحركة، وتعيد تخيّل الحركة، وبالتالي تفتح المجال لتأويل معنى الحركة وفق شروط المستعمَرين. بتعبير آخر، ترفض هذه الأعمال أن يحدّ الحصار كافة آفاق الحركة الممكنة.

تتكوّن مجموعة أكتيف ستيلز من مصوّرين إسرائيليين وفلسطينيين يعملون على توثيق عنف الاستعمار الاستيطاني الإسرائيلي منذ العام 2005.[9] في عملهم داخل حدود الخط الأخضر وضدّه، شكّلت أعمال أكتيف ستيلز أرشيفًا متعدد الأوجه سمح لنا بتقييم العلاقات بين الرتيب والمشهدي، وتمييز أيّ الصور يمكنها أن تحقّق رواجًا. بعد مراجعة آلاف الصور، اخترنا 31 صورة تنقل العادي عوضًا عن الاستثنائي: المشافي الميدانية وأشجار الزيتون المُقتلعة والمنازل المهدمة والكرسي المُدولب المتروك عند الحاجز والفعاليات الصاخبة لمسيرة العودة الكبرى وحضور الناشطات البارز في التظاهرات.

إلا أنّ النقد اللاذع للمشهدية لا يمنع عودتها المسرحية، فنحن في النهاية بصدد إعداد معرض يحفل بكل المعضلات التي يفرضها الاقتصاد الاستنزافي لآلية العرض. اخترنا صورة من الصور التي كانت قد حصدت الجوائز وذاع صيتها في الأشهر الأولى للمسيرة الكبرى، هي صورة صابر الأشقر التي التُقطت في الحادي عشر من أيار/مايو 2018. يتوسّط الأشقر الصورة، وهو جالس على كرسي مدولب، بساقيه المبتورين، ويقذف المقلاع بيمناه، بينما تتصاعد خلفه سحب الدخان أمام متظاهرتين من النساء. حقّقت هذه الصورة انتشارًا واسعًا بسبب توظيفها لمفردات خطاب التمكين: الجسد المقعد الذي يمكنه التظاهر والذي يتمتع بالحميّة والقدرة على الفعل. إلا أنّ هذا المشهد ليس بالضرورة استثنائيًّا في غزة، لذا عطفنا هذه الصورة على صور أخرى لمشاهد الحياة اليومية التي يؤطرها التعجيز الجسدي. إعادة تموضع الصور ذائعة الانتشار، بالأحرى إعادة تموضع المشهدي في سياق من الرتابة والاعتيادية، استراتيجية مهمة يسمّيها إدوار غليسان بـ«حق المستعمَر في الغموض».[10] ولأنها تفضح الميل

للتركيز على «الأيقونات التراجيدية» للإعاقة الجسدية، تدحض إعادةُ التموضع هذه الحالةَ الاستثنائية التي ترغب النظرة الإنسانية إسباغها على الصورة: ما يبدو مشهديًّا من الخارج هو في واقع الحال حدثٌ عادي ومتكرر.[11] ولأنّ الكرسي المدولب أصبح رمزًا عامًّا للإعاقة الجسدية حول العالم، تزيح إعادة التموضع هذه أيضًا الكرسي المدولب بوصفه الطرف الاصطناعي الأساسي وربما الوحيد بالصورة التي يتصدّرها، لصالح المقلاع الذي يمكّن صاحبه جسديًّا.

ينتبهنا الانتقال من سردية الأزمة الإنسانية إلى سردية التحرر الفلسطيني إلى البعد الزمني الطويل لفعل التشويه والإعاقة، خصوصًا على طول الفترة الممتدة قبل وبعد اصطدام رصاصة القناص باللحم والعظم. ويلفت إلى مخزون الخيال السياسي الممتدّ إلى ما هو أبعد من طائلة الدولة الحياسية وقوالبها التمثيلية السائدة. كما يكشف أيضًا أنّ إقدام المتظاهرين على التعرّض للقتل والتشويه ليس مردّه «حافز الموت والتدمير الذاتي» عند فرويد كما يعزوه بعض الصحافيين إجحافًا. كما أنه ليس تعبيرًا عن فيتيشية الاستشهاد (والمُستقاة ولو جزئيًّا من معادلة الحياة والموت عند الفدائيين الاستشهاديين والتي لا يُمكن قياسها على سواها). واقع الحال أن هذا الإقدام ما هو إلا صنو السعي لحياةٍ أكثر عدلًا؛ إقدام يرفض بعناده أوهام الدولة الحياسية عن إمكانية القضاء على المقاومة يومًا ما.

التشويه

يمكننا النظر إلى التشويه على مستويين متمايزين وإن تقاطعا أو تداخلا أحيانًا: أحدهما حرفي والآخر مجازي. يحدث التعجيز الحرفي للأجساد عبر أشكال عدّة سواء عبر استهداف القناصة للأطراف أو تعيير الحصص اليومية من السعرات الحرارية لسكان غزة المحاصَرين أو إنتاج وإعادة إنتاج الصدمة دون توقف. بالمقابل يوظّف التشويه المجازي — وإن بشكلٍ غير مدروس بالضرورة — تعبيرات الإنهاك والضعضعة لوصف حالة التخريب، كأن يُقال مثلًا «شلّ اقتصاد غزة». يندمج المستويان معًا فيما يبدو وكأنه «حدث» التشويه، إلا أنّ شروطهما قد أُوجدت قبل هذا الحدث بأمدٍ طويل جرّاء الظروف البيئية والبنيوية للإنهاك. فالتشويه يتجاوز «آماد الدورة الإعلامية» لتسجيل الحدث وانتشاره.[12] وبالتراوح بين الخنق والاختناق، تشغل مفاعيل التشويه في غزة مستويات عدّة مكانيًّا وزمنيًّا، ما يدفعنا للتساؤل حول ماهيّة ومكان الجرح «الحقيقي؟» بهذا الشكل المزدوج، لا ينحصر التشويه بانتهاك بيولوجيا الحياة البشرية، بل يمتدّ ليُملي الشروط المسبقة لإسباغ صفة الإنسانية على الأجساد والجماعات، أو حجبها عنها. التشويه إذًا ليس شيئًا «يحدث» للجسد؛ بل هو من صميم أنطولوجيا المقاومة، هو جزءٌ لا يتجزأ ممّا تعنيه الحياة «تحت الاحتلال».

من جانبٍ آخر، تضبط الحواجز حركة الأفراد فحسب، بل تضبط أو بالأحرى تُعاير [titrate] دخول المواد الطبية والمياه والأسمنت وغيره من موادّ البناء، كما تعرقل تأشيرات دخول الأطباء والعاملين بمجالات الإغاثة الإنسانية وبُناها التحتية. تمثّل المعلومات التي تُجمع على الحواجز عن كميات هذه المواد والأشخاص أداةً قياسيةً للاستفراد [13].[dividualization] المُستفرَد هو دالةٌ رقمية بطبيعة الحال؛ تكوينٌ من نقاط البيانات الرقمية التي لا تولي اعتبارًا خاصًّا للثنائيات عاديةً كانت أم استثنائية. عوضًا عن ذلك يمثّل المُستفرَد العلاقات بدلالة معايير إحصائية لإدارة المعايرة كتقنية للتحكم. يجبر هذا سكان غزة على اختبار الحياة من خلال معايير إمبريقية رتيبة ولكنها كذلك وحشية، تشمل الصحة والبُنى التحتية والتكاثر وأي شيء يمكن تمكينه أو تعجيزه عبر الإحصاء والمراقبة والنُّظم.[14] المعايرة إذًا هي نوع من «الآليات الأمنية» تولّد «الشيفرة الخاصة بمادة الاستفراد» وتعيد توزيع ونَظْم الزمن وعناصر الحياة الأساسية مرارًا، وهي ظاهريًّا ما «ينظّم الحياة على الوجه الأمثل».[15] إلا أنه في حالة غزة تحديدًا (وفلسطين عمومًا) لا تتمحور الآليات الأمنية التي تغذّي لوجستيات الاحتواء تلك حول الشكل الأمثل للحياة، بل حول «إبقاء قابلية الحركة غير المرغوب فيها عند حدّها الأدنى».[16] بهذا الشكل يصبح استبقاء سكان دولة بأكملها في حالة من الإصابة المستمرّة، واستحكام القبضة الخانقة لتقنيات الإغلاق والحصار، وحساب الأدوات القياسية للتشويه والإحداثيات الرقمية للمُستفرَد، لا الفرد، هو الهدف الأساسي للحياسة اللاإنسانية. تشير تقديرات تعود إلى عام 2012 إلى أنّ غزة ستصبح مدينةً غير صالحة للعيش بحلول العام2020. [17] الآن وقد حلّ العام 2020 وهناك قرابة 1.8 مليون نسمة باقون في غزة، يتضح لنا أنّ قابلية الحياة لا تتعلّق بفهمٍ عامّ لمقوّمات البقاء على قيد الحياة بقدر ما تتعلق بإعادة التعريف المستمرة لماهيّة ما هو قابل للحياة. المعايرة هي شكلٌ من النَّظْم الكمّي يستحثّ تغيرًا نوعيًّا يكسر حدودًا مفاهيمية لا يمكن جبرها إلا بأثرٍ رجعي.

تتراجع ثنائية ما هو قابل/غير قابل للحياة لصالح إنتاجٍ تراكمي لتدرّجات الوجود. لكي نوضح بشكل أفضل كيفية عمل المعايرة، قدّمنا سلسلة رسوم بيانية مستوحاة من البحث الهامّ والحصيف لعالِم الاجتماع و. إ. ب. دوبويس «بورتريهات البيانات».[18] لخّصت رسومنا البيانية كثافة الإحصاءات التي أصدرتها المنظمات العاملة بمجالات الإغاثة وحقوق الإنسان حول الحصار. أعادت الرسومات الأربع والعشرون تمثيل معلومات حول توفّر مياه الشرب وساعات تقنين الكهرباء يوميًّا ونسب الجرحى إلى القتلى خلال السنوات الماضية وعدد المستشفيات المدّمرة وتوافر وسائل نقل وإسعاف المصابين ومنح ومنع تأشيرات الأطباء

وتنظيم مناطق الصيد وحركة البضائع وإتلاف المزروعات وإطلاق وحصر سعات الإنترنت.

لذا يمكننا القول إنّ حصار غزة هو حصارٌ مطاطي الطابع. لا يعمل فقط عبر احتواء الحركة، بل عبر التحكم في ما تعنيه الحركة وما يمكن أن تكونه. أما حدود ما هو قابل أو غير قابل للحياة فتُعاد معايرتها باستمرار وفق مساميّة الحصار وعبر الحوكمة اللوجستية التي تسعى لتنظيم مفهوم الحركة ذاته. وبإعادة تعريف الحركة من خلال، لا رغمًا عن، ضبابية هذا الحصار الخانق، يعيد الغزّاويون تعريف قابلية الحركة كواجهةٍ بينية تفصل الداخل عن الخارج، تمامًا كشريط موبيوس.

من الاحتلال عن بعد إلى القنص عن قرب

عادةً ما تُترجَم قدرة المستعمِر على التشويه بمدى تمكّنه من «لا أنسنة» المستعمَر. إلا أنّ هذا يفترض إنتاج المستعمَر كـ«آخر» طوال الوقت، وهي عمليةٌ شاقّة على الفرد السامي خصوصًا، الذي يمكن القول إنه يستبطن بداخله ذلك الآخر الذي ينتمي لعرقٍ مختلف. تشير التعبيرات التي يصف بها الجنود الإسرائيليون قنص أهدافهم إلى عملية ذاتية التحفيز، أشبه بالاستشعار والغربلة والترتيب.[19] فالاستفراد لا يقطّع أو يقسّم الجسد —إلى ركبة وكاحل وساق وهلمّ جرا — بل يعمد أساسًا إلى تجاهل كون هذه الأجزاء مكوّنات لجسد الفرد المتكامل. ليس الهدف هو الفلسطيني، أو حتى طرف من جسد الفلسطيني، بل ببساطة هو ال/طرف دون توصيف. ثمّة قرب حميمي هنا — فالقناصة ليسوا على مبعدة كبيرة من المتظاهرين، قد تتقابل وجوههم وأحيانًا أعينهم. يبقى أن يتعلم المرء كيف يرى الطرف متصلًا بباقي الجسد. هذا القرب هو تحديدًا ما يسمح، عوضًا عن أن يمنع، برؤية الذراع أو الساق أعضاءً طافية ومستقلة عن باقي الأعضاء؛ بشكل يسمح للقناص بإدراكها كأعضاء مفصولة عن الجسد. يستلزم هذا القرب من الطرف بديهيًّا حضور باقي الجسد كمكمّل له لا العكس. ينتج هذا الإطار العلائقي لرؤية الهدف استفرادًا للجسد عن طريق تعميته بوصفه كلًّا يتألف من أجزاء، ما يخوّل الجنود أن يحصوا كم حصدوا من الأطراف عند نهاية كل نهار.[20]

تتمّ أنسنة الفرد كي يتسنّى النظر في مظالمه ضمن إطارٍ حقوقي (وهو أمرٌ غير متاح أو فعّال بالنسبة للفلسطينيين) وبالمقابل تتمّ لا أنسنته كي يتسنّى قتله. يُشكّل المستفرَد نقطة صفر تحليلية لأجزاء لا تؤلّف كلًّا مكتملًا، ولأدوات حسابية تقيس الأجساد، ولكميات خصائص تُحصى على مستوى ما هو شبه ودون الجسد الفرد. ما من حيثية هنا لتعقيد الجسد البشري المركب، بل لا حيثية لوجوده أصلًا. وبينما يُعتبر (أو يُشتهى أن يكون) جسد المشوّه مساحةً سائغة لطرح خطاب التمكين وعمل التقنيات والأجهزة التعويضية كالأطراف الاصطناعية، يشكّل المستفرَد توقعًّا محسوبًا، لا كائنًا تحدوه الإيديولوجيا، يستند على قابلية أعضاء الجسد للتشويه والاجتزاء. الاستفراد هنا عاملٌ مهم في تحديد كيفية استهداف الفلسطينيين. فالمستفرَد، لا الفرد، هو ما يدفع ممارسات حياسية وحشية تنبني على الحسابات القياسية المحضة بدل الإنسانية.

يعيد هذا الاقتصاد الشهواني لقطف الأجسام واحدًا تلو الآخر — بالأحرى قطف الأطراف السفلى منها — شحن الذات الاستيطانية عاطفيًّا، في ساديةٍ تستمتع بالتكرار الأدائي للمذبحة. يعني ذلك أنه ارتكاب المذبحة لمرة واحدة، أو تكرارها بين الفينة والاخرى، ليس كافيًا. فإشباع هذه السادية لا يتطلب فقط أن تكون أعداد الضحايا كبيرة بما يكفي لتسميتها مذبحة، بل يجب أن يكون كل فعلِ قنصٍ بمثابة مذبحةٍ قائمة بذاتها.

لذا يمثّل القنص مادةً لتجدّد استحقاق ذاتٍ استيطانيةٍ استعمارية استنفذت، ولو مؤقتًا، نفعية القصف الجوي والطائرات المسيّرة وغيرها من أشكال ممارسة العنف عن بعد. يشير التراوح بين صيغتيْ العنف المسيّر عن قرب وعن بعد إلى تأرجح المستعمِر إزاء التقارب مع المستعمَر أو التمايز عنه. التشويه هو إعادةٌ أدائية للحدث (التأسيسي؟) للاستعمار الاستيطاني والذي يسهم في ترسيخ بنية هذا الاستعمار. يعود هنا صدى كلمات غسان كنفاني: «كانت تلوح لي أنها....أنها بدايةٌ فقط».[21] يمكننا أن نخلُص إلى أنه في حالة فلسطين يمثّل الحق في التشويه شرطًا لازمًا للاحتلال الاستعماري الاستيطاني. تجدر الإشارة هنا إلى ملاحظة باتريك وولف الهامّة إلى أنّ الاستعمار الاستيطاني هو في واقع الحال منظومة، وليس حدثًا، مشيرًا إلى أنّ إبادة السكان الأصليين لا يمكن أن تتحقق عبر مذبحة عرقية واحدة.[22] ويوضّح التكرار المتواصل للمذبحة التأسيسية مساميّة حدود الحدث، أي حدث ارتكابها في الزمن، بما يزيل التناقض بين الحدث والمنظومة دون أن يلغي أحدهما الآخر. إذًا تشكّل حوادث التشويه هذه السمة التعجيزية والمتكرّرة لمنظومة الاستعمار الاستيطاني.

اختُبرت أساليب القناصة بانتظام في مخيّمات اللاجئين بالضفة الغربية منذ الانتفاضة الأولى بأقلّ تقدير، لكن ما هي القيمة التكتيكية لاستعمال القنص الآن؟ في سياق الاحتلال عن بعد في غزة، يطلق القنص العنان لسيادةٍ تشرّع وتُمارَس دون مساءلة، وعلى مرأى من جمهورٍ دولي غير مكترث. يمثّل هذا تحوّلًا عمّا كان عليه الوضع عام 2014. أصبح القنص حالة متفاقمة للقوة المتجدّدة لهذه السيادة التي لا ينفكّ بحثها عن جذور لها حتى أقصى الحدود. التشويه في هذا المثال ليس استراتيجية لتجنّب استنكار المجتمع الدولي بإبقاء حصيلة القتلى منخفضة، كما كان الحال سابقًا. واقع الحال أنه يستهدف إنتاج

مشهد من الإعاقة (بتشويه الفلسطينيين) يحيل لحياة لا تستحقّ أن تُعاش، على عكس الفانتازيا الليبرالية حول صورة المُقعَد المُقبِل على الحياة. إنها وقاحة الدولة الإسرائيلية الحياسية حين تُظهر التشويه، لا القتل (وحسب)، كعنوان للسيادة. القنص هو فعلٌ دقيق، لذا ودون أي ادعاء بأنّ التشويه هو عاقبة حتمية للحرب، فإنّ هذه الدقة تحوّل الإصابة من خانة الحتمي إلى القصدي.

يستخدم القناصة الإسرائيليون تشكيلة من الذخيرة الحيّة والرصاص المطاطي ورصاص الدمدم المتشظي والمحرّم دوليًّا، والتي تُعتبر كلها نظريًّا أسلحة غير قاتلة،[23] علمًا أنّ عبارة «غير قاتلة» هنا هي توصيف أقرب إلى الوهميٍّ ويخدّر وقْع العنف علينا أو يسكّنه عند الحد الأدنى. يمكن لهذا التوصيف أن يتغير استنادًا لهوية حامل السلاح والمسافة بينه وبين الهدف وكيفية استعماله للذخيرة. يخضع تصنيف ما هو قاتل وما هو غير قاتل من الأسلحة إلى التقييم التقني والقانوني، إلا أنه أيضًا يُنظّم الكيفية التي تُروى بها سردية الأذى في المكان والزمان. يُبقي هذا التصنيف انتباهنا معلقًّا بتمييز الحد الفاصل بين الحياة والموت، فيتيح بذلك تسخير واستغلال المساحة المخفية الواقعة بين الإصابة والموت. ويُبقينا منشغلين بما إذا كان السلاح قاتلًا أم لا، في محاولةٍ لتفادي السؤال حول مصير من أصيبوا ولم يُقتلوا. يقلل هذا التصنيف أيضًا من شأن الإصابة نفسه كحدث، بحيث يمّحي أثر ما قبل التشويه وما بعده. ما معنى استعمال أسلحة غير قاتلة في غزة في ظلّ دمار البنية التحتية الطبية؟ يمكن للإصابات غير القاتلة، إذا لم تصبح قاتلة بالفعل، أن تتحوّل في فلسطين إلى ما صار يُعرَف بالـ«العاهات المستديمة» — وهي عبارة ملطّفة تقصد الجرح المستديم الذي لا يلتئم. هناك أيضًا تصنيفات أدقّ للأسلحة تشمل ما يُطلق عليه أسلحة قاتلة بدرجة أقلّ وأسلحة ما دون القاتلة وأسلحة غير فاتكة وأسلحة مؤلمة. الغاز المسيّل للدموع على سبيل المثال هو سلاحٌ غير قاتل، إلا أنّ التعرّض له لفترات طويلة قد يجعل منه سلاحًا «ما دون القاتل». تستدعي هذه التدرّجات توترًا زمنيًّا: أي ساعة يحين الموت وكم هو قريبٌ منا الآن؟

غزو المنازل

تقع مسألة الجندر في صميم قضية التشويه. إلا أنها عادةً ما تمرّ مرور الكرام في أغلب المواد التي تتناول مسيرة العودة، سواء أظهرت تلك المواد على منصات إخبارية تقدّمية أو تجارية، أو في تقارير منظمات غير حكومية، أو حتى ضمن البيانات الطبية. لماذا تقتصر كل الصور والأخبار الواردة من غزة على تصوير مشاهد لجموع الرجال؟ هل يرمي ذلك إلى حذف من يشغل مواقع التظاهر من المشهد؟ يعيد تأطير الصّور على هذه الشاكلة إحياء الفصل بين العام والخاص الذي طالما سلّطت الضوء عليه نسويات الموجة الثانية وفكّكته مليًّا النسويات غير البيضاوات. يصبح التداخل المعقّد بين الشأن العامّ في بعده التظاهراتي من جانب والشأن الخاصّ في بعده العائلي من جانب آخر، لا سيما في تجليات الجندر غير المتماثلة لكل منهما، أكثر وضوحًا بفعل آثار التشويه الجسدي.

وبعيدًا عن تأويل سطحي للإخصاء [المعنويٍ]، والحدّ من العمل البدني، و«العبء» الذي يُخلّفه الجسد المعاق على من يحيط به من النساء والبُنى العائلية، فعليًّا ما هي الذكورة المشوّهة، وكيف ترتبط أو تُعفى من سياسات تمثيل الجندر؟ هل توجد بالمقابل أنوثة مشوّهة؟ إذا ما تركنا جانبًا مشهد الجريح الذكر وفيتيشية الاستشهاد، سنجد أنّ أغلب حوادث التشويه في غزة ضحاياها من النساء والفتيات الصغار، بل ومن الأجساد المستعصية على التصنيف في ثنائية الذكورة-الأنوثة. يتكبّد النساء عناء أشكالٍ مزمنةٍ من العنف، منها العنف المنزلي وعنف الاعتداء الجنسي وعنف التعنيف الزوجي. وفي حين يظل مشهد التشويه مذكرًا، فإنّ العنف الواقع على النساء يُقاس بالإصابات والقتلى الناتجة عن الحصار ويزداد ويخفّ مع مدى تشويه أجساد الرجال وإعاقتهم، في علاقة شاذة بين العائلي والعسكري. من وجهة النظر النسوية، لا تعني نهاية الحصار/العدوان/التشويه بالضرورة نهاية العنف ضد النساء. بطريقة أخرى، يمكننا القول إنّ العنف المنزلي يبدأ في واقع الحال مع نهاية التظاهرة.[24] مشهدا العنف، الأول مع القناص والثاني مع الشريك، كلاهما مشهد للألفة والحميمية.

الجرح هنا هو سردية المقاومة التي تحكي عن العائلة والقربى والتقارب الاجتماعي أحادي الجنس. يتمحور التفاعل الاجتماعي في مجتمع الرجال مع مفهوم الجرح حول ميراث الانتصارات البطولية التي تخلق انتماءات أخوية مشتركة، تأتي على حساب الروابط العائلية. بالمقابل يختلف الأمر في مجتمع النساء. فمفاهيم البطولة والعار والتضحية ليست على القدر ذاته من الأهمية في التقارب الاجتماعي الأحادي النسائي. أَوَليست هذه المفاهيم نفسها وليدة الذكورة القومية؟ هناك أكثر من سبب يدفعنا للاقتناع بأنّ تفاعل مجتمع النساء مع الجرح يتخطّى هذه المفاهيم بأشواط. فخلف صور البطولة الذكورية هذه تقبع مساحات وافرة ترفض فيها «البضائع» — اصطلاح طوّره كلاود ليفي شتراوس لوصف النساء كسلعٍ للمقايضة بين الرجال — «العرض في السوق». ما الذي يمكن أن يحدث عندما «تقرر البضائع التضافر؟» بطريقة أخرى، ما نوع علاقات القربى والنسب التي يُمكن أن تنشأ عندما تشتدّ حدود المعيارية الغيرية الجنسية إلى الحد الذي تعجز معه عن رؤية ما هو أبعد من نفسها؛ إلى الحد الذي تعجز فيه عن أن تفطن إلى أنّ «النساء/البضائع يُدرنَ/تدير فيما بينها نوعًا مكتفيًا ذاتيًّا من المقايضة»؟[25]

تشويه أجساد الرجال هو بالمحصّلة محوٌ مضاعف للنساء يفاقم ويراكم العنف الواقع على أجسادهنّ في خضم النضال الثوري كزوجات وأمهات وبنات. فبالرغم من حضورهنّ الرمزي لا تزال النساء تحت نيّر القهر المادي.[26] يضيف التشويه المتعمد على هذا المأزق «أعباء إضافية مضنية» من العمل المنزلي والإنجابي، من الناحيتين العاطفية والعملانية، إذ يقع عبء رعاية المصابين والأسرى على عاتق نساء الأسرة.[27] يحصر ذلك مشاركة النساء السياسية في التنظيم والتظاهر، ويعيد تكريس ذكورية النضال الوطني ويعيد معها تكريس الأدوار الجندرية التقليدية.[28] في الوقت ذاته فإنّ المفعول الإيديولوجي للتشويه كجزء من مكافحة التمرّد هو مفعول في غاية العمق. فإذا كانت العائلة هي وحدة للمقاومة، يصبح التشويه بمثابة انتهاك للعائلة ليس بوصفها تكوينًا ثقافيًّا وحسب، بل بوصفها تكوينًا اقتصاديًّا أيضًا، ما يُحكم تبعيّتها الاقتصادية للمستعمِر ويفاقم من هشاشتها.[29] يعمّق التشويه تقسيم المكان والزمان اللازمين لإعادة إنتاج البُنى الاجتماعية، ما يضطرّ النساء إلى المزيد من العمل المأجور وغير المأجور خصوصًا مع نضوب سوق العمل من الشباب. يقوّض ذلك من بنية الأسرة المعيارية ولكن لجهة تعزيز الأدوار الجندرية التقليدية فيها، خصوصًا على خلفية شعارات الشهادة و«البطولة الوطنية».[30] تسهم هذه الأوضاع في إنتاج البيئة السياسية والاجتماعية المواتية لحدوث العنف على خلفية الجندر وتحصينه من المساءلة أحيانًا.[31]

في هذه الدائرة من إعادة الإنتاج المُجندَرة للبُنى الاجتماعية والعنف المترتب عليها، يشكّل التشويه في حالة الرجال اعتداءً على رجولتهم. إلا أنه يمثل أيضًا اعتداءً مضاعفًا على النساء اللاتي سيضطررن للمزيد من العمل وربما سيتعرّضن بسبب ذلك (للمزيد من) العنف الجنسي. هذا إذا ما تغاضينا عن الإعاقة الجسدية الناتج عن إنهاك أجساد العاملات. فضلًا عن ذلك، تستفيد الدولة الإسرائيلية من إخضاع الفلسطينيات (ربما من المفيد أن نتذكر قضية المرأة إبان حقبة مناهضة الاستعمار) والكويريين(ات) (ولا ننسى توظيف الدفاع عن قضايا المثلية كأداة في خطاب الغسيل الوردي الإسرائيلي) لتبرر ولو جزئيًّا ضرورة الاحتلال الاستعماري.[32] إنْ كان أحد أوجه الدولة الاستعمارية يعطف استعلاءه على افتراض تخلف المرأة الفلسطينية ومجتمعها (من الرجال) الذي يقمعها، فإنها في وجهها الآخر وكما توضح هديل بدارنة تعمد إلى «تفكيك اللُّحمة الاجتماعية لهذا المجتمع لصالحها الديموغرافي، وتحول دون التئامه بهدف خفض معدلات المواليد».[33] وبهذا يستغلّ الاستعمار العلاقة الديالكتيكية بين انفراط عقد الأسرة النواتية المعيارية وإعادة تكريس الثنائيات الجندرية الجامدة.

لذا، ليس التشويه محض اعتداء على الجسد، بل هو أيضًا ظاهرة تعيد ترتيب أنساق المجتمع. لا تحدّ فقط من قدرة المجتمع على المقاومة بأجساده (بمحاولة نزع المقاومة الأنطولوجية للجسد الفرد) بل تعمد أيضًا إلى سدّ آفاق التحرر عبر تقويض الحيوية التنظيمية وإمكانيات النمو. لكن عندما نركّز فقط على كيفية استنزاف قدرة الجسد العامل على التنظيم وممارسة السياسة والمقاومة، فإننا نرسّخ أنطولوجيا تموضع المقاومة خارج الجسد. من الناحية البنيوية، لا تتمايز اقتصادات الرعاية والدعم المتبادل بالضرورة عن شبكات الدعم والعمل على إعادة إنتاج البنى الاجتماعية، بل تأتي هذه الاقتصادات عادةً مشمولة بهذه الشبكات ومفاعيلها من أشكال المقاومة التي تُمكّن استدامة الحياة اليومية.

«التقزّم» هو اصطلاحٌ طبّي يصف تباطؤ النمو عند الأطفال عن المعدلات المعيارية لمن هم في عمرهم، ويصف أيضًا عمليةً لنزع الهوية الجندرية عنهم، ما تسمّيه نادرة شلهوب كيفوركيان بـ«نزع الطفولة»[34]. [unchilding] تعطّل ممارسات نزع الطفولة هذه تطوّر الخصائص المعيارية المميزة لكل من الذكر («الرجل») والأنثى («المرأة») فتعيد بذلك ترتيب العلاقة بين الذكورة والأنوثة وتفتح المجال في الوقت ذاته على طيفٍ متعدد من إمكانات الجندرة.[35] هل الأجساد المستفرَدة هي بالمثل أجسادٌ منزوعة الجندر؟ هل يُمكن أن ننظر للاستفراد كآلية سلطوية لطمس أو تعطيل الهويات الجندرية؟ يشكّل تقاطع التقزّم مع التشويه أيضًا عملية لنزع الهوية الجندرية. فمسار حياة الشاب المشوّه جسده بسبب التقزم يتماثل مع مسار جروحه التي تتطور مع نمو الجسم وتقدمه في العمر، ما يترتب عليه «الحاجة إلى تدخل جراحي مستمر». تنمو الإصابة مع نمو «الجسد المقزّم».[36] لا يندمل الجرح أو يلتئم بل يكبر ويغور مع نمو الجسد.

يشبّع الاحتلال ثنايا المكان والزمان الفلسطينيين ولو جزئيًّا بتقنيات مصمّمة لإنتاج احتلالٍ «يُمكن التحكم به عن بعد». عوضًا عن التهجير القسري والمداهمات وهدم المنازل، تعمل هذه النسخة من الغزو الإسرائيلي للمنازل عبر تشويه الفضاء المنزلي وتقزيم العائلة المعيارية التي تسكن داخل حدوده.[37] تستهدف النسخة الجديدة حيّز الشأن العام، بتعريفه الكلاسيكي، كموقعٍ لمعايرة ونَظْم الحياة نفسها ومقايسة طواعيتها: حيّز الشأن العام بوصفه العتبة الفاصلة لما هو قابل للإبقاء على قيد الحياة. يُعاد هنا تشكيل العائلي عبر تمزيق الوشائج الموصلة بين الخاص والعام. وفي هذا الصدد لا يمكن النظر إلى ترسيخ الثنائيات الجندرية الجامدة كمحض نتاج عارض أو تكتيكي للتشويه، بل هو بالأحرى هدفه الأبعد التشويه هنا هو إخضاعٌ النسيج الاجتماعي للحياة الفلسطينية كلها ولقدراتها الجمعية على المقاومة والاستمتاع والحلم.

تنفس قتالي

لقد خرجت إلى شوارع غزة، شوارع يملؤها ضوء الشمس الساطع، لقد قالوا لي إنّ نادية فقدت ساقها عندما ألقتْ بنفسها فوق اخوتها الصغار تحميهم من القنابل واللهب وقد أنشبا أظفارهما في الدار، كان يمكن لناديا أن تنجو بنفسها، أن تهرب.... أن تنقذ ساقها، لكنها لم تفعل.[38]

لا يستقيم احتلال الأرض مع استقلال أهلها. فالبلد بأكمله، بتاريخه ونبضه اليومي موضوعٌ تحت مطرقة الاحتلال. يضعضعه شيئًا فشيئًا على أمل تدميره نهائيًا. في ظل هذه الظروف تصبح أنفاس المرء مراقبةً ومحسوبة، ويصبح التنفس نفسه محتلًا. هذا هو التنفس القتالي.[39]

يذكّرنا فرانتز فانون مجدّدًا أننا سبق أن كنا هنا، وأننا نعرف التنفس القتالي هذا، حيث تصبح «مجرد إمكانية التنفس هي التحدي الأكبر».[40] وهل كان التنفس القتالي استعارة أصلًا؟ ما يعنينا هو أنه في حالتنا اليوم يُمكن أن يكون أي شيء سوى استعارة. فكوكبنا المحتضر يختنق تحت ضباب التلوث، في نيو دلهي المغلقة بسبب التغير المناخي، وفي أراضي السكان الأصليين المشتعلة في أستراليا، وفي خليج سان فرانسيسكو التي تستيقظ إلى سماء قانية، إنها أجواء الاختناق. إنها في القبضة الخانقة للحصار على غزة وعند حواجز الاحتلال في كل فلسطين وفي ركبة الشرطي الأبيض الضاغطة على العنق الأسود وفي نهش الكورونا لمجتمعات السود. «لا أستطيع التنفس» هي تفصيلةٌ في المسرحة الشنيعة لعنف الشرطة ضدّ الجسد الأسود والوعي الجمعي لسكان الكوكب الواقف على شفير ثورات عدّة. القناع والركبة والقبضة الخانقة وعوادم ثاني أكسيد الكربون ورصاص الخردق وغيره من الأسلحة «غير القاتلة» هي الأطراف الاصطناعية؛ هي الشهود، وهي من يقف وراء التنفس القتالي. ساق ناديا أيضًا ليست بمعزل عن التمرّد الجماعي ضد الحصار على غزة. في الطب الصيني، الرئتان هما بيت الأحزان. تعملان كوسيط بين ما هو داخلي وما هو خارجي بحيث يزول الفرق بينهما. إنهما شريط الموبيوس الخاص بالجسد. وبالتالي «لا أستطيع التنفس» هي عويل وصرخة لوعة وحزن على توقف الحياة والحركة. مشهد التشويه ليس مشهدًا خاصًا بغزة وحدها. فدائرة التشويه حول العالم تكتمل بعنفٍ مماثل في فقأ عيون المتحجين في كشمير برصاص الخردق وفي إمطارهم بقنابل الغاز المسيّل للدموع على الحدود المكسيكية-الأميركية. واقع الحال أنّ نفي حالة الاستثناء عن فلسطين يظهر صلتها ببويرتوريكو وبلدة فلينت بميشيغان ونيو أورليانز وغيرها من المواقع، حيث، وكما في غزة، لا تعود «الكارثة الطبيعية» مجرّد فرصة لوضع خطط تجارية وحسب، بل تصبح هي بحدّ ذاتها خطة المتاجرة.

بالنسبة لمن يراقب العالم من غزة ومن كل مناطق الصراع، وربما من أي موقع بالجنوب العالمي، لا يبدو العالم كما لو كانت تملؤه الأجساد السليمة، إذ لا تنطبق عليه تضاريس المعيارية الجسدية العالمية هنا. هل تدفع تواريخ العنف التي تتمحور حول الموت سرديات بعينها إلى الظهور؟ أي تواريخ أخرى مغايرة من شأنها أن تُكتب بالتمحور حول الجرح عوضًا عن الموت؟ ستقتفي هذه التواريخ أثر التشويه، وتحديدًا على التقاطع بين التشويه والموت، لتظهر استغلال الأول إلى أقصى حدّ كتقنية دولتية. في العام 2010 غيّرت الحكومة الهندية الذخيرة المستعملة في كشمير المحتلة برصاص الخردق «غير القاتل». وفي تشيلي أصيب أكثر من 300 متظاهر في عيونهم برصاص الشرطة بين تشرين الأول/أكتوبر وآذار/مارس 2020. وفي حزيران/يونيو 2020 استهدفت الشرطة بالولايات المتحدة أعين الصحفيين والمتظاهرين عشوائيًا في المظاهرات التي خرجت احتجاجًا على مقتل جورج فلويد. أن نستوعب ونفضح الحق السيادي للدولة في التشويه وفضحه، هو أن ندرك أنه من وجهة نظر دولة الاستعمار الاستيطاني الحياسي، الأمور تجري بالضبط كما ينبغي لها أن تكون.

يجدر بنا التفكّر في الاقتصادين الرمزيين المتشابكين لاستهداف الأعين واستهداف الأطراف السفلى. ففي حين يُمكن قراءة الأول كتدمير حرفي للقدرة على الإبصار، ومعها القدرة على إبصار آفاق سياسية جديدة، يتولّى الثاني تعطيل القدرة على الحركة اللازمة لإعادة إنتاج الاجتماع الإنساني والمقاومة، والحدّ من قدرة المشاركة في الحراك، بحيث يتحكم هذا التعطيل في ماهيّة الحركة وما يُمكن أن تكونه. من الملهم هنا النظر إلى حراكات التضامن من مختلف أرجاء العالم والتي تردّ مشهدية التشويه على المتسببين فيه، وتسترجع من المستعمِر حقه في التشويه كحقٍّ يعود للمستعمَر في استعداده ليشوّه جسده. ردًا على استهداف الجيش الإسرائيلي لعين الصحفي معاذ عمارنة، انتشرت صور المتضامنين مع عمارنة من طلاب وصحفيين ومتظاهرين وهم يغطون إحدى عيونهم بالأيادي واللافتات وعُصابات العين. أتت هذه الصور من كل أرجاء العالم، من شيلي وبوليفيا وهونغ كونغ كما من فلسطين. أظهر الرواج الواسع لهذه الصور مدى انفضاح الحق السيادي في التشويه أمام العالم، وأشّر على أنّ الاستمرار في إصابة أطراف المتظاهرين عوضًا عن قتلهم بذريعة «صون الحياة» لم يعد مقبولًا.

«لا أستطيع التنفس» هي صرخة الجسد المشوّه الذي لا يزال يقاوم أملًا في أن يعود مكتملًا. من مظاهرات

فيرغسون تضامنًا مع غزة عام 2014، شعارنا واحد «عندما تتنفّس، فإننا نتنفّس معًا». وحدة الشعار هنا ليست مجرد رمز للتضامن بين نضالات السود والفلسطينيين فحسب، بل هي بالأحرى مطالبة بعالمٍ لا تراتبية فيه بين من يحقّ لهم التنفس أولًا، ومن لا يحق لهم التنفس إلا أنفاسهم الأخيرة.

1 غسان كنفاني، "ورقة من غزة" في أرض البرتقال الحزين (1962). قبرص: دار منشورات الرمال (2013)، ص. 71-63.

2 تجدر الإشارة بأنّ نص كنفاني ليس رسالة حقيقية منه إلى صديق حقيقي إنما هي قصة قصيرة مكتوبة بصيغة رسالة بضمير المتكلم. [المحرّرات]

3 كنفاني، "ورقة من غزة."

4 * "حياْسة" هي مفردة منحوتة من مفردتيْ "حيوية" و"سياسة". بحسب عالم السياسة السويدي روبرت كيلين، أول من صاغ مفردة biopolitics، لا تشير السياسات الحيوية لنوع من السياسة تمارسه الدولة وحسب، بل أن الدولة في تصوره هي أصلًا وحصرًا كيان حيوي يقوم على هذه الممارسة. لذا ارتأينا ترجمة المفردة الإنكليزية بكلمة واحدة غير منسوبة. [المترجم]
ظهرت نفس العبارة في نص الندوة "الغلاف الحيويّ للحرب" الوارد في هذا الكتاب بترجمة مغايرة - سياسة حيوية. [المحرّرات]

5 انظروا Jasbir K. Puar, *The Right to Maim: Debility, Capacity, Disability* (Durham, NC: Duke Univ. Press, 2017).

6 Nitasha Dhillon, *From Occupation to Decolonization*, Ph.D diss. (University of Buffalo, 2020), p.36.

7 MTL Collective, *Filming as Training in the Practice of Freedom*, YouTube video, 1:25:29 min., uploaded by IRI Institute of Radical Imagination (November 2, 2020), https://instituteofradicalimagination.org/2020/11/02/filming-as-training-in-the-practice-of-freedom-mao-mollona-mtl-collective-amin-husain-nitasha-dhillon (accessed November 17, 2020).

8 Nasser Abourahme, "'Nothing to Lose but Our Tents': The Camp, the Revolution, the Novel," *Journal of Palestine Studies* vol. 48, no. 1 (Autumn 2018).

9 انظروا https://www.activestills.org

10 Édouard Glissant, *Poetics of Relation*, trans. Betsy Wing (Michigan, 2006), p. 189.

11 Neel Ahuja, "Animal Death as National Debility: Climate, Agriculture, and Syrian War Narrative," *New Literary Studies* (forthcoming, 2020).

12 عن جهان بسيسو في ندوة الغلاف الحيوي للحرب، ص. 225 من هذا الكتاب

13 يشير مصدر "استفراد" ومشتقاته في هذا النص إلى الاصطلاح dividual الذي طوّره جيل دولوز وفيليكس غوتاري للإشارة إلى ذات إنسانية يُمكن فرزها وضمّها وتمثيلها بيانيًّا وإحصائيًّا بشكل متكرر ولا متناهٍ عبر التقنيات الحديثة للتحكم الرقمي. [المترجم]

14 Ghassan Abu Sittah, *The Virus, the Settler, and the Siege: Gaza in the Age of Corona*, (Institute for Palestine Studies, 2020).

15 Michel Foucault, *Security, Territory, Population: Lectures at the Collège de France 1977–78*, trans. Graham Burchell (London, 2011), p. 246.

16 Francesco Sebregondi, "Power, Logistics, Interface: The Case of Gaza," *Research Values 2018*, (December 13, 2017) https://researchvalues2018.wordpress.com/2017/12/13/francesco-sebregondi-power-logistics-interface-the-case-of-gaza (accessed November 17, 2020).

17 "Gaza in 2020: A Liveable Place?," Report by the United Nations Country Team in the occupied Palestinian territory (August 2012), https://www.unrwa.org/userfiles/file/publications/gaza/Gaza%20in%202020.pdf (accessed January 20, 2021).

18 انظروا Whitney Battle-Baptiste and Britt Rusert, *W. E. B. Du Bois's Data Portraits: Visualizing Black America* (New York, 2018).

19 انظروا Hilo Glazer, "'42 Knees in One Day': Israeli Snipers Open Up About Shooting Gaza Protesters," *Haaretz*, March 6, 2020, https://www.haaretz.com/israel-news/.premium.MAGAZINE-42-knees-in-one-day-israeli-snipers-open-up-about-shooting-gaza-protesters-1.8632555 (accessed November 17, 2020).

20 Dr. Ghassan Abu Sittah, interview by Perla Issa, "There Is No International Community," *Journal of Palestine Studies* vol. 47 no. 4 (Summer 2018).

21 كنفاني، "ورقة من غزة".

22 Rema Hammami, Andaleeb A. Shehadah, eds., "Navigating Through Shattered Paths: NGO Service Providers and Women Survivors of Gender-Based Violence," UN Women Research Paper (September 2017), https://palestine.unwomen.org/en/digital-library/publications/2017/12/gbv-research17.

23 انظروا Paul Rocher, *Gazer, mutiler, soumettre. Politique de l'arme non létale* (Paris, 2020).

24 Hammani, Shehadah, eds., "Navigating Through Shattered Paths".

25 Luce Irigaray, *This Sex Which Is Not One* (Ithaca, 1985), p. 196.

26 Ann McClintock, "The Angel of Progress: Pitfalls of the Term 'Post-Colonialism,'" *Social Text* (1992).

27 "On the Media of Counterinsurgency and the Targeting of Decolonize this Place," Verso Books Blog (March 11, 2020), https://www.versobooks.com/blogs/4593-on-the-media-of-counterinsurgency-and-the-targeting-of-decolonize-this-place (accessed January 9, 2021).

28 Dhillon, *From Occupation to Decolonization*.

29 Hadeel Badarneh, "The Economy of Desires in Late Capitalism: Reading in the American and Palestinian Context," *Anemones* (2018). يقدّم هذا المقال تحليلًا أكثر تعمّقًا للجندر والقومية والاستعمار

30 المرجع نفسه

31 Hammani, Shehadah, eds., "Navigating Through Shattered Paths".

32 Jasbir K. Puar, "Rethinking Homonationalism," International Journal of Middle East Studies (April 2013); see also *The Journal of Palestine Studies Special Issue: Queering Palestine* (2018).

33 Badarneh, "The Economy of Desires."

34 Nadera Shalhoub-Kevorkian, *Incarcerated Childhood and the Politics of Unchilding* (Cambridge, 2019). في كتابها "طفولة سجينة وسياسات نزع الطفولة" تسائل نادرة شلهوب كيفوركيان مفهوم الطفولة كرأسمال سياسي في يد السلطة عبر طرح مفهوم نزع الطفولة. يتناول مفهوم نزع الطفولة الأثر السياسي لنوع من العنف الاستعماري يهدف إلى إعادة إنتاج الأطفال المستعمَرين كآخرين إثنيًا، أو بعبارةٍ أخرى كجماعةٍ مارقةٍ تشكّل خطرًا جسيمًا على دولة الاحتلال، مما يستلزم نزع صفة الطفولة عن تلك الجماعة كي يتسنّى للاحتلال إخضاعها عبر السجن والتشويه. [المترجم]

35 تقتفي هذه الأسئلة أثر عمل هورتنس سبيلرز حول "لاجندرة" النساء السوداوات وإعادة قراءة س. رايلي سنورتون لها. بطرقٍ مختلفة، يسائل الباحثان ما ينتجه إبطال الجندرة عن الجسد الأسود كنتيجة لمعاداة السود. تفسّر سبيلرز ذلك من خلال عجز ما تسميه "الآجرّومية الأميركية" عن التعرف على صلات القربى التي تتشكل عبر الاستعباد. بينما يشير سنورتون بالمقابل إلى المرونة والسيولة الجندرية الذي يمكن أن تنتج عن هذا الإبطال، والذي يفتح الطريق أمام أشكال متنوعة من تمثلات جسدية متعدية ومتبدّلة ولاثنائية الجندر. تدفعنا سبيلرز، التي تناقش كيف يُزاح الجندر من الفضاء العائلي إلى سفينة لتجارة العبيد، إلى التفكر في ماهية الجندر تحت الحصار والحجر، حيث يلتغي وجود الفضاء العائلي. انظروا Hortense Spillers, "Mama's Baby, Papa's Maybe: An American Grammar Book," *Diacritics* (Summer 1987); C. Riley Snorton, *Black on Both Sides: A Racial History of Trans Identity*. (New York, 2017)

36 Abu Sittah and Issa, "There is No International Community."(انظروا هامش رقم 16)

37 للمزيد حول أثر هدم المنازل على النساء والعنف الجندري، راجعوا Hanan Abu Ghosh, "The Impact of House Demolitions on Gender Roles and Relations: We Will Come Back to Build in the Same Place, We Are Here and We Will Stay Here," *Women's Affairs Technical Committee – Ramallah* (2014)

38 كنفاني، "ورقة من غزة".

39 Frantz Fanon, *A Dying Colonialism*, trans. Haakon Chevalier (New York, 1965), p. 65.

40 Joseph Pugliese and Suvendrini Perera, "Combat Breathing: State Violence and the Body in Question," *Somatechnics* (2011).

تقبُّـــــــل الدمــــــار

نادــــيـــــــة
أبـــو الحــــاج

ترجمه عن الإنكليزية فريق الأركِلوغ

القدس، بُعيد حرب 1967: عمّال يحفرون موقعًا لبناء فندق جدّي. يشقّون التربة فتتكشّف تحت أقدامهم أرضيةٍ من الفسيفساء الأثريّة. إنْ علِمت هيئة الآثار الإسرائيليّة بوجودها فستأمر بوقف أعمال البناء، أقلّه بصورة مؤقّتة. وقد يقع الأسوأ وتُصادر أرض جدّي. فالمكان يقع في القدس الشرقية حيث تصنيف الأراضي كـ «موقع أثري» ليس سوى ذريعة لانتزاع ملكيّتها. ولذا طلب جدّي من العمال طمر ما عثروا عليه بالإسمنت فورًا.

أخبرني والدي هذه القصة حسبما أذكر وإنْ كنت غير متأكدة تمامًا. قد لا تكون لجدّي علاقة بهذه الحكاية على الإطلاق، وقد تكون حدثت لصديق من أصدقاء العائلة. في أيّ حال، ليست القصّة غريبة أو غير محتملة في القدس الشرقيّة. فبالنسبة للفلسطينيّين القاطنين هناك تحت الحكم الإسرائيلي، تُمثّل الأشياء المطمورة في جوف الأرض تهديدًا وجوديًّا. هذا التهديد هو موضوع العمل الفني التركيبيّ بعنوان «العمق غير المعروف» لديمة سروجي ضمن الدورة الأولى لترينالي الشارقة للعمارة في تشرين الثاني/نوفمبر 2019.[1] يتناول العمل من خلال تسليطه الضوء على قرية سبَسطية في فلسطين والمواقع الأثرية فيها ظاهرةً لطالما كانت أحد أقوى الأسلحة في ترسانة صنّاع الأمة الاستيطانية الصهيونية.

انطلقت أعمال التنقيب في سبَسطية — التي يُعتقد أنّها مبنيّة فوق أطلال مدينة السامرة الواردة في الكتاب المقدّس والتي كانت عاصمةً للمملكة الشمالية خلال العصر الحديدي الثاني — في مطلع القرن العشرين تحت إشراف طاقم من جامعة هارفارد.[2] لم تكن حفريات سبَسطية إلّا مثالًا واحدًا لمبحثٍ علمي أوسع جاء بحلّة الدين. فقد توافد المستكشفون الجغرافيون الأميركيّون والأوروبيّون إلى فلسطين في أواخر القرن التاسع عشر بحثًا عن التاريخ التوراتي مدفوعين بمخيال لاهوتي بروتستانتي. وقد جهد هؤلاء لإثبات تاريخيّة الكتاب المقدس فاضطلعوا بترسيم الأحداث والوقائع اللاهوتية على الجغرافيا الفلسطينية المعاصرة. فطرحت هذه الممارسات الخرائطية فلسطين بوصفها كتلة ملموسة ومتماسكة من التاريخ محوّلةً إياها إلى مادّةٍ خاضعة للبحث العلمي المتجدّد، كما أرست المنطلق الفكري لما سيأتي تباعًا من حفريات. بحلول القرن العشرين كانت المسوحات الطبوغرافية قد تراجعت لمصلحة الأركيولوجيا التوراتية التي أصبحت بدورها تخصّصًا قائمًا بذاته. تحوّل باطن الأرض إلى مكمن الحقيقة — بأشكالها المختلفة؛ الحقيقة الممحوّة أو غير المتاحة على السطح.

وإذا كان المرسلون البروتستانت قد سعوا إلى التنقيب عن الآثار لإثبات سلامة العقيدة المسيحيّة، فإنّ الجمعية الاستكشافية الفلسطينيّة اليهوديّة (إبان الانتداب البريطاني) و علماء الآثار الإسرائيليين (بعد عام 1948) عمدوا إلى التنقيب بهدف البحث عن دليلٍ مادي يثبت الرواية التوراتية عن وجود مجتمعات عبرانية[3]* ذات سيادة في فلسطين القديمة. اُستُخدمت الحقائق الأركيولوجية في الحالة الأخيرة لتعضيد رواية المشروع القومي، أو بالأحرى لترجيح العقيدة الإيديولوجية التي سعت لتأطير الاستعمار الاستيطاني في فلسطين كمشروعٍ لعودة اليهود إلى وطنهم الأصلي. وكانت الحفريّات الأثرية جزءًا لا يتجزّأ من غزوٍ مستمرٍّ يؤسّس لوجود يهودي ذي سيادة على الأرض يُمكن رؤيته وتلمّسه في كلّ من التاريخ والحاضر. إذ يجمع ترسيم الخرائط والمسوحات والحفريات مواداً رمزية «تكشف» هوية الأرض كوطن قومي لليهود تعريفاً مستبقًا في أغلب الأحيان وتحسبًا للاستيطان في جزءٍ معيّن من هذه الأرض أو لانتزاع ملكيته.

كان التاريخ بطابعه الأخلاقي المنظور إليه بحماس فائق ويُتناول كسعي مستمرّ عاملًا أساسيًّا في (ولادة) الإيديولوجيّات القوميّة في القرن التاسع عشر، ولم تكن الصهيونية استثناءًا لذلك.[4] من جانبها كانت الأركيولوجيا تعبيرًا فريدًا من إنتاج الحداثة للمخيّلة التاريخية وممارسة التأريخ نفسه، الأمر الذي وافَق إلى حدّ كبير ومؤثّر متطلّبات مشروع صناعة الأمّة الاستيطانية. إذ لا يقتصر عمَل علماء الآثار على إنتاج سرديّات محتملة للماضي، فهم لا «يذهبون» إلى الأرشيف بحثًا عن مواد ووثائق وجدت طريقها إليه عمدًا أو اعتباطًا.[5] بل على العكس، يقوم الأركيولوجي بإنتاج الأرشيف الذي تستند إليه سرديّاته، شأنه شأن الباحث الإثنوغرافي في تعليمات برونيسلاف مالينوفسكي المنهجيّة.[6] بعبارةٍ أدقّ، يُنتج الأركيولوجي موادًّا ملموسةً لا يقتصر فعلها على صياغة الرواية التاريخية فحسب، بل يتجاوزها لاستحداث عمارة وطبيعة جديدتين.[7]

من خلال التنقيب في تاريخ فلسطين القديم، سعت جمعية استكشاف فلسطين اليهودية، ولاحقًا المؤسسات الأثرية الإسرائيلية، إلى تثبيت روايةٍ بعينها عن نشأة الأمّة اليهودية وحقّها في السيادة على فلسطين بالذات. تم ذلك عبر تجميع موادّ أثرية يُمكن استعمالها كأدلّةٍ على وجود مجتمعات عبرانية قديمة وذات سيادة على هذه الأرض. لم تكن هويّة اليهود كشعبٍ تاريخي

وحدها على المحكّ، بل كذلك هويّة الأرض نفسها. من هنا استند علماء الآثار إلى معايير للبحث العلمي مستقاة من القصص التوراتية لإسباغ هويّة عبرانيّة/عبريّة على أرضٍ متنازع على ملكيّتها في الأساس. وبدأت/أعادت الأركيولوجيا كتابة سيرة بعينها للأرض؛ سيرة عن ماضٍ عبراني وعبريّ مفقود يُعاد إحياؤه. وأصبح للأرض، وليس لمستوطنيها فحسب، الحقّ في أن يستعيدوا مجدّدًا ما كانوا عليه في الماضي حسبما «تثبته» هذه السيرة التاريخيّة.

تخيّل المستوطنون المستعمِرون الأرضَ التي غزوها أرضًا بلا شعب؛ ما يُسمّى باللاتيني terra nullius أي فضاءًا مُفرَغًا. وعليه أصبحت إعادة امتلاك الماضي والتثبّت من تاريخ «السابق» عملًا هامًّا لمناهضة الاستعمار، أي البحث عن الجماعات والأمم والتواريخ التي تشكّلت واستقرّت على هذه الأرض التي يدّعي المستوطِنون خلوّها من السكّان. فلطالما شكّلت عمليّة إبراز الدلائل على وجود بشري متجذّر ومستدام في أرضٍ ما خلال النزاعات القانونية على ملكية الأرض لسكانها الأصليين أو في خضمّ النضالات السياسية لمقاومة نزع ملكيّات الأراضي من أصحابها لصالح شركات تعدين على سبيل المثال واحدة من أهمّ سبل التصدي لممارسات التعدّي. وفي هذا الصدد تقف الأعمال الفنيّة والمشاريع المساحيّة المعاكسة في وجه إيديولوجية الفضاء المفرغ.[8] وعلى غرار ذلك، يمكن لمفهوم ضد- أركيولوجي أن يساهم في «ترسيم المخيّلة المعمارية للأرض الفلسطينية الدائمة التحوّل وأن يعيد تسليط الضوء على ما سبق إهماله أو إزاحته من سرديات متشابكة عن فلسطين.» أو كما يسائل مشروع ديمة سروجي «لو كان لأرض فلسطين صوتها المستقل فماذا عساها أن تقول؟»[9] إلا أنّ تصوّر المخيّلة الاستعمارية لفلسطين كأرض بلا شعب يختلف أيضًا عن تصوّر مخيّلات استعماريّة أخرى. فحين يتكلّم المستوطِن الصهيوني باسم الأرض يضع على لسانها تخيّله لقصّة السكان العبرانيين الأصليين.[10] وهو يرسّخ بذلك استثنائيّة الحدث الاستيطاني بوصفه مشروعًا غير استعماريّ استنادًا إلى حجّة مبدئيّة يدفعها (تصورٌ عن) وجود عبراني قديم ذي سيادة وسلطة. وقد انتُحل الدليل على هذا الوجود بالتنقيب عميقًا جدًّا في باطن الأرض. وإذا كان سطح الأرض في فلسطين بلا شعب، فإنّ باطنها يحوي تاريخ حضارتها.

إذًا يثير السعي إلى تفنيد هذا المشروع الاستعماري الاستيطاني معضلةً من نوع خاصّ. فحين ينتحل المستعمِر لنفسه صفة السكان الأصليين، بأي صفة يمكن للسكان الأصليين مُحاجّته؟ قد يركن المرء إلى تاريخ أقدم من التاريخ الذي انتحله المستعمِر وصولًا إلى سردية تسبق سرديته، كأن نقول مثلًا: هذه أرض بني كنعان قبل أن تكون للعبرانيين. ويُمكن له أن يؤطّر تاريخ فلسطين السحيق كلّه لا بصفته جزءًا من تاريخ الذات الفلسطينية حصرًا بل من التراث الحضاري الإنساني.[11] وفي المقابل، يمكن رفض أطروحة التراث الإنساني والالتفات عوضًا عن ذلك إلى تواريخ القرى الفلسطينيّة المدمّرة في العام 1948 والتي وُثّقتْ ولو جزئيًّا بواسطة الشهادات الشفهيّة.[12] أو قد يقتدي المرء بنزعة المؤرّخ نحو الأرشفة من أجل توثيق عمليّة سلب الأرض الفلسطينيّة وممارسة المقاومة.[13]

في تسعينيّات القرن الماضي تحرّى الأنثروبولوجي الراحل ميشال رولف ترويو أمثلة أسكتَ فيها «الأرشيفُ» التاريخَ، مساهمًا بذلك في تعميق النقاش الذي كان سائدًا آنذاك في دوائر دراسات ما بعد الاستعمار.[14] فقد رأى باحثو دراسات ما بعد الاستعمار أنّ الأرشيف (الاستعماري) يحذف صوت المستعمَرين من الرواية التاريخيّة. من جهته، اعتبر ترويو أن الأرشيف يمارس هذا الفعل بأكثر من طريقة وأنّه لا بدّ من التمعّن في كلّ منها على حدة والتصدّي لها بالأساليب التي تتوافق وإيّاها. في كتابه *Silencing the Past* (إسكات الماضي) يروي ترويو قصّة «عبدٍ مُحرَّر أصبح كولونيلًا، شخص منسي في مخاض الثورة الهاييتيّة» وهي قصّةٌ يُمكن من خلالها إعادة «موضعة» الأدلّة المتاحة في الأرشيف لإنتاج سرديّات جديدة. يُعيد ترويو قراءة سرديّة «اكتشاف أميركا» ويوضّح «كيف يُخفي الاتفاق الظاهري حول كولومبوس تاريخًا معقّدًا من الصراعات،» بحيث إذا ما كُشف عن تلك الصراعات في الأرشيف يُصبح من الممكن إعادة صياغة قصّة اكتشاف أميركا كسيرورة مستمرّة لا كـ «حدثٍ» استثنائي. أمّا في حالة الثورة الهاييتية، فيشير ترويو إلى نمط مختلف من الإسكات، لا بأثر رجعي فحسب بل في ذلك الحين نفسها. فكما تُظهر الوقائع، لم تكن الثورة الهاييتية قط أمراً «قابلًا للتخيّل» من وجهة نظر الأوروبيين، كانت «تاريخًا مستحيلًا». فالثورة فعلٌ سياسي يشترط إنسانيّة فاعله. وعليه لم يكن واردًا أن يكون للهايتيّين القدرة على الإتيان بفعل بشري كالثورة باعتبار أنّهم في مرتبة دون «الإنسان» من المنظور الأوروبي. يؤشّر هذا النوع من الإسكات على مأزقٍ أنطولوجي يترتّب على حصر استحقاقات معيّنة بكينونات دون غيرها.[15]

في كل مرة يُطرَح فيها مشروع الاستيطان اليهودي في فلسطين للنقاش، يتردّد سؤالٌ عمّا إذا كان الفلسطينيون مُتحضّرين بما فيه الكفاية لامتلاك وعيٍ وطني — أي إذا ما كان لديهم الحقّ في دولة وطنيّة خاصّة بهم — وإنْ كان هذا السؤال لا يرقى إلى المأزق الأنطولوجي الذي يصفه ترويو.[16] لذا أودّ أخذ مسألة الأنطولوجيا في اتجاه آخر: ماذا لو مددنا سؤال الإمكانية والاستحالة الأنطولوجية إلى ما هو أبعد من مبحث ترويو عن الفاعلين التاريخيين؛ ماذا لو مددناه ليسائل الطبيعة الأنطولوجية للدليل التاريخي نفسه؟ بالأحرى، أودّ أن أفكر في العلاقة بين

الطبيعة الإبستمولوجيّة للدليل — ما مدى موثوقيّة الدليل وسلطويته وقابليّته للتصديق؟ — وأشكاله المتعدّدة، سواء إن كانت وثائقيّة أو ماديّة أو ذكريات أو شهادات شفهية على سبيل المثال. ما هو الدليل، أو ما هو الشيء الذي يمكن اعتباره (أو اعتماده رسميًّا) كدليل على وجود عربي/فلسطيني (غير منقطع) في هذا المكان؟ يشير إيال فايتسمان إلى أنّ «نمط عمل الاستعمار المعاصر يرتكز على محو آثار عنفه،» وهو أمرٌ صحيح دون شكّ في حالة الدولة الإسرائيلية خلال وبعد حرب 1948 حين دُمّرت 472 قرية فلسطينية. إذ لم يهدف التدمير إلى جعل العودة مستحيلة بقدر ما هدف إلى تطهير الأرض من الآثار الماديّة التي يُمكن أن تدلّ على حقّ الانتماء أو الملكيّة أو السيادة. كذلك دمّرت الأركيولوجيا الإسرائيلية في طريقها لتأسيس المشهد التوراتي الإرثَ الثقافي المادّي للآخرين عن طريق التنقيب في طبقة بعد أخرى في جوف الأرض — دمّرت آثارًا دينيّة أو ثقافيّة أو حضاريّة أو أيّ آثار أخرى للوجود البشري — مخلّفة في سبيلها «الخواء» بحسب تعبير ديمة سروجي.

ويسأل المؤرّخ حاييم يروشالمي «هل يمكننا القول إنّ 'النسيان' هو نقيض 'العدالة' بدلًا من 'التذكّر'؟»[17] نلامس في سؤال يروشالمي وطأة الإدراك الحداثي للتاريخ، ذلك الإدراك الذي نشأ وتطوّر في القرن التاسع عشر حيث لم يعد الماضي وحده — الذكريات والوثائق والموادّ التاريخية أو حتى الجينات — هو ما يحدّد هويّتنا الحقيقيّة.[18] في نهاية القرن العشرين وبداية الحادي والعشرين، بات تذكّر الماضي فعلًا أخلاقيًّا يشير بالضرورة إلى بروز وعي أورو-أميركي ما بعد هولوكوستي: أي أنّنا يجب ألا ننسى كي لا تتكرّر شرور الماضي/الهولوكوست.[19] ما من إمكانيةٍ لتخيّل مستقبلٍ — مستقبلٍ مختلف جذريًّا — دون العودة إلى الوراء لاسترداد آثار ماضٍ (تمّ إسكاته أو قمعه أو محوه) بحسب إيال فايتسمان، «فمواجهة الإنكار مهمّة لأنّ الإنكار بكلّ أشكاله هو ظرفٌ يُمهّد لتكرار العنف في المستقبل.»[20]

بالتأكيد ليس التاريخ مسألةً تتعلّق بـ«ما حدث» فحسب، فالتاريخ يتزامن مع تواتر العمليّات الاجتماعيّة-التاريخيّة وتحويلها بشكل مستمرّ إلى سرد كما يشير ترويو. وبالرجوع إلى فلسطين، لفت إدوارد سعيد في عام 1984 إلى أنّ الصراع المستمرّ حول «الحقّ في السرد» هو محور النضال ضدّ الصهيونية. لذا ليس مستغربًا أن تكون النكبة — تهجير 750 ألف فلسطيني من قراهم وبلداتهم خلال حرب 1948 — موضوعًا للنقاش بين الفلسطينيين أنفسهم. ففي الذاكرة الحيّة يُدرك الناس ما حدث هم ولآبائهم ولأجدادهم ولقراهم ولبلداتهم ولأوجه الحياة فيها بينما يُنكر السياسيون الإسرائيليون هذه الحقيقة. ومع أنّ النكبة وُثّقت ورُويت مرارًا من قِبَل باحثين فلسطينيين عديدين على مدى العقود اللاحقة لحرب 1948، فإنّ تاريخ هذه الحقيقة لم يُمحَ من على الأرض وحسب، بل تمّ إسكاته وإقصاؤه — ليس فقط في إسرائيل وحدها وإنما أيضًا في أوروبا وأميركا.

عام 1978، عندما رُفِعت السريّة في عن مجموعةٍ وثائق تتعلّق بما يُعرف إسرائيليًّا بـ«حرب الاستقلال» تغيّرت الحقائق،[21] تمكّن مؤرّخون إسرائيليون من الوصول إلى أدلّة لم تكن متاحة من قبل وبدأ نفرٌ منهم في إعادة كتابة تاريخ بلدهم. واستندوا إلى هذه الأدلّة الوثائقية في التصدّي للسردية السائدة عن تأسيس دولة إسرائيل. والأهمّ من ذلك، فقد أفاد مؤرّخون أمثال بيني موريس وإيلان بابيه بأنّ الفلسطينيّين، وعلى عكس الرواية الإسرائيليّة الرسميّة، لم يغادروا قراهم طواعية أو بأمرٍ من الأنظمة العربية آنذاك، بل طُردوا وهُجّروا بالقوة على يد الميليشيات الصهيونية خلال الحرب. وأثار ذلك خلافاتٍ في أوساط «المؤرخين الجُدُد» (كما أصبح يُطلق عليهم) من جانب، وبينهم وبين الباحثين الفلسطينيين من جانب آخر، حول ما إذا كان التهجير متعمّدًا ومخطّطًا له وأساسيًّا في مسار تأسيس الدولة اليهودية؟ أم أنه «حدثٌ» عارضٌ خلّفته فوضى الحرب؟ في كل الأحوال أصبحتْ المعايير الجديدة التي أرساها هذا التأريخ «الجديد» مقبولة في عُرف المجتمع الأكاديمي وحتى لدى الرأي العامّ الإسرائيلي. ألحقت الميليشيات الصهيونية خلال «حرب الاستقلال» أضرارًا فادحة وارتكبت فظائع عديدة بحقّ السكّان الفلسطينيين، وهم في أغلبهم مدنيّون هُجّروا قسرًا بغرض تأسيس الدولة الإسرائيلية وتوسيع حدودها. وبحلول منتصف الثمانينيّات بدا ذلك المسار البحثي واعدًا. كانت الحقائق متاحةً أمام الباحثين والدليل الأرشيفي على العنف المرتكَب بحقّ الفلسطينيين قد أصبح معلومًا لدى للجميع. ودخل إلى القاموس السياسي اصطلاح جديد هو «ما بعد الصهيونية» ليصف تيّارًا يضمّ في أوساطه هؤلاء المؤرخين الجدد. لكن هل كان ذلك كفيلًا بتغيير الواقع على الأرض؟ هل كان ممكنًا لسرديّة تاريخيّة فلسطينية أن تحظى بقبول واعتبار واسعين؟ هل كنّا على مفترق طرق في مسار الصراع الفلسطيني ضدّ دولة الاستيطان؟[22]

في السنوات الأولى من الألفية انكبّت فرق من فرع الأمن في وزارة الدفاع الإسرائيلية على تمحيص محتويات الأرشيفات الحكومية في جوّ تلفّه السرّية بغرض حجب وثائق منها عن مجال الاطلاع العام. عادت الوثائق التي كان قد طُرحت إلى العلن سابقًا إلى خزائن أمن الدولة الحديديّة.[23] تُشير هاجر شيزاف الصحافية في هآرتس إلى أنّه «أُخفيتْ مئات الوثائق بشكلٍ منهجي لمحو أي دليلٍ على النكبة.»[24] واقع الحال أنّ الوثيقة الأساسيّة التي يستند إليها مقال بيني موريس الشهير والذي صدر عام 1986 تحت عنوان «نشأة مشكلة اللاجئين الفلسطينيين، 1949-1947» قد اختفت هي أيضًا. سألتْ شيزاف المدير السابق لفرع الأمن بوزارة الدفاع الإسرائيلية يحيئيل حوريف: «إذا كان بيني موريس

سبق أن كتب عن الوثيقة عينها فما فائدة إبقاء الحجب عليها؟»، أجابها حوريف:

«لا أتذكّر الوثيقة التي تشيرين إليها، وإنْ كان موريس قد اقتبس منها وهي غير موجودة [أي غير موجودة حيث يزعم هو] فاستنتاجاته محلّ شكّ. إنْ قال 'نعم، لدي الوثيقة، فلا حرج عليه. ولكن ما يزعمه عما يرد في تلك الوثيقة قد يكون حقيقيًّا وقد لا يكون. أما حجب وثيقة كانت متاحةً ثم حُجبت مجدّدًا فهذه كذبة من الأساس وبالتالي الاقتباس منها يطعن في مصداقية الأدلّة التي يقدّمها.»[25]

تعود هنا سلطة الكلمة المكتوبة للانتقام بضراوة. فماذا عساه أن يكون الدليل في غياب الوثيقة الأصليّة؟ إذ الوثائق بحسب هذه الأنطولوجيا أغراض تتغيّر قيمتها بغيابها أو حضورها، فهي وحدها ما يحوّل الشك إلى يقين.[26]

لم يخطئ حوريف فالوثائق الرسمية باعتبارها أغراضًا ماديّة يُفترض فيها الحياد الموضوعي تمتلك سلطةً إبستمولوجيّة لا يُمنح مثيلها للشهادات والذكريات والحكايا الفلسطينيّة. بل إنّ الفلسطينيين أنفسهم وبمحض وجودهم غير جديرين بأن يكونوا شهودًا على معاناتهم تحت الاستعمار والحرب. إلا أنّ العلاقة بين ما يخصّ الحقائق وما يخصّ السلطة أكثر تعقيد مما يظهر في تصريح حوريف. فحتى في وجه الحقائق، سواء أوثّقتها ذكريات اللجوء الفلسطيني وحكاياته أم وثائق رسمية رُفعت السرّية عنها، تظلّ النكبة تاريخًا مستحيلًا: فقد تكون الحقائق ظاهرةً للعيان إلا أنّ الاعتراف بفداحة أثرها السياسي، وبالتالي قدرتها على تغيير موازين السياسة، ليست كذلك. لذا ليس من المُستغرب أن يتحوّل بيني موريس في مطلع الألفيّة من ما بعد-صهيوني متردّد إلى مدافعٍ شرس عن حرب 1948. وبحسب شهادته فقد كان ذلك تحوّلًا لابدّ منه، وبالتأكيد لم يكن هو الوحيد في هذا الصدد.[27]

بعد ارتكاس موريس بسنوات، نشر الكاتب الصحافي الإسرائيلي اليساري الهوى آري شافيت كتابًا بعنوان «أرضي الموعودة» يتناول فيه ماضي وحاضر إسرائيل، مُركّزًا على لحظة تأسيسها وأزماتها السياسية الراهنة. كان المقال أشبه بجردة حساب للعنف ضدّ الفلسطينيين الذي تأسّست عليه دولة إسرائيل.[28] يتمحور الكتاب حول اللدّ، تلك المدينة الصغيرة في الداخل الفلسطيني، التي هُجّر سكانها قسريًا خلال حرب 1948 وباتت لاحقًا كغيرها من المدن الفلسطينية جزءًا مما يُعرف اليوم بدولة إسرائيل. إلا أنّ لمدينة اللدّ قصة أكثر تعقيدًا على المستوى الأخلاقي، إذ شهدت المدينة مذبحةً دامية. كيف يُمكن لشخص ليبرالي أن يتعامل مع حقيقة كهذه، بل وأن يتصالح معها؟[29]

اللدّ في رواية شافيت هي مأساةٌ لا مفرّ منها ولم يَتمكّن المستوطنون الإسرائيليون من إدراكها إلا بعد فوات الأوان. «اللدّ هي صندوقنا الأسود» يستطرد شافيت. «صندوقٌ يقبع بداخله سرّ الصهيونية القاتم، في الحقيقة الصهيونية لم تكن لتتحمّل [واقعة] اللدّ. ولكي تبقى الصهيونية لا بدّ للدّ أن تَبيد. ولكي تبقى اللدّ يتحتّم على الصهيونية أن تفنى.» على مدى السنوات الخمسين الماضية، «نجحت الصهيونية في أن تُخفي عن نفسها التناقض الجوهري بين الحركة القوميّة اليهوديّة وبين اللدّ... ثمّ وفي ثلاثة أيام من صيف العام 1948 الفاجع، اجتاح التناقض كل شيء وكشفت المأساة عن وجهها.»[30] أُجبِر الفلسطينيون على الرحيل كي تُولَد الدولة اليهودية.

لكن هذه الحقيقة بذاتها لا تُفضي بالضرورة إلى أي نقدٍ (ذاتي) سياسيٍ جوهري، إذ لا تتعدّى كونها مجرّد حقيقة مشؤومة لا مخرج سياسي منها. تمثّل اللدّ لشافيت «مأساة»، فهي الحتميّة من ناحية والدلالة من ناحية أخرى على السقوط الأخلاقي للمستوطنين (ولو جزئيًا)؛ هي لحظة فقدان الصهيونية لبراءتها. ولكن بالرغم من اختيار شافيت التركيز على اللدّ بسبب المذبحة، فإنّ عنفها المُفرط لا يمثّل في حدّ ذاته لبّ الموضوع. فإنْ كان تجنُّب المذبحة ممكنًا بشكل أو بآخر، إلا أنّ شروط حدوثها (أي الغزو والتهجير) كانت موجودةً لا محالة. «أيمكنني أن أتنكّر للحركة القوميّة اليهوديّة التي ارتكبت الفِعلة في اللدّ؟» يسأل شافيت نفسه.

«مثل قائد السِرية، أجد نفسي مواجهًا أمرًا يفوق قدرتي على مواجهته فحين يفتح المرء هذا الصندوق الأسود يدرك أنّه في حين كانت مذبحة المسجد الصغير نتاج سلسلة مأساوية من الحوادث العارضة، كان غزو اللدّ وتهجير أهلها منها مخطّطًا عمديًّا... الخيار واضح، إمّا أن نرفض الصهيونية بسبب ما حدث في اللدّ أو نقبل الصهيونية ومعها اللدّ.»[31] وكان خيار شافيت «أن يقف في صفّ الملعونين.»[32]

ربما كان يحيئيل حوريف متخوّفًا أكثر من اللازم من قوّة الوثائق. فإعادة استنطاق الأرشيف الصامت قد لا يُحدث أي تغيير فعلي. فبحسب الفيلسوف ستانلي كافل هنالك فارقٌ بين «العلم» بالشيء و«الإقرار» به. لقد باتت القصص الواردة في الوثائق الإسرائيلية التي رُفعت عنها السريّة (ثم ما لبث وأن حُجبت مجدّدًا) «معلومة» على نطاق واسع، كما ترسّخت الحقائق والأحداث الواردة فيها الآن في وعي الرأي العامّ الإسرائيلي والمؤسسات الليبرالية في الولايات المتحدة التي استقبلت كتاب

شافيت بحفاوة. إلا أنّها لم يُعترف بها ولم يودّ كشفها إلى المساءلة أو التحرّك السياسي حيالها في المجال العام.[33] فقصّة اللدّ تبيّن أنّ إسرائيل تأسست على غزو وتهجير (وإبادة) السكان الفلسطينيين (استنادًا إلى الذاكرة الحيّة للشعب الفلسطيني) في الوقت الذي تصرّ فيه أنّه لم يكن لديها خيار آخر.

لا علاقة للتذكر بالعدالة هنا. فرغم كسرها حواجز الصمت والنسيان والمحو (لا أدلّة ماديّة على وقوعها بطبيعة الحال)، تفتقر نكبة 1948 إلى الزخم السياسي أو الأخلاقي. وإنْ كان ثمّة مسارٌ تاريخيٌ لمراجعات شافيت وموريس، فإنّه ودون شكّ لا يميل نحو العدالة. صحيحٌ أنّ الحرب التي يتذكرها ويوثّقها المؤرّخون الفلسطيّنيون استنادًا إلى الذاكرة والشهادات الشفهيّة للذين نجوا منها وقعت بالفعل. إلا أنّ تاريخ النكبة لا يزال غير جدير بالجبر. بعبارةٍ أخرى، حتى وإنْ توصّل المرء لاتفاقٍ ما حول «الحقائق» وحتى وإنْ تمكّن من تأويل «ما حدث» أو على الأقل تأويل جانب منه، فإنّ هذه الحقائق ستظلّ عاجزةً عن أن تكون مادّةً للشأن العام. إذ يتطلّب ذلك خيارًا سياسيًّا وأخلاقيًّا أقلّ ارتباطًا بمسائل الإپستمولوجيا (بأن نعرف، وبكيف نعرف) ممّا يحلو لنا أن نظنّ، نحن معشر اليسار.

أحيانًا يكون النسيان نقيض العدالة. وفي أحيانٍ أخرى، يكون محو الأثر التاريخي هو تحديدًا ما قد تتطلبه العدالة كي تتحقّق. فلو لم يلجأ جدّي لطمر أرضيّة الفسيفساء الأثريّة التي عثر عليها بالإسمنت، لكان خسر أرضه ومورد رزقه للمرّة الثانية على التوالي.[34] ولو أنّ علماء الآثار فشلوا في تحديد موقع السامرة والتنقيب عنه لكانت سبسطيّة اليوم مجرّد قرية فلسطينيّة أخرى لا أهميّة توراتيّة لها ولكانت غير محاصرة بالمستوطنات كما هي اليوم أو حتّى غير خاضعة للحكم الإسرائيلي المباشر.[35] باختصار، ليس الخواء أمرًا مكروهًا في جميع الأحوال. فتحقيق العدالة قد يتطلّب أحيانًا المحو والنسيان.

لربما كانت هناك أسبابٌ أخلاقيةٌ جذرية للإصرار على استعادة الآثار والتواريخ الأخرى السابقة وربما ستظلّ هناك رغبةٌ في استرداد التاريخ بصرف النظر عن العواقب. إلا أنّ الإصرار على أنّ النسيان هو نقيض العدالة يعني العمل وفق منطق سياسي لا يعي التركيب المعقّد لمنظومة السلطة (الاستعمارية). في فلسطين/ إسرائيل لم تعد صناعة الأمّة الاستيطانية تستند على طمس الأثر التاريخي لل«حقيقة». بل تعمل على اعتناق أكثر جهرًا وسافرًا لمنطق الحيازة: نعم نعلم بأمر النكبة، لكن نحن — الإسرائيليون — لا نبالي.

1 انظروا
https://depthunknown.com (accessed
(November 5, 2020

2 قاد جروج أندرو رايزنر الكشوف الحفريّة في السامرة بين عامي 1910-1908 وهي الفترة التي عمل فيها كأستاذ مساعد للمصريّات في جامعة هارفارد. تمّ استئناف هذه الكشوف الحفريّة بين عامي1935-1931 بقيادة ج. و. كروفوت رئيس كلية الآثار بالقدس. أُجريت هذه الكشوف بالتعاون بين كلية الآثار وصندوق استكشاف فلسطين بلندن وجامعة هارفارد والجامعة العبرية. انظروا
William F. Albright, *The Archaeology of Palestine* (New York, 1960)

3 * ارتأينا استعمال كلمة "عبراني" خلال النص لوصف جماعات يهودية قديمة حقيقية أو مُتخيّلة عوضًا عن "بني إسرائيل" لاقتصار الأخيرة على مجال دلالي محدود بالقصص الإبراهيمي. [المترجم]

4 انظروا
Benedict Anderson, *Imagined Communities: Reflections on Origin and Spread of Nationalism* (New York, 2006).
وحول الصهيونية، انظروا
Yael Zerubavel, *Recovered Roots: Collective Memory and the Making of Israeli National Tradition* (Chicago, 1994)

5 لقراءة أكثر استفاضة حول الأرشيف والممارسات الأرشيفيّة، انظروا
Carolyn Steedman, *Dust: The Archive and (Cultural History* (New Brunswick, NJ, 2002

6 في مقدمة كتابه *Argonauts of the Western Pacific* يُفصّل مالينوفسكي منهجًا علميًّا لعمل الإثنوغرافي، ويلقي على عاتقه مسؤولية جمع أنواع بعينها من البيانات، وكذلك حفظ تفاصيلها في سجل يمكّن من سيلحقه من أنثروبولوجيين من مراجعة البيانات في مرحلة لاحقة، بنفس الطريقة التي يعيد بها (فرضيًّا) العلماء إجراء التجارب المخبرية مرارًا. انظروا
Bronislav Malinowski, *Argonauts of the Western Pacific* (Long Grove, IL, 1984)

7 انظروا
Nadia Abu El-Haj, *Facts on the Ground: Archaeological Practice and Territorial Self-Fashioning in Israeli Society* (Chicago, 2001), Chapter 7.

8 انظروا على سبيل المثال حالة "نغورارا كانفاس II" والتي عُرضت في ترينالي الشارقة للعمارة ومشروع "Ground Truth" الضد-خرائطي من إنتاج منظّمة زوخروت غير الحكومية الإسرائيلية بالتعاون مع مكتب العمارة الجنائية. استعمال مفردات "ضد-خرائطي" و"ضد- أركيولوجي" يحيل هنا إلى مفردة "ضد-جنائي" في أعمال إيال فايتسمان. بمعنى أنّه إذا ما كان تاريخ التحقيقات الجنائية هو مشروعٌ دولتي، فإنّ الدولة في المنطق الضد-جنائي "هي المتّهم." انظروا
Eyal Weizman, *Forensic Architecture: Violence at the Threshold of Detectability* (New York, 2018), p.30.

9 Dima Srouji, https://depthunknown.com
(accessed November 5, 2020)).
عادة ما تذهب الممارسات النقدية المعاصرة المتعلقة بحقوق السكان الأصليين لما هو أبعد من هذا النوع من الممارسات الضدّية، حيث تسعى لإنتاج أشكالٍ جديدة كليًا من المعرفة والحياة. ومن هذه الزاوية تضع بعض المشاريع النقدية للسكان الأصليين منطق "الذوق العام" في مأزق أنطولوجي وإبستمولوجي، وهو ما يغيب عن الممارسات الضدّية التي تسعى فقط لقلب زاوية النظر بين المستعمِر والمستعمَر دون دحض البنية العلمية أو السياسية لهذا النظر. انظروا
Elizabeth Povinelli, *The Cunning of Recognition: Indigenous Alterities and the Making of Australian Multiculturalism* (Durham and London, 2002) and Vanessa Agard-Jones, "What the Sands Remember," *GLQ* (June 2010), pp. 325-346.

10 انظروا على سبيل المثال
Marc Daadler, "Jews as an Indeginous People," *Jewish Currents* (August 28, 2017), https://jewishcurrents.org/jews-as-an-indigenous-people (accessed November 5, 2020);
وانظروا أيضاً
Matthew Gindin , "Are Both Jews and Palestinians Indigenous to Israel?" *Forward* (May 24, 2017), https://forward.com/scribe/372978/are-both-jews-and-palestinians-indigenous-to-israel (accessed November 5, 2020).

11 سعت السلطة الفلسطينية على سبيل المثال لحضّ اليونسكو على تصنيف سبسطية كمركز للتراث العالمي وهو الأمر الذي يخضع للدراسة حالياً. انظروا http:// whc.unesco.org/en/tentativelists/5718 وهي طريقة لدحض الزعم الإسرائيلي حول أهمية الموقع التراثي بالنسبة للدولة العبرية الحديثة.

12 انظروا
Walid Khalidi, All that Remains: The Palestinian Villages Occupied and Depopulated by Israel in 1948 (Washington, D.C., 1992).
وانظروا ايضاً مجموعة "memorial books" حول القرى الفلسطينية لدى مركز جامعة كولومبيا للدراسات الفلسطينية..http://palestine.mei.columbia. edu/palestinian-village-histories-geographies-of-the-displaced.

13 انظروا على سبيل المثال
Walid Khalidi , *From Haven to Conquest: Readings in Zionism and the Palestine Problem until 1948* (Beirut, 1972); Ibrahim Abu Lughod, *The Transformation of Palestine: Essays on the Origin and Development of the Arab-Israeli Conflict* (Chicago, 1971), and Yazid Sayigh, *Armed Struggle and the Search for State: the Palestinian National Movement, 1949-1993* (New York, 1997).

14 Michel-Rolph Trouillot, *Silencing the Past: Power and the Production of History* (Boston, 1995).

15 يوضّح ترويو أنّ هذه الاستحالة مستمرّة في بعض أوجهها. لا تأتي الروايات التاريخية المعتمدة عما يُعرف بـ"عصر الثورات" - وهي الفترة الممتدّة بين عامي 1776 و1843 على أي ذكر للثورة الهايتية كنقطة تحوّل محوريّة في تاريخ أوروبا والعالم:
"What we are observing is archival power at its strongest, the power to define what is and what is not a serious object of research and, therefore, of mention" (ibid, p. 99).

16 ممّا لا شكّ فيه أنّ السؤال حول قدرة شعوب المستعمرات على الحكم الذاتي قد ساد على منطق القوى الاستعمارية خلال القرنين التاسع عشر والعشرين. مهما كان الأمر فحق ولو كانت هذه القوى ترى شعوب المستعمرات أقل تحضّرًا فهي لم تكن تعتبرها ملكًا لها إنّما كانت بنظرتها وبعبارة أدقّ أقل بشرًا/لا تحمل صفة البشرية.

17 Yosef Hayim Yerushalmi, *Zakhor: Jewish History and Jewish Memory* (Seattle, 1996), p. 117.

18 انظروا
Nadia Abu El-Haj, *The Genealogical Science: The Search for Jewish Origins and the Politics of Epistemology* (Chicago, 2012).

19 كما تشير جوان سكوت "تعهّد روبرت جاكسون المدعي العامّ الأميركي في محكمة نورمبرغ لجرائم النازية بمعاقبة وتوثيق ما سمّاه الآثار المشؤومة للنازية بطريقة تجعلها غير قابلة للنسيان أو التكرار."
The Judgment of History (New York, forthcoming)

20 Eyal Weizman, *Forensic Architecture: Violence at the Threshold of Detectability* (New York, 2017), p. 134.

21 وفق القوانين الإسرائيلية، تُتاح الوثائق السريّة للإطّلاع العام بعد انقضاء 30 عامًا على تصنيفها.

22 شهدت أواخر الثمانينيّات اندلاع الانتفاضة الأولى في 1987، والتي ولّدت المزيد من التفاؤل بين الفلسطينيين حول إمكانية حلّ سياسي (على أساس الدولتين).

23 في تجربة مماثلة لحجب وثائق سبق وأن رُفعت عنها السرية في سياق ما بعد أحداث الحادي عشر من أيلول / سبتمبر: Joseph Masco, *The Theater of Operations: National Security Affect from the Cold War to the War on Terror* (Durham, NC, 2014).

24 Hagar Shezaf, "Burying the Nakba: How Israel Systematically Hides Evidence of 1948 Expulsion of Arabs," *Haaretz* (July 5, 2019), https://www.haaretz.com/israel-news/.premium.MAGAZINE-how-israel-systematically-hides-evidence-of-1948-expulsion-of-arabs-1.7435103 (accessed November 5, 2020).

25 المرجع نفسه

26 في لحظة ما بين رفع السريّة عن الوثائق – التي واكبت مطالبة إدوارد سعيد بمنح الفلسطينيين الحقّ في السرد – وبين قرار إعادة حجب "الحقائق"، تحديدًا في التسعينيّات عندما كان يوسي ساريد وزيرًا للتعليم، كانت هناك دعوة، وإن لم تستمر طويلًا، لتضمين المناهج الدراسية الإسرائيلية الرواية الفلسطينية عن تاريخ فلسطين بالتوازي مع الرواية الإسرائيلية. بحيث يكون لكل طرف روايته عن الأحداث دون تسييد واحدة على الأخرى.

27 انظروا
Ari Shavit, "Survival of the Fittest? An Interview with Benny Morris," reprinted on *Counterpunch* (January 16, 2004), https://www.counterpunch.org/2004/01/16/an-interview-with-benny-morris (accessed November 5, 2020).

28 عمل آري شافيت كاتباً بهآرتس بين أعوام 1995 و2016 واضطر إلى الاستقالة بعد ادعاءات بالتحرش الجنسي كجزء من حراك MeToo.

29 ذاع صيت الكتاب في الولايات المتحدة بعد نشر فصل منه في مجلة النيويوركر في تشرين أول/أكتوبر 2014 بعنوان "Lydda, 1948: A City, A Massacre, and the Middle East Today" للمزيد انظروا
Leon Wiesseltier, "The State of Israel," *The New York Times* (November 21, 2013), https://www.nytimes.com/2013/11/24/books/review/my-promised-land-by-ari-shavit.html (accessed November 5, 2020), and Jonathan Freedland, "The Liberal Zionists," *The New York Times* (August 14, 2014), https://www.nybooks.com/articles/2014/08/14/liberal-zionists (accessed November 5, 2020).

30 Shavit, ibid, pp. 108-109.

31 المرجع نفسه، ص. 131

32 المرجع نفسه

33 Stanley Cavell, *Must We Mean What We Say? A Book of Essays* (New York, 1969)

34 كان جدي يعمل أساسًا فيما أصبح يُعرف منذ 1948 بالقدس الغربية. إلا أنّه فقد كل شيء واضطرّ للبدء من الصفر. لحسن حظّه تمكن أحد موظفيه من التسلّل عبر خطّ وقف إطلاق النار لتحصيل إيصال بيع سجّادٍ تم تصديره إلى ميناء العقبة. وبفضل ذلك الإيصال استطاع البدء من جديد في القدس الشرقيّة بعد الحرب.

35 وفق اتفاقية أوسلو، فُرزت سبسطية إلى المنطقة "ج" وهي منطقة من الضفة الغربية تخضع للحكم الإسرائيلي المباشر. فُرزت المناطق هكذا لحماية المستوطنات اليهودية.

ندوة: أشكال الحياة الآجلة

سِپاكيه أنغياما وكودووو إِشون وإِسي إِشون ودينيز فِريرا دا سيلفا وصلاح حسن وأنجاليكا ساغار.

ترجمه عن الإنكليزية فريق الأركلوغ

في 10 تشرين الثاني/نوفمبر 2019 اجتمعت أنجاليكا ساغار وكودووو إِشون (من مجموعة أوتولِث)[1] بكلٍّ من إِسي إِشون ودينيز فِريرا دا سيلفا وصلاح حسن في حوار أدارته سِپاكيه أنغياما.

سِپاكيه أنغياما

تعرّفت إلى صلاح حسن أوّل مرّةٍ من خلال كتاباته في مجلّة *Nka – Journal of Contemporary African Art* [مجلة الفنون الإفريقية المعاصرة] التي كانت قد لعبت دورًا مهمًّا بالنسبة إلى منتجةٍ للثقافة في لندن شابّةٍ مثلي تسعى إلى تكوين فهمها المستقلّ لمعارض فنية أمثال Africa 95 [إفريقيا 95] وإلى إيجاد سبيل للإبقاء على الصلة بمكان لم أولد فيه إلا أني أشعر بالانتماء إليه. سيصطحبنا صلاح في جولة بين ثلاث محطّات مهمّة في التاريخ السوداني ترتبط بالتقاليد الراديكالية للسود.

المحطّات الثلاث هذه كانت أيضًا محورَ الفيلم الذي أنجزته مجموعة أوتولِث التي تأسست عام 2002. تأخذنا ممارسات هذه المجموعة الفنية في جولةٍ على عدد من الوسائط المختلفة منها السينما والأداء، مُستخدمةً جماليّات الخيال العلمي لاستكشاف أماكن أو خيالات لم تتكوّن في أذهاننا بعد. تخوض المجموعة من خلال هذا المشروع الذي يحمل عنوان *Infinity Minus Infinity* [اللانهاية ناقص اللانهاية] حوارًا لا يزال جاريًا مع دينيز فِريرا دا سيلفا التي تنضمّ إلينا أيضًا في هذه الجلسة. كلي الحماس لمناقشة الأنماط التي يشدّد عليها الفيلم وأيضًا التفكير المعمّق حيال مفهوم السواد. كما تنضمّ إلينا إِسي إِشون التي شاركت مجموعة أوتولِث في بناء الإطار المفاهيمي للفيلم ومساره السردي.

صلاح حسن

جوابًا عن سؤال أدريان لحود عن كيف يدعي المرء التماهي مع أشخاص آخرين، كيف يعيد استملاك إنسانيته الإنسانية — في إحالة إلى س. ل. ر. جيمس — كنت قد فكرت بدايةً، في أن أقدّم ورقة بحثية كنت قد كتبتها بعنوان *The Caribbean In Me* [الكاريبيّ داخلي]. فقد كان من الطبيعي بالنسبة إليّ، كسودانيّ أمضى أكثر من نصف حياته البالغة مقيمًا في الولايات المتحدة الأميركية ومنخرطًا في الدراسات الإفريقية والإفريقية-الأميركية، أن أنجذب إلى التقاليد الراديكالية للسود من خلال أعلام كجيمس وفرانتز فانون وجورج پادمور وسيلفيا وينترز وإِريك ويليامز وإيميه سيزير وإدوار غليسان وسيدرِك روبنسون. معظم هؤلاء يتحدّرون من جزر الكاريبي أو من أصول كاريبية في المهجر. وقد قادني هذا الانجذاب إلى السؤال: لِمَ الكاريب؟ ما الذي جعل هذه الجزر الصغيرة تنتج هؤلاء المفكرين والمفكرات العمالقة الذين واللواتي تأثّرت بهم(ن). لقد وجدت الإجابة في كتابات غليسان حين يتحدّث عن جزر الكاريبي كملتقىً لجميع ثقافات العالم — الإمبراطورية البريطانية والسكّان المُستعبَدين والأصليين — ما يجعلها أكثر عالميةً من أوروبا ذاتها. واقترح غليسان نبذ رؤية العالم من المنظور القارّي وتبنّي ما أسماه المنظور «الأرخبيلي» أي أن ننظر إلى العالم ككوكبة من الأرخبيلات.

يتيح لنا هذا التفكير المجال لإعادة استملاك الإنسانية بطريقة ما. فلسنا وحدنا أبناءَ العالم الثالث المتأثّرين بالأوروبيين، بل إننا أجمعين كلما ابتعدنا عن الوحدة الجغرافية الشكلية واقتربنا من النظر إلى العالم من منطلق ما يصفه غليسان «بالكَرْيَلة» أو التهجين اللغوي [creolization]، تبيّن لنا أنّ الحداثة الأوروبية مدينة بمقدار كبير من إرثها للشعوب الأخرى.[2] يقول غليسان إنّ الإمبراطوريات الكبرى دومًا تنهار فيما البلدان الصغيرة تستمر في البقاء، وهذا أمر مثير للاهتمام لا سيّما ونحن نشهد أزمة الرأسمالية وسعيها لإعادة إنتاج ذاتها. إذًا، ماذا تعلمتُ من التقاليد الراديكالية للسود في ما يخص مسار الثورة السودانية الأخيرة ومغزاها في هذا العالم؟

منذ نشأتها، كانت الرأسمالية نظامًا قائمًا على التمييز العرقي، الأمر الذي يلفت نظري. وقد قال إيميه سيزير في معرض نقده للكونية [universalism] أنّ المرء يفقد ذاته بطريقة من اثنتين: «إما الانكفاء خلف جدران الفصل العنصري أو الذوبان في الكوني». (كمثال على ذلك من الشرق الأوسط نتساءل: ما هو منطق الرأسمالية في تركيزها على دولة واحدة مثل إسرائيل على حساب الشعوب العربية كلها والاستمرار في معاملة الفلسطينيين بأقصى درجات العنف، إنْ لم يكن إمعانًا في التمييز العنصري؟)

لقد مثّلت الثورة السودانية بين 2018 و2019 حدثًا استثنائيًا للكثيرين في العالم العربي وبقية العالم. فما الذي جذب انتباه العالم إلى السودان فجأةً هكذا؟ أولًا كانت الثورة بالغة التنظيم. وثانيًا كانت سلمية لاعنفية على نسق الكثير من حركات النضال اللاعنفي وعلى رأسها حركة الحقوق المدنية [في أمريكا الستينيات]. ثمّ كانت مشاركة النساء فاعلة ومؤثرة فقد شكلت النساء نصف المحتجّين في الشوارع. في الواقع، لا يعدّ أيٌّ من

هذه العوامل استثناءً نظرًا لتاريخ حركات المقاومة والمجتمع المدني في السودان. بل إنّ العامل المفاجئ في هذه الثورة يعود إلى ما أسماه الباحث الكيني الراحل علي مزروعي «تعدّد الهامشيات».[3] فالسودان دولة تقع على طرفيْ العَالَمَيْن العربي والإفريقي؛ نحن على هامش كلاهما، إلّا أننا إذا طبّقنا المنظور الأرخبيلي فعندئذ نكون مركز المحور واللقاء بينهما.

شهد السودان تاريخًا حافلًا من الراديكالية والحراكات الاجتماعية. فقد عمل الحزب الشيوعي في السودان على تنظيم نقابات المهن والمجتمع المدني منذ الأربعينيات من القرن الماضي. وقد تمايزت قيادات هذه المجموعات الراديكالية عن الماركسية الراديكالية في بقية العالم من خلال المجاهرة بنقدها للشيوعية بنسختها السوفياتية. بل إنها اتصلت فكريًا بالسود والعرب — كتب القائد الشيوعي عبد الخالق محجوب عن الاشتراكية الإفريقية وترجم شعر إيميه سيزير — ولعبت دورًا بارزًا في صياغة التقاليد الراديكالية باللغات الدارجة وملاءمتها للسياقات المحلية.

تَرِد أنماط الاشتباك المتّبعة اليوم من قبل المتظاهرين والمتظاهرات في كتاب صدر عام 1964 بعنوان «ست سنوات تحت الأرض»، منها الإضراب العام والعصيان المدني اللذان نُظّر لهما وجُرّبا لا في العام 1964 فحسب بل أيضًا خلال أحداث الثورة اللاحقة عام 1985. بهذا المعنى، نستطيع أن نزعم أنّ الملكية الفكرية للربيع العربي تعود إلى السودان لاعتباره قاعدة حراكات شعبية جماهيرية ابتكر أسلحته وتكتيكاته الخاصة.

ولكن ما أهمية مشاركة النساء؟ شهدت السودان حراكًا نسائيًا فعالًا منذ الأربعينيات من القرن الماضي. ولعلكم(ن) سمعتم(ن) بفاطمة أحمد إبراهيم أو بنشأة الاتحاد النسائي السوداني بين أواخر الأربعينيات ومطلع الخمسينيات. ثم إنّ السودان بات أول دولة عربية حصدت المرأة فيها حق الاقتراع وقد انتخب العديد من النساء نائبات في البرلمانين الأول والثاني (بينما تصل النساء في العالم العربي إلى مقاعد البرلمان بالتعيين بدلًا من الانتخاب). لذا يمكن القول إنّ النضالات من أجل الديموقراطية والحرية وحقوق الإنسان في السودان لها جذورٌ ممتدةٌ في تاريخٍ من الحراكات التي كانت أقلّ إقصاءً من غيرها.

سأختم بالإشارة إلى أنّ الوجه الاستثنائي الفعلي لهذا الحراك بالمقارنة مع بقية العالم العربي في رأيي هو مناهضته للإخوان المسلمين. في السودان، نفّذ الإخوان المسلمون انقلابًا أتى بنظامٍ ديكتاتوريٍ استمر ثلاثين عامًا، أي أنّ وجوه السلطة كانوا في الأصل من جماعة الإخوان، في حين أنّ الإخوان في البلدان العربية الأخرى لازموا الهامش أو انضموا إلى صفوف المعارضة. (في مصر، على سبيل المثال، برّرت السلطة قمع أي شكلٍ من أشكال الاحتجاج أو الانتفاضة بالترهيب والتهديد من عودة سيطرة الإخوان المسلمين على غرار ما شهدته البلاد إثر انتخاب محمد مرسي الذي كان أول رئيسٍ مصري منتخَب ديموقراطيًا).

هذه هي حكاية شعبي وها هي بين أيديكم(ن) ولكم(ن) أن تستملكوها، فهي تفيض بالعِبر، لا سيّما أنّ الحراكات الاجتماعية تتوالى مثل أحجار الدومينو بفضل الترابطات والتفاعلات (لننظر إلى ما يحدث اليوم في العراق ولبنان وتشيلي وغيرها من البلدان). وثورة السودان تمتاز بكونها منظّمة بالغ التنظيم بقيادة جمعية المهنيين السودانيين التي تضمّ الأطباء والمهندسين وأساتذة الجامعات وتجمّعاتٍ من الطبقة العاملة. وقد اجتمع هؤلاء عام 2013 وتنبّؤوا بتغيير قادم ولم يشأ أيٌ منهم أن يباغته هذا التحوّل فبادروا مجتمعين إلى صياغة مسودةٍ لبرنامجٍ انتقاليٍ مفصّلٍ. هناك نقاط ضعف فيه، ولكنني أكتفي هنا بهذا القدر.

سِپاكيه أنغياما

حديثنا اليوم يأتي تحت عنوان «أشكال الحياة الآجلة». سبق وأشرتَ إلى الكاتب الترينيداديّ س.ل.ر. جيمس كأحد مراجعك الفكرية، وهو الذي كتب بإسهابٍ عن تاريخ الأفعال الراديكالية للسود وعن الحركة الشيوعية الأممية. وتلمّح أنت إلى تأطير الجنوب العالمي كأرخبيل حيث الجزر مساحاتٌ للكَرْيلة. أودّ أن أسألك إذا ما كنتَ ترى السودان ينشئ لنفسه عقلية الجزيرة — أي أنه لا يفرض نفسه بالضرورة جزءًا من إفريقيا. وهل هذا هو مقصدك من طرح الأرخبيل كمنحى للتفكير؟

صلاح حسن

كثيرًا ما يسألونني في الغرب: «هل أنت إفريقيٌ أم عربيٌ؟» أفضّل التنقّل بين الاثنين. فأنا فخور بالموروثات الإيجابية للعالم العربي وبالتراث الفكري للسود. وقد احتلتْ هذه المسألة مكانةً مهمةً لدى الفنانين والكتاب. فمعظم المتحدرين من تراث اليسار يعرفون أنفسهم كأفارقة-عرب باعتبار أنهم ينتمون إلى هوية هجينة. كما أنّ في السودان مذهبًا فلسفيًا وشعريًا وأدبيًا يُسمّى مذهب الغاب والصحراء، في إشارة إلى العناصر الجغرافية المتنوعة في السودان كرمزٍ لتهجّنه إذ تتنوع رقعة السودان من البيئة الصحراوية إلى الغابة الاستوائية.

من أولى القصائد الملحمية للشاعر السوداني محمد عبد الحي قصيدةٌ بعنوان «العودة إلى سِنّار»، وهي على ما أعتقد مستوحاة من «كراس العودة إلى الوطن» لإيميه سيزير. ونتعرف في «العودة إلى سنار» إلى أوّل مملكةٍ إسلاميةٍ في جنوب السودان حيث تتلاق التقاليد العربية والإفريقية والإسلامية. وهذه هي البوتقة التي انبثقت منها لاحقًا الحركة القومية السودانية.

سِپاكيه أنغياما

أودّ أن أنتقل الآن إلى الحديث عن مشروع Infinity Minus Infinity. أنجاليكا، هلّا حدّثتِنا عن مفهوم المادة في معرض الحديث سمات الفيلم المادية؟

أنجاليكا ساغار

سأستعرض بعضًا من مناحي التفكير المختلفة حول السياسة التي مهّدت لصنع هذا الفيلم. وكان الهدف من صنعه خلق فضاءٍ يكون بمثابة بيئةٍ أو استشعارٍ للماهية السوداء، بأسلوب أقرب إلى حالة من الهذيان متداخل الثنايا حيث الوقت يتحرك ويشكّل ذاته وفقًا لاختلاف أساليب النظر والإحساس والسمع. كما أودّ أن أعرج على الخوف الذي دفعنا إلى اتّخاذ الخيار بصنع هذا الفيلم.

في لندن، كنت قد بدأت أعي معنى أن نكون مستعمَرين في ظل ما نتعرض له في العالم بشكل عام ومن جراء الطوق الذي تحاصرنا به الفاشية التقنية على مستويات عدّة — في أجسادنا وحيواتنا وعواطفنا وعقولنا. أوصلني هذا الشعور وسط هذه اللندن التي يُطلق عليها التقدمية، والتي حسبتني أعيش في رحابها، إلى الوعي بضرورة فعل شيءٍ في حدود قدراتنا بصفتنا فنانين وفنانات. رأيتُ الكاريبيين من جيل «وِندرَش»[4] يتعرّضون للترحيل بعدما استقدمتهم بريطانيا خلال عهد الكومنولث للعمل. تحدثتُ إلى أشخاص «يُعادون» اليوم إلى الكاريبي بعدما عملوا أربعين سنةً في شبكة أنفاق المترو وأسسوا عائلاتهم في إنكلترا. يضرب هذا الواقع في صميم عمل أشخاصٍ أمثال ستوارت هول ومارغريت باسبي (التي كانت أول من نشر أعمال س.ل.ر. جيمس) وأوليف موريس وديان آبوت وجون لا روز وغيرهم. فالنضال المناهض للعنصرية في بريطانيا وليدٌ لتاريخٍ طويلٍ من التمردات متعددة الإثنيات التي خرجت على الرأسمالية العرقية منذ لحظة نشأتها. كيف يتمثّل هذا النضال كجماليةٍ مقاومةٍ؟ أي نوعٍ من الجماليات المقاوِمة يمكّننا من تأمل عملٍ فني ما بطريقة تحررنا من القيود المتنوعة التي تفرضها علينا سلسلات متكاملة من التطويقات المحاصِرة [enclosures]؟

ومن جانب آخر، يثير الفيلم على الصعيد الشكلي مسألة حواسّنا المستعمَرة (بمعنى علاقتنا الحسيّة بالعالم) بفعل اقتحام الرأسمالية المعرفية لأجسادنا. ما معنى أن يكون الجسد مستعمَرًا بواسطة التكنو-فاشية؟ كيف نعيد إحياء الحواس ونظهر واقعها السليب في الوقت عينه؟ تخرج هذه الأسئلة من فيلمنا السابق بعنوان O Horizon [يا أيها الأفق] الذي يعاين العلاقة الطاغورية بين البيداغوجيا والتحرر من الاستعمار في البنغال في مطلع العقد الأول من القرن العشرين. كان طاغور [في مدرسته البديلة] قد حثّ طلابه على إعمال أيديهم وأجسادهم كما عقولهم في فضاء التفكر حول الصوتي والمادي كوسيلة لبعث روح الثورة على قرنين من الاحتلال البريطاني للهند.

وهنالك الجانب المتعلّق بالتعاطي مع فكرة الفيلم المقالي كموسيقى جاز مرتَجلة (أعتقد أنّ آرثر جافا هو صاحب هذه المقولة) ما دفعني إلى البحث عن مقاربة مختلفة للمونتاج – المرور عبر الجسد بدلًا من التسلسل المونتاجي للصورة تلو الأخرى. كما شغلتني فكرة التعدد الصوتي (البوليفونيا) وأسلوب غليسان في توظيف الغناء والصوتية والشاعرية فوجدتُ أنّ وضع فقراتٍ من أعمال غليسان في حوارٍ بين إلين ميتشرنر ودانتي ميشو حيث يتناوبان عليها يضفي مستوىً آخر من التهجين فيفتح المجال لتهجين الفيلم نفسه. ويضاهي التعدد الصوتي في أهميته الطبقة والعرق والجندر والبعد الكوكبي. وكنت أتساءل حول كيفية توعية البعد الكوكبي بحيث لا يكون السواد مرتبطًا بالهوية المصنفة بل بالفكاك من التصنيف.

إسي إشون

سأتطرق إلى بعض القضايا المتقاطعة التي شغلت تفكيرنا أثناء العمل على الفيلم إلى جانب قضية وِندرَش. إننا نتحدث عن لحظاتٍ بيّنة من الثورة والتحرر وعن كيفية ورودها إلينا اليوم، وكيف تتداخل درجات المعنى والتفسير في طرائق تلقّينا للمعلومات من فئات المجتمع المهيمنة. حين وُلدت فكرة الفيلم كنا جميعًا بصدد قراءة كتاب كاثرين يوسف *A Billion Black Anthropocenes or None* [مليار أنثروبوسين أسود أو لا شيء] الذي بات أحد أهمّ مصادر الإلهام لعملنا. يقارن الكتاب بين ولادة علم الجيولوجيا ونشأة الاستعمار ويتناول ارتباط المادة بالبشر السود، أي الأجساد السوداء، والمعادن المُستخرَجة من الأرض. وتذهب يوسف إلى أنّ الاثنين خاضعان لتكنولوجيات الاستخراج عينها وتوضّح ارتباط هذين العاملَيْن بالتغير المناخي.

تركّز يوسف اهتمامها على لحظة زمنية محددة يطلق عليها علماء الجيولوجيا تسمية «طفرة أوربيس». وقعت هذه الطفرة عام 1610 مع إبادة قوم الكاريب وهم السكان الأصليين لجزر الكاريبي، وتوطين العبيد السود بدلًا منهم. تزعم يوسف أنّ التغيّرات التي طرأت على النبات والحيوان في تلك المنطقة جراء وصول مجموعات جديدة من البشر وأجناس غير مألوفة من النباتات والحيوانات أدتْ إلى تغيير طبيعة الغلاف الحيوي لبيئة المنطقة. ومن الأوجه الأخرى الأساسية في الفيلم مسألة العبودية ومفهوم تحرير العبيد مقابل تعويض مادي [لمالكيهم].

شكلت المزارع المشغولة بكدح العبيد مختبرات وحشية لقياس قدرات الجسد البشري على العمل كبطاريات حيوية أو بيوكيميائية أو مُهندسة حيويًّا مهمتها تغذية نظام جائر

من الإنتاج والتدمير بواسطة آليات عنف منهجية. وكان العبيد بمثابة المواد الخامة شأنهم في ذلك شأن المعادن المُستخدَمة في مكثّفات البطاريات، وقد أُستنفذوا وقودًا لاقتصاد المزارع وبالتالي المنظومة الصناعية الأشمل التي شكلوا جزءًا منها.

وكان العبيد النظيرَ الحيوي للعناصر العِدانية [mineralogical] التي شكّل التنقيب عنها واستخراجها الحافز للرأسمالية ومن ثمّ العبودية، فكانوا في نظر النظام الذي استعبدهم مادةً جامدة لا قدرة لها على التعبير أو التفكير المجرد الذي يخوّلهم للارتقاء إلى مصافّ البشر مكتملي الإنسانية. وللمحافظة على دوام خرافة لاإنسانية العبيد، أُبْتُدِعَت هياكلُ تنظيمية للتطويق والتحكم بمقدراتهم الزَمَكانية تقوم على نظام من العنف الجسدي والنفسي والسيكولوجي والفلسفي والقانوني الذي تطبّقه وترسّخه أجهزة الدولة المتعددة ومتفرعاتها.

أتت النهاية المزعومة لهذا النظام عام 1833 مع إلغاء العبودية في أنحاء الإمبراطورية [البريطانية] كافةً ولا سيّما في جزر الكاريبي إضافة إلى كندا وجنوب إفريقيا وإنْ كان على نطاقٍ أضيق. وبينما تحتفي السردية المهيمنة المقترنة بتاريخ إلغاء العبودية بدور مجموعة من الدعاة المسيحيين الذين نجحوا متسلحين بسلطتهم الأخلاقية فحسب في إقناع البرلمان بإعتاق العبيد، فالحقيقة أشدّ تعقيدًا من ذلك بكثير. لم يكن الانتصار الذي أحرزه الدعاة بالتفاوض والإقناع سوى انتصارًا جزئيًا ساهم فيه إلى حد كبير الإقرار لوبي من قبل مالكي العبيد المتنفذ في الهند الغربية بتراجع الجدوى الاقتصادية لامتلاك العبيد إزاء أنماط أخرى من التجارة الحرة أكثر إدرارًا للربح.

وحقيقة الأمر، وفق ما بات معروفًا حديثًا (والفضل في ذلك يعود إلى العمل الأرشيفي الذي قام به كل من كاثرين هول ونيكولاس درابر في كلية لندن الجامعية)، أنّ مالكي العبيد تقاضوا تعويضات بقيمة 20 مليون جنيه استرليني كي يرضوا بإعتاق عبيدهم، ما يوازي اليوم 16 إلى 17 مليار جنيه إسترليني. ومن نافل القول إنّ مالكي العبيد كانوا من أغنى عائلات بريطانيا والعالم آنذاك وهي عائلات ضاربة جذورها في الأرستقراطية التي كانت تتحكم بتدفقات رأس المال حول العالم ولا تزال إلى يومنا هذا. ومن بين هذه العائلات بارينغز وباركليز.

تلقى مالكو العبيد مبالغ مالية فاحشة التضخم كتعويضاتٍ عن خسارة ملكياتهم من العبيد واحتفظوا بجردات بتلك الملكيات في سجلات حسابية بالغة الدقة بهدف المطالبة بالأرباح المستقبلية التي لن يتمكنوا من تحصيلها من ذلك الحين فصاعدًا. في المقابل، لم يحصل العبيد بالطبع على أي تعويضات مقابل الأضرار التي تكبدوها طوال قرون من الاستعباد، بل أُجبِروا على الخضوع لـ«التدريب المهني» بلا مقابل حيث أُلزِموا بالعمل بلا أجرٍ لستّ سنوات إضافية لدى مالكيهم السابقين وإنما تحت مسمى أرباب العمل. وبلغت الثروات التي راكمتها عائلات مالكي العبيد السابقين حدًّا من اللاتكافؤ بحيث عندما تبين في العام 2017 حجم الأموال التي يدفعها البريطانيون كجزء من ضرائبهم لتسديد فوائد متراكمة على الدين من تلك المرحلة وحتى يومنا هذا أذهل الرأي العام إلا أنّه لم يفاجئ أحدًا.

سِپاكيه أنغياما

أعتقد أنّ لمسألتيْ القيمة والمادة صلةً وثيقةً بما يقدمه الفيلم لجهة التفكير في النضالات الاجتماعية والسياسية التي نشهدها في عددٍ من الانتفاضات حول العالم. كما تتطرقون في الفيلم إلى العلاقة بين الانهيار البيئي والانهيار المالي ومفهوم «إعادة» الأشخاص الذين استقرّوا في بريطانيا. حبّذا لو توسع قليلًا في الحديث عن هذا الجانب، يا كودوو.

كودوو إشون

بعضٌ مما نشهده اليوم لا علاقة له بصنع شعوب الكاريبي بل بتفكيك هذه الشعوب. تتساءل دينيز فِريرا دا سيلفا في مقالٍ صدر عام 2017 وقد أثّر تأثيرًا بالغًا على مسار تفكيرنا: «Why? don't black lives matter» [لماذا حيوات السود غير مهمة؟][5] السؤال هنا كيف نفهم السواد، وكيف نفهم الحيوات، وكيف نفهم المادة؟ ما هي المادة التي لا أهمية لها؟[6]

تمهّد سياسة «البيئة المعادية» المزعومة التي انتهجتها الحكومة [البريطانية] المحافِظة في قانون الهجرة لعام 2014 لمجموعةٍ من الممارسات التشريعية التي تهدف إلى نزع المواطنة. وما يتعرض له اليوم أبناء جيل وندرَش الذين وفدوا إلى المملكة المتحدة أربعينيات وخمسينيات القرن الماضي لإعادة إعمار البنية التحتية الصناعية المتهالكة للإمبراطورية هو النزع المنهج لمواطنتهم. وهو جزء لا يتجزّأ من عمليات صنع المواطنة وتفكيكها في إطار المشروع الإمبريالي الأشمل والذي يتضمن ترحيل اللاجئين العراقيين والسوريين والأفغان والسريلانكيين. إنه بمثابة مشروع إيبريالي متواصل منذ أحداث 11 أيلول/سبتمبر يقوم على الترحيل والاعتقال والعقوبات والحرمان والسلب على نطاق واسع يشمل كامل رقعة المملكة المتحدة وإن كان بشكل خفيّ.

تفضي مسألة البيئة المعادية إلى السؤال الأشمل: لماذا حيوات السود غير مهمة؟ سَعَيْنَا إلى إيجاد لغة محددة تتيح التفكير بمادة حياة السود وأهميتها وبالبيئة المعادية، لغة تستطيع أن توفي هذه الأسئلة مقدارها من الخطورة وحقها من الأهمية. لقد شهدنا بالأمس عرضًا مثيرًا للفرقة المصرية «حَ رَ كَ» يطرح مسألة العدالة الجمالية. ما هي الجماليات التي يمكن أن توفي هذه

الأسئلة حقها؟ فنحن بصدد الحديث عن نمط الحياة الآجلة أو عن حياة أنماط الحياة ما قبل العبودية وما بعدها.

في العام 1960 نوّه الكاتب الأفرو-أمريكي ريتشارد رايت إلى أنّ ظروف العبودية والفصل العنصري كانت هي ما منح الفنان الزنجي وجاهةً فكرية وأخلاقية ناقمة. وأظن أنّ سؤال حيوات السود التي لا تهمّ والبيئة المعادية تمنح عددًا من النسويات السوداوات وجاهة أخلاقية ناقمة على نحو مماثل. ففي ظل البيئة المعادية، تكتسب أفكار وكتابات وأبحاث قامات على شاكلة دينيز فِريرا دا سيلفا وسعدية هارتمان وكرستينا شارب وهورتنس سپيلرز وسيلفيا وِنتر وغيرهن الكثيرات زخمًا استثنائيًا، لأنها تسلط الضوء على الأفكار الملقّنة واللازمة لفهم ما هو على المحكّ، كما تمكننا من بناء جماليات قادرة على الاستجابة للأزمة الراهنة. وكان أحد مساعي هذا المشروع هو مَسرحة هذه الأسئلة.

كان أحد المفاهيم التي تناولها الفيلم هو مفهوم سعدية هارتمان للجوقة [chorus]. في كتابها الجديد *Wayward Lives, Beautiful Experiments* [حيوات شقيّة، تجارب جميلة] تقول إنه بالعودة إلى إتيمولوجيا لفظة chorus بالإغريقية القديمة، سنجد أنّ أصلها يفيد معنى الرقص داخل حيّزٍ مسيّج. تقول كذلك إنّ الجوقة، لا سيّما الجوقة النسائية، تعيد بشكلٍ من الأشكال إحياء التقاليد الراديكالية للسود على مستويَيْ الجماعي والجمعي.[7] وهذا ما حاولنا فعله؛ حاولنا بحث مسألة مادة حيوات السود وحيثيتها من منظار جماليات الجوقة.

سِپاكيه أنغياما

أتوجه بالحديث الآن إلى دينيز: قرب نهاية الفيلم يُؤخذ المشاهدون إلى معادلةٍ دائمًا ما تأتي نتيجتها محايدة أو صفرية بالأحرى. هلا شرحتِ لنا المزيد حول هذه المعادلات وعلاقتها بالسواد وأفكارك حول السبب الذي يجعل حياة السود غير مهمة؟

دينيز فِريرا دا سيلفا

قبل أن أتناول معادلة القيمة، أودّ أن أحيل إلى اقتباسين عادةً ما أستند إليهما في كتاباتي. الاقتباس الأول من الإعلان الثاني لحركة الزاپاتيستا من غابة لاكاندون الذي يذكرون فيه أنهم يتواجدون في الجبال ويناجون موتاهم. يتساءلون أي الطرق يسلكون فيجيبهم الموتى: «كل شيءٍ لكل الناس... وإلى أن يتحقق ذلك، لن يكون ثمّة شيء لنا»[8]. أما الاقتباس الثاني فيعود إلى فرانتز فانون الذي يقول: «مهمتنا التاريخية هي دعم كل احتجاجٍ وكل فعلٍ يائسٍ وكل محاولةٍ مجهَضةٍ مغرَقةٍ في أنهار الدم والمصادقة عليها»[9]. أرجو أن يلاقي هذين الاقتباسين بعض الصدى عندنا وأنا أتحدث عن معادلة القيمة وغيرها من الأمور التي كانت تشغلني وأنا أكتب عنها.

إنّ معادلة القيمة هي بالأساس طريقة أحاول من خلالها تفعيل قدرة مفهوم السواد على الإرباك والتقويض، لا سيّما مع ما يحمله هذا المفهوم من تحديات للفكر الحداثي ولأنماط العيش في ظله، والتي أراها ثغراتٍ مفاهيميةٍ تعمل ضمن مفهوم السواد دون أن يطمسها هذا المفهوم. إنها قدرة هذا المفهوم على نسف كل القوالب والتصنيفات الرياضية والمفاهيمية وربما أيضًا المؤسساتية والعملية. المعادلة هي أداة لما أسميه «آدابيّات النسوية السوداء»[10] والتي أدرجها في صميم تقاليد التراث الراديكالي للسود، وذلك لعددٍ من الأسباب أهمها هو اضطلاعها بمهمة الدراسات السوداء، بحسب صياغة س. ل. ر. جيمس وسدريك روبنسون، ألا وهي تقويض الحضارة الغربية.

أسمّي هذه المهمة أيضًا الديكولونيالية، أو إنهاء العالم كما نعرفه اليوم. تتطلّب هذه المهمة استعادة القيمة الإجمالية التي استخرجها المستعمر الأوروبي من أراضي السكان الأصليين وصادرها من عمالة أجسامهم المستعبدة. (استعمل هنا صفة «الأصليين» للإشارة إلى علاقة هذه المهمة بمشروع مناهضة الاستعمار، والذي يمكن اقتفاء أثره إلى اللحظة التي بدأ فيها السكان الأصليون لأمريكا والسكان الأصليون لجزر مالوكو، التي هي جزء من دولة موزمبيق اليوم، مقاومة المحاولات الأوروبية للاستيلاء على أراضيهم وأجسامهم قبل خمسمائة عام). هذه القيمة الإجمالية لما صادره واستخرجه المستعمِر الأوروبي ليست قابلة للحساب أو القياس أو التحديد بأي طريقة — فهي تساوي المجموع الكلي للأشياء جمعاء. ولا يقتصر ذلك على قيمة الأشياء التي كانت يومًا ما أو حدثت بالماضي، بل يشمل كل ما ترتّب على هذه المصادرة وكل ما جعلته هذه المصادرة ممكنًا في الحاضر والمستقبل؛ كل قرشٍ وكل بنايةٍ وكل خليةٍ وكل حجرٍ وكل ذرةٍ من قوام أي نظامٍ يوجد حاليًا ويسهم في إعادة إنتاج ومراكمة رأس المال على ظهر هذا الكوكب. هذا هو ما أعنيه أي أنه كذلك إنهاء العالم كما نعرفه اليوم. لكن ما علاقة كل هذا بالسواد؟

أنطلق هنا ممّا لا يسعنا حصره من الحالات التي تقترف فيها الدولة عنفًا شاملًا — أقصد هنا العنف العرقي — ضد الأفراد السود. أنظر إلى هذا الاستخدام المفرط وغير المقبول للعنف بوصفه علامة على كون السواد أنبوبًا ساحبًا قادرًا على استبقاء كل الطرق البديلة للتفكير والوجود التي يتوجب سحقها كي يتسنّى إفساح الطريق أمام أنماط التفكير والعيش الحداثية. تبعًا لذلك، يحيلنا السواد إلى أنماط من الحياة الآجلة تتجاوز صلات الدم والقربى. كما يؤشّر على طرقٍ أخرى للتفكير تسبق وتناهض وتتجاوز التصنيفات، وتتصل بما تحدّث عنه صلاح بخصوص السودان. هذا هو نفسه التصنيف المرفوض في ما زعمه الموتى في خطاب الزاپاتيستا، وهو ما يشير فانون أيضًا إلى رفضه وهو يفصح عن «مهمتنا التاريخية».

يعود هذا الالتفات إلى ما يمكن أن يعتنقه خطاب السواد من طرقٍ أخرى للتفكير في شؤون العالم ليستلهم مداخلات عدة في الفكر النسوي الأسود، وأخص بالذكر تأويل هورتنس سبيلرز لفكرة «نزع الجندرة عن اللحم الأنثوي». تشير سبيلرز إلى الجسد الأسود الأنثوي الأصلاني، الجريح والمعذّب، بوصفه موقعًا لترسيم معالم إجرام الاستعباد والغزو وانتهاكاته الأخلاقية. وبشكلٍ أدقّ، أستدعي هنا تساؤل سبيلرز حيال توارث الأجيال القادمة تلك الجراح، والتي هي آثار للانتهاك. من هذا المَعين استقيتُ أفكاري حول معادلة القيمة وغيرها من التجارب التي أعمل عليها مؤخرًا.

تشكّل قضية القيمة مواجهةً غير مستغرقة في لحظة التضاد وبالتالي تفارق الجدلية الماركسية. وعليه، عندما أضع السواد في مواجهة الحياة، تكون المحصلة أقرب إلى الإفناء، أو كما أصفها في موضعٍ آخر، «المُسالَبة»[11]. تتيح لحظة المسالبة تلك إمكاناتٍ أخرى دون تسميتها، بما فيها الحياة نفسها. والحياة أهمّ الدوالّ على الإشكالية الأخلاقية السائدة في عصر التنوير. إنها لحظة كسر المحدّدات التي تمنح للحياة تفوقها الأخلاقي، تلك المحدّدات التي صُمّمت خصيصًا لتفرض صورة معينة عن العالم سابقة لأي تصورٍ أو ممارسةٍ للعيش لا يعيدان إنتاج نقطة الانطلاق الحداثية. هذه النقطة التي تنطوي بدورها على فصل الإنسان عن العالم، والتي تجعل من العالم شيئًا قابلًا للغزو والترسيم والاستيلاء ومن ثمّ تضع الممارسات والمناهج التي تُمكّن استخراج وانقراض كل ما لا يُعَد «بشريًا».

سِباكيه أنغياما

تثيرين مسألةً مهمّةً هي في صميم ثقافة السكان الأصليين وهي مسألة انعدام الفصل بين جسد الإنسان والأرض كمادة — وقد لمستها في الفيلم بذاته. أردت هنا التعقيب على أنسجة الجيولوجيا ضمن الفيلم. أتوقّف عندها في كل مرة أشاهد الفيلم لأنها لحظة التفكير عينها في الترابط بين الأرض والمادة المكوّنة للأرض وبين الجسد. أودّ أن أعرف المزيد عن سبب التحول في رؤيتك للمادة بصفتها لا تنفصل عن الأرض بما عليها من البشري وغير البشري.

أنجاليكا ساغار

ترتكز فلسفة أدفايتا ڤيدانتا على فكرة اللافصل بين الذات والشيء، وهي فكرةٌ متجذرة المنطق التانتري الذي يرى العالم المادي وكأنه في حالة تواشج دائمة مع حناياه. فالمرء يتعلم من خلال علاقاته بكل ما يوجد في حيطه الكوني، لأننا كلنا في الأصل كينونة واحدة. نجد تلك الممارسة في الحِكم الخاصّة باليوغا وطبّ الأيورفيدا والفلسفات الهندوسية. كنتُ مهتمة بفهم هذه الممارسة في إطار حياتي وفي العموم. في حالة الفيلم، أردتُ أيضًا أن اتأمل في ماهية تقمص أرواحنا ماديًا في الحاضر، وأردتُ أن أفهم كيف نحقق ذلك على نطاق الكوكب مع الإحساس بالمسؤولية والاستدامة؟

إسي إشون

في نظري، إحدى النقاط الأساسيّة التي يضمرها الفيلم هي السعي لإبراز المبدأ الذي تعتنقه الفلسفة الأرواحية والقائلة بأنّ كل ما في الطبيعة حيّ وهو مزيج من المادة والطاقة. لدينا في الفيلم أجسامٌ تتحوّر من هيئة إلى أخرى. لا تتّبع أي تصنيفٍ للأفراد أو للفئات الاجتماعية وتستطيع اختراق أبعادٍ وأُطرٍ زمنية متعدّدة في آن واحد. تتكلّم هذه الشخوص من موقع «الذات الجيولوجيّة» [geologic subjectivity] كما تسميها كاثرين يوسُف، أي من حيثية متطابقة مع قضايا الأرض. إحدى الشخصيّات التي أؤدّيها [في الفيلم] لها رؤوسٌ عدّة وهي، في جوانب عدّة، تجسيد للأرض. كما لا يتوانى الفيلم عن طرح مسألة وجود استمرارية بين المادة والطاقة من خلال القالب الذي يتبنّاه. تنفرد أطر التفكير اللاغربية بهذه الأنماط والقوالب في حين يرمقها الغرب بنظرة دونية. ولكن عندما تجعلينها محور الفيلم ينتفي منطق التشكيك حيالها أو الداعي لتبريرها، بل تنغمسين في هذا العالم وداخل هذا الإطار. إذًا، من مهمّات هذا الفيلم أن يجعلكِ تُلقين تصوّراتك المسبَقة جانبًا للحظة وتدخلين فضاءً قد لا تودّين دخوله في العادة.

سِباكيه أنغياما

لقد دعانا أدريان [لحود] إلى وضع توصيف لما أسماه «الحياة في الآجل» وللحظة التي تسبق هذا «الآجل». ما هي الحياة، هذه القوة الحيوية، هذا النَفَس، بالنسبة إلينا؟ ولقد دعانا الترينالي ككلّ إلى التفكير في السَّلَف، بل وفي الأجيال المستقبليّة الملتفتة إلى الماضي من منظور يتجاوز اللحظة الراهنة أو المستقبل المنظور، بهدف إعادة تشكيل اللحظة المستقبلية المحتملة. أودّ أن أشكر متحدّثينا ومتحدّثاتنا في هذه الأمسية على مداخلاتهم(ن) التي ساهمت في استعراض طرق التفكير في الحياة على أشكالها.

1 otoliths، أي الحُصيّات الأذنية هي بنيات صغيرة من كربون الكالسيوم في كُييس الأذن الوسطى تساهم في توازن وقد اكتُشفت في كل من الحيوانات الفقارية المنقرضة وغير المنقرضة: https://www.marefa.org/حصية_أذنية [المحرّرات]

2 Édouard Glissant, *Poetics of Relation* (Ann Arbor, MI, 1997).
بتعريف المترجمة مايا زبداوي، "الكَرْيَلة هي شكل من أشكال التهجين اللغوي، وهي عملية تقضي بتطوير اللغة من خلال تبسيط وخلط لغات مختلفة فيها. تحاول هذه العملية خلق نظام نحوي جديد خاص بها، وهذا ما يميّزها عن أنماط تهجين مختلفة [...] واللغات المُكَريَلة تتأثر بموازين القوى التي تجمع شعوب وسلطات اللغات المتلاقحة. أي أننا لا بد أن نتيقّن من واقع أنّ ثمة لغات تقع في موقع المهيمِن وأخرى المهيمَن عليه، في سياق عملية التهجين هذه". انظروا https://kohljournal.press/ar/node/340 [المحرّرات]

3 Ali Al'Amin Mazrui, "The Multiple Marginality of the Sudan," in *Sudan in Africa*, ed. Yusuf Fadl Hasan (Khartoum, 1969).

4 Windrush Generation هي التسمية التي تطلق على جيل من الكاريبيين الذين استقدمتهم الإمبراطورية البريطانية من مستعمرات الكومنولث في الكاريبي ابتداء من عام 8491 لتغطية الحاجة في سوق العمل عقب انتهاء الحرب العالمية الثانية ولغاية العام 1791. وتُنسَب هذه التسمية إلى السفينة "إمپاير ونِدرَش" التي حملت إحدى أكبر مجموعات المهاجرين والمهاجرات من جامايكا وترينداد وتوباغو وبربادوس والجزر الكاريبية الأخرى إلى لندن عام 8491. وقد منح قانون الجنسية البريطاني هؤلاء المهاجرين الحق في السفر إلى بريطانيا والحصول على جنسيتها والاستقرار فيها. جدير بالذكر أنّ المهاجرين الجدد واجهوا لدى وصولهم نقصًا فادحًا في فرص التعليم والطبابة والعمل والسكن، كما لم تلتفت الحكومة البريطانية إلى تقنين أوضاعهم ومنح كلهم الوثائق الثبوتية اللازمة مّما أدى إلى تهميشهم اجتماعيًّا على نطاق واسع. [المترجم]

5 Denise Ferreira da Silva, "1 (life) ÷ 0 (blackness) = − or / : On Matter Beyond the Equation of Value," *e-flux Journal* 79, February 2017, https://www.e-flux.com/journal/79/94686/1-life-0-blackness-or-on-matter-beyond-the-equation-of-value (accessed November 22, 2020).

6 في النص الأصلي تَرد كلمة matter مرة بصيغة الاسم ومعناها "المادة" أي كل جسم ذي وزن ويشغل حيّزًا في الفراغ، ومرة بصيغة الفعل وتفيد كون الشيء "ذا شأن". ويفيد استخدام اللفظة في المنحيين اللعب على الكلام في سؤال دا سيلفا ?Why don't black lives matter في مقالها المذكور. وإذ لا توجد في اللغة العربية لفظةٌ واحدة تفيد كلا المعنيين، وجبت الإشارة. [المترجم]

7 Saidiya Hartman, *Wayward Lives, Beautiful Experiments: Intimate Histories of Riotous Black Girls, Troublesome Women and Queer Radicals* (London, 2019).

8 EZLN, "Segunda Declaración de la Selva Lacandona," June 1994. English translation, Wikisource, https://en.wikisource.org/wiki/Second_Declaration_of_the_Lacandon_Jungle (accessed April 19, 2021).

9 Frantz Fanon, *The Wretched of the Earth* (New York, 1963), 207.

10 وفاءً للمصطلح المنحوت باللغة الإنكليزية poethics والذي يجمع بين الحقلين الفلسفيين poetics و ethics والذي تسعى من خلاله المؤلفة إلى البحث عن الممارسة النسوية السوداء [black feminist praxis] يجيب عن سؤال: هل يستطيع ضمير الأديبة/الشاعرة تحرير أقوال العرق الأسود كشيء وسلعة وحقيقة من غير دليل من أساليب المعرفة العلميّة والتاريخية التي أنتجت هذه المقولة في المقام الاوّل؟ ارتأينا استخدام كلمة "آدابيّات" التي تجمع بين الإشارة إلى الأدب والآداب بمعنى الأخلاق. لقراءة المزيد عن هذا المبحث، يُرجى الاطلاع على نصّ مقال دا سيلفا "Toward a Black Feminist Poethics: The Quest(ion) of Blackness Toward the End of the World," *The Black Scholar*, vol. 44 no.2 (2014), pp. 81–97.
[المترجم]

11 تستعمل دا سيلفا لفظة "المُسالَبة" [Negativation] لوصف موقف نقدي يصبح فيه السواد مرآة نقدية تهشّم ذاتَ الناظر إليها، وهو في هذه الحالة الأوروبي الأبيض الذي ينظر إلى السواد كمرآة اعتاد تاريخيًا أن يطالع من خلالها كماله وتفوّقه على كل من/ما هو أسود. [المترجم]
للمزيد انظروا
Denise Ferreira da Silva, *Unpayable Debt* (Berlin, 2021).

التأريخ النوبي ونهر العودة الدافق أبدًا

علیا مسلّم

ترجمه عن الإنكليزية فريق الأركلوغ

في حفلٍ موسيقي قدّمه بولاية كاليفورنيا عام 1987، تطرّق المطرب النوبي الشهير حمزة علاء الدين إلى جانبٍ من جوانب العلاقة الدقيقة بين الطبيعة ودقّات إيقاع الدَّف.[1] يقول ممسكًا الدَّفّ لعرض توضيحي:

«أعتقد أنّ كلّ دقّةٍ على الطبلة تنطوي على أصواتٍ أربعة. هذا هو الماء»،

ثم نقر وسط دَفّه ليهتزّ بصوتٍ رخيمٍ.

«هذه هي الأرض»،

ثم صَفَق طرف الدَّفّ بيده ليصدر إيقاعًا جافًّا مكتومًا.

«وهذه هي النار»،

ثم نَقَر حوافّ الدَّفّ بأنامله ليقعقع بنغماتٍ متسارعة.

«وهذا هو الهواء»،

ثم مسح بباطن كفّه على الدَّفّ ليصدر حفيفًا خافتًا.

«عندما تدع طبلتك تدق لحنَك، يمكنك أن تشعر بالعناصر الأربع معًا. دعوني أعرض لكم ذلك الآن»[2].

ثم شرع بالعزف على الدَّفّ والجمهور يصغي إلى كلّ من العناصر الأربع، ويختبر حينًا تراكبها وحينًا آخر تضاعفها كموجاتٍ متتالية في لحن أنشودة الأطفال البديعة «هِمَايَلا».

بين كانون الثاني/يناير 2010 و2018 سجّلتُ مقابلات واجتماعات وفعاليات ولقاءات مختلفة في قرىً نوبية عدّة ضمن محاولتي لفهم وتوثيق كيف يُمكن «غناء» التاريخ. أشير هنا إلى كلّ من محتوى هذه الأغاني — أي ما تخبرنا به هذه الأغاني من تجارب التهجير، وفعل الغناء ذاته بوصفه منهجًا — أي كيف تخبرنا الأغاني بتواريخ هذا التهجير.

أثناء بناء السّدّ العالي بأسوان — والذي اكتمل بناؤه عام 1970، مشكّلًا حجر الزاويةِ في النسخة الناصرية من الاشتراكية العربية — هُجّر قرابة 100 ألف نوبي من قراهم، وأُعيد توطين حوالي 48 ألف منهم شماليَّ السّدّ في صحراء كوم أمبو. طُمِر تاريخ هذا التهجير تحت زخم الإيديولوجيا الناصرية وبروباغندا التحديث التي صوّرت بناء السّدّ كضرورةٍ مُلحّة في المخيّلة الشعبية. رُوّج للسّدّ على أنه رمز الحدث الثوري في ستينيات ما بعد الاستعمار باعتباره مصدرًا للماء والكهرباء وبوابة عبور إلى حداثة ينعم بها الجميع وهي مقولات تمثّل فحوى خطابٍ مستتر استهدف به جمال عبد الناصر المجتمعات النوبية نفسها، واعدًا إياهم برفاهٍ آتٍ بعد إتمام السّدّ.[3]

كادت عملية تهجير المجتمعات النوبية نفسها تُطمَر تحت زخم الجهود الدولية لنقل المعابد المصرية القديمة التي توزعت على أراضي القرى النوبية حينها. وفي حين أنّ التهجير يغيب عن السرديات الرسمية للتاريخ، لا تزال آثاره من حكايات ومشاعر وحيوات قبل التهجير وبعده حاضرةً في الأغاني النوبية. حفظت العائلات ومجتمعات القرى هذا التاريخ فيما بينها، وتُعيده على الأسماع في اللقاءات والمناسبات وحكايات للأطفال قبل النوم. يشكّل هذا التاريخ تركةً مجبولةً بعلاقة هذه المجتمعات بالطبيعة والموسيقى.

الماء: التاريخ نهرًا

عند دراسة التأريخ الشعبي، خصوصًا فيما يتعلّق بإنشاء السّدّ، يجدر تناول النهر بوصفه مجازًا لتدفّق التاريخ. يتدفّق التأريخ الشعبي، كما النهر، عبر الحدود. كما يؤخذ بالحسبان أنّ الحكايات النوبية قد سادت في المنطقة الواقعة بين مصر والسودان لعهودٍ طويلة سبقت ترسيم الحدود بين شمال وجنوب السّدّ العالي. كذلك لم تتوقّف حكايات الهجرة عند حدود التسلسل الزمني ولم تتقيّد بترتيبها. إذ إنّ أغاني الهجرة تعود إلى بناء خزّان أسوان عام 1902 وتخبر عن مُجمل تجارب التهجير والفقدان المتراكمة دون أن تميّز منه أحداثًا وأزمنة بعينها.

من المهمّ هنا أن نتذكّر أنّ النهر، ورغم ما يبدو عليه ظاهر الأمر، ليس عدوًّا للسّدّ، ولا هو محبوسٌ خلفه ومحكومٌ عليه بالركود. فالحكايات التاريخية الشعبية تتدفّق «عبر» السّدّ وتقدّم لنا في بعض الأحيان تواريخ مضادّة (قصصٌ تناقض السردية الرسمية عن تجربة إنشاء السّدّ)، وفي أحيان أخرى تربط التجربة المُعاشة بالسّدّ نفسه (نوبيون كُثُر عملوا في إنشاء السّدّ، أو آمنوا بصدق ما يحمله من وعود لمجتمعاتهم). ومن هنا نرى كيف تسري الأفكار عبر الحدود وكيف تُتناقل السرديات عبر الأجيال. نلمس تاريخًا يجسّد الانسياب والتأويل المتعدّد، عوضًا عن التأريخ الزمني المتسلسل الذي يُقدّم لنا سرديةً نهائيةً مُحكَمة.

في زيارتي الأولى لقرية غرب سهيل النوبية في العام 2010، تعرّفت على الشيف شعبان، الموسيقي والطبّاخ، والذي يصادف أن يكون ابن أخت أحمد صدقي سليم، المطرب المعروف الذي وضع غرب سهيل على خارطة الثقافة النوبية. برأي شعبان، كان لزامًا عليّ الاستماع إلى أغاني صدقي لكي أفهم ما عناه إنشاء السّدّ للنوبيين في حينه.

أول ما غنّاه لي الشيف شعبان كان أغنيةً تتناول النيل كمجاز، عنوانها «دايمن نصريبو وو نيل» والتي تعني بالعربية «منتصرٌ دائمًا يا نيل». كان صدقي مطربًا فذًّا يغنّي بلغة الكنزي المحليّة، وطبعت أغانيه ذاكرة المرحلة أثناء إنشاء السدّ فيما قبل التهجير.[4] بلغت شهرته أوجَها خلال ستينيات القرن الماضي وناهزت عبد الحليم حافظ وأم كلثوم في تغنيّه بالمشاريع القومية التي أعقبت الثورة الناصرية عام 1952. تُذكَر أغانيه اليوم على أنها كانت ما «مَهّد» النوبة لاستقبال السدّ.

يستهلّ صدقي «دايمن نصريبو وو نيل» (1960) قائلًا:

منتصرٌ دائمًا يا نيل
دوماً ما غلّبتنا (أي نحن النوبيين)
وكنت مصدر حياتنا
كُن في عون ناصر كما كنت في عوننا
لا تخذله يا نيل

يصدح صدقي بهذا المطلع كنداءٍ مُرسَل لا تصحبه الموسيقى. ومن ثمّ تلحقه أصوات الجوقة كما هي سمة الغناء النوبي الجماعي ودقّات الدَفّ العميقة التي يصفها حمزة علاء الدين في مطلع هذا النص. يشبه الإيقاع تدفّقًا منتظمًا، تحثّه كلمات الأغنية وتسترسله أصوات الجوقة التي تدعو النيل إلى مواصلة التدفق وبالتالي الانتصار، بينما تتسارع وتعلو دقّات الدفوف وأصوات الجوقة بالتناغم مع اقتراب نهاية الأغنية. بدعوته للنيل إلى مؤازرة النوبيين، يستدعي صدقي تاريخ الهجرات النوبية قبل إنشاء السدّ، وهي هجرات أعوام 1902 و1913 و1933، التي وقعت إما أثناء بناء خزان أسوان أو عقب تعليته لاحقًا. يدعو صدقي النيل أيضًا إلى مؤازرة جمال عبد الناصر، الذي - ويا للمفارقة - تحتفي به الأغنية كغيرها من أغاني صدقي.

النيل في هذه الأغنية هو قوةٌ غلبت بالفعل النوبيين رغم الهجرات المتتالية. الوعد الباقي هنا هو أنه مع هذه الهجرة تحديدًا، والتي ستقع عام 1964، قد يحمل النيل للنوبيين خيرات السدّ:

أنت، يا من يبدّل شربُ مائك حالَ المرء
اغلبنا كما فعلت دائمًا
ولتحمل معك الخصوبة والنور والمعادن...

تحمل أغاني صدقي الأخرى أفكارًا كثيرة من أفكار ثورة 1952 وشعاراتها. تحثّ أغنية «تاي تاي تاي» مستمعيها على أن يخبروا العالم بأنّ النوبيين اليوم قد أضحوا جزءًا من الوحدة العربية وصار لهم في كل بلاد العرب وطن. تظهر الوحدة العربية، وغيرها من المفاهيم والمصطلحات الأساسية في الخطاب الثوري الناصري العروبي، في أغاني صدقي بنطقها العربي بدلًا من لغة الكنزي.

يجري النيل إذًا بأكثر من الماء القادم من الجنوب. في تلك الفترة تحديدًا، حمل النيل معه أيضًا أفكارًا من الشمال (كفكرة إنشاء السدّ). أنتجت فلسفة الثورة الناصرية لغةً تتمثّل في ما يُسمّيه غرامشي «الحسّ المشترك» والذي يتحوّل مع الوقت ليصبح فكرةً مهيمنة فيسوّغ مبررات السدّ للجميع.[5] حمل النيل معه مصطلحات مثل الاشتراكية والنصر لوصف العالم الذي سيصنعه السدّ، وأسهم في الإيمان بكون السدّ سببًا للتحديث الحضري والاندماج والرفاه الموعود. حملت هذه الأغاني ما لم يعد الآن مرئيًا: كيف انتقلت المجتمعات القروية من العيش على ضفاف النيل إلى صحراء كوم أمبو القاحلة في ليسكنوا في بيوتٍ بدون أسقف. في ذلك الوقت وُزّعت منشورات على الأهالي تتضمّن صورًا مغرية لبيوتٍ تحوي أفرانًا وحنفيات حديثة تتدفق منها مياه عذبة. كذلك تضمّنت مجلات القصص المصوّرة منذ مطلع الستينيات حكايات أبطالها أطفال نوبيون، وتجري أحداثها في قرىً عامرة ومزدهرة بعد الهجرة المنتظرة. توجّه عبد الناصر نفسه بخطابٍ إلى النوبيين في زيارةٍ ميدانية للقرى القديمة مع بداية أعمال إنشاء السدّ في كانون الثاني/يناير 1960. في هذا الخطاب الشهير (كان عبد الناصر هو آخر رئيس مصري يزور النوبة ويتوجه للنوبيين بخطاب)، وعد النوبيين أنه ومع اكتمال السدّ بعد هجرتهم لن يعود ثمة فلاحٍ مهمّش في النوبة. سيصبح النوبيون عُمّالًا يشيّدون بأنفسهم صرح الأمة الجديدة. سيحصلون على فرصٍ أفضل للتعليم ويلتحقون بركب الثورة. وقع التهجير الواعد بالخير إلا أن أحدًا لم يذكر للنوبيين أنّ هذا التهجير سيحملهم بعيدًا عن النيل بمائه الجاري إلى شظف العيش في بيوتٍ دون أسقف. اختلطت المشاعر إزاء الحياة الجديدة. كان الانتقال نكبةً على الأغلبية التي مع ذلك، شعرت بضرورته. بالمقابل اعتقدت أقليةٌ من الشباب أنّ الانتقال قد يحمل معه حياةً أفضل للمجتمع. أما الوصول إلى كوم أمبو فكان كارثةً على الجميع. بينما كانوا في السابق بجانب ماء غزير فوجدوا أنفسهم الآن في صحارى لا نهاية لها وعراء مكشوف تحت الشمس. وحيث كان يُفترض أن يأتي الاندماج، أتت العزلة المفرطة.

الأرض: خرائط الغناء وسِيَر الارتحال

تمّ نقل قُرابة أربعين قريةٍ نوبية إلى كوم أمبو خلال إنشاء السدّ العالي. إلا أنّ هذه القرى لم يُعاد توطينها بحسب النسق الجغرافي في مواقع تواجدها السابقة، بل اعتُمِد لذلك منطقٌ عشوائي، فتقاطعت التجمعات الجديدة مع قرىً صعيدية وتجمّعاتٍ قَبَليّة كانت تسكن كوم أمبو سلفًا. احتفظت القرى «الجديدة» بأسمائها

الأصلية وأُلحقت بها كلمة «تهجير». مثلاً أصبحت قرية «عنيبة» تُدعى «عنيبة-تهجير» وقرية «أدندان» تُدعى «أدندان-تهجير». تُحيل الصيغة المصدرية «تهجير» لفعلٍ مضارعٍ متعدٍ يفترض وجود فاعلٍ ومفعولٍ به لفعل التهجير. مع كل ذكرٍ لاسم القرية، نفهم ضمنًا أن هذه ليست القرية الأصلية وإنما هي نسخةٌ عنها أعيد توطينها قسرًا في هذا المكان، وأنّ لساكنيها الحق الدستوري في العودة إلى قراهم الأصلية.

في زيارة إلى عنيبة-تهجير عام 2018، سألتُ وجيه حسن، وهو مثقفٌ وناشطٌ محلي عاصرَ الانتقال إلى القرية الجديدة في أواخر مراهقته، عن استخدام كلمة تهجير. كنت أتساءل عمّا إذا كان استخدام الكلمة بصيغتها المصدرية المضارعة سببه امتداد آثار التهجير إلى الزمن الحاضر. أجاب بأن ذلك محتمل، إلا أنه أضاف أنّ السبب الأرجح قد يكون انعدام وجود مثيلٍ لكلمة «تهجير» في اللغات النوبية. عبّرت الكلمة ببساطة عن التجربة كما اختبرها النوبيون وكما أُبلغوا بوقوعها. تسبّب تهجير بلاد النوبة في نقل الأهالي من عنيبة إلى عنيبة-تهجير، إلى أرضٍ أخرى وربما حتى أرض مؤقتة. حافظ ذلك على هوية ومعنى عنيبة الأصلية كأرض سيعودون إليها.

تتضمّن بعض أغاني التهجير قائمةً بأسماء القرى المُهَجّرة بترتيب مواقعها الأصلية على ضفاف النيل، وكأنها خارطةٌ غنائية يُمكِن تذكّرها غيبًا. واحدة من هذه الأغاني هي «صندلة» والتي تصف رحلة أهالي القرى على متن مركب يحملهم إلى الأرض الجديدة. يستهلّ الأغنية نداءٌ يردد أسماء القرى، كلّ منها متبوعٌ بعبارة «قُبلّه آيوه» والتي تعني «إلى هناك، نعم!» في إشارة إلى وجهة الصندل (وهو المركب النيلي). عند سماعي الأغنية للمرة الأولى، دقّقت في أوصاف القرى التي كنت أعلم أنها لم يُعد توطينها في كوم أمبو، شمال السدّ، بل جنوبًا في السودان. أُخبرت حينها أنّ الأغنية تلمّح أيضًا إلى هجرات سابقة خلال تعلية خزان أسوان عامَي 1912 و1933 قبل ترسيم الحدود المصرية السودانية بشكل نهائي. في بادئ الأمر تصوّرت هذه الأغاني أرشيفًا، وسألت عن الأغاني التي «تناولت تهجير عام 1964 فقط»، فأُخبرت حينها أنه ليس ثمّة من طريقةٍ للتحقّق من أنّ أيًّا من أغاني التهجير كانت قد كُتبت حصرًا عن تهجير عام 1964. كانت أغاني التهجير تحمل بداخلها تجربة التهجير بمعزل عن الظرف التاريخي الذي حدثت فيه.

تواصل أغنية «صندلة» فتصف ركّاب الصندل يودّعون النخيل ملوّحين، والذي يبادلهم الوداع بعدما هجرته الطيور، يودّعون الكلاب والقطط التي لم يتمكنّوا من اصطحابها والتي احتمت في البيوت التي هجرها الأهالي. يُغنّي صدقي «تجري الدموع كالنهر»، قبل أن يقاطعه النداء على أسماء قرى التهجير، ثم لا يلبث أن يعود صوته لنبرة الفقد مجددًا.

تستحضر هذه الأغاني، إذًا، خارطةً تُمكّن أيّ طفلٍ من تذكّر ترتيب القرى النوبية على النيل قبل التهجير. وهي أيضًا خارطة لسيرة أهالي النوبة، لا تُظهِر فقط من أين جاء المجتمع النوبي، بل أيضًا التجارب الحياتية التي تَشَكّل من خلال الخوض فيها. تتعدّد طبقات المعنى في هذه الأغاني، ولدى غناء وسماع التهجير تلو التهجير، ندرك أنّ أهمية هذا التاريخ لا تكمن في أنه حدثٌ مضى، بل في استمراره حتى الآن.

النار: إيقاع الغضب المتماوج

خلال رحلتي إلى غرب سهيل، تعرّفت على زيزي وهي فتاةٌ من جيلي كانت دائمًا ما تهتم بسماع الأغاني التي كنت أسجّلها وبالتفكّر معي فيها. صرت أنا وزيزي صديقتين، واستضافتني عائلتها في القرية الصغيرة حيث أقمت أغلب فترة البحث عام 2010.[6] لم تُهجّر هذه القرية قط، وينتمي كلّ أهاليها إلى عشيرة واحدة، هي عشيرة أمّ زيزي. بينما انحدر والد زيزي من أبو سمبل، والتي أغرِقت بالكامل عام 1964. وقد عرض اصطحابي في رحلة إلى القريتين المُهجّرتين أبو سمبل وبلانة-تهجير، إلا أنه قبل ذلك، كانت هناك رحلة أخرى أهم. اصطحبني أبو زيزي في رحلةٍ نهرية إلى الخزان خلف السدّ، أي بحيرة ناصر أو بحيرة النوبة كما يسمّيها النوبيون. ونحن بالقارب أخذ يحدّد مواقع القرى السابقة بيده، وطلب مني أن أرسم خريطة لهذه القرى التي تقبع الآن أسفل القارب في قاع البحيرة. في بعض المواقع لم يكن ثمّة أثرٍ باق، في مواقع أخرى كانت هناك وِهادٌ أسفل الماء، أشار إلى أنها كانت يومًا قمم جبال. كان أبو زيزي مقتنعًا أنه قبل زيارة قرى التهجير في كوم أمبو، ينبغي عليّ أن أفهم موقع هذه القرى في السابق. لاحقًا، عندما ذهبت أنا وزيزي في رحلة إلى أبو سمبل-تهجير وسألت عن أغاني التهجير، أُخبرت أنه ينبغي عليّ البحث عن أغانٍ على شاكلة أغنية «وو حَنِينا». بدأنا بزيارة أكبر خالات زيزي التي دعت نسوة أخريات لمشاركة قصصهنّ. عَرّفَت عنّي إحدى الخالات لأخرى قائلة «هي باحثة، تبحث عن أغانٍ مثل وو حَنِينا». إلا أيًّا من النسوة لم تُغنّ الأغنية نفسها. أصبحت وو حَنِينا مثل شيفرةٍ أو لونٍ غنائي خاصّ أبحث عنه، يصف تجربة التهجير نفسها أو يرثي الحياة السابقة للانتقال.

تمكّنت من العثور على الأغنية في نهاية المطاف.

كانت الأغنية بلغة الفَدْجيكي، وهي لغة أغلب النوبيين المهجّرين، ويغنّيها سيد جَبِير من مواليد أبو سمبل في ثلاثينيات القرن العشرين. تحكي الأغنية عن رجلٍ عاد لزيارة قريته الغارقة ولا يبصر سوى قمم جباها فوق سطح الماء. بينما يقف على ما تبقى من قريته، يأتيه طائر ويسأله لائمًا «لِمَ عُدت أيّها الغريب؟» ألهبت الأغنية العواطف وأثارت الشجون. أُخْبِرتُ أنّ أجهزة عبد الناصر

الأمنية منعت الأهالي حينذاك من غنائها في اللقاءات والتجمعات خوفًا من حراكٍ محتمل قد تثيره الأغنية. لاحظت أثناء البحث وعند الحديث عن التهجير أنّ الشعور بالذنب كان الغالب دائمًا على كل شيء، وحتى على الشعور بالفقدان. بدت هناك فجوة بين إيمان البعض بإمكانية الانتقال وبين إدراك أنهم خُدعوا، وكأنهم يتساءلون إذا ما كان عليهم أن يقاوموا الانتقال. كان الغضب على التهجير أكثر وضوحًا عند الأجيال الأصغر ممن وُلدوا ونشأوا في الأرض الجديدة، وكان لزامًا عليهم مواصلة الحياة وتكوين هويةٍ جديدة رغم التهجير. كان على هؤلاء تخطّي عقبتين هما الانتماء لأقلية مهمّشة والانتماء لثقافة نيلية انقطع اتصالها بالنيل.

في أواخر التسعينيات، قدّم المطرب خضر العطار (مواليد 1962 في قرية إبريم) أغنيةً جريئة هي «اسمي هناك». لم تكن الأغنية صِدامية وحسب، بل كانت ناطقة بالعربية أيضًا، ما سمح للعطار بمخاطبة جمهورٍ جديد كليًا من شباب النوبيين الذين توحّدهم اللغة العربية، كما غيرهم من الجمهور المصري العريض.

اسمي هناك، بلدي هناك
ذاتي هناك والنوبة هناك
شاهدة يا ناس، خلف السّدّ
...
شطبوا يا ناس حضارة كاملة
واغتالوا آمال النوبة السمرا
بتنادي علينا أنين الساقية
طحنوا عظام أجدادنا الباقية
...
فرضوا علينا الهجرة المُرّة
قالوا كوم أمبو الجنة الخضرا
عشنا فيها ليالي حزينة ومشينا سنين في الغربة
طويلة
...
تاريخنا قديم منحوت في الصخرة
كانوا ملوك في الوادي السمحة
هزوا الكون بإرادة قوية حتى الآن معابدهم شامخة
...
يوم فراق النوبة الغالية وصمة عار على جبين أجيالنا
...
هيا يا نوبي ويا نوبية
دقوا طبول العودة الجاية
نحن متين [متى] للذل ركعنا؟ مهما يكون النوبة لينا

بدا أنّ اختيار اللغة العربية لأداء هذه الأغنية لم يكن اعتباطيًا. فالعربية هنا هي صوتٌ جامعٌ لاحتجاج الأجيال الأصغر ينقل حنقهم إلى المجال العام ويطالب بعودة النوبيين لأرضهم الأصلية. تتحوّل الأغنية إلى صرخة في وجه تهجير ظالم لجيل تعرّض لذلّ شائن في الماضي ومستقبل غائم.

تختلف هذه الأغنية عن سواها في اللغة والنبرة والمواجهة. يغنّي خضر العطار عن «وصمة عار على جبين أجيالنا»، في إشارةٍ للأجيال التي هجرت قراها. لا تسترسل هذه الأغنية كما أغاني أحمد صديق، ولا تلتزم رتابة الإيقاع الشجيّ للدّفّ كسائر الأغاني النوبية الشعبية كما في «وو حنينا» أو «وو صندليا» على سبيل المثال. بالعكس، تشمل الأغنية طيفًا متنوعًا من الآلات وأدوات المزج الموسيقي الأكثر شبهًا بالإنتاج الموسيقي المعاصر، بشكل يعكس انفتاحًا على العالم — على مصر في اللغة وعلى السودان في اللون الموسيقي والتقنية.

بعد ثورة عام 2011، سُمع قرع طبول العودة أعلى وأعلى. أسفرت الحراكات التي بدأت منذ أواخر التسعينيات عن ضغطٍ شعبي منظّم إلى جانب تغييرات في الخطاب العام بمطلع الألفينات مع تصاعد دعوات «الحق في العودة»، جميعها أفضت إلى الاعتراف بالحق في العودة كحقٍ دستوري عام 2013. إذ جاءت المادة 236 من الدستور المصري المقَر عام 2014 لتثبّت حق أهالي النوبة في العودة إلى أرضهم، ومسؤولية الدولة عن إعادة تطوير القرى الأصلية وتأسيس هيئة حكومية تُناط بها هذه المهمة. إلا أنه وفي العام ذاته أعلن النظام العسكري في مصر عن ضمّ المناطق المحاذية للحدود المصرية السودانية، بما فيها القرى النوبية، إلى عهدته. ما سمح له عام 2016 باستصدار مرسوم يخوّله بيع أراضي هذه القرى بما فيها قرية توشكى. في اللحظة التي بات فيها حق العودة مكفولًا بالدستور أصبحت الأرض نفسها عصية على المنال.

نظّم الناشطون النوبيون «قوافل العودة» اعتراضًا على المرسوم، وقادوا مسيرات احتجاجية باتجاه قريتيْ توشكى وفرخند. وواجهتهم الدولة بحصار المشاركين في المسيرات وحجزهم على مدى أسبوع. في أيلول/سبتمبر 2017، تجدّدت الدعوة إلى التظاهر تحت شعار «العيد في النوبة أحلى». قاد الحراك مجموعةٌ من الفنانين والمفكرين ووجهوا دعوةً عامةً لمشاركتهم في مسيرةٍ غنائيةٍ سلمية بمدينة أسوان تطالب بحق العودة. جاء الرد هذه المرة عنيفًا، اعتُقل المنظمون فيما أصبح يُعرف لاحقًا باسم قضية «معتقلي الدفوف». شكّل الغناء عن العودة على وقع الدفوف التي تردّد صداها في شوارع أسوان تهديدًا لم تكن الدولة لتتساهل معه.

الريح: نضالات حميمة وعميقة

لم تكن هذه المرة الأولى التي يهبّ فيها أهالي النوبة للمطالبة

بحقوقهم. فقد أعطتني عائلة نفيسة زرّار، والتي التقيتها بقرية أبو سمبل-تهجير، مسحًا ضوئيًّا لأوراق تعود لأخيها المتوفّى، والتي أصرّت نفيسة أنها ستساعدني في بحثي. في شبابه عمل أخوها في بناء خزان أسوان، قبل أن يرتحل إلى الأسكندرية ويصبح واحدًا من الفاعلين الأساسيين خلف حراكٍ للمطالبة بتعويض أهالي النوبة ماديًّا عن أراضيهم التي غرقت بعد تعلية خزان أسوان عام 1933.

اشتملت الأوراق على محاضر اجتماعات حضرها أو نظّمها الرجل لتطوير مقاربات لمواجهة الدولة. نعرف من خلال الأوراق أنه عقد اجتماعات عام 1933 لتحرير عرائض تطالب بتعويض أهالي النوبة عن أراضيهم المغرقة. لم يُعرَف الكثير عن مصير هذه العرائض ومثيلاتها خارج ما تيسّر من المصادر الأكاديمية. كما لم يُعرف الكثير عن مآل حراك 1933 أو محاولات تنظيم حراك مماثل عام 1967 و1968 للمطالبة بحق أهالي النوبة في العودة، والتي طمرها شعار «لا صوت يعلو فوق صوت المعركة»، أثناء حرب الاستنزاف بعد حرب 1967. (بعد الحرب أصبح مصطلح «تهجير» يُستخدم حصرًا لوصف وضع المهجّرين من مدن قناة السويس بعد ترحيل ثلاثة أرباع المليون منهم وإعادة توطينهم بمدنٍ مختلفة في أنحاء البلاد بسبب العمليات العسكرية الجارية. وبذلك محا تهجيرٌ لاحق تهجيرًا سابقًا).

ورغم تعذّر الوصول إلى أرشيف العرائض المُقدّمة عام 1933، يمكن للمرء اقتفاء آثار تلك العرائض وأصحابها في قصص ذويهم كما في حالة نفيسة وأخيها. قد يبدو هذا التاريخ مبعثرًا في ظل غياب أرشيف مركزي، إلا أنّ هذا التاريخ هو محور حياة المجتمعات النوبية، وهو حاضرٌ على الدوام في وعي كل نوبي. من كل ما سجلته خلال لقاءاتي في زياراتي المختلفة إلى النوبة، كانت المقابلة الأقرب إلى قلبي هي مقابلتي مع نفيسة، التي لم تحُل أعوامها التسعون دون بديهةٍ حاضرة وحسّ فكاهي. كعادة مقابلاتي مع كبار السن كان تواجد عدة أفراد من العائلة أثناء المقابلة أمرًا طبيعيًّا. كان شريط التسجيل الصوتي للمقابلة مليئًا بضحكات العائلة ورياح آذار التي تتحرّك وتمور كستارةٍ رقيقة تحفّ حديثنا باستمرار. كانت حميمية التاريخ الذي تشير إليه الأغاني هي السمة الغالبة على الحديث الدافئ.

في إحدى المقابلات، أعادت نفيسة عليّ تهويدة كانت تغنّيها في السابق لطفلها الصغير، تطمئنه بأن ليس من ثمّة ما يخافه في أرض التهجير، فأرواح النيل ترعاه وتحفظه عند السباحة ليلًا. كانت أرواح النيل أسطورةً نوبية تشكّل العلاقة مع النيل. تقول نفيسة، إنه رغم التبرّك بهذه الأرواح لجلب الحظ والرزق في الزواج والولادة وحتى عند الممات، فإنّ للنيل أيضًا أرواحًا شريرة ومؤذية. على سبيل المثال، يعتبر بعض النوبيين السير ليلًا على ضفاف النيل أمرًا خطيرًا من شأنه أن يزعج أرواح النيل الشريرة التي قد تخطف أو تغرق السائر. على صعيدٍ آخر، هنا في أبو سمبل-تهجير، لا وجود لأرواح النيل. ما يوجد هنا هو الجنّ فقط. والجن هو روحٌ تعيش على البرّ وهو مسلمٌ مثلنا نحن الإنس بحسب رواية نفيسة التي تتعجّب إنه «ورغم إسلامه لا يؤمَن جانبه ولا خيرَ فيه». العلاقة المركّبة بأرواح النيل - الخوف منها والاعتماد عليها في ذات الوقت لا يُمكن تعميمها على أرواح البرّ.

كان ذلك الحديث عن الأرواح مبعثًا على استهزاء الصغيرات في مجلسنا. تشكّل الماورائيات والخوارق تجربة نفيسة في علاقتها بقريتها القديمة، إلا أنها أيضًا تشكل الروافد الأساسية لإحساسها بالانتماء إلى المكان. لا تتمتع هذه التواريخ بنفس الحضور البصري للسدّ، إلا أنّ أثرها المادي يناهز السّدّ. تشكّل العلاقة بأرواح النيل مادة القصص الشعبي النوبي، كما تشكّل أيضًا طريقة حياة الأهالي في القرى وإيمانهم بتقاسم هذه الحياة مع كائنات أخرى. حدّدت العلاقة بالأرواح علاقة الأهالي بالأرض وطقوسهم اليومية وأعرافهم غير المنطوقة، مثلًا أين ومتى يمشون، ما معناه تشارك الأهالي هذه الحياة مع مجتمع أوسع.

عودةً إلى التسجيلات، أستمع إلى صوت نفيسة «المتغضّن» المتقطع وهي تحاول استطالة مقاطعها بطريقةٍ منغّمة، وأتذكّر على الفور وجهها الجميل ورائحة المسك وصوت الريح في باحة منزلها. على صعيد ماورائيٍ، أصبحت ذكريات نفيسة هي أيضًا ذكرياتي. من الصعب أن يتخيّل المرء كيف يمكن لمعاناة التعايش مع أرواحٍ أخرى أن تكون طريقة للتنفيس عن وطأة تجربة التهجير. غلبت ضحكات نفيسة وروحها المرحة وصوت الريح على المقابلة، تلك المقابلة التي طبعت مجمل تجربتي البحثية، وبطريقةٍ غامضة، جعلت من تجربة التهجير جزءًا من تكويني، ومن فهمي للنضال والحياة والموسيقى وللتاريخ، جزءًا من تقديري لقيمة الرياح والضحك والدفء والصحبة الرائعة كزاد لمواصلة النضال.

كان نقل تجربة تهجير المجتمعات النوبية دون التعريج على تجربتي الشخصية مع ذلك المجتمع أشبه بإغفال نصف ما تعلمت. لا يُمكن الحديث عن نضال أحمد شوكت ضد تعلية خزان أسوان عام 1933 دون المرور بخسارة نفيسة الروحانية جرّاء التهجير، ولا يمكن ذلك أيضًا دون الحديث عن علاقتي بزيزي التي أمضيتُ برفقتها أشهرًا من بحثي الإثنوغرافي. قصة السّدّ كما أنقلها هي قصةٌ ضمن قصة ضمن قصة. تُتوارث هذه القصص وتُروى من خلال العلاقات عبر الأجيال وتتماوج عموديًّا عبر الزمن، كما تُتناقل عبر العلاقات، كتاريخٍ يتحرك من داخل العلاقات العائلية ومن خارجها، تمامًا كما تناهت إلى مسامعي وتحوّلت من خلالي إلى صيغة مكتوبة. فالقصة لا تنسلخ عن راويها، كما لا تنسلخ عن سياق روايتها الذي هو بحد ذاته طريقة للتعليم والتعلم.

الآن، دعْ طبلتك تدقّ لحنك أنت...

نظرًا إلى كيفية توثيق الناس لتجاربهم إزاء الأحداث التاريخية الكبرى، نلحظ حضورًا لتاريخٍ مُعارضٍ إلا أنه ليس بالضرورة تاريخًا مناقضًا. تجري أحداث هذا التاريخ المعارض لا بالتوازي بل بالاشتباك والتقاطع مع السرديات الكبرى للتاريخ المهيمن. تمثّل الأغاني النوبية التدفّق تمامًا كتدفق نهر النيل، وتجسّد هذا التدفّق بالغناء عن جغرافيات تتجاوز الحدود القطرية. تتناول الأغاني تجربةً تقع خارج تقسيم العصور وتتحدّث عن قوةٍ طبيعية لم تعد تسري في القرى المهجّرة. ينبغي التفكّر في هذه الأغاني بوصفها رابطًا بين الماضي والحاضر، وقناة يستمرّ من خلالها بثّ تجارب الماضي عبر الزمن، ومصدرًا للتاريخ يُروى بلغات مختلفة، وطريقة للسرد القصصي واستحضارًا للأرواح. تخبرنا الأغاني بما يتجاوز الأحداث والتحوّلات التاريخية «الهامة». بل تحمل معها بذور الإيديولوجيات وصوت النهر المغيّب والمشاعر الفيّاضة التي حملها التهجير. تُحرّك الأغاني مستمعيها وتدفعهم باتجاه مستقبلٍ أكثر عدالةً. وتسمح بُنية الصوت في أي أغنية لتكوّن مشاعر كثيرة تؤشّر على تاريخٍ متنوّع الأوجه لا يمكن اختزاله بسرديةٍ واحدة. إلا أنّ هذا التاريخ لا يُتاح فهمه فقط عبر استقراء الأغاني، بل يجب أن يُحَسّ به. بعبارة أخرى عليكِ أن تدعي الموسيقى تعزفك أنت.

1 الدَّفّ هو أحد أعمدة الموسيقى النوبية التقليدية ويُعرف أيضًا بالدُّفّ والتار.

2 *Hamza El Din, concert in Petaluma, CA, February 15, 1987*, YouTube video, 12:13 min., uploaded by “Dano Sediq,” October 17, 2012, https://www.youtube.com/watch?v=eQo1g-6CMBKI (accessed March 25, 2020).

3 في خطاب توجه به إليهم في كانون الثاني/يناير 1960 يَعِد عبد الناصر أهالي النوبة "بالسعادة والحرية والرفاه" بعد بناء السّدّ. يمكن الاطلاع على الخطاب من الرابط التالي: http://www.nasser.bibalex.org (accessed March 5, 2021).

4 يتحدّث أهالي النوبة لغة الكنزي، والتي تُعرف أيضًا بالمتوكي (الشائعة في القرى الأقرب إلى أسوان) والفدجيكي (الشائعة في القرى الأقرب إلى السودان جنوبًا والتي هُجّر أغلب سكانها بعد السّدّ)، وقلة منهم فقط تتحدث العربية.

5 ترتبط فلسفة عبد الناصر بما يسميه أنطونيو غرامشي بـ"العفوية" spontaneous philosophy والتي تتجاوز كونها نظامًا عقائديًّا يعكس تصورات طبقة اجتماعية بعينها أو رغبات الجماعة الحاكمة، إلى كونها فلسفة "تناسب الجميع".هذه الفلسفة كامنة في 1) اللغة نفسها وهي منظومة شاملة لمفاهيم بعينها لا كلمات مجردة من معانيها، 2) "الحسّ المشترك" common sense أو good sense "الحس السليم(3 ،" في التدين الشعبي والتبعية في بنية النظام العقائدي برمته شاملًا الهواجس والآراء والخرافات و طرق النظر إلى الأشياء والحكم عليها والتصرف حيالها والتي يمكن جمعها كلها عنوان "الفولكلور". اعتمدت إيديولوجية عبد الناصر وخطابه على عناصر الفلسفة العفوية وتمّ تذويتها لاحقًا كمصدر للشعور العام بحسب تسمية غرامشي. انظروا Antonio Gramsci, *Selections from the Prison Notebooks* (New York, 1971), p. 323.

6 حُجب اسم القرية المذكورة للحفاظ على السرية.

النكروفاجيا الصوتية
معـــاذ مصبـــاحي

ترجمه عن الإنكليزية فريق الأركِلوغ

إبّان الاحتلال الفرنسي للجزائر، شهدت قرية الهامل أواخر القرن التاسع عشر صراعًا بلغت أصداؤه مقرّ سلطة الاستعمار في الجزائر العاصمة على بعد مائتي كيلومتر شمالًا. نشب الصراع إثر خلاف على ميراث مشيخة زاوية الهامل خلفًا لشيخ الطريقة الولي سيدي محمّد بن أبي القاسم بين ابنته لالّة زينب[1] وابن عمّها محمّد بن الحاج محمّد. ومشيخة الزاوية هي منصب دينيّ ذو امتيازات روحيّة ودنيويّة، وكان شيخ الزاوية الهامليّة في ذلك الزمان يشرف على ثلاث دوائر إداريّة تمتدّ على مساحة شاسعة وتضمّ كتلة سكانيّة ضخمة، ما دفع سلطات الاستعمار إلى إيلائها أهميّة بالغة. انقسم أهالي المنطقة بين أنصار هذه وذاك، واعتبر الكثيرون منهم محمّدًا غير صالح لتولّي المشيخة لضعف تورّعه وانصرافه إلى ملذات الدنيا. وفي معرض الطعن على تولّي ابن عمّها لمشيخة الهامل، سخّرت لالّة زينب جميع صِلاتها بأهل الدين والعلماء المحلّيين ومعارفها الواسعة داخل المنظومة البيروقراطيّة الفرنسيّة فسطّرت مجموعة من الرسائل إلى أصحاب الرأي تبيّن فيها سوء سمعة ابن عمّها وتحذّر من الفوضى التي قد تنشأ حال تولّيه مشيخة الزاوية.[2]

من جهته، كان المسؤول الفرنسي المحلّي، الرائد كروشار، ميّالًا إلى خلافة ابن العمّ بسبب معارضته تولّي امرأة لهذا المنصب. فكتب في العام 1897 أنّ أنوثتها ستؤجّج المشاعر المعارضة للسلطات الفرنسيّة كما ستحول دون إمساكها بزمام الإدارة.[3] عبّرت هذه النزعة عن موقف السلطات الاستعماريّة التي كانت تواجه صعوبات عدّة في السيطرة على المراكز الصوفيّة الخاضعة لولاية النساء.[4] تناهت قضيّة الخلاف إلى مسامع رئيس المحكمة الفرنسيّة، المدّعي العام، بعدما وكّلت لالّة زينب المحامي الفرنسي موريس لادميرال التماسًا لترؤّس هرم السلطة من أجل إدانة سوء تصرّف المكتب العربي (وعلى رأسه كروشار).[5] أفصحت هذه الجرأة في التعامل مع القضية عن الحنكة التي اكتسبتها لالّة زينب من جرّاء تجوالها مع أبيها ومن الأحاديث مع اللاجئين السياسيّين والحجّاج الذين مرّوا بالزاوية وأووا إليها على مرّ السنوات (فعلى الرغم من موقعها النائي، كانت الهامل تقاطعًا هامًّا لتبادل المعارف وكسب المعلومات). فشكّلت الأخبار الواردة من الخارج مصدرًا ثمينًا للمعرفة تمكّنت لالّة زينب من استغلاله لقلب التحدّيات لصالح تحصين موقعها في تراتبيّة السلطة الروحيّة.

غير أنّ الحدث الحاسم الذي ساهم في التفاف المجتمع المحلّي حول لالّة زينب لم يتعلق بالنظام الاستعماري، بل من حدث صوتيّ لا يزال يتردّد في الذاكرة الشعبيّة إلى يومنا هذا، حدث اكتسح المجتمع وضخّم قاعدة أنصارها. إذ يُروى عن لالّة زينب أنّها قصدت ضريح والدها في لحظة حزن وقنوط شديدين وانهارت فوق قبره دامعة متوسّلة، وهي في حالة من الانفعال الوجداني الشديد، ما أجهد حنجرتها إلى حدّ انقلب نشيجها إلى صرخة حادّة مرتفعة. وتقول الرواية إنّ روح الوالد المتوفّى لبّت صراخ ابنته، فخاطبت الحشود وأعلنت لالّة زينب وريثة شرعيّة للمشيخة. هكذا تحقّقت الخلافة لِلالّة زينب التي استنفرت مكانتها كوَليّة تقيّة خاشعة وابنة تنعم بالامتياز الجينيّ وصوت يردّد الوحي الربّاني. هذا الصوت ومنزلة الجسد وإمكانياته الموسيقية هي موضوع هذا النص.

حسم صوت الميّت الخلافة لمصلحة لالّة زينب وهو ما لم يكن ممكنًا لولا الصرخة التي أطلقتها حنجرتها المتقرّحة جرّاء الصدمة.[6] يبيّن هذا الحدث كيف يمكن للجسد أن يؤدّي وظيفة الوسيط الصوتيّ. وإنْ كانت قدرة الجسد على حمل التركيبة الصوتية محكومة بمحدوديته الفيزيائية، فإنّ تجاوز الجسد لنفسه كأضحية، كما حدث في صرخة لالّة زينب، ينفي عنه سلطة الزمن.[7] يكشف الصراخ الطقوسي عن الطرق التي يحمل الفضاء والصوت بها أحدهما الآخر ضمن تفعيلاتهما الإقحامية وتشكيلاتهما البنيوية. عُرفت لالّة زينب خلال فترة ولايتها اللاحقة على رأس الزاوية ببحّة صوتها الذي يعتبره الطب الحديث اليوم أحد عوارض خلل التصويت [dysphonia] الذي يترافق مع عجز عن إخراج الأصوات بشكل طبيعي وكأنّ المتكلّم شخص آخر. وقد توفّيت بعد ذلك بسنوات جرّاء نزيف داخلي في الحنجرة. كانت تلك أضحيتها الأخيرة: بذلت حياتها بعدما قدمت صوتها قربانًا إلهيًّا.

الرقبة

تتقارب اشتقاقيًّا كلمتا «رقبة»، أي المسافة بين الرأس والصدر، و«قرابة» التي تفيد بنوع الصلة الاجتماعية بين الناس. وتربط الرقبة تشريحيًّا الأعضاء المناط بها الإبصار والنطق، أي العينين والفم، بالعضوين اللذين يغذّيانهما أي القلب والرئتين. فالرقبة تختلف عن بقيّة العمود الفقري من ناحية التشريح الهيكلي كون فقراتها السبع تتيح لها قدرة أكبر على الحركة المفصليّة. وكان يُقال في زمن الرقيق المقيت في شبه جزيرة العرب «فكّ الرقبة» للدلالة على الحقوق التي يكسبها العبد عند إعتاقه.[8] والمرء يخفض رأسه علامةَ احترام للأكبر منه سنًّا أو لمن له سلطان عليه. وتدلّ حدّة انحناء الرقبة على اختلاف المراتب بين الناس في حين يتيح اشرئبابها ترصّد المحيط (من المراقبة والرقيب). بذلك تجتمع في الرقبة وظائف الرابط الحيوي والسدّة المرتفعة والحاجب على الباب.

يقسّم علم التشريح الحديث الرقبة إلى مناطق تسمّى «مثلّثات» وتتضمّن كتلًا معقّدة من الأعصاب والأوعية الدموية والعضلات والغدد اللمفاوية في شكل عناقيد يمكن معاينتها أو سبرها جراحيًّا كل على حدة.[9] و من الناحية المفاهيمية، تجد هذه المثلثات مرادفاتها في الوحدة الأنثروپولوجيّة للعائلة الغيرية البحتة، حيث تمثّل النقاط الثلاث الأم والأب والولد الأكبر. ومن هذه الوحدة النواتية يُجمع النسل وتُقسّم المواريث. أمّا علم الأسلاف فيُعرف بعلم الأصول ومفردها أصل. والأصل هو الشيء أو الشخص الذي يُرتقب تأصيله، أي أنه يرتقب لحظة مستقبلية يُوضع فيها موضع النسبة والمقارنة أمام أشياء أخرى. وأمّا حيازة الأصل فهو القدرة على تعيين مواضع الأشياء أو الأشخاص في علاقة كونية.

ولا تكفي معرفة الأصل لنظم التاريخ، بل لا بدّ أن يحرّكه الوعي التاريخي لدى المعنيين به. لذلك يتوجّب على كلّ من تحلّى بالباعث الأخلاقي على التذكّر أن يكثر من زيارة القبور وسرد القصص بغية صوغ التواريخ وتجميع الأصول. تتألّف هذه التواريخ من لوائح من الأسماء والمواقع الواردة في تراجم الأسلاف ومعاجم الأنساب. وبما أنّ التواريخ موصولة بالسفر والتواصل مع الآخرين، فإنّ معرفة المرء بأصوله محكومة بالقدرة على الحركة من أجل دخول التاريخ أو حشد واستضافة أولئك المخوّلين بنقله. فالأصول إذًا ليست مجرّد سجلّ للماضي — وتكاد لا تكون سجلًّا على الإطلاق — بل هي عُرف يستشرف كيفيّة توخّي الفعل المستقبلي. وقد أفضت التواريخ بصفتها كُتُبًا ذات قيمة أثرية وطقوس السرد الشفوي المصاحبة لها إلى نشوء عمارة هدفها الحفظ واستعراض ما يقتضيه أداء تلك الطقوس؛ عمارة يؤمّها الناس من أماكن نائية، قاصدين استعادة تلك التواريخ عبر الذاكرة العابرة للأجيال. وقد يقصد المرء استعادة أصوله التي تعود إلى مئات من السنين الخالية فيحضر أجداده معًا دفعة واحدة ويجاورونه لحظة استدعائهم.

وبالرغم من أهمية هذا النوع من الكتب، إلا أنّ العلاقة مع الأسلاف تُستَمَدّ من الذاكرة أيضًا. فيحافظ المرء على ذاكرة سلالية لتاريخه من خلال ممارسة شكل من أشكال الضيافة غير المشروطة. وتمتزج العمارة المرتبطة بهذا النوع من استضافة الناس واستذكار الأشخاص واستجلاب البضائع والبركات في منظومة عابرة للحدود والأجيال في أبلغ معانيها – فتشكّل مقصدًا تاريخيًّا ومصدرًا استشرافيًّا.

الكفّ

انطوى عبور الصحراء الكبرى على مجازفات حتّمت الاستعانة بما يعصم الراكب من مخاطر الطريق ويشمله بالرفقة والرعاية. وعليه، أنيط بالزوايا الوقوف على آداب السفر وإقرار الضمانات اللازمة لسلامة المسافرين. فشُيّدت كحصون لتأمين قاطنيها والمسافرين النازلين بها. تتسّم مثلًا زاوية عمورة في مدينة جنزور الواقعة غرب العاصمة الليبية طرابلس بخصائص عدّة من هذا الطراز المعماري. بُنيت الزاوية في العام 1228 هـ. (1823 م.)، وتمنحها سماكة حائطها الخارجي الصمود في وجه الغارات من الجهات الأربع وتزوّدها بعزل طبيعي يقيها قيظ الصحراء. واجهاتها الخارجيّة مُجرّدة من الزخرف فيما عدا قشرة لامعة من اللبن أو الطلاء الأبيض في بعض الأحيان تكسو حوائط الأسوار حتى منتصف علوّها. ويستدلّ الزوّار الغرباء على وجود أهل الزاوية من الصيانة المستمرّة لهذه الجدران. أمّا مدخلها فيُزدان بالخطوط ويرتفع على شكل انفراجة في الواجهة الأمامية المصمتة تفوق مستوى ارتفاع السور المحيط، في وسطها باب منخفض منيع يفتح على ممر صغير يفضي إلى رواق طويل في آخره فناء رئيسي.[10]

يعدّ وجود الزاوية أيضاً دليلًا على توافر الماء. يدخلها الضيف فيروي عطشه وإنْ كان تصميم الرواق والفناء يحدّان من مقدار الماء المتاح لاستخدام الفرد. أمّا طائفة التجّار ذات الصلة الطيّبة بأمناء الزاوية فلها فناء ثانٍ يتّسع لقافلة بحاشيتها ودوابّها لتستريح وترتوي. يتّسم هذا البناء المحاذي بسقف أخفض وأرضيّة غائرة ويحتوي على غرف لتخزين الحبوب موزّعة على أطراف الفناء. تُقسّم كل غرفة إلى عدّة حجرات بعضها بفتحات صغيرة للتهوية وبعضها الآخر مغلق بإحكام لحفظ البضاعة القابلة للتلف. كان حجم هذه الحجرات يُقاس بالوحدة الإسلاميّة الصاع التي توازي أربعة أمداد (حفنات) من الحبوب. وكان الصاع الواحد كذلك يساوي مقدار الزكاة المفروض في العيدين. إذًا فعرض الكفّ هو مقياس سعة المخزن ولهذا النوع من الحساب البدني أثر في هندسة المبنى. فالكفّ محرّك لفعلين نقيضين هما تسديد المال وعدّ الغلّة مقابل فعل الدعاء: أي الإمداد مقابل التوسّل. أمّا الزواية فهي تحيي الماضي باستمرار، من خلال تجسّدها كمحطّة في شبكة تنسيق وتجارة وتوسّط بين الناس، مواضي كل من حطّ رحاله بين أسوارها.

كانت الزاوية تستضيف الزوّار والمسافرين في غرف مخصّصة لهم كما تحتوي على قاعة كبيرة للصلاة جماعة. يدور الفناء الرئيسي حول شجرة منفردة عادة ما تكون شجرة لوز أو برتقال كمؤشّر بيّن على دورة الفصول وكمستراح مظلّل تُقام فيه الأنشطة على مرأى من الجميع. وكانت تُدار كمنزل أسريّ مصمّم ليعتني به أهله والمهاجرون المارّون به على السواء. وكانت الأرض المحيطة به توضع تحت رعاية شيخ الزاوية بالتوافق مع عائلات الناحية، أمّا قسمة الميراث وولاءات الأُرومة والأنساب فقد كانت محطّ نزاعات شديدة. وكان شيخ الزاوية الحكم في مسائل الأوقاف ومصلح النزاعات المحليّة بين الأفرقاء المتخاصمين.[11] وكان الطامحون إلى إجازة الإفتاء يسافرون إلى الزاوية لتلقّي العلم

عن شيوخها الأجلّاء (الإجازة بإصدار الفتوى لا تُمنح إلّا عن قاضٍ مرجعي معروف). فالزاوية إذًا تثبّت القانون بالمكان من حيث هي مساحة للتماسّ بين الدولة أو الجهاز الحاكم العابر للأمم وبين السكان المحليين. في هذا السياق، يسجّل الالتقاء بهذه العمارة بوصفه لحظة واحدة ضمن شبكة شاسعة ومتشعّبة ومتعددة الأزمان من الأمكنة والأزمنة عبر سيادات وصلاحيات متداخلة.

اللسان

لطالما كان اكتشاف نبع أو بئر مياه منسوبًا إلى الوحي الإلهي وكان الشاهد على هكذا أحداث أو المقترن بها يُعتبر من الأولياء الصالحين، وكانت هذه الأحداث قصصًا تتناقلها الأجيال بدقّة وتفصيل. ويتمحور تقليد إنشاء الزاوية حول شخصيّة العالم الذي يمتح المقدّر الهيدرولوجي للأرض ومن ثم ينصرف إلى تعليم مريديه الجدد. وليس التوزّع الجغرافي للزوايا سوى معيارًا أو ناموسًا للأرض وظروفها البيئية المواتية للبشر.[12] ويُدفن المؤسّس بعد وفاته عند موقع نذر الزاوية الذي يتحوّل إلى ضريح وموضع لتذكّر منهاج الولي وتعاليمه. ومع موارة جثمان الولي في التراب يتحوّل المكان من فضاء بلا معالم أو زوايا إلى وجهة ذات مغزى تربوي، إلى مساحة تحدّها مجموعة من الزوايا فترسي مقياسًا لما هو مقدّس: خط يمتدّ فترسم ثناياه وتعرّجاته الحدّ الفاصل بين الداخل والخارج. وتتضاعف أهميّة الزاوية من الناحية الدينية باكتساب ضريح المؤسّس قوّة البركة، التي إنْ تُرجمت إلى الإنجليزية blessing لَفقدت بُعدها المادي، فالبركة لا تُلتَمَس إلّا في الحضور الجسدي قُرب الجثمان. وحتى إنْ تعذّرت رؤية الجثمان أو ملامسته مباشرة، فإنّ الإيمان بالحضور المادي يبقى الرابط الذي يوثق أواصر الجماعة من المؤمنين والمريدين. إذًا، فالزاوية هي المصطلح الهندسي الذي يفيد بالدرجة الأولى العمارة التي تغلّف الضريح وتستضيفه. يوطّد هذا الصرح طقوس التضرّع والصلاة نظرًا لكونها فضاءً لتلقّي التعليم الديني الموروث عن الأموات والموجّه من قِبلهم فتدبّ الحياة في مراقدهم. يعلي هذا الجانب البيداغوجي من شأن الرفات فوق الحدّ السماعي المحسوس فيتّخذ وظيفة غرفة الصدى، ما يتيح سماع الأموات.

نشأت أهمية التلقين الشفوي في التقليد العربي عن القرآن، أي النص الموحى والمحكي الذي بات نموذج البرهنة الشرعية في الإسلام. وتقوم قوة النص القرآني وسلطته، بصفته الركن الأساس لمجمل العلوم الإسلامية، على مبدأ الثبات وعدم قابليته للتغيير. ولم يُثبّت القرآن نصًّا مدوّنًا إلا بعد وفاة النبي محمد عام 632 م. بسنوات، وكان الهدف من تدوينه إعداده كنصّ للتلاوة لا القراءة الصامتة، ما يجعله دليلًا ممنهجًا في أصول النطق من خلال تعاليمه الصارمة لكيفية استخدام النَّفَس وتموضع اللسان.

وقد لبث الكلام الذي أوحى به الملاك جبريل على النبي محمد يُتناقل عبر الألسنة منذ عهد النبي إلى أن تكرّم الخليفة عمر بن الخطاب فأمر بتدوينه في مصحف مكتوب.

ويمكن الاستدلال على وسْع انتشار القرآن كأداة إمبريالية للتوحيد الزماني من شواهد القبور، إذ يمكن تتبّع علامات التجويد في الآيات ولحظ التنافر والتعدد بين ما يُتلى كما مواضع التطابق على امتداد الحقبة بين القرنين السادس والثامن.[13] وتساهم النقوش في تقييم مدى انتشار الإسلام إبان الفتوحات الأولى لكونها تأتي على ذكر المؤمنين الذين دُفنوا وفق التعاليم والشريعة الإسلامية في الأماكن التي انتشرت إليها الدعوة وبالتالي كم ابتعدوا عن مهبط الوحي. وتتضمّن هذه النقوش آيات وسيرة المدفون ونصوص لأدعية مكتوبة غالبًا بصيغة الأمر مشيرة على الزائر بوجوب أداء فروض معيّنة.[14] إذًا، لا تكتفي هذه الشواهد بقراءة عابرة وإنما تتضمن دليلًا لكيفية أداء الطقوس التي يجب على الزائر اتّباعها طلبًا للشفاعة والرحمة الإلهية للموتى. ينطق الضريح فيخلق مساحة صوتية لبثّ التعاليم الإلهية: «هو الذي خلقكم من طين ثم قضى أجلًا وأجلٌ مسمى عنده»[15] ويُستحضَر الموت في شعائرية السجود، عن طريق طيّ الساق في زاوية تشريحية. تشدّ الركبة الجسد فتعيده إلى التراب. وتتوثّق القربى بين جسد المعرفة المتمثّل بالجثّمان المدفون وجسد العالم الرحّالة في فضاء الذبذبات المنطوقة التي تترجع فيما بينهما. إذًا، فالزاوية دالّة لا على الهيكل المبنيّ فحسب بل على تراكم التعاليم المنقوشة على الأضرحة ونشرها. فمع أنها بدت نمطًا عمرانيًا جامدًا ومعزولًا، فهي على العكس من ذلك تحاكي نوعًا من الترابط الجغرافي والزماني. أي أنها فضاء ملموس تتلاقى فيه عملية التعلم وتجلّي مآلاتها.

الركبة

الركبة، وهي مشتقّة من الجذر ر-ك-ب هي المفصل الذي يمنح الساق القدرة على الحركة والتنقل: ثنية مكتنزة تنتج الحركة، إنها آلية الارتحال الأساسية. مجموعة من العظام والغضاريف العائمة في بحر مطّاط من الأربطة، تنقل قامة الجسم من وضعية الانتصاب إلى وضعية الخشوع سجودًا أمام الرحمن. وتُستخدَم وضعية الركبة في احتساب الصلوات: فيقال ركعة للإشارة إلى مجموع الحركات التي يؤدّيها المؤمن أثناء أدائه فروض الصلوات الخمس اليومية. وتختلف هذه الفروض بحسب طول مسافة الرحلة التي يقطعها المؤمن: فإنْ كان على سفَر أُنقِص عدد الركعات المفروضة عليه. وهكذا تختزن الأنسجة العضلية ذاكرة الركوع فتصبح وتيرة الركعات دلالة على تاريخ الجسد في الارتحال.

تتيح الساق المحنيّة الفعل المزدوج للاستغفار (بالصلاة) والاستجارة (بعد عناء السفر) في صيغة فعل التضرّع

والتوسّل، فتلقي هذه الممارسة الشعائرية الضوء على البعد المادي للصلاة وموضع أدائها. فهي ترتبط بهيئة المتضرّع في المأساة الإغريقية: عندما يجثم المرء متذلّلًا فيدخل في حالة «خُثونية»[16] على شفا الموت. فتكشف وضعية الخشوع من خلال محاكاتها للموتى عن «موضع» الخشوع كمكان يختزن الرعب اللساني-البدني [glosso-somatic] في عتبة التجربة البرزخية أو تجربة الميت الحيّ الاستثنائي، ذلك الذعر الرهيب لحظة التقاء المرء بالمجهول وكأنه نابع من صلبه.[17] إذًا، فالحدث اللساني-البدني هو الحدث الذي يحدّد مجال التلاقي بين هذا العالم والعالم الآخر. وتحظى هذه الوضعية البرزخية التي تُتّخَذ بانحناء الركبة، بمكانة مقدّسة في الإسلام بصفتها الشكل الأسمى للصلاة الذي لا يمكن أداؤه إلا في حضرة الأموات. وللخشوع بُعدان، الأول هو الدعاء طلبًا للمغفرة والبركة، والثاني التوسل التماسًا للتعرف إلى شخص غريب في زمان ومكان محددين. يتلقي المعنيان عند الزاوية التي تمنح الضيافة وترسي اقتصادًا ثلاثيًّا ضلاعه الضيف (المريد) والمضيف (الشيخ) والفضاء (المدرسة). وتنطوي الزاوية على ممارسة تربوية قوامها المتكلّم والمخاطَب، ويقسّم منهجها إلى فئتين: الدراسات القرآنية و«العِلم» (أي الدراسات العلمية) ولكلتاهما مساحة منفصلة: «القرآنية» و«العالمية». أمّا الاختلاف بينهما فهو ذو بعد صوتي، أي أنه يستند إلى القواعد التي تتحكّم بالكلام المُباح في كل واحدة من هاتين المساحتين. تتّبع الأولى أسلوب «القراءة»، وهو نظام من التلاوة الصوتية يمنع المتكلّم من تعديل أيّ حرف من الكلام الذي يتلّقنه، أي أنه نظام من الترديد الحرفي الدقيق. أمّا الثانية، فتعتمد أسلوب «الرواية» حيث يجاز لناقل الكلام التصرّف بالنص. ويقول المثل المنقول عن الشاعر ابن مقبل:

"I sent out the verses crooked so that the transmitters can straighten them out for their delivery."

وتشكّل «الزاوية» عند التقاء أسلوبيْ الكلام معمارًا للاختلاف الصوتي حيث يخطّ التعدّد الصوتي للمكان والذات معالمَ ما هو مسموع. وكأنّ «الزاوية»، في معناها المكاني هندسة للتضخيم الصوتي، وبوصفها ركنًا ناتجًا عن من التقاء خطيْن، حيث الزاوية الحادة تعكس الصوت وتكثّفه، موجِّهَةً إياها نحو جمهور من المتلقّين فتؤذن هم بسماع التاريخ ومحاورة الموتى.

خاتمة

يُدفن الميّت في العديد من مذاهب الإسلام في وضعية السجود مستلقيًا على جنبه الأيمن بحيث يكون كتفه الأيسر مسنودًا باتجاه الأعلى. وكما يقف المصلّي مواجهًا، مكّة كذلك يُمدّد الميّت في اتجاه القِبلة. هكذا يُسجّى الجثمان في وضعيّته الصحيحة استعدادًا لمراحل الموت – مثبّتًا دومًا نحو القِبلة المقدّسة في انتظار التحلّل. وبعد أن تُوارى الجثّة الثرى تبدأ السوائل ذات التركيز العالي من الأمونيا بالتسرّب منها فتفتك بالغطاء النباتي المحيط بموضع الدفن – وهذا هو الفعل المدمّر للرفات المطمورة في المرحلة الأولى. تحدّد مساحة انتشار هذه السوائل ما يسمّى في الأنثروبولوجيا الجنائيّة «رقعة التحلّل الجيفي» وهي عبارة عن ترسيم أولي لمدى التأثير البيئي لجثمان الميّت. ومن ثمّ تبدأ البكتيريا والفطريات والحشرات بنخر الجثّة. ومن العادات المتّبعة في ليبيا وتونس نثر الأرز أو حبوب اليقطين وغيرها من المأكولات المجففة فوق تربة الميت كجزء من طقوس زيارة قبور الأسلاف المفروضة في الإسلام لاجتذاب مجموعة كائنات أكثر تنوّعًا إلى موضع الدفن. توجد تنويعات لهذه العادة في مختلف أنحاء العالم الإسلامي.

تشقّ هذه الصيرورة فضاء للممكن يوازي بطقسيّته فكرة البركة التي يلتمس من خلالها المتوسّل عند الميّت فَرجًا لهمومه الدنيوية. تمثّل دورة الإسكان في الجسد هذه انبثاق الحياة من صلب الموت في صيرورة مطّردة. تُسمّى الأجناس التي تتغذّى على الجثث المتحلّلة «الحيّوم المَواتي» [necrobiome] وهي عبارة عن كتلة من الكائنات الحيّة التي تحجّ بلا انقطاع إلى جغرافيا معروفة ومجزية لها. تساهم هذه الكتلة في الحفاظ على النسق الجوهري والمقدّس للأيْض الغذائي المَواتي للعالم وتجدّده الحيوي في صيغة تتناسج وتتواشج فيها مختلف أوجه الوجود ومستوياته البشريّة والأبعد من بشرية والجغرافية والبيئية.

يحرّض المفهوم الصوتي لما يسمّى النكروفاجيا [necrophagy]، أي التغذي على الجِيَف، على النظر بجدّية إلى التداخل بين الأجسام بعيدًا عن تصنيفاتها المعيارية أو وظائفها النمطية كما يحثّ على عدم النظر إلى الدنيوي كنقيض للمقدّس وإلى تلمّس السماعي في البصري وإلى الماضي في الحاضر. إنّها طريقة «لنقض التنظيم والتشكيل والتفكير في العالم سعيًا إلى المَلاء».[18] والملاء [plenum] عند لايبنتز هو بمثابة مذهب من التفكير يأخذ في الاعتبار أنّ «لكل حادث في الكون أثرًا على سواه، إلى الحد الذي يمكن معه لمن يبصر الأشياء كلها أن يقتفي فيها أثر كل ما حدث ويحدث وسيحدث في كل مكان، فيرى ما انقضى زمانه ومكانه أو لما ينقضِ في الحاضر».[19] فالملاء نظريّة تنفي وجود الخلاء المطلق وتصوّر العالم ممتلئًا بالكامل. يوحي الملاء «بتوصيف افتراضي للوجود تتّسم المادة فيه بالعرضية والاحتمالية بدلًا من الضرورة والحتمية».[20] يقوّض هذا التصوّر ثنائية الزمان والمكان من خلال النظر إلى العالم كطاقة مكنونة في كل الأجسام ومحدّدة بجميع الأجسام الأخرى الممتدّة على الزمن كلّه. يقابل الملاء في الفيزياء الكميّة الفونون [phonon] وهو مقياس اهتزاز الذرّات

التي تتكوّن منها المادة جمعاء. ويُصاغ الفونون كشبه جُسيم، أي كأصغر وحدة صوتية؛ تنشأ الأصوات المسموعة للأذن البشرية عن الفونونات طويلة الموجة.

يعيّن الفونون الصوتَ أساسًا مشتركًا للتبادل ووسيطًا حيويًا يتيح إمكانيّة تخيّل الكون بكليّته. كتب الفيلسوف الشاعر ابن عربي: «كقيثارة يُضرب على وتر منها فتهتز باقي الأوتار، فتبوح بتآلف خفي بين المعاني المتّصلة».[21] لقد سبق ابن عربي الفيزياء الكمية ولايبنيتز بأجيال إلا أنّ التشابه بين الاثنين مدهش. فقد قام فكر ابن عربي على نظرية صوفية إسلامية تقول بأنّ العالم بموجوداته هو النَّفَس الفلكيّ المنبعث من «كائن غير منطوق»، طنين سماويّ لا ينقطع. وأنّ النَّفَس الإلهي هو الوجود المطلق وأنّ الموجودات كلها الكلام الإلهي، أي نظم سماوي للكلمات، وأنّ الكلام البشري ما هو إلا ترديد منفرد ومحدود لهذا النفَس.[22]

وكما أشرنا آنفًا، القرآن إنما هو حدث صوتي، وَحيٌ مرقوم على لوح محفوظ انقلب شاهدًا ناطقًا يسبّح بوجود الخالق وحدته. إنه الفعل الخطابي الذي تُستنبط عنه الموجودات من العدم وتنتظم، وهو الموشورالمؤسّس الذي تُجترح من خلاله الأصوات أفكارًا ومفاهيم. وهو الذي ينتمي إلى الفلسفة القائلة بأنّ الذات ما هي إلا كلمة ينطقها الخالق، في عالم منطوق يتشكّل فاعلوه نطقًا ويترابط بالنطق: «مدار جميع الخلائق على هذه الحقائق والعالم كله مربوط الرويّ على الصراط السويّ».[23]

أهمية الصوتانيّ [vocalic] كصيغة للوجود تقدّم لنا مفتاحًا لفهم فضاء من طراز «الزاوية». فمن خلال الصوت، يتكشّف المبنى عما يتعدّى كونه حيازة أو شكلًا إلى نقطة وصل تُدني ما يبدو للوهلة الأولى بعيدَ المنال. يُموضع الوسيط الصوتي الجسدَ في الفضاء ومن ثمّ يخصّصه كحيّز للسيرورات الاجتماعية المتجاوزة له في حدود بينية بين مجالات متعددة للوجود. تحدد الممارسة الصوتية النكروفاجية إحداث الأصوات كفعل لسبر أعماق الإدراك أو كعملية مستمرة من الإصغاء إلى هذه الكوكبة التي تغمرنا جميعًا. تعبير يتحدّى قيود الصمت التاريخي. وبناء على ذلك، تصبح «الزاوية» ركنًا لسانيًّا-بدنيًّا للرعاية يخترق الزمن أو بالأحرى يقوّض الزمنية على نفسها، أي أنها اقتصاد مثلّث يوفّر الحماية والضيافة والتربية ويتمظهر كقدرة عمرانية كامنة لإرساء حوار أكثر إنصافًا بين الأجيال.

1 "لالّة" لفظة أمازيغية للتوقير والاحترام تعني "مولاتي".
2 من رسالة من الرائد كروشار من العام 1897 واردة في Julia A. Clancy-Smith, *Rebel and Saint: Muslim Notables, Populist Protest, Colonial Encounters (Algeria and Tunisia, 1800–1904)* (Berkeley, CA, 1994), p. 340, note 91.
3 المصدر نفسه، ص. 96
4 Jamil M. Abun-Nasr, *The Tijaniyya: A Sufi Order in the Modern World* (Oxford, 1965), p. 88.
بيّن أوّل مسح فرنسيّ في هذا المجال في العام 1917 أنّ عدد النساء اللواتي تولّين مواقع القيادة الروحيّة في منطقة تونس كان قد بلغ 18 امرأة. والجدير بالذكر أنّ أنوثة لالّة زينب لم تكن من العوامل الفاصلة في تأييد الأهالي لولايتها.
5 Allan Christelow, "Algerian Islam in a Time of Transition," *Maghreb Review* 8, nos. 5–6 (1983): 125
6 Clark Rosen and Thomas Murry, "Phonotrauma Associated with Crying," *Journal of Voice* 14, no. 4 (2001): 575–80
7 يماثله في الإغريقيّة القديمة الأورغانون organon وهو الكلمة التي تحمل معنيَيْن هما "الجسد [بالمفهوم الأحيائي]" و"الآلة [الموسيقية]".
8 القرآن، سورة البلد الآية 13.
9 على سبيل المثال هنالك المثلّث السُباتي والمثلث الأمامي والمثلث تحت الذقني والمثلث الرُغامي. مع ملاحظة أنّ الأخير بين هذه المثلثات هو في واقع الحال مربع الأضلاع، إلا أنّ ذلك لم يحل دون تسميته بالمثلث.
10 أشكر ناصر زحاف ومعشر "أبناء عمومتي" على مساعدتهم لي والذين لولاهم لما كانت الجولة الميدانية في جنزور والدخول إلى زاويتها ممكنة.
11 للمزيد حول النزاعات القانونية على ملكية الزاوية انظروا: Judith Scheele, *Smugglers and Saints of the Sahara: Regional Connectivity in the Twentieth Century* (Cambridge, 2012).
12 الناموس كلمة عربية فصيحة مشتقّة من اللفظ الإغريقي nomos، إلا أنها في العربية تمتّ أكثر إلى الأخلاق منها إلى الجغرافيا بصلة وإنْ كانت تشير إلى هذه الأخيرة. يرجى مراجعة النقاش حولها لدى: Rana Issa, "The Arabic Language and Syro-Lebanese National Identity Searching in Burus al-Bustānī's Muḥīṭ al-Muḥīṭ," *Journal of Semitic Studies* 62, no. 2 (Autumn 2017): 465–84.
13 انظروا حسن الفقيه، "مواقع أثرية في تهامة"، المجلد الأول، مخلاف عشم (الرياض، 1992)، ص. 353 وص.388، وأيضًا Arthur Jeffery, *Materials for the History of the Text of the Qur'an* (Leiden, 1937), p. 76 and p. 262.
يُقصَد بالتعدّد هنا كل ما شذّ عن "مصحف عثمان" بفعل تأثير اللهجات والاختلافات المحلية، لا فرضية الأصول اللغوية المتعددة للقرآن، التي تمّ دحضها بشكل قاطع في عدد من الدراسات الحديثة.
14 Abd al-Tawab, *Steles islamiques*, vol 1 لأمثلة عديدة انظروا باب أسوان بين حوالي عام 820 و 870 م.
15 القرآن، سورة الأنعام الآية 2
16 اللفظة معربة عن اليونانية "خثونيوس" χθόνιος والتي تعني العالم السفلي. وتشير عادةً إلى العوالم السفلية في الميثولوجيا الإغريقية. [المترجم]
17 Thanos Zartaloudis, "*Hieros anthropos* – An Inquiry into the Practices of Archaic Greek Supplication," *Law and Humanities* 13, no. 1 (2019): 63.
18 Denise Ferreira da Silva, "Toward a Black Feminist Poethics: The Quest(ion) of Blackness Toward the End of the World," *The Black Scholar* 44, no. 2 (2014): 86.
19 Gottfried Wilhelm Leibniz, *Leibniz: Philosophical Essays* (Indianapolis, 1989), p. 221.
تستلهم دا سيلفا من لايبنتز مفهوم الملاء للاستدلال على قوة السوادية blackness وانتهاكها المستمرّ.
20 da Silva 2014 (see note 19), p. 94.
21 ابن عربي كما ورد في Annemarie Schimmel, *As Through a Veil* (New York, 1982), p. 16.
22 Oludamini Ogunnaike, "The Presence of Poetry, the Poetry of Presence," *Journal of Sufi Studies* 5, no. 1 (2016): 58–97, 68.
23 ابن عربي كما ورد في Denis McAuley, *Ibn Arabi's Mystical Poetics* (Oxford, 2012), p. 45.

استحقاقات الأسلاف

دينيز فِريرا دا سيلفا

ترجمه عن الإنكليزية فريق الأركِلوغ

ليس للجنس البشري يدٌ في تعيين الظروف المؤدّية إلى نشوء العصر الكربوني الثالث أو العصر النووي. وكل ما يُروى عن ضلوعه في نشأة الأنثروبوسين [anthropocene] ما هو إلا استعادة هزلية للمغامرة القضيبية الكبرى المؤنسِنة والحداثية التي يكتسب فيها الإنسان، المخلوق في صورة إله تلاشى، قوىً خارقة في صعوده الدنيوي المقدّس ليؤول به الحال مجدّدًا إلى الهمود المأساوي. ثمّ هوى الإنسان ذاتيّ التكوين والقادر على إعادة إنتاج نفسه ثانيةً، هذه المرّة جرّاء خللٍ مأساوي في النظام أدّى إلى تحويل النُظم البيئية ذات التنوّع الحيويّ إلى صحارى منبوشة موحلة تعجّ بالرخويات اللزجة وقناديل البحر اللادغة. كذلك لم تكن الحتمية التكنولوجية مُنشئة العصر الكربوني الثالث، فلا الفحم ولا المحرّك البخاري أبطال هذه الحكاية. زدْ على ذلك أنّ جميع التواريخ خاطئة، ليس لأنّه علينا أن نبدأ الحساب من العصر الجليدي الأخير، إنّما لأنّ التأريخ لا يستوي أقلّه دون ذكر التحوّلات البالغة في تصوّر العالم من منطلق السوق والسلعة، ذلك التصوّر الذي ساد خلال القرنين السادس عشر والسابع عشر من عصرنا الراهن، حتى وإنْ اعتقدنا (واهمين) أنّه في استطاعتنا الاستمرار في مقاربة التحوّلات «العولميّة» التي تَسِم الكابيتالوسين [Capitalocene] من منظور المركزية الأوروبية.

دونا هاراواي، التفكير المجساتي: الأنثروبوسين، الكابيتالوسين، الكَثولوسين *Tentacular Thinking: Anthropocene, Capitalocene, Chthulucene"*

فلو سلّمنا إذن أنّه يجب الخروج من الأُفهوم المعطى لمقارنته تأليفيًّا بآخر؛ لاحتجنا إلى ثالث يصدر عنه، وحدَه، تأليف الأُفهومين. لكن ما هو هذا الثالث الذي بمثابة وسط لكل الأحكام التأليفية؟ إنه فقط «جملة» تتضمّن كل تصوّراتنا، أعني إنّه الحسّ الباطن وصورته القَبلية: الزمان. ويستند تأليف التصوّرات إلى المخيّلة، وتستند وحدتها التأليفيّة (اللازمة في الحُكم) إلى وحدة الإبصار. ففي الثلاثة {يُقصَد بالثلاثة: الزمان والمخيّلة ووِحدة الإبصار، وهي مصادر أو أصول التصوّرات القَبلية} إنّما علينا أن نبحث عن إمكان الأحكام التأليفية بل، لأنّها كلها تتضمّن مصادر التصوّرات القَبلية، أن نبحث عن إمكان الأحكام التأليفية القَبلية التي ستكون ضرورية بناءً على تلك الأصول حتى لو كانت ستؤدّي إلى معرفة بالموضوعات المستندة إلى تأليف التصوّرات وحسب.[1] عمانوئيل كانط، *Critique of Pure Reason*

عندما أفكّر في الكوارث التي عصفت بالكوكب طوال العقد الماضي، أجد أنّ لا وسيلة للتصدّي لها سوى بتعديل الوجهة. إذ وحدها الخلخلة الجذرية (وربما الهدم) للبنى التحتية والبينية [intra-structures] للفكر قادر على إحداث التحوّل النوعي المطلوب لإدراك وفهم حجم التحدّيات التي تنتظر الأجيال القادمة. أمّا نقطة انطلاقي في هذا السعي — مسترشدةً بالمسار الذي رسمت لنا معالمه آدابيّات[2] النسوية السوداء [Black Feminist Poethics]، فهي الديكولونياليّة أي الاستعادة الكاملة للقيمة المُستخرَجة من أراضي السكان الأصليين ومُصادَرة عمالة المستعبَدين من قِبل الاستعمار.[3] فالديكولونياليّة هي الدالّ والمدلول الوحيدين لكل ما يُمكِن اعتباره وصفًا لمذهب كثيرين في تعريف مفاهيم مثل «العدالة الاجتماعية» أو «العدالة الكَونية»، أو بتعبيرٍ أوضح، الديكولونياليّة هي المطلب الذي تجتمع فيه القضايا الأخلاقية السياسية الأكثر إلحاحًا. فإذًا، لا بدّ لأيّ تحوّل فكريّ يمهّد لبروز توصيفات للوجود قادرة على معالجة الكوارث الكونيّة الراهنة أن ينطلق من الديكولونياليّة، أي أنّه يجب أن يبدأ بالاعتراف بالإخضاع الكولونيالي والعرقي ومجابهته بوصفه عنصرًا مكوّنًا ومؤثّرًا في ظروف العالم الراهنة، لا بوصفه حدثًا تُسفر هذه الكوارث عنه — لا بوصفه الماضي لحاضرنا ولا بوصفه السبب لما نشهده من آثار — بل باعتباره مكوّنًا فعّالًا على كل مستوى في إنتاج هذه الظروف.

عن أيّ كوارث أتحدّث؟ وعن أيّ قضايا أخلاقية سياسية؟ سأذكر أربعًا منها. أوّلًا، هنالك استراتيجية قانونية-اقتصادية قائمة أصفها بالـ«جنوحية» [criminality] تُمارَس منذ عقود وتظهر في تكثيف عمليات الاعتقال والقتل التي تُجيزها الدولة وتُيسّرها كيانات اقتصادية خاصة (تشمل السجون ومراكز الاحتجاز المدارة من قبل شركات خاصة والمقاتلين المرتزقة وبناة الأسوار) بحجّة مكافحة «الجنوح» (أي إجرام «زُعران العصابات» و«الإرهابيين» و«المهاجرين غير الشرعيين»). الفئات المستقصدة

هنا برأيي هي السود واللاتينيين(ات) في الولايات المتحدة الأميركية إضافةً إلى سكان البلدان الإسلامية الرازحين تحت وطأة الحروب المشتعلة في الشرق الأوسط والقارّة الإفريقية، من دون أن أستثني الصراع المسلّح المتصل بحروب المخدّرات على امتداد رقعة أميركا اللاتينية وجزر الكاريبي. ثانيًا، وفي إطارٍ متّصل، هنالك موجة التهجير غير المسبوقة لشعوب الجنوب العالميّ على غرار ما يُسمّى «أزمة اللاجئين» في أوروبا التي بدأ العالم بالالتفات إليها منذ نحو خمس سنوات رغم قِدم عهدها. ويكاد معظم الناس ينسى الصلة المباشرة لهذه «الأزمة» بالصراعات المسلّحة المحلّية والإقليمية التي ذكرتُها أعلاه — وهي صراعات لا تتعارض مع استمرار مصادرة حقوق العمال [labor expropriation] وبالتالي الإمعان في المزيد من مصادرة الأراضي واستخراج المعادن العزيزة جدًّا على الرأسمال العالميّ. ولا تنفصل هذه «الأزمة» عن استراتيجيات التنمية المدمِّرة لسبل الرزق في الجنوب العالميّ الذي يبدو كأنّها تعيد تشكيل اقتصاداته إلى طور التعدين والزراعة تحت إمرة الشركات متعدّدة الجنسيات. ولا ننسى أنّ ردّ الفعل الأوروبي على «أزمة اللاجئين» والمسؤول عن مصرع جموع من السود والسُّمر من مواطني المستعمَرات الأوروبية السابقة قد ساهم في تكريس وجه الدولة الشركاتية-الأمنية ومهّد الطريق لصعود الهوياتية البيضاء القاتلة من جديد. ثالثًا، لدينا جائحة كوفيد-19، آخر فصل لأزمة كوكبنا والتي أثبتت في أقلّ من عام واحد أنّ أثرها أشدّ فتكًا بالسود والأميركيين اللاتينيين والشعوب الأصلية في شمال أميركا وأنّها بلا شكّ ستعيث فسادًا في مستعمَرات الجنوب العالميّ السابقة. رابعًا، وليس أخيرًا هناك الاحتباس الحراريّ الذي تجلّى مؤخّرًا تجلّيًا مريعًا في سلسلة الحرائق التي عمّتْ الساحل الغربي للولايات المتحدة الأميركية وعجزُنا الكامل عن إدراك أبعاده. برأيي، لا بدّ لأيّ تفكير يسعى إلى أخذ هذه التطوّرات الأربعة بالحسبان — الجنوحية والتهجير والجائحة والاحتباس الحراريّ — وإلى موضعتها معًا في السياق العالميّ الراهن أن ينطلق من المنظور الديكولونيالي بصفتها المبدأ الأخلاقي الوحيد الملائم للتعاطي مع أزمات هذا العصر.

لماذا؟ لمَ لا يتجلّى الترابط بين هذه القضايا الأربع بديهيًّا؟ وما الذي يجعل الديكولونياليّة في منزلة المقاربة الأخلاقية السياسية الوحيدة الملائمة للردّ على هذه القضايا؟[4] يقتضي الاهتمام بمطلب التحرّر من الاستعمار وتقدير زخمه الأخلاقيّ إحراز تحوّل على مستوى المبادئ أو إعادة تشكيل «الأنا الشقّافة» بنيويًّا على المستويين التحتانيّ والبينيّ. سأقدّم هنا توصيفًا للحالات التي يجب أن تُستهلّ عندها هكذا عملية من باب المساهمة في إرساء الأسس الضروريّة لتكوين الوعي اللازم بأهميّة المطلب الديكولونياليّ وللنظر في ما يستدعيه من تصويب جوهري لوجهتنا أي أنني سأوصّف تحديدًا حال الوجود (أو التشابك السحيق [deep implicancy])[5].

وأسوةً بما قمت به في السابق، بدلًا من صياغة تعريف للتشابك العميق سأعمد من خلال هذا التعقيب على الاحتباس الحراريّ إلى وضع ملامح لما يمكن أن يحدث لمسار التفكير عندما يدخل مفهوم «التشابك العميق» على توصيف بنيته على المستوى البينيّ، أي على الأساس غير المنطوق للإلمام بما يحدث وما هو موجود.

نسق الطبيعة

نقطة انطلاقي هنا هي كيفية تغلغل «الأنا المفكّرة» لدى كانط، أي «وحدة الإبصار» الوارد في الاقتباس الافتتاحي، في معجم ونحو التوصيفات الدالّة على ما يحدث وما هو موجود على الصعيدين البشري وما بعد البشري. وفي ضوء تصوّر كانط للذات وكيف تؤدّي دور المحدِّد، لا بدّ من الإشارة إلى أنّ هذه الذات تؤدّي هذا الدور على مستويَي البُنى التحتانية والبينية — أي ضمن الركائز الأنطو-إبستمولوجية (الانفصالية والتحديدية [determinacy] والتتابعية) وواصفاتها (الشكلانية والنجاعة [formality and efficacy]). وهي تقوم بذلك كنتيجةٍ للشرط المسبق للمعرفة الذي هو النسق المُعطى (أي الطبيعة) الذي يقوم على أساسه المشروع الكانطي. الإحالة هنا إلى ما يسمّيه كانط «قانون تخصيص الطبيعة» الذي «يفترضه [الحكم] بغية جعل نسق الطبيعة مفهومًا من لدن فهمنا حين يصنّف قوانين الطبيعة العامّة ويُخضِع لها كثرة القوانين الجزئية».[6] ومن حيث هو الركيزة الوحيدة والأساسية للحكم، يشكّل هذا المبدأ الشرطَ المسبقَ للأحكام العلمية المحدِّدة والأحكام الجمالية التأمّلية والأحكام الأخلاقية المُلزِمة. ويتتبع تحويل مسار الفكر نحو تحليل مناهض للاستعمار وافٍ للسياق العالميّ خطوةً أساسيّة ألا وهي الكشفُ عن كيف تعتمل «الأنا المفكّرة» في صميم المصطلحات الواصفة التي تؤلّف خطابنا.

لننظر إلى المقاربات النقدية لمسألة الاحتباس الحراريّ التي تلقي اللائمة على التعدين الاستعماري والممارسات الزراعيّة واسعة النطاق ومتطلبات الرأسمال الصناعي. وهي في ذلك محقّة، بوصف هذه العناصر سببًا رئيسيًا للظروف المساهمة في ارتفاع معدّلات غازات الدفيئة. ويهدف صوابًا المصطلحان «الأنثروبوسين» [العصر الجيولوجي البشري] و«الكابيتالوسين» [العصر الجيولوجي الرأسمالي]، واللذان تعقّب عليهما دونا هاراواي في اقتباس الافتتاح أعلاه، إلى إسناد ظاهرة الاحتباس الحراريّ إلى الإنسان، أي إلى أوجه تأثّر الكوكب بالأحوال والظروف المرتبطة بالوجود البشري. غير أنّ هذيْن المصطلحين ومن خلال وظيفتهما التحديديّة يكرّسان سلسلةً من التأثيرات لا تسمح باستبيان كيفية عمل ممارسات التعدين والمصادرة [extraction and expropriation] الاستعماريّيْن. يعود ذلك إلى الطريقة التي

يعتمل من خلالها عنصرا الشكلانية والنجاعة على المستوى الما بين بنيوي، وذلك في الظروف «الإمبريقيّة» أو «المادّية» التي نُحتَ مصطلحا الأنثروبوسين والكابيتالوسين من أجل ضبطها. فمن الناحية الأولى، تتمثّل الشكلانية في نموذج «الأنا المفكّرة» الكانطيّة المفترَض في منهجية تحديد العصور الجيولوجية لكوكب الأرض والتي تقيّد الكوكب بزمن خطّي، ما يسمح بتسمية أطواره التاريخية. وتقدّر التقنيات والأدوات المتوفّرة عمر الأرض بنحو 4.6 مليارات سنة، لا تزال الستمائة مليون سنة الأولى منها بلا تسمية رسمية على ما يبدو بسبب غياب الأدلّة (وجود الحياة البكتيرية) التي أجازت تسمية الأربعة مليارات سنة اللاحقة. وترسّم الشكلانية، لكونها إحدى الواصفات الأنطو-إبستمولوجية التي تثبّت مزاعم المعرفة اليقينية، خارطة «الأنا المفكّرة» فوق خارطة الكوكب لأنّ عملية التسمية توظّف مناهج علم الأحياء ومفاهيمه وصياغاته.[7] ومن الناحية الثانية، تستند التحليلات المتعلقة بظاهرة الاحتباس الحراريّ إلى النجاعة باعتبارها الواصفة الأنطو-إبستمولوجية الرئيسية الموثّقة لبداية طور جديد من عمر كوكب الأرض سواء أأطلقنا عليها تسمية «الأنثروبوسين» أم «الكابيتالوسين»، أي سواء أكان نتيجة للتحوّلات الناجمة عن الأنشطة الاقتصادية واسعة النطاق القائمة بمجملها على استخراج الموارد ومصادرة حقوق العمال أم لا. بعبارة أخرى، يُعَدّ النشاط الاقتصادي البشري المسبّب الفاعل في كلتا الحالتين، مع فارق أنّ تسمية «الكابيتالوسين»، بحسب هاراواي، تقارب «الأنا المفكّرة» مقاربة نقدية، الأمر الذي تغفله «الأنثروبوسين».

بدلًا من تسمية عصر جيولوجي جديد يكرّس الاستثنائية البشرية بوصفها تفسيرًا نهائيًّا لما نعرفه عن تأثير الأنشطة الاقتصادية، هبْنا أمعنّا النظر هذه الأنشطة نفسها. لا شكّ أنّ الجنس البشري كان ولا يزال يساهم في ارتفاع الحرارة إلى معدّلات قادرة على إبادة الكائنات الحية على هذا الكوكب أو دفعها نحو الانقراض. فالطعام الذي نأكله والوقود الأحفوري الذي نستهلكه في مركباتنا مسؤولان في أقلّ تقدير عن تدفّق الطاقة المميت والمتمثّل في ظاهرة الاحترار. إذًا، الحرارة، والتي يعرّفها العلم كتحويل الطاقة الداخلية الناشئة عن الحركة، هي العامل المسبّب للاحتباس الحراريّ. تسري الحرارة من جسم إلى آخر عبر اللمس أو الإشعاع أو التدخّل الوسائطي. كلّ ما في الوجود يبثّ الأشعّة الكهرومغناطيسية طالما أنّ حرارتها الداخليّة — أو بالأحرى قياس معدّل حرارتها الداخلية، أعلى من الصفر المطلق (الذي لم يتحقق قطّ خارج نطاق التجارب العلمية المخبرية حسب علمي). بالمقابل يمكن تحويل الطاقة الحركية الداخلية، المعتمِدة على الكتلة والسرعة، إلى أيّ شكل آخر من أشكال الطاقة. إذًا، كيف نتناول هذه الأنشطة الاقتصادية من دون أن نغفل تلك البنى الأنطو-إبستمولوجية البينيّة لـ«أنا المفكّرة» وعالها المتناسق وبدلًا من توصيف الأنشطة الاقتصادية المسبّبة للاحتباس الحراريّ من حيث النجاعة، ماذا لو أخذت مقاربتنا بعين الاعتبار كل ما تنطوي عليه هذه الأنشطة من الناحية المادية كالعمالة والموادّ الخامّة وأدوات الإنتاج؟ بعبارة أدقّ، أنا معنيّة بطرح توصيف لما يحدث في صميم عملية انبعاث غازات الدفيئة، أي في تحوّل طاقة الوضع (الشغل) أو الطاقة الحركية الداخلية (الحرارة) عند استخدام شيء لاستثارة تغيير في شيء ثانٍ (الشغل) أو عندما يتمّ إيجاد شيء يُضاف إلى كل ما سبق ووُجد (الحرارة).

الأرض

بهذه الفرضية أنتقل إلى الخطوط العريضة لطرحي: الديكولونيالية تمدّنا بالأسس الأخلاقية للمطالبة بالتغيير القانوني والاقتصادي اللازم لمواجهة هيمنة رأس المال الدولي والحثّ على تجنّب الاستغلال (للأراضي والموارد) الذي أنزل التهجير والسلب والقتل بغير الأوروبيين على خلفيات عرقية وأجبرهم على ترك أوطانهم. إذ يعرف الجميع، وإنْ لم يكونوا ملمّين بآليّة الاحتباس الحراريّ، أنّ الظاهرة ناجمة عن انبعاث غازات الدفيئة وتراكمها، كثاني أكسيد الكربون والميثان وأكسيد النيتروجين، من دون الحاجة إلى إلمام بآلية الظاهرة، ما أدّى إلى ارتفاع حرارة طبقة التروبوسفير (السفلى من الغلاف الجوّي لكوكب الأرض). وينتج ارتفاع الحرارة هذا من امتصاص هذه الغازات بثّ الأشعّة تحت الحمراء الناجم عنها. ويرتبط التراكم المتسارع لغازات الدفيئة بالتنقيب المتزايد لتوفير الوقود الأحفوري ومغذّيات التربة لإنبات المحاصيل الزراعية وتربية الماشية. إذًا، يتلازم تراكم الانبعاثات الغازية مع مصادرة الأراضي ومصادرة حقوق العمال الضرورية للوصول إلى موارد الوقود الأحفوري والتربة. وسواء أرجعنا السبب الفاعل إلى نشأة الزراعة في القِدَم أم أرجعناه إلى الثورة الصناعية في القرن الثامن عشر، فلا شكّ أنّ تركيز وسائل الإنتاج والاستحصال على الموادّ الخامّة مرتبط بالانبعاثات المفرطة لغازات الدفيئة. ومن نافل القول إنّ الاستعمار، بما هو عليه كنسق من أنساق الحكم والذي يتوسّل العنف الشامل لبسط الهيمنة على الطاقات الداخليّة للأرض والأجساد ومصادرتها، قد يَسّر هذا التركيز طوالَ أكثر من خمسمائة عام خلتْ. لذا بإمكاننا تتبّع هذا المنطق للإشارة إلى أنّ تراكم هذه الغازات يعبّر (بصورة ماديّة) عن مدى وشدّة تركّز الطاقة (الحركية) الداخلية المصادرة بتيسير من الحكم الاستعماري والآليّات القانونية والاقتصادية لرأس المال الدولي. ويكفي أن نستذكر مدى الحرمان في الجنوب العالميّ أو الحروب التي لا تنتهي في القارّة الإفريقية وفي الشرق الأوسط وأفغانستان — تلك الصراعات الاستعمارية التي لا تتعارض مع استمرار استخراج الموارد الطبيعية، لنستدلّ على حجم نهب الطاقة الداخلية وكثافة مصادرتها.

الأرض بما عليها من مياه ومخلوقات سوى البشر موجودة في شكل طاقة الوضع (كيميائية أو جاذبية، إلخ). كيف السبيل إذًا إلى التفكير بأسلوب يُخلّ بالفصل والتعاقب الخطّيين اللذين يمليهما المكان والزمان؟ دعونا ننظر إلى كيف تجسّد التعادل بين المادّة والطاقة بحسب ألبرت أينشتاين في القنابل التي اختُبرت في جزر مارشال. باعتقادي أنّ الأمر ينطوي على تصوّر مغاير للوجود خالٍ من فرضية الاستقلالية. في الوقت عينه، لو وضعنا نصب أعيننا فكرة أنّ شيئًا ما قد تمّ استخراجه وأنّ مطالب السكان الأصليين بأحقّيتهم في أرضهم ليست مجرّد دعاوى للملكية (بحسب منطق القيمة الاقتصادية التي ذكرتها آنفًا) بل لأحقّيتهم في الموروث (الذي تكفله إپستمولوجياتهم الأصلية)، فلعلّنا نستطيع أن نرى عندئذٍ أنّ الأصليين هم الماء (الأجساد المكوّنة من الماء ومن كل ما أحياه وأنبته الماء على هذه الأرض من زرع وسمك وطير). يمكننا أيضًا التوصّل إلى أنّه ليس كل ما يُستَخرج عرضةً للتلاشي أثناء الاستهلاك وبالتالي. واقع الحال هو أنّنا لو فكّرنا بمفهوم «التغيير» من منطلق التحوّل الطوريّ (الأطوار الصلبة والسائلة والغازية والپلازميّة للمادّة الواحدة) ومفهوم نقل الطاقة (تحوّل الطاقة من صورة إلى أخرى مثلما يحوّل مكبّر الصوت الموجات الصوتية إلى موجات كهربائية) يمكننا الخلوص إلى أنّ أجساد أجدادهم قد تكوّنت ممّا أنبتته تلك المياه، وعند استخراج الماء انتقلت معه جزيئات من أجسادهم إلى أماكن أخرى. هذه هي أحقّية الأصليين التي لا تقبل القياس لأنّها كلّ شيء.

ثمّة مبحثان متعلّقان بمسألة سحب المياه: الأول يخصّ السحب تحت غطاء من العنف الشامل (النهب المتواصل والحرمان الاقتصادي)، والثاني يرتبط بما أسمّيه إعادة التركيب/التحلّل حيث يبقى الماء المكوّن المادّي للأجسام والشجر وكل ما في الوجود. يمكننا أن نعتبر الماء مكوّنًا للثروة التي راكمتها ذرّية المستعمرين والمستوطنين في هذه الأراضي، تلك الثروة التي أُرسلت إلى مواطنهم في أوروبا على شكل أشياء وموادّ أوليّة دخلت نطاق مراكمة الأوّلى لرأس المال في صورة رأسمال صناعي؛ تلك الثروة المسلوبة التي شهدت أطوارًا عدّة من التحوّلات. قد تمّ «نقل طاقة» جميع هذه المستَخرجات، أي أنها تحوّلت إلى أموال وإلى بضائع مالية افتراضية مما يسود الرأسمالية العالمية اليوم.

لو أخذنا المادّة والطاقة كلتاهما في الحسبان لأمكننا أن نقارب مفهوم تعويض مجمل القيمة المسلوبة بشكل مختلف، فلا ننظر إلى هذا التعويض كاستعادة الممتلكات القابلة للتسييل بل كعودة أحد المكوّنات الحيوية لمجتمع السكان الأصليين الذي أُخضع للنهب (أشبه باستعادة طرف من أطراف الجسم). وبما أنّ الثروة التي تدرّها عمليات التنقيب والاستخراج جزء من تركيب كل ما يوجد لا في أوروبا فحسب بل في كل مكان، فإنّ الاستعادة هي أشبه بالرجوع إلى الوطن وهذا هو التحقيق الفعلي للتشابك السحيق.

إذًا، فالتعويض غير قابل للتسييل كما لا يمكن احتسابه أو وضعه في ميزان الخسارة (أو الربح). والتحرّر من التفكير الخطّي ومن أسسه الأنطو-إپستِمولوجية (الاستقلالية والتحديد والتتابعية) وواصفاته (الشكلانية والنجاعة) وأساليبه في تكوين المعنى، يفسح المجال لإدراك مطلب السكان الأصليين للتحرّر من الاستعمار ومطلب ذوي (ذوات) البشرة السوداء للتعويضات [عن الاستعباد] بصورة مغايرة. فما كان مطلوبًا ولا يزال هو استعادة شيء لم يتلاشَ كلّيًا، شيء جعلهم (نا) جزءًا من كل ما في الوجود.

1 نقلًا عن الترجمة العربية لموسى وهبة، نقد العقل المحض. بيروت/باريس: منشورات مركز الإنماء القومي، 1990 (ص. 125). [المترجم]

2 وفاءً للمصطلح المنحوت باللغة الإنكليزية poethics والذي يجمع من الحقليْن الفلسفيين poetics و ethics والذي تسعى من خلاله المؤلّفة إلى البحث عن الممارسة النسوية السوداء [black feminist praxis] يجيب عن سؤال: هل يستطيع ضمير الأديبة/الشاعرة تحرير أقوال العرق الأسود كشيء وسلعة وحقيقة من غير دليل من أساليب المعرفة العلميّة والتاريخية التي أنتجت هذه المقولة في المقام الاوّل؟ ارتأينا استخدام كلمة "آدابيّات" التي تجمع بين الإشارة إلى الأدب والآداب بمعنى الأخلاق. لقراءة المزيد عن هذا المبحث، يُرجى الاطلاع على نصّ مقال دا سيلفا "Toward a Black Feminist Poethics: The Quest(ion) of Blackness Toward the End of the World," *The Black Scholar*, vol. 44 no. 2 (2014), pp. 81–97. [المترجم]

3 يتوافق هذا التوصيف للتحرّر من الاستعمار مع كلا المنظورين الليبرالي والمادي التاريخي للعمل والإنتاج. وأقدّم منظورًا في كتابي *Unpayable Debt* ("دين غير قابل للتسديد" كامبريدج/برلين، 2021)

4 ثمّة أسباب عدّة بلا شك. سأعلّق باختصار على أحد الأسباب النظرية وهو أنّ التوزيع والعرفان يشكّلان ركنَيْ المنطق السائد في المحاججة دفاعًا عن كل ما يستوفي مفهوم العدالة الجوهرية (التصويبيّة لا الحمائيّة فحسب)، سواء أكانت "اجتماعيّة" أم "عالمية". للأسف لا مجال هنا للعودة إلى نظرية جون راولز عن العدالة التوزيعيّة ولا إلى مفهوم تشارلز تايلور عن العرفان كأحد المبادئ تحت مظلّة التعددية الثقافية ولا إلى منتقديهما. ولكنّني سأنوّه بأنّ ألذع الانتقادات التي تلقّتها هاتان النظريّتان هي تلك التي تعمد تحديدًا إلى تصويب الانتباه على مسألة الإخضاع الاجتماعي (العرقي، الجندري، الجنسي) والاستعماري. للمزيد حول الإخضاع الاجتماعي، راجعوا أيريس ماريون يونغ، *Justice and the Politics of Difference* (پرِنستون، 2012)، وحول الإخضاع الاستعماري راجعوا غلِين كولتهارد، *Red Skin, White Masks* (مينياپوليس، 2014).

5 تطرح دا سيلفا هذا المفهوم في فيلمها المشترك مع أرجونا نيومن بعنوان *4 Waters: Deep Implicancy* (2018) يستعرض هذا التجهيز السينمائي القضايا العالمية الملحّة كالهجرة والنزوح وموروثات الاستعمار والدمار البيئي ويتساءل عن الاحتمالات التي يمكن أن يوجدها فعل تجريد الفكر الأخلاقي من مفاهيم القيمة والأفضلية. ويسعى هذا الفيلم لتكوين تصوّر لحظة التشابك الابتدائيّة التي سبقت استقلالية المادّة التي ستطوَّر لاحقًا لتصبح الكوكب الذي نعرفه، وهو ما تطلق عليه دا سيلفا deep implicancy والتي آثرنا ترجمتها التشابك السحيق. تستمدّ دا سيلفا هذا العنوان من مفاهيم فيزياء الكمّ حيث يُستَخدَم وصف التشابك الكمّي للتعبير عن ظاهرة تولّد زوج أو مجموعة من الجُسيمات أو تفاعل الجسيمات ذات التقارب المكاني أو تشابكها بحيثٍ لا يمكن وصف الحالة الكميّة لجسيم معيّن مستقلًا عن الجسيمات الأخرى، حتى لو فصلت مسافة كبيرة بين هذه الجسيمات. للمزيد عن التشابك السحيق. انظروا: https://www.e-flux.com/announcements/251881/denise-ferreira-da-silva-and-arjuna-neuman4-waters-deep-implicancy/ https://vimeo.com/289292003 [المترجم]

6 عمانوئيل كانط، *Critique of the Power of Judgement*، كامبريدج، 2000، ص.72. ترجمة سعيد الغانمي، "نقد ملكة الحكم"، منشورات الجمل، 2009، ص.107.

7 تستخدم الشكلانية نظام التصنيف الأحيائي الذي وضعه عالم الطبيعة الفرنسي جورج كوفييه في مطلع القرن التاسع عشر. يهيمن من خلاله التكوين العضوي لل"عرق" الأوروبي (القوقازي) - باعتباره النموذج الأمثل والأكمل لتشكّلات الكائنات الحية - على تصوّرات تكوين مجمل الكائنات الحية الأخرى ووظائفها. من هنا، تبقى الأطوار/الطبقات غير المسمّاة من عمر الأرض كذلك نتيجة تعذّر فرزها عن بعضها البعض بحسب الكائنات الحية التي عاشت خلالها والتي بدورها يُستدَّل عليها من مدى تعقيد بنيتها العضوية، الأمر الذي يتيح تحديد الأجناس والأنواع وإلى ما هنالك. أما وبعد أن أُدمِج تشريح كوفييه المقارن مع نظرية داروين للاصطفاء الطبيعي، فقد حازت الكائنات الحية ما فوق-الإنسانية على موقعها أيضًا في التسلسل الزمني الذي يرسم المسار التطوّري للحياة بوصفه المسبّب الفاعل والنهائي، وفقًا لتمثّل الروح عند هيغل، في تكوّن خصوصية أعضاء الكائنات الحية وحركاتها. لتحليل معمّق لعلم الحياة وللمزيد حول هذا النقاش، انظروا كتابي *Toward a Global Idea of Race*, Minneapolis: Univ. of Minnesota Press, 2007.

3L

ا

Sharjah Architecture Triennial 2019

November 9, 2019 – February 8, 2020

Exhibition

Al-Qasimiyah School
7 Sheikh Saqr Bin Khalid Al Qasimi Street

all(zone)
Alonso Barros, Gonzalo Pimentel, Juan Gili, and Mauricio Hidalgo
CCCP/2020
Cooking Sections with AKT II
Dogma
Farzin Lotfi-Jam, Felicity Scott, and Mark Wasiuta
Feral Atlas Collective
Francesco Sebregondi and Jasbir K. Puar
Hamed Khosravi and Roozbeh Elias-Azar with Nazgol Ansarinia
HaRaKa Platform/Adham Hafez Company
Ibiye Camp with Emmy Bacharach and David Killingsworth
Informal Collective on Western Sahara
Jamon Van Den Hoek and Steve Salembier
Lina Ghotmeh Architecture
Marina Tabassum Architects
Mohamed Elshahed with Farida Makar
Ola Hassanain
Public Works
Studio Bound (Hussam Dakkak and Basmah Kaki)
The Otolith Group

Old Al Jubail Fruit and Vegetable Market
Bujair Bin Abi Bujair Street

Adam Jasper with Li Tavor, Alessandro Bosshard, Matthew van der Ploeg, Max Kriegleder, Vivian Wang, Dewa Alit, Vibeke Sorensen, and U5
Civil Architecture
Dima Srouji with Dirar Kalash, Silvia Truini, Nadia Abu El-Haj, and Omar Jabareen
L.E.FT
Marwa Arsanios
Nidhi Mahajan
Samaneh Moafi with WORKNOT!, Mhamad Safa, Maria Bessarabova, Platform 28, and residents of Mehr in Dowlatabad, Esfahan
Studio Anne Holtrop

Al Mureijah Art Spaces, Gallery 5
Al Mureijah Square

Manmarriya Daisy Andrews, Milyinti Dorothy May, Kulyukulyu Trixie Shaw Ngarralja Tommy May, Ngumumpa Walter Rose, Jukuja Dolly Snell, Ngirlpirr Spider Snell, Yirrpura Jinny James, Purlta Maryanne Downs, Jijijar Molly Dededar, Kurtiji Peter Goodijie, Mayapu Elsie Thomas, Waninya Biddy Bonney, Kuji Rosie Goodjie, George Tuckerbox, Nyuju Stumpy Brown, Luurn Willie Kew, Nanjarn Charlie Nunjun, Nyangarni Penny K-Lyon, Nada Rawlins, Yukarla Hitler Pamba, Miltja Thursday Pindan, Killer Pindan, Terry Murray, Monday Kunga, Wajinya Paji Honeychild Yankarr, Kurnti Jimmy Pike, Pijaji Peter Skipper, Raraj David Chuguna, Parlun Harry Bullen, Tapiri Peter Clancy, Mawukura Jimmy Nerrimah, Jukuna Mona Chuguna, Jinny Bent, Munangu Huey Bent, Kapi Lucy Cubby, Pulukarti Honey Bulagardie, Pajiman Warford Budgieman, Ngurnta Amy Nuggett, Japarti Joseph Nuggett

Tuan Andrew Nguyen

Platform
Opposite Al Arouba Street, Um Al Tarafa

Dogma

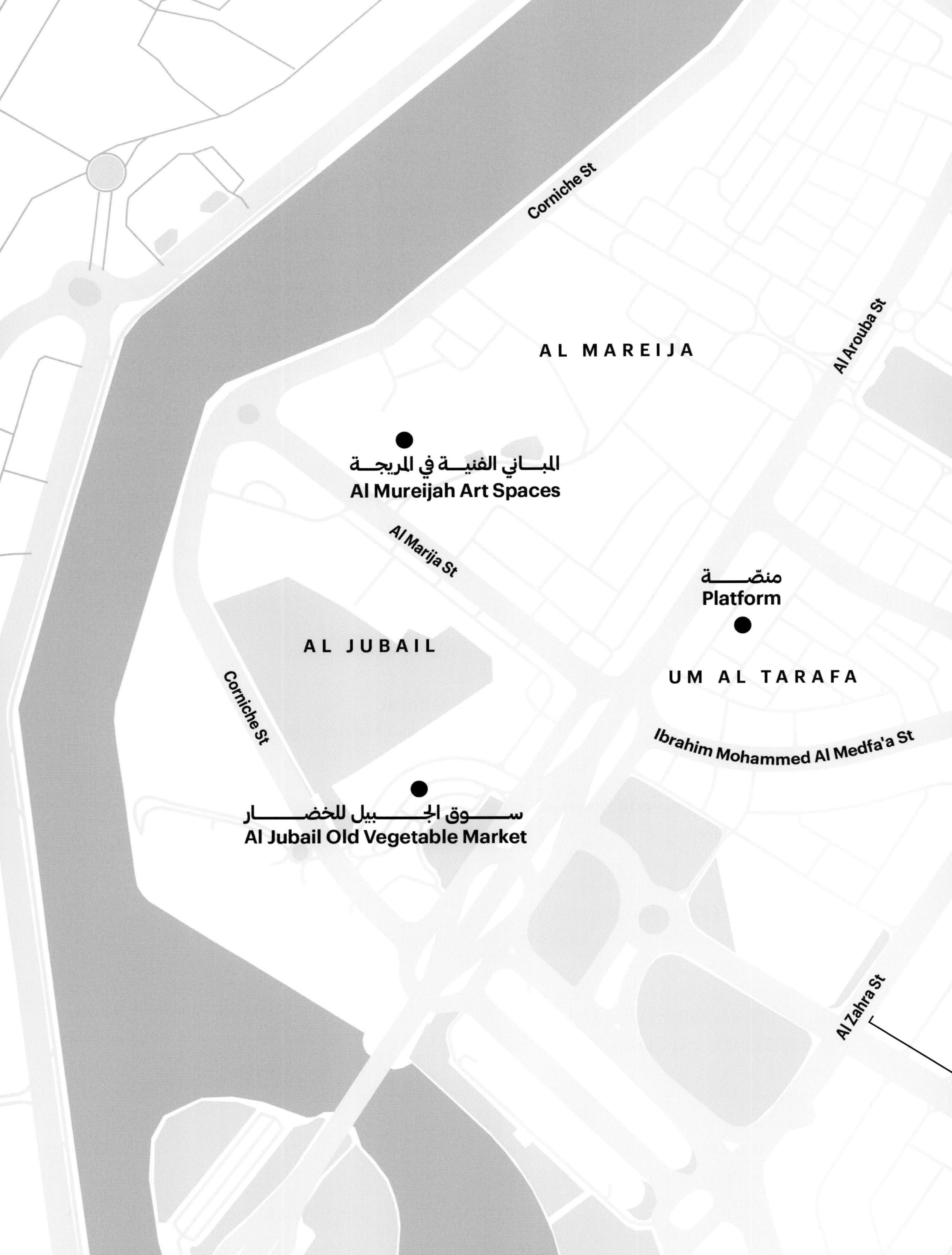
Corniche St
AL MAREIJA
Al Arouba St
المبـــاني الفنيـــة في المريجـــة
Al Mureijah Art Spaces
Al Marija St
منصّـــة
Platform
AL JUBAIL
UM AL TARAFA
Corniche St
Ibrahim Mohammed Al Medfa'a St
ســـوق الجـــبيل للخضـــار
Al Jubail Old Vegetable Market
Al Zahra St

Ibrahim Mohammed Al Medfa'a St

قاعة إفريقيا
Africa Hall

AL MANAKH

مدرســـة القـــاسميـــة
Al-Qasimiyah School

Sheikh Saqr Bin Khalid Al Qasimi St

SHARJAH 150m N

Al-Qasimiyah School

Cooking Sections with AKT II, *Becoming Xerophile*, 2019.
Soil, rubble, bricks, desert plants, 65 × 50 × 50 m.

Facing page: Hamed Khosravi and Roozbeh Elias-Azar with Nazgol Ansarinia, *Revolution Begins at Home*, 2019. Mixed-media installation, dimensions variable.

Farzin Lotfi-Jam, Felicity Scott, and Mark Wasiuta, *Media Habitat*, c. 1975, 2019. Multichannel video installation, 2.4 × 4.4 × 19.2 m.

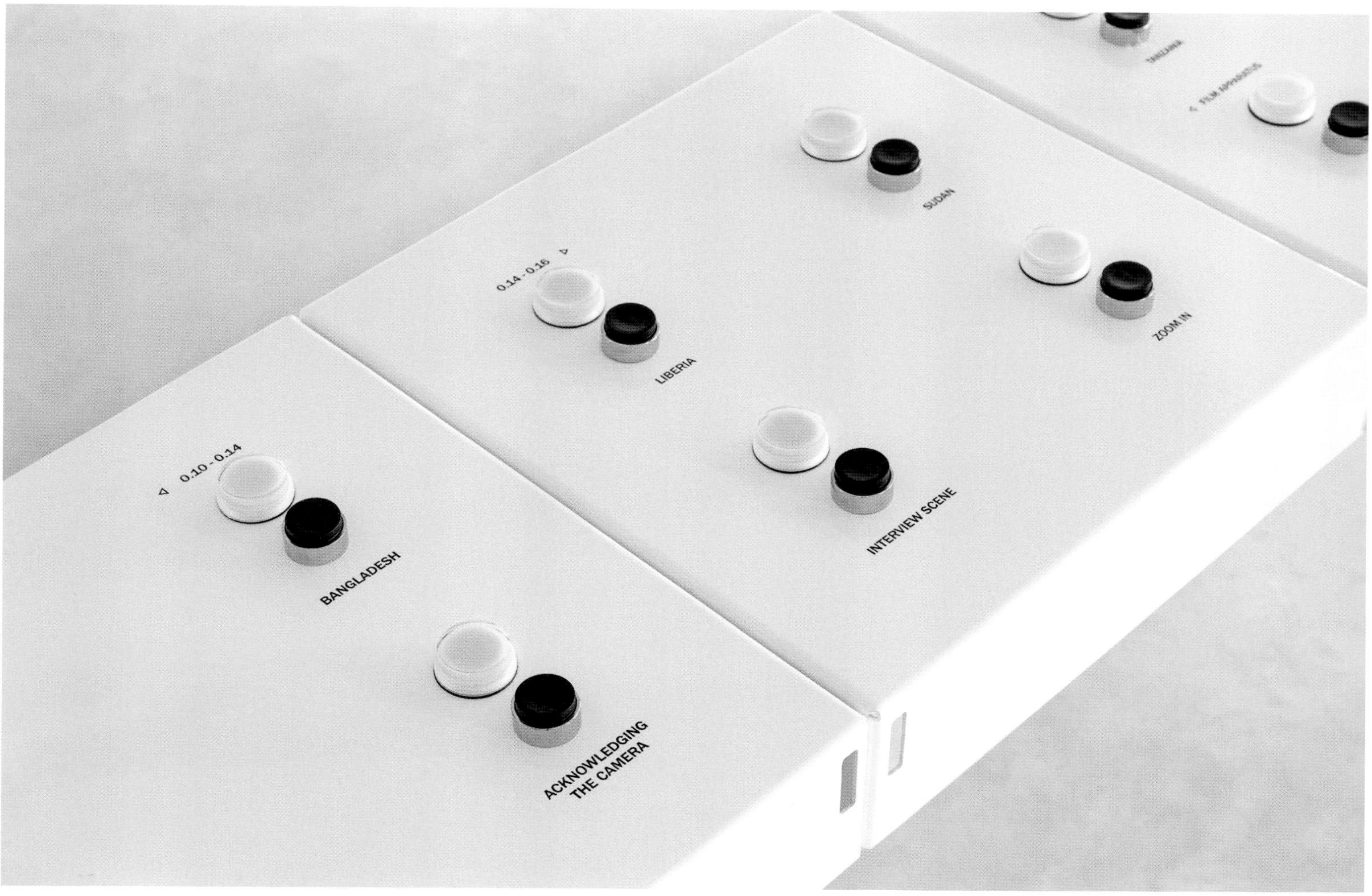

CCCP/2020, *Curricular Exchange*, 2019. Thermal printer, paper, dimensions variable.

Facing page (top): Jamon Van Den Hoek and Steve Salembier, *Satellite Disparities*, 2019. Multichannel video installation, 24 hours.

Facing page (bottom): all(zone), *Set the Controls for the Heart of the Sun*, 2019. Sunshade net, aluminium pipe, nylon rope, plywood, 0.48 × 9 × 19.2 m.

Public Works , *The Architect, the Law, the Sponsor, and their Maid's Room*, 2019. Model, archival documents, five-channel audio installation, dimensions variable.

Facing page: Francesco Sebregondi and Jasbir K. Puar, *Future Lives of Return*, 2019. Mixed-media installation, dimensions variable.

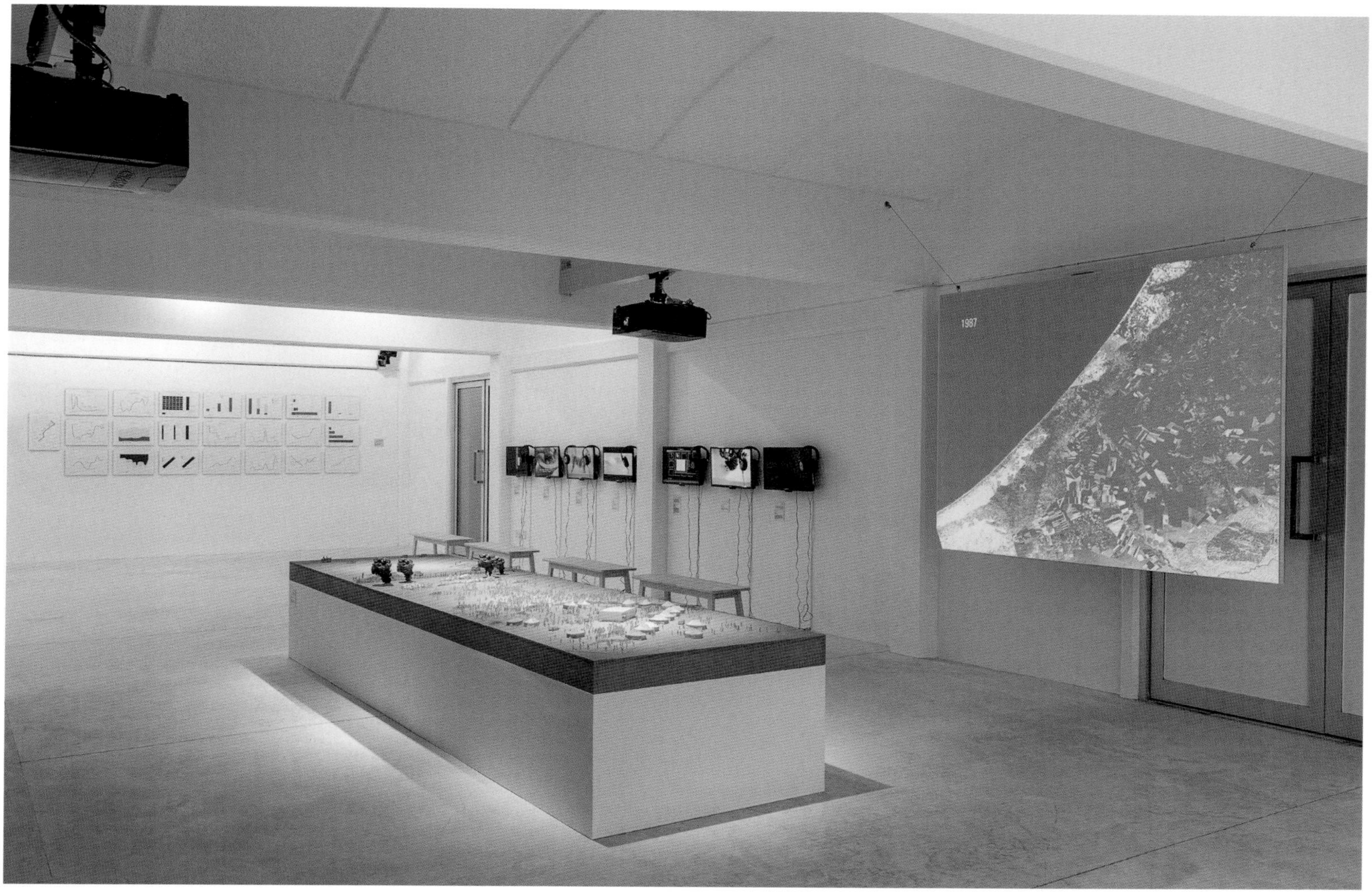

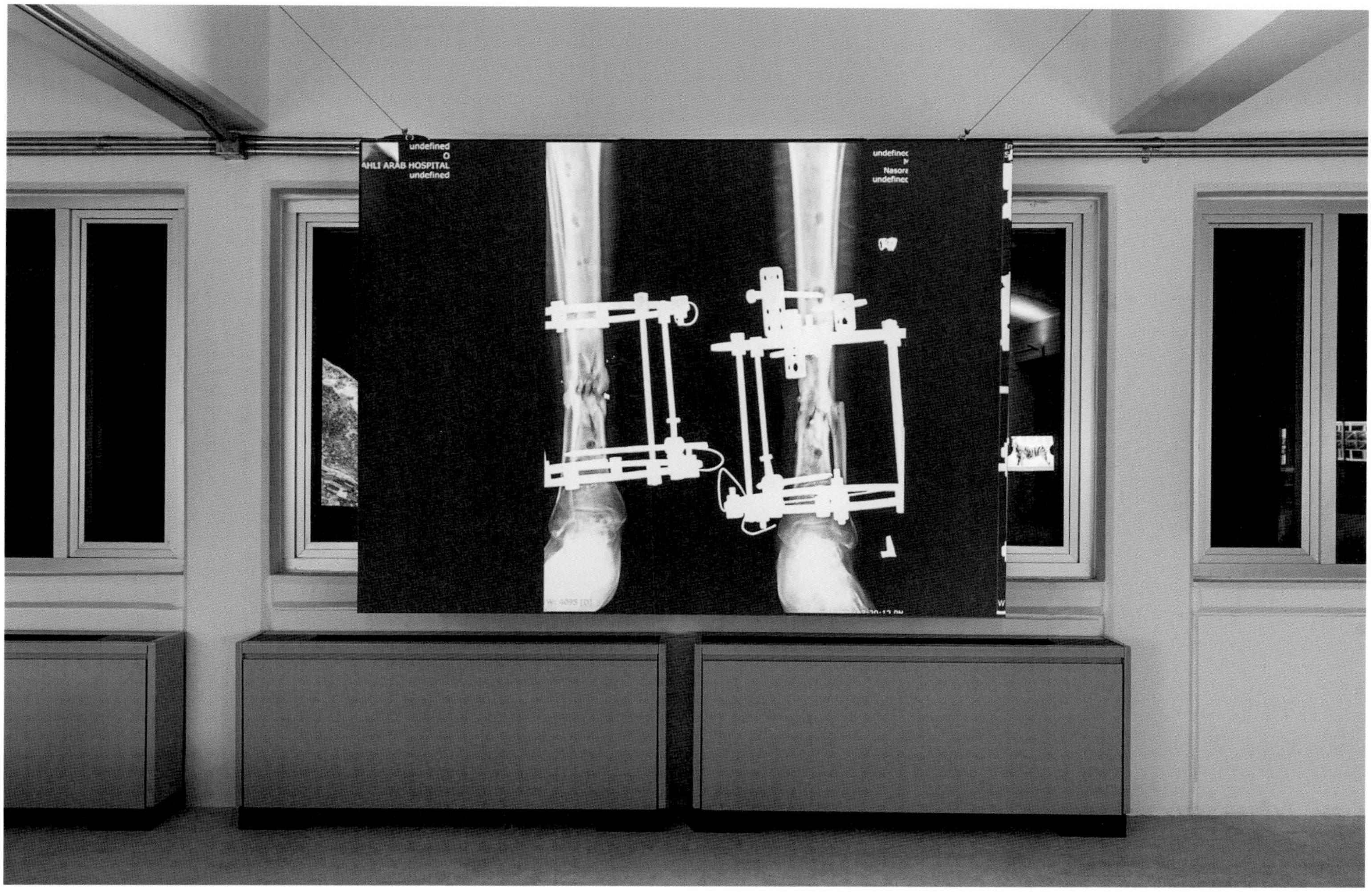

Feral Atlas Collective, *Feral Atlas*, 2019. Mixed-media installation, dimensions variable.

Next page: The Otolith Group, *Infinity minus Infinity*, 2019. Video, 50 min.

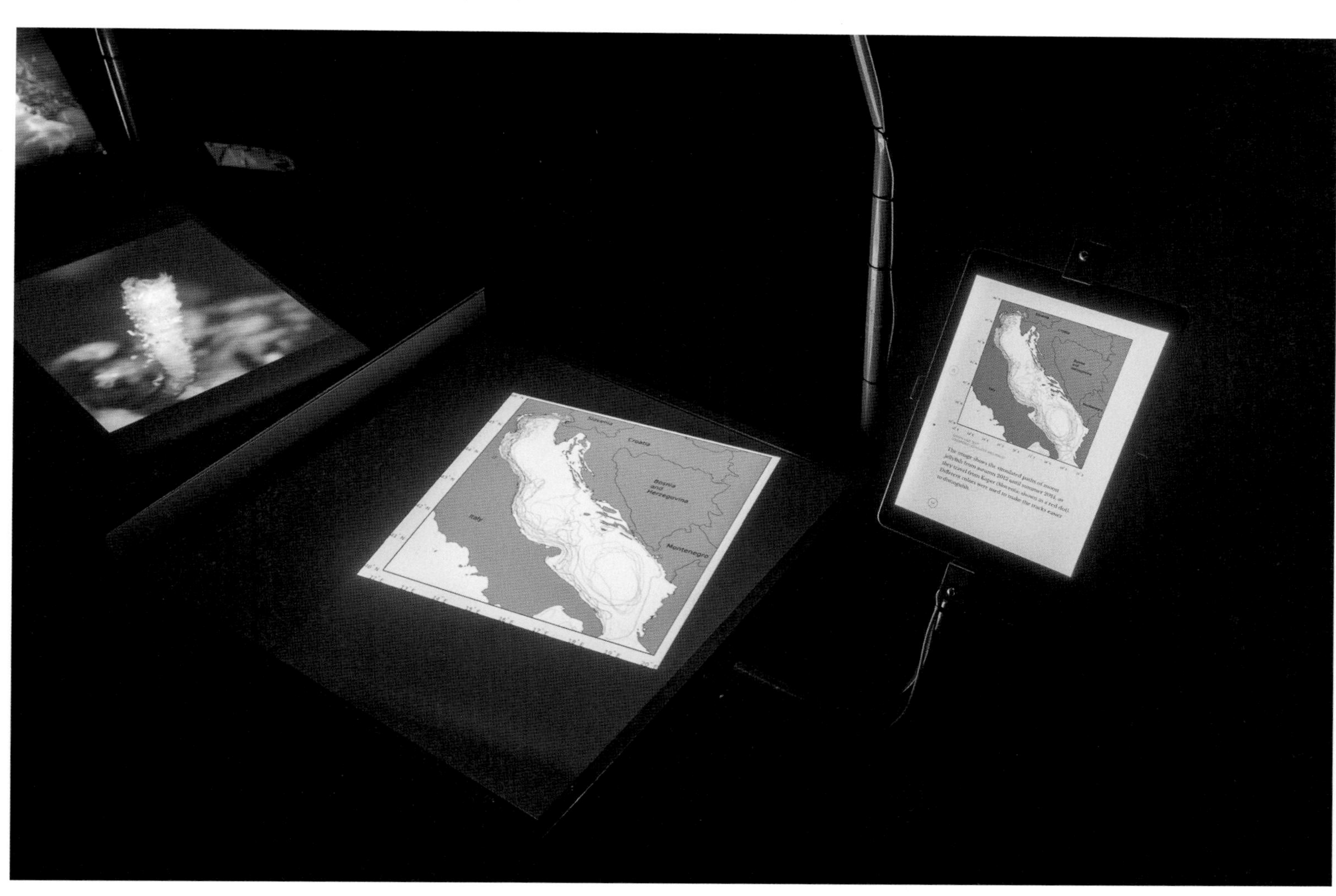
Slovenia
Croatia
Bosnia and Herzegovina
Italy
Montenegro

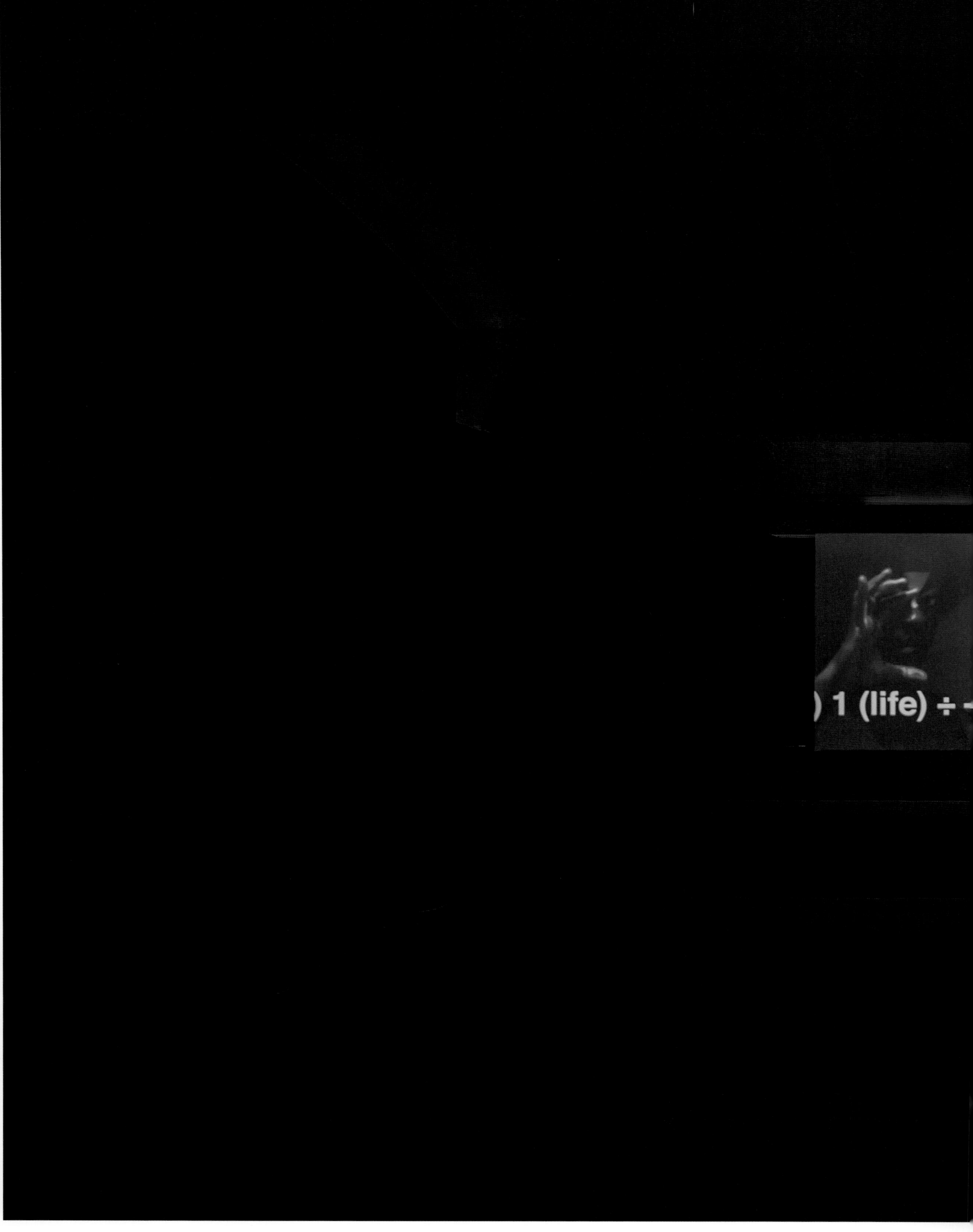
) 1 (life) ÷

ackness) =

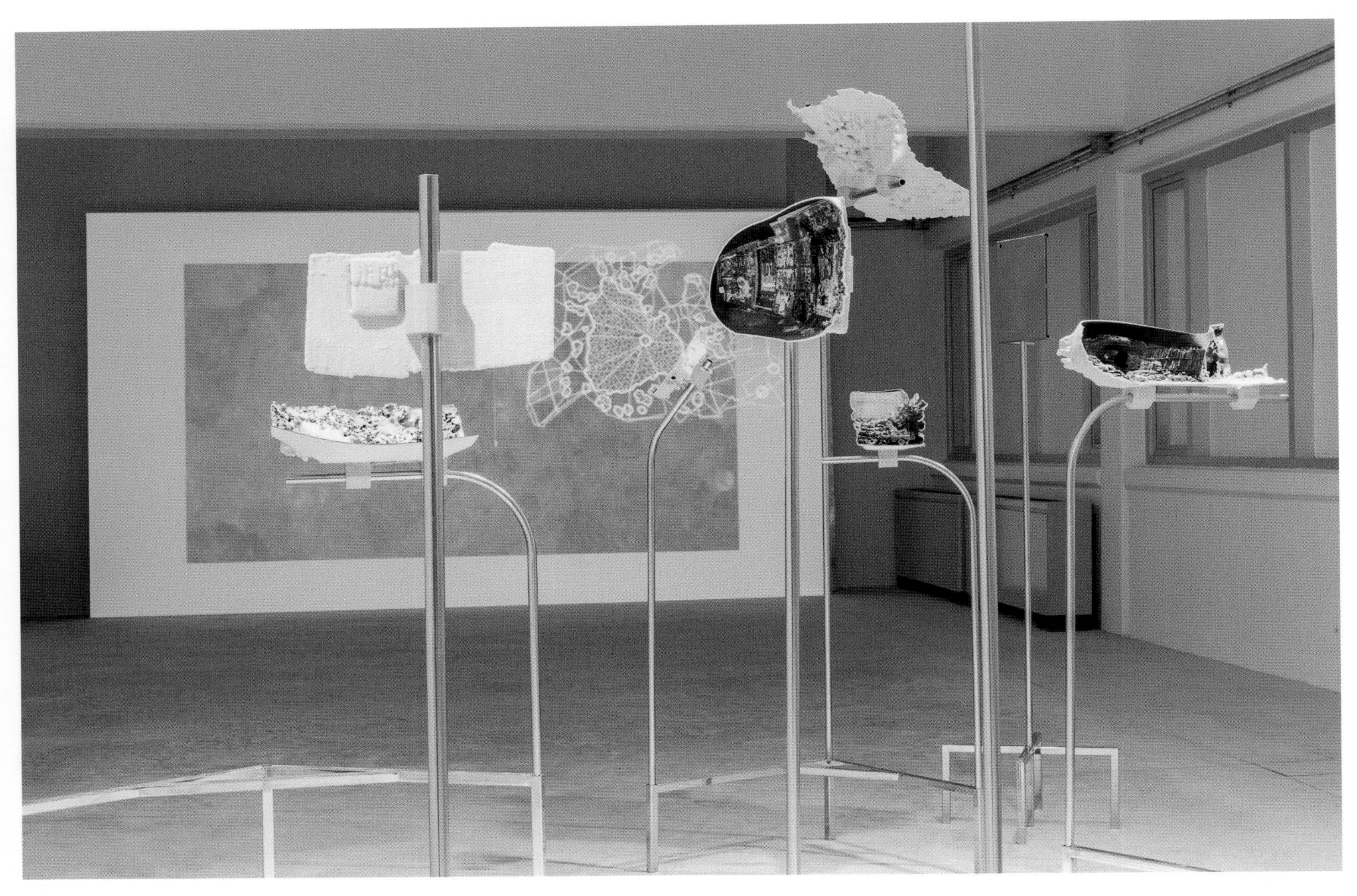

Ibiye Camp with Emmy Bacharach and David Killingsworth, *The Sacred Forests of Ethiopia*, 2019. Photogrammetry, video, audio recordings, dimensions variable.

Marina Tabassum Architects, *Inheriting Wetness*, 2019. Three prefabricated houses, each 3.35 × 6.4 × 5 m.

Dogma, *Platforms*, 2019. Ink-jet prints, bound book, model, dimensions variable.

Facing page: Ola Hassanain, *Gathering Space*, 2019. Mixed-media installation, dimensions variable.

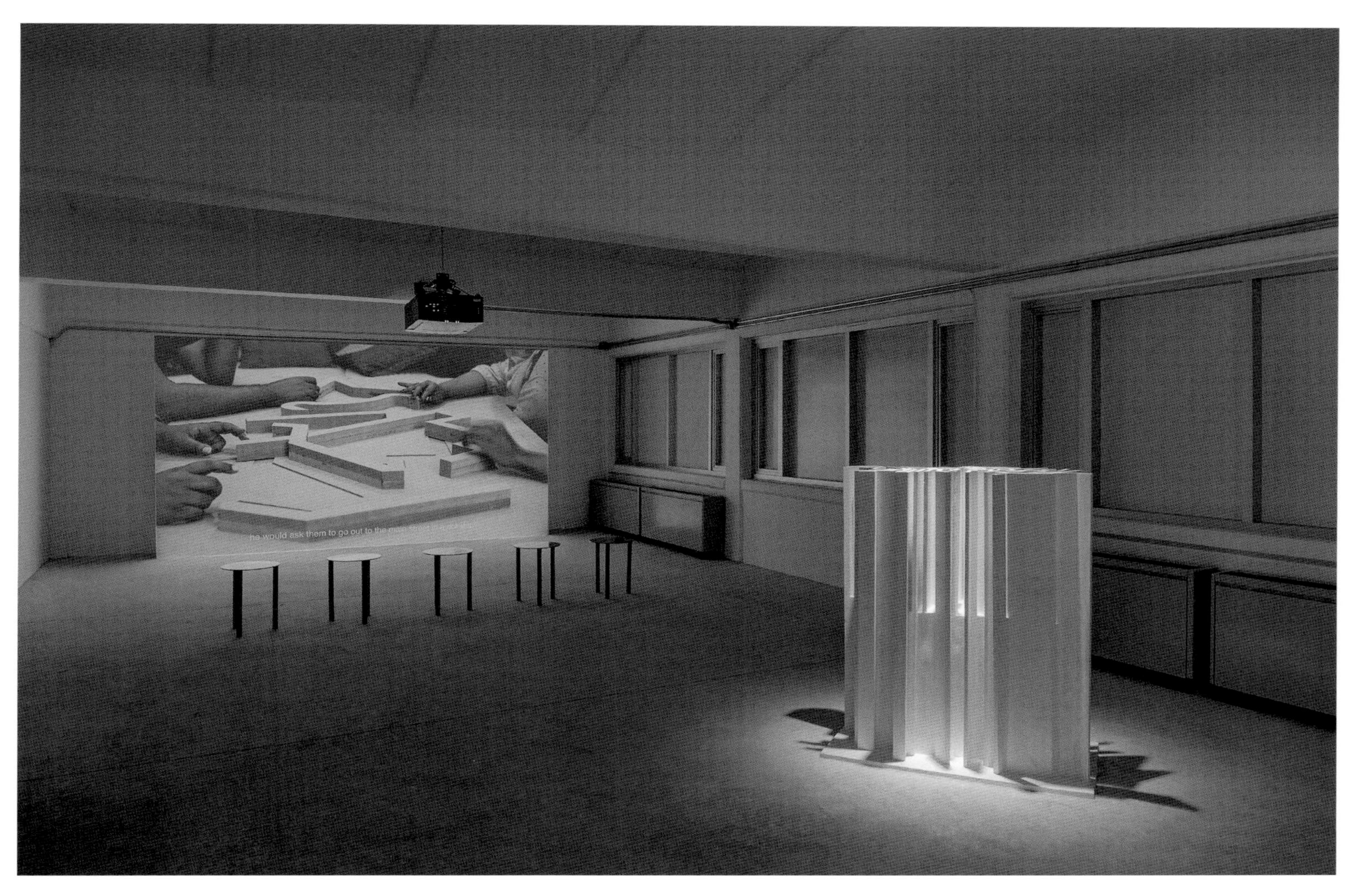
he would ask them to go out to the

Studio Bound (Hussam Dakkak and Basmah Kaki), *Sacred Landscapes*, 2019. Mixed-media installation, dimensions variable.

Facing page: Informal Collective on Western Sahara, *Necessità dei volti – Fourth Extension,* 1999–2019. Sound, video, postcards, dimensions variable.

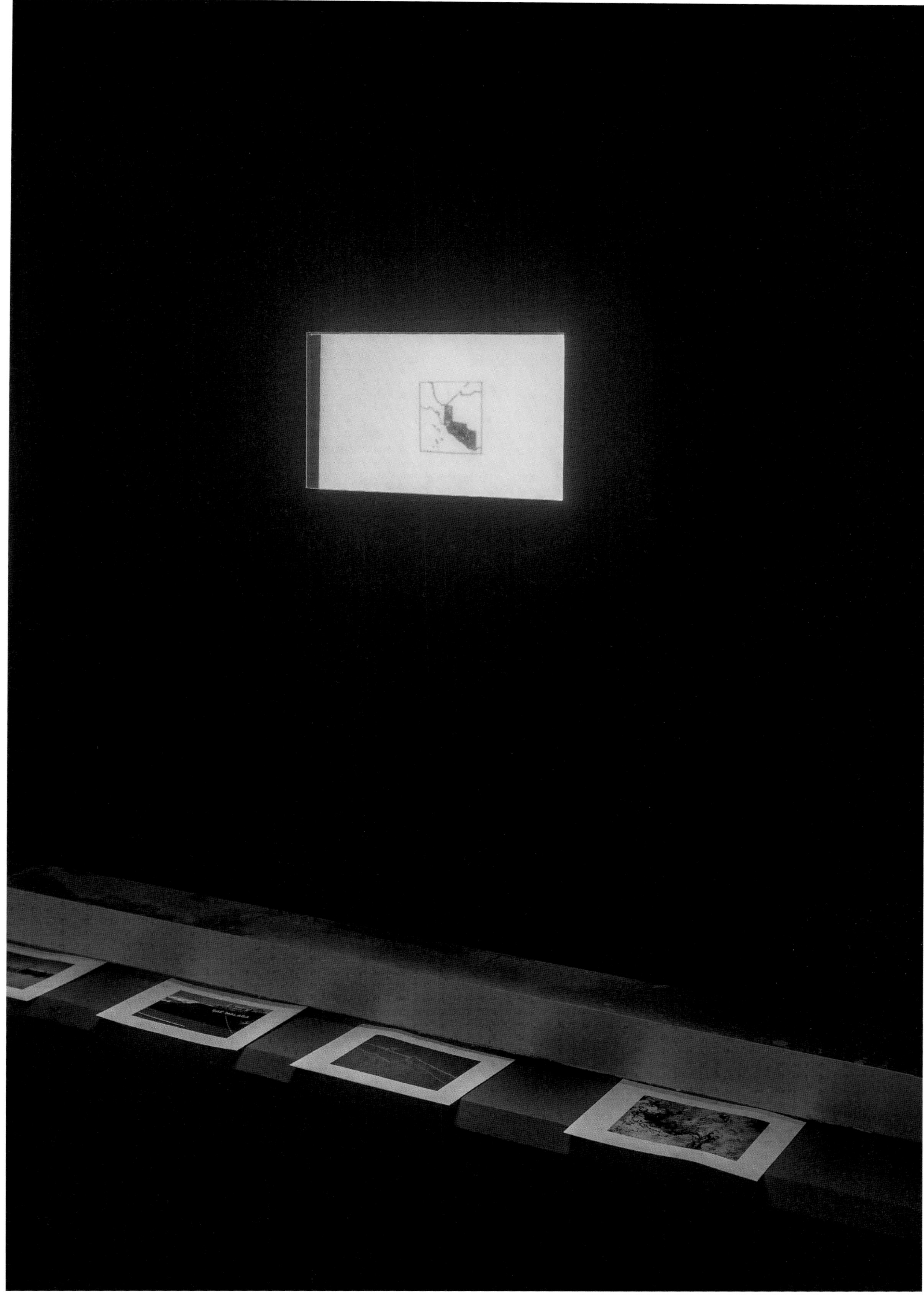

Alonso Barros, Gonzalo Pimentel, Juan Gili, and Mauricio Hidalgo, *The Atacama Lines*, 2019. Light boxes, foam models, video, dimensions variable.

Facing page (top): Lina Ghotmeh Architecture, *Inclusive Living* , 2019. Model, 0.2 × 0.6 × 10 m.

Facing page (bottom): Mohamed Elshahed with Farida Makar, *New School/ Future Egyptians*, 2019. Mixed-media installation, dimensions variable.

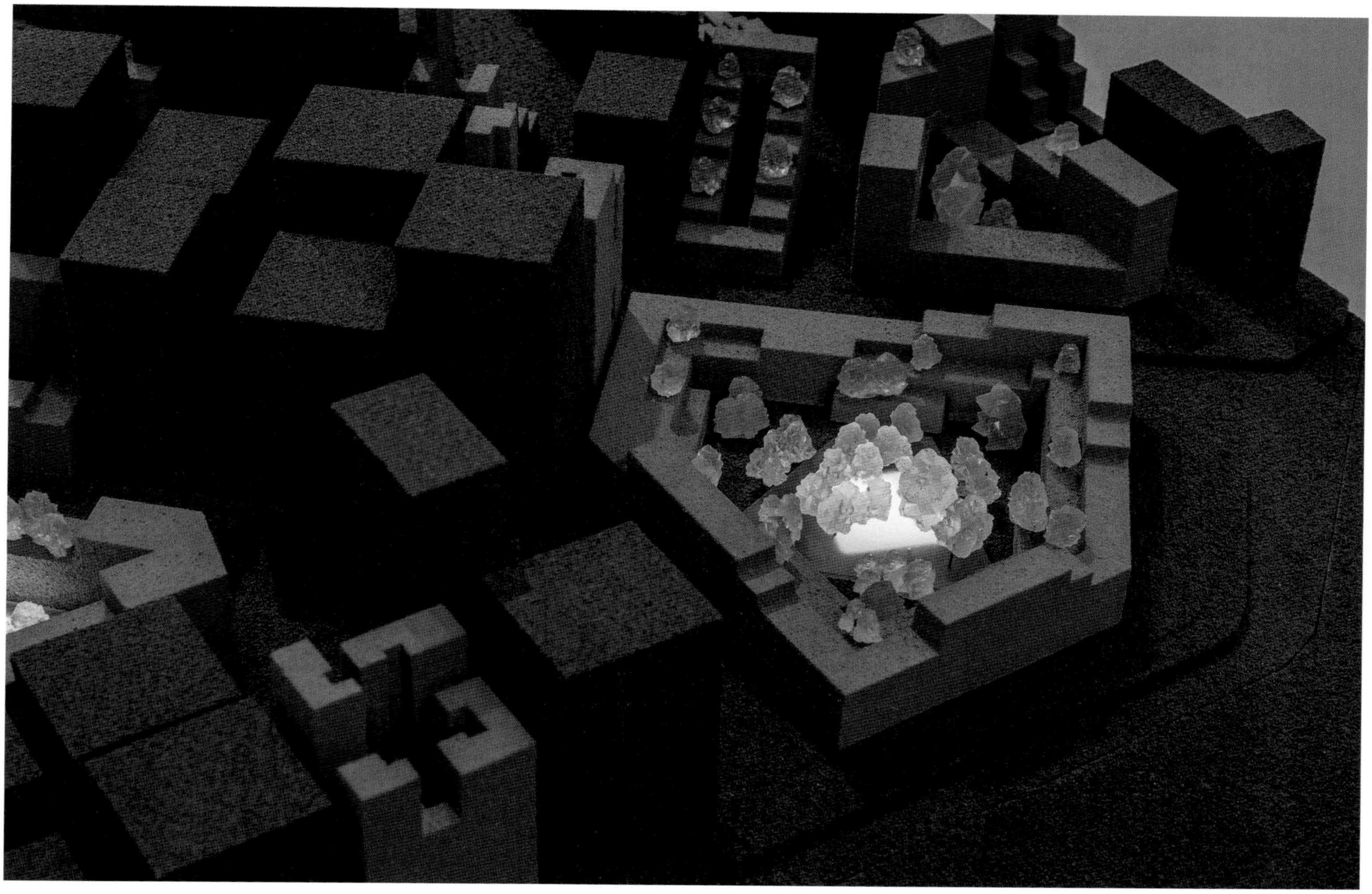

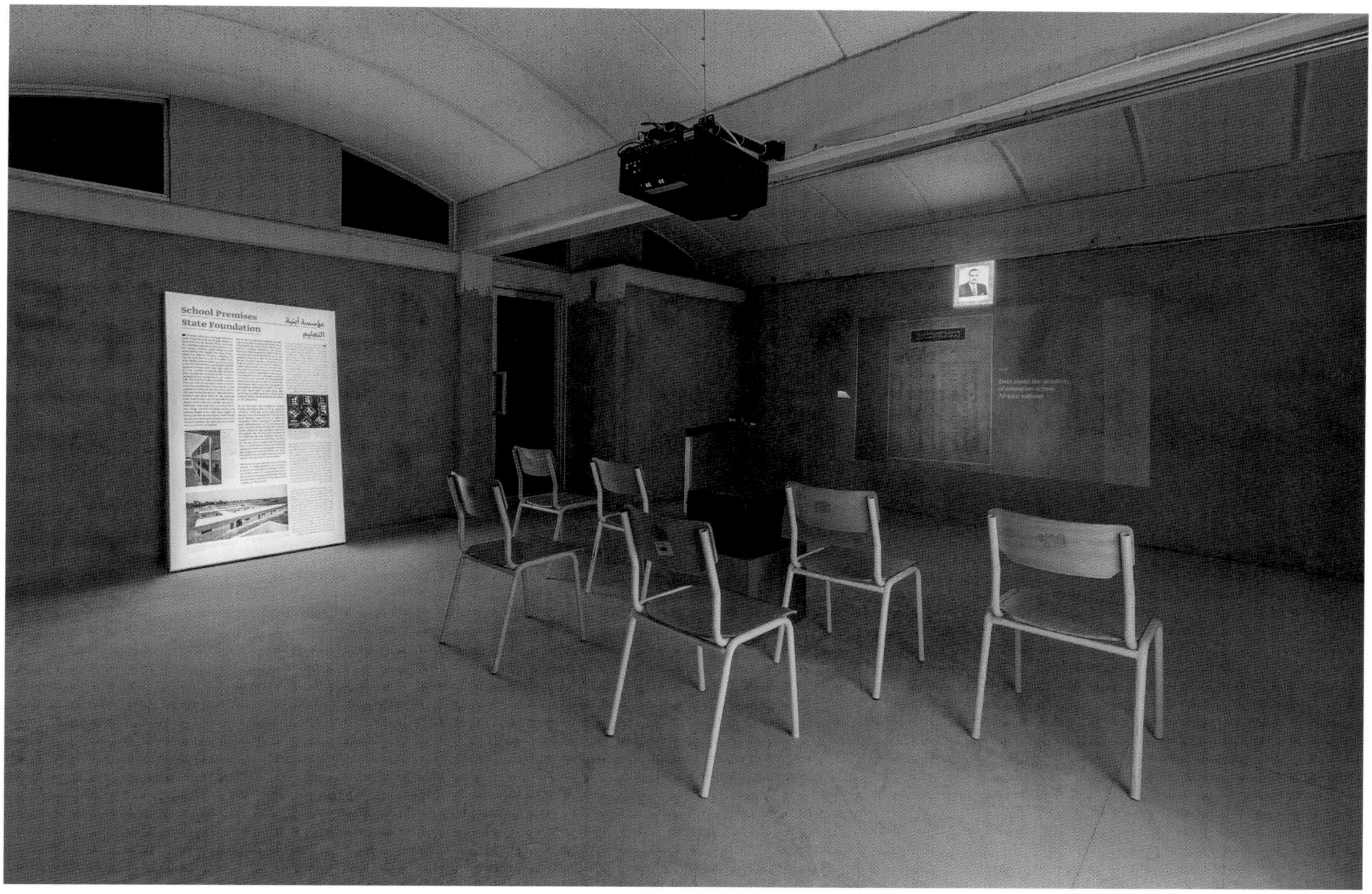
School Premises
State Foundation
مؤسسة أبنية
التعليم

Old Al Jubail Fruit and Vegetable Market

Facing page: Civil Architecture, *Three Ideal Mounds*, 2019.
Photographic prints, video, carpet, dimensions variable.

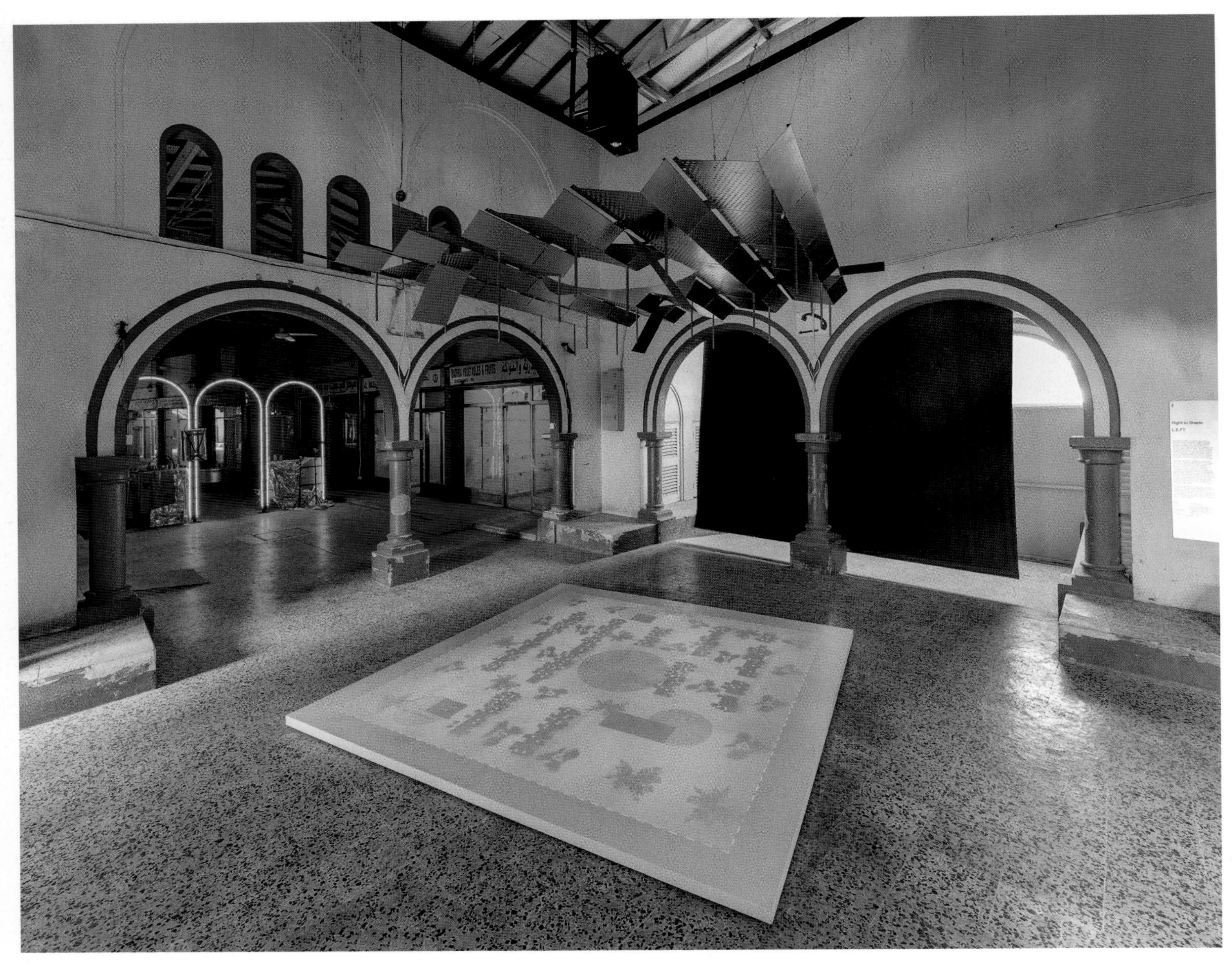

L.E.FT, *Right to Shade*, 2019. Mixed-media installation, dimensions variable.

Facing page: Marwa Arsanios with Vinita Gatne, *Micro-Resistances*, 2019. Mixed-media installation, dimensions variable.

This land is
very fertile
Yes in some cases we have to,
but they are not chemical

Samaneh Moafi with WORKNOT!, Mhamad Safa, Maria Bessarabova, Platform 28, and residents of Mehr in Dowlatabad, Esfahan, *Parable of Mehr*, 2019. Mixed-media installation, dimensions variable.

محل محمد عبدالله احمد للخضروات
91 MOHD. ABDULLA AHMED VEG. SHOP
انصار لتجارة المواد الغذائية
AL JASAR
VEGETABLE CENTRE
95 مركز الجسر للخضروات

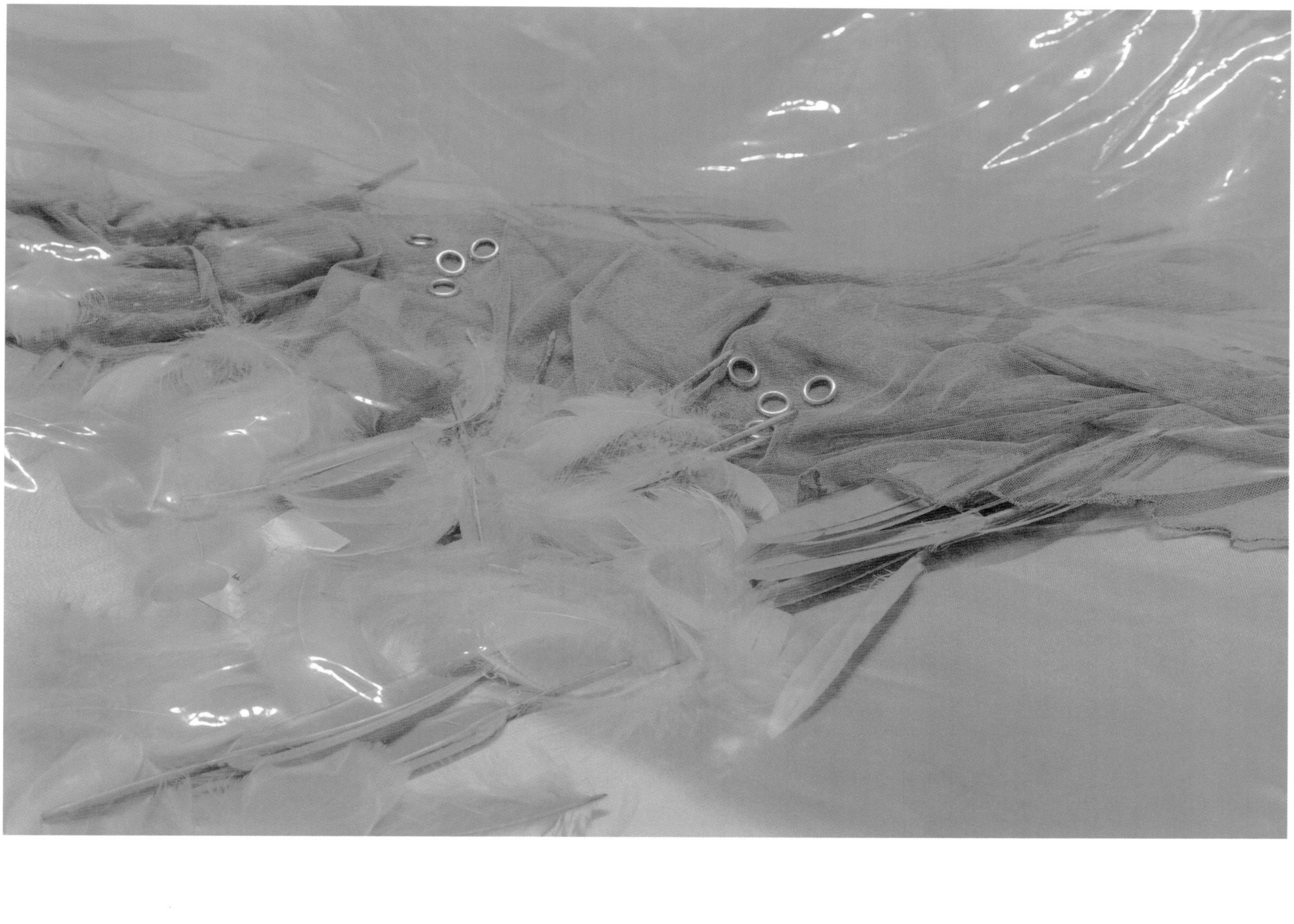

Dima Srouji with Dirar Kalash, Silvia Truini, Nadia Abu El-Haj, and Omar Jabareen, *Depth Unknown*, 2019. Mixed-media installation, dimensions variable.

Next page: Nidhi Mahajan, *Silences and Spectres of the Indian Ocean*, 2019. Models, video, dimensions variable.

لتجارة الخضروات
AL MUDHIA
55
of the smiling face that welcomes

L MANAR
للخضروات والفواكه
VEG. & FRUIT
SHOP

MOHD. AL QASEER HEIR VEG. SHOP
AL HAJIR
VEG. & FRUITS

Studio Anne Holtrop, *Material Gesture: Gypsum*, 2017–2019.
Models and photographic prints, dimensions variable.

EST.
(BRANCH 3)

البيت الاخضر للخضروات د
AL BAIT AL AKHDAR VEG LLC
Shop No.16
للخضروات و الفواكة
RHIFAIYA VEG. & FRUITSCENTRE
محمد شافي

This and previous page: Adam Jasper with Li Tavor, Alessandro Bosshard, Matthew van der Ploeg, Max Kriegleder, Vivian Wang, Dewa Alit, Vibeke Sorensen, and U5, *Priests and Programmers*, 2019. Mixed-media installation, dimensions variable.

Al Mureijah Art Spaces

Tuan Andrew Nguyen, *We Were Lost in Our Country*, 2019.
Three-channel video installation, 35 min.

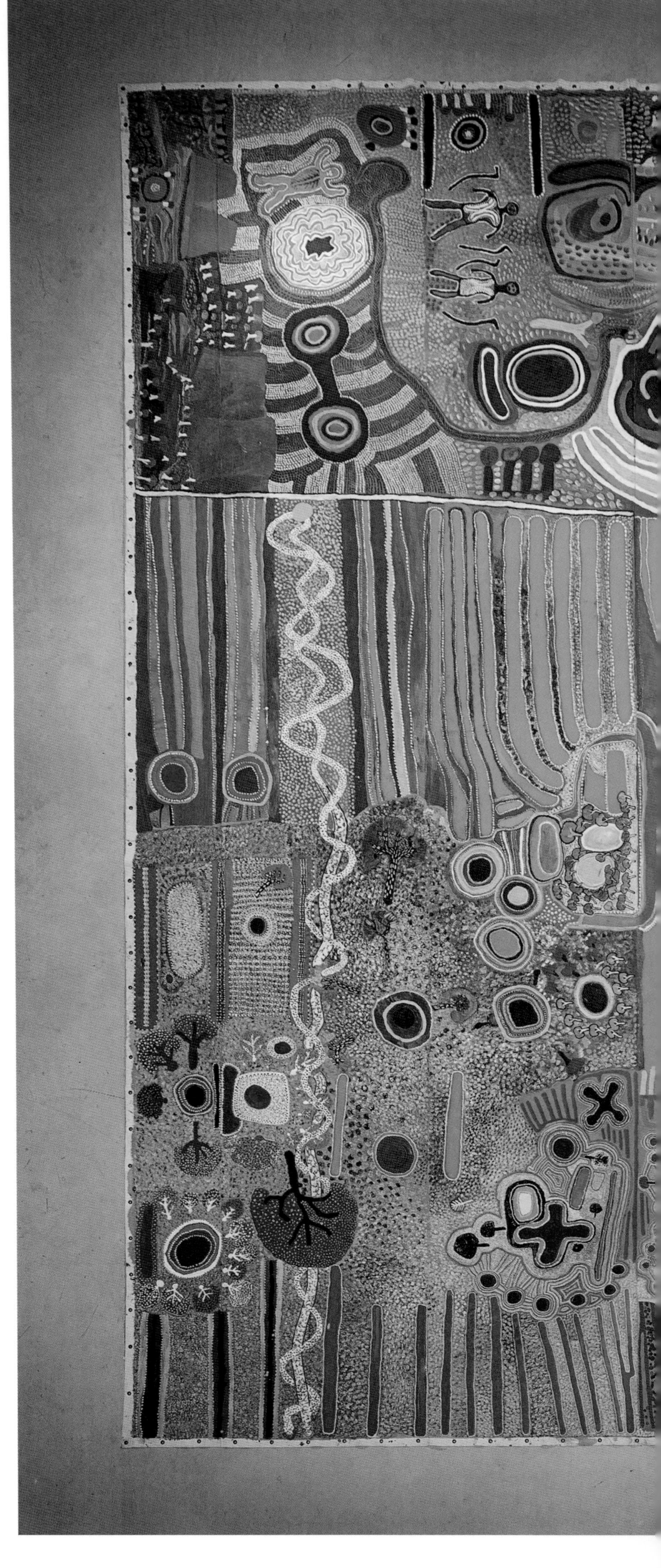

Manmarriya Daisy Andrews, Milyinti Dorothy May, Kulyukulyu Trixie Shaw Ngarralja Tommy May, Ngumumpa Walter Rose, Jukuja Dolly Snell, Ngirlpirr Spider Snell, Yirrpura Jinny James, Purlta Maryanne Downs, Jijijar Molly Dededar, Kurtiji Peter Goodijie, Mayapu Elsie Thomas, Waninya Biddy Bonney, Kuji Rosie Goodjie, George Tuckerbox, Nyuju Stumpy Brown, Luurn Willie Kew, Nanjarn Charlie Nunjun, Nyangarni Penny K-Lyon, Nada Rawlins, Yukarla Hitler Pamba, Miltja Thursday Pindan, Killer Pindan, Terry Murray, Monday Kunga, Wajinya Paji Honeychild Yankarr, Kurnti Jimmy Pike, Pijaji Peter Skipper, Raraj David Chuguna, Parlun Harry Bullen, Tapiri Peter Clancy, Mawukura Jimmy Nerrimah, Jukuna Mona Chuguna, Jinny Bent, Munangu Huey Bent, Kapi Lucy Cubby, Pulukarti Honey Bulagardie, Pajiman Warford Budgieman, Ngurnta Amy Nuggett, Japarti Joseph Nuggett; *Ngurrara Canvas II*; 1997. Synthetic polymer on two-pass rubber cloth, 10 x 8 m.

Dogma, Platform, 2019. Tinted concrete,
0.5 × 20 × 20 m.

Sharjah Architecture Triennial 2019

November 9, 2019 – February 8, 2020

Public Program and Working Group

Performative Work

Lawrence Abu Hamdan
HaRaKa Platform/Adham Hafez Company
Godofredo Pereira
Stefan Tarnowski
Bouchra Ouizguen

Forums

Ghassan Abu-Sittah
Sepake Angiama
Samanta Arango Orozco
María Estela Barco
Jehan Bseiso
John Carty
Esi Eshun
José Esparza Chong Cuy
Denise Ferreira da Silva
Salah Hassan
Mauricio Hidalgo
María Claudina Loaiza
Maha Maamoun
Paulo Tavares
Helga Tawil-Souri
Sónia Vaz Borges
Nicole Wolf
Ala Younis
Members of the Ngurrara Canvas II Artists' Group

Music

Al Ahly Thikr Jamaah
Dewa Alit and Gamelan Salukat
Kelman Duran
Abdullah Ibrahim
Nicolas Jaar
DJ Kampire
Mazaher
Shabjdeed + Al Nather (BLTNM)
Shabmouri (BLTNM)
Slikback
ZULI

Rights of Future Generations Working Group

Gayatri Chakravorty Spivak
Ha-Joon Chang
Lumumba Di-Aping (chair)
María Fernanda Espinosa
Denise Ferreira da Silva
Richard Flanagan
Hoesung Lee
Thabo Mbeki
Dilma Rousseff
Youba Sokona
Peter Turkson
Françoise Vergès

Saturday, November 9, 2019
Devotional Practices

Old Al Jubail Fruit & Vegetable Market

11:30
Opening Procession

A model dhow and flags are carried from the Port of Sharjah to Nidhi Mahajan's installation

13:00–13:30
Procession to Platform

Led by
Al Ahly Thikr Jamaah

Platform

13:30–14:40
Forum 1
Repetition and Recital—*p.68*

Nazgol Ansarinia, Roozbeh Elias-Azar, Hamed Khosravi, Nidhi Mahajan, Samaneh Moafi, Abir Saksouk, Pier Vittorio Aureli and Martino Tattara (Dogma); moderated by Paulo Tavares

Al-Qasimiyah School

14:40–16:00	17:00–17:30	19:30–20:30
Procession to Al-Qasimiyah School	Music Performance	Performance “In 50 Years Or So (Act I)”
Led by Al Ahly Thikr Jamaah	Dewa Alit and Gamelan Salukat	HaRaKa Platform/Adham Hafez Company

Al-Qasimiyah School

21:00–Late
Music Performance

Mazaher

consents to be prosaic. But it is precisely
because this prosaic character is a
triumphant reason for its existence: for the
first time, artifice aims at something
common, not rare. And as an immediate
ronsequence, the age-old function of
nature is modified: it is no longer the Idea,
the pure Substance to be regained or
imitated: an artificial Matter, more bountiful
than all the natural deposits, is about to
replace her, and to determine the very
invention of forms.
A luxurious object is still of this earth, it still
نعرف أن التقليد [...] ظل مطبوعاً بطابع الادعاء، وكان جزءاً من
عالم المظاهر وليس من عالم الاستعمال، وكان يهدف إلى إعادة
إنتاج المواد الأكثر نُدرة بأقل التكاليف كالماس، والريش، والفراء
، والفضة وكل لمعان العالم الباذخ. البلاستيك المطوي هو مادة
منزلية. وهو المادة السحرية الأولى التي ترضخ للابتذال. ذلك
لأن هذه التفاهة تشكل سبب وجوده المنتصر. وللمرة الأولى
تسعى الخدعة لتكون عامة وليس نادرة، وفي الوقت نفسه تغيرت
الوظيفة السلفية للطبيعة: فلم تعد هي الفكرة والجوهر الصافي
الذي نسعى للعثور عليه أو تقليده. إذ هناك مادة مصطنعة

Sunday, November 10, 2019
Signs and Transmission

Al-Qasimiyah School

09:00–10:00
Sharjah Architecture Triennial Press Conference

Hoor Al Qasimi, Adrian Lahoud

10:00–11:00
Atacama Press Conference

Mauricio Hidalgo (Huatacondo community), Alonso Barros, Claudia Montero, & Gonzalo Pimentel (Fundación Desierto de Atacama)

11:00–12:00
Forum 2
Biospheres of War—*p.76*

Ghassan Abu Sitta, Jehan Bseiso, Jasbir Puar, Francesco Sebregondi; moderated by Helga Tawil Souri

Al-Qasimiyah School

13:00–14:00	14:20–15:00	15:30–16:30
Forum 3 Micro-Resistances	Lecture Performance "Syria Revolution Media"	Forum 4 Signal
Samanta Arango Orozco, Marwa Arsanios, María Claudina Loaiza, María Estela Barco, Nicole Wolf; moderated by Sónia Vaz Borges	Stefan Tarnowski	Adam Jasper, Farzin Lotfi-Jam, Felicity D. Scott, Dima Srouji, Jamon Van Den Hoek, Mark Wasiuta; moderated by José Esparza Chong Cuy

Africa Hall

17:00–17:30	18:00–19:00	19:30–21:00
Music Performance	Lecture Performance “Natq”	Performance “In 50 Years Or So (Acts II and III)”
Dewa Alit and Gamelan Salukat	Lawrence Abu Hamdan	HaRaKa Platform/Adham Hafez Company

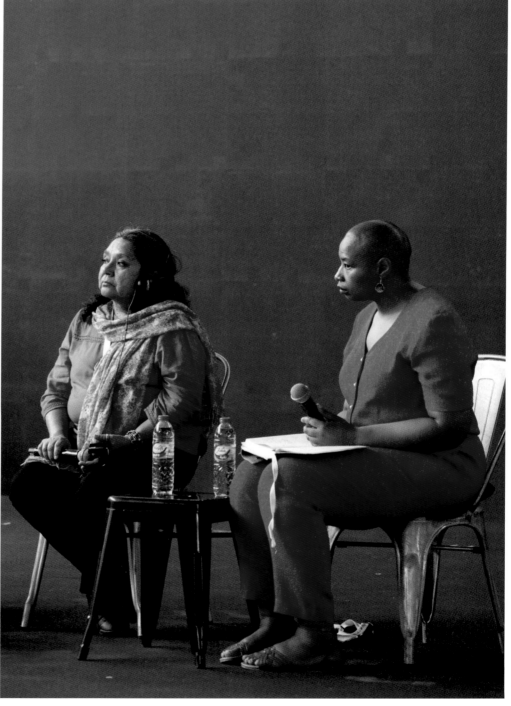

Old Al Jubail Fruit & Vegetable Market

21:30–late

Music Performances

Shabjdeed + Al Nather (BLTNM), Shabmouri (BLTNM), DJ Kampire

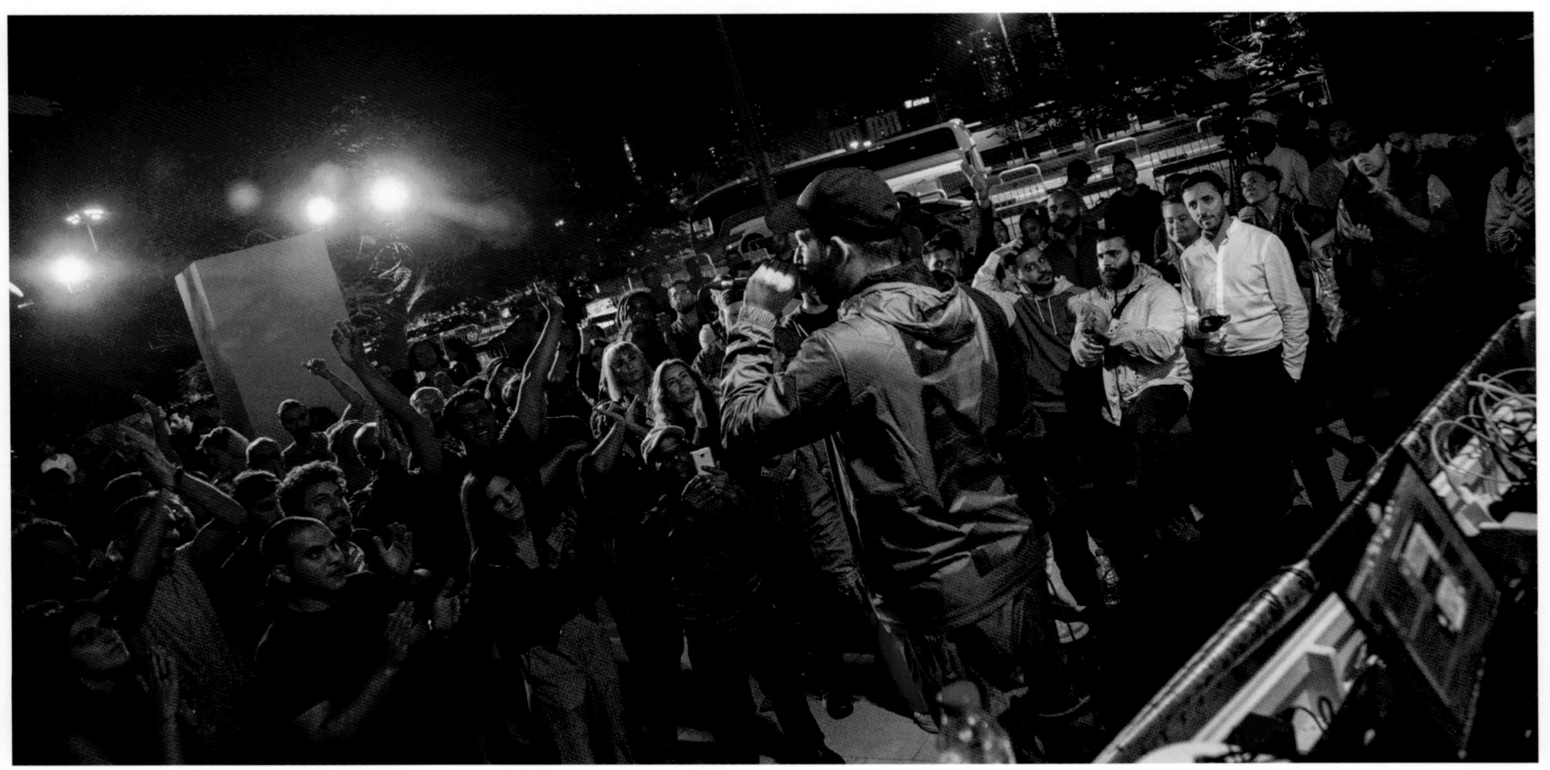

Monday, November 11, 2019
Forms of Afterlife

Al Muraijah Art Spaces

10:00–10:40

Ngurrara Canvas II Awakening Ceremony

11:00–12:00

Forum 5
The World as Green Archipelago

Members of the Ngurrara Canvas II Artists' Group, John Carty, Michael McMahon, Tuan Andrew Nguyen; moderated by Adrian Lahoud

Al-Qasimiyah School

13:00–14:00

Forum 6
Forms of Afterlife

Denise Ferreira da Silva, Salah Hassan, Anjalika Sagar and Kodwo Eshun (The Otolith Group), Esi Eshun; moderated by Sepake Angiama

Mleiha Fort

14:00–15:00	16:45–18:00	18:30–19:50
Conditions Book Launch	Music Performance	Screening O Horizon
Maha Maamoun and Ala Younis (Kayfa-ta), Andrea Bagnato	Nicolas Jaar	The Otolith Group

20:00–20:40
Lecture Performance
"Ex-humus"

Godofredo Pereira

21:00–00:30
Music Performance

Slikback

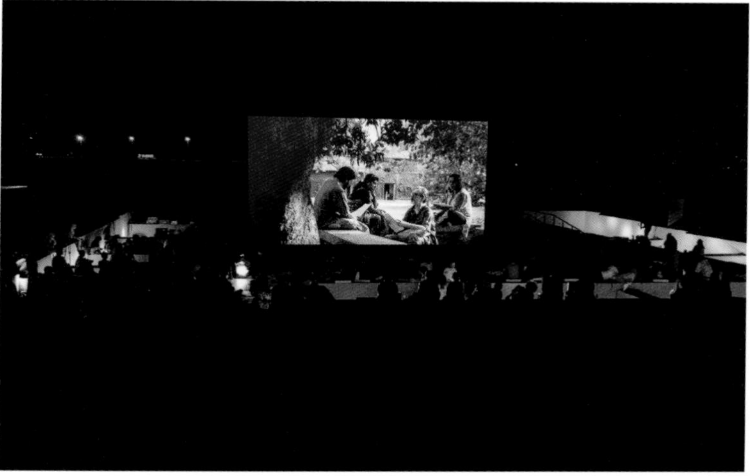

Tuesday, November 12, 2019
Rights of Future Generations Working Group

Africa Hall	Al-Qasimiyah School	Africa Hall
09:00–13:00 Working Group Session 1	14:00–14:35 Performance "Corbeaux"	14:45–16:45 Working Group Session 2
H. H. Sheikh Dr. Sultan Al Qasimi (opening address) Thabo Mbeki Dilma Rousseff Card. Peter Turkson	Bouchra Ouizguen	Hoesung Lee and Youba Sokona Maria Fernanda Espinosa Ha-Joon Chang

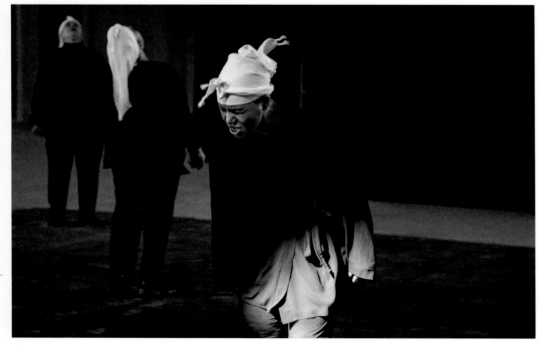

Bassata Village, Ras Al-Khaimah

20:00–22:00

Music Performance

Abdullah Ibrahim

23:00–Late

Music Performances

ZULI
Kelman Duran

بينما كانوا في السـابق بجانب مـاء غزير
فوجدوا أنفسهم الآن في صحارى لا نهاية لها
وعراء مكشوف تحت الشمس.
وحيث كان يُفترض أن يـأتي الاندمـاج،
أتت العزلة المفرطـة

عليـا مسـلّم

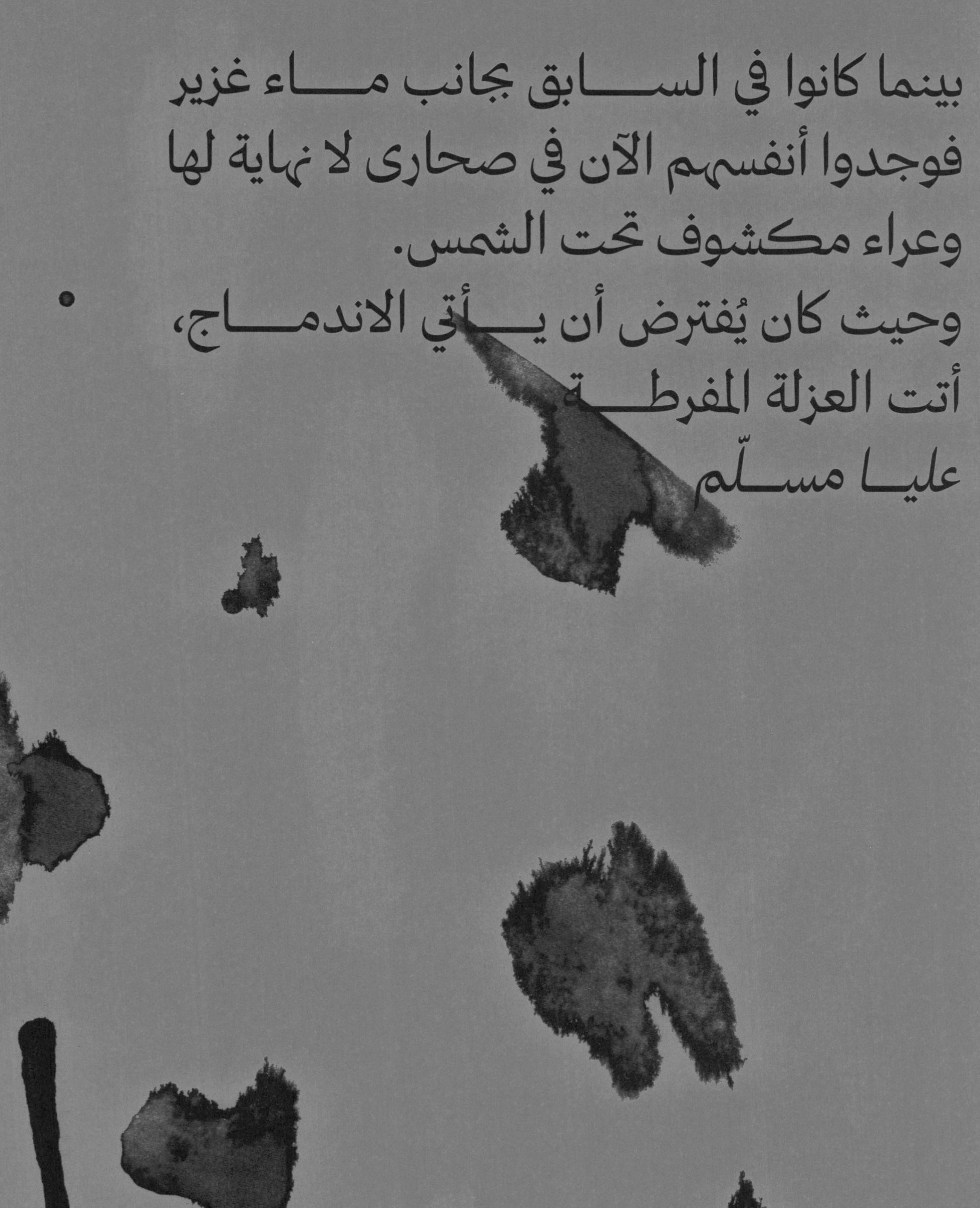

SHARJAH ARCHITECTURE TRIENNIAL

Advisor
Mona El Mousfy

Communications and External Relations Manager
Mahnaz Fancy

Project Coordinators
Farah Alkhoury
Hatem Hatem
Diane Mehanna

Production Coordinator
Tamara Barrage

Communications and Programs Assistant
Anum Laghari

Senior Graphic Designer
Fermin Guerrero

Senior Administrative Coordinator
Rowaida Badawieh

Travel and Hospitality Coordinator
Shereeja Majeed

Government Relations and Communications Consultant
Asma Mohammad Hassouni

Founder
Khalid bin Sultan Al Qasimi

Board
Hoor Al Qasimi (chairperson)
Khalid Al Ali
Khalid Bin Butti Al Muhairi
Khaled Al Huraimel
George Katodrytis

Partners
Sharjah Urban Planning Council (SUPC)
Sharjah Art Foundation (SAF)
Directorate of Town Planning and Survey (DTPS)
Bee'ah
College of Architecture, Art and Design (CAAD), American University of Sharjah

SHARJAH ARCHITECTURE TRIENNIAL 2019
Rights of Future Generations
November 9, 2019 –
February 8, 2020

Curator
Adrian Lahoud

Curatorial Team
Moad Musbahi, Kasia Wlaszczyk

Publications
Andrea Bagnato

Curatorial Research
Kamil Dalkir, David Kim,
Michael McMahon

Working Group
Lumumba Di-Aping

Exhibition Design
Dyvik Kahlen

Graphic Design
Michael Oswell
with photography
by Satoshi Fujiwara

Digital Design and Development
PWR Studio

Publications Design
Morcos Key

Editorial Partners
Africa Is a Country
Ajam Media Collective
ArtReview
e-flux Architecture
Jadaliyya
Mada Masr

Music Program
Ma3azef

Strategic Positioning
Rival Strategy

Public Relations
Pelham Communications

Exhibition Support
Royal College of Art, London

Project Support
AFAC (Arab Fund for Arts and Culture)
AKT II
Embassy of Switzerland in the United Arab Emirates
ETH Zurich
Dr. Georg und Josi Guggenheim Stiftung
Graduate School of Architecture, Planning and Preservation, Columbia University
Graham Foundation for Advanced Studies in the Fine Arts
Hilal Foundation
National Arts Council Singapore
Pro Helvetia
School of Architecture, University of Technology Sydney
Swissquote

Research Consultants
Sharmeen Azam Inayat
Faysal Tabbarah

Events Management
Miral Tamimi
Mridula Rawat
Igor Ilic
Ola Mahmood

Graphic Design Support
Tayma Bittard

Translations
Yazan Ashqar
Jacques Aswad
Adil Babikir
Armin Dwairy
Mahmoud Hossam
Nour Irfai

Interns
Raghad Al Ali
Abanob Ataia
Mariam AbdelAziz
Muhammad Aziz
Mariam Arwa Al-Hachami
Farah Hamdan
Mohammad Ramez El-Jachi
Reem Jeghel
Maitha Lootah
Eman Shafiq
Adomas Zein Eldin

Sharjah Art Foundation
Hassan Ali Al Joudi
Hassan Ali Mahmood
Saira Ansari
Mariam Al Askari
Najeeba Aslam
Humaid Ayesh
Aya Azad
Kashif Hasnain
Zahra Al Hassan
Shaima Hussain
Fatma Al Jasmi
Maria Kalaiji
Hinjal Kumar
Mahesh Kumar
Naveed Majeed
Nitin Mathais
Younus Mohammad
Nawar Al Qassimi
Mohamad Rida Al Saadei
Reem Shadid
Asad Siddique
Younus Suliman
Wasan Yousif

Technical and Production Team
Masroof Ahmed
Muhammad Atif
Amin Ul Haq Abdul Rauf
Fazel Rahman
Joy Pulikkottil
Sunil Mathew
Muhammad Farooq
Hassan Darwish Haikal
Habib Akhtar Hameed
AbdulGhaffar Fazal Hussain
Arshad Khalil
Mahesh Dharmmarajan
Atlas Khan Amir Dawar Khan
Ibrahim Khan Qadeem Khan
Muhammad Khan Mira Khan
Muslim Khan Shah Bazir Khan
Wasim Khan
Zabit Ullah Wilayat Khan
Abid Amir Dawar Khan
Noufal Muhammed Koya
Aswani Kummar
Abdul Rahman Mavila Kandy
Sudheersha Mohamed
Salil Abdul Salam
Abdul Khaliq Shan Muhammad
Safdar Khan Sher Muhammad
Satheesh Mundeerath
Shakir Mohmood Nasir
Moidu Koroth Saidalu
Khalid Sami
Shajahan Kannokaran Sulaiman
Ayoub Khan Gul Sultan

Acknowledgments
Rahel Aima
Nora Akawi
Lucia Alonso
Dalal Alsayer
Amale Andraos
Kirsten Anker
Lina Attalah
Sahar Attia
Muhammad Aziz
Salma Belal
Ahmad Borham
Charlotte Bouckaert
Abboudi Bou Jaoude
David Burns
Mark Campbell
John Carty
Max Celar
Tony Chakar
Yasmina El Chami
Fred Chaney
Belinda Cook
Louise Darblay
Karen Dayman
Jawad Dukhgan
Ben Eastham
Mohamed Elshahed
Hannah Elsisi
Ghalia Elsrakbi
Bassem Fahmy
Heba Farid
Nadine Fattaleh
Fehras Publishing Practices
Marco Ferrari
Tarek Abou El Fetouh
Tarsha Finney
Marco Galofaro
Bassam Haddad
Nabeel El Hadi
Monika Halkort
Mona Harb
Salah M. Hassan
Samia Henni
Beth Hughes
Kareem Ibrahim
May Al-Ibrashy
Saba Innab
Raghda Jaber
Sean Jacobs
Sam Jacoby
Rowan Kandil
Farhan Karim
Amr Abdel Kawi
Maher Kayyali
Omnia Khalil
Jessika Khazrik
David Kim
Tigran Kostandyan
Clara Kraft
Maha Maamoun
Ahmad Makia
Fadi Mansour
Mahy Mourad
Omar Nagati
Edwin Nasr
Michael O'Donnell
Marina Otero Verzier
Frans Parthesius
Ippolito Pestellini Laparelli
Asseel Al-Ragam
Mark Rappolt
Vincent de Rijk
Bassem Saad
Ali Q. Al Sagban
Steve Salembier
Mohammad Bassam Samara
Eman Shafiq
Alex Shams
Robin Snowdon
Amira el Solh
Beth Stryker
Ala Tannir
Tasnim Tinawi
Christine Tohme
Sonia Vaz Borges
Eric Verdeil
Lawrence Wallen
Tarek Waly
Ala Younis
Nabeela Zeitou
Ashkal Alwan, Beirut
Mangkaja Arts Resource Agency
Sarab Project, Jordan
Startup Haus, Cairo
Studio X Amman, Jordan
Zawya Cinema, Cairo

RIGHTS OF FUTURE GENERATIONS:
PROPOSITIONS

This is the second volume to be published in conjunction with the Sharjah Architecture Triennial 2019. The first volume, *Rights of Future Generations: Conditions,* was published by Hatje Cantz in 2019.

Editor
Adrian Lahoud

Coeditor
Andrea Bagnato

Associate Editors
Edwin Nasr, Jumanah Younis, Kasia Wlaszczyk

Book Design
Morcos Key
(Wael Morcos, Jon Key,
Rouba Yammine)

Arabic Translations
The Archilogue
Ziad Dallal

Arabic Copyediting and Proofreading
Suneela Mubayi, Bekriah Mawasi

English Proofreading
Aaron Bogart

Transcriptions
Ines Tazi

Project Management
Claire Cichy, Hatje Cantz
Dorothee Hahn

Production
Stefanie Kruszyk, Hatje Cantz

Printing and Binding
GRASPO CZ, A.S.

Printed on Munken Polar 100 g/m², Munken Lynx 90 g/m², Arctic Volume White 130 g/m²

Published by Hatje Cantz Verlag GmbH
Mommsenstrasse 27
10629 Berlin, Germany
www.hatjecantz.com
A Ganske Publishing Group Company

Sharjah Architecture Triennial
Sharjah, United Arab Emirates
www.sharjaharchitecture.org

ISBN 978-3-7757-4872-8

Printed in the Czech Republic

Image Credits

Rights of Future Generations Artwork
(pp. 6–7, 184, 249, 313)
Michael Oswell

Rights of Future Generations Photography
(pp. 32–33, 46–47, 62–63, 74–75, 88–89, 106–107, 118–119, 132–133, 146–147, 160–161, 174–175)
Satoshi Fujiwara

Exhibition Photography (pp. 254–297)
Marco Cappelletti with Flavio Pescatori

Public Program Photography (pp. 300–311)
Talie Eigeland
Matthew Twaddell
Sharjah Architecture Triennial

Cover Image: Satoshi Fujiwara, 2019

CW00919788

Palazzo Versace

The culinary stylings and splendour of an inspirational hotel

Chef – Steve Szabo

"Where there is no extravagance there is no love,
and where there is no love there is no understanding."

Oscar Wilde

RECIPES BY STEVE SZABO
PHOTOGRAPHY BY DEAN CAMBRAY

Gastronomy

From the Ancient Greek words for stomach (gastros) and knowledge (nomos), gastronomy is the study of the relationship between culture and food. Because around great food there exists dance, drama, painting, sculpture, literature, architecture and music.

PALAZZO VERSAC
Steve Sza

Around the celebrated food at Palazzo Versace, also, there exists a fiery, fun-loving Welshman called Steve Szabo who, as one of his most devoted Gold Coast colleagues once said in a moment of glorious understatement, "takes a bit of getting used to". Which he does. Quite a bit. But unquestionably, it is worth the effort.

Szabo joined Palazzo Versace in December, 2001, some months after the hotel had opened for business, and quickly showed himself to be a man able to create and deliver food that would satisfy the stratospheric expectations imposed on the hotel by the presence of the Versace brand.

Szabo is a thoughtful chef. Since he was 15, he has thought of little else but mastering and developing his craft. He began his training in a kitchen in Swansea. He excelled and, within years, had been snapped up by a London establishment in which he continued to learn, listen and create. It soon became evident, however, that Szabo was a man with his own approach to the culinary arts. He was, and remains, a rugged outdoorsman with a wicked wit – an enthusiastic hunter, a fine wing shot, a practical joker and a man not afraid to speak his mind. With Szabo, what you see, and what you hear, is what you get. While his food can be spectacular, what you taste is as direct, honest and to the point as the man himself.

Among his many responsibilities, Szabo has had to assemble, and maintain, a top brigade of chefs at Palazzo Versace.

"Things you look for in someone you hope will develop into a great chef are the ability to teach themselves, and enough passion to ensure they do it without considering the personal cost.

"I look for the young chef who sees a more accomplished chef making puff pastry, while he has only ever used frozen. His reaction will not be to wonder why anyone would bother, but to learn how to do it. He will buy his own butter and flour and try to make it at home. And if it doesn't work, he will go on making it, and making it, until it does."

From the time Szabo came to Australia in 1988, aged 27 and fresh from his London experiences, he showed himself to be a man of extraordinary determination and ability. He settled in Melbourne where he had accepted a position at the new Grand Hyatt and, after adjusting to the pace and rhythms of the city, he opened two spectacular restaurants of his own – Roses and Olive, both of which dazzled the critics, and both of which offered an approach to the use of fresh ingredients that broke new ground in a city regarded by many as the nation's gastronomic capital.

And then, the opportunity arose for Szabo to revamp an iconic Melbourne establishment with a national following. That establishment was Jimmy Watson's, the iconic Carlton wine bar which, in the hands of Alan Watson, son of the legendary wine merchant Jimmy, was ready to spread its culinary wings.

"Jimmy's was more famous for its incomparable range of museum wines than for its food. The idea was to reshape the upstairs area of the old, heritage building into a unique restaurant in which we would offer fine dining and, where possible, match dishes to heritage wines no longer available anywhere else but here."

Jimmy Watson's was declared a sensation. It was awarded Two Hats in the *Melbourne Good Food Guide*, and remained at that exalted level while Szabo remained at the stoves.

But sadly for Jimmy's, and for Melbourne, the Gold Coast called. Szabo had met, and fallen in love with Zorica, also a fine chef. They married and Zorica raised the possibility of a move, even for a short time, to the Gold Coast, where her parents had settled.

"To be honest, I heard about the job in Vanitas at Palazzo Versace and I took it, purely because of Zorica. But it has turned out to be just about the best move I have ever made in my life.

"The way my role at the hotel has grown has played a large part in my satisfaction with life up here. We work hard in these kitchens, but we all love it, and we have a great time. We know that what we are doing is good, very good. But then, we also know that what we are expected to do has to be good."

As a hotel, Palazzo Versace is uniquely attuned to a lifestyle, an approach, a set of values and an insistence upon elegance, beauty and measured extravagance at all times. No corners were cut, no refinement overlooked, no expense spared in the development of this establishment. But has this set the tone for the food, also?

"The owners and operators recognise and understand quality. But also, they want things to be distinctive, cutting edge. And that was my brief," says Szabo.

"They have given me freedom to do things the way I think they should be done. It's a huge responsibility, but I thrive on that sort of challenge."

As executive chef, Szabo shoulders an awesome load: there always seem to be new restaurants opening under the Sunland banner and lavish dinner parties masterminded on hotel-managed properties.

"There is always something to be thought about," says Szabo. *"It might be VIP guests, complicated requests, or something completely new. The work load is heavy, but always interesting and stimulating.*

"I have always believed that when a chef gets bored, that's when they should move on because, inevitably, their inspiration will die and their food will become routine."

Clearly, there is little chance of this happening at Palazzo Versace where, according to Szabo, the one thing that every chef knows for sure is that he, or she, will never be bored.

The design concepts in place at the hotel – the requirement for every meal to look, as well as taste, like a Versace creation – could frustrate, even infuriate, an inflexible chef. But not Szabo.

"When I started, I would have given anything for a couple of white plates on which to serve dishes. But that just shows how easy it is for chefs to become blinkered, too set in their ways.

"The more I worked with the Versace china, the more I came to understand it and appreciate it. I have not had to make any concessions to accommodate the plate designs – a chef has to be able to put food on anything. But putting food on plates that are beautiful to start with, how hard is that?"

Szabo's unique approach to life, and his earthy charm, have stood him in good stead at Palazzo Versace.

"We get famous people through constantly, but I treat them all the same, and they seem to accept it. They know that with me, what they see is what they get. I have neither the time nor the inclination to adjust the way I go about my business."

Szabo's other great strength, as he is quick to acknowledge, is his support staff, and in particular the quartet of accomplished chefs with which he has surrounded himself – Brett Hobson, Charles Duffin, Christopher Smith and Martin Glutz, the incomparable chef de cuisine at Vanitas, Palazzo Versace's signature restaurant. Even in this distinguished company, Glutz stands out.

"He's my rock," admits Szabo. *"I would have to say he is the calmest chef I have ever met, and one of the very best. He has worked in some extraordinary places around the world, he is passionate about food and he is a good friend.*

"His thought processes are frighteningly like mine. He thinks outside the square and if something is not quite working, he soon works out why. And fixes it. He understands things."

He understands, for example, Szabo's eccentricities – like the fact that this man who works daily with lobsters, caviar, foie gras and the like insists that his favourite food in the world is a bacon and marmalade sandwich: he eats several daily.

"But then, I am a very simple eater. I will eat anything in the world, and appreciate extraordinary food and exotic ingredients, but I prefer simplicity," he says.

"When I was an apprentice in Wales, we would go down to the beach and collect periwinkles. We would fill a kettle with them, boil them, and sit picking them out with needles. I loved that.

"But it's all to do with the mood I am in, and I think that is true of everyone who understands fine food. In Vanitas, it is up to us to set the mood, and then satisfy it. When I go out, I want to be served food I would not cook at home, and I think that is true of everyone."

And is there one very special dish that appears on the menu at Vanitas that, in the opinion of the man who created it, defines the place and adds to the Palazzo Versace experience?

"Possibly, yes. It is a prawn version of chicken Kiev, bursting with garlic butter. Very Queensland, very decadent and very Versace. Nobody can resist that dish. And nobody should try."

vanitas

VANITAS – LATIN FOR VANITY – REFERS TO A TYPE OF STILL-LIFE PAINTING CONSISTING OF A COLLECTION OF OBJECTS THAT SYMBOLISE THE BREVITY OF HUMAN LIFE AND THE TRANSIENCE OF EARTHLY PLEASURES AND ACHIEVEMENTS (E.G., A HUMAN SKULL, A MIRROR, BROKEN POTTERY).

Fine word, Vanitas – a word alive with artistic endeavour and philosophical conclusions and possibilities. A word tinged with the exotic and the macabre and also, therefore, a word imbued with inspiration for suitable discourse and eternal debate.

Is life too short? Do we devote too much time and attention to the pursuit of earthly pleasure and too little to achieving greatness, or is it the other way around? Does anything about our lives make sense, or carry weight? Or, indeed, is life the only thing that makes sense and carries weight?

Vanitas is a word that tells stories and prompts questions. It is a word alive with imagery – part of the title of a haunting work by 17th century Dutch master Pieter Claesz, Vanitas Still Life with the Spinario, 1628, which resides, solemnly, in Amsterdam's incomparable Rijksmuseum. And which, once viewed, is something that will remain with you. *Always.*

Vanitas, therefore, is an inspired name for a restaurant which, once patronised, will not easily be forgotten – a place that celebrates the earthly pleasures of food and wine and offers an exquisite canvas for the artistry of a master chef. A restaurant that is part of a refined and inspired hotel in an exquisite setting in a glorious location: a place that makes absolute sense of enlightened indulgence.

Now, a meal in Vanitas might be expected to begin as all great meals should begin – with a tall flute of perfectly chilled Champagne, perhaps the house offering here, which is the crisp and elegant Louis Roederer non-vintage. Or, should a more ornate overture be called for, a suitable beginning might be a Versace kir royale which is, essentially, a flute of this same Champagne, judiciously stained and elevated with a splash of Crème de Cassis. Either way, you will discover that in the blink of an eye, or perhaps two, your appetite has been sharpened to a razor's edge and that you, fortuitously, are in just the right frame of mind to make those vital decisions that can no longer be sidestepped.

You may, of course, choose to embark upon the degustation menu of the day, devised by the restaurant's chef de cuisine. This could mean you would begin with a modicum of foie gras mousse on a fragment of toasted, house-made brioche with a dried apricot relish before being further transported by a sliver or two of meticulously cured Atlantic salmon supporting a tian of crab, served with a scattering of risoni pasta and touched with a maple and dill dressing.

And, from there, you might progress to a gruyere and goat's cheese soufflé flanked by a segment of potato and prosciutto terrine, shavings of baby fennel and a dollop of cumin jam, all united at plate level with a measure of port wine reduction. By which time, I dare say, you would have concluded that you were in the very best of hands.

Alternatively, you may choose to construct a meal all of your own, as many of us do when we dine in Vanitas. On one memorable visit, for example, a meal unfolded, with the occasional murmur of approval and perhaps admiration from my dining companion, rather like this…

We had chosen to dine early enough to peer over the rims of our Champagne flutes into the remains of the golden evening light – just sufficient to highlight the ripples imposed by a gentle sea breeze that moved towards us, across the surface of the lagoon that laps at the restaurant's balcony on which we had chosen to take our aperitifs while we wrestled, contentedly and with surrender in our hearts, with the gastronomic options.

Finally, we made our choices and, as the night temperature began its descent to roughly the same level as the last of our fizz, we moved inside to a table from which we would be able to bask in the charm of the restaurant's signature mural, executed in the instantly recognisable style of legendary fashion illustrator Gladys Perint Palmer. We were eased into our seats and invited to make our choices from the warm, house-made rolls – paninni for me, the sourdough for her – served with discs of cultured French butter. Whereupon our amuse bouches arrived and invited our full and undivided attention.

For these, trunks of a richly flavoured blood sausage or black pudding had been marooned in a bowl of glorious New Caledonian prawn bisque touched with cognac. The trunks had been topped, first with a small, roasted scallop and then a delicate slice of black truffle, the whole mounted with a crisp aerofoil of pancetta. Small, certainly, but exquisite. The stage was set.

We had drained our flutes before embarking on the amuses bouches and, in their places, came glasses of a lightly oaked, '04 Wills Domain chardonnay that aligned perfectly with both the amuses bouches and, perhaps even more stylishly, with the dish that followed – a tile of pork belly, twice cooked, infused with anise flavours and accompanied, shyly, by poached and dangerously fresh Moreton Bay bugs, a few bullets of basil gnocchi and a flimsy shrapnel of bok choy.

Then, a hint of Japanoise – a cleansing jelly of traditional plum wine that worked admirably and warned us of impending extravagances of flavour, which was hardly bad news.

Next, main courses: these were, for her, of milk-fed Tamworth lamb, braised and then roasted with shimeji mushrooms, green olives, beans and couscous – silky, delicate meat with a hint of pink, delicately sauced, immensely satisfying.

And for me, a roasted loin of venison, dark without and deepest burgundy within, served with a carrot puree, onion marmalade, and wallowing in a dark jus dotted with chestnuts and infused with juniper berries. Glorious, also. And, with the lamb, elegantly matched to a '04 Scorpo shiraz from Victoria's Mornington Peninsula. Perfect, yet again.

My bread and butter pudding, perhaps the greatest of all retro desserts, was a thick disc of silken opulence, given an additional hint of olde English extravagance with a globe of nutmeg ice-cream. Gorgeous, and demonstrating rather more restraint than her surprising light, but suitably decadent chocolate fondant that paddled in the lightest and purest of raspberry sauces.

With these, we shared a half-bottle of crisp, deeply refreshing, tantalisingly sweet Scrapona Moscato d'Asti. More of that confounded perfection.

It was left, then, for us simply to digest our meals, both physically and philosophically, as we returned our gazes to the lagoon which, with the demise of the sea breeze, had regained its glassy composure. Beyond it, the star-flecked night sky provided an ideal place into which to gaze, pleasantly unfocused, as we sipped ancient Calvados and inhaled its aroma of fresh-picked apples, released by the warmth of our hands around the fragile snifters into which it had been splashed.

Memorable? Vanitas? You tell me…

BOB HART
Melbourne Food Critic

RECIPE

From the Latin "recipe" meaning to take back, suggesting that listed ingredients should be taken out of storage. In modern usage, a recipe is a set of instructions telling how to replicate any dish.

There are as many recipes in the world as there are golden leaves in a temperate Autumn. All attempt to add to the general fund of culinary knowledge, but the vast majority simply build upon, or occasionally detract from, recipes that have come before.

There are, however, recipe collections that offer something new, distinctive and original. And in terms of the recipes that follow, written by Palazzo Versace executive chef Steve Szabo, you are dealing with such a collection.

Szabo, as is to be expected of a man who has risen to such a rank in one of the world's leading hotels, is a master craftsman and an innovative and highly creative chef.

His recipes build upon mainly European gastronomic traditions, but are set apart through the use of some of the finest and freshest raw ingredients in the world – ingredients readily available to a chef who has chosen to live and work in a subtropical, oceanic paradise in the southern hemisphere, and who has adapted to his idyllic surroundings.

But while Szabo's creations are spectacular, they are inevitably delicious, easy to eat, and comparatively straight forward to replicate for the competent home cook. The recipes are precise, explicit and easy to follow. Every recipe has been painstakingly tested, and then exquisitely photographed to show the reader exactly how the finished product should look.

The rest, now, is up to you...

150g (5 1/2oz) A-grade tuna

Tuna Marinade
1/4 cup mirin
1/4 cup sake
1/4 cup soy sauce
1 small red chilli, deseeded and sliced
1cm (1/2in) piece ginger, cut into julienne*
2 garlic cloves, finely chopped

Dukkah
90g (3 1/4oz) black sesame seeds
90g (3 1/4oz) sesame seeds
1 1/2 tbsp cumin seeds
100g (3 1/2oz) hazelnuts, roasted, skinned* and very finely chopped
2 tsp sea salt
1 1/2 tsp cracked black peppercorns

DUKKAH TUNA

This tuna can be served with any type of salad, pickled vegetable or salsa. You could use some of the marinade as a dipping sauce or as a salad dressing. The excess dukkah can be kept in a sealed container in the refrigerator for up to a year.

To make tuna marinade, bring mirin and sake to the boil in a small saucepan and flambé* to burn off alcohol. Remove from heat and add soy sauce, chilli, ginger and garlic. Set aside to cool and allow flavours to infuse.

To make dukkah, combine all ingredients in a bowl and mix well.

Cut tuna into three 3 x 10cm (1 1/4 x 4in) logs. Arrange tuna logs on a bamboo steamer tray. Steam for 3 minutes, remove from steamer and place in marinade. Cover and marinate overnight in refrigerator.

Cut tuna logs into 1cm (1/2in) thick slices and roll outer edges in dukkah. Arrange on a plate and serve.

Serves 3

Definitions can be found in the Glossary (see page 190).

4 yellow golf-ball sized
vine-ripened tomatoes
1 cup mixed baby salad leaves
120g (4 1/4oz) celeriac, cut into batons
1 granny smith apple, cut into batons
4 tbsp sevruga caviar
1/3 cup extra virgin olive oil
sea salt and cracked black pepper

Gazpacho
1/3 cup olive oil
5 yellow vine-ripened tomatoes,
deseeded and roughly diced
1/2 telegraph cucumber, peeled,
deseeded and roughly diced
1/2 white onion, diced
1 yellow capsicum (pepper),
deseeded and diced
1 garlic clove, finely chopped
2 tbsp white wine vinegar
4 fresh basil leaves
splash of Tabasco sauce
sea salt
celery salt*

Yellow Tomato Gazpacho

To make gazpacho, heat olive oil in a large saucepan over medium heat and lightly sauté tomatoes, cucumber, onion, capsicum and garlic until softened. Deglaze* with vinegar and continue to cook for 5 minutes or until vegetables are tender. Add basil and season with Tabasco, sea salt and celery salt. Purée in a blender and pass through a fine chinois*. Allow to cool, then check for correct seasoning.

Score base of each tomato and blanch for 30 seconds in rapidly boiling water. Refresh in iced water and peel skin away from flesh. Cut top off each tomato and scrape out membrane and seeds with a small spoon.

Combine salad leaves, celeriac and apple in a small bowl and gently mix. Spoon into cavity of each tomato and place a quenelle* of caviar on top.

Place a stuffed tomato in centre of each serving bowl and pour gazpacho around tomato. Drizzle over extra virgin olive oil, season with salt and pepper and serve.

Serves 4

2 tbsp olive oil
1kg (2lb 4oz) fresh black mussels, cleaned and debearded*
1/2 onion, cut into julienne*
1 carrot, cut into julienne*
2 garlic cloves, finely sliced
1 tbsp baby capers, rinsed and drained
1 small red chilli, deseeded and cut into thin strips
1/2 cup riesling
1/2 cup double chicken stock *(see page 186)*
100g (3 1/2oz) butter
4 tbsp finely chopped fresh flat leaf (Italian) parsley
cracked black pepper

STEAMED MUSSELS

Only use the freshest mussels for this recipe. If any do not open once cooked, do not use them as this means that the mussels were dead before cooking. It is better to discard one or two unopened mussels than to continue cooking them in the pot and risk having the rest overcooked.

Heat a large, heavy-based saucepan over high heat until it gives off a haze. Add olive oil, mussels, onion, carrot, garlic, capers and chilli and sauté for 30 seconds. Add riesling, chicken stock and butter, cover with a lid, and cook, shaking pan every now and then, for 1-2 minutes or until mussels have opened. Remove from heat and place mussels in a large serving dish. Return pan to high heat and reduce cooking liquid by one-third, add parsley and season with pepper. Pour cooking liquid over mussels and serve with crusty bread.

Serves 4

4 whole large quails
5 egg yolks, lightly beaten

Salt Crust
1/2 cup fresh thyme leaves
1/2 cup fresh rosemary leaves
4 garlic cloves, chopped
600g (1lb 5oz) table salt
14 egg whites
1.2kg (2lb 12oz) plain (all-purpose) flour
150ml (5fl oz) water

Preheat oven to 190°C (375°F/Gas 5)

SALT-CRUSTED QUAILS

This dish is also fantastic if you substitute poussins (spatchcocks or baby chickens) for the quail.

Line two baking trays with baking paper.

To make salt crust, place thyme, rosemary, garlic and salt in a food processor and blitz. Combine egg whites, flour and water in a separate bowl and mix well. Add flour mixture to herb mixture and blitz to form a smooth dough.

Divide dough into 10 even pieces. Roll out 8 portions of dough to a thickness of 5mm (1/4in) on a lightly floured work surface. Place one piece on a prepared baking tray and place a quail in centre. Cover quail with a second piece of dough, brush edges with egg yolks and firmly seal using your fingers. You can then use your artistic flair to create the shape of a quail by attaching a head and wings using the two reserved pieces of salt dough. Brush dough with egg yolks. Repeat with remaining dough and quails. Place in oven for 20 minutes or until golden.

Serve by breaking salt crust at the dinner table and releasing the succulent quail from the crust. Serve with your choice of vegetables.

Serves 4

BEEF TARTARE WITH QUAIL EGGS & BABY HERBS

160g (5 3/4oz) beef tenderloin, trimmed
sea salt and cracked black pepper
2 hard-boiled eggs, shelled
1 tbsp aioli *(see page 186)*
1 tbsp baby capers
8 fresh chive tips
4 quail eggs
1/2 cup baby herbs, such as
fresh chives, basil and cress
2 tbsp extra virgin olive oil
4 white anchovy fillets

Very finely chop beef and season with salt and pepper.

Separate egg whites from yolks and finely grate yolks then finely grate whites.

To serve, smear some aioli on each serving plate. Divide beef into four portions, press each portion into a 5 x 10cm (2 x 4in) rectangle and arrange on aioli. Garnish each plate with egg white and yolk, capers, aioli, 2 chive tips and salt. Carefully remove top third of shell from each raw quail egg. Spoon a mound of grated egg yolk on to a teaspoon, stand quail egg in shell on top, sprinkle with pepper and place to one side on plate. Dress herbs with olive oil. Form anchovy into a ring around salad leaves and place on top of beef tartare.

Serves 4

SAUTÉED VEAL KIDNEYS & SWEETBREADS

8 x 30g (1oz) veal kidneys*, cleaned
4 x 50g (1 3/4oz) sweetbreads*, membrane removed
sea salt and cracked black pepper
1 cup plain (all-purpose) flour
3 tbsp peanut oil
4 French shallots, finely chopped
1 garlic clove, finely chopped
150g (5 1/2oz) oyster mushrooms, trimmed
120g (4 1/4oz) butter, chopped into dice
1/4 cup finely chopped fresh
flat leaf (Italian) parsley
2 tbsp chopped fresh thyme leaves
juice of 1 lemon

Season kidneys and sweetbreads with salt and pepper, dust with flour and shake off excess.

To an extremely hot, heavy-based frying pan, add oil, kidneys and sweetbreads and sauté for 1 minute or until beginning to caramelize. Add shallots, garlic and mushrooms, toss or stir to combine, and cook for a further 30 seconds. Add butter, parsley and thyme and cook until butter has melted and starts to bubble. Add lemon juice and remove from heat.

Arrange kidneys, sweetbreads and mushrooms on serving plates and serve with cooking juices.

Serves 4

POLYNESIAN BARRAMUNDI

The red wine fish sauce used in this dish is relatively easy to make and it goes with many varieties of fish: including monkfish (angler fish), red mullet, salmon and jewfish.

8 x 90g (3 1/4oz) barramundi fillets, with skin on
sea salt and cracked black pepper
10g (1/4oz) butter
32 shimeji mushrooms
baby chives, to garnish
12 baby fresh flat leaf (Italian) parsley leaves
12 shiso* leaves
12 tatsoi* leaves

Red Wine Fish Sauce
300g (10 1/2oz) salmon bones, cleaned and chopped
1/2 celery stalk, finely chopped
1/2 medium onion, finely chopped
1/2 small leek, cleaned and finely chopped
2 French shallots, finely chopped
4 button mushrooms, sliced
1 cup red wine
1 cup double chicken stock *(see page 186)*
3 sprigs fresh thyme
20g (3/4oz) unsalted butter, chopped into dice

Crumb Mixture
100g (3 1/2oz) butter
4 French shallots, finely chopped
250g (9oz) fresh breadcrumbs
2 hard-boiled eggs, shelled
2 tbsp finely chopped fresh flat leaf (Italian) parsley
sea salt and cracked black pepper
4 tsp truffle oil

Preheat oven to 190°C (375°F/Gas 5).

To make red wine fish sauce, combine salmon bones, celery, onion, leek, shallots and mushrooms in a heavy-based saucepan and sauté over medium heat for 5-7 minutes or until just beginning to brown. Deglaze* with red wine and reduce to about 2 tablespoons of glaze. Add chicken stock and thyme and simmer for 15 minutes or until reduced by two-thirds. Strain into a container, cover and chill in refrigerator. To finish, reheat sauce in a saucepan over low heat and monter* in butter, whisking until emulsified.

To make crumb mixture, melt butter in a frying pan, add shallots and sauté over medium heat for 2 minutes or until transparent. Add breadcrumbs and cook for 5 minutes or until a light golden colour. Remove and place on a tray. Separate egg whites from yolks and finely grate yolks then egg whites on to crumb mixture. Add parsley, season with salt and pepper, drizzle over truffle oil and gently toss to combine.

Season barramundi with salt and pepper. Heat a large, non-stick frying pan over high heat, add barramundi and sear, skin-side down, for 3 minutes or until skin is crisp. Turn and transfer to oven for 6 minutes or until just cooked. Remove from oven and press crumb mixture on to crisped skin of each piece of barramundi. Place barramundi, crumb-side up, under preheated grill *(broiler)* for 30 seconds or until golden brown.

Meanwhile, heat a large frying pan over high heat, add butter and mushrooms and sauté for 3 minutes or until mushrooms are golden.

Place barramundi on serving plates, being careful not to tip off crumb mixture. Garnish with mushrooms, chives, parsley, shiso and tatsoi, drizzle over a little red wine fish sauce and serve.

Serves 4

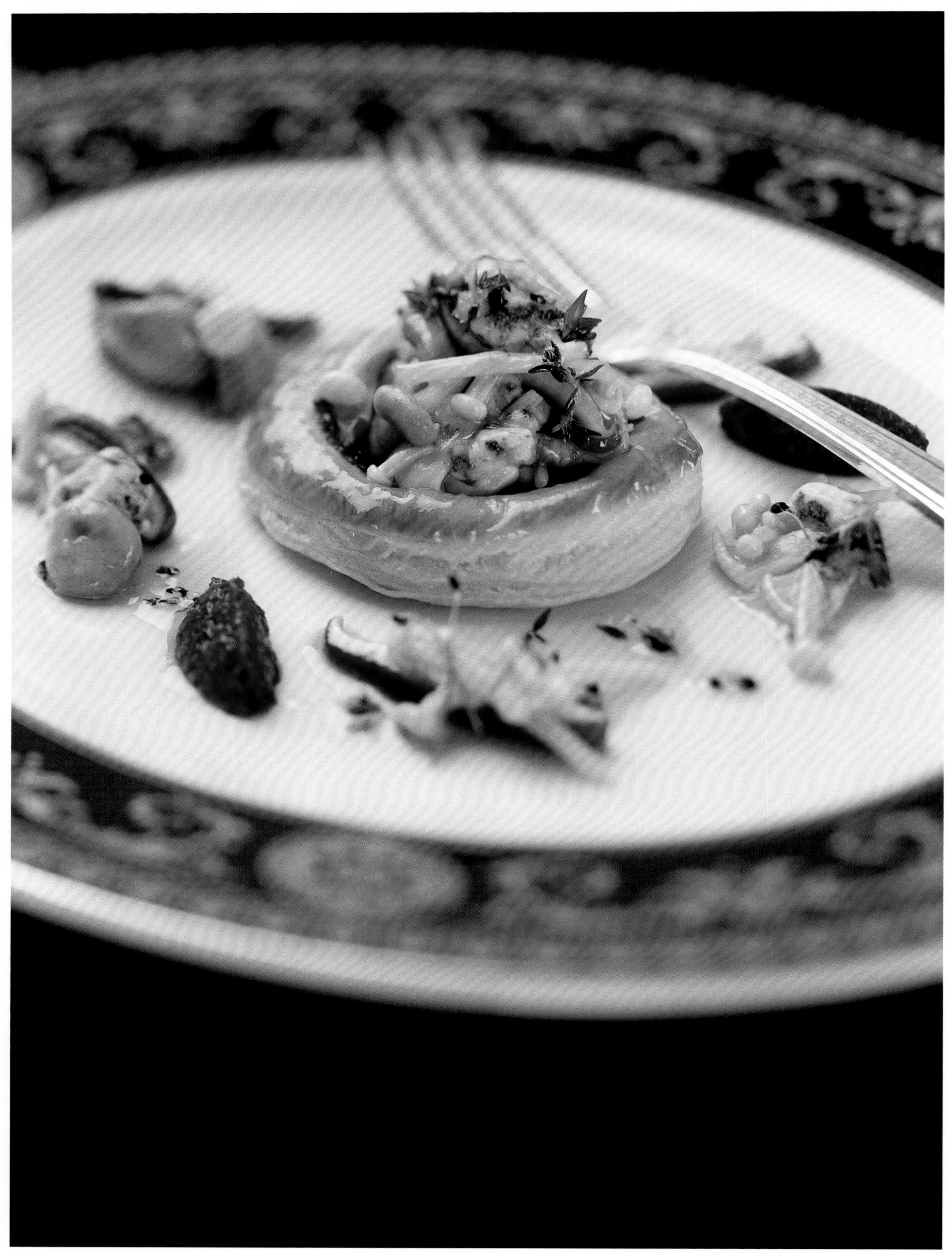

Mushroom Tart

200g (7oz) puff pastry *(see page 189)*
2 tbsp olive oil
2 French shallots, finely chopped
300g (10 1/2oz) mixed mushrooms, shiitake, enoki, shimeji, oyster, pine, baby button, field, sliced
30g (1oz) gorgonzola dolce
2 tbsp fresh thyme leaves
sea salt and cracked black pepper
40g (1 1/2oz) butter
2 tbsp extra virgin olive oil, to garnish

Black Olive Tapenade
1/3 cup olive oil
2 French shallots, finely chopped
100g (3 1/2oz) Ligurian olives
6 anchovy fillets
1 tbsp chopped fresh chives
1 tbsp fresh lemon juice
sea salt and cracked black pepper

Pastry Glaze
1 egg yolk
4 drops of olive oil
pinch of sea salt

Preheat oven to 200°C (400°F/Gas 6)

To make black olive tapenade, heat olive oil in a large frying pan over medium heat, add shallots and sauté over medium heat for 3 minutes or until softened. Add olives, anchovies and chives and sauté gently for 10 minutes to allow flavours to develop. Blitz in a food processor or chop by hand into a fine paste. Add lemon juice and season with salt and pepper.

To make pastry glaze, combine egg yolk, olive oil and salt in a small bowl and mix together with a whisk.

To make pastry cases, roll out puff pastry on a lightly floured work surface to a thickness of 5mm (1/4in). Cut pastry into four 8cm (3 1/4in) rounds and place on a baking tray lined with baking paper. Prick base of each pastry case with tines of a fork – this will prevent pastry from rising too much. Spread a 1cm (1/2in) thick layer of tapenade in centre of each pastry disc, leaving a 1cm (1/2in) rim around edge. Then using a pastry brush, brush pastry glaze over exposed pastry at rim. Transfer pastry cases to oven for 4-5 minutes or until golden.

Heat olive oil in a large frying pan, add shallots and mushrooms and sauté over high heat for 2-3 minutes or until coloured. Add gorgonzola and 1 1/2 tablespoons of thyme. Season with salt and pepper and finish by gently stirring in butter until melted and well combined.

Place each pastry case on a serving plate and top with sautéed mushroom mixture. Place 2 or 3 quenelles* of tapenade around each mushroom tart and drizzle over mushroom juices remaining in pan. Sprinkle over remaining thyme, drizzle over extra virgin olive oil and serve.

Serves 4

This tapenade recipe can be adjusted by adding chillies or other spices of your choice to create your own version.

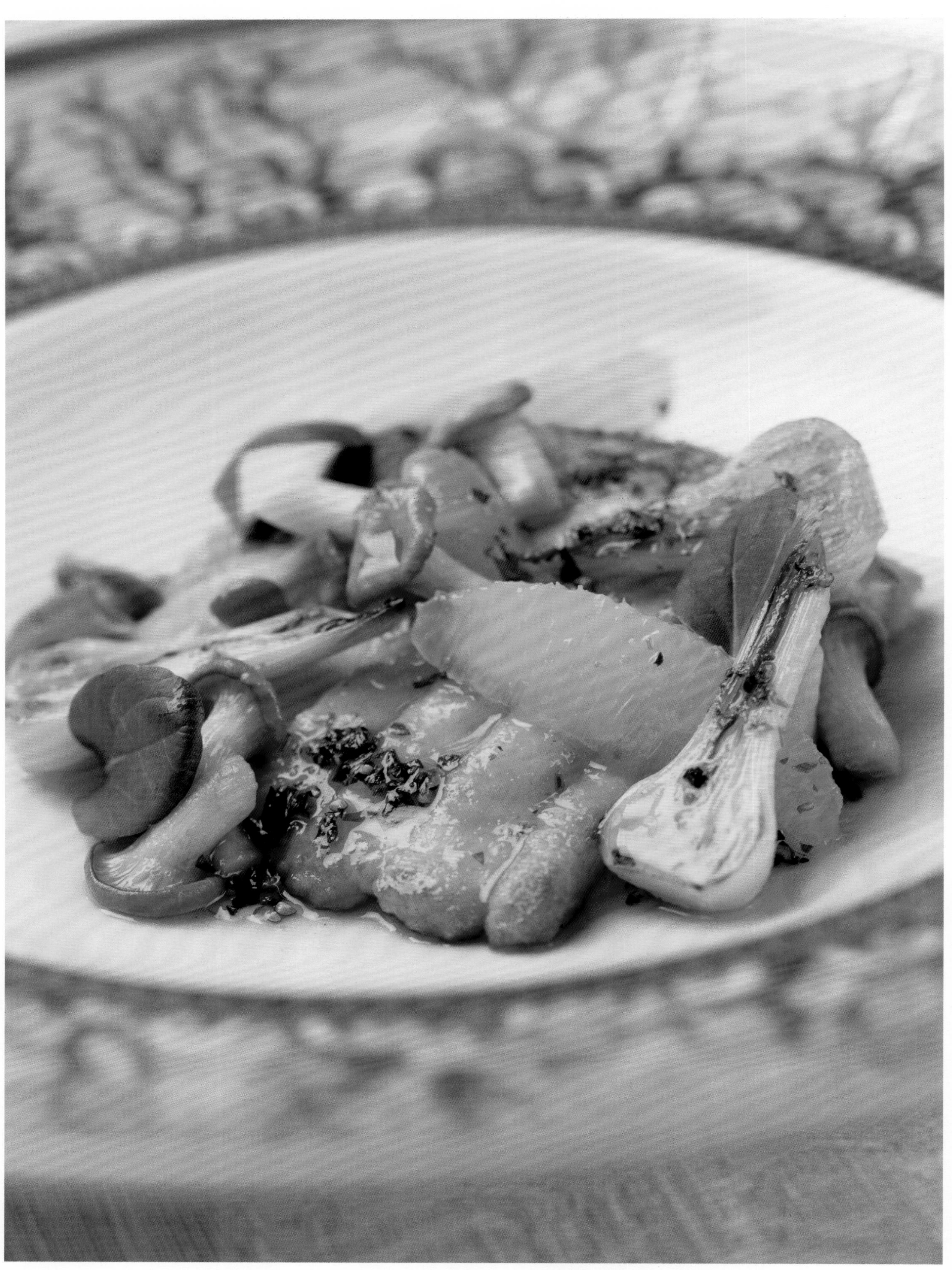

4 x 180g (6 1/2oz) skate wings
2 tsp salt
1 tbsp white vinegar
3 tbsp olive oil
200g (7oz) unsalted butter, chopped into dice
8 small wild garlic* cloves,
blanched and halved lengthways
40 shimeji mushrooms
4 tsp fresh thyme leaves
16 lime segments
16 lemon segments
16-20 mâche* (lamb's lettuce) leaves

Seasoned Flour
100g (3 1/2oz) plain (all-purpose) flour
1 tsp cayenne pepper
1 tsp paprika
2 tsp salt
2 tsp cracked black pepper
1 tbsp garlic powder*
2 tbsp finely chopped fresh marjoram,
thyme and flat leaf (Italian) parsley

Skate Wings with Sautéed Shimeji Mushrooms

To make seasoned flour, combine all ingredients in a shallow bowl and mix well.

Rub skate wings with salt and vinegar to remove slime, rinse in cold water, drain and pat dry with paper towel. Dust skate wings in seasoned flour, gently shaking off excess.

Heat olive oil in a large frying pan over medium heat, add skate wings, in batches if necessary, and sauté on each side for 1 1/2 minutes or until golden brown. Add butter and cook for 30 seconds or until butter starts to colour. Transfer skate to a warmed serving plate and set aside. Add garlic, mushrooms and thyme to pan and sauté for 30 seconds. Add lime and lemon segments and allow to heat through. Spoon over skate, garnish with mâche leaves and serve.

Serves 4

1 sheet gold leaf*
25g (1oz) unsalted pistachio nuts,
blanched, peeled and chopped

Vanilla Panna Cotta
2 gelatine sheets
300ml (10 1/2fl oz) pouring cream
150ml (5fl oz) milk
125g (4 1/2oz) vanilla sugar*
1 vanilla bean, split lengthways
and seeds scraped

Malted Vanilla Milkshake
2 scoops vanilla ice-cream *(see page 186)*
1 tbsp malt powder
100ml (3 1/2fl oz) milk
honey, to taste (optional)

Vanilla Panna Cotta with Pistachio Nuts

To make vanilla panna cotta, soak gelatine sheets in cold water for 2 minutes or until softened. Combine cream, milk, half of the vanilla sugar and the vanilla bean in a saucepan and bring just to the boil. Whisk in remaining vanilla sugar and softened gelatine sheets. Strain through a muslin-lined strainer or a fine chinois* and set aside to cool. When cool, pour into four 100ml (3 1/2fl oz) dariole moulds *(or something similar)* and place in refrigerator for 2-3 hours to set.

To make malted vanilla milkshake, place all ingredients in a blender and blend until frothy.

Unmould panna cottas by dipping moulds in hot water and inverting on to serving plates. Pour milkshake into shot glasses and top with gold leaf. Decorate plate with remaining milkshake froth. Sprinkle pistachio nuts around plate and serve with a teaspoon topped with remaining pistachio nuts.

Serves 4

1 vanilla bean, split lengthways
and seeds scraped
2 tbsp maple syrup
2 tbsp chopped walnuts
1 dragon fruit (strawberry pear), peeled and diced
8 fresh mint leaves, cut into julienne*

Fig and Almond Torte
250g (9oz) dried figs, roughly chopped
1/4 cup whisky
4 egg whites
1 1/2 cups icing (confectioners') sugar
250g (9oz) dark couverture chocolate, finely chopped
250g (9oz) flaked almonds

Preheat oven to 150°C (300°F/Gas 2)

Fig & Almond Choc Chip Torte

Line a 15cm (6in) square cake tin with foil.

To make fig and almond torte, place figs and whisky in an airtight container and set aside to soak overnight. Transfer to a food processor and blitz to break down slightly. Whisk egg whites in a large mixing bowl until soft peaks form, add sugar and whisk to a firm meringue. Fold in chocolate and almonds with a large metal spoon, then fold in figs and whisky. Spoon mixture into prepared cake tin and bake for 40 minutes or until firm to touch.

Combine vanilla seeds and maple syrup in a small mixing bowl and set aside.

Cut fig and almond torte into 4 portions. Place a portion on each serving plate and top with walnuts. Decorate plate with vanilla maple syrup, dragon fruit and mint and serve.

Serves 4

Pigeon with Soba Noodles

125g (4 1/2oz) soba noodles*
2 pigeons, legs removed
and kept for another use
sea salt and cracked black pepper
1 tsp ground turmeric
4 tbsp peanut oil
6 baby shiitake mushrooms
2 tbsp trimmed enoki mushrooms
2 baby bok choy (pak choy), trimmed
2 French shallots, finely chopped
1 tbsp julienne* of nori
1 tbsp sesame seeds
1/2 cup baby watercress leaves
12 lime segments

Dressing
2 tbsp cider vinegar
1 tbsp wholegrain mustard
2 tsp ground turmeric
5 tbsp olive oil
sea salt and cracked black pepper

Preheat oven to 200°C (400°F/Gas 6)

Place soba noodles in a large saucepan of boiling salted water and cook for 4 minutes. Refresh in cold water and drain.

Rub skin of each pigeon with salt, pepper and turmeric.

Heat 2 tablespoons of peanut oil in a large pan until very hot, add pigeons and seal on all sides for 30 seconds or until golden brown. Transfer to oven for 7 minutes. Remove and rest in a warm place for 10-15 minutes.

In a separate pan, heat remaining 2 tablespoons of peanut oil over high heat and quickly sauté shiitake mushrooms, enoki mushrooms and bok choy for 2-3 minutes or until wilted. Remove from pan and set aside. Add shallots and cook for 2 minutes or until transparent *(residue heat and oil in pan will be enough to finish cooking shallots).* Remove shallots from pan.

To make dressing, deglaze* pan with cider vinegar, then add mustard and turmeric. Reduce to a paste, add olive oil and season with salt and pepper. Remove from heat.

Place noodles in a small bowl and season with a little dressing. Scatter over nori and sesame seeds.

To serve, twist a quarter of the noodles around a fork and place in centre of each serving plate. Repeat with remaining noodles. Remove pigeon breasts from bone, cut each into 6 slices and arrange around soba noodles. Scatter mushrooms and bok choy neatly around plate. Drizzle remaining dressing over pigeon, garnish with watercress and lime segments and serve.

Serves 4

30g (1oz) white chocolate
2 cups pouring cream
175g (6oz) dark couverture chocolate,
roughly chopped
90g (3 1/4oz) caster (superfine) sugar
4 egg yolks
1 tsp vanilla extract

Preheat oven to 170°C (325°F/Gas 3)

POT O' CHOCOLATE

This dish can be served with ice-cream – such as hazelnut, vanilla or honey – or whatever matches your personal taste. Fresh berries are a great addition in the summer months.

To make white chocolate curls, melt white chocolate in a heatproof bowl over a saucepan of simmering water. Thinly spread chocolate on to a marble board using a palette knife. When set, use a knife to scrape chocolate from marble so it forms curls.

Bring cream to a simmer in a saucepan over medium heat. Add dark chocolate and stir until melted. Remove from heat, add sugar, egg yolks and vanilla and strain through a fine chinois*. Pour mixture into 4 demitasse cups. Place cups in a bain-marie*, and fill with warm water two-thirds of the way up sides of each cup, transfer to oven for 20 minutes or until just set. Allow to cool down a little.

Decorate each pot o' chocolate with white chocolate curls and serve.

Serves 4

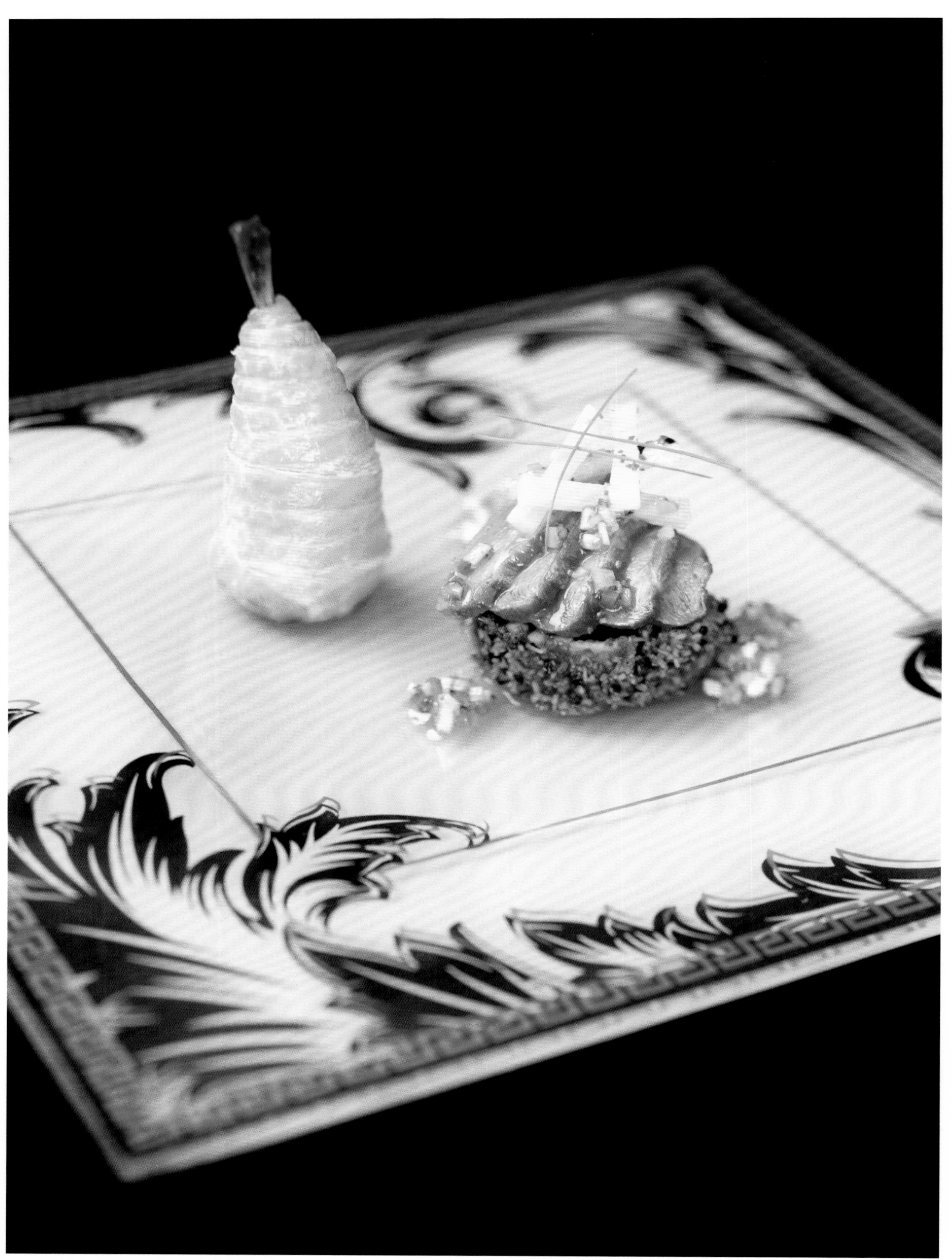

Braised Artichoke & Pigeon Salad

2 pigeons
sea salt and cracked black pepper
2 tbsp finely chopped blanched almonds
2 tbsp finely chopped dried apricots
150g (5 1/2oz) puff pastry *(see page 189)*
4 tbsp finely chopped chives
1 small potato, cooked and thinly sliced
4 chive stems, chopped into batons
4 tbsp vegetable and vanilla vinaigrette

Vegetable and Vanilla Vinaigrette
100ml (3 1/2fl oz) olive oil
2 French shallots, cut into fine brunoise*
1 carrot, cut into fine brunoise*
1 zucchini (courgette), skin cut into fine brunoise*
1/4 celeriac, cut into fine brunoise*
1 vanilla bean, split in half lengthways and seeds scraped
1 tbsp Champagne vinegar
sea salt and cracked black pepper

Blanc*
2 cups chicken stock *(see page 186)*
2 star anise
1 onion, chopped
2 sprigs fresh thyme
50g (1 3/4oz) plain (all-purpose) flour
juice of 1 lemon
salt
4 globe artichokes, prepared and cooked*

Pastry Glaze
1 egg yolk
4 drops of olive oil
pinch of salt

To make blanc, bring chicken stock to the boil, add star anise, onion and thyme, reduce heat and simmer for 30 minutes. Mix flour with just enough water to make a paste then add to stock. Return to the boil and add lemon juice, salt and artichokes, reduce heat and simmer for 20 minutes. Set aside to cool down in cooking liquid. This can be kept, covered with plastic wrap or baking paper, for several days in refrigerator; just make sure that artichokes are submerged in liquid.

To make vegetable and vanilla vinaigrette, heat 2 tablespoons of olive oil in a frying pan over medium heat, add shallots, carrot, zucchini, celeriac and vanilla bean and seeds and lightly sweat. Deglaze* with Champagne vinegar, add remaining olive oil and season with salt and pepper. Remove vanilla bean and slice into slivers.

Preheat oven to 180°C (350°F/Gas 4) and line a baking tray with baking paper.

To make pastry glaze, combine egg yolk, olive oil and salt in a small bowl and mix together with a whisk.

To prepare pigeons, cut skin between each leg and breast, twist legs to break the joint and remove legs. Remove thighbone from legs, season with salt and pepper and roll in almonds and apricots. Roll out puff pastry on a lightly floured work surface to a thickness of 5mm (1/4in) and cut into 1 x 30cm (1/2 x 12in) strips. Starting at the top of each leg, wrap pastry, overlapping it a little, around until you reach the end of the bone. Trim off excess pastry allowing bone to protrude a little and place on prepared baking tray. Brush pastry with pastry glaze and transfer to oven for 12 minutes or until golden brown. Cook breasts on bone in oven for 7 minutes for rare, then set aside to rest in a warm place for 5 minutes before slicing.

To serve, remove artichokes from blanc and pat dry with paper towel. Roll artichokes in finely chopped chives and place to one side on each serving plate. Fan sliced pigeon breast on top and garnish with potato slices and chive batons. Drizzle over vegetable and vanilla vinaigrette and position pigeon leg next to artichoke.

Serves 4

2 tbsp olive oil
4 x 180g (6 1/2oz) wild barramundi fillets, with skin on
100ml (3 1/2fl oz) double chicken stock *(see page 186)*
80g (2 3/4oz) unsalted butter, chopped into dice
sea salt and cracked black pepper
4 roma (plum) tomatoes, peeled*, deseeded and diced
2 tbsp picked fresh tarragon leaves

Pommes Fondantes
4 large desiree potatoes, peeled
2 cups double chicken stock *(see page 186)*
50g (1 3/4oz) unsalted butter

Preheat oven to 200°C (400°F/Gas 6)

Wild Barramundi with Pommes Fondantes

To make pommes fondantes, shape potatoes into cylinders 3cm (1 1/4in) high with a diameter of 7cm (2 3/4in). Place potato cylinders in a saucepan that is big enough to fit them in one layer. Just cover with stock and bring to the boil. Reduce heat to low, add butter, cover, and cook for 40 minutes or until all stock is absorbed. Reduce heat to low and continue to cook until butter has fried underside of potato cylinders a beautiful golden brown.

Heat olive oil in a large frying pan over high heat, add barramundi, in batches if necessary, and sear, skin-side down, for 1-2 minutes or until golden and crisp. Transfer to oven and cook for 4-5 minutes, depending on thickness. Remove barramundi from pan and set aside to rest in a warm place for 5 minutes. Return pan to high heat, deglaze* with stock and bring to the boil. Reduce heat to low and monter* by whisking in butter, a little at a time, until butter sauce is emulsified and consistency is very thick. Season with salt and pepper, add tomatoes and toss to combine.

To serve, arrange pommes fondantes in centre of each serving plate, place barramundi skin-side up on top and season with salt and pepper. Arrange tomatoes and butter sauce around barramundi then sprinkle over tarragon.

Serves 4

Nero Pasta Marinara

300g (10 1/2oz) Atlantic salmon fillet
1 tbsp olive oil
12 fresh diver scallops
4 fresh baby octopus, cleaned and beak removed
2 fresh cuttlefish, cleaned and scored
2 garlic cloves, thinly sliced
2 garlic cloves, finely chopped
sea salt and cracked black pepper
50g (1 3/4oz) butter
fresh baby tarragon leaves, to garnish
snow pea (mangetout) sprouts, to garnish

Nero Pasta
4 cups plain (all-purpose) flour
pinch of salt
25ml (1fl oz) olive oil
1 tbsp squid ink
2 eggs
6 egg yolks
50g (1 3/4oz) butter
sea salt and cracked black pepper

To make nero pasta, sift flour and salt on to a clean work surface and make a well in centre. Mix olive oil and squid ink together, combine with eggs and egg yolks and pour into well. Incorporate flour from sides with your hands and work mixture for 3-4 minutes, being careful not to overwork, to form a smooth dough. Cover with plastic wrap and refrigerate for 1-2 hours. To finish, divide dough into four portions and run through thickest setting on a pasta machine. Fold dough in half lengthways, dust both sides with a little flour and repeat. Continue dusting with flour and running through progressively thinner settings on pasta machine until pasta sheet is about 2mm (1/16in) thick. Repeat for each dough portion. Run through fettuccine cutter and hang over a long wooden spoon or something similar to dry. If you do not have a pasta machine you can roll the dough out by hand as thinly as possible and then cut into fine strips or small sheets. Cook pasta in boiling salted water for 1 1/2 minutes. Refresh in iced water and drain well. Melt butter in a large frying pan over medium heat, add pasta, toss and season with salt and pepper.

Cut salmon into twelve 3cm (1 1/4in) cubes.

Heat olive oil in a large non-stick pan over high heat, add seafood and sauté for 3-4 minutes or until beginning to caramelize. Add sliced and chopped garlic, salt, pepper and butter and sauté for 30 seconds or until garlic is soft.

To serve, twist a portion of pasta around a large fork and place in centre of each plate. Arrange cooked seafood around pasta, dress with pan juices and sprinkle over tarragon leaves and snow pea sprouts.

Serves 4

This beautiful yet simple dish should not be overcooked – it's all about the freshness of the seafood and the sumptuous Nero pasta. Do not attempt to cook this dish with anything other than fresh seafood or you will be disappointed.

POACHED CHICKEN SALAD WITH BABY COS

2 cups chicken stock *(see page 186)*
2 chicken breast fillets, trimmed
1 baby cos (romaine) lettuce, trimmed
12 slices papaya, cut into 2 x 4cm (3/4 x1 1/2in) chunks
8 slices mozzarella cheese
baby fresh basil leaves, to garnish
2 tbsp pepitas (pumpkin seeds)

Dressing
100ml (3 1/2fl oz) olive oil
1 French shallot, finely diced
1/4 cup cider vinegar
pinch of ground turmeric
sea salt and cracked black pepper

To make dressing, heat a little of the olive oil in a frying pan, add shallot and sauté over medium heat for 2-3 minutes or until transparent. Deglaze* with vinegar, add turmeric, remaining olive oil and salt and pepper to taste and set aside until required.

Bring chicken stock to a simmer in a saucepan over low heat, add chicken and poach, ensuring stock doesn't boil, for 8-10 minutes or until cooked through. Drain and allow chicken to rest in a warm place for 5 minutes.

While chicken is poaching, arrange cos leaves, papaya and mozzarella on serving plates. Thinly slice warm chicken breasts and arrange on top of salad. Drizzle over dressing, garnish with basil leaves and pepitas and serve.

Serves 4

SEARED SCALLOPS WITH CAVIAR

12 fresh diver scallops
sea salt and cracked black pepper
1/4 cup olive oil
20g (3/4oz) butter
1/2 cup chopped Chinese white coral mushrooms
4 tbsp sevruga caviar
1/2 pink lady apple, peeled and cut into julienne*
12-15 baby mâche* (lamb's lettuce) leaves

Port Reduction
150ml (5fl oz) port
30g (1oz) caster (superfine) sugar
2 1/2 tbsp red wine vinegar

To make port reduction, combine port, sugar and vinegar in a small saucepan over medium-high heat and reduce to a syrup consistency.

Season scallops with salt and pepper. Heat 1 1/2 tablespoons of olive oil in a frying pan over high heat, add scallops and sear for 30 seconds on one side only, turn, add butter and remove from pan immediately. Set aside.

Season mushrooms with salt and pepper and dress with remaining 1 1/2 tablespoons of olive oil.

To serve, drizzle port reduction on to each serving plate, arrange 3 scallops and the mushrooms on top and garnish with caviar, apple and mâche leaves.

Serves 4

4 quails, with legs and breasts removed
sea salt and cracked black pepper
1/2 tbsp olive oil
60g (2 1/4oz) Persian feta
25g (1oz) panko (Japanese) breadcrumbs
1 tbsp truffle oil
1/3 cup pouring cream
120g (4 1/4oz) goat's cheese, such as Bourdin
2 tbsp finely chopped fresh
flat leaf (Italian) parsley
1/2 cup baby watercress leaves
2 French shallots, cut into rings

Mustard Vinaigrette
1 garlic clove, finely chopped
2 French shallots, finely chopped
1 tbsp dijon mustard
2 tbsp wholegrain mustard
juice and zest of 1 lime
75ml (2 1/4fl oz) extra virgin olive oil
cracked black pepper

Preheat oven to 200°C (400°F/Gas 6).

Quail, Feta & Goat's Cheese Salad

To make mustard vinaigrette, combine garlic, shallots, mustards and lime juice and zest in a small bowl, add oil and pepper and whisk until emulsified. Cover and place in refrigerator for at least 1 hour. This dressing can be stored in a sealed container for up to 2 weeks and is fantastic for charcuterie*.

Season quail legs and breasts with salt and pepper. Heat olive oil in a large frying pan over medium heat, add legs and breasts and quickly sear on all sides for 3-5 minutes or until golden brown. Sprinkle over feta and breadcrumbs, and place in oven for 2-3 minutes or until crumbs start to turn golden brown. Set aside to rest in a warm place for 5 minutes.

For goat's cheese mixture, in a small bowl combine truffle oil, cream and goat's cheese. Form into 12-16 quenelles using 2 teaspoons to shape mixture into small lozenges.

To serve, arrange quail on serving plates and sprinkle over parsley and salt. Garnish with 3 or 4 goat's cheese quenelles and scatter watercress and shallots around plate. Liberally pour mustard vinaigrette over quail and watercress.

Serves 4

VERSACE

Poached Western Australian Marron with Champagne & Star Anise Cream

4 x 300g (10 1/2oz) live
Western Australian marron (crayfish)
100g (3 1/2oz) enoki mushrooms, trimmed
200g (7oz) broad beans, cooked and shelled
1 tbsp truffle oil

Marron Poaching Liquor
2 tbsp peanut oil
5 French shallots, sliced into rounds
2 medium carrots, thinly sliced into rounds
juice and zest of 1 lemon
8 star anise
2 bay leaves
10 black peppercorns, crushed
100ml (3 1/2fl oz) dry vermouth (Noilly Prat)
2 litres (8 cups/70fl oz) fish stock
1 cup fresh orange juice

Champagne and Star Anise Cream
25ml (1fl oz) olive oil
50g (1 3/4oz) button mushrooms, washed
4 French shallots, peeled and quartered
3 garlic cloves, peeled and quartered
75g (2 3/4oz) jewfish or flathead fillet
2 sprigs fresh thyme
1/2 cup white wine
1/3 cup dry vermouth (Noilly Prat)
1/3 cup dry sherry
3 cups fish stock
zest and juice 1 lemon
4 cups pouring cream
8 star anise
1 tsp arrowroot
1/2 cup flat leaf (Italian) parsley
stems and leaves, for infusing
1/2 cup chervil, for infusing
2 sprigs fresh thyme, for infusing
2 1/2 tbsp Champagne
sea salt and cracked black pepper

To make marron poaching liquor, put shallots, carrots, lemon zest, star anise, bay leaves and peppercorns in a pot with the oil and sweat for 5 minutes or until they are starting to soften. Add vermouth and reduce by one-quarter. Add fish stock and orange and lemon juice and simmer gently for 15 minutes, skimming regularly.

Place marron in freezer until they've dropped off to sleep. Plunge them gently into simmering cooking liquor and cook for 4 minutes. Lift from liquor and, while warm, remove head *(keep antennae)* and peel off shell.
Keep peeled marron warm in a little poaching liquid. Remove some carrot, shallot and four star anise from poaching liquor and reserve for garnish.

To make Champagne and star anise cream, heat olive oil in a heavy-based saucepan over medium heat, add mushrooms, shallots, garlic, fish trimmings and thyme and sweat for 5 minutes or until shallots are softened but not coloured. Deglaze* with white wine, vermouth, sherry and reduce to 2 tablespoons of liquid forming a glaze. Add fish stock and reduce by two-thirds. Stir in cream and star anise, and return to the boil. In a stainless-steel bowl, mix arrowroot with just enough water to form a thin paste and whisk into boiling stock until thickened. Skim surface, remove from heat, plunge in herbs for infusing and set aside for 3-4 minutes, before passing through a fine chinois*. To finish sauce, add Champagne, correct consistency and seasoning, if necessary, and keep warm.

Blanch enoki mushrooms in a little marron poaching liquor for 30 seconds. Drain well.

To serve, cut marrons in half and devein. Arrange on each serving plate with broad beans, carrot, shallot, enoki mushrooms and star anise. Drizzle over Champagne cream sauce and a little truffle oil. Finish by strategically placing antennae on top for final effect.

Serves 4

Carpaccio of Venison

4 x 140g (5oz) venison loins, trimmed of sinew and fat
4 tbsp dijon mustard
2 tbsp ground sumac
1 tbsp peanut oil
1 cup mixed baby salad leaves, such as mizuna, cress and mâche* (lamb's lettuce)
80g (2 3/4oz) Parmigiano Reggiano or soft goat's cheese
30g (1oz) yellow enoki mushrooms, trimmed
4 tbsp sweet corn kernels

Aioli
1 tbsp olive oil
10 garlic cloves, peeled
25ml (1fl oz) fresh lemon juice
zest of 1 lemon
3 egg yolks
600ml (21fl oz) Tuscan oil*

Truffle Oil Dressing
3 1/2 tbsp olive oil
1 French shallot, finely chopped
1 tsp dijon mustard
2 tbsp sherry vinegar
1 tsp truffle oil
2 tbsp Madeira
sea salt and cracked white pepper
2 slices black truffle, finely chopped

To make aioli, heat olive oil in a heavy-based frying pan, add garlic and fry over low heat until golden. Place garlic and lemon juice and zest in a food processor and blitz to combine. Add egg yolks and blitz. With motor running, slowly drizzle in Tuscan oil and process until incorporated and thick. This dressing can be stored in a sealed container in refrigerator for up to 4 weeks.

To make truffle oil dressing, heat 1 tablespoon of olive oil in a saucepan over medium heat, add shallot and sauté for 3 minutes or until starting to colour. Stir in mustard and vinegar and remove from heat. Add truffle oil, then whisk in olive oil and Madeira until emulsified. Season with salt and pepper and add truffle.

Coat venison with a thin layer of mustard, roll in sumac and rest for 1 hour in refrigerator. Heat oil in a heavy-based frying pan over high heat, add venison and quickly sear on all sides until browned. Cool slightly before tightly wrapping in plastic wrap to form a cylinder about 4cm (1 1/2in) in diameter. Place venison in freezer until just frozen then thinly slice.

To serve, arrange venison carpaccio on each serving plate and pipe aioli on to plate. Dress salad leaves with truffle oil dressing and place on plate. Top salad with freshly shaved Reggiano or a quenelle* of goat's cheese. Scatter mushrooms and corn kernels over carpaccio and drizzle over truffle oil dressing.

Serves 4

Vanitas – a place that celebrates the earthly pleasures of food and wine,
and offers an exquisite canvas for the artistry of a master chef.

SAUTÉED BUG TAILS WITH HERBED BEIGNETS

12 Moreton Bay bug tails, meat removed from shells
sea salt and cracked black pepper
1 tbsp olive oil
10g (1/4oz) butter
200ml (7fl oz) veal jus *(see page 187)*, warmed
2 x 5g (1/8oz) truffles, cut into julienne*
2 tbsp finely chopped fresh flat leaf (Italian) parsley

Beignets
200g (7oz) peeled and deveined New Caledonian prawns
2 garlic cloves, finely chopped
pinch of cayenne pepper
pinch of ground cumin
1 tbsp finely chopped fines herbes*, such as fresh tarragon, chives, flat leaf (Italian) parsley and chervil
1 tbsp hot English mustard
sea salt
100g (3 1/2oz) unsalted butter, softened

Pane Mixture
100g (3 1/2oz) plain (all-purpose) flour
sea salt and cracked black pepper
4 eggs, lightly beaten
200g (7oz) panko (Japanese) breadcrumbs
2 cups peanut oil, for deep frying

To make beignets, roughly chop prawns and place in a bowl. Add garlic, cayenne pepper, cumin, fines herbes and mustard and season with salt. Mix in butter and shape into 8 quenelles*. Place in freezer for 30 minutes.

To make pane mixture, season flour with salt and pepper. Place flour in a shallow bowl, eggs in another bowl and breadcrumbs in a third bowl. First dust beignets with flour, then dip in egg and finally coat well with breadcrumbs. Place in freezer for 30 minutes and repeat crumbing steps. The idea of doing this is to get a crust around the garlic butter so that when the beignets have been pan-fried to golden brown, you can cut them in half and garlic butter will weep out as a luscious sauce.

Season bug tails with salt and pepper. Heat oil and butter in a frying pan, add bug tails and sauté over high heat for 2 minutes on each side or until just cooked.

Arrange 3 bug tails and 2 beignets on each serving plate and drizzle over warmed veal jus. Dress bug tails with truffles and parsley and serve.

Serves 4

You may like to vary this dish by using ground almonds or hazelnuts. This dish uses panko (Japanese) breadcrumbs, which can be bought at most Asian grocers. They are a little coarser than most breadcrumbs, but always have a crisp white finish.

Pressed Tomato Terrine

1 granny smith apple, cut into batons
2 slices black truffle, cut into julienne*
5 fresh basil leaves, cut into julienne*
extra virgin olive oil, to garnish

Pressed Tomato Terrine
1 cup fresh basil leaves
3 cups Tuscan oil*
300ml (10 1/2fl oz) aged balsamic vinegar
4 garlic cloves, peeled and sliced
5 French shallots, peeled and sliced
sea salt and cracked white pepper
1.5kg (3lb 5oz) tomatoes, peeled, deseeded and sliced into segments (petals)

Vegetable Salsa
1/3 cup extra virgin olive oil
1 carrot, cut into brunoise*
1 red capsicum (pepper), cut into brunoise*
1 yellow capsicum (pepper), cut into brunoise*
1 zucchini (courgette), cut into brunoise*
1/2 eggplant (aubergine), skin only, cut into brunoise*
sea salt and cracked black pepper

To make pressed tomato terrine, prepare marinade for tomatoes by combining basil with oil, vinegar, garlic, shallots and salt and pepper. Place tomatoes in a bowl and pour over marinade. Cover and leave tomatoes overnight in refrigerator. Lift tomato petals out of marinade and press flesh into four 6cm (2 1/2in) ring moulds, allowing about 1cm (1/2in) of flesh to protrude from top of moulds. Place a weight over top of each mould and refrigerate for at least 2-3 hours before serving.

To make vegetable salsa, heat oil in a large saucepan, add carrot and sauté over medium heat for 2 minutes. Add capsicums, zucchini and eggplant and cook for a further 3-4 minutes; the vegetables shouldn't be too soft. Season with salt and pepper and remove from heat.

Unmould tomato terrines on to serving plates and garnish with apple, truffle and basil. Make a ring of vegetable salsa around each terrine, drizzle with extra virgin olive oil and serve with crusty bread.

Serves 4

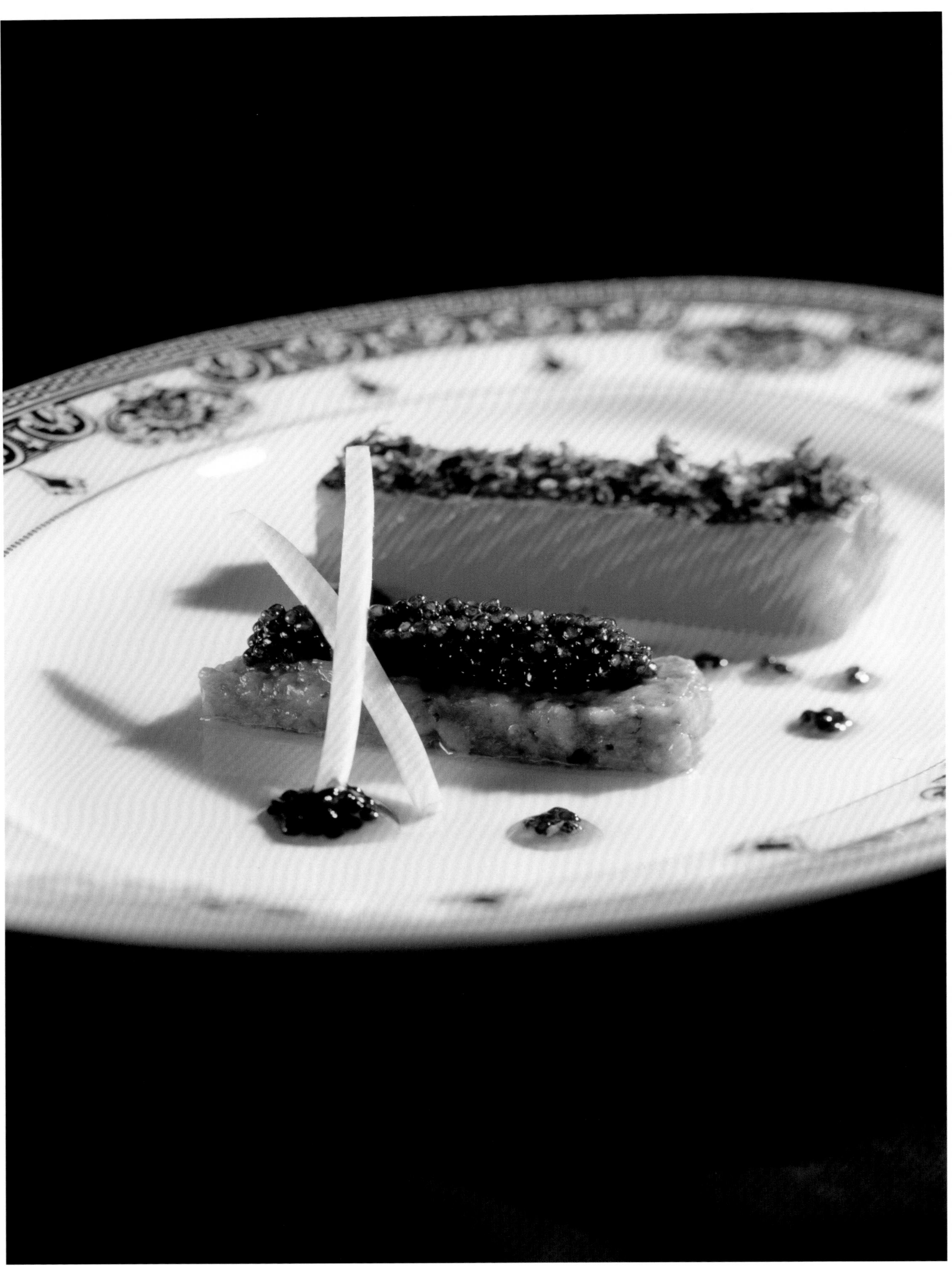

SALMON CONFIT WITH MAPLE CAVIAR DRESSING

300g (10 1/2oz) Atlantic salmon fillet, skin on
200g (7oz) fine rock salt
50g (1 3/4oz) celery salt*
3 star anise
50g (1 3/4oz) Szechuan pepper
50g (1 3/4oz) white peppercorns
4 cups duck fat or extra virgin olive oil
1/3 cup finely chopped fresh flat leaf (Italian) parsley
8 tbsp black caviar
8 witlof (chicory/Belgian endive) batons

Maple Caviar Dressing
2 tbsp finely chopped fresh dill
2 1/2 tbsp extra virgin olive oil
1 tbsp maple syrup
2 tbsp black caviar
sea salt and cracked black pepper

Eggplant Caviar
1 eggplant (aubergine), cut in half lengthways
1 tbsp fresh thyme leaves
2 garlic cloves, thinly sliced
sea salt and cracked black pepper
100ml (3 1/2fl oz) olive oil

Preheat oven to 180°C (350°F/Gas 4)

To make maple caviar dressing, combine ingredients in a bowl and mix with a small whisk. Taste and adjust seasoning if necessary. Chill in refrigerator until needed.

To make eggplant caviar, cut slits in flesh of each eggplant half. Insert thyme, garlic, salt and pepper in each slit and drizzle over olive oil. Wrap in foil and place on a baking tray. Bake in oven for 30 minutes or until soft. Remove from oven and set aside to cool. Scrape out flesh and chop up finely. Check seasoning. *(For something different, make smoky-flavoured eggplant caviar by holding whole eggplant with a pair of tongs or a roasting fork over an open flame until skin is charred black all over, then proceed to cut eggplant in half and insert herbs into flesh.)*

Cut salmon into four 2.5 x 8cm (1 x 3 1/4in) fingers. Blend rock salt, celery salt, star anise, Szechuan pepper and white peppercorns in a blender to a fine salt. Rub this salt into salmon, cover in plastic wrap and refrigerate for 40 minutes.

Heat oil to 60°C (140°F) in a saucepan, add salmon fingers and gently cook for 14 minutes. It is critical to this dish that temperature of oil and cooking time be exact. Remove from heat and let salmon cool in oil. Drain well on a drainage tray.

Place each confit salmon finger on a serving plate and scatter over parsley. Place a thick row of eggplant caviar next to salmon, top with a line of black caviar and garnish with 2 witlof batons. Dress with maple caviar dressing and serve.

Serves 4

This dish is fantastic cooked in extra virgin olive oil. The confit fat can be strained, refrigerated and used again.

PRAWN TARTARE WITH GREEN BEAN SOUP

50g (1 3/4oz) plain (all-purpose) flour
100ml (3 1/2fl oz) iced water
4 green New Caledonian prawns, peeled and deveined, tails intact
200ml (7fl oz) peanut oil, for frying
sea salt

Green Bean Soup
1/2 tbsp olive oil
1/2 onion, chopped into dice
2 garlic cloves, finely chopped
1/4 leek, cleaned and roughly chopped
1/4 celery stalk, diced
1 potato, peeled and diced
sea salt and cracked black pepper
1 cup chicken stock *(see page 186)*
200g (7oz) green beans, topped and tailed
100ml (3 1/2fl oz) pouring cream

Dressing
10g (1/4oz) ginger, chopped
10g (1/4oz) onion, chopped
20g (1/2oz) tomato, chopped
140ml (4 3/4fl oz) grape seed oil
3 1/2 tbsp soy sauce
juice of 1/2 lime
cracked black pepper
1/2 granny smith apple, cut into brunoise*
1/2 red capsicum (pepper), cut into brunoise*

Prawn Tartare
8 green New Caledonian prawns, peeled, deveined and finely chopped

To make green bean soup, heat oil in a saucepan over medium heat, add onion, garlic, leek, celery and potato, then sauté for 6-8 minutes or until tender. Season with salt and pepper, add stock and bring to the boil. Add beans and boil for 4 minutes or until beans are tender. Add cream and return to the boil. Blend and pass through a fine chinois*. Taste and adjust seasoning if necessary, then chill down immediately to keep rich green colour.

To make dressing, blend ginger, onion, tomato, grape seed oil, soy sauce, lime juice and pepper until smooth. Add apple and capsicum and stir to combine.

To make prawn tartare, combine prawns with half of the dressing. Press one-quarter of the prawn tartare into a 10cm (4in) ring mould placed in middle of each serving plate. Repeat until all of the prawn tartare mixture has been used. Pour green bean soup into four shot glasses and place in centre of each prawn tartare round.

Combine flour and just enough water to make a light batter, it does not matter if there are a few lumps. Dip prawns in batter, lightly shaking off excess. Heat oil in a deep frying pan over medium-high heat, add prawns and pan-fry until golden brown. Season with salt and place a prawn on top of each shot glass. Finally, dress plate with remaining dressing and serve.

Serves 4

SAGO PUDDING WITH NUTMEG ICE-CREAM & HAZELNUT BISCOTTI

4 sprigs fresh mint

Sago Pudding
2 cups milk
30g (1oz) caster (superfine) sugar
1 vanilla bean, split lengthways
80g (2 3/4oz) sago
2 egg yolks
3 egg whites
2/3 cup icing (confectioners') sugar

Nutmeg Ice-cream
300ml (10 1/2fl oz) pouring cream
300ml (10 1/2fl oz) milk
1 whole nutmeg, grated
6 egg yolks
3/4 cup caster (superfine) sugar

Hazelnut Biscotti
400g (14oz) plain (all-purpose) flour
320g (11 1/4oz) caster (superfine) sugar
200g (7oz) hazelnuts, lightly toasted and chopped
pinch of salt
1 tsp baking powder
1 vanilla bean, split lengthways and seeds scraped
1 tbsp espresso coffee
3 eggs
3 egg yolks

To make sago pudding, bring milk, caster sugar and vanilla bean to the boil in a saucepan over medium heat. Add sago, stirring constantly, and cook for 20-30 minutes or until sago still has a little bit of bite. Remove from heat and discard vanilla bean, and while still warm, stir in egg yolks. Whisk egg whites and icing sugar until soft peaks form. Fold in cooled sago mixture. Pour into desired moulds (I use demitasse cups) and refrigerate until set.

To make nutmeg ice-cream, bring cream, milk and nutmeg to the boil over medium heat. Whisk egg yolks and sugar until pale and thick. Pour cream into egg mixture and mix to combine. Pour into a clean saucepan and cook over low heat for about 10 minutes, stirring constantly with a wooden spoon, until mixture coats back of spoon. Remove from heat and cool down over iced water. Churn in an ice-cream machine following manufacturer's directions and freeze.

Preheat oven to 160°C (315°F/Gas 2-3).
Line a baking tray with baking paper.

To make hazelnut biscotti, in a large bowl combine flour, sugar, hazelnuts, salt, baking powder and seeds from vanilla bean *(cut rest of vanilla bean into thin strips for use as part of decoration)*. Add coffee, eggs and egg yolks and mix to form a smooth dough. Divide into two, roll into log shapes and transfer to prepared baking tray. Place in oven and bake for 30-40 minutes or until golden. Place on a wire rack to cool. Cut into 3mm (1/8in) thick slices, transfer to baking trays lined with baking paper and return to oven for 15-20 minutes or until crispy.

Spoon a quenelle* of nutmeg ice-cream on top of each pudding, decorate with a sprig of mint and a sliver of vanilla bean and serve with crisp hazelnut biscotti.

Serves 4

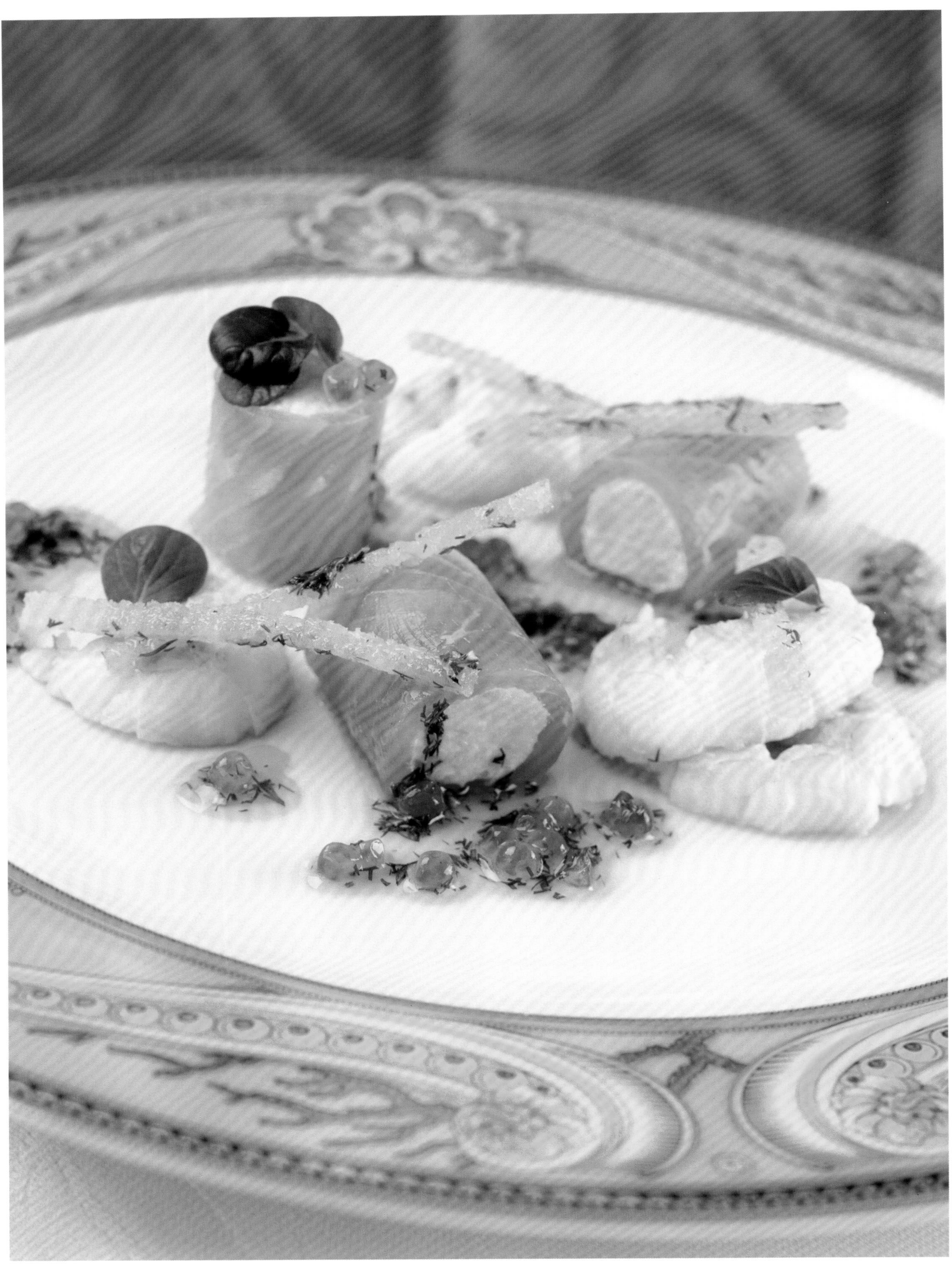

Smoked Salmon Roulade with Yabbies

8 x 120g (4 1/4oz) live yabbies (crayfish)
12-16 baby mâche* (lamb's lettuce) leaves

Salmon Caviar Dressing
2 tbsp finely chopped fresh dill
2 tbsp salmon caviar
1 1/2 tbsp extra virgin olive oil
1 tbsp maple syrup
sea salt and cracked black pepper

Smoked Salmon Roulade
200g (7oz) picked crabmeat
4 tbsp mayonnaise *(see page 186)*
8 slices smoked salmon

Crouton Sticks
2 slices white bread, crusts removed
1 tbsp olive oil
sea salt

Preheat oven to 180°C (350°F/Gas 4)

To make salmon caviar dressing, place all ingredients in a bowl and whisk until emulsified. Taste and season accordingly. Chill until needed.

To make smoked salmon roulade, combine crabmeat and mayonnaise in a small bowl, mix well and spoon into a piping bag. Place two slices of smoked salmon, overlapping on the bloodline, on a piece of plastic wrap. Pipe crab mixture in the shape of a log on top of salmon. Roll up tightly to form a cylinder, twist ends and place in refrigerator. Repeat this process for remaining smoked salmon and crab mixture so that you have four roulades in total.

To make crouton sticks, cut bread into thin sticks, drizzle over olive oil and scatter over sea salt. Place on a baking tray and bake in oven for 5 minutes or until golden brown.

Place yabbies in the freezer for about 15 minutes to send them to sleep before cooking them. Cook yabbies in a large saucepan of boiling salted water for 3-4 minutes. Drain and set aside to cool a little before removing flesh from shells.

To serve, slice each roulade at 3cm (1 1/4in) intervals and arrange on serving plates. Cut yabbie tails in half and arrange next to roulade. Drizzle dressing around plate and garnish with crouton sticks and mâche.

Serves 4

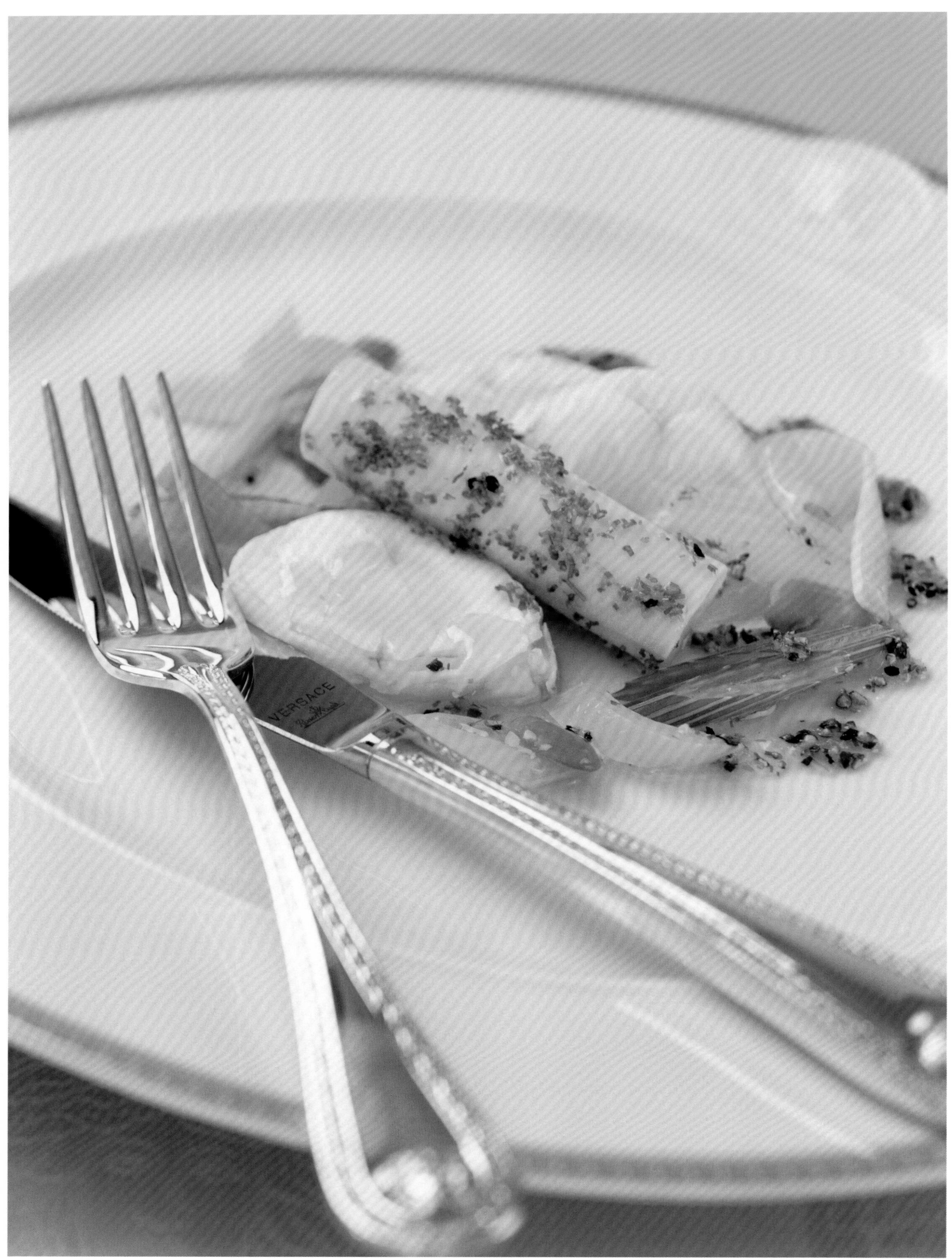
VERSACE

POELE OF VEGETABLES WITH PRAWN CANNELLONI

The vegetables in this dish are left to marinate in their own juices to allow the flavours to infuse. You may choose to add other vegetables, such as peas and green beans, towards the end of cooking so that they do not lose their colour.

2 x 600g (1lb 5oz) live lobsters
1 tbsp finely chopped fresh flat leaf (Italian) parsley

Poele of Vegetables
1/3 cup olive oil
4 baby carrots, peeled and cut into rounds
4 French shallots, quartered
1 celery stalk, sliced
4 star anise
2 1/2 tbsp white wine
4 baby pencil leeks, cleaned and sliced
1/2 baby fennel bulb, sliced
12 shelled broad beans, blanched and grey outer skin removed

Filling for Cannelloni
150g (5 1/2oz) green prawn meat, cleaned and finely diced
1 tbsp finely chopped coriander (cilantro)
juice and zest of 1 lime
sea salt and cracked black pepper

Cannelloni
250g (9oz) strong flour
1 tbsp olive oil
2 eggs
1 egg yolk
salt
2 tbsp cold water

To make poele of vegetables, heat 2 tablespoons of olive oil in a frying pan over medium heat, add carrots, shallots, celery and star anise and lightly sauté for 3 minutes without colouring. Deglaze* with wine and reduce by half. Add leeks, fennel and remaining 2 tablespoons of olive oil and cook for about 10 minutes or until wine is reduced to 1 tablespoon. Add broad beans and allow them to heat through.

To make filling for cannelloni, mix prawn meat with coriander and lime juice and zest and season with salt and pepper. Spoon into a piping bag.

To make cannelloni, place flour in a mixing bowl. Whisk oil, eggs, egg yolk and salt until combined in a separate bowl. Add to flour while beating with an electric mixer using a paddle attachment. Knead dough on low speed until dough starts to come together. Add just enough water to form a firm dough and continue kneading for 1-2 minutes or until dough is smooth and elastic. Divide into two portions, roll into balls, wrap in plastic wrap and rest in refrigerator for 1 hour. Dust one ball with a little flour and run dough through thickest setting on a pasta machine. Continue dusting with flour and running through progressively thinner settings on pasta machine until pasta sheet is about 46cm (18in) long and 2mm (1/16in) thick. Repeat with remaining dough. Pipe a line of filling lengthways down the centre of each sheet of dough. Roll dough over to cover filling and form a cylinder shape. Brush edge of pasta sheet with a little water, press to seal closed and cut into 10cm (4in) lengths. Blanch in boiling salted water for 2 minutes, remove with a slotted spoon and drain well.

Place lobsters in freezer for 20 minutes before cooking to send them to sleep. For me, the best way to cook lobsters is in a large pot of boiling seawater. If this is not available, a large pot of boiling salted water is just as good. A 600g (1lb 5oz) lobster will cook in 6-8 minutes *(allow a little more time for heavier lobsters)*, remove from water and allow to cool.

To serve, remove lobster meat from shell, cut each tail into six medallions. Put 3 medallions on each plate and place cannelloni alongside. Garnish with poele of vegetables and parsley and drizzle over vegetable juices.

Serves 4

PEKING DUCK BROTH

1/2 barbecued Peking duck*
1/2 onion, chopped
1 garlic clove, sliced
1/2 lemon grass stalk, bruised
10 star anise
30g (1oz) ginger, chopped
650ml (22 1/2fl oz) chicken stock *(see page 186)*
1/2 tbsp nam pla (fish sauce)
25ml (1fl oz) hoisin sauce
25ml (1fl oz) kecap manis (sweet soy sauce)
25ml (1fl oz) oyster sauce
2 1/2 tbsp green ginger wine*
1/2 cup fresh mint leaves
juice and zest of 1/2 lime
2 kaffir lime leaves
4 asparagus spears, trimmed
2 nori sheets, cut in half
1 tsp black sesame seeds
1 tsp sesame seeds

Remove all flesh from duck carcass and chop into dice.

Chop duck bones into pieces and place in a heavy-based saucepan with onion, garlic, lemon grass, star anise, ginger and chicken stock and simmer for 1 hour to extract maximum flavour from duck bones. Add nam pla, hoisin sauce, kecap manis, oyster sauce and ginger wine. Bring to the boil and skim surface well. Line a fine chinois* with muslin, mint, lime zest and kaffir lime leaves. Strain broth through chinois, leave to infuse for 3 minutes and strain again. Finish with lime juice. Serve straight away or refrigerate and reheat when required.

Blanch asparagus in boiling salted water for 3 minutes, refresh in iced water and drain. Roll each asparagus spear in a sheet of nori.

Pour broth into 4 demitasse cups or shot glasses, garnish with sesame seeds and diced Peking duck and top with nori-wrapped asparagus spears.

Serves 4

Chocolate & Blueberry Fondants with Sugar Pencils

100ml (3 1/2fl oz) pouring cream
1 vanilla bean, split lengthways and seeds scraped
150g (5 1/2oz) blueberries
4 sprigs fresh mint

Raspberry Coulis
150g (5 1/2oz) raspberries
50g (1 3/4oz) caster (superfine) sugar

Chocolate fondant
1 gelatine sheet
1/2 cup milk
1/2 cup pouring cream
4 egg yolks
50g (1 3/4oz) caster (superfine) sugar
200g (7oz) dark couverture chocolate, roughly chopped

Sugar Pencils
200g (7oz) sugar

To make raspberry coulis, place raspberries and sugar in a saucepan over medium heat and cook for 4 minutes or until sugar is dissolved and raspberries softened. Transfer to a blender, blend until smooth and pass through a fine chinois*. Set aside to cool.

To make chocolate fondant, soak gelatine sheet in cold water for 2 minutes or until softened. Combine milk and cream in a saucepan and bring just to the boil. Beat egg yolks and sugar until pale and thick. Pour milk and cream into egg mixture and beat to combine. Transfer to a clean saucepan and cook over a low heat, stirring constantly with a wooden spoon, until mixture coats back of spoon. Add chocolate and stir until melted. Stir in softened gelatine and 2 tablespoons of raspberry coulis and pour into four 4 x 6cm (1 1/2 x 2 1/2in) ring moulds. Cover and place in refrigerator for 1 hour or until set.

To make sugar pencils, boil sugar in a heavy-based saucepan over high heat until golden brown: watching carefully as at this high temperature caramel will burn easily. Remove from heat and using the back of a metal spoon quickly drizzle toffee in long thin strands over a piece of baking paper.

Whip cream until soft peaks form and add vanilla seeds.

Unmould chocolate fondants by running a small knife around inside of each ring mould and place in centre of each serving plate. Arrange blueberries on top and place a quenelle* of vanilla cream alongside. Decorate with raspberry coulis, mint and sugar pencils and serve.

Serves 4

DRAGON FRUIT & RASPBERRY STACK

1 large dragon fruit (strawberry pear)
150g (5 1/2oz) raspberries
1 cup finely diced watermelon, strawberries, pineapple and pear
5 fresh mint leaves, cut into julienne*

Vanilla Mascarpone
100g (3 1/2oz) mascarpone
20g (3/4oz) icing (confectioners') sugar
1 tsp vanilla extract

Passionfruit Coulis
50g (1 3/4oz) sugar
25ml (1fl oz) water
pulp of 5-6 passionfruit

To make vanilla mascarpone, whisk mascarpone, sugar and vanilla in a bowl.

To make passionfruit coulis, combine sugar and water in a saucepan, bring to the boil and continue to boil for 3 minutes. Add passionfruit pulp and boil for a further 30 seconds. Allow to cool. Place in a blender and pulse for 5 seconds. Strain through a coarse strainer and return one-quarter of the passionfruit seeds to syrup.

Peel and cut dragon fruit into 5mm (1/4in) slices. Cut slices into discs about 7cm (2 3/4in) in diameter.

Arrange raspberries, dragon fruit and vanilla mascarpone in layers to form a stack on each serving plate. Decorate plate with passionfruit coulis, diced fruit and mint. Pipe remaining vanilla mascarpone on top of each stack and serve.

Serves 4

APPLE SORBET

1-2 granny smith apples, peeled and diced
1/3 cup vodka

Apple Sorbet
500g (1lb 2oz) caster (superfine) sugar
500ml (20fl oz) water
1kg (2lb 4oz) granny smith apples, quartered and cored
juice of 4-5 lemons
1 1/2 tbsp Calvados

Apple Crisps
2 granny smith apples, very finely sliced
100g (3 1/2oz) icing (confectioners') sugar

Preheat oven to 160°C (315°F/Gas 2–3)

To make apple sorbet, combine sugar and water in a large saucepan, bring to the boil and cook for 10 minutes or until sugar is dissolved and syrup is transparent. Allow to cool. Place apples and lemon juice, to taste, in a blender and purée. Mix apple purée and Calvados with sugar syrup. Transfer to an ice-cream machine, churn following manufacturer's directions and freeze.

To make apple crisps, dust apple slices with sugar, place between two sheets of baking paper and sandwich between two baking trays. Bake in oven for 30 minutes or until crisp.

To serve, place 1 dessertspoon of diced apple and a scoop of apple sorbet in the base of each martini glass, pour over 1 tablespoon of vodka and place an apple crisp on top.

Makes 1 Litre

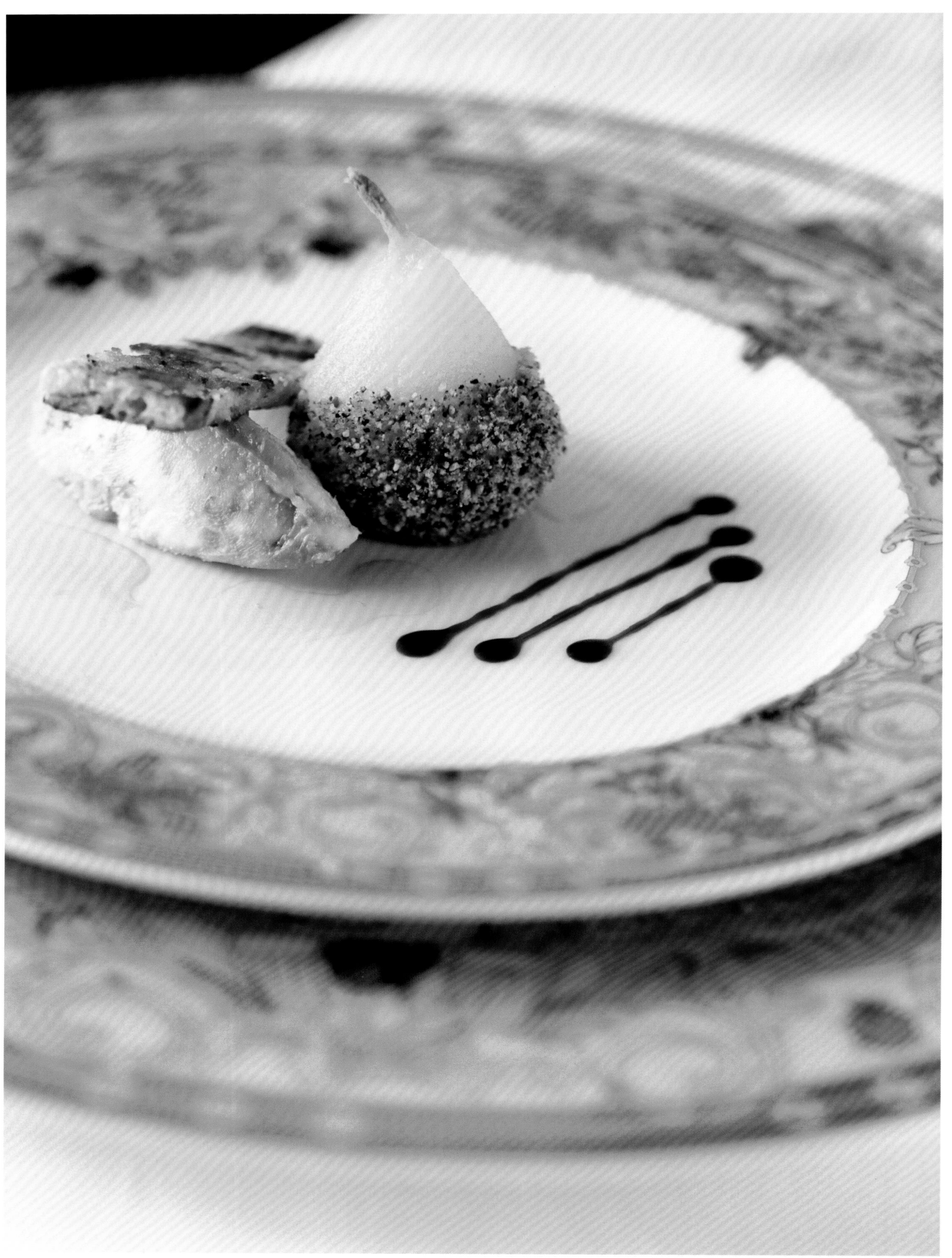

POACHED PEARS WITH GORGONZOLA & WALNUT BISCOTTI

500g (1lb 2oz) sugar
2 cups water
2 star anise
1 cinnamon stick
2 cloves
4 paradise pears, peeled, stem left on
120g (4 1/4oz) gorgonzola dolce
1 tbsp extra virgin olive oil

Walnut Biscotti
400g (14oz) plain (all-purpose) flour
320g (11 1/4oz) caster (superfine) sugar
pinch of salt
1 tsp baking powder
200g (7oz) walnuts, lightly toasted and roughly chopped
1 vanilla bean, split lengthways and seeds scraped
1 tbsp espresso coffee
3 eggs
3 egg yolks

Port Reduction
150ml (5fl oz) port
30g (1oz) sugar
2 1/2 tbsp red wine vinegar

Walnut Biscotti Crumbs
2 walnut biscotti
10 blanched almonds
1/2 tsp cracked black pepper

Preheat oven to 160°C (315°F/Gas 2–3)

Line a baking tray with baking paper.

Combine sugar, water, star anise, cinnamon and cloves in a saucepan and bring to the boil. Reduce to a simmer, add pears, cover with baking paper and cook for 10 minutes or until pears are tender. Leave pears in syrup to cool. Drain well.

To make walnut biscotti, combine flour, sugar, salt and baking powder in a large bowl and mix well. Add walnuts, vanilla seeds, coffee, eggs and egg yolks and mix until a smooth dough is formed. Divide dough into two and roll into loaves. Place on prepared baking tray and transfer to oven for 30-40 minutes or until deep golden brown in colour. Place on a wire rack to cool. Cut into 3mm (1/8in) thick slices and place on baking paper-lined baking trays. Return to oven for 15-20 minutes or until crisp.

To make port reduction, combine port, sugar and vinegar in a saucepan over high heat and reduce by two-thirds to a syrup consistency.

To make walnut biscotti crumbs, crush biscotti, almonds and pepper using a mortar and pestle. Press walnut biscotti crumbs around bottom third of each pear to create a crust.

Place a pear on each serving plate. Spoon a quenelle* of gorgonzola next to each pear and top with walnut biscotti. Decorate plate with port reduction, drizzle over a little extra virgin olive oil and serve.

Serves 4

Caramel Pecan Slice

1 fig, quartered
4 fresh mint tips

Sweet Pastry
75g (2 1/2oz) butter, softened
30g (1oz) caster (superfine) sugar
1 egg
1 cup plain (all-purpose) flour

Caramel Topping
1/4 cup golden syrup
75g (2 1/2oz) unsalted butter
395g (13 3/4oz) tin condensed milk
50g (1 3/4oz) pecans, lightly toasted and roughly chopped

Pecan Praline
100g (3 1/2oz) sugar
1/2 tbsp water
30g (1oz) pecans, lightly toasted

Vanilla Syrup
100g (3 1/2oz) sugar
2 1/2 tbsp water
1/2 tbsp honey
1 vanilla bean, split lengthways, seeds removed, and cut in half to make 4 batons
1/4 cup caster (superfine) sugar

Preheat oven to 160°C (315°F/Gas 2–3)

Lightly grease and line a 20 x 30cm (8 x 12in) baking tin with baking paper.

To make sweet pastry, cream butter and sugar in a mixing bowl. Slowly add egg and flour and bring together, being careful not to overwork dough. Wrap in plastic wrap and refrigerate for 20 minutes. When chilled, on a lightly floured work surface, work dough gently with your hands for 1-2 minutes or until soft enough to roll. Roll out to a thickness of 5mm (1/4in) and place in prepared baking tin, making sure that dough is pushed well into corners and comes about 1cm (1/2in) up sides of tin – this is to allow for shrinkage. The aim is to have a flat pastry base that covers base of baking tin only. Chill for another 20 minutes then transfer to oven for 10 minutes or until pastry is firm but not coloured.

Increase oven temperature to 170°C (325°F/Gas 3).

To make caramel topping, combine golden syrup and butter in a saucepan and bring to the boil. Remove from heat, add condensed milk and pecans and mix well. Pour caramel over pastry base and place in oven for 10 minutes or until set firm. Return to refrigerator to chill for at least 2 hours and slice into 8cm (3 1/4in) squares using a knife dipped in hot water.

Line a baking tray with baking paper.

To make pecan praline, melt sugar and water in a heavy-based saucepan over low heat for 10-20 minutes or until golden brown. Remove from heat, add pecans, coat well with caramel and pour on to prepared baking tray. Allow to set at room temperature. Once cold, chop into small pieces or place in a food processor and blitz until fine. Be careful not to over-process as praline will heat up and stick together. Praline can be kept in an airtight container for 1 month in pantry.

To make vanilla syrup, bring sugar and water to the boil, add honey and cook for 5 minutes or until golden. Remove from heat and carefully dip vanilla bean lengths in syrup for about 20 seconds. Remove and roll in caster sugar. To finish syrup, add seeds scraped from vanilla bean and allow to cool.

To serve, sprinkle crushed pecan praline on top of 4 portions of caramel slice. Place each slice on a serving plate. Stand a fig quarter beside caramel slice and decorate with crystallized vanilla bean baton, mint and vanilla syrup.

Serves 4

CRISPY GARLIC PRAWNS & BUG TAILS

2 tbsp peanut oil
8 Moreton Bay bug tails,
meat removed from shells
8 green New Caledonian prawns,
peeled and deveined, tails intact
4 shiitake mushrooms, sliced
2 garlic cloves, thinly sliced
sea salt and cracked black pepper
30g (1oz) butter
1 tbsp finely chopped fresh
flat leaf (Italian) parsley
1 tbsp crushed unsalted peanuts
1/2 cup bull's blood leaves*

Heat a large frying pan over high heat, add peanut oil and bug tails and sauté for 2 minutes on each side or until just starting to colour. Add prawns, mushrooms and garlic and sauté for 3-5 minutes or until just cooked. Season with salt and pepper. Add butter and sauté for 3 minutes or until butter is nut brown. Finish by adding parsley and peanuts.

Spoon into small serving bowls, garnish with bull's blood leaves and serve immediately.

Serves 4

CAVIAR & OYSTER APPETIZER

50g (1 3/4oz) salmon roe
16 freshly shucked oysters
30g (1oz) sevruga or osetra caviar
1 sheet gold leaf*, to garnish

In four shot glasses, layer salmon roe, 2 oysters, caviar, 2 oysters and salmon roe. Finish with a quenelle* of caviar on top. Garnish with gold leaf and serve.

Serves 4

Rich treasures from the depths of the sea, golden statues, shells,
pearls and corals, the fascination of glamorous epochs
turned into an imaginative experience...

4 x 180g (6 1/2oz) monkfish fillets
sea salt and cracked black pepper
4 slices pancetta
2 spring onions (scallions), cut into batons and blanched
1/2 cup baby bull's blood* leaves
2 medium kipfler potatoes, cooked and cut into 5mm (1/4in) slices

Croutons
1 slice white bread, crusts removed
10g (1/4oz) butter

Turmeric Vinaigrette
1/3 cup olive oil
2 French shallots, finely chopped
1/2 tsp ground turmeric
1/2 cup white wine
sea salt and cracked black pepper

Preheat oven to 180°C (350°F/Gas 4)

POACHED MONKFISH WITH TURMERIC VINAIGRETTE

To make croutons, cut bread into four 1 x 8cm (1/2 x 3 1/4in) rectangles. Melt butter in a frying pan over medium heat, add bread and fry until golden brown.

To make turmeric vinaigrette, heat 1 tablespoon of olive oil in a frying pan over medium heat, add shallots and sauté for 2 minutes or until soft. Add turmeric and deglaze* with wine. Reduce by half, add remaining 1/4 cup of olive oil and season with salt and pepper.

Season monkfish with salt and pepper and tightly wrap each fillet in a sheet of plastic wrap to form a cylinder shape. Poach in simmering water for 4-5 minutes. Leave in water to cool.

Place pancetta between 2 sheets of baking paper and sandwich between 2 baking trays. Place in oven for 8-10 minutes or until crisp.

Slice monkfish in half and place in centre of each serving plate. Garnish with spring onion batons, bull's blood leaves, kipfler potatoes, crouton and pancetta. Drizzle turmeric vinaigrette around plate and serve.

Serves 4

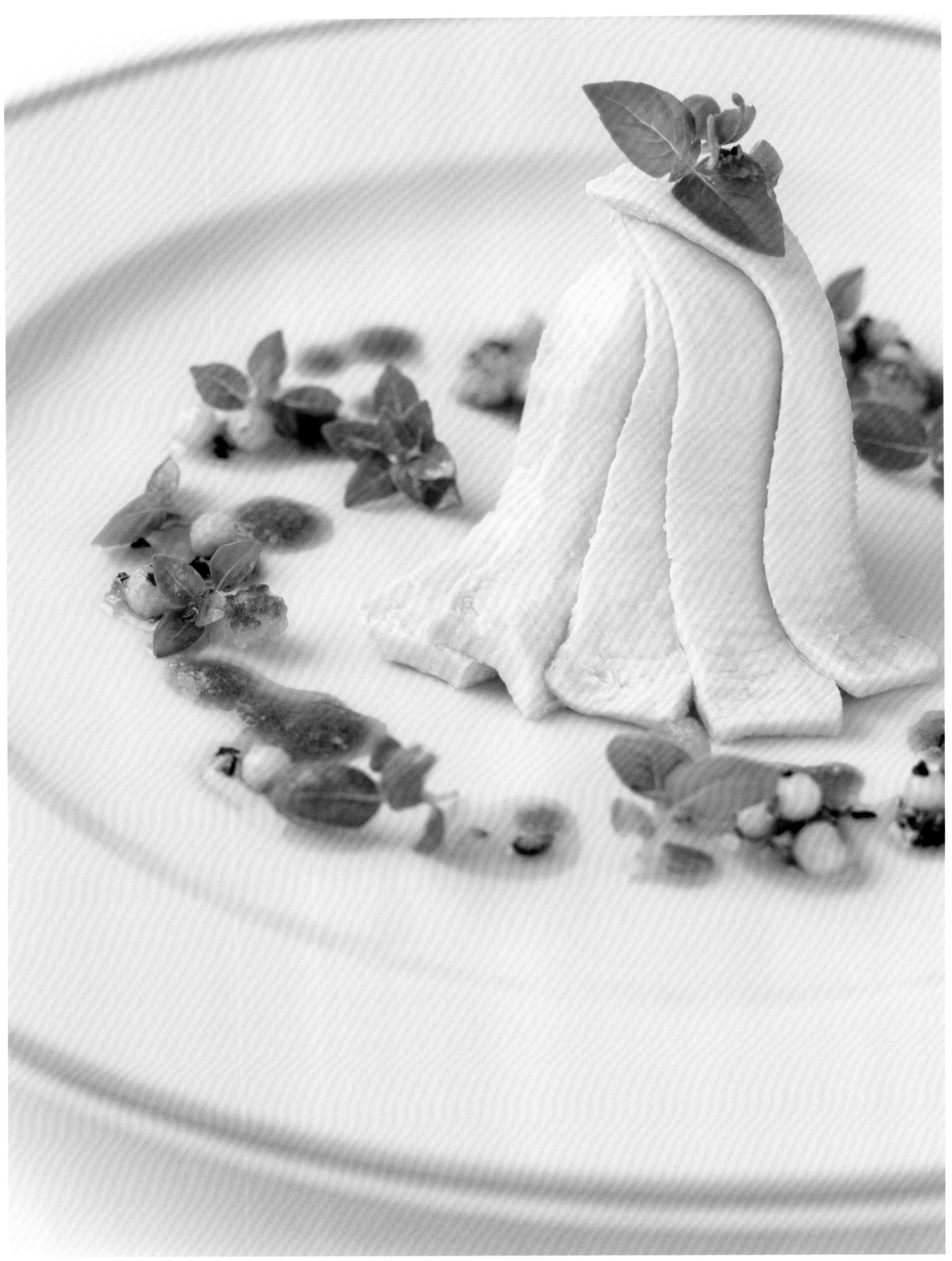

POACHED LOIN OF RABBIT WITH CRESS PESTO & COUSCOUS

2 carrots, peeled and cut into 5cm (2in) lengths
300ml (10 1/2fl oz) chicken stock *(see page 186)*
20g (3/4oz) butter
4 rabbit loins, trimmed of fat and sinew
sea salt and cracked black pepper

50g (1 3/4oz) mograbieh (Israeli) couscous*
24-32 bush basil* tips
4 tbsp black pepper dressing *(see page 187)*

Cress Pesto
1 cup baby watercress
2 1/2 tbsp olive oil
1 garlic clove, chopped
1 tbsp pinenuts, toasted
sea salt and cracked black pepper

Croutons
2 slices white bread, crusts removed
40g (1 1/2oz) butter

Preheat oven to 170°C (325°F/Gas 3)

Combine carrots, 1 cup of chicken stock and the butter in an ovenproof dish and cook, uncovered, in oven for 15 minutes or until tender.

Season rabbit loins with salt and pepper, place in a zip-lock bag with remaining 2 1/2 tablespoons of chicken stock and seal. Place bag in a saucepan of simmering water for 5 minutes. Remove bag and allow rabbit to cool in bag.

Combine couscous and plenty of salted water in a large saucepan. Bring to the boil, reduce heat to low, cover, and simmer for 10 minutes. Remove from heat and break up any clumps of couscous with a fork.

To make cress pesto, combine all ingredients in a food processor and blitz until smooth.

To make croutons, cut bread into 5mm (1/4in) dice. Melt butter in a frying pan over medium heat, add bread and fry until golden. Strain and dry on paper towel.

To serve, carve rabbit loins lengthways into long strips. Place carrot in centre of each serving plate and arrange rabbit slices on top. Dress plate with couscous, croutons and bush basil. Drizzle over black pepper dressing and dot with cress pesto.

Serves 4

Roasted Quail with Gnocchi & Parsnip

2 quails
1/3 cup finely chopped fresh tarragon, flat leaf (Italian) parsley and thyme
1/3 cup extra virgin olive oil
1 parsnip, peeled and cut into batons
sea salt and cracked black pepper
1/2 cup peas, blanched
1 tbsp fresh mint leaves, cut into julienne*

Gnocchi
250g (9oz) desiree potatoes, peeled and chopped into even-sized pieces
sea salt
70g (2 1/2oz) plain (all-purpose) flour

Preheat oven to 180°C (350°F/Gas 4)

Place quail, breast-side up, on a clean work surface. Cut skin between each leg and breast. Twist legs to break joint. Remove legs. Cut along breastbone and through wishbone. Split quail open and cut out backbone. Remove wings. Repeat for remaining quail. Place breasts on the bone on a baking tray, season well and roast in oven for 6 minutes or until golden. Set aside to rest in a warm place for 5 minutes before slicing breasts carefully off bone. Clean legs by removing thighbones and cleaning meat from shinbone. Roast in oven for 3 minutes or until tender and roll thigh meat in chopped herbs.

Place 2 tablespoons of extra virgin olive oil and the parsnip in a baking tray and roast in oven for 10-12 minutes or until golden, season well.

To make gnocchi, cook potatoes by boiling in lightly salted water until just cooked. Strain, allow to steam to reduce water content before mashing, this will help to create a dry mash, and season with salt. Lightly knead flour into warm mashed potato. Roll out into a long sausage shape about 1.5cm (5/8in) in diameter and cut into lozenges 2-3cm (3/4–1 1/4in) in length. Cook in boiling salted water until gnocchi float to surface, remove with a slotted spoon, refresh in iced water and drain well.

Place some parsnip to one side on each serving plate and top with a quail breast. Toss gnocchi, peas and mint in remaining extra virgin olive oil, season and arrange on each plate. Add quail leg and serve.

Serves 4

1 Chinese barbecued duck
4 witlof (chicory/Belgian endive) leaves
1 frisée heart leaves
4 tbsp trimmed enoki mushrooms
24 Vietnamese mint leaves
1/3 cup house dressing *(see page 189)*
1/3 cup black beans, soaked in water for 30 minutes
sea salt and cracked black pepper

House Dressing
200ml (7fl oz) grape seed oil
2 tbsp walnut oil
1 tbsp sherry vinegar
1 tsp wholegrain mustard
1 tbsp port
1 tbsp Madeira
sea salt and cracked black pepper

Place all ingredients in a bowl and whisk until well combined. Check seasoning and adjust if necessary. Refrigerate until required.

Makes 300ml (10 1/2fl oz)

Preheat oven to 170°C (325°F/Gas 3)

Peking Duck Salad with Black Beans

It is best if duck is still warm for this dish: so, if necessary, warm duck in oven for 15 minutes. Remove meat from carcass and thickly slice. Keep warm.

Combine witlof, frisée, mushrooms and 12 mint leaves in a bowl with house dressing. Remove black beans from soaking liquid and squeeze lightly. Add black beans to dressed salad and season with salt and pepper.

Arrange salad and still slightly warm sliced duck in centre of each plate, garnish with remaining mint leaves and serve.

Serves 4

1 tbsp olive oil
4 fresh diver scallops
4 baby squid tubes, skinned and cut into 5mm (1/4in) thick slices
4 baby octopus, beaks removed
sea salt and cracked black pepper
4 x 150g (5 1/2oz) live marron (crayfish), placed in freezer for 20 minutes
1/2 telegraph cucumber, sliced thinly and cut into long spaghetti-like strips
1/4 cup baby mizuna and bull's blood* leaves
4 tbsp Champagne cream sauce *(see page 189)*

Ravioli
120g (4 1/4oz) lobster meat, chopped
juice and zest of 1 lemon
2 tbsp finely chopped fresh tarragon
sea salt and cracked black pepper
4 sheets squid ink pasta *(see page 188)*

Squid Ink & Lobster Ravioli

To make ravioli, combine lobster meat with lemon juice and zest, tarragon and salt and pepper. Place pasta on a lightly floured work surface. Spoon 1 dessertspoon of lobster mixture in centre of pasta sheet about 6cm (2 1/2in) from one end and repeat at 12cm (4 1/2in) intervals. Brush exposed pasta with a little water and place a second pasta sheet over the first, carefully pressing dough around lobster mixture to form a tight seal. Cut out ravioli using a 10cm (4in) round pastry cutter. Repeat with remaining pasta and lobster mixture. Blanch in boiling salted water for 4 minutes, remove with a slotted spoon, drain well and set aside.

Heat olive oil in a large frying pan, add scallops, squid and octopus and sauté over high heat for 5 minutes or until tender. Season with salt and pepper. Cook marron in boiling salted water for 3-4 minutes. Drain, allow to cool a little and remove meat from shell.

To serve, twirl a quarter of the cucumber spaghetti around a fork and place in centre of each serving plate. Place ravioli on top and arrange seafood around plate. Garnish with mizuna and bull's blood leaves and finish with Champagne cream sauce.

Serves 4

Opulent and elegant acanthus motifs conjure up the luxury lifestyle of the baroque and ideally represent the embodiment of passion and boldness.

Goat's Cheese & Spinach Pithivier with Truffle Vinaigrette

1 witlof (chicory/Belgian endive), cut into julienne*
1/2 cup baby bull's blood* leaves

Egg wash
2 egg yolks
pinch of salt

Pithivier
10g (1/4oz) butter
300g (10 1/2oz) baby spinach leaves, washed and dried
sea salt and cracked black pepper
250g (9oz) soft goat's cheese
250g (9oz) goat's curd
1/2 tsp grated nutmeg
1 tbsp black truffle oil
10g (1/4oz) black truffle, very finely diced (optional)
500g (1lb 2oz) puff pastry *(see page 189)*

Truffle Vinaigrette
100ml (3 1/2fl oz) extra virgin olive oil
5 French shallots, finely diced
5 tsp dijon mustard
1 1/2 tbsp redcurrant jelly
2 tbsp sherry vinegar
2 1/2 tbsp black truffle oil
2 tbsp hazelnut oil
1 1/2 tbsp fino sherry
1 tbsp cognac
1 tbsp Madeira
sea salt and cracked black pepper

Preheat oven to 170°C (325°F/Gas 3)

Line a baking tray with baking paper.

To make egg wash, combine egg yolks and salt in a bowl and lightly beat.

To make pithivier, melt butter in a saucepan, add spinach and cook over medium heat until wilted. Season with salt and pepper and remove from pan. Strain in a colander and squeeze out as much liquid as possible. Allow to cool, then finely chop. Combine goat's cheese with goat's curd in a bowl, add nutmeg, spinach, truffle oil and truffle, if using, and season well. Form into four balls, wrap in plastic wrap and refrigerate until required. Roll out puff pastry on a lightly floured work surface to a thickness of 3mm (1/8in) and cut into eight 15cm (6in) squares. Place a ball of goat's cheese mixture in the centre of one puff pastry square. Brush some egg wash around pastry edge and place another sheet of pastry on top. Gently press both pieces of pastry together without trapping any air. Place a 10cm (4in) round pastry cutter over pithivier and press down firmly to cut away excess pastry, leaving a border about 5mm (1/4in) wide. Using a small, sharp paring knife, lightly score a pattern into the pastry 'dome' starting in the centre and bringing the knife down to the base to form a C shape. Repeat these cuts, taking care not to puncture the pastry, until all pithivier is scored. The scoring needs to be at about 5cm (2in) intervals. Repeat process with remaining pastry and goat's cheese mixture so that you have four pithiviers in total. Brush pithiviers with egg wash, place on prepared baking tray and transfer to oven for 25 minutes or until golden.

To make truffle vinaigrette, heat 1 tablespoon of extra virgin olive oil in a frying pan over medium heat, add shallots and sauté for 2 minutes or until soft. Transfer shallots to a small bowl. Add redcurrant jelly to pan and allow to caramelize until nearly burnt. Remove from heat and carefully pour in sherry vinegar to deglaze* pan. Add to shallots and whisk in remaining ingredients. Season and refrigerate until required. This dressing needs to be at room temperature for serving.

Place a warm pithivier in centre of each serving plate and dress plate with some truffle vinaigrette. Garnish with witlof and bull's blood leaves and serve.

Serves 4

Chocolate Semifreddo with Mango & Hazelnut

Meringue
2 mango cheeks
8 dried rose petals
1 tbsp julienne* of fresh mint
1 mango cheek, chopped into dice
1 1/2 tbsp sugar syrup *(see page 188)*

Chocolate Semifreddo
120g (4 1/4oz) dark couverture chocolate, roughly chopped
120g (4 1/4oz) milk chocolate, roughly chopped
1/4 cup caster (superfine) sugar
3 eggs, separated
100ml (3 1/2fl oz) double (thick) cream
150ml (5fl oz) pouring cream

Tuiles
100ml (3 1/2fl oz) fresh orange juice
200g (7oz) caster (superfine) sugar
100g (3 1/2oz) plain (all-purpose) flour
100g (3 1/2oz) butter, melted
1/2 tsp ground cinnamon
100g (3 1/2oz) pistachio nuts, crushed

Hazelnut Meringues
4 egg whites
160g (5 3/4oz) caster (superfine) sugar
1/2 tsp vanilla extract
1/2 tsp white vinegar
1 tsp powdered gelatine
50g (1 3/4oz) ground hazelnuts

To make chocolate semifreddo, melt dark and milk chocolate in a heatproof bowl over a saucepan of simmering water. In a separate bowl, whisk half of the sugar with egg yolks until pale and thick and fold into chocolate. Gradually fold in double cream. Whisk pouring cream in another bowl until soft peaks form and fold into chocolate mixture. Whisk egg whites with remaining sugar until stiff and glossy. Gently fold egg whites into chocolate mixture and spoon into 10cm (4in) ring moulds. Cover with plastic wrap and freeze for at least 2 hours.

Preheat oven to 180°C (350°F/Gas 4).
Line a baking tray with baking paper.

To make tuiles, mix orange juice, sugar, flour, butter and cinnamon in a bowl until combined. Place four spoonfuls of mixture on prepared baking tray and spread to form 12cm (4 1/2in) discs. Sprinkle over pistachio nuts and bake in oven for 5-6 minutes or until golden. Set aside to cool and harden.

Decrease oven temperature to 100°C (200°F/Gas 1/2).
Line a baking tray with baking paper.

To make hazelnut meringues, whisk egg whites and sugar in a heatproof bowl over a saucepan of simmering water until light and fluffy. Remove from heat and whisk until cold. Gently fold in vanilla, vinegar, gelatine and hazelnuts, trying not to knock out too much air. Spoon into a piping bag and pipe 12cm (4 1/2in) discs about 1.5cm (5/8in) thick on to prepared baking tray. Place in oven and bake for 2 hours.

Slice mango cheeks very thinly and fold into a circle shape.

To serve, place a hazelnut meringue on each serving plate. Top with chocolate semifreddo, mango cheek slices and a tuile. Decorate plate with rose petals, mint, diced mango and sugar syrup.

Serves 4

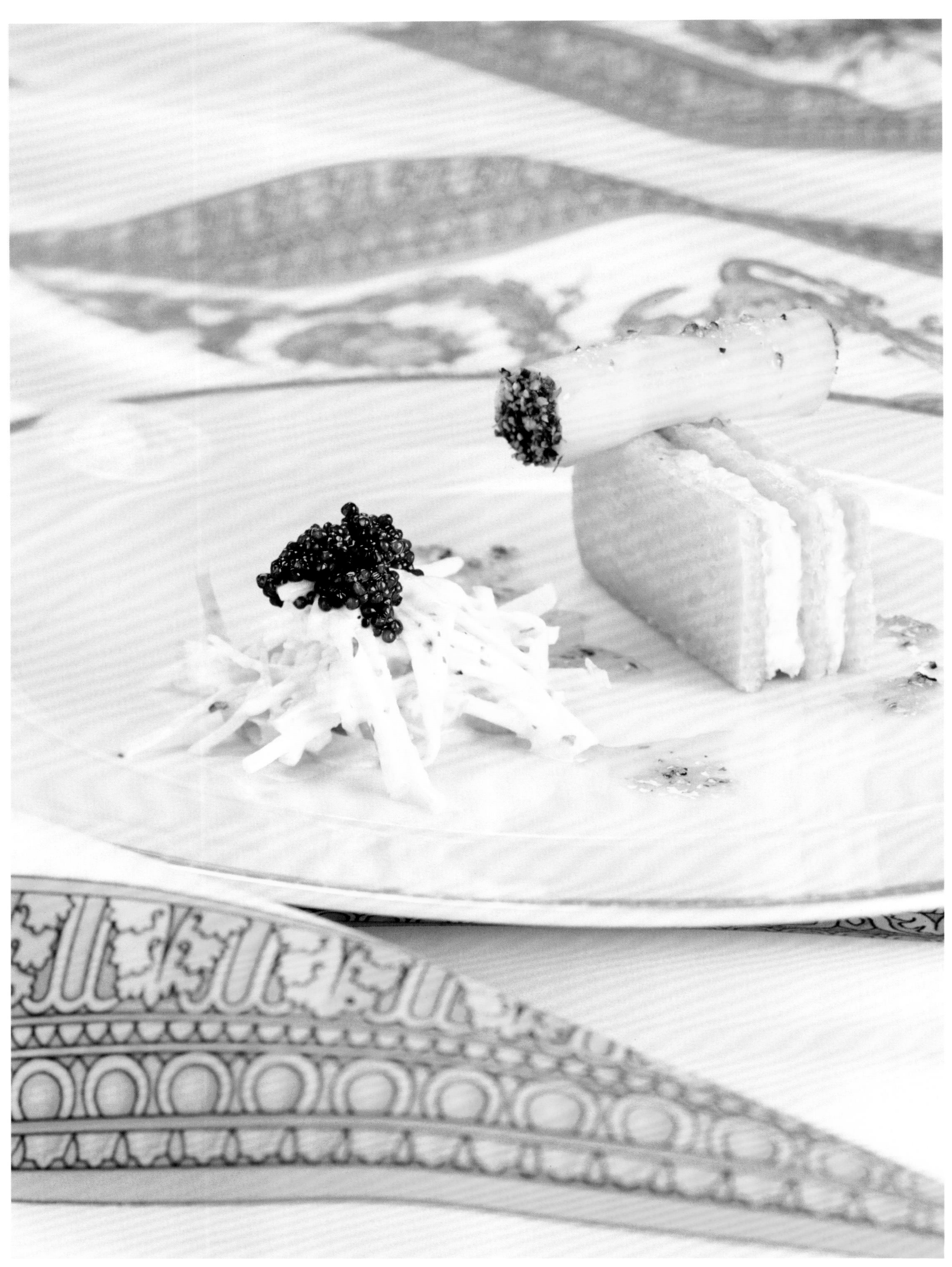

SAND CRAB SANDWICH WITH CANNELLONI, WITLOF & CELERIAC REMOULADE

Celeriac Remoulade
1 tbsp sevruga or osetra caviar
1/3 cup olive oil
cracked black pepper

Sand Crab Sandwich
12 thin slices brioche *(see page 187)*, toasted
180g (6 1/2oz) sand crabmeat
1/4 cup aioli *(see page 186)*
sea salt and cracked black pepper

Cannelloni
6 green New Caledonian prawns, peeled, deveined and finely chopped
juice and zest of 1 lemon
2 tbsp finely chopped fines herbes*, fresh flat leaf (Italian) parsley, chervil, tarragon and chives
sea salt and cracked black pepper
4 sheets pasta dough *(see page 188)*

Witlof and Celeriac Remoulade
60g (2 1/4oz) celeriac, cut into julienne*
1 tbsp aioli *(see page 186)*
1 witlof (chicory/Belgian endive), sliced

To make sand crab sandwich, cut brioche slices into 3 x 8cm (1 1/4 x 3 1/2in) fingers. Mix crabmeat with aioli and season with salt and pepper. Make a triple-decker sandwich with crab mixture and brioche and repeat this process until all brioche and crab mixture is used.

To make cannelloni, combine prawns, lemon juice and zest, 1 1/2 tablespoons of fines herbes and season with salt and pepper. Spoon prawn mixture into a piping bag. Place pasta sheets on a lightly floured work surface and pipe a line of filling lengthways down centre of each sheet of dough. Brush edge with a little water, roll into cigar shapes and press to seal edge closed. Blanch in boiling salted water for 3 minutes, remove with a slotted spoon and drain well. Trim ends and dip into remaining fines herbes.

To make witlof and celeriac remoulade, dress celeriac with aioli and mix well. Add witlof and mix to combine.

Place a sand crab sandwich on each serving plate and arrange cannelloni on top. Arrange remoulade on plate and garnish with caviar. Drizzle plate with olive oil, scatter over pepper and serve.

Serves 4

Cheesecake Slice

4 tbsp mascarpone
1 vanilla bean, split lengthways, seeds removed, and cut in half to make 4 batons
4 fresh mint tips

Tuiles
100ml (3 1/2fl oz) fresh orange juice
200g (7oz) caster (superfine) sugar
100g (3 1/2oz) plain (all-purpose) flour, sifted
100g (3 1/2oz) butter, melted
1/2 tsp ground cinnamon

Sponge Base
4 eggs
120g (4 1/4oz) caster (superfine) sugar
1 tsp vanilla extract
120g (4 1/4oz) plain (all-purpose) flour
1 tbsp milk

Cream Cheese Topping
300g (10 1/2oz) cream cheese
225ml (7 3/4fl oz) pouring cream, semi-whipped*
2 tsp powdered gelatine
1/3 cup hot water
125g (4 1/2oz) caster (superfine) sugar
1 1/2 tbsp water
3 egg whites
1 tsp vanilla extract
1 1/2 tbsp lemon juice
pinch of salt

Orange Gel
1 cup water
250g (9oz) sugar
100ml (3 1/2fl oz) fresh orange juice
2 gelatine sheets, soaked in cold water for 2 minutes or until soft

Orange Candy
1 orange
1 cup water, for blanching zest
1 cup sugar
1 cup water, for syrup
1 tbsp caster (superfine) sugar

Preheat oven to 180°C (350°F/Gas 4)

Line a baking tray with baking paper. Grease inside and line base of a 15cm (6in) square cake tin with baking paper.

To make tuiles, mix orange juice, sugar, flour, butter and cinnamon in a bowl until combined. Place spoonfuls on prepared baking tray and spread to form triangles. Bake in oven for 5-6 minutes or until golden.

To make sponge base, lightly whisk eggs in a large mixing bowl. Add sugar, whisk until pale and thick and stir in vanilla. Fold in flour alternately with milk, using a large metal spoon, until thoroughly combined and free of lumps. Pour into prepared cake tin, place in oven and bake for 8-10 minutes or until lightly coloured and firm to touch.

To make cream cheese topping, place cream cheese in a large mixing bowl and beat until smooth using a paddle attachment. Scrape down side of bowl often during this process. Fold in cream and set aside. Combine gelatine and hot water in a bowl, stir well and leave for 5 minutes. Place sugar and water in a saucepan and boil until temperature reaches 120°C (235°F) on a sugar thermometer. Whisk egg whites until soft peaks form. Slowly pour in sugar syrup and whisk until thick and glossy. Fold in gelatine mixture, then fold in vanilla, lemon and salt. Lastly add cream cheese mixture, mixing quickly and gently by hand to retain volume. Pour over sponge base and place in freezer for 30 minutes or until cold.

To make orange gel, bring water and sugar to the boil in a heavy-based saucepan and add orange juice. Remove from heat, add softened gelatine and stir until dissolved. When nearly cold, pour over cheesecake and return to freezer for 15 minutes or until set. Slice into 8 portions using a knife dipped in hot water.

To make orange candy, using a paring knife, remove skin from orange, avoiding white pith, and cut into 4 pieces. Combine orange zest and 1/4 cup of water in a saucepan over high heat, bring to the boil and strain. Repeat process 3 more times until all water is used. Then make sugar syrup by bringing sugar and water to the boil, add zest and boil for 10 minutes until zest is transparent and soft. Roll each piece of zest in caster sugar.

Combine mascarpone and vanilla seeds in a small bowl and set aside.

Place 2 portions of cheesecake and a quenelle* of vanilla mascarpone on each serving plate. Arrange tuile, vanilla bean baton, mint and orange candy on top of vanilla mascarpone and serve.

Serves 4

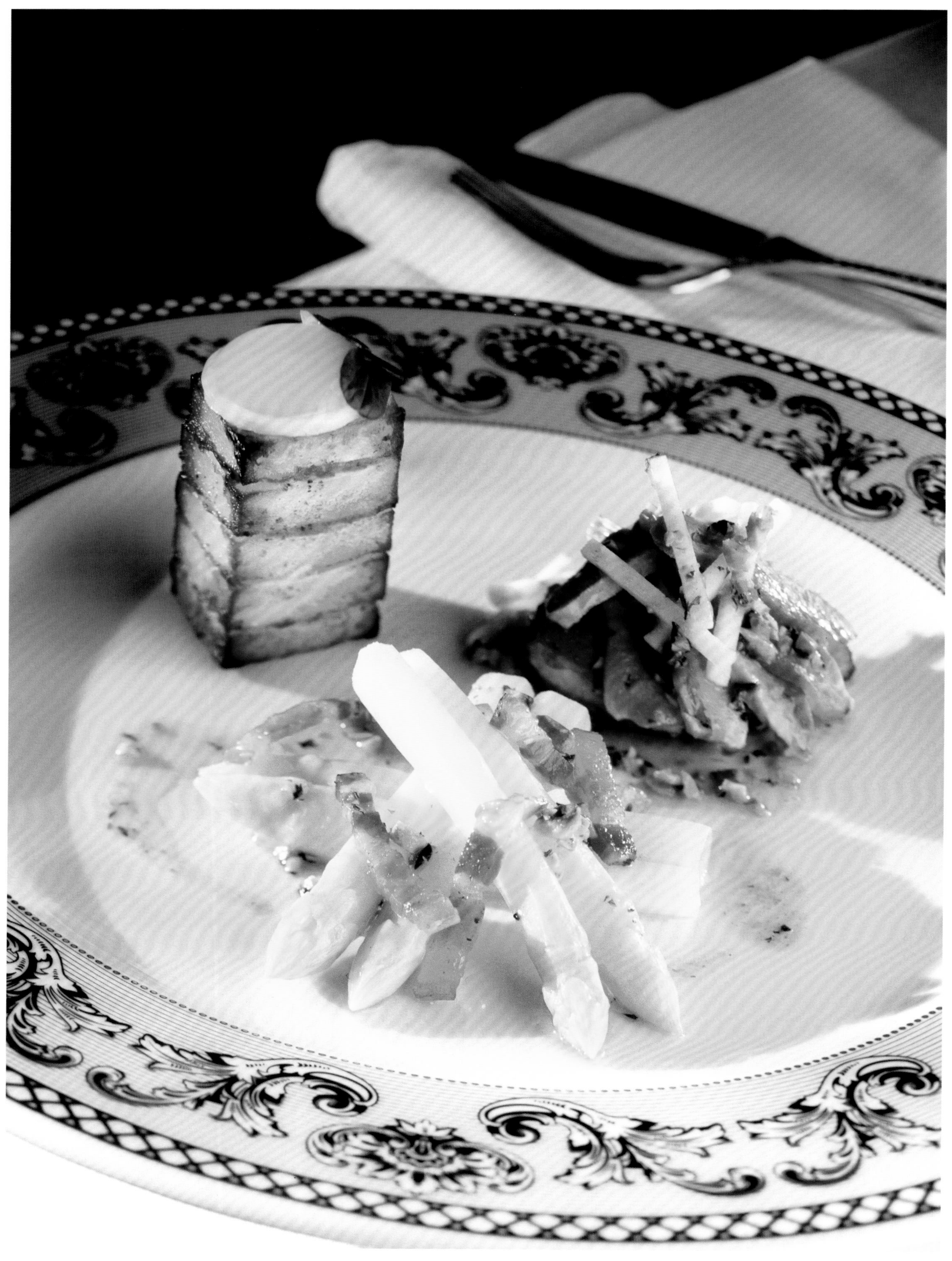

Smoked Duck Salad with White Asparagus

2 duck breast fillets
sea salt and cracked black pepper
1/2 cup olive oil
16 white asparagus spears, trimmed
4 quail eggs
40g (1 1/2oz) butter
2 tbsp chopped walnuts
4 tbsp bacon lardons*
1/2 red apple, cut into julienne*

Potato Terrine
4 large desiree potatoes, peeled
400ml (14fl oz) duck fat
sea salt and cracked black pepper
4 slices prosciutto

Preheat oven to 180°C (350°F/Gas 4)

If you don't have a smoker you can use the stovetop and a perforated tray with a lid.

To make potato terrine, cut potatoes into perfect 2.5 x 4cm (1 x 1 1/2in) rectangles. Warm duck fat in a roasting tin, add potatoes and toss well. Transfer to oven and roast for 12-15 minutes or until potatoes are soft. Strain duck fat into a container and reserve for later use. Line a 20 x 5cm (8 x 2in) terrine mould with two layers of plastic wrap, making sure you press it into corners. Layer and press potatoes into terrine mould, adding seasoning and prosciutto between each layer. Cover in plastic wrap, cut out a piece of Styrofoam or thick cardboard that is same size as top of terrine and tie in place with butchers' twine. Refrigerate for a minimum of 2 hours or until needed.

To smoke duck breasts, season with salt and pepper and set aside for 30 minutes. Get smoker really hot, add hickory wood chips and duck breasts and smoke duck on each side for about 5 minutes. Remove breasts from smoker.

Heat 2 tablespoons of olive oil in a frying pan over high heat and sear duck, breast-side down, for 3 minutes, turn and pan-fry for 4 minutes for medium-rare. Set aside to rest for 5-10 minutes in a warm place and slice into slivers.

Cook asparagus in boiling salted water until just tender.

Fry quail eggs in 2 tablespoons of olive oil in a frying pan over low heat. Drain on paper towel and cut around each quail egg with a 3cm (1 1/4in) round cutter.

When ready to plate up, cut potato terrine into four 5cm (2in) squares. Heat remaining 2 tablespoons of olive oil in a frying pan over medium heat, add potato terrine squares and sauté on each side until golden.

In a separate frying pan, melt butter until nut brown, add walnuts and sauté for 20 seconds. Season with salt and pepper.

To serve, place potato terrine on each serving plate and top with a quail egg. Arrange duck, asparagus and bacon lardons on plate, garnish duck with apple and dress plate with butter and walnut sauce.

Serves 4

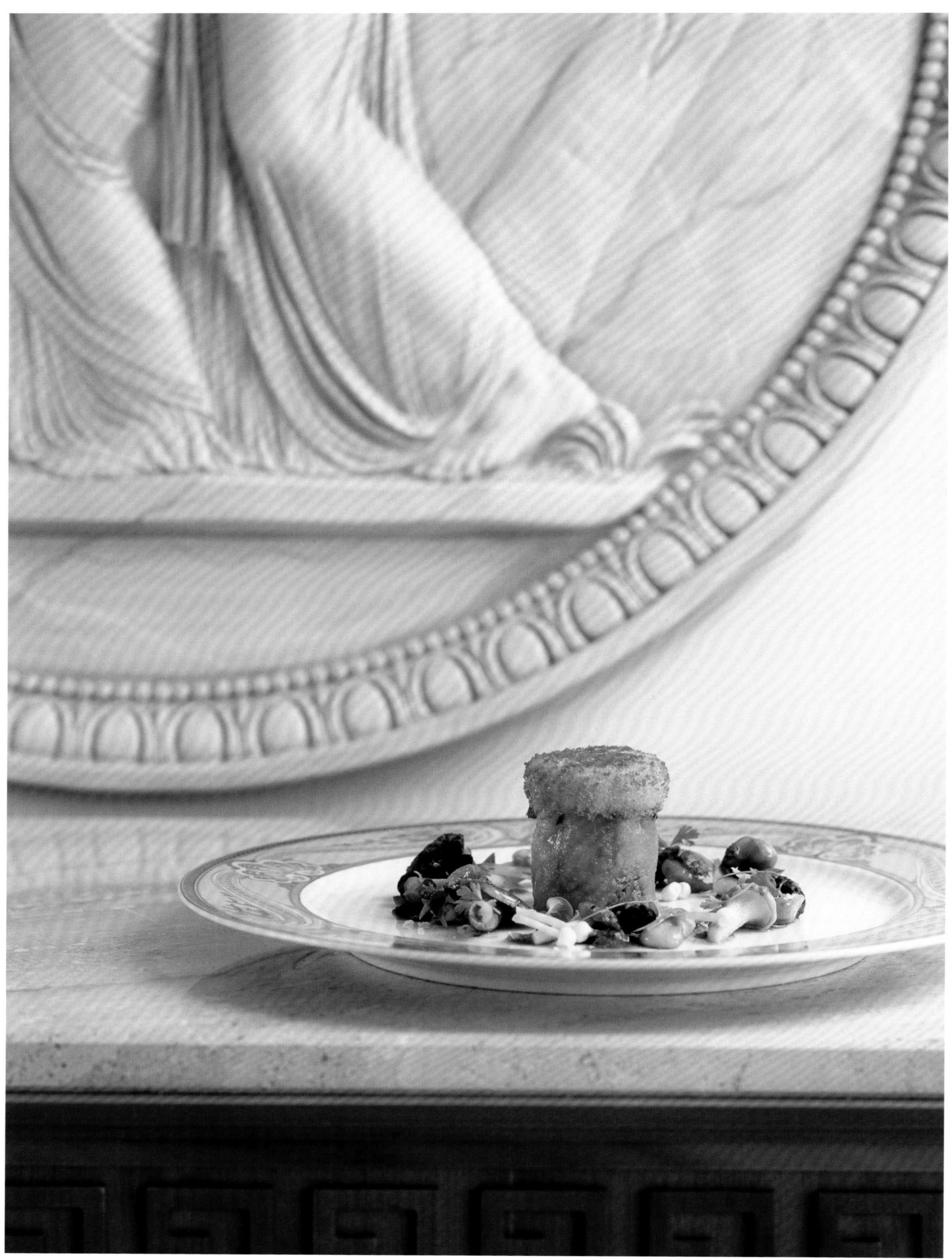

1 kg (2lb 4oz) oxtail, cut into 6 pieces
600ml (21fl oz) red wine
6 cups beef stock *(see page 187)*
1 large onion, peeled and chopped
1 carrot, peeled and chopped
1 celery stalk, peeled and chopped
1 medium leek, washed and chopped
3 bay leaves
2 sprigs fresh thyme
cracked black pepper
4 egg yolks, lightly beaten
200g (7oz) fresh brioche *(see page 187)* crumbs
20 chervil leaves, to garnish
1/3 cup extra virgin olive oil

Mushroom Salad
1/3 cup olive oil
180g (6 1/2oz) mixed mushrooms,
such as shimeji, enoki, shiitake (quartered), oyster (sliced) and Swiss brown (quartered)
sea salt and cracked black pepper

Preheat oven to 180°C (350°F/Gas 4)

Braised Oxtail with Mushroom Salad

Combine oxtail, wine, stock, onion, carrot, celery, leek, bay leaves, thyme and pepper in a large saucepan, bring to the boil. Reduce heat to low, cover, and braise for 3-4 hours. Allow to cool a little and remove meat from bones. Place meat in a sheet of plastic wrap, tightly roll into a cylinder and set aside to cool completely. Cut into 4 portions and unwrap from plastic.

Crumb top of each oxtail cylinder by dipping into egg yolks and then coating with brioche crumbs. Repeat this procedure three times. Place in a roasting tin and roast in oven for 8-10 minutes or until crust is golden brown.

To make mushroom salad, heat olive oil in a frying pan and sauté mushrooms over high heat for 5-8 minutes or until cooked, season with salt and pepper.

To serve, place oxtail in centre of each serving plate, arrange mushroom salad around oxtail and garnish with chervil and a drizzle of extra virgin olive oil.

Serves 4

Partridge on Puff Pastry

4 sheets puff pastry *(see page 189)*
4 tbsp black olive tapenade *(see page 186)*
2 egg yolks, lightly beaten
2 partridge breast fillets
sea salt and cracked black pepper
1/2 cup olive oil
1 French shallot, finely chopped
1 garlic clove, finely chopped
1 cup mixed sliced mushrooms, such as oyster, chestnut and Swiss brown
1 medium carrot, chopped into dice
1 small potato, peeled and chopped into dice
1/2 small celeriac, peeled and chopped into dice
2/3 cup veal jus *(see page 187)*
8 fresh chive tips
1/4 cup baby bull's blood* leaves

Preheat oven to 220°C (425°F/Gas 7)

Cut puff pastry sheets into four 7 x 12cm (2 3/4 x 4 1/2in) rectangles and prick with tines of a fork. Spread 1/2 tablespoon of tapenade in centre of each puff pastry rectangle. Using a pastry brush, lightly brush egg yolks around edge of each rectangle. Place on a baking tray and bake in oven for 4-5 minutes or until golden.

Season partridge breasts with salt and pepper. Heat 1 tablespoon of olive oil in a frying pan, add partridge breasts and pan-fry over high heat for 3 minutes on each side, then set aside to rest for 5-10 minutes.

In another frying pan, heat 3 tablespoons of olive oil, add shallot and garlic and sauté over medium heat for 2 minutes. Add mushrooms and sauté for 6-8 minutes or until soft. Season and place on pastry cases. Slice partridge into slivers and arrange on top of mushrooms.

In a separate pan, heat 2 tablespoons of olive oil over medium heat, add carrot, potato and celeriac, season with salt and pepper, and sauté for 5 minutes. Deglaze* with veal jus and continue to cook for 6-8 minutes or until vegetables are tender.

Place a pastry case in centre of each serving plate. Make a quenelle* of remaining tapenade and place on top of partridge. Garnish plate with vegetables in veal jus, chive tips and bull's blood leaves and serve.

Serves 4

4 cups veal stock *(see page 187)*
sea salt and cracked black pepper
100ml (3 1/2fl oz) Madeira or port (optional)
12 thin slices truffle
1 tsp truffle oil

Raft
400g (14oz) minced (ground) beef
1 medium carrot, peeled and finely chopped
1 small onion, peeled and finely chopped
1 celery stalk, finely chopped
1 garlic clove, peeled and finely chopped
5 egg whites

Vegetable Garnish
1 potato, chopped into dice
1 spring onion (scallion), finely chopped
4 shiitake mushrooms, thinly sliced
2 baby carrots, sliced
50g (1 3/4oz) enoki mushrooms, trimmed

BEEF CONSOMMÉ WITH TRUFFLES

You can use other types of vegetables for this dish – cabbage, celeriac, leek, peas and different mushrooms. Those in season usually are the best.

To make raft, in a large bowl mix beef, carrot, onion, celery, garlic and egg whites with a wooden spoon.

Transfer raft mixture to a large saucepan, add veal stock and whisk to combine. Bring to a simmer, stirring occasionally, making sure raft doesn't catch on base of pan, and cook until raft is floating on top. Continue to simmer gently for 10 minutes or until a clear consommé forms. Very gently strain through a muslin cloth or coffee filter. Season to taste and add Madeira or port, if desired.

To make vegetable garnish, individually blanch potato, spring onion, shiitake mushrooms, carrots and enoki mushrooms in boiling salted water until tender.

To serve, place vegetable garnish and truffle slices in each serving bowl, pour over hot consommé and drizzle over a few drops of truffle oil.

Serves 4

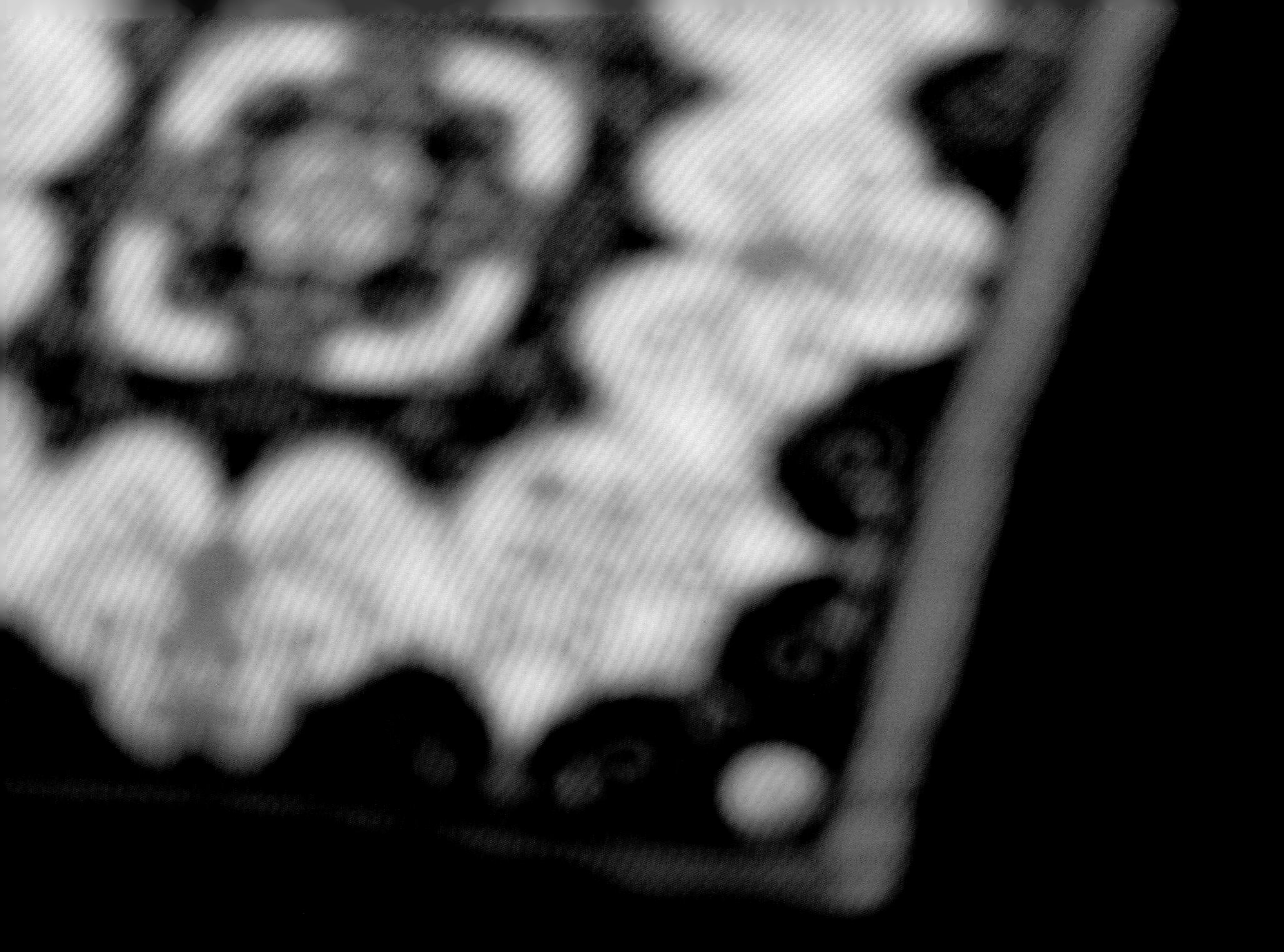

A great way to augment this dish is to add some finely chopped jalopena peppers (chillies), which will give it a lively kick.

ASPARAGUS PANNA COTTA

1 telegraph cucumber
8 asparagus tips, to garnish
1/2 cup baby cress leaves
1 pear cheek, cut into batons
1 spring onion (scallion), cut into slivers
1/3 cup extra virgin olive oil
sea salt and cracked black pepper

Asparagus Panna Cotta
1/3 cup olive oil
1/2 small onion, finely chopped
1 garlic clove, finely chopped
200ml (7fl oz) chicken stock *(see page 186)*
2 bunches (350g/12oz) asparagus, trimmed and chopped
1 gelatine sheet, softened in cold water for 5 minutes
2 1/2 tbsp pouring cream
sea salt and cracked black pepper

To make asparagus panna cotta, heat olive oil in a large saucepan, add onion and garlic and sauté gently for 4 minutes or until soft. Add chicken stock and bring to the boil. Add asparagus and cook for 15 minutes or until tender. Purée in a blender, add soaked gelatine sheet while still hot and pulse to combine. Add cream and season with salt and pepper.

Cut 4 long, thin slices from cucumber. Line four 6cm (2 1/2in) ring moulds with a slice of cucumber and pour over asparagus mixture. Place in refrigerator for 2 hours or until set.

Blanch asparagus tips in boiling salted water until just tender.

Unmould asparagus panna cotta in middle of each serving plate. Arrange cress leaves, pear batons and spring onion slivers around panna cotta. Use 2 asparagus tips to garnish each panna cotta. Dress cress with extra virgin olive oil, salt and pepper and serve.

Serves 4

VEAL LIVER WITH RÖSTI POTATO

1/3 cup olive oil
4 x 180g (6 1/2oz) veal livers, skin removed, cut into goujons*
1 French shallot, finely diced
2 garlic cloves, thinly sliced
4 tbsp pancetta lardons*
1/3 cup apple cider
30g (1oz) butter, chopped into dice
sea salt and cracked black pepper
1 green apple, peeled and diced
1 green apple, peeled and chopped into julienne*

Rösti Potato
2 large desiree potatoes, scrubbed
2 tbsp olive oil
sea salt and cracked black pepper
20g (3/4oz) butter

To make rösti potato, cook potatoes in their skin in boiling salted water until tender. Drain and set aside to cool completely, then peel and coarsely grate. Form into four 10cm (4in) cakes. In a hot, non-stick frying pan over medium heat, add olive oil and potato cakes and brown on one side. Turn, season with salt and pepper, add butter and continue cooking until potato is caramelized and golden underneath. Invert on to a warmed plate and set aside.

Heat olive oil in a separate frying pan over medium-high heat, add veal liver goujons and sauté on both sides for 4 minutes or until golden brown and medium-rare. Remove liver from pan, reduce heat, add shallot, garlic and pancetta lardons and sauté for 3 minutes or until pancetta is starting to brown. Deglaze* pan with apple cider, reduce by one-third and monter* butter into pan to make a butter sauce. Season with salt and pepper.

To serve, in centre of each serving plate, place a rösti potato and pile veal liver goujons on top. Dress with butter sauce and diced apple and arrange apple julienne on top of goujons.

Serves 4

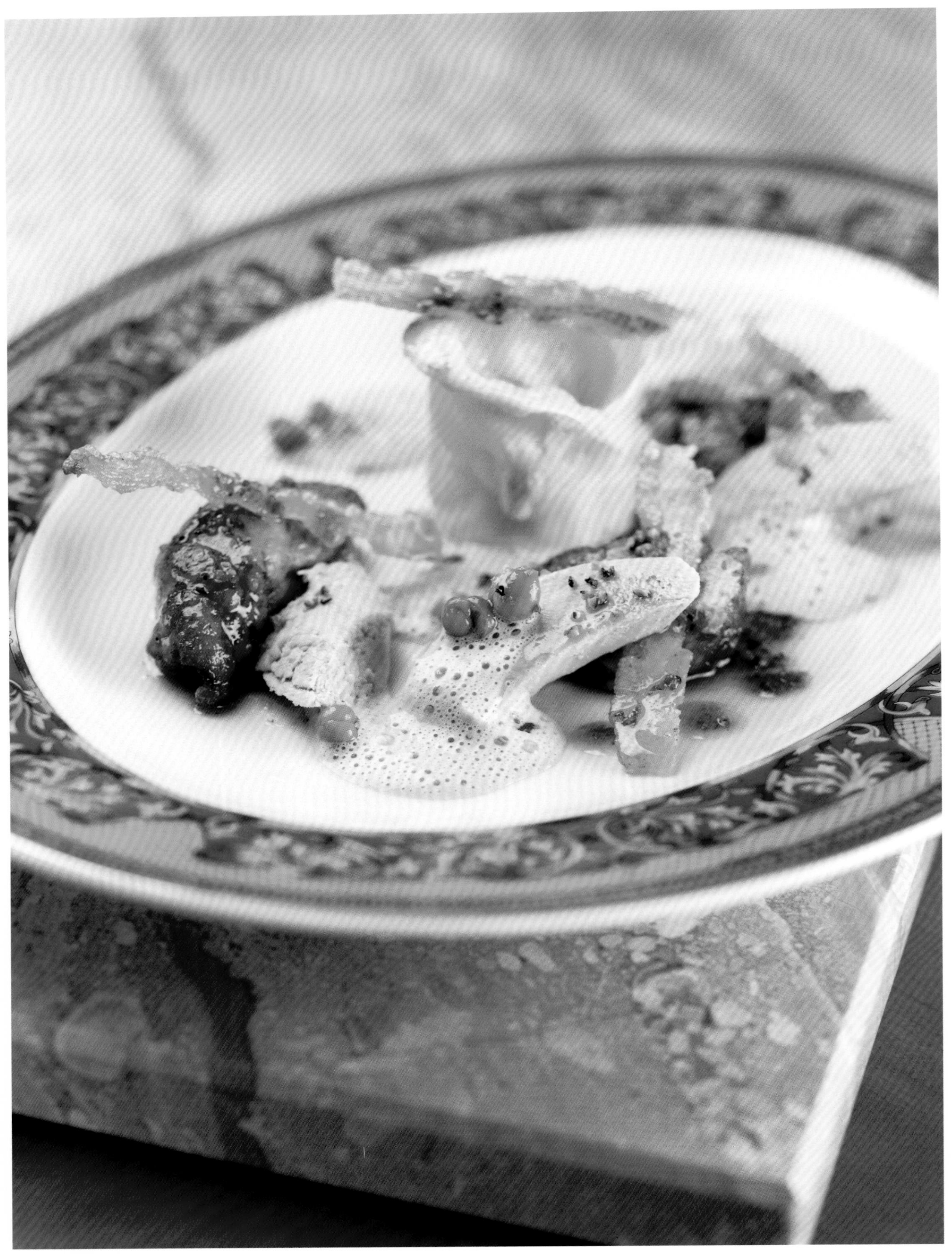

Pasta & Sweetbreads

4 sheets pasta dough *(see page 188)*
12 slices flat pancetta
2 pheasant breast fillets
sea salt and cracked black pepper
1/2 tbsp olive oil
240g (8 1/2oz) sweetbreads*, skinned
20g (3/4oz) butter
4 tbsp peas, blanched

Duxelles
3 tbsp olive oil
1 cup sliced mixed mushrooms, such as enoki, shimeji and oyster
3 French shallots, finely chopped
1 tsp fresh thyme leaves
3 garlic cloves, finely chopped
sea salt and cracked black pepper

Red Wine Froth
2 French shallots, finely chopped
1 tbsp olive oil
1/3 cup red wine
1/3 cup veal stock *(see page 187)*
2 1/2 tbsp pouring cream

You could also use chicken breast, guinea fowl or partridge.

To make duxelles, heat olive oil in a frying pan, add mushrooms, shallots, thyme and garlic, season with salt and pepper and sauté over medium heat until mushrooms are tender. Set aside to cool down.

Place pasta sheets on a lightly floured work surface and cut out four 10cm (4in) discs. Place a good teaspoon of duxelles in centre of each disc and shape into tortellini by brushing edge of pasta disc with a little water, fold disc in half to enclose filling and seal edge well. Now bring two outer points together to form a tight ring and seal with a little water. Finally, roll curved flap of pasta over to back of now-formed tortellini. Blanch tortellini in boiling salted water for 5 minutes or until pasta is cooked, remove with a slotted spoon, drain and set aside.

Preheat oven to 180°C (350°F/Gas 4).

Place pancetta slices between two sheets of baking paper and sandwich between two baking trays. Transfer to oven for 8-10 minutes or until crisp.

Season pheasant breasts with salt and pepper. Heat olive oil in a frying pan, add pheasant and sear on each side for 3 minutes or until nicely browned. Transfer to oven to roast for 6 minutes for medium-rare. Leave to rest for 10 minutes and slice into slivers.

Season sweetbreads with salt and pepper. Melt butter in a separate frying pan, add sweetbreads and sear for 4-7 minutes or until caramelized.

To make red wine froth, heat olive oil in a saucepan, add shallots and sauté for 2 minutes or until tender. Deglaze* with red wine and reduce by half. Add veal stock and reduce by half again. Add cream and froth up using a hand blender.

To serve, re-blanch tortellini and peas in boiling salted water for 1 minute, remove with a slotted spoon and drain well. Arrange pheasant slices and sweetbreads on each serving plate. Place tortellini in the middle of each plate and garnish with peas, pepper, crisp pancetta and red wine froth.

Serves 4

RABBIT CHOPS WITH TOMATO TERRINE

1 rabbit saddle with best end, from 2.5kg (5lb 8oz) rabbit
2 1/2 tbsp pouring cream
sea salt and cracked black pepper
12 fresh baby basil leaves
12 small pieces caul*, soaked in water for 24 hours
2 tbsp olive oil
4 tbsp bacon lardons*
8 dried baby figs, soaked in warm water until soft
16-20 mâche* (lamb's lettuce) leaves

Tomato Terrine
8 vine-ripened tomatoes, blanched and peeled*, with stalk
200ml (7fl oz) olive oil
50ml (1 1/2fl oz) aged balsamic vinegar
2 garlic cloves, finely chopped
1/2 cup fresh basil leaves
2 sprigs fresh thyme
sea salt and cracked black pepper

Preheat oven to 180°C (350°F/Gas 4)

To make tomato terrine, carefully cut top from each tomato. To make tomato petals, quarter tomatoes and remove seeds. Place tomato petals and tops in a shallow bowl and add olive oil, balsamic vinegar, garlic, basil, thyme, salt and pepper. Cover and transfer to refrigerator to marinate for 2 hours. Strain and press tomato petals into eight 4cm (1 1/2in) ring moulds and top with a tomato lid.

Cut 12 rib bones from best end into cutlets. Remove all sinew and clean bones well. Make a farce* using 100g (4oz) of remaining meat that has also been well trimmed. Blend in a food processor with cream, salt and pepper. Place 1 dessertspoon of farce on each rabbit cutlet and garnish with a basil leaf. Wrap each cutlet individually in caul* and season. Heat olive oil in a frying pan, add cutlets and sear on each side for 3 minutes or until golden. Place in oven for 3-4 minutes and set aside to rest in a warm place. Using same pan, sauté bacon lardons in residual oil until crisp.

To serve, place 3 rabbit cutlets, two tomato terrines and 2 figs on each serving plate. Scatter over bacon lardons, drizzle over pan juices and garnish with mâche leaves.

Serves 4

Venison Loin with Marmalade

2 cups baby spinach
600g (1lb 5oz) venison loin, trimmed of sinew
sea salt and cracked black pepper
2 tbsp olive oil
4 tbsp good-quality marmalade, plus extra to garnish
40g (1 1/2oz) butter
100ml (3 1/2fl oz) veal jus *(see page 187)*
1 tbsp finely chopped fines herbes*, fresh flat leaf (Italian) parsley, chives, chervil and tarragon
4 slices truffle, cut into julienne*
16-20 baby mâche* (lamb's lettuce) leaves

Spaetzle
2 cups plain (all-purpose) flour, sifted
5 eggs
100ml (3 1/2fl oz) milk
sea salt and cracked black pepper
pinch of grated nutmeg

Cauliflower Purée
2 tbsp olive oil
1/4 onion, finely diced
2 garlic cloves, finely chopped
300g (10 1/2oz) cauliflower, cut into florets
100ml (3 1/2fl oz) chicken stock *(see page 186)*
sea salt and cracked black pepper
1/2 cup pouring cream

Blanch spinach for 30 seconds or until wilted, strain and squeeze dry.

Season venison loin with salt and pepper. Heat olive oil in a frying pan over high heat, add venison and sear on all sides for 3-5 minutes for medium-rare.

Place two sheets of plastic wrap on a work surface and spread out spinach to form a 15 x 20cm (6 x 8in) rectangle. Spread marmalade over spinach and place venison in centre. Tightly roll up into a cylinder and, while still wrapped in plastic, slice into four equal portions and carefully unwrap.

To make spaetzle*, combine flour, eggs and milk in a mixing bowl and mix until smooth. Season with salt, pepper and nutmeg. Push through a spaetzle sieve or a small colander into salted boiling water and cook for 2-3 minutes or until they float to surface, drain and refresh.

To make cauliflower purée, heat olive oil in a saucepan over medium heat, add onion, garlic and cauliflower, cover, and sweat for 5 minutes. Add chicken stock, season and cook for 6 minutes or until cauliflower is tender. Transfer to a blender and purée until smooth. Add just enough cream to thin purée a little and check seasoning.

Heat a frying pan until hot, add butter and a handful of spaetzle and sauté until just golden. Add veal jus, reduce until a sauce consistency and add fines herbes.

Place venison in centre of each serving plate and garnish with marmalade and truffle julienne. Garnish plate with spaetzle, cauliflower purée and mâche leaves.

Serves 4

LAMINGTON WITH MINT OIL & MAPLE SYRUP

50g (1 3/4oz) desiccated coconut
1/2 granny smith apple, peeled and cut into julienne*
1/2 tbsp julienne* of mint
1/2 granny smith apple, peeled and chopped into dice
4 tbsp maple syrup

Mint Oil
1 cup fresh mint leaves, cut into julienne*
150ml (5fl oz) grape seed oil

Lamington Sponge
10 eggs
200g (7oz) caster (superfine) sugar
1 tsp vanilla extract
200g (7oz) plain (all-purpose) flour, sifted
1/3 cup milk

Chocolate Sauce
300ml (10 1/2fl oz) hot water
250g (9oz) brown sugar
2 tbsp maple syrup
2 tbsp raspberry jam
225g (8oz) icing (confectioners') sugar, sifted
55g (2oz) cocoa powder, sifted

To make mint oil, blanch mint leaves in boiling water for 15 seconds, refresh in iced water and dry on paper towel. Transfer to a blender, slowly add grape seed oil and purée until smooth. Let mint oil stand for 2 hours or until colour has seeped out of mint. Strain through muslin or a coffee filter and set aside.

Preheat oven to 180°C (350°F/Gas 4).
Grease a 20 x 20cm (8 x 8in) cake tin.

To make lamington sponge, whisk eggs lightly in a large mixing bowl until fluffy. Add sugar, beat until pale and thick and stir in vanilla. Fold in flour alternately with milk, being sure to remove all lumps. Pour into prepared cake tin and place in oven for 10 minutes or until firm to touch. Allow to stand in tin for 5 minutes before turning out on to a wire rack to cool. Cut sponge into 5cm (2in) cubes and place in freezer until ready to use.

To make chocolate sauce, place hot water, brown sugar, maple syrup and jam in a saucepan over low heat. Combine icing sugar and cocoa powder and whisk into jam mixture. Bring to the boil and remove from heat immediately.
Cool mixture slightly.

To assemble lamingtons, set up a lamington station with frozen sponge cubes, warm chocolate sauce and coconut on hand. Dip sponge cubes quickly into chocolate sauce and coat in coconut. Repeat until all lamington cubes are covered. Place on a tray and transfer to refrigerator for 20 minutes.

Place a lamington in centre of each dessert plate and arrange apple julienne and mint julienne on top. Garnish plate with diced apple, mint oil and maple syrup and serve.

Serves 4

½ cup snow pea (mangetout) sprouts
2 cups chicken stock *(see page 186)*
100g (3 ½oz) cannellini beans,
soaked in cold water overnight
2 tbsp olive oil
1 tomato, peeled*, deseeded and diced
½ telegraph cucumber

Ravioli
1 Chinese barbecued duck*
2 tbsp hoisin sauce
1 tbsp julienne* of ginger
sea salt and cracked black pepper
4 sheets pasta dough *(see page 188)*

Ravioli of Duck with Cannellini Beans

To make ravioli, carefully remove skin from duck carcass, cut out four 10cm (4in) square pieces of skin, and shred meat. Place half of the duck meat in a bowl, add hoisin sauce, ginger and salt and pepper and toss to combine. Place pasta dough on a lightly floured work surface and using a 10cm (4in) round cutter, cut out 8 discs. Place a heaped teaspoon of duck mixture in centre of 4 discs. Brush a little water around edge of pasta, place another pasta disc on top and gently press around filling to remove air bubbles and to seal edges. Blanch ravioli in salted gently boiling water for 4 minutes. Remove with a slotted spoon, drain well and season with salt and pepper.

Wrap reserved pieces of duck skin around small bundles of snow pea sprouts and roll into 4 cigars.

Bring chicken stock to the boil, add cannellini beans and simmer for 40 minutes or until tender. Drain and set aside.

To make salsa, heat olive oil in a frying pan over medium heat, add cannellini beans, tomato and remaining duck meat and cook for 5 minutes or until heated through.

Thinly slice cucumber lengthways and cut into long spaghetti-like strips to make cucumber spaghetti.

To serve, twist a portion of cucumber spaghetti around a fork, place in centre of each plate and top with ravioli and a duck-skin cigar. Arrange warm salsa around plate and garnish with remaining snow pea sprouts.

Serves 4

Try filling the tuna roulade, as an alternative, with chopped green beans, crushed potatoes, black olives and diced tomatoes to create a nicoise version of the dish.

TUNA & AVOCADO ROULADE WITH CAVIAR

2 tbsp mayonnaise *(see page 186)*
1 tbsp sevruga caviar

Roulade
320g (11 1/4oz) A-grade sashimi tuna
2 avocados, finely sliced lengthways
200g (7oz) sand crabmeat, picked
4 tbsp mayonnaise *(see page 186)*
sea salt and cracked black pepper
1 tbsp finely chopped fresh chives

Dressing
2cm (3/4in) piece fresh ginger, chopped
1/2 tomato, peeled* and deseeded
1 French shallot, peeled
140ml (4 3/4fl oz) grape seed oil
3 1/2 tbsp soy sauce
juice of 1 lime
cracked black pepper

To make roulade, cut tuna into eight 4 x 5cm (1 1/2 x 2in) slices. Place a sheet of plastic wrap on a work surface and slightly overlap one-quarter of the avocado slices to form an 8 x 10cm (3 1/4 x 4in) rectangle. Place 2 slices of tuna on top of avocado. Combine crabmeat, mayonnaise, salt, pepper and chives in a small bowl and mix well. Spoon into a piping bag and pipe crabmeat mixture down centre of tuna. Tightly roll avocado around tuna to form a cylinder. Repeat process until all avocado, tuna and crabmeat mixture is used. Refrigerate for 30 minutes or until needed.

To make dressing, blend all ingredients in a blender and adjust seasoning if necessary.

Carefully unwrap roulades and trim each end. Place a roulade in centre of each serving plate, pipe a thin line of mayonnaise along roulade and arrange caviar on top. Dress plate with ample dressing and serve.

Serves 4

TUNA, PISTACHIO NUTS AND QUAIL EGGS

16 green beans, topped and tailed
4 quail eggs
480g (1lb 1oz) A-grade sashimi tuna
2 tbsp roughly chopped unsalted pistachio nuts, to garnish

Pistachio Vinaigrette
1 1/2 tbsp extra virgin olive oil
1/2 tbsp fresh lemon juice
sea salt and cracked black pepper
2 tbsp roughly chopped unsalted pistachio nuts, blanched

Blanch beans in boiling salted water until just tender, refresh in iced water and drain well.

Cook quail eggs in boiling water for 3-4 minutes and refresh in iced water. Remove shell and slice each egg in half.

Cut tuna into 3 x 8cm (1 1/4 x 3 1/4in) fingers.

To make pistachio vinaigrette, combine olive oil, lemon juice and salt and pepper in a bowl and whisk until emulsified. Add pistachio nuts and set aside.

To serve, arrange green beans on each serving plate, place tuna on top and garnish with pistachio nuts. Add a quail egg and drizzle over pistachio vinaigrette.

Serves 4

A turquoise ocean and the elegance of magnificent arabesques merge
into a harmonious play of opulence and sophisticated translucency.

3 tbsp olive oil
8 poussin breast fillets, skin on
16 white asparagus spears, trimmed
100g (3 1/2oz) somen noodles
4 tbsp julienne* of nori
2 tbsp fresh chervil tips

Spice Mixture
50g (1 3/4oz) crispy fried onion
30g (1oz) crispy fried garlic
1 tsp dried chilli flakes
1 tsp sea salt

Butter Sauce
1/2 cup double chicken stock *(see page 186)*
60g (2 1/4oz) butter, chopped into dice
2 tbsp finely chopped fresh chervil

Preheat oven to 200°C (400°F/Gas 6)

POUSSIN WITH WHITE ASPARAGUS & WHITE SOMEN NOODLES

To make spice mixture, place all ingredients in a food processor and blitz until well combined.

To make butter sauce, bring stock to the boil, monter* butter into stock and add chervil.

Heat olive oil in a large frying pan, add poussin, in batches, and pan-fry on each side for 3-5 minutes or until golden. Press spice mixture on to poussin skin and place in oven, skin-side up, for 6-8 minutes or until crisp. Set aside to rest in a warm place for 10 minutes.

Blanch asparagus in boiling salted water until tender and drain well.

Soften noodles in boiling water for 4 minutes or until al dente. Refresh in iced water and drain. Just before serving, blanch noodles in boiling water for 30 seconds and drain well.

To serve, place 2 poussin breasts and 2 stacks of noodles on each serving plate. Garnish noodle stacks with nori julienne. Arrange asparagus spears around plate, dress with butter sauce and scatter over chervil.

Serves 4

Seared scallops with watermelon and persian fetta: This dish is also fantastic made with fresh yabbies or scampi (langoustines) instead of the scallops.

SEARED SCALLOPS WITH WATERMELON & PERSIAN FETA

400g (14oz) watermelon
20 fresh diver scallops
sea salt and cracked black pepper
2 tbsp olive oil
40g (1 1/2oz) butter
50g (1 3/4oz) Persian feta, crumbled
1/3 cup extra virgin olive oil
20 baby mâche* (lamb's lettuce) leaves
1 tsp fresh thyme leaves

Dice watermelon into 1.5cm (5/8in) cubes.

Season scallops with salt and pepper. Heat olive oil in a frying pan, add scallops and sear for 30 seconds on one side. Add butter and allow it to turn nut brown, quickly toss scallops once and remove from pan immediately.

To serve, arrange one-quarter of the feta, watermelon and scallops on each serving plate and dress with extra virgin olive oil, pepper, mâche and thyme leaves.

Serves 4

SCALLOP CARPACCIO

12 fresh diver scallops, thinly sliced
juice of 2 limes
1/2 cup extra virgin olive oil
sea salt and cracked black pepper
8 baby zucchini (courgettes)
segments of 2 limes
4 tbsp goat's cheese
24 baby fresh chives

Marinate scallops in lime juice, extra virgin olive oil, salt and pepper for 2-3 minutes. Strain, reserving marinade.

Blanch zucchini in boiling salted water for 1 minute, refresh in iced water, drain and slice into thin rounds. Place zucchini rounds and lime segments in a bowl, add reserved scallop marinade and set aside.

Arrange scallop slices, 2 quenelles* of goat's cheese, the zucchini rounds and lime segments on each serving plate. Scatter over chives and dress with marinade and pepper.

Serves 4

CHOCOLATE SOUFFLÉ WITH PISTACHIO NUT ICE-CREAM

4 tbsp pistachio nuts, chopped icing (confectioners') sugar, for dusting

Pistachio Nut Ice-cream
2 cups milk
5 egg yolks
90g (3 1/4oz) caster (superfine) sugar
100ml (3 1/2fl oz) pouring cream
40g (1 1/2oz) pistachio paste
1 1/2 tbsp kirsch
150g (5 1/2oz) pistachio nuts, toasted and crushed

Sponge Base
2 eggs
40g (1 1/2oz) caster (superfine) sugar
40g (1 1/2oz) plain (all-purpose) flour
2 tbsp milk
1/2 tsp vanilla extract

Chocolate Soufflé
100ml (3 1/2fl oz) water
500g (1lb 2oz) sugar
170g (6oz) cocoa powder
1 cup water
8 egg whites

To make pistachio nut ice-cream, bring milk to the boil in a saucepan over medium-high heat. Whisk egg yolks and sugar until pale and thick. Add milk and mix well. Pour this mixture into a clean saucepan and cook, stirring constantly, over low heat until anglaise coats back of a wooden spoon. Remove from heat. In a separate saucepan, warm cream and pistachio paste and stir into anglaise. Fold in kirsch and pistachio nuts, allow to cool over some iced water. Transfer to an ice-cream machine and churn following manufacturer's instructions. Freeze in a sealed container.

Preheat oven to 180°C (350°F/Gas 4).
Grease and line a 12cm (4 1/2in) square cake tin.

To make sponge base, lightly whisk eggs in a mixing bowl. Add sugar and whisk until pale and thick. Fold in flour with a metal spoon. Fold in milk, ensuring no lumps remain. Pour into prepared cake tin and bake for 8-10 minutes or until firm to touch. Allow to cool and cut out four 4cm (1 1/2in) discs.

Preheat oven to 220°C (425°F/Gas 7). Butter four, 1-cup capacity, soufflé moulds and dust with a little caster (superfine) sugar, tipping out excess.

To make chocolate soufflé, combine 100ml (3 1/2fl oz) water and sugar in a heavy-based saucepan and bring to the boil. Cook to hard-ball stage or until temperature of sugar syrup is between 130-135°F (250-265°F) on a sugar (candy) thermometer. Remove from heat. Whisk cocoa powder with 1 cup of water until smooth. Carefully combine sugar syrup with cocoa mixture and allow to cool in refrigerator. This soufflé base can be stored for up to 1 week in refrigerator. Whisk egg whites in a mixing bowl until stiff peaks form. In a separate bowl, combine 1 tablespoon of soufflé base with 3 tablespoons of egg white, this gives you one portion of soufflé, and spoon into a prepared mould. Repeat with remaining soufflé base and egg whites. Place soufflés in oven and bake for 8 minutes or until risen. Serve immediately.

Meanwhile, place a sponge disc on each serving plate and top with a scoop of pistachio nut ice-cream. Arrange pistachio nuts in a semi-circle on each plate and, at the last second before serving, dust each soufflé with icing sugar, place on plate and serve.

Serves 4

LOBSTER & OYSTERS WITH SOMEN NOODLE SALAD

100g (3 1/2oz) somen noodles
2 x 650g (1lb 7oz) lobsters
12 freshly shucked oysters
1 granny smith apple,
  peeled and finely diced
juice and segments of 2 limes
1/2 cup baby watercress
4 tbsp extra virgin olive oil
sea salt and cracked black pepper

Cook somen noodles in boiling salted water for 4 minutes and refresh in iced water and drain.

Place lobsters in freezer for 20 minutes to send them to sleep before cooking. Cook lobsters in a large saucepan of boiling salted water for 7 minutes. Refresh in iced water. Remove meat from shell and slice each lobster into 6 even medallions.

To serve, place 3 lobster medallions on each serving plate and top each medallion with a stack of somen noodles. Place an oyster on each noodle stack and garnish with a little diced apple. Garnish plate with lime segments, remaining diced apple and watercress. Dress plate with extra virgin olive oil, lime juice and salt and pepper.

Serves 4

BRAISED BEEF CHEEKS

4 x 180g (6 1/4oz) beef cheeks
600ml (21fl oz) red wine
1 medium carrot, roughly chopped
1 medium onion, roughly chopped
1 celery stalk, roughly chopped
2 garlic cloves, chopped
3 bay leaves
2 sprigs fresh thyme
1/3 cup olive oil
6 cups beef stock *(see page 187)*
sea salt and cracked black pepper

Combine beef cheeks, red wine, carrot, onion, celery, garlic, bay leaves and thyme in a shallow bowl, cover, and place in refrigerator overnight to marinate. The following day, strain and reserve marinade.

Preheat oven to 130°C (250°F/Gas 1).

Heat olive oil in a large flameproof casserole over medium heat, add beef cheeks and sauté for 10 minutes or until browned all over. Add reserved marinade and beef stock and bring to the boil. Cover and transfer to oven for 3-4 hours or until beef is very tender and almost falling apart. Season with salt and pepper and serve with crusty bread, mash or roasted root vegetables.

Serves 4

ETUVÉE OF VEGETABLES WITH CRISP EGG

120g (4 1/4oz) goat's cheese
1/4 cup finely chopped fines herbes*, fresh flat leaf (Italian) parsley, chives, tarragon and chervil
dash of white vinegar
4 very fresh eggs

Egg wash
2 egg yolks
pinch of salt

200g (7oz) panko (Japanese) breadcrumbs
2 cups peanut oil, for deep frying
2 cups chicken stock *(see page 186)*
2 baby golden beetroot (beets), peeled and cut into quarters
8 zucchini (courgette) flowers, pistils removed
1 carrot, cut into batons
2 tomatoes, peeled*, deseeded and cut into batons
4 tbsp peas
8 shimeji mushrooms
1 baby fennel bulb, sliced
100ml (3 1/2fl oz) extra virgin olive oil
sea salt and cracked black pepper

Mould goat's cheese into four 7cm (2 3/4in) discs, roll in fines herbes and set aside.

To make egg wash, combine egg yolks and salt in a bowl and lightly beat.

Bring some water and the vinegar to a simmer in a saucepan, make a whirlpool in water and crack an egg into centre. Cook for 4-5 minutes for soft poached. Remove egg with a slotted spoon, chill in iced water, drain well and dry on paper towel. Repeat with remaining eggs. Dip each poached egg in egg wash and coat in breadcrumbs. Heat oil to 180°C (350°F) in a large saucepan over high heat and deep fry eggs in batches for 1-2 minutes or until crisp. Centre should still be soft and runny.

Bring stock to the boil, add beetroot, zucchini flowers and carrot and cook for 5 minutes or until tender. Add tomatoes and cook for 1 minute, then add peas, shimeji mushrooms and fennel and cook for a further minute or until tender. Strain, return stock to pan and reduce by three-quarters. Add extra virgin olive oil, season accordingly and return vegetables to sauce to heat through.

To serve, place a goat's cheese disc in centre of each serving plate and top with a crisp egg. Arrange vegetables around plate and drizzle over sauce.

Serves 4

For an interesting flavour twist, use fresh duck eggs instead of the hens' eggs.

12 fresh chive tips
20 baby bull's blood* leaves

Veal Tartare
300g (10 1/2oz) veal tenderloins,
trimmed and finely diced
2 tbsp baby capers, rinsed and chopped
2 tbsp chopped cornichons (baby gherkins)
2 tbsp fresh chives, finely chopped
sea salt and cracked black pepper
pinch of paprika

Croutons
brioche *(see page 187)*
80g (2 3/4oz) butter
sea salt

Dressing
2 hard-boiled eggs, shelled
1/2 cup extra virgin olive oil
1 tbsp chopped fresh chives
sea salt and cracked black pepper

VEAL TARTARE WITH BRIOCHE CROUTONS

Interesting variations of this dish can be made using beef fillet or fresh Atlantic salmon instead of the veal.

To make veal tartare, combine veal, capers, cornichons, chives, salt, pepper and paprika in a bowl and mix well.

To make croutons, cut 8 slices from brioche, remove crusts and trim into 7cm (2 3/4in) equilateral triangles. Cut remaining brioche into 1cm (1/2in) dice. Melt butter in a frying pan over medium heat, add croutons, sauté until lightly coloured and remove. Repeat with diced brioche and season with salt.

To make dressing, separate egg whites from yolks and finely grate yolks, then finely grate whites. Combine egg white and yolk, extra virgin olive oil, chives, salt and pepper in a small bowl and mix together.

To serve, shape veal tartare into 4 pyramids and place on each serving plate. Rest 2 triangular croutons on opposite sides against veal tartare and arrange diced croutons around plate. Garnish with chive tips and bull's blood leaves and scatter dressing around plate.

Serves 4

2 tbsp peanut oil
1/2 onion, finely chopped
1 celery stalk, finely chopped
1 carrot, chopped into dice
2 garlic cloves, finely chopped
2 star anise
2 sprigs fresh thyme
2 bay leaves
100g (3 1/2oz) yellow lentils
2 litres (8 cups/70fl oz) chicken stock *(see page 186)*
2 smoked ham hocks
2 celery stalks, cut into julienne*
sea salt and cracked black pepper

Braised Smoked Ham Hock

Heat oil in a large saucepan over medium heat, add onion, finely chopped celery, carrot and garlic and sauté for 3-4 minutes or until softened. Add star anise, thyme, bay leaves, lentils and chicken stock and bring to the boil. Add ham hocks and simmer for 1-2 hours or until meat falls off the bone. Remove meat from bone, keeping pieces as large as possible, and portion into eight pieces. Discard bones.

Blanch julienne of celery in boiling salted water for 30 seconds and refresh in iced water. Drain well.

Place 2 pieces of ham hock in centre of each serving plate and dress with lentils and julienne of celery. Season with salt and pepper and serve.

Serves 4

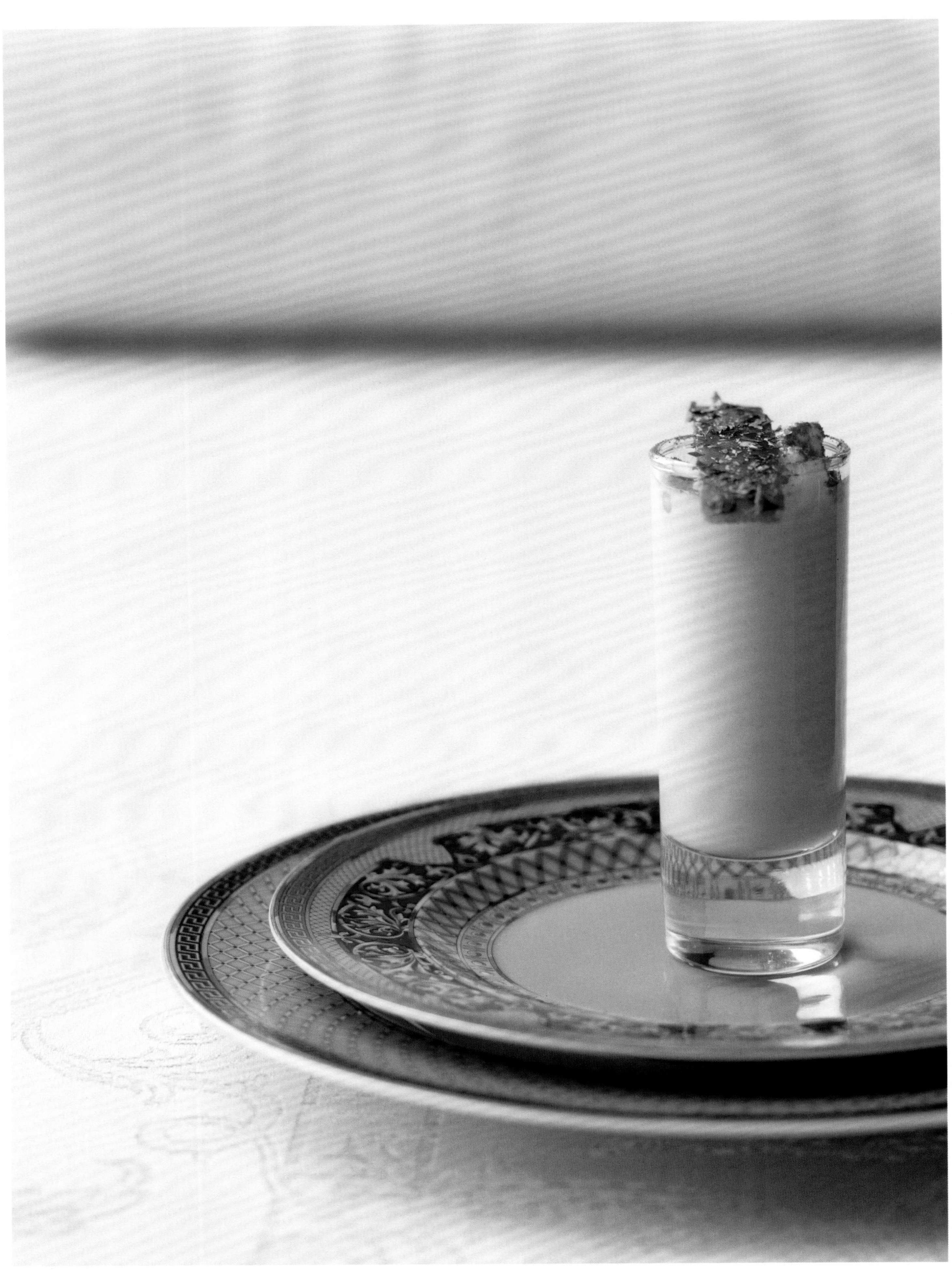

Cappuccino of Borlotti Beans with Pancetta

100g (3 1/2oz) flat pancetta, thinly sliced
2 dried porcini

Soup Base
1kg (2lb 4oz) borlotti beans
1/3 cup olive oil
4 brown onions, peeled and diced
10 French shallots, peeled and sliced
3 celery stalks, chopped into dice
2 leeks, washed and sliced
125g (4 1/2oz) button mushrooms, sliced
2 garlic cloves, finely chopped
2 parsnips, peeled and chopped into dice
100ml (3 1/2fl oz) dry sherry
100ml (3 1/2fl oz) white wine
2 1/2 tbsp Madeira
3 cups veal stock *(see page 187)*
2 litres (8 cups/70fl oz) chicken stock *(see page 186)*
sea salt and cracked black pepper
20g (3/4oz) mixed dried mushrooms
(porcini, chanterelles, morels)
6 sprigs fresh thyme

Cappuccino
1 tbsp olive oil
12 French shallots, peeled and sliced
125g (4 1/2oz) button mushrooms, sliced
100ml (3 1/2fl oz) dry sherry
150ml (5fl oz) white wine
100ml (3 1/2fl oz) Madeira
2 cups chicken stock *(see page 186)*
2 cups pouring cream
2 cups soup base
30g (1oz) mixed dried mushrooms
(porcini, chanterelles, morels), soaked
for 8 hours in 150ml (5fl oz) water
150ml (5fl oz) fino sherry
4 fresh thyme sprigs
1/2 cup flat leaf (Italian)
parsley stalks and leaves
1 1/2 tsp salt
90ml (3fl oz) truffle oil

Preheat oven to 190°C (375°F/Gas 5)

Place pancetta slices on a baking tray and transfer to oven for 5-10 minutes or until crisp. Drain on paper towel and set aside until required.

To make porcini dust, place porcini in a blender and process to a powder. Transfer to an airtight container.

To make soup base, soak borlotti beans in 3 litres (12 cups/104fl oz) of water overnight, rinse and drain well. Heat olive oil in a heavy-based saucepan over medium heat, add onions, shallots, celery and leeks and sweat for 5 minutes or until softened but not browned. Add button mushrooms, garlic and parsnip and sauté for 5 minutes or until starting to soften. Deglaze with sherry, white wine and Madeira and reduce to 1 tablespoon. Add veal and chicken stocks, dried mushrooms and borlotti beans and cook for 1 hour or until borlotti beans are tender. Season, blend in a food processor and pass through a conical strainer. Refrigerate until required.

To make cappuccino, heat olive oil in a heavy-based saucepan over medium heat, add shallots and mushrooms and sweat for 5 minutes or until soft. Deglaze with dry sherry, white wine and Madeira and reduce to 1 tablespoon. Add chicken stock, cream and soup base, bring to the boil and skim scum that rises to surface. Add soaked dried mushrooms and fino sherry, thyme and parsley, season with salt and finish with truffle oil. Pass through a fine strainer. The finished soup can be frothed with a hand blender before serving to give it a more authentic cappuccino appearance.

Pour into demitasse cups and, using a small, fine sieve, sprinkle a little porcini dust on top, garnish with a strip of crisp pancetta and serve.

Serves 16

Roasted Beef Tenderloin with Tempura Oysters

200g (7oz) rice flour
sea salt and cracked black pepper
iced water
4 x 180g (6 1/2oz) beef tenderloins, trimmed of sinew
1/4 cup olive oil
1 cup peanut oil
1 potato, peeled and cut into julienne*
12 freshly shucked oysters
100g (4oz) plain (all purpose) flour, for coating oysters
2 French shallots, finely chopped
200ml (7fl oz) red wine
150ml (5fl oz) veal jus *(see page 187)*
1/2 cup baby watercress leaves

Parsnip Purée
1 tbsp olive oil
1 onion, finely chopped
2 garlic cloves, finely chopped
2 parsnips, peeled and chopped
1 cup chicken stock *(see page 186)*
sea salt and cracked black pepper
100ml (3 1/2fl oz) pouring cream

To make parsnip purée, heat olive oil in a saucepan over medium heat, add onion, garlic and parsnips and gently sauté, without colouring, for 10 minutes or until starting to soften. Add chicken stock, season with salt and pepper and cook until parsnip is tender. Strain and transfer to a blender and process until smooth. Add the cream and adjust seasoning if necessary.

Combine rice flour, salt and pepper and just enough iced water in a bowl to make a lumpy batter the consistency of double (thick) cream.

Season beef tenderloins with salt and pepper. Heat 2 tablespoons of olive oil in a frying pan over high heat, add beef and sear on each side for 5 minutes or until cooked to your liking. Set aside to rest for at least 10 minutes.

Heat peanut oil in a large saucepan over medium heat, add potato and fry until crisp and golden brown. Remove with a slotted spoon, drain on paper towel and season with sea salt. Reserve oil to fry oysters.

To make tempura oysters, coat each oyster in flour and dip in tempura batter, shaking off excess. Heat reserved oil until hot, add oysters in batches and fry for 30 seconds or until golden and crisp. Drain on paper towel.

Heat remaining olive oil in a small saucepan, add shallots and sauté for 3 minutes or until soft. Deglaze* with red wine and cook for 4-5 minutes or until reduced by half. Add veal jus and reduce by two-thirds, season with salt and pepper.

Place a dollop of parsnip purée on each warmed serving plate and, using the back of a spoon, smear it across plate. Arrange 3 oysters on each plate and garnish with potato julienne and watercress leaves. Place beef tenderloin on top, dress plate with red wine jus and serve.

Serves 4

Gruyere & Goat's Cheese Soufflé

4 tbsp finely grated parmesan cheese
1/2 cup baby lettuce leaves, such as rocket (arugula), mizuna and bull's blood*

Red Wine Reduction
300ml (10 1/2fl oz) red wine
1 1/2 tbsp red wine vinegar
100g (3 1/2oz) brown sugar

Cheese Soufflé
50g (1 3/4oz) butter
50g (1 3/4oz) plain (all-purpose) flour
pinch of cayenne pepper
1/2 tsp mustard powder
1 cup milk
90g (3 1/4oz) gruyere cheese, grated
50g (1 3/4oz) goat's cheese
4 eggs, separated
sea salt and cracked black pepper
1 egg white, extra

Preheat oven to 160°C (315°F/Gas 2–3)

Liberally butter four, 1-cup capacity metal dariole moulds, line a baking tray with baking paper and lightly grease another baking tray.

Sprinkle parmesan on to paper-lined baking tray and place in oven for 6-7 minutes or until golden. Cool down on tray and when cold, crumble now-crisp parmesan crumbs into an airtight container.

To make red wine reduction, bring wine, vinegar and sugar to the boil and simmer until reduced by at least two-thirds and of a syrup consistency. Set aside to cool.

To make cheese soufflé, make a roux by melting butter in a saucepan and stirring in flour, cayenne pepper and mustard powder. Cook for about 10 minutes over a low heat. Bring milk to the boil in another saucepan and slowly add to roux, stirring constantly. Once milk has been added, simmer for 10 minutes then turn off heat and add gruyere and goat's cheese. Cool mixture slightly, stir in egg yolks and season. Whisk egg whites to soft peaks and gently fold through mixture. Pour batter into prepared moulds and bake in oven for 30 minutes or until well-risen and golden brown. Allow to cool completely before turning out on to greased baking tray.

Increase oven temperature to 200°C (400°F/Gas 6) and return soufflés to oven for 5 minutes.

Spoon a line of red wine reduction and a line of toasted parmesan crumbs on each serving plate. Garnish with baby herbs and, seconds before serving, place a soufflé on each plate.

Serves 4

There is no art where there is no style,
and there is no style where there is no harmony,
and harmony comes from the individual.

Oscar Wilde

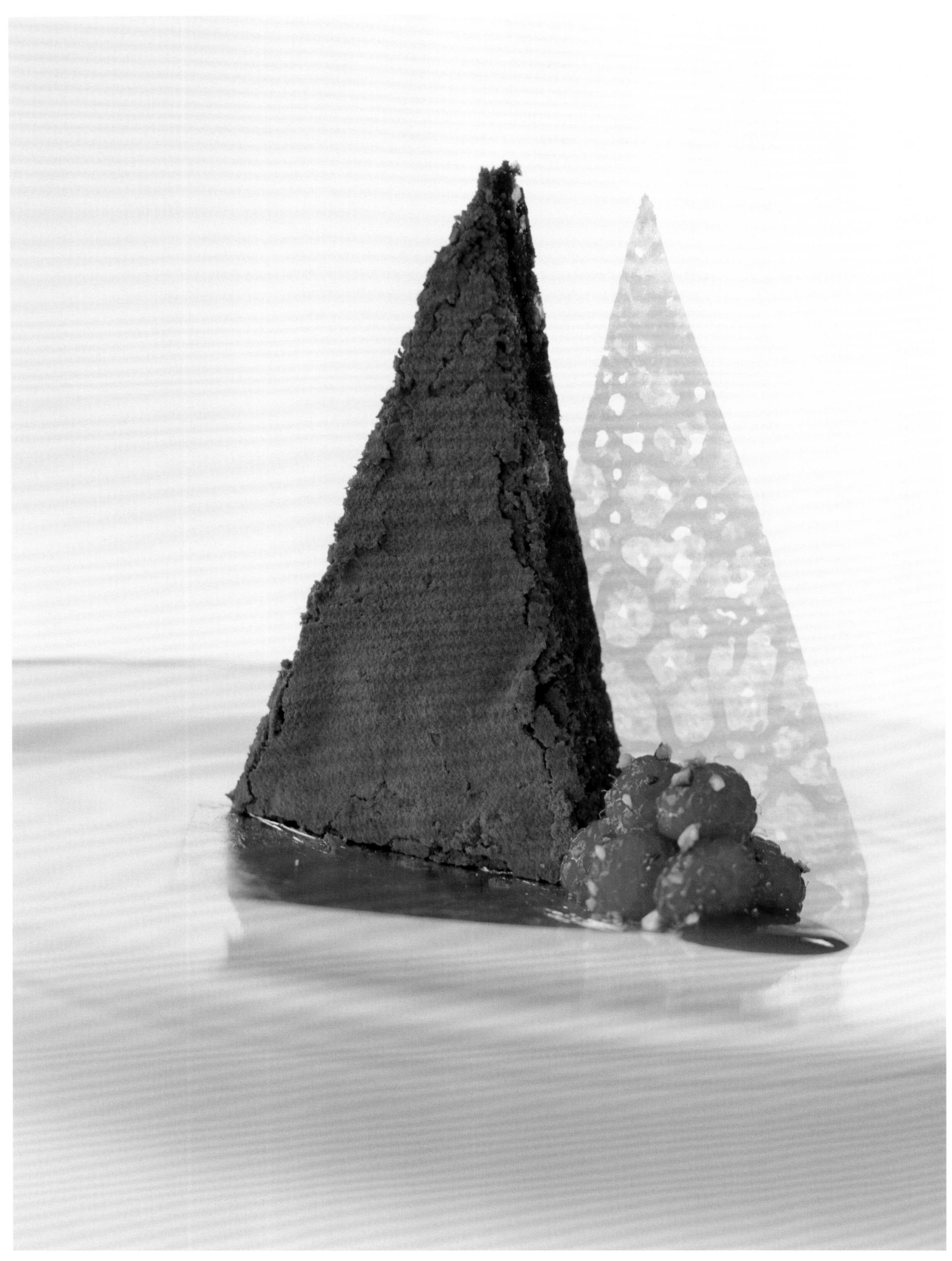

Chocolate Brownies with Raspberries

4 sheets gold leaf
24 raspberries
8 unsalted pistachios, blanched, peeled and chopped

Lace Wafers
1/2 cup caster (superfine) sugar
1/4 cup fresh orange juice, heated
1/2 cup plain (all-purpose) flour, sifted
80g (2 3/4oz) unsalted butter, melted and cooled

Chocolate Brownies
150g (5 1/2oz) unsalted butter, melted
3 eggs
300g (10 1/2oz) caster (superfine) sugar
1 cup plain (all-purpose) flour
1/4 cup cocoa powder
100g (3 1/2oz) gianduja (hazelnut-flavoured chocolate), chopped
140g (5oz) dark couverture chocolate, chopped
80g (2 3/4oz) hazelnuts, toasted and skinned*
cocoa powder, for dusting

Raspberry Coulis
150g (5 1/2oz) raspberries
1/4 cup caster (superfine) sugar

Preheat oven to 160°C (315°F/Gas 2-3) and line a baking tray with baking paper.

To make lace wafers, whisk sugar and orange juice in a bowl until sugar is dissolved. Slowly whisk in flour. Ensure melted butter is cool before whisking into batter. Refrigerate for 2 hours. Using a 2mm (1/16in) thick plastic sheet, cut out a triangle template 12cm (4 1/2in) high with a 7cm (2 3/4in) base. Place template on baking paper, trace around outline, remove template and evenly spread lace wafer mixture inside triangle outline. Repeat with remaining mixture. Place in oven and bake for 5 minutes or until golden brown. Set aside to cool. Place in an airtight container until ready to use.

Preheat oven to 180°C (350°F/Gas 4) and grease and line a 15 x 25cm (6 x 10in) rectangular cake tin with baking paper.

To make chocolate brownies, place melted butter, eggs and sugar in a bowl. Sift in flour and cocoa powder and stir to combine. Fold in gianduja, chocolate and hazelnuts and pour mixture into prepared cake tin. Place in oven and bake for 30 minutes. Allow to cool in tin before turning out and cutting into four triangles with a base of 8cm (3 1/4in) and a height of 13cm (5in). Dust with cocoa powder.

To make raspberry coulis, place raspberries and sugar in a saucepan over medium heat and cook for 4 minutes or until sugar dissolves and raspberries are soft. Transfer to a blender, blend until smooth and pass through a fine chinois*. Set aside to cool.

To serve, carefully place a sheet of gold leaf on each plate, stand a brownie triangle on top. Spoon a little coulis to one side, arrange 6 raspberries on coulis and sprinkle over pistachios. Finish by leaning a lace wafer against each brownie.

Serves 4

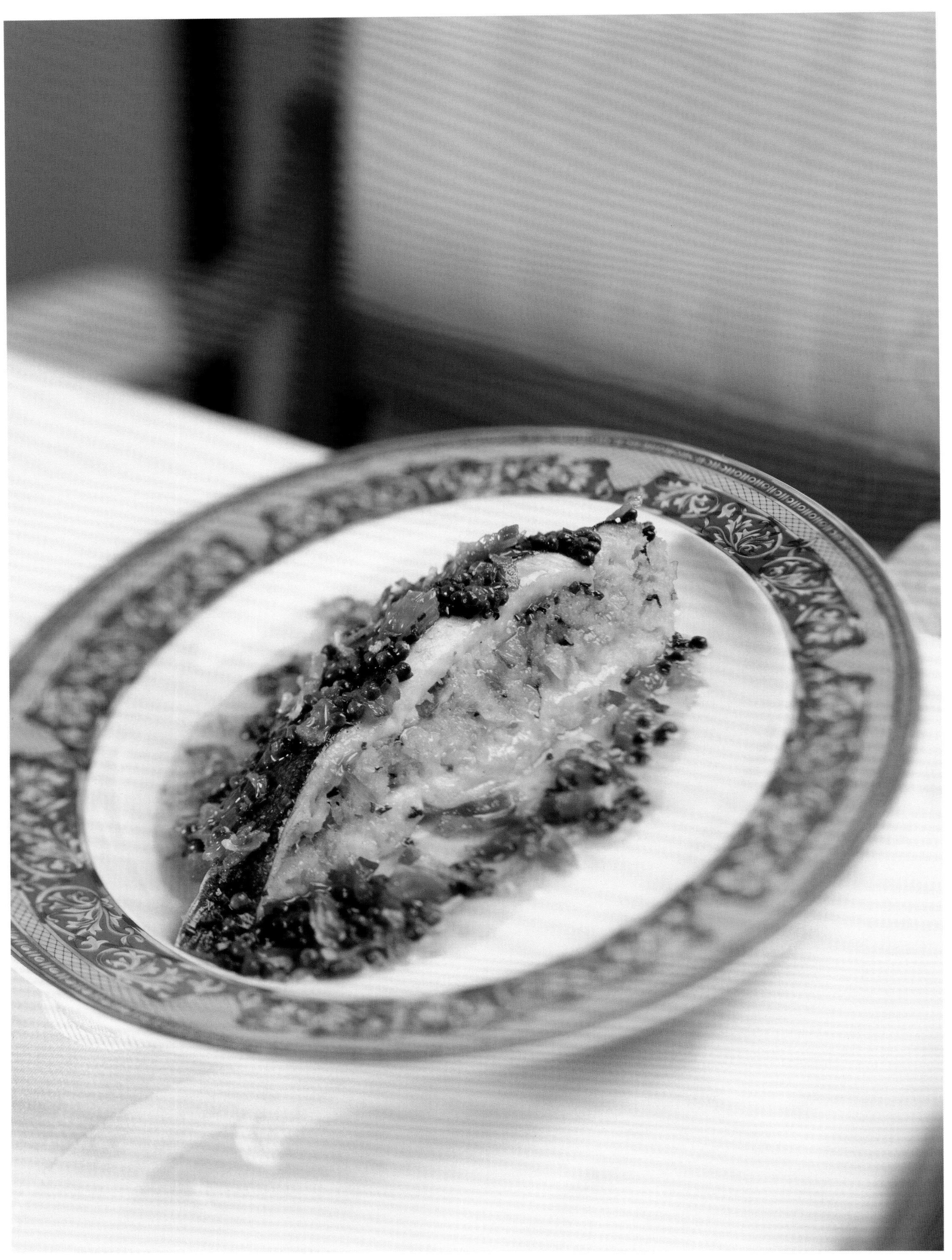

Stuffed Flounder

2 x 700g (1lb 9oz) whole flounder, scaled and gutted
1/3 cup peanut oil

Stuffing
100g (3 1/2oz) butter
2 tsp fresh thyme leaves
1/2 onion, finely chopped
2 garlic cloves, crushed
4 sage leaves, finely chopped
150g (5 1/2oz) panko (Japanese) breadcrumbs
sea salt and cracked black pepper

Butter Sauce
75g (2 1/2oz) butter
2 garlic cloves, cut into slivers
4 tbsp bacon lardons*
1 pink grapefruit, segmented
2 tbsp baby capers, rinsed
4 tbsp finely chopped flat leaf (Italian) parsley
sea salt and cracked black pepper

To prepare flounder, cut off head, tail and fins, keeping skin on. Cut each fish in half lengthways and, using a filleting knife, remove bones from each flounder half by cutting along backbone, from head to tail end, being careful not to cut completely through to other side. Prise flesh away from either side of backbone with tip of knife. Cut out backbone and remove so that you have created a pocket.

Preheat oven to 200°C (400°F/Gas 6).

To make stuffing, melt butter in a frying pan over medium heat, add thyme, onion, garlic and sage and sweat for 5 minutes or until onion is transparent. Add breadcrumbs, season with salt and pepper and stir to combine. Spoon stuffing into pocket in each piece of flounder and season outside of fish. Heat 1 tablespoon of peanut oil in an ovenproof frying pan and sear 1 stuffed flounder fillet for 30 seconds on each side. Repeat with remaining fillets. Transfer to oven for 5-10 minutes or until the flesh is white and soft to the touch.

To make butter sauce, melt butter in a frying pan over medium heat, add garlic, bacon, grapefruit, capers and parsley and cook for 3 minutes or until butter is golden. Season with salt and pepper.

Place flounder in centre of each warmed serving plate, garnish with butter sauce and serve.

Serves 4

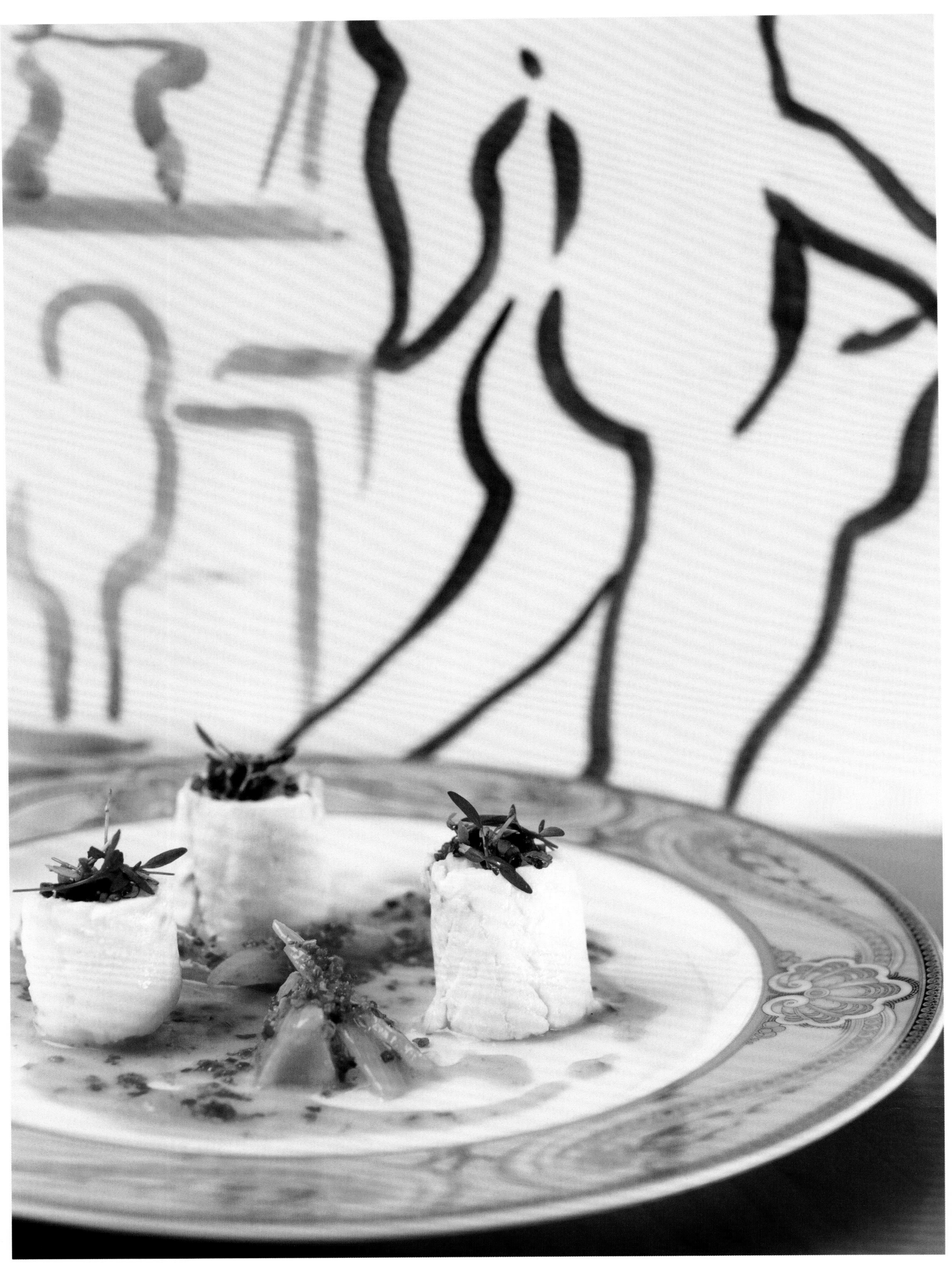

4 x 180g (6 1/4oz) monkfish fillets, trimmed
1 fennel bulb
1 cup chicken stock *(see page 186)*
1 cup beef stock *(see page 187)*
100g (3 1/2oz) butter
sea salt and cracked black pepper
1 tsp aniseed
2 rashers bacon, finely chopped
2 tbsp fried onion *Fried onion can be purchased from Asian supermarkets.*
1/2 cup baby cress and bull's blood* leaves

Preheat oven to 170°C (325°F/Gas 3)

Monkfish with Braised Fennel

Place each portion of monkfish on a piece of plastic wrap, presentation-side down, and roll into a cylinder shape. Tightly twist plastic wrap ends to ensure that no water will be able to get to fish. Place monkfish rolls in a saucepan of simmering water for 5 minutes or until cooked – or alternatively cook in a steamer for 5 minutes. Set aside to rest for 5 minutes and cut each cylinder into 3 pieces.

Cut fennel into wedges, place on a roasting tray and add chicken stock, beef stock, half of the butter, salt and pepper and aniseed. Place in oven to braise for 20 minutes or until fennel is tender.

Heat a frying pan over medium heat, add bacon and sauté until crisp. Remove and drain on paper towel. Return pan to high heat, deglaze* with 1 cup of stock from braised fennel, bring to the boil and reduce by two-thirds. Reduce heat to low and monter* by whisking in remaining butter, a little at a time, until butter sauce is emulsified and consistency is very thick. Season with salt and pepper.

Combine bacon and fried onion in a small bowl and mix well.

In centre of each serving plate, arrange 3 pieces of braised fennel and 3 monkfish discs. Spoon butter sauce over monkfish and fennel, garnish with bacon and fried onion mixture and cress and bull's blood leaves and serve.

Serves 4

650g (1lb 7oz) salmon belly fillets, pin-boned
sea salt and cracked black pepper
1 telegraph cucumber, peeled
2 tbsp extra virgin olive oil
1/2 tsp smoked Danish sea salt
3 tbsp crème fraîche

Dill Yoghurt Dressing
3 tbsp natural yoghurt
1 tbsp dill, finely chopped
juice of 1/2 lemon
1 tbsp honey
sea salt and cracked black pepper

Smoked Salmon Belly with Dill Yoghurt Dressing

To make dill yoghurt dressing, combine yoghurt, dill, lemon juice and honey in a bowl and season accordingly.

Trim salmon into four log-shaped portions and season with salt and pepper. Have your smoker hot and ready to go with some hickory woodchips, add salmon and smoke for 6-8 minutes. While salmon is still warm, wrap each portion tightly in plastic wrap to form a cylinder and set aside to cool in refrigerator.

Slice cucumber into 5mm x 10cm (1/4 x 4in) batons and marinate in salt, pepper and olive oil for 10 minutes. Remove from marinade.

Cut two 5mm (1/4in) presentation slices from each salmon portion and unwrap from plastic. Place cucumber and larger piece of salmon in centre of each serving plate and sprinkle Danish sea salt over salmon. Arrange 2 salmon presentation slices and a quenelle* of crème fraîche on each plate. Drizzle over dill yoghurt dressing and serve.

Serves 4

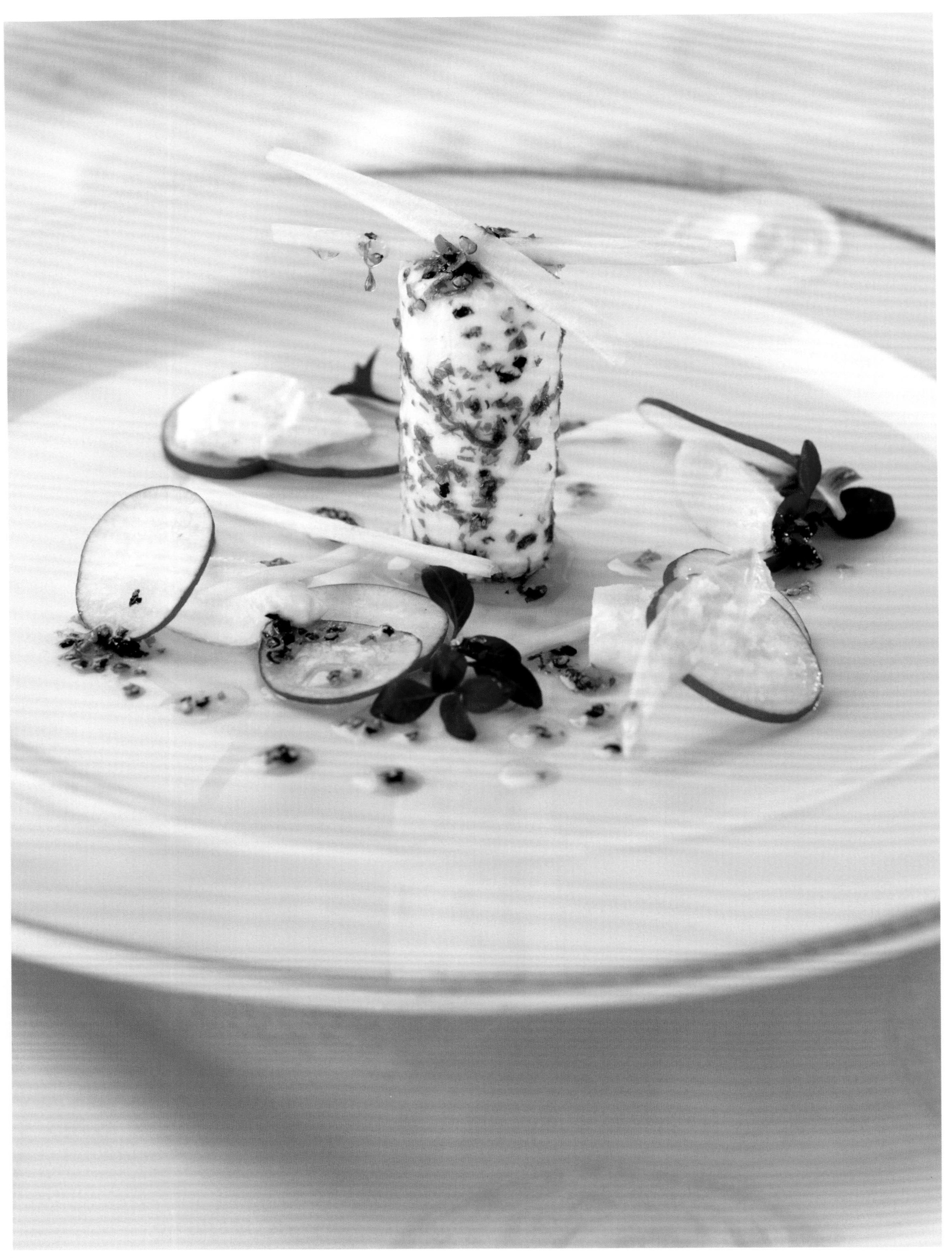

4 radishes
300g (10 1/2oz) soft goat's cheese
1/4 cup truffle oil
sea salt
1 tbsp cracked black pepper
1/4 cup fresh grapefruit juice
2 tbsp finely chopped chervil, flat leaf (Italian) parsley, tarragon and chives
1 witlof (chicory/Belgian endive), cut into 5cm (2in) batons
1 cup baby salad leaves, such as rocket, mizuna or bull's blood*
1/2 cup extra virgin olive oil
Very finely dice two radishes.

HERB-CRUSTED GOAT'S CHEESE

A delectable addition to this dish is a garnish of peeled, halved and seeded muscatel grapes. An important part of this dish is that you use the best olive oil that you can afford.

Place goat's cheese in a bowl, add diced radishes, truffle oil, salt, pepper, grapefruit juice and a quarter of the chopped herbs. Mix well and spoon two-thirds of the goat's cheese mixture into a piping bag *(reserve remaining mixture to make 16 quenelles* to garnish).*

Place 4 sheets of plastic wrap on a clean work surface. Arrange the remaining chopped herbs in an 8cm (3 1/4in) square on each sheet of plastic wrap. Pipe the goat's cheese mixture in the shape of a log on top of herbs. Tightly roll in plastic wrap to form 4 cylinder shapes, twist ends and chill in refrigerator.

Cut remaining radishes into thin slices.

Carefully remove goat's cheese cylinders from plastic wrap and stand upright in the centre of each serving plate. Arrange sliced radish, witlof and baby salad leaves around goat's cheese. Garnish with goat's cheese quenelles, drizzle over extra virgin olive oil and season with salt and pepper.

Serve with good crusty bread or crisp croutons.

Serves 4

Lustruous blue and the classic Medusa head give an inimitable character to the table.

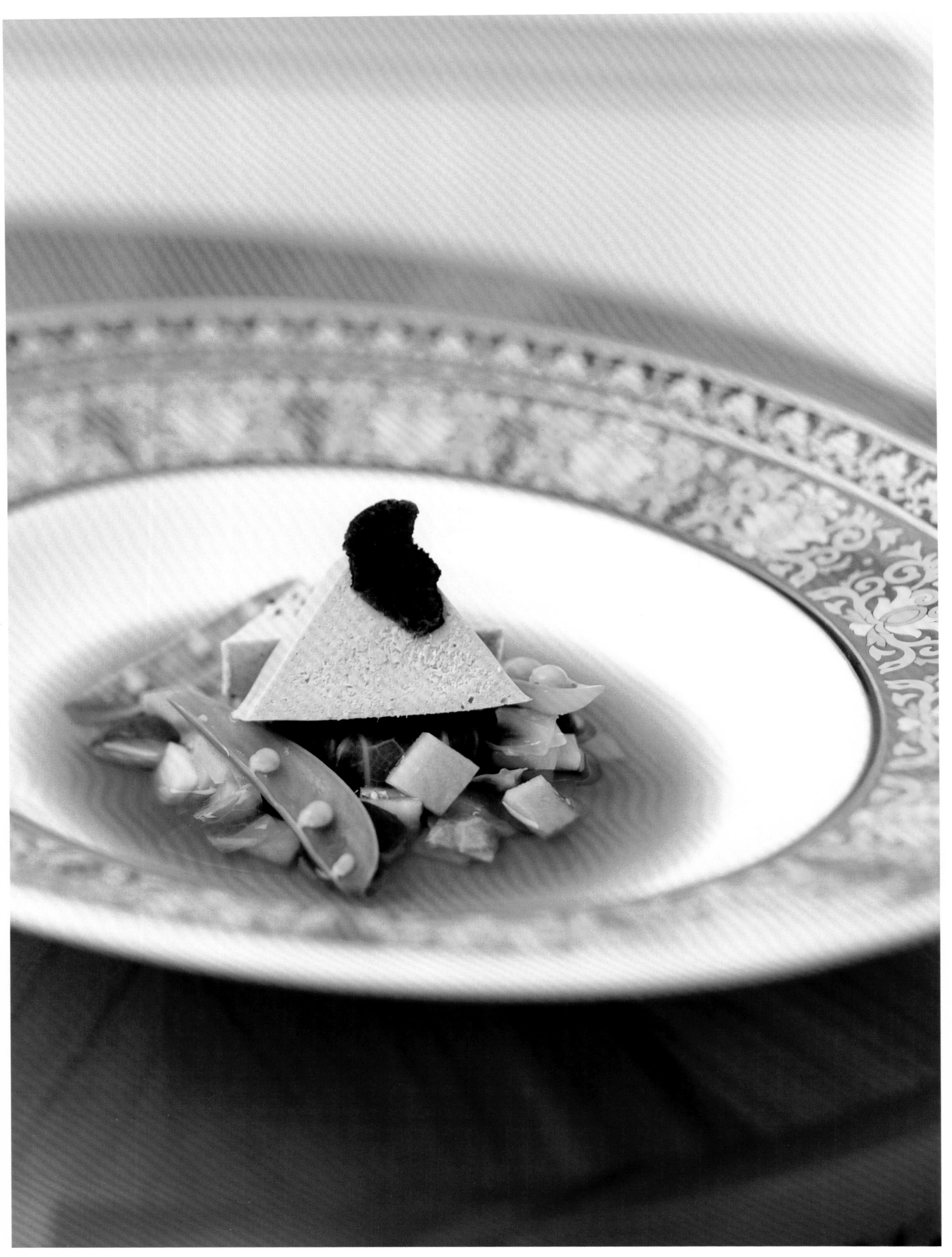

Stuffed Cabbage with Duck Liver Parfait

4 truffle slices

Duck Liver Parfait
170g (6oz) duck livers, trimmed
1 tbsp brandy
1 tbsp Madeira
1 tbsp port
1 egg
100g (3 1/2oz) butter, melted
sea salt and cracked black pepper

Consommé
400g (14oz) minced (ground) shin of beef
1 carrot, finely chopped
1 onion, finely chopped
2 celery stalks, finely chopped
2 garlic cloves, finely chopped
5 egg whites
sea salt and cracked black pepper
4 cups beef stock *(see page 187)*
shot of Madeira or port (optional)

Stuffed Cabbage
250g (9oz) duck breast fillets
40 duck livers, trimmed
2 tsp brandy
2 sprigs fresh thyme
50g (1 3/4oz) pork fat
sea salt and cracked black pepper
pinch of ground mace
pinch of ground star anise
pinch of ground cloves
4 large cabbage leaves

Garnish
6 snow peas (mangetout), trimmed, cut in half and blanched
1 medium potato, peeled, cooked and chopped into 1cm (1/2in) dice
1 spring onion (scallion) cut into 1cm (1/2in) lengths
1 tbsp olive oil
4 shiitake mushrooms, quartered
2 baby carrots, cut into 1cm (1/2in) lengths
2 savoy cabbage leaves

Preheat oven to 160°C (315°F/Gas 2–3).

To make duck liver parfait, place duck livers in a shallow dish, add brandy, Madeira and port, cover, place in refrigerator and allow to marinate for 2 hours. Transfer to a food processor and blend to a purée. Add egg and, with motor still running, slowly add butter. Season with salt and pepper and strain through a fine chinois*. Line a 15cm (6in) wide x 8cm (3 1/4in) deep triangular mould with plastic wrap, spoon in parfait mixture and cover with plastic wrap. Cook parfait in a bain-marie* with the water halfway up the sides of the mould for 10-12 minutes or until a metal skewer comes out clean after it has been inserted into centre of parfait. Allow to cool a little and place in refrigerator for 2 hours or until set. To remove parfait from the mould, invert mould on to a chopping board and pull gently on plastic wrap to release parfait. Carefully remove plastic wrap and, using a hot knife, cut parfait into eight slices about 1cm (1/2in) thick.

To make consommé, combine beef, carrot, onion, celery, garlic, egg whites and salt and pepper in a large bowl to make raft mixture. Transfer raft mixture to a large saucepan, add cold beef stock and whisk to combine. Bring to a fast simmer, making sure raft doesn't catch on base of pan. Once raft is floating on top, do not stir again, reduce heat to low and simmer gently for 10 minutes or until a clear consommé forms. Very gently strain through a muslin-cloth or coffee-filter lined strainer. Season to taste and add Madeira or port if you like.

To make stuffed cabbage, combine duck breast and livers in a shallow bowl, add brandy and thyme and marinate for 2 hours. Remove thyme and discard. Force duck meat, livers and pork fat through a medium-sized mincer and season well with salt and pepper, mace, star anise and cloves. Blanch cabbage leaves in boiling salted water for 40 seconds and refresh in cold water. Line a 1/2-cup capacity ladle with a cabbage leaf, add a small spoonful of minced duck mixture and wrap excess part of cabbage leaf around duck mixture to enclose. Seal to form a small package. Repeat this process to make 4 parcels. Place cabbage leaf parcels in a steamer over a saucepan of simmering water, cover and steam for 6-8 minutes. Remove from steamer and drain on paper towel.

To make garnish, blanch snow peas in boiling salted water for 30 seconds, refresh in cold water and drain well. Cook potato in boiling salted water for 15 minutes or until tender and drain well. Blanch spring onion in boiling water for 1 minute and refresh in cold water. Drain well. Heat olive oil in a frying pan over medium-high heat, add mushrooms and sauté for 2 minutes or until lightly browned. Drain on some paper towels. Cook carrots in boiling salted water for 6 minutes or until tender and drain well. Blanch cabbage in boiling salted water for 1 minute, refresh in cold water, drain well and finely chop.

To serve, gently reheat consommé in a saucepan over low heat. Place a stuffed cabbage leaf in centre of each serving bowl and garnish with snow peas, spring onion, carrot, shiitake mushrooms, cabbage and potato. Top with 2 slices of duck liver parfait, a slice of truffle and pour over consommé.

Serves 4

4 x 150g (5 1/2oz) soft-shell crabs
3 cups peanut oil, for frying
1/2 cup baby mizuna and
bull's blood* leaves
1/3 cup extra virgin olive oil
sea salt and cracked black pepper

Tomato and Chilli Jam
500g (1lb 2oz) tomatoes
4 large red chillies, finely sliced
4 garlic cloves, finely chopped
2cm (3/4in) piece ginger,
peeled and chopped
1 1/2 tbsp fish sauce
100ml (3 1/2fl oz) red wine vinegar
300g (10 1/2oz) sugar

Tempura Batter
200g (7oz) rice flour
iced water

Tempura of Soft-Shell Crabs

To make tomato and chilli jam, chop tomatoes into 5mm (1/4in) dice and set aside. Combine chillies, garlic, ginger, fish sauce and red wine vinegar in a food processor and blend to a purée. Transfer to a saucepan, add sugar and bring to the boil over medium heat. Add tomatoes and simmer for 30-40 minutes or until jam starts to thicken. Set aside for later use.

To make tempura batter, combine flour and just enough iced water to make a lumpy batter the consistency of double (thick) cream.

Dip each crab in tempura batter and shake off any excess. Heat peanut oil in a deep frying pan over medium heat, add crabs, in batches, and fry until crisp and golden brown. Season with salt and pepper and cut each crab in half.

To serve, arrange baby herbs and soft shell crab halves in centre of each serving plate. Garnish with tomato and chilli jam, drizzle over extra virgin olive oil and season with salt and pepper.

Serves 4

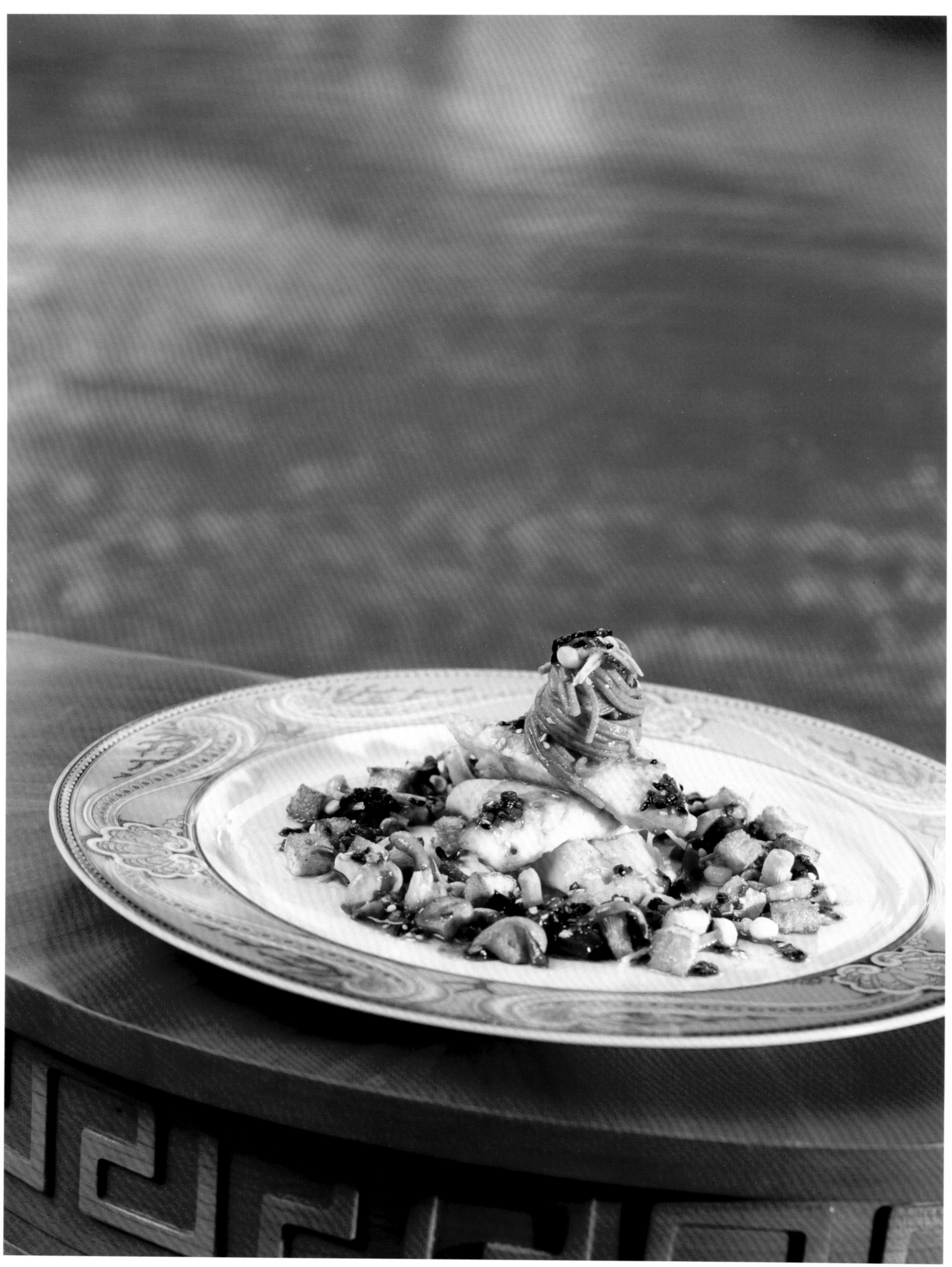

John Dory with Soba Noodles

4 x 180g (6 1/4oz) John Dory fillets
sea salt and cracked black pepper
1/4 cup olive oil
100g (3 1/2oz) enoki mushrooms, trimmed
50g (2oz) shimeji mushrooms
100ml (3 1/2fl oz) veal jus *(see page 187)*
50g (1 3/4oz) butter, chopped into dice
100g (3 1/2oz) soba noodles
1/2 cup bull's blood* leaves
1 tsp black sesame seeds
1 tsp sesame seeds

Croutons
2 slices sourdough bread, crusts removed
50g (1 3/4oz) butter
sea salt and cracked black pepper

Pesto
3 tbsp fresh tarragon leaves
3 tbsp flat leaf (Italian) parsley leaves
2 garlic cloves, peeled
30g (1oz) grated parmesan cheese
1 tbsp pine nuts, toasted
200ml (7fl oz) olive oil
sea salt and cracked black pepper

To make croutons, cut bread into 1cm (1/2in) dice. Melt butter in a frying pan over medium heat, add bread and cook until golden brown. Drain on paper towel and season with salt and pepper.

To make pesto, place tarragon, parsley, garlic, parmesan and pine nuts in a food processor and blitz for 30 seconds. With motor running, slowly drizzle in olive oil and process until well combined. Season with salt and pepper.

Preheat oven to 220°C (425°F/Gas 7).

Cut each John Dory fillet in half lengthways and season with salt and pepper. Heat 1 tablespoon of olive oil in an ovenproof frying pan over medium-high heat and sauté fish, skin-side down, in batches for 3 minutes or until skin is starting to crisp. Turn and transfer to oven for 3-4 minutes or until just cooked.

To make garnish, heat remaining olive oil in a frying pan, add enoki and shimeji mushrooms and sauté for 2 minutes or until they start to colour. Deglaze* with veal jus, bring to the boil and reduce by two-thirds. Reduce heat to low and monter* by whisking in butter, a little bit at a time, until butter sauce is emulsified and consistency is very thick. Season with salt and pepper.

Cook soba noodles in boiling salted water for 3-4 minutes or until tender. Drain well.

Place 2 John Dory pieces in centre of each serving plate and dress with enoki and shimeji mushrooms, butter sauce, pesto and bull's blood leaves. Twirl soba noodles around a fork to form a stack and place on top of John Dory. To finish, sprinkle sesame seeds around plate and serve.

Serves 4

4 ripe figs, cut in half
olive oil, for brushing
icing (confectioners') sugar, for dusting
80g (2 3/4oz) goat's cheese
20g (3/4oz) chopped unsalted pistachio nuts
12 mâche* (lamb's lettuce) leaves

Gluhwein Reduction
100ml (3 1/2fl oz) port
25ml (1fl oz) brandy
2 1/2 tbsp fresh orange juice
25g (1oz) caster (superfine) sugar
1/4 lemon
1/4 orange
1/2 cinnamon stick
1/2 vanilla bean
1 star anise
1 clove
1 cardamom pod

Glazed Figs with Goat's Cheese & Gluhwein

To make gluhwein reduction, combine ingredients in a heavy-based saucepan over medium heat, bring to the boil, reduce heat and simmer for 5 minutes. Remove from heat, pass through a chinois* and return to pan. Return to the boil, reduce heat and simmer until gluhwein is reduced by half. Set aside to cool.

Lightly brush figs with olive oil and dust with icing sugar. Place a little goat's cheese on the cut side of each fig half, and place under preheated grill (broiler) for 2-3 minutes or until figs and goat's cheese colour a little.

To serve, place 2 fig halves in the centre of each serving plate and drizzle around some gluhwein reduction. Sprinkle over pistachio nuts and garnish with mâche leaves.

Serves 4

Shellfish & Cognac Bisque

500g (1lb 2oz) prawn, crab and/or lobster shells
4 hard-boiled eggs, shelled
80g (2 3/4oz) crabmeat
4 slices truffle
1 tbsp truffle oil
16 bush basil* tips

Crustacean Stock
2 tbsp olive oil
1 onion, finely chopped
1 celery stalk, finely chopped
1 leek, finely sliced
2 garlic cloves, finely chopped
500g (1lb 2 oz) salmon bones
(excluding head), chopped
2 1/2 tbsp dry sherry
100ml (3 1/2fl oz) white wine
10 sprigs thyme
20 stalks parsley
2 litres (8 cups/70fl oz)
chicken stock *(see page 186)*

Bisque
50g (1 3/4oz) butter
1 onion, finely chopped
1 celery stalk, finely chopped
1 leek, finely sliced
1 carrot, finely chopped
1 1/2 tbsp tomato paste
1/2 cup plain (all-purpose) flour
2 1/2tbsp white wine
100ml (3 1/2fl oz) cognac
400g (14oz) tin peeled roma (plum) tomatoes
400g (14oz) tomato-based pasta sauce
3 garlic cloves
1/3 bunch thyme
300ml (10 1/2fl oz) pouring cream
sea salt and cracked black pepper

Preheat oven to 220°C (425°F/Gas 7).

Place prawn, crab and/or lobster shells on a roasting tin and bake in oven for 30 minutes or until dry and starting to colour. Set aside until required.

To make crustacean stock, heat olive oil in a heavy-based saucepan over low heat, add onion, celery, leek and garlic and sweat for 5 minutes or until softened but not coloured. Add salmon bones and half of the roasted prawn, crab and/or lobster shells *(remaining shells are to be used in bisque)*, deglaze* with sherry and white wine and add thyme and parsley. Add chicken stock and bring to the boil, skim surface and simmer for 35 minutes or until reduced to 2 litres (8 cups/70fl oz). Pass through a chinois* and set aside until required for bisque.

To make bisque, melt 25g (1oz) butter in a large ovenproof saucepan over medium heat, add onion, celery, leek and carrot and sauté for 5 minutes or until onion is golden. Remove half of the vegetables and transfer to a roasting tin. Spread over tomato paste, bake in 220°C (425°F/Gas 7) oven for 30 minutes, or until tomato paste starts to brown, and return to saucepan. Add remaining butter and remaining roasted prawn, crab and/or lobster shells and cook until butter is melted. Add flour and stir until mixture is the consistency of wet sand. Transfer to oven for 40 minutes to cook out the flour. Remove from oven, return to medium heat and deglaze* with white wine and 2 1/2 tablespoons of cognac. Slowly add half of the crustacean stock. Add tomatoes, pasta sauce, garlic, thyme and remaining crustacean stock and simmer for 20 minutes. Blend *(shells and all)*, pass through a chinois* and return to pan. Bring to the boil, add as much cream as needed to make a good consistency, season with salt and pepper to taste and finish with remaining cognac.

Separate egg whites from yolks and finely grate yolks, then finely grate whites.

Place a 3cm (1 1/4in) ring mould in the centre of each serving bowl, lightly press in a little crabmeat, some egg yolk, egg white, then a little more crabmeat. Place a slice of truffle on top and garnish with a tiny mound of egg white and a bush basil tip. Remove ring mould and carefully ladle bisque around crabmeat and egg pillar, Drizzle over a little truffle oil, garnish with 3 bush basil tips and serve.

Serves 4

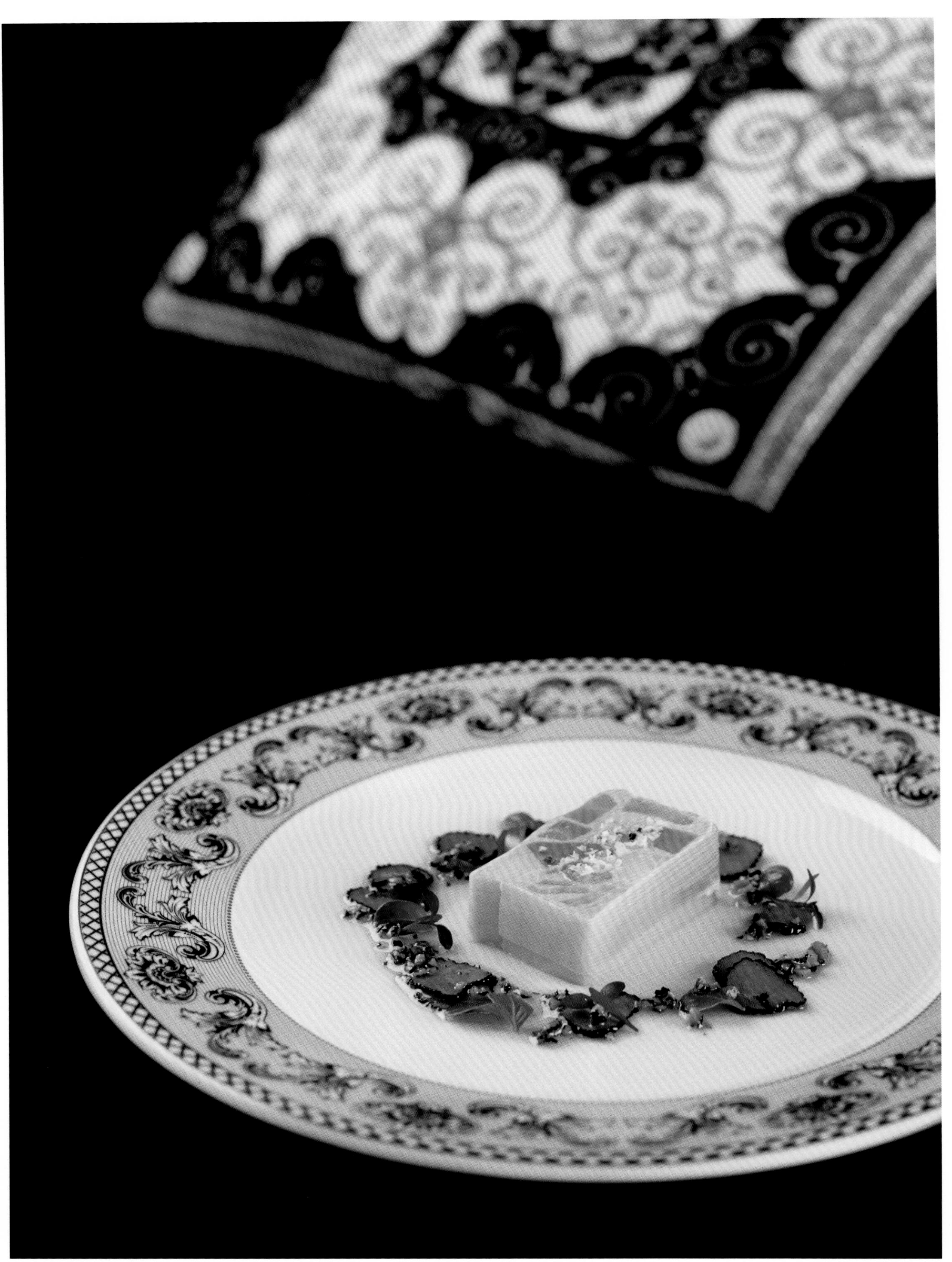

FOIE GRAS & VEGETABLE TERRINE

300g (10 1/2oz) foie gras, cooked
100g (3 1/2oz) butter, melted
1 1/2 tbsp brandy
150ml (5fl oz) pouring cream
sea salt and cracked black pepper
300ml (10 1/2fl oz) vegetable stock
30g (1oz) butter
1 carrot, cut into batons
1 celery stalk, cut into batons
2 baby leeks, cut into batons
150g (5 1/2oz) celeriac, cut into batons
1 baby fennel bulb, cut into batons
1 leek, white part only, trimmed and leaves separated
16 thin truffle slices
1/2 cup baby herb leaves, such as mâche* (lamb's lettuce), bull's blood* and rocket (arugula) leaves
1/3 cup extra virgin olive oil
2 tbsp truffle juice

To make mousse, blend foie gras in a food processor until smooth. Add butter and brandy and, with the motor running, pour in cream and process until combined and mixture is smooth. Season with salt and pepper.

Bring stock and butter to the boil in a heavy-based saucepan, add carrot, celery, baby leeks, celeriac and fennel and cook for 10 minutes or until tender.

Blanch leek leaves in boiling water for 40 seconds, refresh in iced water and drain well.

Line a small 7 x 15cm (2 3/4 x 6in) terrine mould with 2 sheets of plastic wrap and cover with half of the leek leaves, ensuring that they overlap slightly. Arrange layers of mousse and vegetables on leek leaves, making sure there are no air pockets, finishing with a layer of mousse. Top with a layer of remaining leek leaves and cover with plastic wrap. Place in refrigerator for 3 hours or until set.

Invert terrine on to a chopping board and carefully remove plastic wrap. Using a warm, sharp knife, slice terrine into 4 portions and season surface with salt and pepper.

Place a terrine portion on each serving plate. Arrange truffle slices and baby herbs around terrine, drizzle over extra virgin olive oil and truffle juice and serve.

Serves 4

LOBSTER SALAD WITH ZUCCHINI FLOWERS

2 x 650g (1 lb 7oz) lobsters

Stuffed Zucchini Flowers
8 tbsp goat's cheese
2 tbsp finely chopped fresh chives
1 tbsp truffle oil
sea salt and cracked black pepper
8 zucchini (courgette) flowers, pistils removed

Vegetable and Vanilla Vinaigrette
100ml (3 1/2fl oz) olive oil
2 French shallots, cut into fine brunoise*
1 carrot, cut into fine brunoise*
1 zucchini (courgette), skin cut into fine brunoise*
1/4 celeriac, cut into fine brunoise*
1 vanilla bean, split in half lengthways and seeds scraped
1 tbsp Champagne vinegar
sea salt and cracked black pepper

Place lobsters in freezer for 20 minutes to send them to sleep before cooking. Cook lobsters in a large saucepan of boiling salted water for 7 minutes. Refresh in iced water. Remove meat from shell and slice each lobster into 4 nice medallions.

To make stuffed zucchini flowers, combine goat's cheese, chives, truffle oil and salt and pepper in a bowl and mix well. Prise open zucchini flower petals with your fingers and spoon in 1 tablespoon of goat's cheese stuffing. Gently twist petals closed to hold stuffing in place. Score each zucchini 3 times from base to 5mm (1/4in) from flower end, being careful not to break flower. Poach zucchini flowers in boiling salted water for 2 minutes, remove with a slotted spoon and drain on paper towel.

To make vegetable and vanilla vinaigrette, heat 2 tablespoons of olive oil in a frying pan over medium heat, add shallots, carrot, zucchini, celeriac and vanilla bean and seeds and lightly sweat. Deglaze* with Champagne vinegar, add remaining olive oil and season with salt and pepper. Remove vanilla bean and slice into slivers.

Arrange 2 lobster medallions and 2 zucchini flowers on each serving plate. Drizzle vegetable and vanilla vinaigrette around plate, garnish with a few vanilla bean slivers and serve.

Serves 4

VERSACE KIR ROYALE

Our red Champagne cocktail!
150ml (5fl oz) Louis Roederer non-vintage Champagne, chilled
15ml (1/2fl oz) crème de cassis

Pour Champagne into a champagne flute, gently add crème de cassis to glass and serve.

Makes 1

FRESH KIWI & PASSIONFRUIT CAIPRIOSKA

1 glass crushed ice
45ml (1 1/2fl oz) Belvedere vodka
15ml 42 Below passionfruit-infused vodka
1 kiwifruit, peeled and chopped
2 lime wedges
passionfruit pulp, to decorate
1 tsp icing (confectioners') sugar, to dust

Muddle ice, vodkas, kiwifruit and lime wedges in an old-fashioned glass to extract as much flavour as possible. Decorate with passionfruit pulp, dust with sugar and serve.

Makes 1

LUXURY GOLD MARTINI

$^{1}/_{4}$ cup Belvedere vodka
1 glass crushed ice
vermouth
gold leaf* flakes, to garnish
1 stuffed olive, to garnish

Place a martini glass in freezer to chill. Combine vodka and ice in a cocktail shaker, shake and leave to sit for 5 minutes. Remove glass from freezer and lightly skim inside of glass with vermouth. Strain vodka into glass, garnish with gold leaf and olive and serve.

Makes 1

VERSACE BLOODY MARY

Dedicated to Mary Queen of Scots!
$^{1}/_{2}$ small red chilli, deseeded and finely sliced
5 small fresh coriander (cilantro) leaves, chopped
1 tsp julienne* of celery
$^{1}/_{2}$ tsp Tabasco sauce
1 tsp Worcestershire sauce
zest of $^{1}/_{2}$ lemon
sea salt and cracked black pepper
2 lemon slivers
45ml (1 $^{1}/_{2}$fl oz) Belvedere chilli-infused vodka
15ml ($^{1}/_{2}$fl oz) Grey Goose vodka
90ml (3fl oz) tomato puree, chilled
1 tbsp julienne* of celery, to garnish

Combine chilli, coriander, celery, Tabasco and Worcestershire sauces and lemon zest in a small bowl and mix well. Place in ice-cube trays and freeze. Place ice cubes in a chilled cocktail glass and season with salt, pepper and lemon slivers. Pour over vodkas and top with pureed tomatoes. Garnish with julienne of celery and serve.

Makes 1

ARCTIC KISS

Our blue Champagne cocktail!
150ml (5fl oz) Louis Roederer
non-vintage Champagne, chilled
15ml (1/2fl oz) Marie Brizard blue curaçao

Pour Champagne into a champagne flute and very gently add curaçao. Serve at once.

Makes 1

LIME & SWEET MELON MARTINI

15ml (1/2fl oz) Midori
juice of 1/2 lime
honey, to taste
2 tsp Marie Brizard blue curaçao
1 glass crushed ice
apple fan, to decorate
1 green grape, to decorate

Combine Midori, lime juice and honey in a cocktail shaker. Shake well and strain into a chilled martini glass. Combine curaçao with ice in a cocktail shaker and shake well. Strain curaçao and delicately pour over Midori mixture so that curaçao floats on top. Garnish with apple fan and grape and serve.

Makes 1

COGNAC CAFÉ ROYALE

45ml (1 1/2fl oz) Hennessy VSOP cognac
1/4 cup hot espresso coffee
2 tsp sugar syrup, chilled
1/4 cup pouring cream
gold leaf* dust, to garnish

Gently heat cognac, add coffee and set aside to infuse. Decant into a warmed cognac or martini glass. Gently pour in sugar syrup and cream to float on top, dust with gold leaf and serve.

Makes 1

LUXURIOUS VERSACE COWBOY

15ml (1/2fl oz) melted dark couverture chocolate
15ml (1/2fl oz) Baileys
1 1/2 tbsp butterscotch schnapps
15ml (1/2fl oz) Belvedere vodka
45ml (1 1/2fl oz) pouring cream
drinking chocolate, to dust
white chocolate shavings, to decorate
mint tip, to decorate

Drag a wine-knife dipped in melted chocolate up the inside of a chilled cocktail glass. Combine Baileys, butterscotch schnapps and vodka in a cocktail shaker and shake well. Add cream, shake and gently strain into centre of prepared glass. Dust with drinking chocolate and decorate with white chocolate shavings and mint.

Makes 1

VANILLA ICE-CREAM

8 egg yolks
170g (6oz) caster (superfine) sugar
300ml (10 1/2fl oz) milk
300ml (10 1/2fl oz) pouring cream
1 vanilla bean, split lengthways and seeds scraped

Whisk egg yolks and sugar in a bowl until pale and fluffy.

Bring milk, cream and vanilla seeds to a rolling boil in a heavy-based saucepan and remove from heat. Pour hot milk mixture over egg yolk mixture, whisking constantly to prevent egg yolks from becoming cooked and lumpy. Return egg yolk and milk mixture to cleaned saucepan and cook on a low heat, stirring constantly with a wooden spoon, until custard becomes thick enough to coat back of spoon without running off. It is important that the custard does not boil. Strain through a fine chinois*, refrigerate for 2 hours or until cool and churn in an ice-cream machine following manufacturer's instructions. Keep in a sealed container in freezer until required.

Makes 900ml (31fl oz)

BLACK OLIVE TAPENADE

250g (9oz) black olives, pitted
50g (1 3/4oz) anchovies
1 tbsp capers
1 garlic clove
2 tbsp extra virgin olive oil
1 tbsp finely chopped chives
1 tsp cracked black pepper

Separately chop olives, anchovies, capers and garlic until very fine. Place in a small bowl, add oil and chives, mix to combine and season with pepper. Refrigerate until required.

Makes 350g (12oz)

AIOLI

4 egg yolks
1 garlic clove, finely chopped
pinch of cayenne pepper
1 tsp dijon mustard
150 ml (5fl oz) fresh lemon juice
100ml (3 1/2fl oz) olive oil
300ml (10 1/2fl oz) grape seed oil
1 tsp sea salt

Place egg yolks, garlic, cayenne pepper, mustard and juice in a food processor and blitz to combine. With motor running, slowly drizzle in olive and grape seed oils and process until thick and well combined. Season with salt, transfer to a container, cover, and refrigerate until required.

Makes 650ml (22 1/2fl oz)

MAYONNAISE

4 egg yolks
1 tsp dijon mustard
75ml (2 1/2fl oz) fresh lemon juice
75ml (2 1/2fl oz) white wine vinegar
100ml (3 1/2fl oz) olive oil
300ml (10 1/2fl oz) grape seed oil
1 tsp sea salt

Place egg yolks, mustard, juice and vinegar in a food processor and blitz. With motor running, slowly drizzle in olive and grape seed oils and process until thick and well combined. Season with salt, transfer to a container, cover, and refrigerate until required.

Makes 650ml (22 1/2fl oz)

CHICKEN STOCK

1kg (2lb 4oz) chicken bones
1 small onion, roughly chopped
1 medium carrot, roughly chopped
1 celery stalk, roughly chopped
2 garlic cloves, peeled
2 sprigs thyme
3 bay leaves
1 tsp black peppercorns
3 litres (12 cups/104fl oz) water

Place all ingredients in a large heavy-based saucepan and bring to the boil. Reduce heat to low and simmer for 2 hours, skimming surface often. Strain through a fine chinois*, cool and refrigerate or freeze until required.

Makes 2 litres (8 cups/70fl oz)

DOUBLE CHICKEN STOCK

1kg (2lb 4oz) chicken bones, roasted until golden
2 litres (8 cups/70fl oz) chicken stock *(see page 186)*
1 small onion, roughly chopped
1 medium carrot, roughly chopped
1 celery stalk, roughly chopped
2 garlic cloves, peeled
2 sprigs thyme

Place all ingredients in a large, heavy-based saucepan and bring to the boil. Reduce heat to low and simmer, skimming surface often, until reduced to half its original volume. Strain through a fine chinois*, cool and refrigerate or freeze until required.

Makes 4 cups

BEEF STOCK

2kg (4lb 8oz) tomatoes, cut in half
1kg (2lb 4oz) beef bones, roasted until dark brown
1 pig's trotter or calf's foot
1 small onion, roughly chopped
1 medium carrot, roughly chopped
1 celery stalk, roughly chopped
2 garlic cloves, peeled
1 tsp black peppercorns
3 litres (12 cups/104fl oz) water
2 sprigs thyme
3 bay leaves

Preheat oven to 130°C (250°F/Gas 1).

Place tomatoes, cut-side up, on a baking tray, place in oven and bake for 1 hour or until dry and soft.

Combine tomatoes and remaining ingredients in a large, heavy-based saucepan and bring to the boil. Reduce heat to low and simmer, skimming surface often, for 6 hours. Strain through a fine chinois*, cool and refrigerate or freeze until required.

Makes 2 litres (8 cups/70fl oz)

VEAL STOCK

2kg (4lb 8oz) tomatoes, cut in half
1kg (2lb 4oz) veal bones, roasted until dark brown
1 pig's trotter or calf's foot
1 medium carrot, roughly chopped
1 celery stalk, roughly chopped
1 small onion, roughly chopped
2 garlic cloves, peeled
1 tsp black peppercorns
3 litres (12 cups/104fl oz) water
2 sprigs thyme
3 bay leaves

Preheat oven to 130°C (250°F/Gas 1).

Place tomatoes, cut-side up, on a baking tray, place in oven and bake for 1 hour or until dry and soft.

Combine tomatoes and remaining ingredients in a large, heavy-based saucepan and bring to the boil. Reduce heat to low and simmer, skimming surface often, for 6 hours. Strain through a fine chinois*, cool and refrigerate or freeze until required.

Makes 2 litres (8 cups/70fl oz)

BLACK PEPPER DRESSING

300ml (10 1/2fl oz) house dressing *(see page 189)*
2 tsp coarsely cracked black pepper
sea salt

Place house dressing and pepper in a bowl, whisk until well combined and season to taste. Refrigerate until required.

Makes 300ml (10 1/2fl oz)

VEAL JUS

2 tbsp vegetable oil
600g (1lb 5oz) raw veal or beef off-cuts
1 small onion, roughly chopped
1 medium carrot, roughly chopped
1 celery stalk, roughly chopped
6 button mushrooms, roughly chopped
2 garlic cloves, peeled
300ml (10 1/2fl oz) red wine
1 tbsp tomato paste
2 litres (8 cups/70fl oz) veal stock *(see page 187)*
sea salt and cracked black pepper

Heat oil in a large, heavy-based saucepan over medium heat, add veal or beef and fry until dark brown all over. Add onion, carrot, celery, mushrooms and garlic and fry for a further 2 minutes. Deglaze* pan with red wine and reduce to 1 tablespoon. Stir in tomato paste, add stock and bring to the boil. Reduce heat to low and simmer, skimming surface often, until reduced by three-quarters. Season with salt and pepper and strain through a fine chinois*. Cool and refrigerate until required.

Makes 2 cups

BRIOCHE

290g (10 1/4oz) plain (all-purpose) flour
1/2 tsp salt
1 tsp caster (superfine) sugar
1/2 cup milk
15g (1/2oz) dried yeast
1 egg
70g (2 1/2oz) unsalted butter, softened

Combine flour, salt and sugar in a large bowl.

Lightly warm milk and add yeast. Stand for 10 minutes to allow yeast to start working.

Add egg and milk mixture to dry ingredients and mix to form a smooth dough. Place in a lightly floured bowl, cover and stand in a warm place to prove. The dough needs to double in size.

Cut butter into 1cm (1/2in) dice and gently work into dough until about 90 per cent absorbed. Shape dough and put into a buttered and floured loaf tin. Again allow dough to double in size.

Preheat oven to 180°C (350°F/Gas 4).

Place brioche in oven for 30-40 minutes or until golden and firm to touch.

Makes 1 loaf

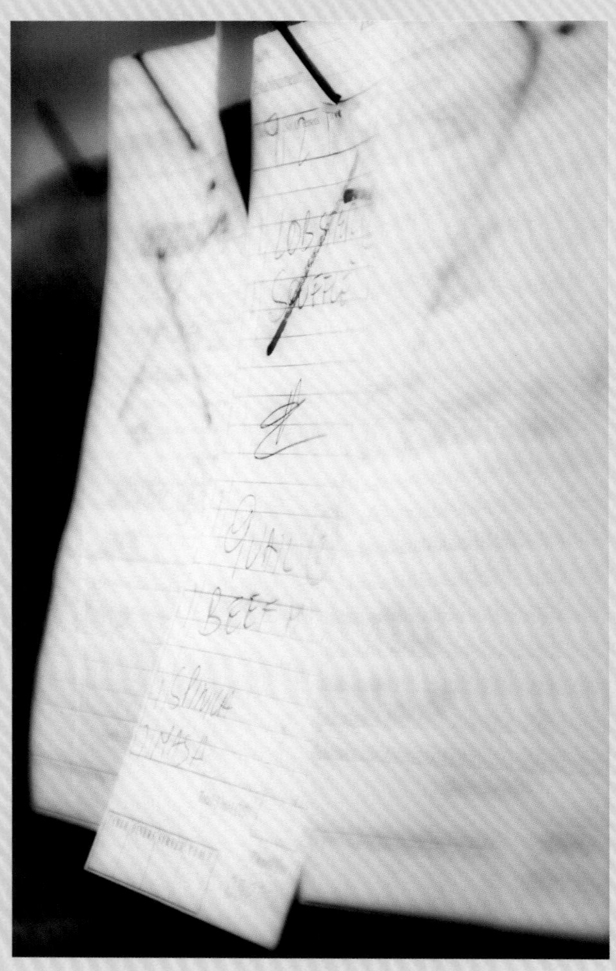

PASTA DOUGH

250g (9oz) bakers flour
2 eggs whole
1 egg yolk
1 tbsp olive oil
1 tbsp water
salt

Place the flour in a mixing bowl with a paddle attachment. Whisk the oil, water and eggs together and add to the flour on the machine. Knead the dough on a low speed until it comes together – continue for a further 3-4 minutes. Portion into 2 equal amounts, wrap in cling film and rest in fridge for at least an hour.

SUGAR SYRUP

100g (3 ½oz) caster (superfine) sugar
100ml (3 ½fl oz) water
4 star anise
1 cinnamon stick
segments and zest of 1 lemon
segments and zest of 1 lime

To make sugar syrup, combine sugar, water, star anise and cinnamon in a saucepan and bring to the boil. Continue to boil gently for 15 minutes. Remove syrup from heat and add lemon and lime segments and zest. Set aside until required.

SQUID INK PASTA

4 cups plain (all-purpose) flour
pinch of salt
25ml (1fl oz) olive oil
1 tbsp squid ink
2 eggs
6 egg yolks
50g (1 ¾oz) butter
sea salt and cracked black pepper

To make squid ink pasta, sift flour and salt on to a clean work surface and make a well in centre. Mix olive oil and squid ink together, combine with eggs and egg yolks and pour into well. Incorporate flour from sides with your hands and work mixture for 3-4 minutes, being careful not to overwork, to form a smooth dough. Cover with plastic wrap and refrigerate for 1-2 hours. To finish, divide dough into 4 portions and run through thickest setting on a pasta machine. Fold dough in half lengthways, dust both sides with a little flour and repeat. Continue dusting with flour and running through progressively thinner settings on pasta machine until pasta sheet is about 2mm (1/16in) thick. Repeat for each dough portion.

PUFF PASTRY

500g (1lb 2oz) plain (all purpose) flour
20g (3/4oz) salt
200ml (7fl oz) water
1 tbsp lemon juice
50g (1 3/4oz) unsalted butter, melted
400g (14oz) unsalted butter

Sift flour and salt on to a clean, cold work surface, make a well in centre and pour in water, lemon juice and melted butter. Gradually bring in flour to centre of the well and work with your fingertips to create a paste. Continue to work gently with fingertips until a smooth, elastic dough forms. Roll dough into a ball, wrap tightly in plastic wrap and refrigerate for at least 2 hours.

Place butter between two sheets of baking paper and pound with a rolling pin to soften slightly. Shape butter into a 1cm (1/2in) thick square and return to refrigerator to chill.

Flour work surface and roll out dough into a square twice as big as the square of cold butter. With pastry in front of you, with corners running north and south, place butter in middle on the opposite angle. Fold in the four triangular – shaped sides so that they all meet in middle. Wrap in plastic wrap and refrigerate for a further 40 minutes.

Lightly flour work surface and roll out dough into a rectangle three times longer than its width. Take one end of the length of dough and fold it to a point two-thirds along the rectangle of dough, then fold the last flap back over top. This is the first turn.

Turn rectangle through 90 degrees, Roll and fold dough as before, making two small dimples in dough with the tip of a finger. This represents the second turn. Wrap in plastic wrap and rest in refrigerator for at least 30 minutes.

You must now repeat these 2 turns twice more, making 6 turns in total. Don't forget to mark the number of turns and to rest the dough after each set of 2 turns. Dough is now ready to roll out as instructed in recipe.

Makes 1kg (2lb 4oz)

HOUSE DRESSING

200ml (7fl oz) grape seed oil
2 tbsp walnut oil
1 tbsp sherry vinegar
1 tsp wholegrain mustard
1 tbsp port
1 tbsp Madeira
sea salt and cracked black pepper

Place all ingredients in a bowl and whisk until well combined. Check seasoning and adjust if necessary. Refrigerate until required.

Makes 300ml (10 1/2fl oz)

BALSAMIC JUS

2 1/2 tbsp vegetable oil
1kg (2lb 4oz) raw lamb off-cuts or bones
1 small onion, roughly chopped
1 medium carrot, roughly chopped
1 celery stalk, roughly chopped
2 tomatoes, roughly chopped
2 garlic cloves, peeled
200ml (7fl oz) red wine
100ml (3 1/2fl oz) aged balsamic vinegar
2 cups chicken stock *(see page 186)*
2 cups veal stock *(see page 187)*
1 sprig rosemary
sea salt and cracked black pepper

Heat oil in a large heavy-based pot over medium heat, add lamb and fry until dark brown all over. Add onion, carrot, celery, tomatoes and garlic and fry for a further 2 minutes. Deglaze* with red wine and balsamic vinegar and reduce to 1 tablespoon. Add chicken and veal stocks and rosemary and bring to the boil. Reduce heat to low and simmer, skimming surface often, until reduced by three-quarters. Season with salt and pepper and strain through a fine chinois*. Set aside to cool then refrigerate until required.

Makes 300ml (10 1/2fl oz)

CHAMPAGNE CREAM SAUCE

2 cups chicken stock
2 cups veal stock
1kg (2lb 4oz) chicken bones
2 sprigs thyme
1 small onion, roughly chopped
1 medium carrot, roughly chopped
1 celery stalk, roughly chopped
6 button mushrooms
2 garlic cloves, peeled
300ml (10 1/2fl oz) Champagne
or dry sparkling white wine
1 cup pouring cream
1 tsp sea salt
1/2 tsp cracked black pepper

Combine chicken and veal stocks, chicken bones, thyme, onion, carrot, celery, mushrooms and garlic in a large, heavy-based saucepan and bring to the boil. Reduce heat to low and simmer, skimming surface often, until reduced by half. Strain into a clean saucepan, add Champagne or wine and reduce by half. Add cream, reduce by half again and season with salt and pepper. Refrigerate until required.

Makes 300ml (10 1/2fl oz)

GLOSSARY

bain-marie
The French term for double boiler or water bath.

blanc
A term used for a white acidic cooking liquor used to prevent discolouring in certain vegetables, such as artichoke hearts, salsify and witlof *(chicory/Belgian endive)*, during and after cooking. It is made by mixing 200g (7oz) plain (all-purpose) flour with 4 cups of any white stock or water, salt and the juice of 4 lemons. Bring all the ingredients to the boil, stirring constantly to get a smooth soup-like product, add the desired vegetable and cook, cool and store in the blanc until required.

brunoise
A neat, fine, perfect 3mm (1/8in) dice. To achieve the best results, shape what you are going to dice into a square or rectangular piece, cut off 3mm (1/8in) slices, cut them into 3mm (1/8in) strips and finally cut the strips into 3mm (1/8in) dice. This method works well for most vegetables and fruit.

bull's blood leaves
The young, deep-red tips that have been picked from the tops of organic bull's blood beetroot (beet).

bush basil
A small shrub *(Ocimum basilicum var. minimum)* that has a basil-like fragrance and small leaves, it is used in any dish that would suit sweet basil. It is also used to make a tea-like drink that is supposed to help flatulence.

caul
The lining of a pig's stomach, sometimes referred to as crepinette. It is used to wrap loose meats, such as mousses, to keep them from moving when being cooked. The best thing about using caul is that it melts during the cooking process and leaves a perfect finish.

celery salt
A seasoning made from mixing ground celery seeds and salt, available in any good grocery store.

charcuterie
Cooked and cured meats, terrines, pâtés, sausages, etc.

chinois
A very fine-meshed metal conical strainer.

crepinette
See caul.

deglaze
Means to loosen the glaze (pan residue) at the bottom of a cooking vessel. This is usually done by adding a liquor, such as wine, sherry, stock or even water, to the pan after food has been sautéed and removed. The residue at the base of the pan is stirred until loosened and this mixture may be used as the base for a sauce to accompany the food cooked in the pan.

farce
Another word for stuffing.

fines herbes
Equal quantities of finely chopped chervil, tarragon, chives and flat leaf (Italian) parsley.

flambé
To flame a savoury or sweet dish by adding a high-alcohol content liquor, such as brandy, and burning off the alcohol leaving the subtle flavour of the alcohol used. The best example of this is orange curaçao in crêpes suzette.

garlic powder
Ground dried garlic, available in any good grocery store.

globe artichokes
To choose globe artichokes, make sure they are firm at the base, unbruised and have a nice deep-green colour. To prepare the artichokes, peel back the outer leaves and bend downwards until they snap. Do this until you reach the core. Cut very gently around the outside of the artichoke until you reach the heart. Clean the artichoke heart by removing the soft cottonwool-like centre *(the choke)* with your fingers or by scraping it out with a small spoon. Cut off the pointed top and trim the stem to 2cm (3/4in) from base. Place the artichokes in a boiling blanc for about 15 minutes and allow to cool in the blanc. Thoroughly wash your hands and utensils after preparing the artichokes, as they leave a very bitter residue on anything they come into contact with.

gold leaf
Real gold that has been flattened to just a few micrometres in thickness. Take care to use only food-grade gold leaf as copper is often alloyed with gold for decoration purposes. Can be purchased from any good delicatessen.

goujons
Small strips of fish or meat 1.5 x 7cm (5/8 x 2 3/4in) in size.

green ginger wine
An interesting drink made from fresh ginger. I use Stone's Original Green Ginger Wine, which can be purchased from any good alcohol retailer.

hazelnuts
To roast and skin hazelnuts, preheat the oven to 170°C (325°F/Gas 3). Spread the hazelnuts on a baking tray, place in the oven and bake for 5 minutes or until the skin is dark brown and cracking. Transfer the hazelnuts to a clean tea towel and rub to remove the skins.

julienne
Thin matchstick-shaped strips. To achieve the best results, shape what you are going to slice into a square or rectangular piece, cut off 3mm (1/8in) slices, cut them into 3mm (1/8in) strips and finally cut the strips into 4cm (1 1/2in) lengths. This method works well for most vegetables and fruit.

lardons
Batons cut from whole smoked pork belly, sometimes referred to as speck or kaiserfleisch. Lardons are cut about 5mm x 3cm (1/4 x 1 1/4in) in size and are often cooked first before adding to the recipe by frying in a little vegetable oil until they have good all-over colour, Cooking first helps to render out excess fat and develops that unique, crispy, smoky, bacon taste, which can then be absorbed into the dish.

mâche
Also called lamb's lettuce, lamb's tongue, corn salad, field salad and field lettuce. Mâche is a tender salad green with a nutty flavour that is common in Europe. A good substitute is tatsoi.

mograbieh couscous
Also known as Israeli couscous, maftoul or pearl couscous. Mograbieh is the Lebanese name for giant pearl-sized couscous.

monter
To lift with butter by whisking or stirring small pieces of cold butter into a sauce to give it a richer, glossy and slightly thicker finish.

mouli
A food mill with interchangeable discs of varying diameters that allow you to purée cooked vegetables, soups, etc. Moulis come in a range of sizes.

mussels
To clean and debeard mussels, the easiest and best way to do this is to hold the mussel in a cloth and gently pull the beard until it is released. These days there are machines that debeard mussels. You may ask your fishmonger for this to be done, but I prefer to do this myself to ensure freshness.

pane mix
A basic pane mix is flour, breadcrumbs and egg wash.

peking duck
I always buy my ducks from the experts who know what it takes. A good Chinese barbecued meats retailer in your local Chinese district is the best place to go. The ducks can be bought as a half or a whole. Be warned – the head is still very much attached.

quail
It is possible to buy quail that are already tunnel boned or butterflied from a good butcher. To do this yourself, stand the quail on a chopping board with the breast uppermost. Remove the backbone by inserting a sharp knife through the opening at the tail end to the neck end and cutting firmly through the bones on either side of the backbone. Now that is done, fold out the quail and carefully remove the remaining breast bones with a small knife. Finish by taking out the thighbone, taking care to leave in the shinbone by cutting through at the knee.

quenelle
A light mousse-style dumpling usually of fish or poultry, shaped like a tiny rugby ball, that is poached and served in a rich sauce. To form quenelle shapes, place the mixture on one spoon and shape into small ovals using a second spoon.

semi-whipped
Sometimes referred to as soft peaks, the cream is whipped until it has body.

shiso
An Asian herb often used by Japanese chefs to wrap sushi. It is close to sweet basil in flavour. Purple basil would make a great substitute.

soba noodles
These dusky brown-grey noodles are made from wheat flour, buckwheat and yam. I find the best variety to use is Ishiguro Yamaimo Soba. These noodles do not need a lot of cooking, can be served hot or cold and have a multitude of uses. They can be flavoured with different oils, mustards and herbs or eaten simply and plainly on their own.

somen noodles
A thin, round white noodle made from wheat flour. They are similar to vermicelli and are often served cold or added to soups.

spaetzle
'Little sparrows' are a soft freeform noodle from German cuisine.

sweetbreads
The pancreatic glands from lambs and calves. They can be obtained from any good butcher, if ordered in advance. Freshest is best, but if you can't obtain fresh sweetbreads, most butchers will have a frozen supply. Sweetbreads have a light membrane covering the outside, which is chewy and unappetizing. Carefully remove this membrane and cut sweetbreads into 2cm (3/4in) portions.

tatsoi
An Asian salad green used in salads, soups and stir-fry dishes. Tatsoi has small, dark-green, spoon-shaped leaves with a mild mustard flavour. Watercress can be used as an alternative.

tomatoes, peeled
To peel tomatoes, cut a cross in the base of each tomato then plunge into boiling water for 30 seconds. Drain and transfer to a bowl of cold water. Peel skin away from the cross when the tomato is cool enough to handle.

tuscan oil
A less expensive blend of Italian olive oil and good vegetable oils that can be used freely in place of olive oil when flavour is still important.

wild garlic
A fresh, light garlic with usually only three cloves making up the bulb stock. It is often cooked whole because of its subtle flavour.

vanilla sugar
Simply vanilla-flavoured sugar, which is available to buy but is easy to make and should always be on your shelf. Just fill a storage jar with caster (superfine) sugar and push 2 or 3 vanilla beans into it. They will impart their flavour to the sugar. Vanilla sugar can be used in recipes such as mousses, ice-creams and custards.

veal kidneys
Select beautiful fresh veal kidneys. To prepare kidneys, cut them in half and remove any suet (fat) and white elastic membrane inside. Cut into the desired size, about 2cm (3/4in).

Vanitas Gourmet Collection – Palazzo Versace

First published in 2007 by Palazzo Versace

Palazzo Versace
94 Sea World Drive, Main Beach,
Queensland 4217 Australia
PO Box 137, Main Beach,
Queensland 4217 Australia
Telephone +61 7 5509 8000
Facsimile +61 7 5509 8888
www.palazzoversace.com

National Library of Australia.

Our catalogue record is available from
The National Library of Australia.

1st edition.
Includes index.
ISBN 978 0 9804293 0 5

Designed and produced by
Peter Sexty Graphic Design
Peter Sexty *Art Director*
Danielle Towill *Senior Designer*

Edited by Megan Johnston

Printed in Australia by Printpoint